An outline of

The Law of Contract

An outline of
The Law of Contract

Sixth edition

Sir Guenter Treitel QC, DCL, FBA

Honorary Bencher of Gray's Inn,
Formerly Vinerian Professor of English Law

OXFORD
UNIVERSITY PRESS

OXFORD

UNIVERSITY PRESS

Great Clarendon Street, Oxford OX2 6DP

Oxford University Press is a department of the University of Oxford.
It furthers the University's objective of excellence in research, scholarship,
and education by publishing worldwide in

Oxford New York

Auckland Bangkok Buenos Aires Cape Town Chennai
Dar es Salaam Delhi Hong Kong Istanbul Karachi Kolkata
Kuala Lumpur Madrid Melbourne Mexico City Mumbai Nairobi
São Paulo Shanghai Taipei Tokyo Toronto

Oxford is a registered trade mark of Oxford University Press
in the UK and in certain other countries

Published in the United States
by Oxford University Press Inc., New York

British Library Cataloguing in Publication Data
Data available

Library of Congress Cataloging in Publication Data
Data available

ISBN 0 406 97268 0

10 9 8 7 6 5 4 3 2 1

Typeset in New Baskerville
by Doyle & Co, Colchester

Printed in Great Britain
on acid-free paper by
William Clowes Ltd, Beccles and London

Preface

This edition takes account of the many important changes in the law of contract brought about by legislation and case law since the last edition, published nine years ago. At the same time, the new edition seeks to preserve the character of the book as one which provides an account of the main principles of the law of contract in the light of often conflicting policies, and which, by avoiding technical detail as much as possible, remains intelligible to readers without specialist legal training.

So far as new primary legislation is concerned, the most important changes are those brought about by the Contracts (Rights of Third Parties) Act 1999. The Act not only affects the structure of the chapter on parties but also has repercussions on many other parts of the book. Other significant changes are made in the light of the Arbitration Act 1996, the Competition Act 1998, the Late Payment of Commercial Debts (Interest) Act 1998, the Financial Services and Markets Act 2000 and the Enterprise Act 2002. Further changes have resulted from secondary legislation implementing EC Directives. In particular, the Unfair Terms in Consumer Contracts Regulations 1999 differ significantly from their 1994 precursor; and although a detailed account of the Sale and Supply of Goods to Consumers Regulations 2002 is beyond the scope of this book, account is taken in it of some of the new concepts that they have introduced into English law. This edition also takes account of the legislation which deals with the impact of electronic communications on the law of contract.

Since the last edition there have been over 600 cases relevant to the subject, and in this relatively short book it has been possible to deal only with those of exceptional importance. These include such landmark decisions of the House of Lords as *Director General of Fair Trading v First National Bank* on unfair terms in consumer contracts; *Smith New Court v Srimgeour Vickers* on damages for misrepresentation; *Royal Bank of Scotland v Etridge* on undue influence; *Alfred McAlpine v Panatown* on damages in respect of a third party's loss; *A-G v Blake* on account of profits as a remedy for breach of contract; *South Australia Asset Management Corp v York Montague* on the relevance of the 'scope of duty' test to damages; a number of cases including *Ruxley Electronics v Forsyth* and *Farley v Skinner* on damages for non-pecuniary loss; *Malik v BCCI* on stigma damages; and *Co-operative Insurance v Argyll Stores* on specific performance. Among cases in the lower courts, attention may here be drawn to *Baird Textile v Marks & Spencer*, as one of a group of cases which has led to a recasting of the account of the various kinds of estoppel given in Chapter 3; and the *The Great Peace*, which has led to a considerable rewriting of the account of mistake in Chapter 8.

The above list is far from complete. Many other changes have been made so that more than a quarter of the text is new. To retain the essential character of the book (as described at the beginning of this Preface) compensating deletions have been made, so that the length of the book has increased by less than five per cent.

Work on this edition was completed at the end of May 2004; some later developments have been briefly incorporated at the proof stage. I am grateful for much valuable help provided (as usual) by the staff of the Codrington Library of All Souls College, to LexisNexis UK for their help at various stages in the production of the book, and to OUP for their welcome.

GHT
August 2004

Contents

Table of Statutes

Table of Statutory Instruments

Table of European Legislation

List of Cases

Chapter 1

Introduction

1 DEFINITION OF CONTRACT

A contract may be defined as an agreement which is either enforced by law or recognised by law as affecting the legal rights or duties of the parties. The law of contract is, therefore, primarily concerned with three questions: is there an agreement? is it one which should be legally recognised or enforced? and just how is the agreement enforced, or in other words, what remedies are available to the injured party when a contract has been broken?

This introductory chapter deals with a number of general points arising mainly, though not exclusively, out of the three questions just put.

2 CONTRACT AND CONTRACTS

The subject-matter of this book is 'the law of contract'. It was formerly the fashion, which in some parts of the common law world still persists, to refer to the law of contracts (in the plural). The point of modern references to a law of contract (in the singular) is to indicate that the law has a general or unified theory of contract, that is, one which applies to all contracts irrespective of their content or subject-matter. A contract may relate to any one or more of a large number of transactions, such as sale, employment, carriage, hire, lease, mortgage and so forth. A general theory of contract asserts that there is at least a substantial body of rules which applies to all contracts in common; and that these rules constitute the 'law of contract'. This is the theory of modern English law. On the other hand it has been said that Roman law had 'not a theory of contract, but a theory of contracts'.[1] What is meant is, that the rules which governed the formation and effects of a contract depended either on its content (eg whether it was sale or loan) or on its form (eg whether it was expressed orally or in writing). Neither theory can be accepted without qualification. In most modern systems of law there is, indeed, a body of rules which applies to contracts

1 Buckland and McNair *Roman Law and Common Law* (2nd edn) p 195.

1

generally. These rules may, however, be modified in their application to particular transactions such as sale, employment or carriage; and such transactions may also be governed by special rules peculiar to them, in the sense that they have no close analogy with general rules which apply to other transactions. In this book our concern will be with the general rules, and to some extent with the modified form in which they apply to particular transactions. At the same time, it is necessary to warn the reader that the general 'law of contract' is something of an abstraction, since most contracts obviously concern some particular class of transaction; and since there is always some degree of danger in assuming that a 'general' rule applies (at least without modification) to a contract of the particular type under consideration.

3   AGREEMENT

In the normal case, a contract results from an agreement between the parties to it; but the description of a contract as an agreement is nevertheless subject to a number of important qualifications.

The first of these is that the law generally speaking applies an objective test of agreement. If the words or conduct of the one party, A, are such as to induce the other, B, reasonably to believe that A is assenting to certain terms proposed by B, then A will generally be held so to have assented, whatever his actual state of mind may have been.[2] The law adopts this objective test because, in our example, B might be seriously prejudiced if he could not take A's apparent assent at its face value. The principle is, however, one of convenience only, so that it will not apply where, on balance, the inconvenience to A of applying the objective test exceeds the inconvenience to B of allowing A to rely on his actual intention: for example, where B knew that A's actual state of mind was not in accordance with the objective appearance created by A's conduct.[3] The position is probably the same where, though a reasonable person in B's position would have believed that A was assenting to the terms in question, B actually had no such belief; for in such a case B cannot suffer the prejudice against which the objective test is meant to protect him.

The second qualification is that, even where agreement determines the existence of a contract, it does not necessarily determine all the contents or scope of a contract. These matters are often determined

---

2   *The Hannah Blumenthal* [1983] 1 AC 854, as interpreted in *The Leonidas D* [1985] 2 All ER 796; see post, p 8.

3   See *The Golden Bear* [1987] 1 Lloyd's Rep 330 at 341; and see post, p 137.

by so-called 'implied terms'. These may be divided into terms implied *in fact* and terms applied *in law*: this distinction will be explained in Chapter 6. Only terms implied in fact are truly based on the intention of the parties. Terms implied in law are duties prima facie imposed by law; and with respect to them, the intention of the parties is relevant only insofar as it may be open to the parties to exclude the implied terms by contrary agreement.

Thirdly, there are cases, commonly discussed under the general heading of contract, in which the obligation arises, not out of an agreement between two parties, but rather out of a promise made by one of them. This would be the position where a person made a gratuitous promise in such a form that it was legally binding: for example, in a deed. Such a promise can bind the promisor even before it is communicated to the promisee and hence without any agreement between the parties.

Fourthly, the idea that contract depends on agreement must be qualified in cases in which one party's bargaining position is so much stronger than the other's that the former can in a sense impose his terms on the latter. This possibility is illustrated by the standard form contracts which are used by many commercial suppliers of goods or services. Under such contracts the customer may be bound by terms of which he is not aware because he has taken his chance of whatever terms were contained in the form, or he may have agreed reluctantly, or he may not in truth have 'agreed' at all.

4 FREEDOM OF CONTRACT

In its most obvious sense, the expression 'freedom of contract' refers to the general principle that the law does not restrict the terms on which parties may contract: it will not give relief merely because the terms of the contract are harsh or unfair to one party. Many of the principles of the modern law of contract were settled in the nineteenth century, when, in the light of the prevailing *laissez faire* philosophy, it was thought wrong to interfere with private agreements on such grounds. The present trend is rather to stress abuses to which the principle of 'freedom of contract' can give rise; so that the principle has been considerably restricted, both by legislation and by judicial decision. Very substantial legislative inroads on the principle have, for example, been made in the law relating to consumer contracts; while restrictions on the effectiveness of exemption clauses in standard form contracts are due partly to judicial decisions and partly to legislation.[4] Such

4 See Chapter 7, post.

developments now give a good deal of protection to the person who is assumed to be the weaker party to a contractual relationship. But in most commercial transactions between parties, bargaining at arm's length, the principle of 'freedom of contract' remains an important one.

'Freedom of contract' is also used in another sense, to refer to the principle that, in general, a person is not by law compelled to enter into a contract. Here again the law has from time to time made exceptions to the general rule on grounds of public interest. The earliest exceptions related to the so-called 'common callings' of common carriers and innkeepers. Such persons could not refuse their services as they pleased: they could do so only on certain grounds specified by law. More recently, a similar principle has been extended by legislation over a wider area so that, for example employment, accommodation or certain other facilities may not, in certain circumstances, be refused to a person on grounds of race, sex or disability;[5] it is unlawful to refuse to employ a person 'because he is, or is not, a member of a trade union';[6] and exclusion from a trade union on one of a number of specified grounds gives rise to a claim for compensation.[7] Even at common law there seems to be a remedy for arbitrary exclusion from an association (eg on religious or political grounds), if the exclusion deprives the person in question of the opportunity to exercise a particular profession.[8]

It is obvious that, the more the law interferes with the relationship of the parties, the less important the factor of agreement becomes. In some situations the degree of interference is so large that it becomes improper to describe the relationship between the parties as a contract. One illustration of such a relationship is that of marriage. Once the parties have agreed to enter into the relationship, it creates a status[9] the essential incidents of which are determined by law and cannot be varied by agreement: for example, an agreement that a marriage should last for a trial period of three years would not have any legal effect. In other cases, one of the parties may not have any choice at all: for example where a person's property is compulsorily acquired against his will under statutory powers. These cases differ from those

---

5   Race Relations Act 1976, Pts II and III; Sex Discrimination Act 1975, Pts II and III; Disability Discrimination Act 1995, ss 4, 5, 12 and 19; see also Human Rights Act 1998, s 1 and Sch 1, Pt I, Art 14.
6   Trade Union and Labour Relations (Consolidation) Act 1992, s 137(1)(a).
7   Trade Union and Labour Relations (Consolidation) Act 1992, ss 174–177.
8   See *Nagle v Feilden* [1966] 2 QB 633 (a case of sex discrimination, now unlawful under Sex Discrimination Act 1975, s 13).
9   *Bellinger v Bellinger* [2001] EWCA Civ 1140, [2002] Fam 150 at [99].

described in the preceding paragraph. In those cases, the relationship is contractual because the parties have a considerable degree of legal freedom to decide upon the terms of their relationship, even though they may enter it under some degree of legal compulsion.

5   REASONS FOR ENFORCING CONTRACTS

The legal enforceability of contractual agreements is so well established that a discussion of the reasons for it may seem to be superfluous. Yet such a discussion is important in relation to the topic of remedies for breach of contract, since the principles on which enforcement is based will determine the extent to which enforcement is to be carried. Three reasons for the enforcement of contracts are commonly given,[10] and they may be illustrated by some simple examples. First, A has agreed to buy something from B and paid for it in advance but B has not delivered it. If B could nevertheless keep the advance payment, he would be unjustly enriched; and it is therefore generally agreed that he should at the very least pay back the money to A. This process is sometimes referred to as protecting A's 'restitution interest'. Secondly, A has agreed to render some service to B at a distant place. He incurs travelling expenses in getting to that place but on his arrival there B repudiates the agreement. Here A's expenditure has not enriched B, but A nevertheless generally has a remedy against B, in respect of the wasted expenditure which he has incurred in reliance on the contract. This process is sometimes called the protection of A's 'reliance interest'. But the law of contract goes beyond protecting the restitution and reliance interests, as a third example will show. A offers to buy a picture from B for £20,000 and B accepts the offer. The same day, before A has paid B or incurred any expense in reliance on the contract, B repudiates it by refusing to deliver the picture. There is no doubt that A can enforce the contract; and the reason given is, that A's expectations arising out of the contract have been disappointed. It is said that the law here protects A's *expectation interest*. The protection of such expectations is the characteristic feature of the law of contract. Of course, other expectations are protected by other branches of the law: for example, under the law of torts a person who has been injured by another's negligence may recover damages for loss of his expected earnings. But this expectation exists independently of the negligence giving rise to the legal liability to compensate for its loss.[11] The law of contract,

---

10   See further post, pp 375–378.
11   Cf the explanation of *White v Jones* given post, p 252.

on the other hand, protects expectations which owe their existence solely to the very agreement for breach of which the action is brought. The common explanation of this state of the law is that such protection is necessary in the interests of commercial convenience: that 'business could not go on' unless contractual expectations were protected by law. This is probably too extreme a view. In practice, a good deal of business does go on without the sanction of legal enforceability of expectations. One may instance the very considerable credit betting industry; or business arrangements which are so vague as not to amount to binding contracts, or which are expressed to be 'gentlemen's agreements'. On the other hand the rule of law by which agreements for the sale of homes 'subject to contract' are not legally binding has been criticised precisely because of the inconvenience which it can cause to the disappointed party. The protection of contractual expectations does mitigate such inconvenience and so tends to promote stability; it also provides the legal framework for the operation of share, commodity and similar markets. This is the best explanation for the general principle that the law will protect these expectations, even where there has been no receipt of benefit under the contract and no loss suffered by action in reliance on it.

6   COMMON LAW AND EQUITY

English law recognises a distinction between common law and equity; and hence between legal and equitable rights, remedies and defences. Originally, the distinction was based on the fact that common law and equity were distinct systems of law, administered in separate courts. This separate administration of the two systems was abolished well over a hundred years ago, so that both are now administered in the same courts. Even so, the distinction remains of considerable importance to an understanding of the law of contract. Although generalisations on the point are hazardous, it is broadly speaking true that equity often takes a less rigid or literal approach than the common law to contract problems; that it pays greater regard to substance than to form; and that it often provides more satisfactory remedies than those available at common law. Differences between the common law and equitable approaches to contract problems will therefore have to be discussed at many points in the following chapters.

Chapter 2

Agreement

This chapter is concerned with the process by which the parties to a contract reach agreement. Generally, that process can be analysed into the acceptance by one party of an offer made by another. For example, A may offer to sell B 20 tons of coal for £500; and when B says 'I accept' (or uses words to that effect) a contract is concluded. In practice, the course of contractual negotiations is often much more complex than this. When parties begin to negotiate there may be considerable differences between them as to price, quantity, quality, delivery dates, terms of credit and so forth. Gradually, by a series of concessions, they move towards agreement, and it is often hard to say just when an offer has been accepted. For the purpose of answering this question, the law distinguishes between various steps or stages in negotiations.

1   OFFER AND INVITATION TO TREAT

An offer is a statement to the effect that the person making it (the offeror) is willing to contract on the terms stated, as soon as these are accepted by the person to whom the statement is addressed (the offeree). The offer may be made to one person, or to a group of persons, or to the public at large; it may be made expressly or by conduct. Under the objective test,[1] A's words or conduct can constitute an offer if they induce B reasonably to believe that A intended to make an offer to him, even though A actually had no such intention: for example, where a university offered a place to an intending student as a result of a clerical error.[2] Even failure to act may occasionally amount to an offer: for example, failure to assert a right or remedy may amount to an offer to abandon it.[3] But inactivity is likely to have this effect only when combined with other circumstances indicating

---

1   Ante, p 2.
2   *Moran v University College Salford (No 2)* [1994] ELR 187, CA.
3   *The Splendid Sun* [1981] QB 694 (see now Arbitration Act 1996, s 41(3)); *Collin v Duke of Westminster* [1985] QB 581.

that A has the necessary intention: inactivity *alone* is usually too equivocal to give B reasonable grounds for thinking that A is making an offer to him.[4]

The essential feature of an offer is that the person making it must (actually or objectively) intend to be bound without further negotiation, by a simple acceptance of his terms. Thus there is no offer where the owner of a house, in response to an enquiry from a person who wishes to buy it, states the price at which he might be prepared to sell;[5] nor even where the owner wishes to sell and invites offers at or about a specified price. In the latter case he is said to make an 'invitation to treat', and he is not bound to accept the highest or any other offer. This is also the position where a prospective customer asks a supplier whether he can supply goods suitable for the customer's needs.[6] In border-line cases it is obviously hard to determine with what intention the statement was made; but the difficulty is mitigated in two ways. First, it is enough to show that the statement was reasonably understood by the person to whom it was addressed as indicating an intention to be bound; and secondly, the character of certain frequently-recurring types of statements is settled by rules of law, at any rate in the absence of clear evidence of contrary intention.

Thus it is generally accepted in England that a display of price-marked goods in a shop-window, or on the shelves of a self-service shop, is usually no more than an invitation to treat.[7] The offer in such a case comes from the customer; and where a supplier of goods indicates their availability on a website the offer (if any) is likewise made by the customer.[8] Likewise, advertisements in newspapers or in trade circulars are commonly held not to amount to offers.[9] These rules may apply even though the person making the statement calls it an offer: a shop's 'special offer' may well be nothing more than an invitation to treat. But it should not be supposed that all displays and advertisements are only invitations to treat. They can be offers if the intention to be bound is sufficiently clear: for example, where a notice in a shop window stated that 'we will beat any TV ... price by £20 on the spot'.[10] A notice displayed at the entrance to an automatic car

---

4   *The Hannah Blumenthal* [1983] 1 AC 854; *The Leonidas D* [1985] 2 All ER 796; *The Agrabele* [1987] 2 Lloyd's Rep 223; *The Antclizo* [1988] 2 All ER 513.
5   *Gibson v Manchester City Council* [1979] 1 All ER 972; *Michael Gerson (Leasing) Ltd v Wilkinson* [2001] QB 514 at 530.
6   *Interfoto Picture Library Ltd v Stiletto Visual Programmes Ltd* [1989] QB 433 at 446.
7   *Pharmaceutical Society of Great Britain v Boots Cash Chemists (Southern) Ltd* [1953] 1 QB 401.
8   See below, p 11; cf Electronic Commerce (EC Directive) Regulations 2002, SI 2002/2013, reg 12.
9   *Partridge v Crittenden* [1968] 2 All ER 421.
10   *R v Warwickshire County Council, ex p Johnson* [1993] AC 583 at 588.

park has likewise been described as an offer, presumably because no further act of acceptance on the part of the proprietor was contemplated after the customer had driven in.[11] Similar reasoning seems to apply to the sale of petrol at a self-service filling station; the view that the offer comes from the customer[12] seems to be based on the now uncommon situation in which he is served by a forecourt attendant. Advertisements of rewards for the return of lost property are likewise regarded as offers since they do not envisage further bargaining. For the same reason, advertisements of rewards for the return of (for example) lost property are commonly held to be offers. Similarly, in *Carlill v Carbolic Smoke Ball Co*[13] manufacturers of 'carbolic smoke balls' stated in an advertisement that they would pay £100 to any person who caught influenza after using the appliance as directed, and that they had deposited £1000 with a named bank 'shewing our sincerity in the matter'. It was held that the advertisement was an offer. Certain advertisements relating to the sale or supply of goods can also give rise to liability under legislation for the protection of consumers.[14]

It is a common commercial practice to ask for 'tenders' for the purchase or sale of goods, or for the supply of services. In this situation, the person asking for tenders normally makes an invitation to treat; the offer comes from the person making the tender. The person to whom a tender is made is normally free to accept or reject it as he pleases.[15] These general rules are, however, qualified in a number of ways. First, the invitation for tenders may indicate that the best tender will be accepted: the invitation will then be an offer and the best tender which complies with its terms will amount to an acceptance, giving rise to a contract.[16] Secondly, the terms of the invitation may bind the person making it at least to consider (though not to accept) such a tender.[17] Thirdly, in the case of tenders for certain public works, the freedom of the body seeking the tenders is restricted by legislation, the object of which is to prevent unfair discrimination in the award of such contracts between contractors from member states of the European Union.[18]

---

11 *Thornton v Shoe Lane Parking Ltd* [1971] 2 QB 163 at 169.
12 *Esso Petroleum Ltd v Customs and Excise Comrs* [1976] 1 WLR 1 at 5, 6, 11.
13 [1893] 1 QB 256.
14 Under consumer guarantees: Sale and Supply of Goods to Consumers Regulations 2002, SI 2002/3045, reg 15; and under implied terms in the contract of sale: Sale of Goods Act 1979, s 14(2D).
15 See *Spencer v Harding* (1870) LR 5 CP 561; *William Lacey (Hounslow) Ltd v Davis* [1957] 1 WLR 932 at 939.
16 *Harvela Investments Ltd v Royal Trust Co of Canada (CI) Ltd* [1986] AC 207.
17 *Blackpool and Fylde Aero Club Ltd v Blackpool Borough Council* [1990] 3 All ER 25.
18 SI 1991/2679; SI 1991/2680; SI 1992/3279; SI 2000/2009.

In the case of auction sales, no offer for sale is made by the advertisement of the auction;[19] nor by putting the goods up for bidding. The offer is made by the bidder and accepted by the auctioneer in the customary manner, ie usually by the 'fall of the hammer'.[20] Even where the auction is expressly said to be 'without reserve', there is no contract of *sale* if the auctioneer refuses to knock the goods down to the highest bidder; though in such a case the auctioneer is liable for breach of a separate undertaking that the auction was to be without reserve.[1]

In contracts for the carriage of passengers, many views have been expressed on the question when and by whom the offer is made. At one extreme, a railway time-table has been held to be an offer;[2] and it has been suggested that the act of running a bus constitutes an offer to intending passengers.[3] Another view is that the carrier does not make the offer until he issues the ticket, and that the contract is made when the passenger keeps the ticket without objection,[4] or when he claims his seat.[5] Where a booking is made in advance, the offer may come from the passenger, for it has been said that the contract is made as soon as the carrier 'accepts' the booking,[6] or when he issues the ticket.[7] There is no single rule: the time when the contract is made depends in each case on the wording of the relevant document and on the circumstances in which it was issued.

2   ACCEPTANCE AND COUNTER-OFFER

Assuming that an offer has been made, a contract comes into existence when the offer is accepted. To accept an offer, the offeree must indicate his assent to the terms of the offer. He may do this either expressly (by words of acceptance) or by conduct. An 'acknowledgement' of an offer does not amount to an acceptance if it amounts merely to a confirmation that the offer has been received; but it can amount to an acceptance if by its terms or in a particular context (eg in website

---

19   *Harris v Nickerson* (1873) LR 8 QB 286.
20   Sale of Goods Act 1979, s 57(2).
1   *Warlow v Harrison* (1859) 1 E & E 309; *Barry v Heathcote Ball & Co (Commercial Auctions) Ltd* [2001] 1 All ER 944.
2   *Denton v Great Northern Rly Co* (1856) 5 E & B 860.
3   *Wilkie v London Passenger Transport Board* [1947] 1 All ER 258 at 259.
4   *Thornton v Shoe Lane Parking Ltd* [1971] 2 QB 163 at 169.
5   *MacRobertson Miller Airline Services v Comr of State Taxation of State of Western Australia* (1975) 8 ALR 131.
6   *The Eagle* [1977] 2 Lloyd's Rep 70.
7   *Dillon v Baltic Shipping Co* [1991] 2 Lloyd's Rep 155 at 159, revsd on other grounds (1993) 176 CLR 344.

trading) it means that the person making it has agreed to the terms of the offer.[8]

In most cases, the acceptance, no less than the offer, contains a promise. The contract is then said to be a *bilateral* one, that is, one under which each party undertakes obligations: for example one party agrees to deliver goods and the other to accept and to pay for them. There may also be a *unilateral* contract, under which only one party comes under an obligation. The stock examples are a promise by A to pay £100 to B, if B walks from London to York; or one to pay B £100 if he refrains from smoking until he is 21. Here, only A undertakes an obligation: B does not promise to do, or to refrain from doing, anything.

The most important rule with regard to an acceptance is that it must correspond with the offer. If it seeks to qualify or to vary the offer, it is ineffective as an acceptance: for example, an offer to sell 1,200 tons of iron is not accepted by a reply stating that the offeree will take 800 tons.[9] Trivial variation between the terms of the offer and acceptance may be disregarded; and the same is true of variations which merely make express a term which the law would in any event imply.[10] Subject to these qualifications, a purported acceptance which introduces different terms is not in law an acceptance but a counter-offer. As such it may have two legal consequences. First, it rejects the original offer, so that the original offeree cannot then accept it: eg, in the above example by a further letter purporting to accept the offer to sell 1,200 tons. Secondly, it amounts to a fresh offer, which the original offeror (who has now become the offeree under the counter-offer) may accept. A counter-offer may be followed by a further communication of the same character; and complicated negotiations may take the form of a long series of counter-offers, alleged to have culminated in a concluded agreement when one of the counter-offers is finally accepted without, or with only trivial, variations. In such a situation, the court must look at the whole course of the negotiations[11] to determine whether, and, if so, exactly when the parties have reached agreement.

The rules relating to counter-offers are particularly important in the situation, known as the 'battle of forms', in which each party sends the other a previously prepared form containing the terms on which he is prepared to contract. For example, a buyer offers to buy goods

8   Electronic Communications (EC Directive) Regulations 2002, SI 2002/2013, reg 11 seems to use 'acknowledgement' in this sense.
9   *Tinn v Hoffman & Co* (1873) 29 LT 271.
10 *Lark v Outhwaite* [1991] 2 Lloyd's Rep 132 at 139.
11 *Hussey v Horney-Payne* (1879) 4 App Cas 311.

on the terms of his 'purchase form' and the seller purports to accept the offer on the terms of his 'sales form'. If, as is probable, the terms of the forms differ (since the one is drafted in the buyer's, and the other in the seller's, interest) there is at this stage no contract. All that has happened is that the seller has made a counter-offer. This counter-offer may be accepted by conduct when the buyer takes delivery of the goods. In that event, there will be a contract on the terms of the seller's form.[12] On the other hand, the contract would be on the buyer's terms if the original offer had come from the seller, and had been followed by a buyer's counter-offer which had in turn been accepted by the conduct of the seller. Thus victory in the 'battle of forms' normally goes to the party who fires the last shot, ie to the party by whom the last form in the series is despatched. But this is not invariably true; for if that party has, in his own last communication, indicated his acceptance of the terms stated in the other party's form, the contract will be made on those terms.[13]

3   COMMUNICATION OF ACCEPTANCE

As a general rule, an acceptance has no effect unless and until it is communicated to the offeror.[14] This means that the fact of acceptance must be brought to the notice of the offeror. If the words of acceptance are 'drowned by an aircraft flying overhead', or spoken into a telephone which has gone dead, there is no contract.[15] The reason for this rule is that it might be unjust to the offeror to hold him bound if he did not know that his offer had been accepted. On the other hand, no injustice is normally caused to the offeree by holding that there is no contract. In the cases put, he knows at once that there has been a failure of communication, so that he can take steps to retrieve the situation by making a second attempt to communicate the acceptance. For the purpose of the present rule, the acceptance need not be communicated to the offeror personally. It is sufficient to communicate it to an agent authorised to receive it, such as a company's senior official. Obviously, leaving a message with a porter would not suffice.

---

12   See *British Road Services Ltd v V Crutchley & Co Ltd* [1967] 2 All ER 785 at 787 and [1968] 1 All ER 811 at 817.
13   *Butler Machine Tool Co Ltd v Ex-Cell-O Corpn (England) Ltd* [1979] 1 All ER 965.
14   *Brogden v Metropolitan Rly* (1877) 2 App Cas 666; *Brinkibon Ltd v Stahag Stahl und Stahlwarenhandelsgesellschaft mbH* [1983] 2 AC 34.
15   *Entores Ltd v Miles Far East Corpn* [1955] 2 QB 327 at 333.

There are three exceptions to the general rule that an acceptance must actually be communicated. The first is that there may be a contract when the failure in communication is in some sense due to the fault, or at any rate to the act or omission, of the offeror himself.[16] This would be the position if the offeror did not hear words of acceptance spoken into a telephone simply because, at the crucial point, he had put the telephone down without telling the offeree that he was doing this. The second exception arises where the terms of the offer expressly, or by implication, dispense with communication of acceptance. This is often the position where the offer invites acceptance by conduct. For example the contract which arises between the issuer of a credit card and a retailer to whom the card is presented by a customer is made when the retailer deals with the customer, even though the retailer has not at this stage communicated with the issuer of the card.[17] And where goods are ordered from a supplier, it may be that the offer to buy can be accepted by simply despatching the goods.[18] The third exception relates to acceptances sent through the post. This is a complex subject calling for separate treatment.

4   POSTAL ACCEPTANCE

There are many possible answers to the question when an acceptance sent by post should become operative. At the one extreme, it is possible to take the view that such an acceptance should take effect only when it is actually brought to the notice of the offeror; at the other extreme, there is the view that such an acceptance should take effect as soon as it is posted. Intermediate possibilities are that the acceptance should take effect when it is delivered to the offeror's address, or when it should have arrived there in the ordinary course of post. Any view can give rise to the possibility of some hardship to one or other of the parties, especially where the acceptance is lost or delayed in the post. If the contract is complete on posting, the offeror may be bound before he knows of the acceptance; and this result may be justified by saying that he takes the risk of being placed in such a position by initiating negotiations through the medium of the post. But when it is recalled that a contract may result from a lengthy sequence of counter-offers leading in the end to an acceptance, it will be obvious that the final offeror is not necessarily the person who has initiated the negotiations. If, on the other hand, the contract is not complete

16   *Entores Ltd v Miles Far East Corpn* [1955] 2 QB 327 at 333.
17   *First Sport Ltd v Barclays Bank plc* [1993] 3 All ER 789 at 794.
18   *The Kurnia Dewi* [1997] 1 Lloyd's Rep 553 at 559.

till the acceptance reaches the offeror, then the offeree will find it hard to know exactly when he can rely on having secured a firm contract. There is no way of reconciling these interests. The choice between the various solutions is an arbitrary one and can only be justified on grounds of convenience. Even this justification inevitably takes the point of view of one or other party. English law looks primarily to the convenience of the offeree, and this is best served by holding that the acceptance takes effect as soon as it is posted,[19] for if the letter of acceptance goes astray or is delayed the offeree will usually not know this until it is too late to make a further communication. Where 'instantaneous' means of communications, such as the telephone, telex, fax, email or website trading,[20] are used the rule will not apply if the failure in communication is such that the offeree knows of it in time to retrieve the situation (eg if a telephone goes dead in the course of negotiations);[1] but it should apply where he has no such knowledge or means of knowledge (eg if a faxed acceptance reaches the offeror in a partly illegible form).

The rule with respect to posted acceptances is subject to a number of commonsense limitations. In the first place, it must be reasonable in all the circumstances to use the post.[2] Obviously it would not be reasonable to reply by second class mail to a telexed offer, or to send an acceptance by post on the eve of a postal strike. Secondly, the general rule presupposes that the letter of acceptance is properly addressed and stamped. If this is not the case, any loss due to resulting delay should fall on the party who is responsible for the defect in the communication. This will normally be the offeree; but it may be the offeror: for example, where he sends out an offer in which he fails to give his own correct or complete address. Finally, the general rule can be excluded by the terms of the offer, which may require the acceptance to be actually communicated to the offeror, or at least to be delivered at his address.[3]

Where the general rule does apply, it leads to a number of practical consequences. The first, and by far the most important, is to curtail

---

19   *Adams v Lindsell* (1818) 1 B & Ald 681; *Henthorn v Fraser* [1892] 2 Ch 27 at 33; *Bruner v Moore* [1904] 1 Ch 305 (telegram, now replaced for inland purposes by telemessage).
20   Electronic Commerce (EC Directive) Regulations 2002, SI 2002/2013, reg 11(2)(a) states that such communications are 'received' when the addressee is 'able to access' them; but this does not necessarily answer the question when the contract is concluded.
1   *Entores Ltd v Miles Far East Corpn* [1955] 2 QB 327; *Brinkibon Ltd v Stahag Stahl und Stahlwarenhandelsgesellschaft mbH* [1983] 2 AC 34.
2   *Henthorn v Fraser* [1892] 2 Ch 27.
3   *Holwell Securities Ltd v Hughes* [1974] 1 All ER 161.

the offeror's power to withdraw his offer. The posting of an acceptance concludes the contract even though, after the acceptance has been posted but before it has reached the offeror, he communicates a withdrawal of the offer to the offeree; and even though, before the acceptance was posted, the offeror had posted a withdrawal which had not yet reached the offeree when the latter posted the acceptance.[4] The second consequence of the rule is to put the risk of accidents in the post on the offeror: thus there is a good contract although the acceptance is delayed in the post;[5] and the same is true even if it is lost in the post, so that it never reaches the offeror at all.[6] This is perhaps the case in which the 'posted acceptance' rule can cause the greatest hardship to the offeror; but to hold that there was no contract could cause equal hardship to the offeree, if he had acted in reliance on his posted acceptance. Thirdly, the contract is taken to have been made at the time of posting:[7] this may be important in order to determine the priority of two or more competing claimants each of whom has made a contract affecting the same subject-matter.

It should not be supposed that the 'posted acceptance' rule necessarily applies in all situations to which it could logically be applied. The rule will not be applied where it would lead to 'manifest inconvenience and absurdity':[8] in each new situation the question must be asked whether the rule produces, on balance, a convenient result.[9] This is the test which should be applied to the difficult question whether a posted acceptance can be revoked by the offeree, if he manages actually to communicate the revocation to the offeror before the latter has received the acceptance. One view is that the offeree should be allowed to do this, since the offeror cannot have acted in reliance on an acceptance of which he is as yet unaware. Another view is that, just as the posting of the acceptance curtails the offeror's power to withdraw the offer, so it should curtail the offeree's power to revoke his acceptance. For, if it did not have this effect, an offeree could, on a fluctuating market, post an acceptance and rely on it if the market moved in his favour; while he could revoke it later on the same day, if the market moved against him. Although the rule of convenience exists to protect the offeree, it does not seem that he should be allowed to exploit it in this way.

4   *Byrne & Co v Leon Van Tienhoven & Co* (1880) 5 CPD 344.
5   *Dunlop v Higgins* (1848) 1 HL Cas 381.
6   *Household Fire and Carriage Accident Insurance & Co v Grant* (1879) 4 Ex D 216.
7   *Potter v Sanders* (1846) 6 Hare 1.
8   *Holwell Securities Ltd v Hughes* [1974] 1 All ER 161 at 166.
9   *Brinkibon Ltd v Stahag Stahl und Stahlwarenhandelsgesellschaft mbH* [1983] 2 AC 34 at 41.

A contract for the supply of goods or services between a commercial seller or supplier and a consumer is, if made by (for example) exchange of letters or emails, a 'distance contract' for the purpose of Regulations[10] which give the consumer the 'right to cancel' such a contract by notice within a period specified in the Regulations. The contract, if so cancelled, is, as a general rule, 'treated as if it had not been made'.[11] But this rule is qualified in various ways;[12] and the very concept of the 'right to cancel' assumes that a contract has come into existence under the common law rules of offer and acceptance discussed above. Those rules also continue to govern the question whether the seller or supplier (who has no right to cancel) is bound by the contract.

Under the Vienna Convention on Contracts for the International Sale of Goods (which has not been ratified by the United Kingdom) an offer to enter into such a contract takes effect when it 'reaches' the offeree[13] and an acceptance when it 'reaches' the offeror,[14] ie when it is communicated to the addressee or delivered to his address.[15] Thus there is no contract if the acceptance is lost in the post; but if the acceptance is delayed in transmission, it is effective, unless the offeror informs the offeree promptly on its receipt that he regards the offer as having lapsed.[16] Once an offer has become effective, it cannot be revoked after the offeree had dispatched his acceptance.[17] An acceptance may be withdrawn by a communication which reaches the offeror before (or at the same time as) the acceptance would have become effective[18] if there had been no such withdrawal.

5   METHOD OF ACCEPTANCE PRESCRIBED BY OFFER

An offeror may in his offer expressly require the acceptance to be made in a certain way, eg by letter or telex. Prima facie, the offeree can then accept only in that way, as the offeror has made the requirement for his own protection; an attempt to accept it in some other way

10   Consumer Protection (Distance Selling) Regulations 2000, SI 2000/2334.
11   SI 2000/2334, reg 10(2).
12   See, eg SI 2000/2334, reg 13 (exceptions to right to cancel), reg 17 (restoration of goods to supplier).
13   Article 15(1).
14   Article 18(2)
15   Article 24.
16   Article 21(2).
17   Article 16(1); *cf* the English position stated ante, p 15 at n 4.
18   Article 22.

amounts at most to a counter-offer.[19] To this rule there are, however, two exceptions. First, an acceptance made in a different manner may be effective, if the matter actually adopted is no less efficacious from the offeror's point of view: ie if it is in every way as quick and reliable as the prescribed method.[20] Secondly, allowance must be made for the fact that an offer is often made on a form supplied by the offeree: for example where a customer submits an offer to enter into a hire-purchase agreement on a form provided by the finance company. Here the stipulation as to the manner of acceptance exists for the benefit of the offeree, so that the stipulation can be waived by him, at least so long as this does not prejudice the offeror.[1]

6 SILENCE AS ACCEPTANCE

An offer may stipulate that it can be accepted by silence. If the offeree makes no response to such an offer, the general rule is that he is not bound. For example, A may write to B offering to buy B's car, and adding: 'If I hear no more about it, I shall consider it mine.' There is no contract if B simply ignores the letter.[2] It would obviously be undesirable to enable A to force a contract on B by ultimatum, or to oblige B to take the trouble of rejecting an unsolicited offer. It is by no means equally obvious that, in the above situation, A should not be bound if B has acted in reliance on the offer: for example, if B has turned away another offer to buy the car, thinking that he had a contract with A. If A stood by, knowing that B was about to act in this way in reliance on the offer, he might be estopped from denying that there was a contract.[3]

The rule that there can be no acceptance by 'silence' does not mean that it is always necessary to communicate *words* of acceptance to the offeror. An acceptance may be inferred from the conduct of the offeree, and communication of acceptance may be dispensed with.[4] The acceptance is then said to be by conduct rather than by silence.[5] 'Conduct' here refers to some action on the part of the offeree, so

19 *Wettern Electric Ltd v Welsh Development Agency* [1983] QB 796.
20 *Manchester Diocesan Council for Education v Commercial and General Investments Ltd* [1970] 1 WLR 241.
1 *Carlyle Finance Ltd v Pallas Industrial Finance* [1999] 1 All ER (Comm) 659 at 670.
2 *Felthouse v Bindley*(1862) 11 CBNS 869, (1863) 1 New Rep 401.
3 *Spiro v Lintern* [1973] 1 WLR 1002 at 1011; but see *Fairline Shipping Corpn v Adamson* [1975] QB 180 at 189; for estoppel cf post, p 168.
4 Ante, p. 13.
5 *Roberts v Hayward* (1828) 3 C & P 432.

that mere inaction is not normally sufficient. It can amount to an acceptance only 'in the most exceptional circumstances:'[6] eg where a 'duty to speak'[7] was imposed on the offeree because he had begun the negotiations by soliciting the offer and then failed to reply to it in circumstances leading the offeror reasonably to believe that the offer had been accepted.[8]

7   ACCEPTANCE REQUIRES KNOWLEDGE OF OFFER

A person may do an act which appears to amount to acceptance of an offer but be unaware of the offer: for example, he may give information for which a reward has been advertised without knowing of the advertisement. In such a case there is no agreement, and hence no contract. On the other hand, an act done with knowledge of the offer can amount to an acceptance even though it was done primarily with some motive other than that of claiming the reward. Thus, in *Carlill v Carbolic Smoke Ball Co*,[9] the plaintiff recovered the £100, although she presumably did not use the smoke ball with this aim in view, but rather to stave off the various diseases against which the appliance was meant to give protection.

One application of the rule, that a person can accept an offer only if he knows of it, is also said to apply in cases of so-called identical cross-offers. If A writes to B offering to buy B's car for £5,000 and by the same post B writes to A offering to sell the car for £5,000 there is, it is said, no contract.[10] Yet it could be argued that A and B were in agreement; and the probable reason for the rule is that parties to such a correspondence would be left in some degree of uncertainty. This is best resolved by some further communication between them.

8   UNILATERAL CONTRACTS

In the case of a bilateral contract, acceptance of the offer normally takes the form of a counter-promise from the offeree (though this

---

6   *The Leonidas D* [1985] 2 All ER 796 at 805; *Vitol SA v Norelf Ltd* [1996] AC 800 at 812; so far as contra, *The Golden Bear* [1987] 1 Lloyd's Rep 330 is open to doubt.

7   *Rafsanjan Pistachio Producers Co-operative v Bank Leumi (UK) plc* [1993] 1 Lloyd's Rep 513 at 542.

8   *Rust v Abbey Life Assurance Co Ltd* [1979] 2 Lloyd's Rep 334 at 340; affd [1978] 2 Lloyd's Rep 386 at 393.

9   [1893] 1 QB 256, ante, p 9.

10   *Tinn v Hoffman & Co* (1873) 29 LT 271 at 278.

may be inferred from conduct), and the moment of acceptance is, as a general rule, that of the communication of the counter-promise. Where the contract is unilateral, however, there is no counter-promise. The person to whom £100 is promised if he walks from London to York, or forbears from smoking until he is 21, does not promise to do these things. He can, without breach of contract, give up walking or start smoking at any time after he has begun to engage in the required course of conduct. Hence it could be argued that the person who promised the £100 should likewise have the power to withdraw until the walk had been completed or the abstinence fully accomplished; and in support of this view it was said that there had been no acceptance until the terms of the promise had been fully performed. In some cases such a solution may indeed be in accordance with the intention of the parties and a perfectly fair one. It is, for example, sometimes possible to regard the contract by which a prospective seller of a house engages an estate agent as a unilateral one, by which the agent is to receive his commission if he effects a sale, without promising to do anything to that end.[11] In such a case it might be perfectly reasonable to allow the owner to revoke without liability, even if the agent had taken steps in performance, such as advertising the property. But the ground for this view would be that such a result was in accordance with the intention of the parties, and not that the contract was unilateral: the position would be exactly the same where the agent *had* made some promise (eg to use his best endeavours to effect a sale, or to advertise the property at his own expense[12]), so that the contract would be bilateral. More generally, in the case of a unilateral contract, the parties' intention would not be to allow the promisor to revoke without liability after part-performance by the promisee (eg walking as far as Doncaster); and the general view is that the offer of a unilateral contract cannot be revoked after part-performance by the promisee.[13] This view, however, presupposes that the contract is simply one to pay a lump sum for the performance of the act. It may also amount to a promise to make a number of payments in response to each of a series of acts; and the promise is then revocable, in the sense that the promisor can escape liability in respect of acts done after (but not before) revocation. This possibility is illustrated by so-called

11 See *Luxor (Eastbourne) Ltd v Cooper* [1941] AC 108 at 124.
12 *E Christopher & Co v Essig* [1948] WN 461; *John McCann & Co v Pow* [1974] 1 WLR 1643 at 1647; cf *Bentall, Horsley and Baldry v Vicary* [1931] 1 KB 253.
13 See *Errington v Errington and Woods* [1952] 1 KB 290 at 295; *Daulia Ltd v Four Millbank Nominees Ltd* [1978] Ch 231 at 238; *Harvela Investments Ltd v Royal Trust Co of Canada (CI) Ltd* [1986] AC 207 at 224.

continuing guarantees.[14] These are contracts by which A promises B to guarantee liabilities which C may incur to B. The contract between A and B is unilateral since B does not promise A to give credit to C. If the guarantee is in respect of a single transaction between B and C it is 'indivisible' and A cannot withdraw after B has begun to give credit to C. But if the guarantee is 'divisible', ie given in respect of a series of loans each of which is a separate transaction, then A can revoke it with respect to loans made by B after notice of revocation.

9   TERMINATION OF OFFER

Events may occur after an offer has been made which bring it to an end so that it can no longer be accepted. This happens when the offer is withdrawn by the offeror, or rejected by the offeree; and it may happen by lapse of time, by the occurrence of a condition, or by the death or supervening incapacity of one of the parties.

a   Withdrawal

An offeror may withdraw his offer at any time before the offeree has accepted it.[15] This is so even though the offer expressly states that it will be left open for a fixed time. Generally such a statement is (as we shall see in the next chapter) a promise without consideration and it therefore does not bind the offeror.[16]

The law does, however, limit the offeror's power to withdraw his offer, by insisting that the withdrawal must be communicated to the offeree. Thus if A has offered to sell his car to B, he cannot withdraw the offer simply by changing his mind or by selling the car to C: B must have notice of the withdrawal. B may not actually be able to get the car (if it has in the meanwhile been delivered to C); but if B accepts A's offer before its withdrawal has been communicated to him, he is entitled to damages for breach of contract against A. For the purpose of the present rule, the notice of withdrawal must, as a general rule, actually reach the offeree's address. Once this happens, the withdrawal takes effect, even though the offeree does not actually read it, at least if it arrives during business hours.[17] But a mere posting of the withdrawal is not enough.

14   See *Offord v Davies* (1862) 12 CBNS 748; *Lloyd's v Harper* (1880) 16 Ch D 290.
15   *Offord v Davies* (1862) 12 CBNS 748.
16   *Dickinson v Dodds* (1876) 2 Ch D 463; for criticism, see post, p 56; for exceptions, see Companies Act 1985, s 87(2); Vienna Convention (ante, p 16), art 16(2).
17   Cf *The Brimnes* [1975] QB 929.

Thus, if A posts a withdrawal, and B then posts an acceptance before the withdrawal has reached him, there is a contract between A and B.[18] This is so, even though there may never have been any agreement between them. The rule is an important one: if it did not exist, no offeree could safely act in reliance on his acceptance of an offer; for the possibility that a withdrawal was in the post could not be ruled out. So long as the withdrawal is communicated *to the offeree*, it need not, however, be communicated *by the offeror*. It suffices if the offeree gets to know from a reliable source that the offeror no longer intends to deal with him on the terms of the offer.[19]

In some exceptional cases, a withdrawal may be effective even though it is neither actually communicated to the offeree, nor delivered to his address. For example, a withdrawal delivered to the offeree's last known address would probably be effective if he had moved without notifying the offeror. And where an offer is made by public advertisement, a withdrawal is probably effective if it is published in such a way that it is reasonably likely to come to the attention of those who saw the original advertisement.[20]

b Rejection

Rejection terminates an offer, so that, once an offeree has rejected it, he cannot then change his mind and accept it. In this connection, it is important to recall that a counter-offer amounts to a rejection. Hence an offeree who makes a counter-offer thereby loses the power of accepting the original offer.[1] But an offer is not rejected by a mere enquiry whether the offeror would be prepared to depart from its terms. A distinction is drawn between a rejection (including a counter-offer) and a request for information.[2] For example, an offer to sell at a stated price would not be rejected by an enquiry whether the seller was prepared to give credit, or even whether he was prepared to reduce the price, so long as the enquiry was 'merely exploratory'.[3] The distinction between such a request or enquiry and a rejection depends on the intention of the offeree, as reasonably understood by the offeror.

It seems that a rejection does not take effect on posting, but only when it reaches the offeror. Until this happens, the offeree can still

---

18   *Byrne & Co v Leon Van Tienhoven & Co* (1880) 5 CPD 344.
19   *Dickinson v Dodds* (1876) 2 Ch D 463.
20   Cf *Shuey v US* 92 US 73 (1875).
1   *Hyde v Wrench* (1840) 3 Beav 334.
2   *Stevenson, Jaques & Co v McLean* (1880) 5 QBD 346.
3   *Gibson v Manchester City Council* [1979] 1 All ER 972 at 978.

accept, provided he does so by a communication which overtakes the posted rejection, eg by telephone. The offeror is not prejudiced by this rule, since a rejection gives him no rights and since he cannot act in reliance on it until he actually receives it.

c   Lapse

An offer may come to an end by lapse of time. If a time limit for acceptance is expressly stated in the offer, it cannot be accepted after that time. If no time is stated, the offer lapses at the end of a reasonable time. What is a reasonable time is a question of fact, depending on such circumstances as the nature of the subject-matter and the general market conditions in which the offer is made.[4]

d   Occurrence of condition

An offer may be so expressed as to come to an end on the occurrence of a condition: for example, where a tender to sell goods from time to time is made subject to the seller's being himself able to obtain adequate supplies. Where an offer is made to buy goods, there is an implied term to the effect that it cannot be accepted after the goods have been seriously damaged.[5]

e   Death and incapacity

One possible view is that an offer cannot be accepted after the death of either party, since the fact of death makes it impossible for them to reach agreement. But the strict application of such a rule might cause hardship. Suppose that A makes a continuing offer to B, to guarantee loans to be made by B to C. If A dies and B in ignorance of this fact makes a further loan to C, he might well be prejudiced by a rule that A's death automatically terminated the offer, and it seems that in such a situation B is entitled to sue A's estate on the guarantee.[6] It is always open to A's personal representatives to terminate the offer by giving notice of withdrawal in the ordinary way. Similarly, there seems to be no reason why an offer should necessarily be brought to an end by the death of the offeree, since acceptance by the personal representatives of the offeree would not normally prejudice the offeror. Of course

---

4   *Ramsgate Victoria Hotel Co v Montefiore* (1866) LR 1 Exch 109.
5   *Financings Ltd v Stimson* (1962) 3 All ER 386.
6   See *Coulthart v Clementson* (1879) 5 QBD 42 at 46.

there are certain contracts which are 'personal' in the sense that they would be terminated by the death of either party: for example, contracts of personal service.[7] Offers to enter into such contracts are terminated by the death of either party.

Supervening incapacity may be involuntary, as where one of the parties becomes mentally ill. The question whether an acceptance made after this had happened bound either party, would depend on the general rules governing contracts with mental patients.[8] Supervening incapacity may also be voluntary, as where a company changes its objects so that the contract to which the offer relates is no longer within the powers of the company.[9] Where the company is incorporated under the Companies Act 1985, contracts which fall outside those objects or outside the power of its board of directors are, in general, nevertheless effective in favour of a person who deals with the company in good faith.[10] But a member of the company can bring an action to restrain it from doing an act beyond its capacity.[11] Hence if an offer had been made to the company and it had then changed its objects so that the resulting contract would be beyond its powers, a member could bring an action to restrain the company from accepting the offer. But such an action does not lie to restrain the company from fulfilling legal obligations arising from acts of the company previous to the change of objects.[12] The member's remedy seems therefore not to be available where it is the company which makes an offer and the offer is then accepted after the company had changed its objects so as to put the resulting contract beyond its powers. The company can of course withdraw the offer before acceptance unless it has bound itself not to do so by granting a binding option.[13] Where a corporation is created by Royal Charter, its contractual capacity is not limited by the terms of the Charter, so that alteration of those terms would not affect the legal effects of offers made by or to the corporation.[14] Where a corporation is created by special statute, contracts not authorised by that statute are *ultra vires* and void.[15] Its contractual capacity can be reduced by changes in that statute; and such a change can therefore terminate offers made by or to the company to enter into a contract of the kind in question. Limited

7   See post, p 352.
8   See post, p 234.
9   See post, p 237.
10   Companies Act 1985, ss 35(1) and 35A(1); post, pp 237–238.
11   Companies Act 1985, ss 35(2) and (4); post, p 238.
12   Companies Act 1985, ss 35(2) and (4); post, p 238.
13   Post, p 56.
14   Post, p 235.
15   Post, p 236.

liability partnerships incorporated under the Limited Liability Partnerships Act 2000 are bodies corporate;[16] but problems of the kind discussed above cannot arise with regard to them as they have 'unlimited capacity'.[17]

10 NO IDENTIFIABLE OFFER AND ACCEPTANCE

In certain exceptional situations, there is undoubtedly a contract, but the process of reaching agreements cannot readily be analysed into the normal stages of offer and acceptance.[18] For example, the parties may negotiate through the same broker who eventually obtains their consent to the same terms. Here it is very hard to say which of them has made the offer and which the acceptance.[19] Again, it has been held that the competitors in a regatta enter into a contract, not only with the club which organises the race, but also with each other, to the effect that each will abide by the regatta rules.[20] In this situation, too, it is far from clear exactly when each competitor makes his offer to the others and when that offer is accepted.

11 VAGUE OR INCOMPLETE AGREEMENTS

So far, we have been concerned with what may be called the mechanics of agreement. Even where the rules relating to offer and acceptance are complied with, the agreement may still suffer from defects, making it impossible or very difficult for the courts to determine on exactly what terms the parties were agreed. The task of the courts in this area is a delicate one. They do not, on the one hand, want to impose on the parties terms to which they never agreed, or, as it is put, to 'make a contract for the parties'. On the other hand, they will often do their best to uphold loosely worded agreements. They recognise that businessmen often do not have the time to work out the terms of their agreements in meticulous detail; and that it may be desirable to avoid too much precision and rigidity in commercial agreements, if these are to stand up to the stresses of changing economic circumstances.

---

16   See Limited Liability Partnerships Act 2000, s 1(2).
17   Section 1(3).
18   *New Zealand Shipping Co Ltd v A M Satterthwaite & Co Ltd* [1975] AC 154 at 167; *Gibson v Manchester City Council* [1979] 1 WLR 294 at 297.
19   *Pagnan SpA v Feed Products Ltd* [1987] 2 Lloyd's Rep 601 at 616.
20   *The Satanita* [1895] P 248; affd sub nom *Clarke v Dunraven* [1897] AC 59.

It is common to find in commercial contracts references to 'fair quality' or to terms which are 'usual' in the course of business at a particular place. Such vague terms do not necessarily vitiate the contract: their want of precision may be made good by reference to any relevant trade custom or to the standard of reasonableness.[1] So long as there are 'objective criteria by which the court could assess what would be reasonable',[2] this standard can be applied even to fill gaps on which the contract is completely silent. For example an agreement for the sale or for the supply of goods may amount to a contract even though no price is agreed: in that event, a reasonable price must be paid.[3] On the other hand, failure to agree on such an important point as the amount to be paid may indicate that there was no concluded contract.[4] Even where this is the case, a party doing work under the agreement may be entitled to a reasonable recompense;[5] but, as there is no contract, he would not be liable in damages, eg for delay in doing the work.[6]

Where a contract contains vague or meaningless provisions on matters which are not considered to be of vital importance, those provisions can be ignored and the rest of the contract enforced. But if the vague provisions relate to a vital matter and cannot be resolved in any of the ways described above, there is no contract. This was, for example, held to be the position in a case in which an agreement was made to supply a van 'on hire-purchase terms':[7] an agreement in these terms cannot give rise to a contract if such vital matters as the amount of the deposit and the number of instalments are left unspecified.

Even greater difficulty arises where the parties are unable or unwilling to reach agreement on certain vital points and provide that these are to be settled by future agreement. When long-term contracts are made in times of fluctuating markets, it is natural to find the parties reluctant to bind themselves to fixed prices. But an agreement for the sale of goods 'at a price to be agreed' is in a sense more difficult to enforce than one which simply says nothing about the

1 *Hillas & Co Ltd v Arcos Ltd* (1932) 147 LT 503.
2 *Baird Textile Holdings Ltd v Marks & Spencer plc* [2001] EWCA Civ 274, [2002] 1 All ER (Comm) 737 at [30], where this requirement was not satisfied.
3 Sale of Goods Act 1979, s 8(2); Supply of Goods and Services Act 1982, s 15(1).
4 *Courtney and Fairbairn Ltd v Tolaini Bros (Hotels) Ltd* [1975] 1 All ER 716.
5 Post, p 421.
6 *British Steel Corpn v Cleveland Bridge and Engineering Co Ltd* [1984] 1 All ER 504.
7 *G Scammell and Nephew Ltd v Ouston* [1941] AC 251.

price. In the latter case, the courts can claim merely to be supplementing the agreement of the parties by determining the amount of the reasonable price which the buyer has to pay. In the former case they may be overriding the agreement, if they substitute their own notion of what was reasonable for a figure which the parties might have reached after further bargaining. Nevertheless, the courts will uphold such an agreement where it is clear that the parties intended to be bound by it[8] and they may do so even though so important a matter as the price is left to be decided by subsequent agreement.[9] But where the parties do not intend to be bound before they have agreed some vital outstanding point (such as the price) there is no contract before they have settled that point.[10] Their agreement at this stage is a mere agreement to negotiate or a 'contract to make a contract'; and in law such an agreement is 'too uncertain to have any binding force'.[11] Nor can this defect be cured by implying into the agreement a term to the effect that the parties will negotiate in good faith since such a term is itself too uncertain to be enforced.[12] The uncertainty lies in the fact that a duty to negotiate would be 'inherently inconsistent with the position of a negotiating party'[13] who must be free to advance his own interest; hence it is impossible in this context to define the requirements of 'good faith' with anything like precision.

Parties who cannot agree on all vital points at once may provide some machinery or standard for resolving such matters: eg they may say that prices or rents are to be fixed by reference to market values, or by arbitration, or by the decision of a designated third party, or even by the decision of one of the parties themselves, as where interest rates are left to be fixed by the lender.[14] Such agreements are binding, though they may be avoided if the agreed machinery breaks down: eg if the

---

8   *Pagnan SpA v Feed Products Ltd* [1987] 2 Lloyd's Rep 601.
9   *Foley v Classique Coaches Ltd* [1934] 2 KB 1; *Voest Alpine Intertrading GmbH v Chevron International Oil Co Ltd*[1987] 2 Lloyd's Rep 547; *Didymi Corpn v Atlantic Lines and Navigation Co Inc* [1988] 2 Lloyd's Rep 108 (price *adjustment* to be agreed); *Mamidoil Jetoil Greek Petroleum Co SA v Okta Crude Oil Refinery AD* [2001] EWCA Civ 406, [2001] 2 Lloyd's Rep 76 (price agreed for part of contract period).
10 Eg *May and Butcher Ltd v R* [1934] 2 KB 17n.
11 *Courtney and Fairbairn Ltd v Tolaini Bros (Hotels) Ltd* [1975] 1 All ER 716 at 720.
12 *Walford v Miles* [1992] 2 AC 128.
13 *Walford v Miles* [1992] 2 AC 128 at 138.
14 *Lombard Tricity Finance Ltd v Paton* [1989] 1 All ER 918; the lender must not exercise this power arbitrarily or capriciously: *Paragon Finance plc v Staunton* [2001] EWCA Civ 1466, [2001] 2 All ER (Comm) 1025 at [36].

third party fails to make the valuation.[15] However, if the agreed machinery is merely 'subsidiary and incidental'[16] its failure to operate is not fatal to the formation of a contract. In one such case, a party tried to defeat the agreed machinery by refusing to appoint a valuer. The House of Lords upheld the agreement, construing it as one to sell for a reasonable price which could be determined by the court itself.[17]

There is a further group of cases in which the parties may have reached agreement on all vital terms, but stipulate for the execution of some formal document. Such a stipulation may have a number of different purposes. First, it may be evidence of the intention of the parties not to be bound till the formal document is drawn up and duly executed.[18] This is the purpose of the stipulation commonly found in agreements for the sale of land that the agreement is 'subject to contract'. The normal[19] effect of this phrase is that neither party is bound until formal contracts are 'exchanged',[20] a process that may be completed by telephone.[1] Secondly, the purpose of the stipulation may simply be to provide written evidence of the conclusion of the contract and of its terms. In such a case, there is a good contract even though the formal document is not executed.[2] A third possible purpose of the stipulation is that the parties, having agreed on essentials, look to the formal document for the solution of points of detail which may be quite important, such as the delivery dates, precise technical specifications and terms of payment. At a time of increasing complexity in contractual relations, it is this third purpose which gives rise to the greatest difficulties and as to which the authorities provide no very clear guidance. Probably there are three factors on which the existence of a contract in these cases primarily depends: the intention of the parties, the degree of importance of the terms left to be settled by the formal document, and the extent to which the parties have acted on the informal agreement.[3]

---

15 Sale of Goods Act 1979, s 9(1).
16 *Re Malpass* [1985] Ch 42 at 50.
17 *Sudbrook Trading Estate Ltd v Eggleton* [1983] 1 AC 444.
18 Eg *British Steel Corpn v Cleveland Bridge and Engineering Co Ltd* [1984] 1 All ER 504.
19 Ie unless the contrary intention is made extremely clear, as in *Alpenstow Ltd v Regalian Properties plc* [1985] 2 All ER 545.
20 *Chillingworth v Esche* [1924] 1 Ch 97.
1   *Domb v Isoz* [1980] Ch 548.
2   *Rossiter v Miller* (1878) 3 App Cas 1124.
3   Eg *Pagnan SpA v Feed Products Ltd* [1987] 2 Lloyd's Rep 601; *G Percy Trentham Ltd v Archital Luxfer Ltd* [1993] 1 Lloyd's Rep 25; *The Gladys (No 2)* [1994] 2 Lloyd's Rep 401.

12 CONDITIONAL AGREEMENTS

The expression 'condition' is used in the law of contract in a confusing variety of senses, some of which are discussed later in this book.[4] At this point, we are concerned with a condition in the sense of an event on which the operation of the contract depends, but which neither party is bound to bring about. For example, a person may agree to buy a machine on condition that it proves, on trial, to have a stated capacity; or to buy a house on condition that he can raise a mortgage of a stated amount. In these cases the agreement is said to be subject to a *condition precedent*. The effect of such a condition depends upon its construction. It may mean that, until the event occurs, neither party is bound at all, so that each party is free to withdraw from the transaction without legal liability.[5] A second more common, interpretation would be that until the event occurred neither party was bound to render the principal performance promised by him (eg, to pay the price of goods, or to deliver them) but that, in the meantime he must not deliberately do anything to prevent the occurrence of the event: for example in the first case put above, neither must impede the trial of the machine.[6] It may even be that one party is bound to do his best to bring about the event without absolutely undertaking to do so: for example where goods are sold 'subject to export licence'. In such a case one of the parties (usually the exporter) will have to make reasonable efforts to obtain the licence; but if, in spite of his having done so, no licence is obtained, neither he nor the other party will be under any liability.[7] He will be liable only if the terms of the contract, on their true construction, amount to an absolute undertaking that a licence will be obtained.[8]

A contract may be subject to a *condition subsequent*, that is, it may come to an end when a future event occurs: for example, where a father contracts to pay his daughter an allowance 'until you marry'.

4   See post, pp 320, 327.
5   *Pym v Campbell* (1856) 6 E & B 370.
6   *Mackay v Dick* (1881) 6 App Cas 251.
7   *Re Anglo-Russian Merchant Traders* [1917] 2 KB 679.
8   As in *Pagnan SpA v Tradax Ocean Transportations SA* [1987] 3 All ER 565.

Chapter 3

Consideration

1 DEFINITION

Legal systems do not regard all agreements whatsoever as contracts. They use various devices of limiting the area of enforceable agreements: they may insist on the use of some formality, or on part performance, or on compliance with some other requirement. In English law, an agreement (even if made with the requisite contractual intention),[1] is not a contract unless it is *either* made in a deed *or* supported by some 'consideration'.

The doctrine of consideration is based on the idea of *reciprocity*: that a promisee should not be able to enforce the promise, unless he has given (or promised to give), or unless the promisor has obtained (or been promised), something in exchange for it. This idea underlies the often repeated judicial definition that consideration is a detriment to the promisee or a benefit to the promisor.[2] Only one limb of the definition needs to be satisfied: if there is a detriment to the promisee there is consideration, even though there is no benefit to the promisor; and conversely. In most cases the detriment to the promisee (eg parting with goods under a contract of sale) will also be the benefit to the promisor (ie receipt of the same goods).

Where the contract is bilateral, each party will both make and receive a promise. In such a case, it is the consideration *for each promise* that is under discussion: it is confusing and wrong to think of the consideration *for the contract.* Thus in the case of a contract for the sale of goods, the consideration for the buyer's promise to pay is the seller's promise to deliver the goods, or their actual delivery. This is a detriment to the seller, in that he will part with the goods; and for the purpose of the requirement of consideration, it is quite irrelevant whether he has sold the goods for more, or for less, than they are worth. The question whether he has suffered a detriment is, in other words, determined simply by looking at his performance, without

---

1 See Chapter 4, post.
2 Eg *Currie v Misa* (1875) LR 10 Exch 153, 162; *Midland Bank Trust Co Ltd v Green* [1981] AC 513 at 531.

regard to what he will receive in exchange when the buyer performs his promise to pay. Conversely, the consideration for the seller's promise to deliver is the buyer's promise to pay, or the payment of, the price. The detriment to the buyer is that he will part with his money: again, this is looked at in isolation, irrespective of the exchange which he receives for it.

2   GRATUITOUS AND ONEROUS PROMISES

The idea behind the doctrine of consideration being that of reciprocity, it follows that a gratuitous promise, such as a promise to make a gift to a charity for no return, is not supported by consideration. This does not mean that such a promise cannot be made legally enforceable. To produce this result, it is only necessary to make the promise in a deed. A document will take effect as a deed executed by an individual if it states on its face that it is intended to be a deed, and if it is signed, witnessed and delivered. Delivery here does not mean transfer of possession but merely conduct indicating that the signer intends to be bound by the deed. There is no longer any requirement of 'sealing'.[3] Similar rules apply to deeds executed by most companies.[4] It follows from the availability of these relatively simple formalities that it is only *informal* gratuitous promises which are not binding in English law, as a result of the doctrine of consideration. This fact should be stressed when comparing English law with other systems of law in which there is no doctrine of consideration, but in which gratuitous promises are nevertheless enforceable only if they are made in some special form, eg by a notarised writing.[5] The purpose of such requirements is to provide some safeguard against rash promises to make gifts.

The central idea of a gratuitous promise is easy enough to understand: it is a promise to make a gift, ie one to give or do something of value, for no return. To take the most obvious case, a promise by A to make a present of a car to B is a gratuitous promise; and so is a promise by A to lend B his car for one day without charge, or to give B a free lift from London to Edinburgh. If A goes back on any of these promises, B has in English law no right to damages for breach of contract. The position would be the same if A agreed to undertake

---

3   Law of Property (Miscellaneous Provisions) Act 1989, s 1(1)(b), (2) and (3).
4   Ie by those incorporated under the Companies Acts and under the Charities Acts: Companies Act 1985, s 36A(4); Charities Act 1993, ss 50, 60. For certain electronic documents as deeds, see Land Registration Act 2002, s 91(5) and (9).
5   See, for example, s 518 of the German Civil Code.

the safe-keeping of B's car without reward, or agreed (again without reward) to arrange to insure B's car.[6] If in the first of these cases A withdrew his promise before the car had come into his possession, or if in the second he simply forgot to insure the car, he would not be under any liability to B for breach of contract.[7] But if, instead of simply doing nothing to fulfil the gratuitous promise, A starts to perform it and in the course of so doing negligently causes loss to B, he may be liable to B under the law of tort. This would, for example, be the position where A promised to look after B's car, actually received it and then negligently damaged it,[8] or where he caused loss to B in the course of carelessly rendering some other gratuitous service;[9] but pure omissions do not generally give rise to any such liability in tort.[10] They may, indeed, exceptionally do so where the circumstances give rise to a 'duty to act';[11] but such a duty would not arise merely from the making of a gratuitous promise.

In the above examples, it is assumed that B makes no counter-promise. If he does make such a counter-promise there is usually no difficulty in finding consideration for both promises. Thus if A promised to lend B his car for a week, without charge, and in return B promised to wash the car, there would be a good contract binding both parties.[12] The situation, in which B's counter-promise is simply one not to complain of defects in A's performance, is discussed later in this chapter.[13]

3 BENEFIT AND DETRIMENT

The doctrine of consideration, however, does not prevent the enforcement of all informal promises which, on a commonsense view, are gratuitous; while, on the other hand, it has prevented the enforcement of some promises which are not in any very obvious sense gratuitous at all. The doctrine has from time to time served many different purposes, so that it is almost possible to regard it as a

6   *Argy Trading Development Co Ltd v Lapid Developments Ltd* [1977] 3 All ER 785.
7   *The Zephyr* [1985] 2 Lloyd's Rep 529 at 538.
8   *Coggs v Bernard* (1703) 2 Ld Raym 909; *Mitchell v Ealing London Borough* [1979] QB 1. For possible liability in tort to third parties for omissions, see *White v Jones* [1995] 2 AC 207 (post, p 252), but there the defendant's promise was not gratuitous.
9   *Wilkinson v Coverdale* (1793) 1 Esp 74.
10   *Outram v Academy Plastics* [2001] ICR 367 at 372.
11   *White v Jones* [1995] 2 AC 207 at 261, 268, 295; *Lennon v Metropolitan Police Commissioner* [2004] EWCA Civ 130, [2004] 2 All ER 266.
12   Cf *Bainbridge v Firmstone* (1838) 8 Ad & El 743.
13   See post, p 37.

collection of separate doctrines. The courts have used it as a substitute for other, imperfectly developed, doctrines; they were able to do this because of the essential vagueness of the twin notions of 'benefit' and 'detriment'. They have sometimes taken the view that any 'benefit' or 'detriment' *which could be detected by the court* was sufficient consideration, even though the person suffering the alleged 'detriment' may not have regarded it as such, but rather as a benefit. In one case, for example, a young man was held to have provided consideration for his uncle's promise to pay him an allowance by suffering the 'detriment' of marrying his fiancée.[14] This approach often makes it possible for the courts to 'find' or invent a consideration for a promise which would strike a layman as gratuitous. On the other hand, the courts have sometimes held that acts or promises, which are in fact benefits or detriments, should not be regarded as such in law, simply because the thing done or promised *was already legally due*. For example, the general rule (to be further discussed later in this chapter) is that part payment of a debt is no consideration for a promise by the creditor to forgo the balance. These different shades in the meaning of 'benefit' and 'detriment' make a comprehensive definition of 'consideration' impossible. The precise meaning, or meanings, of the term can be gathered only from a survey of the many varying situations in which it has been applied.

Promises which are not supported by consideration do not give rise to full contractual liability but may nevertheless have certain limited legal effects. The point has already been illustrated in our discussion of liability for defective performance of gratuitous services;[15] and in other cases to be discussed later in this chapter the law provides remedies against a person who goes back on a promise, even though is was not supported by consideration.[16] But such promises are not *binding as contracts*; so that the remedies for their breach are generally less advantageous to the promisee than those available in respect of promises which are supported by consideration.[17]

4   IRRELEVANCE OF ADEQUACY OF CONSIDERATION; NOMINAL CONSIDERATION

Although there must be some consideration for a promise, it is well settled that 'the law will not enter into an enquiry as to the adequacy

14   *Shadwell v Shadwell* (1860) 9 CBNS 159.
15   See ante, pp 30–31.
16   See post, pp 47–49, 54–56.
17   See post, pp 48, 56.

of the consideration'.[18] The doctrine of consideration is not concerned with the question whether the bargain which the parties have made is particularly favourable to one of them, and consequently unfavourable to the other. One striking result of this rule is the device of nominal consideration. An agreement by which A promises to pay B £1,000 in exchange for a peppercorn, or to convey a house in exchange for £1, does not suffer for want of consideration. This device provides a second way (in addition to the promise in a deed) in which a gratuitous promise can be made legally binding. It makes no difference that the thing received by way of nominal consideration is of no use to the recipient and that he in fact throws it away.[19] But if both parties know that one party's performance cannot have any value at all, there would be no consideration: for example, if A agreed to pay B £100 for the contents of B's cellar, which was known by both to be empty. The position would be different if there was a chance, however slight, of the cellar's containing something.

These general rules are well established, but the courts are not insensitive to the problems raised by unequal bargains; so that the general rules are subject to exceptions, to be discussed later in this book.[20] In none of these exceptional cases, however, is a promise held to be invalid *merely* because inadequate value has been given for it: some other factor must be established, such as a relationship enabling one party to take unfair advantage of the other.

Conversely, the courts sometimes feel that promises which are legally enforceable because they are under seal or supported by nominal considerations do not, if they are truly gratuitous, deserve the same degree of enforceability as those for which substantial value has been given. For this reason, equity refuses to aid a 'volunteer', ie a person who has given no *substantial* consideration for a promise of the former kind.[1] The fact that adequate value is not given may also operate to the prejudice of third parties such as the creditors of the promisor or his dependants. The interests of such persons are protected by special statutory rules.[2]

Although a nominal consideration will suffice at law, there are cases in which the act or forbearance, promised or performed, is of

---

18   *Westlake v Adams* (1858) 5 CBNS 248 at 265; cf, in consumer contracts, post, p 112.
19   *Chappell & Co Ltd v Nestlé Co Ltd* [1960] AC 87.
20   See post, pp 181–183, 201, 411.
1   *Jefferys v Jefferys* (1841) Cr & Ph 138; the principle does not apply to completed gifts: *Pennington v Waine* [2002] EWCA Civ 227, [2002] 1 WLR 2075.
2   Eg Inheritance (Provision for Family and Dependants) Act 1975, ss 10, 11; Insolvency Act 1986, ss 238, 339, 423; statements in *Lipkin Gorman v Karpnale Ltd* [1991] 2 AC 548 at 561, 575 and 577 are explicable on similar grounds.

such a trifling character that it becomes doubtful whether it can be regarded as consideration at all. It has, for example, been held that a son did not provide consideration for his father's promise not to enforce a debt, by promising not to bore his father with complaints.[3] It is, moreover, 'no consideration to refrain from a course of action which is was never intended to pursue':[4] eg where a promise to pay £100 is made to a confirmed teetotaller if he will abstain from alcohol for a week. The reason for this rule is, however, not to be found in the trifling value of the consideration, but in the requirement that it must be given in exchange for the promise.

5 PAST CONSIDERATION IS INSUFFICIENT

This last requirement also explains the general rule that 'past consideration' is no consideration. This means that an act done *before* the promise was made cannot normally be the consideration for it.[5] Consideration is, for example, past where goods are sold and at some later time the seller gives a guarantee as to their quality.[6] But there is obviously some elasticity in the notion of past consideration. If the promise and the previous act are substantially one transaction, the consideration is not past merely because there is a (relatively short) interval of time between them. There is quite commonly such an interval in the ordinary case, in which a buyer of goods claims the benefit of a manufacturer's guarantee. Although some days may elapse between the original purchase and the giving of the guarantee, it is not thought that the consideration for such a guarantee would be regarded as past. Where the guarantee is a 'consumer guarantee' within Regulations made for the protection of consumers, it binds the guarantor by force of the Regulations:[7] there is no further requirement of consideration.

An act for which no recompense was fixed before it was done can constitute consideration for a subsequent promise to pay for it if (1) it was done at the request of the promisor, (2) the understanding of the parties when it was done was that it was to be paid for, and (3) a promise to pay for it would, had it been made in advance, have been legally enforceable.[8] The rule covers the common case in which services

3   *White v Bluett* (1853) 23 LJ Ex 36.
4   *Arrale v Costain Civil Engineering Ltd* [1976] 1 Lloyd's Rep 98 at 106.
5   *Eastwood v Kenyon* (1840) 11 Ad & El 438.
6   *Roscorla v Thomas* (1842) 3 QB 234.
7   Sale of Supply of Goods to Consumers Regulations 2002, SI 2002/3045, reg 15.
8   *Re Casey's Patents* [1892] 1 Ch 104 at 115–116.

are rendered on a commercial basis, but the rate of remuneration is only agreed after they have been rendered. On the same principle, a past *promise* made at the request of one party can constitute consideration for a counter-promise later made by that party.[9]

By way of exception to the rule that consideration must not be past, an 'antecedent debt or liability' is good consideration for a bill of exchange;[10] and a promise by an adult to perform an obligation contracted by him during minority is enforceable.[11] Moreover, a debtor who makes a written acknowledgement of a debt may thereby extend the period of limitation during which the debt can be sued for,[12] provided that, when the acknowledgement was made, that period had not already expired.[13]

6 CONSIDERATION MUST MOVE FROM THE PROMISEE

The rule that consideration must 'move from the promisee'[14] means that a person cannot enforce a promise (though made to him) if the consideration for it moved wholly from some other person. If, for example, A promised B to pay £1,000 to B if C did the same, B could not enforce A's promise, since the only possible consideration for it moved from C. But it is not necessary for B to provide the whole consideration, and B may also provide consideration by procuring C to do an act in favour of A. Thus, a promise by A to B to pay B a commission of 5 per cent on any loan which B might persuade C to make to A, would not suffer from lack of consideration.

Although consideration must move from the promisee, it need not move to the promisor. The requirement of consideration may be satisfied by the promisee's conferring a benefit on the promisor, even without suffering any detriment.[15] It may further be satisfied if such a benefit is conferred, not on the promisor, but (at his request) on a third party. This is the position where goods are sold and payment is made by means of a cheque or credit card: the issuer of the card promises the seller that the cheque will be honoured or that the seller will be paid; and the seller provides consideration for this

9   *Pao On v Lau Yiu Long* [1980] AC 614.
10 Bills of Exchange Act 1882, s 27(1)(b).
11 Post, p 229.
12 Limitation Act 1980, ss 29(5), 30(1).
13 Limitation Act 1980, s 29(7).
14 *Thomas v Thomas* (1842) 2 QB 851 at 859.
15 See *Edmonds v Lawson* [2000] QB 501.

promise by delivering the goods to the customer.[16] In the credit-card case, consideration may also move to the promisor (the issuer of the card) in the shape of the discount allowed to him by the seller.[17]

7   MUTUAL PROMISES AS CONSIDERATION

There is no doubt that mutual promises can be, and generally are, consideration for each other: eg where A and B agree today on a sale of goods, to be delivered and paid for tomorrow. Some difficulty has been felt in explaining this rule. Obviously, it will not do to say that each party suffers a detriment because he is bound by his own promise, for this presupposes the conclusion which it is sought to prove, viz the binding force of each promise. Probably the explanation is a simpler one: the making of a promise in fact (and quite apart from legal enforceability) generates a commercial pressure for its performance; and similarly, its receipt generates a commercial expectation that performance will be rendered. This pressure and this expectation are the detriment and benefit by virtue of which one promise can be said to be consideration for another. It is, however, not the case that all mutual promises are consideration for each other. Three qualifications must be made.

First, a promise is consideration only if the thing promised would, if performed, itself amount to consideration. For example, a debtor's promise to pay part of a debt already due would not be consideration for a promise by the creditor to release the balance, since (as we shall see)[18] the actual part payment would not be consideration for such a promise.

Secondly, a promise to accept a gift is not consideration for a promise to make it. Just as the receipt of £100 cannot be regarded as a detriment, so the promise to accept the money cannot be so regarded. Of course, the position is different if burdens are attached to the subject-matter of the gift and the donee promises to discharge them. Thus, a promise to accept a gift of a leasehold house and to perform the donor's obligations (eg to pay rent and to do repairs) is good consideration for the promise to make the gift.[19] A further complication arises if a person to whom a gift is promised makes a counter-promise not to complain, or sue, in respect of defects in the

---

16   See *R v Lambie* [1982] AC 449; *Re Charge Card Services Ltd* [1987] Ch 150; affd [1988] 3 All ER 702.
17   *Customs and Excise Comrs v Diners Club Ltd* [1989] 1 WLR 1196 at 1207.
18   See post, p 46.
19   *Price v Jenkins* (1877) 5 Ch D 619.

gift. Here again, it seems at first sight obvious that the counter-promise is no consideration: it is ridiculous to suppose that a promise to give someone a horse could be made binding by a counter-promise not to look the horse in the mouth. But if performance of the promise has begun, and brought the parties into a relationship in which defective performance would normally give rise to legal liability to the 'donee', a promise by him not to enforce that liability could amount to consideration. This would be the position where A promised to give B a free ride and B promised not to sue A for negligence in the performance of A's promise. There could be a contract, at least once A had begun to perform his promise.[20]

Thirdly, a promise is no consideration for a counter-promise if the former promise is freely revocable at the will of the person making it. This would be the position where a person promised to do something if he felt like it, or unless he cancelled the promise.[1] Such obviously illusory promises are not in practice bargained for, nor do they give rise to any legal difficulty; but more subtle variants do occur and give rise to problems. For example, A may promise to buy from B 'all the coal I require for my works'. Here, if A requires nothing, he is not bound to buy anything, but his promise is nevertheless a real one and so provides consideration for B's promise to supply any coal ordered. As A has promised to buy *all* his requirements from B, he is not at liberty to buy from anyone else and this restriction is a sufficient detriment to satisfy the requirement of consideration.

A further difficulty, which arises where mutual promises are alleged to constitute consideration for each other, is that one of them may not be binding under some rule of law: for example because it was procured by fraud, or because the party giving it lacked contractual capacity, or because the promise was illegal, or because it is void by statute. At first sight it might seem logical to say that a promise which was not binding on a party for such a reason therefore could not be consideration for the counter-promise. Some cases adopt this reasoning. Thus if A promises B a pension in return for B's promise not to compete with him, A can escape liability by showing that B's promise is illegal under the rules relating to restraint of trade.[2] Here B's promise is invalid in the public interest; but where it is invalid in the interest of B or of a class to which he belongs, this invalidity does not prevent it from constituting good consideration for A's counter-promise. Thus, if B is not bound because he is under age and so lacks

---

20   *Gore v Van der Lann* [1967] 2 QB 31; and see next note.
1   See post, p 105, for limitations on the effectiveness of certain provisions of this kind.
2   *Wyatt v Kreglinger and Fernau* [1933] 1 KB 793; post, p 202.

contractual capacity, A is nevertheless bound, ie B's promise, though it does not bind B, is good consideration for A's promise.[3] Similar reasoning applies, where A, by fraud, induces B to enter into a contract with him. Here, B's promise does not bind him in the sense that he can avoid the contract.[4] But if he wishes to enforce A's promise, he is entitled to do so: by affirming the contract, he makes his own promise binding and so supplies consideration for A's promise. The same result will often follow where the party who is not bound actually performs his promise.[5] But this last rule does not apply where the contract is illegal. Thus, in the restraint of trade case put above,[6] the actual performance by B of his promise not to compete does not (any more than the giving of the promise) enable B to enforce A's promise to pay him a pension; for the law must not give the party making the illegal promise any incentive to perform it. Nor will performance of one party's promise constitute consideration where a statute makes the promises of *both* parties void, as in the case of a gaming or wagering contract.[7] The rules stated in this paragraph cannot be logically deduced from the doctrine of consideration. They are based rather on the different policy grounds which, in each of the situations discussed, invalidate the promise or promises in question.

Although mutual promises are sufficient to constitute consideration, they are not necessary. Thus, in the case of a unilateral contract, performance of the requested act, or forbearance, can constitute consideration even though nothing was promised. Probably this is so even where the required performance has only been begun but not completed: this would seem to be a sufficient 'detriment' to satisfy the requirement of consideration.

8   COMPROMISES AND FORBEARANCES

If A has a legal claim against B and promises not to enforce it, there is in general no difficulty in seeing that A thereby provides consideration to a counter-promise by B. For example, if A is owed £100 by B payable today, A's promise not to enforce the debt would be good consideration for B's promise to give security for it. Similarly, if A had suffered loss as a result of B's breach of contract, A's promise not to sue B would be good consideration for B's promise to pay A £5,000 by way of compensation. Such cases may give rise to questions as to the scope of

3   *Holt v Ward Clarencieux* (1732) 2 Stra 937.
4   See post, p 163 et seq.
5   *Fishmongers' Co v Robertson* (1843) 5 Man & G 131.
6   See supra, n 2.
7   Gaming Act 1845, s 18; *Lipkin Gorman v Karpnale Ltd* [1991] 2 AC 548.

the release: for example, whether it covers claims of which A was not and could not have been aware;[8] but questions of this kind do not raise issues of consideration. Such issues can, however, arise in two further situations.

a Doubtful and invalid claims

The claim which A promises to give up in exchange for B's promise may not, in fact or in law, be a good one. If A sued, he would therefore lose his action and have to pay costs, so that it can be argued that he suffers no detriment, but on the contrary gains a benefit, by his forbearance. Nevertheless he provides consideration for B's promise not only where his (A's) claim is good, but also where it is doubtful in law and even where it is clearly bad in law.[9] For this rule to apply, there must be reasonable grounds for the claim; A must honestly believe that it has a fair chance of success; he must seriously intend to prosecute the claim; and he must not conceal from B any facts which would exonerate B.[10] Even where B's *promise* is not legally binding, a *payment* made under it 'to close the transaction'[11] cannot be claimed back. Where A's claim is clearly bad in law, it is hard to see any detriment to A or benefit to B; but the rule that B's promise is binding reflects the desire of the courts to encourage reasonable compromises. It does not apply where A's claim is known to be bad. If A alone knows this, he is guilty of a kind of dishonesty which the law would obviously not want to encourage. The position is sometimes the same even if A's knowledge is shared by B: thus, a 'compromise' of a gambling debt would not be enforced.[12]

b Cases in which there is no promise to forbear

A may not promise to forbear from suing B, but simply forbear in fact. The question whether A's actual forbearance amounts to consideration for a promise from B appears to depend, in the first

---

8 *Bank of Credit and Commerce SA v Ali* [2001] UKHL 8, [2001] ICR 337.
9 *Callisher v Bischoffsheim* (1870) LR 5 QB 449.
10 *Cook v Wright* (1861) 1 B & S 559 at 569; *Miles v New Zealand Alford Estate Co* (1886) 32 Ch D 266 at 284; *The Proodos C* [1980] 2 Lloyd's Rep 390 at 392; *Colchester Borough Council v Smith* [1992] Ch 421 at 425.
11 *Woolwich Equitable Building Society v IRC (No 2)* [1993] AC 70 at 165.
12 *Hyams v Coombes* (1912) 28 TLR 413.

place, on the nature of the claim forborne. In one case[13] a bank was owed £22,000 by one of its customers and pressed him to give security. He promised to do so and it was held that the bank had provided consideration for the customer's promise by forbearing to enforce the claim, even though it had not made any promise to forbear. Here the claim was such that the bank would almost certainly have taken steps to enforce it, if the customer had not made his promise. It was therefore obvious that the bank's forbearance was induced by that promise. In a contrasting case,[14] a seller of land promised to pay certain sums of money to his dissatisfied buyer, who later argued that he had provided consideration for the seller's promise by forbearing to take proceedings to rescind the sale. The argument was rejected because it was not shown that the buyer ever intended to take such proceedings; and it was said that there was nothing (ie no promise by the buyer) to bind him not to do so. The claim to rescind was not such that the buyer would clearly have pursued it; nor was it clear that his forbearance to do so was induced by the seller's promise. In other words, the stronger the claim, the more likely it is that actual forbearance (without a promise to forbear) will be consideration for a promise made by the person liable to the claim.

The need to establish a causal connection between the forbearance and the promise also accounts for the further rule, that the forbearance must occur at the express or implied request of the promisor. Hence the mere fact that B owes a debt to A which A might have, but has not, enforced, is not sufficient to provide consideration for a promise made by B to A.[15] In technical language, the antecedent debt is past consideration, unless A's forbearance to enforce it was induced by B's promise.

9   EXISTING DUTIES AS CONSIDERATION

One of the most troublesome problems in the law of contract is whether a person can provide consideration by performing, or promising to perform, a pre-existing legal duty. In one sense, such a person suffers no detriment as he is already bound to render the performance in question; but he may find it economically expedient to break the duty and pay damages unless he has the benefit of some additional promise. Correspondingly, the person making that

---

13   *Alliance Bank v Broom* (1864) 2 Drew & Sm 289. Cf *R v A-G for England and Wales* [2003] UKPC 22, [2003] EMLR 499 at [31].
14   *Miles v New Zealand Alford Estate Co* (1886) 32 Ch D 266.
15   *Wigan v English and Scottish Law Life Assurance Association* [1909] 1 Ch 291.

additional promise may benefit from the performance of the original duty; for the damages legally recoverable for its breach will not always compensate him fully for the loss which the breach would actually cause.[16] On the other hand, it may sometimes be undesirable to enforce promises made to secure the performance of a pre-existing legal duty. Such a state of the law might encourage the person under the duty to refuse to perform it unless some added inducement were held out to him, and so lead to results that amounted to duress or were contrary to public policy.

a   Public duty

This last argument is particularly strong where the pre-existing duty is one imposed by the general law. It is obvious that a person should not be held to provide consideration by merely forbearing to commit a breach of the criminal law;[17] and that a public officer should not be able to enforce a promise to pay him money for doing nothing more than his public duty.[18] On the other hand, if such an officer is induced by the promise to do more that his public duty he can enforce the promise. Thus, if a person promises to pay the police for providing him with a greater degree of protection than they reasonably think necessary, the promise is not invalid for lack of consideration.[19] By statute, a person is liable to pay for 'special police services' provided at his 'request'.[20] Such a request may be implied where a person organises an event which cannot safely take place without such special services: for this reason a football club has been held liable for the cost of policing matches held on its ground.[1]

Even a promise to do no more than the public duty may be enforceable. Thus in a number of cases, police offers have recovered rewards advertised for information leading to the capture of criminals, even though they were legally bound to transmit or act on such information once they acquired it.[2] The tendency of such promises was to promote the administration of justice by encouraging extra effort, rather than to lead to the corruption of public officers. Although some of the older authorities can be cited in favour of the view that the performance of, or promise to perform, a duty imposed by law is

16   See post, p 389 et seq.
17   *Brown v Brine* (1875) 1 Ex D 5.
18   *Morgan v Palmer* (1824) 2 B & C 729 at 736.
19   *Glasbrook Bros Ltd v Glamorgan County Council* [1925] AC 270.
20   Police Act 1996, s 25.
1   *Harris v Sheffield United Football Club Ltd* [1988] QB 77.
2   Eg *England v Davidson* (1840) 11 Ad & El 856.

no consideration for a counter-promise, the modern view is that the counter-promise is enforceable, unless there are grounds of public policy against its enforcement.[3]

b   Duty imposed by contract with a third party

Where the pre-existing duty is imposed, not by law, but by an earlier contract, a distinction is drawn between two situations. In the first, the duty is imposed on the promisee by an earlier contract between him and the promisor; in the second that duty is imposed by an earlier contract between the promisee and a third party. As the law relating to the latter situation is relatively the more certain, it will be convenient to begin the discussion with cases of this kind.

Most authorities support the view that the performance of a contractual duty owed by A to B can be good consideration for a promise made by C to A.[4] Thus, in one case,[5] A (a stevedore) had contracted with B (a shipowner) to unload goods from B's ship. Some of the goods belonged to C who promised A not to make any claim against him if he damaged the goods while unloading them. It was held that A had provided consideration for C's promise by unloading the goods even though this was something that he was already bound to do under his contract with B. Similarly, B may contract to do building work for C, and C may promise A (one of B's workmen) that he will pay him a bonus on completion of the work. This promise would be binding, even though A was already bound by his contract with B to work on the site. In all these cases it might be argued that A suffered no detriment, as he did no more than he was already bound to do under his contract with B; but the performance of the duty is in fact a benefit to C, and this is sufficient to make C's promise binding. Where performance of the duty owed to the third party would be consideration, the promise to perform it has the same effect. Thus, in the last example, A's promise to C to perform his contract with his employer (B), no less than its actual performance, would constitute consideration for C's promise to A.[6]

In all the above cases, A's performance of the duty imposed on him by his contract with B (or his promise to perform it) does constitute a real benefit to C. It is, however, necessary to guard against the danger that A may bring undue pressure to bear on C; for example, where the workman

3   *Ward v Byham* [1956] 2 All ER 318.
4   See *Shadwell v Shadwell* (1860) 9 CBNS 159, criticised on other grounds in *Jones v Padavatton* [1969] 1 WLR 328 at 333.
5   *The Eurymedon* [1975] AC 154.
6   *Pao On v Lau Yiu Long* [1980] AC 614.

A tells the site-owner C that he will refuse to perform his contract with B unless C pays him a bonus. Such conduct may fall within the now expanding concept of duress.[7] If so, C's promise can be avoided on that ground; but if there is in fact no duress the doctrine of consideration, which was formerly used to protect C against such forms of pressure, no longer presents any bar to the enforceability of the promise.

c Rescission or modification of contract between original parties

After entering into a contract, the parties may agree to abandon (or in technical language to 'rescind') it, or to vary it. An agreement to 'rescind' a contract made before any part of it was (or should have been) performed will generate its own consideration in the sense that each party suffers a detriment in not getting what he bargained for, and gains a benefit in not having to perform what he promised. This reasoning would apply even though the contract had been partly performed, so long as each party was still under some obligation and promised to give up rights under the contract:[8] each of them can then be said to give up and to obtain something, by way of consideration for the promise to release him.

Difficulties begin to arise where a 'rescission' occurs after one party has completely performed (so that only the other is released). Suppose that after a seller has delivered, but before the buyer has paid, the parties agree that nothing more is to be done under the contract. This looks like a promise to make a gift of the price to the buyer, and such a promise to renounce an accrued debt is not binding unless the buyer provides some separate consideration for it, typically by doing something that he was not, under the original contract, bound to do. To this rule there is an exception: if the holder of a bill of exchange or promissory note, after its maturity, unconditionally and in writing renounces his rights against any person liable on it, such a person is discharged.[9] Thus in the case put, the seller could take a bill of exchange or promissory note in payment, and renounce it: in this way it is possible to evade the rule that a release without consideration is of no effect.

There are also many cases in which the *variation* (as opposed to the rescission) of a contract gives rise to no problem of consideration. Suppose that A on 1 May agrees to sell a car to B for £5,000, delivery and payment to take place on 1 June. If subsequently the parties agree to postpone delivery and payment until 1 July, there is no

---

7   See post, pp 178–179.
8   *Collin v Duke of Westminster* [1985] QB 581 at 598.
9   Bills of Exchange Act 1882, s 62.

difficulty in finding consideration for the new promises. A suffers a detriment, in that he gets the money later, but gets a benefit in that he keeps the car for the extra time; and B gets a corresponding benefit and suffers a corresponding detriment. Moreover, as the law takes no account of adequacy of consideration, the same arguments would apply if payment were postponed until 2 June and delivery until 1 July. It is assumed that the variation is in fact made to secure some benefit (however small) for each party. If, though capable of benefiting both, it is in fact made for the benefit of one, there is no consideration for the variation.[10] This would be the position where the place at which a loan is to be repaid was altered at the request, and for the sole convenience, of the debtor. Similarly, there is no consideration for a buyer's promise to accept late delivery of goods (even through the price is only payable on delivery), if the promise was made solely to accommodate the seller.[11]

Further problems arise where the variation affects the obligations of only one of the parties. Sometimes, such a variation can be enforced as a separate contract, collateral to the main contract and supported by separate consideration. Thus in one case[12] the owners of a block of flats had agreed to sell long leases of the flats to tenants. These leases required the tenants to contribute to the cost of roof repairs, but during the negotiations the owners had promised to repair certain existing defects in the roof 'at our own cost'. This promise was held binding as a collateral contract for which the tenants had provided consideration by executing the formal documents in which the leases were embodied.

But a variation cannot take effect as a 'collateral' contract where it purports to alter a term of the main contract itself: eg where a contract to sell a car for £5,000 is varied by an agreement to raise the price to £6,000 or to lower it to £4,000. In such cases, it is hard to find any consideration either for the buyer's promise to pay more or for the seller's promise to accept less, since at first sight the variation seems to be capable of benefiting only the seller in the first and the buyer in the second case. But the buyer who promises to pay more may in fact benefit by securing actual delivery of the car, and the seller who promises to reduce the price similarly benefits by actually being paid a substantial part of the original agreed price. The question whether such a benefit amounts to consideration gives rise in principle to the same difficulty whether the effect of such a one-sided variation is to increase or to reduce the obligation of one party (the buyer) while

10   *Vanbergen v St Edmunds Properties Ltd* [1933] 2 KB 223.
11   *Charles Rickards Ltd v Oppenhaim* [1950] 1 KB 616.
12   *Brikom Investments Ltd v Carr* [1979] QB 467.

that of the other (the seller) remains constant. But for technical reasons the two situations require separate discussion.

d   Variations increasing one party's obligation

Where the effect of the variation is simply to increase the obligation of one party, some cases take the view that there is no consideration for the variation. This position was first established in a case[13] in which sailors, who had signed on for a voyage at a fixed rate of pay, were then promised extra pay for completing it. In a sense they suffered no detriment, as they merely did what they were legally bound to do; and the captain who made the promise got no benefit, since he was already legally entitled to their services. In fact, however, it is arguable that the captain did benefit, since he got the sailors' actual services, and this benefit was almost certainly worth more than the legal right to obtain them.

More recently, this was the argument which prevailed where a builder, who had contracted to refurbish a number of flats, engaged a subcontractor to do the carpentry work for £20,000. Later he promised to pay the carpenter an extra £10,300 for that work; he made this promise because he had recognised that the original sum was too low and because he feared that, without extra pay, the carpenter might not be able to complete his part of the work on time. The 'practical benefits'[14] obtained by the builder in actually getting the carpentry work done were held to satisfy the requirement of consideration, so that the promise of extra pay was enforceable. This conclusion restricts the scope of the earlier cases on sailors' wages; and it seem likely that the benefit of securing actual performance will normally be regarded as consideration, so that the promise of extra pay will be binding unless it was obtained by improper pressure amounting to duress.[15]

Such a promise may also be supported by other consideration. If, for example, the sailors in the above case had undertaken additional duties (not imposed by the original contract) the requirement of consideration would have been satisfied.[16] Even in such cases, the promise may be open to attack on the ground that it had been obtained by improper pressure; but the doctrine of consideration is

13   *Stilk v Myrick* (1809) 2 Camp 317, 6 Esp 129.
14   *Williams v Roffey Bros & Nicholls (Contractors) Ltd* [1991] 1 QB 1 at 11; and cf at 19, 23.
15   Cf *B & S Contracts and Design Ltd v Victor Green Publications Ltd* [1984] ICR 419,
16   Cf *The Atlantic Baron* [1979] QB 705.

no longer needed to provide protection against such pressure now that this function is more satisfactorily performed by the expanding concept of duress.[17]

A promise to pay increased wages to an employee will not suffer from want of consideration where the employment is short-term or terminable by notice. In such cases, the employee is only obliged to work till the end of the agreed term or notice period and provides consideration by staying at work thereafter, or by forbearing to exercise his right to give notice and so to put an end to his original obligation. Alternatively, even a fixed-term contract may be expressly or by implication made at the 'going rate' of pay, whatever it may be from time to time;[18] and in such a case a promise to increase the rate of pay for part of the period would not suffer from lack of consideration.

e   Variations reducing one party's obligation

A variation may simply reduce the obligation of one party: for example, where a landlord promises to relieve his tenant from obligations to repair imposed by the lease; where a buyer, purely for the convenience of the seller, promises to accept delivery at a time later than that agreed; or (in practice the most important case) where a creditor agrees to accept part payment of a debt in full settlement. In all these cases, the starting principle is that there is no consideration for the variation, unless the party whose obligation is reduced also does, or promises, something which he was not by the original contract bound to do. Suppose, for example, that A is owed £100 by B and promises to accept £75 in full settlement. B duly pays the £75, but according to the decision of the House of Lords in *Foakes v Beer*,[19] A is nevertheless entitled to recover the remaining £25 from B. There is said to be no consideration for A's promise to accept the £75 in full settlement since B is already bound to pay A £100. Hence B suffers no detriment by paying less; and, since A is already entitled to £100 from B, he gains no benefit by receiving less. Such reasoning often ignores the commercial reality that part payment from a debtor who is in difficulties is in fact a benefit to the creditor. As we have just seen, similar benefits are now regarded as consideration for promises to pay more for the performance originally undertaken; and the law would be more satisfactory if this reasoning were applied to the part payment cases. For the present, *Foakes v Beer* stands in the way of such a development;[20]

17   See *The Universe Sentinel* [1983] 1 AC 366 and post, p 176.
18   Cf *Lombard Tricity Finance Ltd v Paton* [1989] 1 All ER 918.
19   (1884) 9 App Cas 605.
20   *Re Selectmove Ltd* [1995] 1 WLR 474.

but the law does impose important limitations on the principle that a variation which simply reduces the obligation of one party is not legally binding. Many of these limitations apply specifically to promises to accept part payment of a debt in full settlement but one of them is of a more general character. We shall first consider this general limitation, which is commonly (if not very accurately) referred to as the doctrine of 'promissory estoppel', and then revert to the special rules relating to part payment of a debt.

10 PROMISSORY ESTOPPEL

This doctrine applies where one party to a contract by words or conduct makes a clear and unequivocal[1] promise or representation which leads the other party 'to suppose that the strict rights arising under the contract will not be enforced, or will be kept in suspense or held in abeyance'.[2] Its effect is that 'the person who otherwise might have enforced those rights will not be allowed to enforce them where it would be inequitable having regard to the dealings which have thus taken place between the parties'.[3] Under the doctrine of promissory estoppel, certain limited effects are given to promises without consideration. But there are several crucial differences between the legal effects of such a promise under that doctrine and the effects of a variation which is contractually binding because it is supported by consideration.

i) The first is that a variation alters the relations of the parties once for all; but, in general, promissory estoppel only *suspends*[4] an obligation. For example, a landlord who has promised not to enforce his tenant's obligation to repair cannot then turn around and peremptorily forfeit the lease because the tenant has not repaired; but it would not be equitable (or in accordance with the intention of the parties) to deprive him permanently of the right to require the tenant to do the repairs. He can therefore reassert his rights by giving the tenant notice to repair within a reasonable time, unless later events make it impossible (or highly inequitable) to require the tenant, as it were, to catch up on his original obligation.[5]

---

1   See *The Scaptrade* [1983] 1 All ER 301; affd without reference to this point [1983] 2 AC 694; mere inactivity will not suffice unless exceptional circumstances give rise to a 'duty to speak': *The Leonidas D* [1985] 2 All ER 796 at 805; cf ante, p 18.

2   *Hughes v Metropolitan Rly Co* (1877) 2 App Cas 439 at 448.

3   *Hughes v Metropolitan Rly Co* (1877) 2 App Cas 439 at 448.

4   *Tool Metal Manufacturing Co Ltd v Tungsten Electric Co Ltd* [1955] 2 All ER 657; *Hazel v Akhtar* [2001] EWCA Civ 1883, [2002] 2 P & CR 17 at [43].

5   See *Ogilvy v Hope-Davies* [1976] 1 All ER 683 at 696; *The Ion* [1980] 2 Lloyd's Rep 245 at 251.

Secondly, the principle of promissory estoppel applies only when it would be 'inequitable' for the promisor to go back on his promise without due notice. The notion of what is 'inequitable' cannot be defined with anything approaching precision; but the basic idea is that the promisee must have acted in reliance on the promise so that he cannot be restored to the position in which he was before he acted in this way.[6] For example, he must have continued his attempts to perform the contract (as in the case of the seller who continues to make efforts to perform, in reliance on the buyer's promise that late delivery will be accepted); or he must have refrained from taking steps to safeguard his position (as in the case of the tenant neglecting to repair, in reliance on his landlord's promise that performance of the obligation to repair would not be enforced). Even where there has been such reliance, outside events may justify the promisor in going back on his promise; for example, retraction of a creditor's promise not to insist on punctual payment of a debt, may be justified by the fact that a third party is about to levy execution on the property which formed the security for the debt.[7] Nor will it be inequitable for the promisor to go back on his promise if he does so promptly, while it is still possible to restore the promisee to the position in which he was before the promise was made.[8]

In English law the effect of the doctrine of promissory estoppel is also limited in another way. The doctrine prevents a party from asserting rights which he has under an existing contract; but the general view is that it does not operate so as to create entirely new rights.[9] It would not, for example, apply where A promised B to pay B any expenses which B might incur on a trip to Paris and B then incurred such expenses, or to increase the amount payable by A to B under an earlier contract between them: such promises are binding only if B provides consideration.[10] This limitation on the scope of the doctrine has occasionally been viewed with scepticism by the courts, who have sometimes doubted it, ignored it, or sought to narrow its scope;[11] and it has been rejected in

6   *Maharaj v Chand* [1986] AC 898.
7   *Williams v Stern* (1879) 5 QBD 409.
8   *The Post Chaser* [1981] 2 Lloyd's Rep 695.
9   *Combe v Combe* [1951] 2 KB 215; *Argy Trading Development Co Ltd v Lapid Developments Ltd* [1977] 1 WLR 444 at 456; *Baird Textile Holdings Ltd v Marks & Spencer plc* [2001] EWCA Civ 274, [2002] 1 All ER (Comm) 737 at [34], [87]; contrast *Re Wyvern Developments Ltd* [1974] 1 WLR 1097 at 1104–1105; *The Henrik Sif* [1982] 1 Lloyd's Rep 456 at 466.
10   See ante, pp 45–46; *The Proodos C* [1980] 2 Lloyd's Rep 390.
11   See dicta in *Re Wyvern Developments Ltd* [1974] 1 WLR 1097 at 1104–1105; *The Henrik Sif* [1982] 1 Lloyd's Rep 456 at 466; *Azov Shipping Co v Baltic Shipping Co* [1999] 2 Lloyd's Rep 159 at 175; *Thornton Springer Ltd v NEM Insurance Co Ltd* [2000] 2 All ER 489 at 519; *Baird Textile Holdings Ltd v Marks & Spencer plc* [2001] EWCA Civ 274, [2002] 1 All ER (Comm) 737 at [88].

other common law jurisdictions.[12] In English law, the limitation seems to survive[13] and to be explicable on the ground that it is necessary to prevent a head-on conflict between the two doctrines of promissory estoppel and consideration.

None of the limitations on the scope of the doctrine of promissory estoppel applies where the subsequent promise is supported by consideration and so takes effect as a contractually binding variation. In that case, the promisee can enforce the variation without showing that it would be 'inequitable' for the promisor to go back on it; the effect of the variation will be to alter the rights of the promisor permanently and not merely to suspend them; and the variation can create entirely new rights. The doctrine of promissory estoppel may have reduced, but it has not eliminated, the practical importance of consideration for the modification of contracts.

11 ESTOPPEL BY CONVENTION

Promissory estoppel must be distinguished from so called estoppel by convention. This arises where the parties to a transaction act on a common assumption of fact, that is one shared by both of them or made by one and acquiesced in by the other. Normally, the assumption will be one of fact, but a mistake which is one of law[14] in the sense of being one as to the meaning of a document can also give rise to an estoppel by convention. The effect of such an estoppel is to preclude the parties from denying the truth of the assumption if it would be unjust to allow them (or one of them) to go back on it.[15] For example, in one case[16] the parties to a guarantee assumed that it covered loans made not only by the company to which the guarantee was given, but also by one of its subsidiaries. As the parties had acted on this assumption, it was held that the guarantor could not deny its truth. Estoppel by convention may thus prevent a party from denying that a promise *has been made*, or that it meant what both parties believed it

---

12   See, in the United States, Restatement 2d, Contracts, § 90; and in Australia *Waltons Stores (Interstate) Ltd v Maher* (1988) 164 CLR 387.

13   See the authorities cited in n 9, supra.

14   See (for example) *The Indian Endurance (No 2)* [1998] AC 878 at 913; *Johnson v Gore Wood & Co* [2002] 2 AC 1 at 34; contrast at 40.

15   *The August Leonhardt* [1985] 2 Lloyd's Rep 28; *The Vistafjord* [1988] 2 Lloyd's Rep 343 at 351–352; *Hiscox v Outhwaite* [1992] 1 AC 562; affd [1992] 1 AC 562 at 587.

16   *Amalgamated Investment and Property Co Ltd v Texas Commerce International Bank Ltd* [1982] QB 84.

meant, while promissory estoppel is concerned with the *legal effects* of a promise, the existence and meaning of which are not in doubt, but which is not supported by consideration. In our guarantee case the promise described above was clearly supported by consideration[17] and thus binding: the only issue was whether it could be taken to have been made. Where the assumed promise would, if made, have been *unsupported* by consideration, both types of estoppel may operate in the same case; estoppel by convention to prevent a party from denying that he has made the promise, and promissory estoppel to determine its legal effects. The two types of estoppel resemble each other in that neither can give rise to new rights.[18]

12 PART PAYMENT OF A DEBT

The rule that a variation of a contract is not *prima facie* supported by consideration, if it simply reduces the obligations of one party, has caused most trouble in cases arising out of promises by a creditor to accept part payment of a debt in full settlement. Under the rule in *Foakes v Beer*,[19] a creditor who has made such a promise can nevertheless sue for the balance, but the courts have created many qualifications and exceptions to this rule, so as to bring the law more or less into harmony with commercial needs.

In the first place the rule only applies to 'liquidated' claims,[20] ie to claims for a fixed sum, such as the agreed price for goods or services. It does not apply to unliquidated claims such as claims for damages, or to claims for a reasonable price, where none is fixed by the contract or subsequently agreed. In such cases the claim is of uncertain value, and even though the overwhelming probability may be that it is worth *more* than the agreed settlement figure, the possibility of its being worth *less* is sufficient to provide consideration. There is an intermediate possibility where the creditor has both a liquidated and an unliquidated claim: for example, a dismissed employee may have a liquidated claim for arrears of wages and an unliquidated claim for damages for wrongful dismissal. Here a promise by him to accept the accrued wages in full settlement of both his claims would not be supported by consideration since the employer would, in paying the wages, only be doing what he was already legally bound to do; and the payment could not be worth

17 See ante, p 35.
18 In the cases cited in notes 15 and 16 supra, estoppel by convention operated only by way of defence. Cf also post, p 168.
19 See ante, p 46.
20 *Wilkinson v Byers* (1834) 1 Ad & El 106.

more than the wages plus damages.[1] Secondly, the rule does not apply if the claim is in good faith disputed,[2] or where its extent is not clearly defined by the original contract:[3] again this makes its value uncertain, so that any settlement of it by the parties will be upheld. Thirdly, the rule does not apply if the method of performance is varied so as to benefit the creditor in some way:[4] eg if he agrees to accept part payment in full settlement even a single day before the full sum is due. Fourthly, the debtor might provide consideration for the creditor's promise in some other way. He might, in addition to paying the smaller sum, transfer to the creditor some benefit in kind, such as 'a hawk, horse, or robe':[5] this is sufficient since the thing given *may* be worth more than the balance of the debt. Or he might confer a benefit on the creditor by performing his contractual obligation to take delivery of goods and so increasing the creditor's chance of making further sales. Such a benefit can constitute consideration:[6] it is only the benefit of part payment which must be disregarded under the rule in *Foakes v Beer*. Yet a further possibility is that the debtor might give up some cross-claim against the creditor: thus a seller's promise to accept part of the price in full settlement would be binding if the buyer gave up a claim for damages in respect of defects in the subject matter.[7] Fifthly, a promise to accept part payment in full-settlement may amount to a binding collateral contract reducing the debtor's liability under the principal transaction.[8] Finally, such a promise is binding if it is made in a deed, or if it is supported by a nominal consideration (other than one in money): eg if it is expressed to be made in consideration of the debtor's delivering a peppercorn.

The above exceptions to the general rule can fairly easily be reconciled with the traditional reasoning of the doctrine of consideration. Two further exceptions are well established but harder to reconcile with the orthodox doctrine. First, a creditor who has accepted part payment *from a third party* in full settlement cannot then sue the debtor for the balance.[9] Secondly, a debtor may enter into a composition agreement with several creditors, by which each of

1   Cf *Arrale v Costain Civil Engineering Ltd* [1976] 1 Lloyd's Rep 98.
2   *Cooper v Parker* (1855) 15 CB 822.
3   *Anangel Atlas Compania Naviera SA v Ishikawajima-Harima Heavy Industries Co Ltd (No 2)* [1990] 2 Lloyd's Rep 526 at 564.
4   *Pinnel's Case* (1602) 5 Co Rep 117a.
5   *Pinnel's Case* (1602) 5 Co Rep 117a.
6   *Anangel Atlas* case [1990] 2 Lloyd's Rep 526.
7   Cf *Brikom Investments Ltd v Carr* [1979] QB 467.
8   *Brikom Investments Ltd v Carr* [1979] QB 467, see ante, p 44.
9   *Hirachand Punamchand v Temple* [1911] 2 KB 330.

these creditors agrees with the others and with the debtor to accept part payment in full settlement. A creditor who accepts such part payment cannot later sue the debtor for the balance of the debt.[10] The simplest explanation for these rules may be that a creditor who sues for the balance attempts to break his contract with the third party, or with the other creditors participating in the composition agreement. The court will not assist him in such an attempt and may indeed be able to restrain it: eg by allowing the third party to intervene so as to obtain a stay of the creditor's action against the debtor for the balance[11] or by allowing the debtor to enforce any contractual promise which the creditor may have made to the third party not to sue the debtor for the balance.[12]

A final exception to the general rule in *Foakes v Beer* is more controversial. It arises under the doctrine of promissory estoppel. That doctrine stretches back well into the nineteenth century, and promises to accept part payment of a debt in full settlement were literally within the formulation of the doctrine. Yet no one had thought of applying that doctrine to such promises; on the contrary, the rule that such promises were not binding was settled by the House of Lords *after* the doctrine was first laid down in the terms already quoted.[13] But in the *High Trees* case[14] in 1947 a landlord had promised his tenant to reduce the annual rent due under a 99-year lease of a block of flats by one half for so long as war-time difficulties of sub-letting continued; and it was said that the landlord was bound by the promise under the doctrine of promissory estoppel even though the promise was not supported by consideration. The problem is, how to reconcile this view with the rule in *Foakes v Beer*, that a promise to accept part payment in full settlement is not binding.

Probably the best reconciliation is to say that a promise which gives rise to a promissory estoppel is not binding *as a variation* of the contract, but has a more limited effect. In the first place, it may only suspend the creditor's right and not extinguish it. Sometimes, indeed, suspension may be all that is intended: eg where a debt is payable in instalments and the creditor agrees to reduce the amount of those instalments to tide the debtor over temporary financial difficulties, without intending to reduce the total amount due.[15] But where the

---

10   *Boyd v Hind* (1857) 1 H & N 938.
11   Cf *Snelling v John G Snelling Ltd* [1973] QB 87.
12   Contracts (Rights of Third Parties) Act 1999, s 1, post, p 255. For this purpose, it is the debtor who is the 'third party'.
13   See ante, p 47.
14   *Central London Property Trust Ltd v High Trees House Ltd* [1947] KB 130.
15   Eg *Ajayi v R T Briscoe (Nigeria) Ltd* [1964] 3 All ER 556.

intention is permanently to extinguish part of the debt, that intention would clearly be defeated by allowing the creditor to claim the full amount after reasonable notice.[16] In some cases, such a result could perhaps be avoided by relying on the principle that promissory estoppel can operate extinctively in those exceptional cases where events after the promise make it highly inequitable to allow the promisor, even after reasonable notice, to reassert his original rights.[17] This principle could apply to the part payment of a debt cases: eg where the debtor had, in reliance on the creditor's promise, entered into fresh and irrevocable financial commitments. On the other hand, the creditor would not be acting inequitably in going back on his promise after reasonable notice merely because the debtor had relied on the promise by making the part payment. If, for example, there were a sudden improvement in the debtor's financial position, it might be perfectly reasonable, and in accordance with commercial morality, for the creditor to claim the balance.

The creditor may also be justified in going back on his promise by reason of the debtor's conduct in obtaining it. No doubt a creditor is normally thought of as the stronger party to a contractual relationship; but that position may also be occupied by the debtor who may use undue pressure to extort from the creditor a promise to accept part payment in full settlement. This possibility is illustrated by the *D & C Builders*[18] case, where a houseowner owed a sum of money for work done to a small firm of builders, who were in desperate need of money. He induced them to promise to accept part of that sum in full settlement by threatening that, if they did not give such a promise, he would pay them nothing. It was held that the builders could go back on their promise and sue for the balance.

The purpose of the rule in *Foakes v Beer* was precisely to protect the creditor from this kind of pressure. But unfortunately the rule was explained on the ground that there was no consideration for the creditor's promise; and this reasoning applied even where that promise formed part of a perfectly reasonable variation, as in the *High Trees* case, where it reflected a change in circumstances after the making of the original contract. The protective function of the rule is now more satisfactorily performed by the concept of economic duress;[19] and the rule should be replaced by one which struck only at variations extorted by duress. The doctrine of promissory estoppel

16　Cf *J T Sydenham & Co Ltd v Enichem Elastomers Ltd* [1989] 1 EGLR 257 at 260 (where the debt was *disputed*: cf ante, p 51).
17　Ante, p 47.
18　*D & C Builders Ltd v Rees* [1966] 2 QB 617.
19　See post, pp 176–177.

should not prevent a creditor from going back on a promise obtained in this way. Where, however, the debtor's conduct falls short of duress, the doctrine of promissory estoppel should not be excluded merely because the court views the debtor's conduct with some disapproval: such a vague category of 'improper conduct' is not only unnecessary but also 'unhelpful because it would make the law uncertain'.[20]

13 PROPRIETARY ESTOPPEL

The doctrine of proprietary estoppel applies to many situations, with only one of which we are here concerned. This arises where an owner of property (usually land) makes a representation or promise to another person that the latter has, or will be granted, legal rights in or over the property, and the latter suffers substantial[1] detriment in reliance on that representation or promise. The landowner may then be prevented from denying the existence of those rights, or even be compelled to grant them; and, because the rights in question concern property, the estoppel has come to be known as 'proprietary'. Under this doctrine, some legal effect may be given to a promise even though it is not binding as a contract: eg because it is not intended to have contractual effect, or because it is not supported by consideration.

Typical illustrations of proprietary estoppel are provided by family arrangements between parent (A) and child (B), to the effect that, if B will build a house on land belonging to A, then A will give the land to B,[2] or allow B to stay there for life.[3] Such promises cannot be revoked after B has built the house. Similarly, a promise by A to allow B to live in his house may induce B to believe that B has a legal right to stay there; such a promise cannot be revoked after B has, in reliance on it, made improvements to the house.[4] In these cases, the landowner would be unjustly enriched if he could freely evoke the promise, for he would then have the land together with the improvements made by the promisee. But action in reliance by the promisee can give rise to a proprietary estoppel even though it does not result in any improvement of the land referred to in the promise, for example, where it consists of personal services rendered to the promisor;[5] and detrimental reliance

20 *Pao On v Lau Yiu Long* [1980] AC 614 at 634.
1 *Gillett v Holt* [2001] Ch 210 at 232.
2 *Dillwyn v Llewelyn* (1862) 4 De GF & J 517.
3 *Inwards v Baker* [1965] 2 QB 29.
4 *Hussey v Palmer* [1972] 3 All ER 744; *Eves v Eves* [1975] 3 All ER 768; *Pascoe v Turner* [1979] 1 WLR 431; *Voyce v Voyce* (1991) 62 P & CR 290.
5 Eg *Campbell v Griffin* [2001] EWCA Civ 999, [2001] WTLR 981; *Jennings v Rice* [2002] EWCA Civ 159, [2002] WTLR 367.

may give rise to a proprietary estoppel even where it does not result in any benefit at all to the promisor.[6] The doctrine applies only where the promise relates to *identifiable* property: it is not enough for the promisee to render services to another in the expectation (induced by the promise) of receiving some indeterminate benefit under the latter's will.[7] It is, moreover, necessary for the promisee to believe that the promise gives rise to a *legal* right to the property,[8] and for that belief to be induced by the words or conduct of the other party.[9]

Proprietary estoppel can give rise to a variety of legal consequences. The promisor may be required actually to convey the land to the promisee,[10] or to allow him to stay there for life,[11] or simply to compensate him for his expenditure or in respect of other reliance;[12] the court may also combine an order for the conveyance of some of the relevant land with one for further compensation in money.[13] Although the remedy is thus 'extremely flexible',[14] the court must adopt a 'principled approach',[15] taking into account such factors as the terms of the promise, the extent of the promisee's reliance, the proportion between the promisee's expectations and the extent of his detrimental reliance.[16] In applying this test of 'proportionality' the court may refuse to give full effect to the expectations in fact formed by the promisee and award a sum that is reasonable having regard to the extent of his reliance.[17] This approach may, however, in turn be displaced in the light of the promisor's 'ruthlessness'[18] in seeking to evict the promisee from the property to which the estoppel relates.

Proprietary estoppel resembles promissory estoppel in that the promise remains revocable until the promisee has acted on it[19] or

---

6   *Crabb v Arun District Council* [1976] Ch 179.
7   *Layton v Martin* [1986] 2 FLR 227; contrast *Re Basham* [1987] 1 All ER 405, where the property was more clearly defined.
8   *Coombes v Smith* [1986] 1 WLR 808.
9   *A-G of Hong Kong v Humphreys Estate (Queen's Gardens) Ltd* [1987] AC 114.
10 *Dillwyn v Llewelyn* (1862) 4 De GF & J; *Pascoe v Turner* [1979] 1 WLR 431; *J T Developments Ltd v Quinn* (1990) 62 P & CR 33.
11 *Inwards v Baker* [1965] 2 QB 29.
12 *Dodsworth v Dodsworth* (1973) 228 Estates Gazette 1115; *Burrows and Burrows v Sharp* (1991) 23 HLR 82; *Jennings v Rice* [2002] EWCA Civ 159, [2002] WTLR 367.
13 *Gillett v Holt* [2001] Ch 210.
14 *Roebuck v Mungovin* [1994] 2 AC 224 at 235.
15 *Jennings v Rice* [2002] EWCA Civ 159, [2002] WTLR 367 at [43].
16 [2002] EWCA Civ 159, [2002] WTLR 367 at [36], [56].
17 As in *Jennings v Rice* [2002] EWCA Civ 159, [2002] WTLR 367.
18 *Pascoe v Turner* [1979] 1 WLR 431 at 439; cf *Gillett v Holt* [2001] Ch 210 at 235.
19 *Pascoe v Turner* [1979] 1 WLR 431 at 439; before action in reliance, promisee was said to have only a licence at will.

even thereafter if the promisee can still be restored to the position in which he was before he acted on the promise. On the other hand there are also important differences between them. The first is that promissory estoppel is not, whilst proprietary estoppel is, restricted to promises affecting property. And secondly, promissory estoppel cannot create new rights,[20] while proprietary estoppel can do so:[1] for example, it can give the promisee the right to have land conveyed to him.

A promise which gives rise to a proprietary estoppel is nevertheless less advantageous to the promisee than one which is binding contractually. In cases of proprietary estoppel, the promise may be revocable; the remedy for its breach is not available as of right but only at the discretion of the court; and in exercising that discretion the court may take into account factors other than the terms of the promise. The enforceability of promises which have contractual force is not subject to any of these restrictions.

14 IRREVOCABLE OFFERS

An offer can be withdrawn at any time before it has been accepted. This is so even though the offeror has expressly or by implication promised to hold his offer open for a stated period. Such a promise is not binding unless it is made by deed or unless consideration has been given for it:[2] for example, by the offeree's making some counter-promise, or by his buying an option or by doing some other act at the request of the promisor (such as making efforts to raise the money that will enable the offeree to accept the offer). Such acts may also constitute consideration for a promise by which the offeror undertakes for a specified time not to offer the subject-matter to any person except the offeree,[3] but such a 'lock-out' agreement would not prevent the offeror from withdrawing the offer and simply not selling at all.

In some contexts, the legal position is well understood in the business world, where no-one would, for example, expect to be able to enforce wholly gratuitous share options. But in other commercial contexts reliance is reasonably placed on promises to hold offers open. For example, a builder may base his own offer to a customer on offers for the supply of materials which he himself has received and which are expressed to remain 'firm' for a fixed period; but those

---

20   See ante, p 48.
1   *Crabb v Arun District Council* [1976] Ch 179 at 187.
2   *Dickinson v Dodds* (1876) 2 Ch D 463; see ante, p 20.
3   *Pitt v PHH Asset Management Ltd* [1993] 4 All ER 961.

offers can be withdrawn within that period, even after the builder has bound himself contractually to a customer in reliance on them. Here the rule causes hardship[4] to the builder and proposals for reform have from time to time been made.[5] These proposals have not so far been implemented; but exceptions to the rule have been created in the interests of commercial convenience. One[6] such exception appears to be established where a contract for the sale of goods provides for payment by a banker's irrevocable credit. Under such a provision, the buyer will instruct his bank to notify the seller of the irrevocable credit; and the notification takes the shape of an irrevocable promise by the bank to pay the seller, usually on tender of specified shipping documents relating to the goods. The commercial understanding is that the bank is bound as soon as it notifies the seller of the credit and before the seller has done anything which can be said to amount to acceptance of the bank's offer, or to provide consideration for it. If, as seems likely, the courts accept this commercial view they can be said to enforce a promise not to revoke an offer, even though there is no consideration for it in the traditional sense.[7] The existence of these exceptions provides a final illustration of a point often made in this Chapter: that the doctrine of consideration requires considerable modification to enable the law of contract to remain in touch with modern business needs.

4 Which Canadian courts have managed to avoid: see *Northern Construction Co Ltd v Gloge Heating and Plumbing* (1984) 6 DLR (4th) 450.
5 See Law Commission, Working Paper No 60 (1975).
6 For another, see the Vienna Convention, ante, p 16, Art 16(2).
7 See *Hamzeh Malas & Sons v British Imex Industries Ltd* [1958] 2 QB 127; *The American Accord* [1983] 1 AC 168 at 183.

Chapter 4

Contractual intention

An agreement supported by consideration may not amount to a contract because the agreement was made without any intention to affect legal relations. In deciding whether such an intention exists, a distinction must be drawn between implied agreements and express ones. The former are approached on the basis that 'contracts are not lightly to be implied' and that the court 'must be able to conclude with confidence that the parties intended to create contractual relations'.[1] The burden of proof on this issue is on the party alleging the existence of the contract.[2] But where the claim is based on an express agreement made in an ordinary commercial context, that party does not need to prove affirmatively that there was such an intention. On the contrary, it is up to the party denying the existence of a contract to disprove the intention and the onus of proof which he has to discharge is a heavy one.[3] Moreover, in such cases the courts apply an objective test,[4] so that a party to an ordinary commercial arrangement cannot escape liability merely by showing that he did not, in his own mind, intend the agreement to affect legal relations.[5] In cases of express agreements, the requirement of contractual intention is therefore significant only in a number of somewhat exceptional situations.

1 EXPRESS PROVISIONS

Contractual intention may be negatived by the terms of the agreement. This was, for example, held to be the effect of an 'honour clause'

---

1   *Blackpool and Fylde Aero Club Ltd v Blackpool Borough Council* [1990] 3 All ER 25 at 31.
2   Eg *Baird Textile Holdings Ltd v Marks & Spencer plc* [2001] EWCA Civ 274, [2002] 1 All ER (Comm) 737 (burden not discharged); *Modahl v British Athletics Federation* [2001] EWCA Civ 1477, [2002] 1 WLR 1192 (burden discharged).
3   *Edwards v Skyways Ltd* [1964] 1 WLR 349 at 355; *Orion Insurance Co plc v Sphere Drake Insurance plc* [1992] 1 Lloyd's Rep 239 at 263.
4   *Edmonds v Lawson* [2000] QB 501.
5   *Kingswood Estate Co Ltd v Anderson* [1963] 2 QB 169.

which provided that the agreement was not to be a 'legal agreement'.[6] In an agreement for the sale of land, contractual intention is normally negatived by the words 'subject to contract'.[7] But where these words are omitted from such an agreement, it will amount to a binding contract even though one party subjectively believed that he was not to be bound until the usual 'exchange of contracts' had taken place. The objective test would prevent that party from relying on the belief,[8] unless it was known to the other party.[9]

One important class of agreements which at common law were *prima facie* held to be binding in honour only, were collective agreements between trade unions and employers or associations of employers.[10] Under the Trade Union and Labour Relations (Consolidation) Act 1992 such an agreement is 'conclusively presumed not to have been intended by the parties to be a legally enforceable contract' unless it is in writing and expressly provides that it is intended to be legally enforceable.[11] Whether or not the agreement is legally enforceable between the parties to it (ie the unions and the employer) some of its terms[12] may be incorporated by reference into individual contracts of employment and may then, if so intended, become binding between employers and employees.[13]

2 VAGUE AGREEMENTS

Vagueness may be a ground for concluding that the parties never reached agreement at all;[14] but even where they have reached some agreement, its vagueness may prevent it, for want of contractual intention, from having contractual force. This principle is often applied in order to determine whether a statement forms part of an admitted contract. For this purpose the courts have distinguished between simple 'sales talk' which gives rise to no liability, 'mere

6   *Rose and Frank Co v J R Crompton & Bros Ltd* [1925] AC 445. Contrast *Home Insurance Co and St Paul Fire and Marine Insurance Co v Administration Asigurarilor de Stat* [1983] 2 Lloyd's Rep 674 at 677 where similar words referred only to the *interpretation* of the agreement.
7   See ante, p 27.
8   *Tweddell v Henderson* [1975] 2 All ER 1096.
9   *Pateman v Pay* (1974) 232 Estates Gazette 457.
10 *Ford Motor Co Ltd v Amalgamated Union of Engineering and Foundry Workers* [1969] 2 QB 303.
11 Section 179(1) and (2).
12 See s 180(1) and (2) for restrictions on incorporation of 'no strike' clauses.
13 *Marley v Forward Trust Group Ltd* [1986] ICR 891; *National Coal Board v National Union of Mineworkers* [1986] ICR 736.
14 Ante, p 25.

representations' which have some legal effects without being contractually binding, and statements which are contractual terms.[15] Only statements which are (objectively) *intended* to be contractually binding will fall into the last of these classes. The same requirement may also determine the very existence of a contract. Thus in one case[16] it was held that no contract arose from claims made by a manufacturer in promotional literature that his product was 'foolproof' and that it 'required no maintenance'; and such statements are probably also too vague for the purpose of legislation which makes a seller of goods liable to a buyer who deals as consumer for statements in advertising as to their 'specific characteristics', and a person such as a manufacturer liable if he gives the buyer a 'consumer guarantee' in respect of such goods.[17] The vagueness of the language used may also lead to the conclusion that 'letters of intent' or 'letters of comfort' issued in the course of commercial negotiations do not have contractual force.[18] Two factors which influence the courts in cases of this kind are, on the one hand, the importance of the statement to the person to whom it is addressed[19] and, on the other, the degree of precision with which it is expressed. If A says to B 'You will come to no harm if you buy X's paint to paint your factory', A's statement is unlikely to have contractual force. But the position is different if A says to B 'If you buy X's paint to paint your factory, I guarantee that it will last for seven years'.[20] In the second case the specific terms of A's promise make it highly probable that he intended to be legally bound, or at least that B reasonably received that impression.

3   DISCRETIONARY AGREEMENTS

Contractual intention is most obviously negatived where an argument leaves performance by each party to that party's discretion.[1] The same may be true where the agreement confers a wide discretion on only one of the parties. In an old case, a promise to pay for services 'such remuneration as may be deemed right' was held to be 'merely an

---

15   See post, pp 146–151, 155–157.
16   *Lambert v Lewis* [1982] AC 225, affd on other grounds ibid, at 271.
17   See Sale of Goods Act 1979, s 13 (2D); Sale and Supply of Goods to Consumers Regulations 2002, SI 2002/3045, regs 3 and 15.
18   *J H Milner & Son v Percy Bilton Ltd* [1966] 2 All ER 894; *Kleinwort Benson Ltd v Malaysia Mining Corpn Bhd* [1989] 1 All ER 785.
19   *J Evans & Son (Portsmouth) Ltd v Andrea Merzario Ltd* [1976] 2 All ER 930.
20   Cf *Shanklin Pier Ltd v Detel Products Ltd* [1951] 2 KB 854.
1   *Carmichael v National Power plc* [1999] 1 WLR 2042.

engagement of honour'[2] and thus not legally enforceable. Nowadays the courts are reluctant to reach such a result after work has actually been done under the agreement; but they will still do so where the intention to negative contractual intention is clear.[3]

4 SOCIAL AND DOMESTIC AGREEMENTS

Many everyday social arrangements are obviously not intended to be contractually binding. No one would, for example, suppose that acceptance of an invitation to dinner created a contract. Similarly, most arrangements within the family which relate to the ordinary day-to-day running of the household are not contracts. Where a husband pays his wife a housekeeping allowance, he does not normally contract to do so, any more than the wife contracts to manage the household; nor is an arrangement under which husband and wife draw on a joint bank account normally a contract.[4] This position usually holds good even though the parties are temporarily living apart, eg because the husband's work has taken him abroad.[5] Of course, when the parties live apart because of the break-up of their marriage, any agreement between them regulating the terms of separation is likely to be contractual in nature. Even in such a case, contractual intention may be negatived by the vague or discretionary terms of the arrangement: for example, where a husband, on leaving his wife, promised to pay her £15 per week 'so long as I can manage it'.[6] Similar principles can apply between parent and child, so that a parent's informal promise to pay the child an allowance during study would not normally be a binding contract. But where the promise was made in order to induce the child to give up one occupation and to qualify for another, the promise would *prima facie* be binding, even though this inference could in turn be rebutted by the vagueness of the arrangement.[7] The fact that the promisee has taken some important step in reliance on the promise can also outweigh the significance normally attached to a 'family' relationship in negativing contractual intention. Thus it has been held that there was a contract where a young couple left their home and went to live with elderly relations on the faith of the

2 *Taylor v Brewer* (1813) 1 M & S 290 at 291.
3 *Re Richmond Gate Property Co Ltd* [1964] 3 All ER 936.
4 *Gage v King* [1961] 1 QB 188.
5 *Balfour v Balfour* [1919] 2 KB 571.
6 *Gould v Gould* [1970] 1 QB 275.
7 *Jones v Padavatton* [1969] 2 All ER 616; cf *Hardwick v Johnson* [1978] 2 All ER 935.

latters' promise to provide for them by will.[8] Similar reasoning has been applied to house sharing agreements between persons who lived together as husband and wife without being married.[9] The fact that one of the parties has helped to improve the property is also sometimes relied upon to give such an agreement contractual force.[10]

5   OTHER ILLUSTRATIONS

The categories of cases discussed above, in which there is no contractual intention, are not exhaustive and there are many other factors which may negative contractual intention. Thus, it has been held that an agreement which was intended merely to give effect to rights believed already to exist was not a contract, as the parties had no intention to enter into a new contract;[11] that the relationship between a minister of religion and the church which had appointed him was not a contract as it was not intended to be enforceable in the courts;[12] and that contractual intention may be negatived where a promise is made in jest or anger, at least if this fact is apparent to the person to whom the promise is made.[13] Occasionally, conflicting factors will lead to differences of judicial opinion on the issue of contractual intention;[14] and the type of relationship from which the issue arises is not as a matter of law decisive. The point is illustrated by civil service appointments, which were formerly regarded as non-contractual for want of the necessary intention on the part of the Crown;[15] but evidence of a change in the Crown's position on the point has led the courts to hold that they now have contractual force.[16] This development shows that the categories discussed above are useful only in providing general guidance. They are not decisive since, in the last resort, the question of contractual intention is one of fact in each case.

8   *Parker v Clark* [1960] 1 All ER 93.
9   *Tanner v Tanner* [1975] 3 All ER 776, contrast *Horrocks v Forray* [1976] 1 All ER 737; but such contracts may now fail to satisfy the formal requirements described at post, p 65.
10   *Eves v Eves* [1975] 1 WLR 1338; cf *Grant v Edwards* [1986] Ch 638 (liability based on 'constructive trust').
11   *Harvela Investments Ltd v Royal Trust Co of Canada (CI) Ltd* [1986] AC 207.
12   *President of the Methodist Conference v Parfitt* [1984] QB 368; *Davies v Presbyterian Church of Wales* [1986] 1 All ER 705.
13   *Licences Insurance Corporation v Lawson* (1896) 12 TLR 501.
14   *Esso Petroleum Ltd v Customs and Excise Comrs* [1976] 1 All ER 117.
15   *R v Civil Service Appeal Board, ex p Bruce* [1988] 3 All ER 686.
16   *R v Lord Chancellor's Department, ex p Nangle* [1992] 1 All ER 897.

Chapter 5

Form

1 NATURE AND PURPOSE OF FORMAL REQUIREMENTS

To say that a contract must be in a certain form means that its conclusion must be marked or recorded in a prescribed manner. In modern systems of law, formal requirements invariably call for some kind of written instrument. Normally, such requirements must be satisfied in addition to the ordinary requirements of agreement, consideration and contractual intention, though occasionally form may replace one or more of these requirements. For example, a promise in a deed to make a gift is binding, even in the absence of consideration and of agreement. In this chapter, however, we shall consider cases in which form is an *additional* (and not those in which it is a *substitute*) requirement.

There are several reasons why the law may impose formal requirements. First, the use of a prescribed form leads to greater certainty, making it easier to tell when a contract has been made, what its terms are, and what type of contract it is (eg whether it is sale or hire-purchase). Secondly, a requirement of form acts as a warning against rashly entering into a contract. This was one of the functions of the deed in the days when sealing by an impression on wax was still necessary for its execution; and a modern equivalent can be seen in the formalities required by law for the execution of regulated consumer credit agreements (such as hire-purchase agreements) in which the debtor is an individual and the amount of credit does not exceed £25,000.[1] Here the debtor and creditor must sign a document drawn up in accordance with government regulations. The debtor must sign inside a 'signature box' warning him that he is signing a consumer credit agreement; and the document must specify certain information which has to be given to the debtor. Such requirements also illustrate a third (increasingly important) function of form, which is to protect the weaker party to the transaction by giving him a written

---

1   Consumer Credit Act 1974, ss 8, 55, 60, 61; SI 1998/996.

statement of its terms. Similar legislation exists to protect, for example, certain tenants and employees, who may have to be given written particulars of the terms on which they have contracted.[2]

2   FORM GENERALLY NOT REQUIRED

Although there are thus many and good reasons for imposing formal requirements in certain cases, the general rule is that contracts can be made quite informally. In spite of a popular belief to the contrary, it is not even necessary for a contract to be in writing. Contracts for the sale of goods or shares worth millions of pounds can be made quite informally, by word of mouth. In practice, such contracts are often made in writing, even when there is no such legal requirement; and this practice gives rise to problems which will be discussed in Chapter 6.

The main reason for the general rule is that formal requirements are thought to be commercially inconvenient. The execution of a formal agreement takes time, when speed may be essential; and formal requirements are subject to pitfalls, so that a slip in the execution may enable a party to escape from a transaction on some technical ground. These factors justify the general principle, but there are many exceptions to it. These now all depend on legislation dealing with particular types of contracts. Our concern is with the general principles of the law of contract and it would be impossible in a book of this kind to deal with the rules governing formal requirements in relation to each particular type of contract to which they apply. But two topics of general interest can appropriately be discussed here. The first concerns the difference between various formal requirements imposed by law, and the second, the effects of failing to comply with these requirements.

3   TYPES OF FORMAL REQUIREMENTS

Although all formal requirements involve writing of some kind, the exact nature of the writing required varies from case to case.

At one extreme, the law may require the contract to be made by deed: this is, for example, the position with regard to a lease of land for more than three years.[3]

A second group of contracts must be *in writing*, but the writing does not have to be in the form of a deed. A regulated consumer

2   See pp 65–66, post.
3   Law of Property Act 1925, s 52.

credit agreement is 'not properly executed' unless a document in the required form, containing the express terms of the agreement, is signed by both parties.[4] And most contracts for the sale or disposition of an interest in land must be 'made in writing', ie in a document which incorporates all the terms expressly agreed by the parties and which is signed[5] by or on behalf of both of them.[6]

A third type of requirement is that there must be a *note or memorandum in writing* of the contract. This requirement exists in relation to contracts of guarantee.[7] It differs from the second type in that it is satisfied even though the document comes into existence after the time of contracting, so long as it recognises the existence of the contract[8] and comes into existence before an action is brought. For this reason it is sometimes said that the contract does not have to be *in writing*, but only *evidenced in writing*. The memorandum must identify the parties and the subject-matter of the contract and state its terms (though the consideration for the guarantee need not be stated).[9] It must also be 'signed' by the party to be charged; but this requirement has in the present context[10] been very loosely interpreted, so that initials or a printed signature will do. The signature need not be at the foot of the document, so long as it authenticates the whole document.[11] A memorandum may even be put together from two or more documents, if the document signed by the party to be charged expressly, or by implication, refers to the other or others; or if, by placing the two side by side, their connection becomes obvious and does not have to be established by oral evidence.[12] These lax rules indicate the courts' dislike of the present requirement, which was often used to set up unmeritorious defences based on technical slips.

There is, finally, a fourth group of contracts which do not have to be in, or to be evidenced in, writing, but which are subject to the

---

4   Consumer Credit Act 1974, s 61. See also ss 62, 63, 64 for requirements as to delivery of copies and notice of a 'cooling-off' period.
5   Merely typing a person's name and address on the document does not, for this purpose, amount to a signature: *Firstpost Homes Ltd v Johnson* [1995] 1 WLR 1567.
6   Law of Property (Miscellaneous Provisions) Act 1989, s 2(1) and (3); leases for less than three years, sales by public auction and transactions in certain securities are excluded by s 2(5).
7   Statute of Frauds 1677, s 4, repealed in relation to certain other contracts by Law Reform (Enforcement of Contracts) Act 1954.
8   *Tweddell v Henderson* [1975] 2 All ER 1096 (the contract in this case would now be subject to the more stringent requirement stated at n 5, supra).
9   Mercantile Law Amendment Act 1856, s 3.
10   Contrast the position stated in n 5, supra.
11   *Hill v Hill* [1947] Ch 231 at 240, *Schneider v Norris* (1814) 2 M & S 286.
12   *Stokes v Whicher* [1920] 1 Ch 411; *Elias v George Sahely & Co (Barbados) Ltd* [1983] 1 AC 646.

requirement that one party must (either spontaneously or on request) *supply certain written particulars* to the other: for example, under some tenancies, a landlord is bound to give his tenant a rent-book setting out certain particulars; and an employer is often bound to give his employee a written document setting out the principal terms of the contract.[13]

The above requirements of 'writing', of a 'document' or of 'signature' can be satisfied where contracts are made by email or by trading on a website.[14] Whether the requirement of signature is satisfied by an act such as clicking on a website button depends on the common law test of what amounts to a signature: ie on whether the act was intended to authenticate the document.[15] Some statutory requirements (eg sending particulars of a consumer credit agreement to the debtor by post)[16] can be satisfied only by the use of paper documents; and these may require modification in the light of a provision in an EC Directive requiring member states to ensure that in general, their legal systems allow contracts to be concluded by electronic means.[17] This requirement does not, however, apply to contracts for the sale of interests in land or to contracts of guarantee.[18] It therefore does not affect the existing English legislation specifying the formal requirements of such contracts;[19] nor will it affect any English legislation that may be passed to enable them to be made electronically.[20] The protective function of form would lose much of its efficacy if a guarantor could become liable as such by simply clicking on the appropriate part of a website.

4   EFFECTS OF FAILURE TO USE THE REQUIRED FORM

The effect of failure to comply with a formal requirement imposed by law is hardly ever to make the contract a compete nullity. It varies according to the nature of the formal requirement.

---

13   Landlord and Tenant Act 1985, s 4; Employment Rights Act 1996, ss 1, 2–4, 11.
14   See Law Commission paper on *Electronic Commerce: Formal Requirements in Commercial Contracts* (December 2001). Electronically stored information can be a 'document': *Victor Chandler International Ltd v Customs and Excise Comrs* [2000] 1 WLR 1296.
15   Ante at n 11.
16   Eg Consumer Credit Act 1974, ss 63(3), 64(2).
17   Directive 2000/13/EC, Art 9. Parts of the Directive (but not Art 9) are implemented by Electronic Commerce (EC Directive) Regulations 2002, SI 2002/2013.
18   Art 9(2)(a), (2)(c).
19   Ante, at nn 4 and 6.
20   Eg under Part 8 of the Land Registration Act 2002.

The first possibility is that because of the failure the contract simply does not come into existence. This is the position where a contract for the sale of land is not 'made in writing' in accordance with the requirements just described. Such a conclusion can cause hardship: eg to a purchaser who has partly performed, or otherwise acted in reliance on, the supposed contract. Various legal techniques exist for mitigating this hardship: the purchaser may have a remedy under the doctrine of proprietary estoppel;[1] or, where the writing is defective because it omits one of the agreed terms, he may be able to have the contract rectified (if the omission was due to a mistake in the drawing up of the document)[2] or to enforce an omitted term as a collateral contract, so long as that term is not intended to form an essential part of the main contract.[3]

A second possibility is that the contract may still be binding as such, but that it does not produce all the legal effects which it would have produced, if it had been in the required form. This would, for example, be the position if a lease for over three years were simply in writing but not made by deed. The document would be 'void for the purpose of creating a legal estate'[4] but it would be a perfectly valid agreement for a lease which could be enforced by the tenant.[5] The main difference between such an agreement and a duly executed lease is that the former might not, whereas the latter would, prevail against a third person to whom the landlord had sold the land.

A third possibility is that restrictions may be placed on the right of *one* of the parties to enforce the agreement. For example, a regulated consumer credit agreement cannot be enforced against the debtor if it has not been signed by him; if it suffers from one or more of a number of other formal defects, it can be enforced against the debtor only on an order of the court;[6] and where no such order is made the debtor is under no liability to make restitution to the creditor in respect of any benefits that the debtor may have received under the agreement.[7] In deciding whether to make an enforcement order, the court can take into account factors such as the amount of prejudice caused to the debtor by the formal defect and the degree of culpability of the creditor. The court can also take various intermediate courses

---

1   Ante, p 54; Law of Property (Miscellaneous Provisions) Act 1989, s 2(5) preserves this possibility: *Yaxley v Gotts* [2000] Ch 162 at 193.
2   Post, p 142; Law of Property (Miscellaneous Provisions) Act 1989, s 2(4).
3   Eg, *Record v Bell* [1991] 4 All ER 471; *Grossman v Hooper* [2001] EWCA Civ 615, [2001] EGLR 82 at [21].
4   Law of Property Act 1925, s 52.
5   *Walsh v Lonsdale* (1882) 21 Ch D 9.
6   Consumer Credit Act 1974, ss 65, 127.
7   *Dimond v Lovell* [2002] AC 384 at 398.

between allowing and refusing enforcement: for example it can enforce the contract as if it did not contain a term which should have been, but was not, included in the document signed by the debtor. The result of this judicial discretion will be to prevent a debtor from relying on unmeritorious defences based on technical formal slips. For the purpose of these rules, enforcement includes the retaking of any goods to which the agreement relates. Failure to comply with the statutory formalities has no effect on the right of the debtor to enforce the contract.

A fourth possibility is that the contract is valid but cannot be enforced by action against any party who has not signed a note or memorandum of it. This is the position with regard to contracts of guarantee: if the document has been signed by one party but not by the other, it can be enforced against the former but not the latter. As the contract is not void but only enforceable,[8] a party who has paid money or transferred property under it is not entitled to its return.[9]

A fifth possibility is that a contract is not admissible in evidence at all unless it is embodied in a written document containing certain particulars. Such a rule is laid down by statute for policies of marine insurance.[10]

The final possibility is that the failure may not affect the validity of the contract at all: this is, for example, the position where a landlord fails to give his tenant a rent book in accordance with the relevant legislation. In such a case the landlord commits a criminal offence, but he can nevertheless sue the tenant for rent,[11] and of course the tenant can enforce the lease against the landlord.

5   RESCISSION AND VARIATION OF WRITTEN CONTRACTS

A contract which is subject to a formal requirement can nevertheless be *rescinded* informally: for example, a contract for the disposition of an interest in land or one of guarantee can be rescinded orally.[12] An attempt to vary such a contract orally gives rise to two possibilities. First, the variation may be regarded as a rescission of the old contract,

---

8   *Leroux v Brown* (1852) 12 CB 801.
9   *Thomas v Brown* (1876) 1 QBD 714.
10   Marine Insurance Act 1906, s 22.
11   *Shaw v Groom* [1970] 2 QB 504.
12   Cf *Morris v Baron & Co* [1918] AC 1. Law of Property (Miscellaneous Provisions) Act 1989, s 2(1) does not say anything about how a contract which must be *made* in writing is to be *unmade*.

followed by the substitution of a new one on different terms. In that case the rescission will be effective, but the new contract will not satisfy the formal requirement and so there will be no legally enforceable contract on the new tems.[13] Secondly, the variation may be an attempt to add a term to the original contract, or to strike out or to change one of its terms. In that case, the variation is ineffective and each party can sue (and can sue only) on the original contract.[14] At most, the variation might have a limited effect under the doctrine of a 'waiver', which is substantially similar to the doctrine of promissory estoppel discussed in Chapter 3.[15]

If the contract is not subject to any formal requirement, but happens to have been made in writing or by deed, it may be rescinded or varied without the use of the same formality. For example, where a contract is made by deed (though it is not legally required to be so made), it can be varied by a writing not amounting to a deed.[16]

13 *Morris v Baron & Co* [1918] AC 1.
14 *Goss v Lord Nugent* (1833) 5 B & Ad 58; *Tyers v Rosedale and Ferryhill Iron Co* (1875) LR 10 Exch 195.
15 Ante, pp 47–49; *British and Beningtons Ltd v North Western Cachar Tea Co Ltd* [1923] AC 48.
16 *Berry v Berry* [1929] 2 KB 316.

Chapter 6
The contents of a contract

A contract may contain both express and implied terms. Express terms depend on the words used by the parties in reaching or recording their agreement. Implied terms are included, for various reasons to be discussed in this chapter, even though they have not been expressly stated in words.

1 ASCERTAINMENT OF EXPRESS TERMS

The ascertainment of express terms raises two questions: what words did the parties use and what did those words mean? The first question is simply one of fact, but the second raises issues of law. In answering it, the court applies the objective test: a party cannot enforce the contract in the sense that he gave to the words, if that sense is not one in which a reasonable person would have understood them.[1]

Where the contract is in writing, there is normally no dispute as to the words contained in the document. But some difficulty may arise where a contract is set out in one document, which incorporates another document by express reference: eg where a contract is made subject to the rules of a trade association, or subject to the regulations in a time-table. The document so referred to may be one of great length and complexity, running into many pages and sometimes into literally hundreds of clauses. In that case, the parties will often not be fully aware of the terms of the second document and they may include, in the first, provisions which are inconsistent with those contained in the second. The court then has to resolve the inconsistency as best it can; and, where possible, it will give primacy to the terms actually drawn up by the parties, as these are likely to represent their predominant intention.[2]

A contract may be contained in two documents, even though the principal one does not *expressly* refer to the other, if in the court's view it was the intention of the parties to incorporate the second document.

---

1   *Eyre v Measday* [1986] 1 All ER 488; *Thake v Maurice* [1986] QB 644.
2   See *Adamastos Shipping Co Ltd v Anglo-Saxon Petroleum Co Ltd* [1959] AC 133.

For example, in one case[3] a contract for the sale of certain securities was held to incorporate a term in a prospectus, even though that term was not set out in the contract of sale, while all the other terms in the prospectus were so set out.

Where the contract is in writing, the so-called parol evidence rule may prevent a party from relying on other evidence as to its express terms. This rule will be considered after a discussion of implied terms.

2 IMPLIED TERMS

Implied terms may be divided into (a) terms implied in fact; (b) terms implied in law; and (c) terms implied by custom or usage.

a Terms implied in fact

A term implied in fact is one which was not expressly stated, but which (in the court's view) the parties must have intended to include, because it was 'so obvious that it goes without saying; so that, if while the parties were making their bargain, an officious bystander were to suggest some express provision for it in the agreement, they would testily suppress him with a common "Oh, of course!"'[4] In applying the 'officious bystander' test the courts have insisted that the implication must be obvious to *both* parties, so that if one of them is ignorant of the matter to be implied, or has no view on it, the implication will fail.[5] Similarly, it is not sufficient to show that the parties would have made *some* provision for the matter, if it is not obvious that they would have both agreed to the *same* one.[6]

It is also often said that the term must be 'necessary to give the transaction such business efficacy as the parties must have intended',[7] or (what seems to mean the same thing) that the implication is subject to a test of 'necessity'.[8] But these are not additional requirements: they are, rather, practical tests of intention[9] and are based on the

3   *Jacobs v Batavia and General Plantations Trust Ltd* [1924] 1 Ch 287.
4   *Shirlaw v Southern Foundries (1926) Ltd* [1939] 2 KB 206 at 227; affd [1940] AC 701.
5   *Spring v National Amalgamated Stevedores and Dockers Society* [1956] 2 All ER 221; *K C Sethia (1944) Ltd v Partabmull Rameshwar* [1950] 1 All ER 51; affd [1951] 2 All ER 352n.
6   *Lister v Romford Ice and Cold Storage Co Ltd* [1957] AC 555.
7   *Luxor (Eastbourne) Ltd v Cooper* [1941] AC 108 at 137; *Trollope and Colls Ltd v North West Metropolitan Regional Hospital Board* [1973] 2 All ER 260.
8   Eg *Hughes v Greenwich London Borough Council* [1994] 1 AC 170 at 179.
9   Eg *Ashmore v Corpn of Lloyd's (No 2)* [1992] 2 Lloyd's Rep 620 at 626; *McClory v Post Office* [1993] 1 All ER 457 at 462.

assumption that the parties would have agreed to terms which were necessary to make their agreement work. They also emphasise the point that it is not enough to show that the contract might have been a more reasonable one with the added term; for although the test of reasonableness may be used in *interpreting* express terms,[10] and although the fact that the alleged term was reasonable may help to satisfy the 'officious bystander' test,[11] the court will not normally undertake the task of improving the contract by implying new terms into it.[12] This is particularly true 'where the parties have entered into a carefully drafted written contract containing detailed terms agreed between them'.[13] The judicial attitude is illustrated by a case[14] arising out of a contract by which an oil company undertook to supply petrol and oil to a garage while the garage promised to buy such goods only from the company. One reason why the court refused to imply a term that the company should not 'abnormally discriminate' against the garage in favour of neighbouring retailers was that it was not obvious that the company would have agreed to such a term; another was that the alleged term was too vague.[15]

b   Terms implied in law

Many of the obligations which arise out of certain types of special contracts are said to be based on 'implied terms'. For example, a seller of goods may impliedly undertake that the goods are of satisfactory quality, or fit for the particular purpose for which the buyer requires them;[16] a person who contracts to supply services in the course of a business undertakes that he will carry them out with reasonable care and skill;[17] and an employer impliedly undertakes that he will not require his employee to do any unlawful act, that he will take reasonable care not to endanger the employee's health and that he will not without reasonable cause do anything to destroy or seriously damage the relationship of trust and confidence between the parties.[18] Detailed

---

10   *Paula Lee Ltd v Robert Zehil & Co Ltd* [1983] 2 All ER 390; cf ante, p 25.
11   *Paragon Finance plc v Staunton* [2001] EWCA Civ 1466, [2001] 2 All ER (Comm) 1025 at [36].
12   *Liverpool City Council v Irwin* [1977] AC 239; *Duke of Westminster v Guild* [1985] QB 688 at 700; *The Maira (No 3)* [1988] 2 Lloyd's Rep 126; *McAuley v Bristol City Council* [1992] QB 134 at 146.
13   *Shell UK Ltd v Lostock Garages Ltd* [1976] 1 WLR 1187 at 1200.
14   *Shell UK Ltd v Lostock Garages Ltd* [1976] 1 WLR 1187.
15   Cf *Walford v Miles* [1992] 2 AC 128.
16   Sale of Goods Act 1979, s 14.
17   Supply of Goods and Services Act 1982, s 13.
18   *Johnstone v Bloomsbury Health Authority* [1992] QB 333; *Malik v BCCI SA* [1998] AC 20.

discussion of such terms will be found in works on sale of goods, contracts of employment, and so forth. Some of them are based on judicial decisions (though a number of these have been codified by statute); others owe their origin to statute. At common law, such terms can be excluded by express contrary provision; but the power to exclude them is now restricted by legislation discussed in Chapter 7.[19]

Obviously, an implied term which cannot be excluded has nothing to do with the intention of the parties and is therefore very different in its legal nature from a term implied in fact. Where the implied term can be excluded, the intention of the parties is relevant, in that it may negative the term. But many terms (including those listed in the preceding paragraph) can be, and often are, implied though the 'officious bystander' test is clearly not satisfied.[20] Some of these terms are so complex that it is quite unrealistic to suppose that the parties had any positive common intention with respect to them;[1] they have been described as 'legal incidents of [particular] kinds of contractual relationships'.[2] It has, indeed, been said that the implication rests on 'necessity';[3] but in determining what amounts to necessity the courts do not, in the present context,[4] look for evidence of common intention. They determine the existence, scope and content of terms implied in law rather by the citation of authorities and by reference to general considerations of policy.[5] The distinction between the two processes of implication is illustrated by a case in which it was held to be an implied term of a lease of a maisonette in a council block that the landlord should take reasonable care to keep the 'common parts' of the block in a reasonable state of repair.[6] The implication arose (in spite of the fact that the 'officious bystander' test was not satisfied) because it was thought desirable to impose some obligation on the landlord as to the maintenance of those common parts. In such cases the courts are really laying down, as a matter of law, how the parties to a contract ought to behave;[7] and the parties will be bound by such standards of conduct unless they have effectively excluded or varied them by the terms of the contact.

19   Unfair Contract Terms Act 1977, ss 6(2), 6(3); see post, pp 103–105.
20   *Scally v Southern Health and Social Services Board* [1992] 1 AC 294 at 307.
1   Cf *Ashmore v Corpn of Lloyd's (No 2)* [1992] 2 Lloyd's Rep 620 at 628.
2   *Mears v Safecar Securities Ltd* [1983] QB 54 at 78.
3   *Tai Hing Cotton Mill Ltd v Liu Chong Hing Bank Ltd* [1986] AC 80 at 104–105.
4   Contrast ante, p 71 at n 9.
5   *Crossley v Faithful & Gould Holdings Ltd* [2004] EWCA Civ 293, [2004] IRLR 377 at [36].
6   *Liverpool City Council v Irwin* [1977] AC 239.
7   Cf *Barrett v Lounova (1982) Ltd* [1990] 1 QB 348 at 358–359.

Terms are implied in fact to give effect to the unexpressed intention of both parties, and in law to attach legal incidents to particular types of contracts. There is also the possibility that terms may be implied into an individual contract on the basis of an intention *imputed* to the parties, or held by one of them and imputed to the other. The courts do not normally imply a term into an individual contract where one party would plainly have rejected it;[8] and for this reason a term will be implied on the basis of an imputed (but not actual) intention only where this is 'strictly necessary'.[9] The power to imply terms on these grounds will therefore be 'sparingly and cautiously used'.[10] Its use is illustrated by a case[11] in which a term was implied into a contract of life assurance that the insurer would not use a discretion conferred on it by the terms of one of its policies in such a way as to defeat the reasonable expectations of a policyholder, based on other terms of the contract.

c   **Terms implied by custom or usage**

Where persons deal in a particular market, a custom of that market may be incorporated into their contract, so long as the custom is 'notorious'[12] (ie generally known), not inconsistent with the express terms of the contract, or with terms necessarily implied in the contract otherwise than by custom. In cases of such inconsistency, the custom is said to be 'unreasonable'. This was the position where a custom of the tallow market allowed an agent, who had been engaged to buy goods for his principal, to sell goods of his own to the principal.[13] The custom was inconsistent with the fundamental nature of the agency relationship and therefore unreasonable; for an agent engaged to buy must buy as cheaply as he can, while one who sold his own goods would seek to obtain the highest possible price. Although these rules are most easily illustrated by reference to a custom of a market, they apply equally to customs or usages of a particular locality or trade. For example, where persons engaged in the business of hiring out machinery regularly deal with each other on terms drawn up by a trade association, those terms may be implied in a particular transaction even though no express reference to them was made when that transaction was concluded.[14]

8   The 'officious bystander' test ante, p 71 requires 'a *common* "Oh of course"'.
9   *Equitable Life Assurance Society v Hyman* [2002] 1 AC 408 at 459.
10   Ibid.
11   *Equitable Life Assurance Society v Hyman* [2002] 1 AC 408.
12   See *Turner v Royal Bank of Scotland plc* [1999] 2 All ER (Comm) 664.
13   *Robinson v Mollett* (1875) LR 7 HL 802.
14   *British Crane Hire Corpn Ltd v Ipswich Plant Hire Ltd* [1975] QB 303.

Where the custom is 'reasonable' the parties are bound by it whether they know of it or not. The suggestion that the incorporation of customary terms is based on the presumed common intention of the parties is therefore a somewhat artificial one. It becomes even less plausible in view of the fact that the question, whether a custom is reasonable, is one of law which the parties can scarcely be expected to resolve. Customary terms are best regarded as incorporated on grounds of convenience, irrespective of the intention of the parties.

3 THE PAROL EVIDENCE RULE

Where a contract is reduced to writing, the general rule is that neither party can rely on extrinsic evidence to add to, vary or contradict the written instrument.[15] The rule applies to any contract which is in fact in writing, whether or not it is required by law to be in writing. And although it is commonly called the parol evidence rule, it applies not only to oral evidence, but also to any other forms of evidence extrinsic to the document, such as evidence of another document, unless, of course, that document forms one of the contractual documents under the rules as to incorporation, discussed earlier in this chapter. The purpose of the rule is to promote certainty,[16] and this can most clearly be seen where the parties have put the terms of their agreement into a formal, detailed written document. In such a case, it may often be reasonable to say that the parties intended their relations to be governed by that document and by it alone. On the other hand, a less detailed contractual document may fail fully to express the intention of the parties, and where this is the case, one of the parties could feel reasonably aggrieved by the exclusion of evidence of extrinsic terms. The law has therefore limited the scope of the rule and created exceptions to it, so that in the following situations it does not apply.

(1) The rule relates only to evidence as to the *contents* of a contract. It does not apply where evidence is introduced to show that the contract is not legally binding, eg for lack of consideration, or for mistake or misrepresentation. Nor does the rule prevent a party from relying on evidence to show that the contract is subject to a condition precedent, which is not stated in the written contract,[17]

---

15 *Jacobs v Batavia and General Plantations Trust Ltd* [1924] 1 Ch 287 at 295; *Rabin v Gerson Berger Association Ltd* [1986] 1 All ER 374 at 378, 382; *Orion Insurance Co plc v Sphere Drake Insurance plc* [1992] 1 Lloyd's Rep 239 at 273.
16 *AIB Group (UK) Ltd v Martin* [2001] UKHL 63, [2002] 1 WLR 94 at [4]; *Shogun Finance Ltd v Hudson* [2003] UKHL 62, [2004] 1 AC 919 at [49].
17 *Pym v Campbell* (1856) 6 E & B 370.

or that one of its terms is a 'mere sham', designed to evade the Rent Act.[18]

(2) The written contract may be fully effective at law, but oral evidence may be relied on for the purpose of *establishing an equitable defence*. Thus an agent who, on behalf of his principal, signs a written contract by the terms of which he (the agent) is made personally liable, may be able to rely by way of equitable defence on an oral promise by the other party to hold only the principal liable on the contract.[19]

(3) In general, the rule prevents a buyer from relying on evidence of so-called 'oral warranties' – ie of express undertakings as to the quality of the subject-matter. For example, a buyer of paint under a written contract containing no warranty could not rely on an oral promise by the seller that the paint would last for seven years. But such 'oral warranties' can be relied on for two purposes. First, an oral statement *of fact* (eg one that the paint contained no lead) may, if untrue, amount to a misrepresentation inducing the written contract[20] and so go to the *validity* of the contract and not as to its *contents*. Secondly, extrinsic evidence may be relied on by one party so as to deprive the other of the benefit of an exemption clause set out in the written contract. An oral statement made at an auction sale of cattle has, for example, been admitted so as to prevent the seller from relying on an exemption clause in the written particulars of sale.[1]

(4) The parol evidence rule only prevents a party from relying on extrinsic evidence as to the express terms of a written contract. Such evidence is admissible *to show that a term ought to be implied*. For example, a buyer of paint might have told the seller that he wanted to use the paint on the outside of his house. He could rely on such evidence to raise an implication that the paint was fit for that particular purpose.[2]

(5) The parol evidence rule applies only to evidence of statements made before or at the time of the execution of the written contract. Extrinsic evidence can be used to show that the written contract has been *subsequently varied or rescinded,*[3] or to give rise to an estoppel.[4]

---

18   *AG Securities v Vaughan* [1990] 1 AC 417 at 469, 475; cf *Chase Manhattan Equities Ltd v Goodman* [1991] BCLC 897 at 921.

19   *Wake v Harrop* (1861) 6 H & N 768; 1 H & C 202.

20   See post, p 146.

1   *Couchman v Hill* [1947] KB 554; *Harling v Eddy* [1951] 2 KB 739.

2   Under Sale of Goods Act 1979, s 14(3).

3   *Morris v Baron & Co* [1918] AC 1. For the *validity* of such variations, see ante, p 68.

4   *James Miller & Partners Ltd v Whitworth Street Estates (Manchester) Ltd* [1970] AC 583 at 611, 615.

(6) The parol evidence rule applies to evidence as to what the express terms of a contract are. But extrinsic evidence can often be used to show *what the terms of a written document mean.* Such evidence can thus be used to explain ambiguous or vague expressions and technical terms.[5] On the same principle, evidence of the factual background to the negotiations (though not of the parties' 'subjective intent'[6]) can be used where it sheds light on the meaning of the document[7] for example, to determine the area of land sold,[8] or otherwise to identify the subject-matter of the contract,[9] or the capacity in which the parties contract. In one case,[10] a written contract for the sale of flour failed to make it clear which party was buyer and which was seller, and evidence was admitted to show that one of them was a baker and the other a flour-dealer. But where the document names the parties, evidence is not admissible to *contradict* this provision, ie to show that one (or both) of the parties was (or were) someone else.[11] Nor can evidence be used for the purposes described above of *negotiations before* the document was executed (since the document is *prima facie* taken to supersede them)[12] or of the *conduct* of the parties *thereafter* (since this would change the meaning of the contract in the course of its operation).[13]

(7) Evidence of *custom* can be used for several of the purposes mentioned above: for example, evidence of custom can be used to imply a term, to show whether a person contracting as agent was personally liable on the contract, and as an aid to construction. Such evidence may be used 'to annex incidents to written contracts in matters with respect to which they are silent'.[14] The

---

5   *Bank of New Zealand v Simpson* [1900] AC 182; cf *Mannai Investment Co Ltd v Eagle Star Life Assurance Co* [1997] AC 749.

6   *Investors Compensation Scheme Ltd v West Bromwich Building Society* [1998] 1 WLR 896 at 913; *The Red Sea* [1999] 1 Lloyd's Rep 28 at 30.

7   *Prenn v Simmonds* [1971] 1 WLR 1381; *Reardon Smith Line Ltd v Hansen-Tangen* [1976] 1 WLR 989 at 996.

8   *Scarfe v Adams* [1981] 1 All ER 843; cf *Perrylease Ltd v Imecar AG* [1987] 2 All ER 373.

9   *Macdonald v Longbottom* (1860) 1 E & E 977.

10 *Newell v Radford* (1867) LR 3 CP 52.

11 *Shogun Finance Ltd v Hudson* [2003] UKHL 62, [2004] 1 AC 919 at [49].

12 *Prenn v Simmonds* [1971] 3 All ER 237; contrast *HIH Casualty and General Insurance Ltd v New Hampshire Insurance Co* [2001] EWCA Civ 735, [2001] 2 All ER (Comm) 39 at [83], where the prior contract was *not* intended to be superseded.

13 *James Miller & Partners Ltd v Whitworth Street Estates (Manchester) Ltd* [1970] AC 583.

14 *Hutton v Warren* (1836) 1 M & W 466 at 475.

general rule is that custom may add to, but may not contradict, the written contract. Obviously, in borderline cases it is hard to distinguish between addition and contradiction. A practical test is to suppose that the custom was actually written out in the contract and then to ask whether the resulting document is self-contradictory. In one case, a contract provided that the expenses of unloading goods from a ship should be borne by *one* party (the charterer) 'as customary', and evidence of a custom that those expenses should be borne by the *other* party (the shipowner) was rejected.[15] In another case,[16] a contract provided for payments at a specified rate and it was held that evidence of a customary discount did not contradict the contract, since the discount was calculated on the contract rate.

Evidence of custom can be used for the purpose of interpreting the contact, even though it does contradict the natural meaning of the words used in the contract. Thus evidence has been admitted to prove a local custom by which '1000 rabbits' meant '1200 rabbits'.[17]

(8) A document may fail fully or accurately to record a previous oral agreement, and, where this is due to a mistake in recording a previous oral agreement,[18] the document can be *rectified* ie brought into line with the oral agreement.[19] Rectification is necessarily based on extrinsic evidence; but the remedy is not available where the parties know that the document is at variance with the terms actually agreed.

(9) The mere existence of some document relating to a contract does not necessarily lead to the conclusion that all the terms of the contract are contained in that document. A distinction is drawn between, on the one hand, documents which are only *informal memoranda*, and, on the other, those which were intended as *complete contractual documents*, ie exhaustive records of the terms finally agreed. In one case[20] the seller of a horse gave the buyer a note simply recording the fact of sale and the price; and it was held that evidence of an oral warranty relating to the horse was admissible. In another case,[1] however, a document set out detailed provisions as to the terms on which a business had been sold, and

---

15   *Palgrave, Brown & Son Ltd v SS Turid (Owners)* [1922] 1 AC 397.
16   *Brown v Byrne* (1854) 3 E & B 703.
17   *Smith v Wilson* (1832) 3 B & Ad 728.
18   Cf *Rabin v Gerson Berger Association Ltd* [1986] 1 All ER 374 at 380.
19   Post, pp 142–145.
20   *Allen v Pink* (1838) 4 M & W 140.
1   *Hutton v Watling* [1948] Ch 398.

it was held not to be a mere memorandum, so that extrinsic evidence of other terms was rejected. It has been suggested that this group of cases turns the parol evidence rule into 'no more than a circular statement',[2] which only prevents a party from relying on evidence of extrinsic terms if they were *not* intended to be part of the contract, so that the evidence would have no effect even if it were admitted. But the rule is in practice most likely to be important where one party (A) intended the extrinsic term to be part of the contract while the other (B) relies on the document as an exclusive record. In such a case, B can rely on a presumption[3] that a document which to a reasonable person *looks* like a complete contractual document was indeed intended to be an exclusive record, so that extrinsic evidence of other terms is excluded.[4] The effect of this presumption is that B's view may prevail even though he does not show that he believed the document to contain all the terms of the contract. It is up to A to show that B had no such belief; and, in view of the importance attached (especially by non-lawyers) to writing in a contractual context, this will be no easy task. Where A fails to perform this task, he will be unable to rely on the extrinsic term even though he intended it to form part of the contract and even though B knew this: B will succeed simply because the term was not recorded in the document. In such cases, the parol evidence rule is more than a 'circular statement'; and, while the rule no doubt promotes certainty,[5] it may sometimes do so at the expense of justice.[6]

(10) Although all the terms of a contract are contained in a written document, it may be possible to show that the parties made another, wholly separate contract relating to the same subject-matter; in which case this *collateral contract* can be proved by evidence extrinsic to the main written contract. In one case, for example, a written agreement for a lease did not refer to an oral agreement, made before the written one was executed, that the landlord would do certain specified repairs. It was held that the oral agreement could be enforced as an 'independent agreement'.[7] According to the older authorities,[8] a party could not rely on evidence of a collateral contract which actually

2   Law Commission Paper 154, para 2.7.
3   *Gillespie Bros & Co v Cheney, Eggar & Co* [1896] 2 QB 59 at 62.
4   *Hutton v Watling* [1948] Ch 398 at 406.
5   Ante, p 75.
6   *AIB Group (UK) Ltd v Martin* [2001] UKHL 63, [2002] 1 WLR 94 at [4].
7   *Mann v Nunn* (1874) 30 LT 526 at 527.
8   *Angell v Duke* (1875) 32 LT 320; *Henderson v Arthur* [1907] 1 KB 10.

contradicted the main contract. But a later case[9] rejects this restriction on the scope of the device, holding that a tenant could rely (by way of collateral contract) on an oral assurance that he could reside in the premises which had been let to him, even though the lease expressly provided that they were to be used for business purposes only. The scope of the collateral contract device is, however, restricted in two ways. First, the oral promise must have been intended to operate as a *separate* contract.[10] It could not, therefore, be relied on if it contained a term which one would expect to find in the main contract or which went to the essence of that contract; for in such cases the promise would have been intended as a term of the main contract.[11] Secondly, to take effect as a collateral contract, the promise must be supported by separate consideration: this follows from its nature as a separate contract. These restrictions are necessary to preserve a formal consistency between the parol evidence rule and the collateral contract device; for if extrinsic evidence were always admissible to prove a collateral contract, the parol evidence rule would, in effect, cease to exist. But it must be admitted that the scope of the first restriction is hard to define, so that the courts are left with a large measure of discretion in deciding whether to allow a party to rely on evidence extrinsic to a written contract.

9   *City and Westminster Properties (1934) Ltd v Mudd* [1959] Ch 129; cf *Brikom Investments Ltd v Carr* [1979] QB 467 (where no point as to the admissibility of evidence was taken).
10   Cf *Heilbut, Symons & Co v Buckleton* [1913] AC 30.
11   Cf ante, p 67 at n 3.

Chapter 7

Standard terms and exemption clauses

Contracts are often made on standard terms prepared by one party and presented by him to the other. Usually such terms are set out in a printed form, which is either the contractual document or one to which reference is made at the time of contracting. Such terms are meant to govern a whole class of contracts, only the individual details being completed in each case. The practice has obvious advantages. It saves time; and, by creating a standard pattern of dealing, it enables the parties to know, in general terms, what sort of risks they will probably have to bear, and to cover by insurance. On the other hand, the practice was also open to abuse, particularly in contracts between commercial suppliers of goods or services and private consumers. The supplier could draft the standard terms so as to *exclude or limit* his liability for defective performance, and also so as to *define his rights* in a way highly favourable to himself. The consumer would often be in a weak position to resist the imposition of such terms. For one thing, he would generally not read the printed form: indeed, if he did so, its main purpose (of saving time) would be defeated. For another, he would often not be able to obtain the goods or services except on the standard terms, so that his only choice might be to secure them on these terms or to do without them altogether.

In cases concerning exemption clauses, the courts were to a considerable extent able to redress the balance in favour of the party prejudicially affected by standard terms; but they were less inclined to do so where standard terms conferred rights on the supplier. In both fields, legislative intervention has become increasingly important, the principal legislative provisions being contained in the Unfair Contract Terms Act 1977 and in the Unfair Terms in Consumer Contracts Regulations 1999. But in a significant number of situations standard terms are not affected by this (or other) legislation, so that the common law rules affecting them still call for discussion, even though many of the cases from which they are derived would now be differently decided under such legislation.

1   INCORPORATION OF STANDARD TERMS

A party who wishes to rely on a standard term, must first show that it has become part of the contract. He can do this in one of three ways.

a   Signature

The first is to get the other party to sign the contractual document in which the term is set out. The party signing is then *prima facie* bound,[1] even if he could not read or understand the document, eg because it was in a language which he did not know.[2] In the case of a signed document, it is not necessary to comply with the requirement of notice,[3] discussed below, unless perhaps the term in question is 'particularly onerous or unusual.'[4]

b   Notice

Many contracts are made without being signed by either party. In such cases, standard terms, often including an exemption clause, may be contained in a notice posted up where the contract is made. Alternatively, they may be printed in a document which is simply handed or sent by one party to the other; or in one to which reference is made in the document, which is handed over: for example where a ticket refers to conditions set out in a time-table. In these situations the exemption clause will form part of the contract if the party relying on the clause took reasonable steps to bring it to the other party's attention.[5] The question whether such reasonable steps have been taken is essentially one of fact; but some useful guidelines may be derived from the cases.

First, a distinction is drawn between contractual documents and mere vouchers or receipts. A document is contractual if it is known to contain contractual terms, or if it is of a kind that could normally, in the ordinary course of business, be expected to contain such terms. Thus it has been held that a passenger ticket was a contractual document[5a] but that a receipt given to a person to show

---

1   *L'Estrange v F Graucob Ltd* [1934] 2 KB 394.
2   *The Luna* [1920] P 22.
3   *HIH Casualty and General Insurance Ltd v New Hampshire Insurance Co* [2001] EWCA Civ 735, [2001] 2 All ER (Comm) 39 at [209].
4   *Ocean Chemical Transport Inc v Exnor Craggs Ltd* [2000] 1 Lloyd's Rep 446 at 454.
5   *Parker v South Eastern Rly Co* (1877) 2 CPD 416.
5a   *Thompson v London Midland and Scottish Rly* [1930] 1 KB 41, *Hood v Anchor Line* [1918] AC 837.

that he had paid for the hire of a deck-chair at a seaside resort was a mere voucher.[6]

Secondly, the steps to notify the other party of the terms must be taken at or before the time of contracting. For example, where a contract between a hotel-keeper and a guest was made when the guest booked in at the reception desk, it was held that a printed notice which came to the guest's attention *later*, when he got to his room, did not form part of the contract.[7]

Thirdly, the steps must in all the circumstances be reasonably sufficient to bring the existence of the clause home to the other party. This depends on both the manner in which the term is displayed or set out, and on the nature of the term. It is advisable to draw attention to the term by clear words on the face of any document handed over at the time of contracting, especially if the term is not contained in that document, but in another, which the first document incorporates by reference. Words such as 'For conditions see ...' or 'subject to our conditions of contract, obtainable on request'[8] are commonly used. The degree of notice required increases in proportion to the unusualness of the term. For example, a person who contracts to leave his car in a car-park might expect the proprietors to exclude liability for loss of or damage to the car (which is likely to be insured); but a clause excluding liability for personal injury[9] would be more unusual, so that a higher degree of notice of such a clause would have to be given.[10] This could be done by printing or displaying such a clause in some particularly conspicuous manner: eg in block capitals or in red letters.

If reasonable steps have been taken, the term becomes part of the contract, even though it does not *actually* come to the attention of the party adversely affected. In one case, for example, an exemption clause took effect even though that party could not read it because she was illiterate.[11] However, the position might be different if the party relying on the clause *knew* that the other could not read it: for example, if the clause was in English and the party relying on it was aware of the fact that the other party knew hardly any English.[12]

6   *Chapelton v Barry UDC* [1940] 1 KB 532.
7   *Olley v Marlborough Court Ltd* [1949] 1 KB 532; cf *The Eagle* [1977] 2 Lloyd's Rep 70.
8   *Smith v South Wales Switchgear Ltd* [1978] 1 All ER 18.
9   To the extent that it purported to exclude or restrict liability for personal injury *caused by negligence*, such a clause would now be ineffective; see post, p 103.
10   *Thornton v Shoe Lane Parking Ltd* [1971] 2 QB 163; cf *Interfoto Picture Library Ltd v Stiletto Visual Programmes Ltd* [1989] QB 433.
11   *Thompson v London Midland and Scottish Rly Co* [1930] 1 KB 41.
12   *Geier v Kujawa Weston and Warne Bros (Transport) Ltd* [1970] 1 Lloyd's Rep 364; the clause in that case would now be invalid under the Road Traffic Act 1988, s 149.

c Course of dealing

So far it has been assumed that the contract in question is an isolated transaction. But the parties may have entered into a series of contracts over a period of time; and they may regularly have used a form incorporating the same standard terms. Two problems may arise out of such a course of dealing.

First, the steps normally taken to incorporate the clause may, by some oversight, be omitted on the crucial occasion when something goes wrong: eg a warehouseman may fail to hand over the usual warehouse receipt in relation to a particular consignment of goods, which is then stolen. The position is that the usual terms are nevertheless incorporated in that transaction by course of dealing, even though the customer had never actually read them, so long as reasonable notice of them has been given in the series of transactions as a whole.[13] To bring this rule into operation, there must be an established and regular course of dealing (and not, for example, just half a dozen transactions in the course of five years);[14] and it must be *consistent* (ie the same terms must have been used in all the transactions constituting the course of dealing).[15]

Secondly, the party normally handing over the document may wish to alter its terms in his own favour. That person would then have to take special steps to bring the alteration to the other party's notice, since *prima facie* the latter would be entitled to assume that a consistent course of dealing was continuing without alteration.[16]

In the cases so far considered, the course of dealing is one between the parties to the contract. A term may also be incorporated in a contract because of a general course of dealing amounting to a trade custom or usage.[17] A term can be incorporated in this way even between parties who have not previously dealt with each other.[18]

---

13 *J Spurling Ltd v Bradshaw* [1956] 2 All ER 121.
14 *Hollier v Rambler Motors (AMC) Ltd* [1972] 2 QB 71; *Circle Freight International Ltd v Mideast Gulf Exports Ltd* [1988] 2 Lloyd's Rep 427.
15 See *McCutcheon v David MacBrayne Ltd* [1964] 1 All ER 430; *Mendelssohn v Normand Ltd* [1970] 1 QB 177.
16 See *Pancommerce SA v Veecheema BV* [1983] 2 Lloyd's Rep 304 at 305 ('in bold type').
17 See ante, p 74.
18 See *British Crane Hire Corpn Ltd v Ipswich Plant Hire Ltd* [1975] QB 303.

2 CONSTRUCTION OF STANDARD TERMS

a In general

The primary rule is that standard terms are construed strictly against the party at whose instigation they were included in the contract and who now seeks to rely on them. Most of the cases which illustrate the rule concern exemption clauses. In one such case[19] a hire-purchase agreement provided that 'no warranty, condition or description or representation *is* given'; and it was held that this provision did not exclude liability for an undertaking which had been *previously* given. Although the present rule applies to all exemption clauses, it is less rigorously applied to those which merely limit liability than to those which attempt altogether to exclude it.[20]

Sometimes it is, paradoxically, the party claiming the protection of the clause who will rely on a narrow construction of it. He will do so where, on such a construction, the clause would, but on a wider construction it would not, satisfy the statutory reasonableness test on which the validity of many exemption clauses depends.[1]

b Liability for negligence

Clauses purporting to exempt a contracting party from liability for negligence are now often ineffective under the legislation to be considered later in this chapter.[2] Where these legislative provisions do not apply, liability for negligence can in principle be excluded, but 'clear words'[3] must be used for this purpose. This requirement is most obviously satisfied if the clause refers expressly to 'negligence';[4] but it may also be satisfied by general words[5] of the kind to be discussed below. In deciding whether a party is protected by such general words, the courts distinguish between cases in which that party's liability for breach of contract is strict and those in which it depends on negligence.[6]

---

19   *Webster v Higgin* [1948] 2 All ER 127.
20   *Ailsa Craig Fishing Co Ltd v Malvern Fishing Co Ltd* [1983] 1 All ER 101.
1   See *Watford Electronics Ltd v Sanderson (FL) Ltd* [2001] EWCA Civ 317, [2001] 1 All ER (Comm) 646; for the statutory reasonableness test, see post, p 104.
2   See post, pp 103, 104.
3   *Gillespie Bros & Co Ltd v Roy Bowles Transport Ltd* [1973] QB 400 at 419.
4   Eg, *Monarch Airlines Ltd v Luton Airport Ltd* [1998] 1 Lloyd's Rep 403.
5   *Canada Steamship Lines Ltd v R* [1952] AC 192 at 208; *Smith v South Wales Switchgear Ltd* [1978] 1 All ER 18 at 22, 26.
6   See post, pp 313–315.

Where there is a realistic possibility[7] that a party can be made liable irrespective of negligence, an exemption clause in general terms (eg one simply excluding liability 'for loss or damage') will normally be construed to refer only to his strict liability.[8] If he is in fact negligent, he will therefore not be protected by such a clause. But the rule is one of construction only and will not be applied if the intention to exclude liability even for negligence is made clear.[9] This was, for example, held to be the position where an exemption clause excluded liability for loss or damage 'however caused which can be covered by insurance'.[10] Even in the present group of cases, moreover, general words which merely *limit* liability are more likely to be construed to cover negligence than similar words in a clause which purports altogether to *exclude* liability.[11]

Where the contract is one under which the party relying on the clause is liable *only* if he is negligent, the rule that general words do not normally exclude liability for negligence does not apply. Such words *may* therefore exempt the party in breach from liability for negligence.[12] But it by no means follows that they *will* have this effect: they may be construed simply as a warning to one party that the other is not in law liable except for negligence. Which of these constructions is adopted depends on the court's view as to the more obvious meaning of the clause to the injured party. Thus, in one case[13] a customer left a car with a garage on the terms that 'customers' cars are driven by our staff at customer's sole risk'. It was held that this clause did protect the garage proprietor from liability for loss caused by the negligence of one of his staff, since he was liable only where such loss was due to negligence, and the obvious meaning of the clause was to exclude this liability. But in another similar case,[14] a provision that the garage was 'not responsible for damage caused by fire to customers' cars' was held to be no more than a warning that the garage was not legally liable in the *absence* of negligence. Accordingly it did not protect the garage for liability for damage to a customer's car caused by a fire due to the negligence of the garage.

7   *Smith v South Wales Switchgear Ltd* [1978] 1 All ER 18 at 27.
8   *Canada Steamship Lines Ltd v R* [1952] AC 192 at 208; *Toomey v Eagle Star Insurance Co Ltd* [1995] 2 Lloyd's Rep 88.
9   *The Golden Leader* [1980] 2 Lloyd's Rep 573.
10   *Joseph Travers & Sons Ltd v Cooper* [1915] 1 KB 73.
11   *George Mitchell (Chesterhall) Ltd v Finney Lock Seeds Ltd* [1983] 2 AC 803 at 814.
12   *J Archdale & Co Ltd v Comservices Ltd* [1954] 1 All ER 210; *Smith v Eric S Bush* [1990] 1 AC 831 (as to which see also post, p 150).
13   *Rutter v Palmer* [1922] 2 KB 87.
14   *Hollier v Rambler Motors (AMC) Ltd* [1972] 2 QB 71.

c Seriousness of breach

Traditionally, the courts were not concerned with the fairness of contracts. But they nevertheless resisted attempts by contracting parties to exclude liability for particularly serious breaches; and to this end they developed the so-called doctrine of fundamental breach. According to one view, this doctrine made it impossible as a matter of substantive law to exclude liability for such breaches. This *substantive doctrine* was at one time a useful device for protecting consumers against unfair exemption clauses; but it is no longer needed for this purpose now that such clauses can be dealt with under the legislation to be discussed later in this chapter.[15] Moreover, the substantive doctrine was not restricted to cases involving consumers; and when it was applied to commercial transactions negotiated between parties bargaining on equal terms it could create uncertainty and upset perfectly fair arrangements for allocating risks and the burden of insuring against them. For these reasons the House of Lords has rejected the substantive doctrine and has held that the doctrine of fundamental breach is a rule of construction only.[16] That rule amounts to a presumption that general words in an exemption clause will not normally cover certain very serious breaches; but the presumption can be overcome if the words of the clause are sufficiently clear. Viewed in this way, the doctrine of fundamental breach can be regarded simply as an aspect of the principle that exemption clauses are to be construed strictly against parties who rely on them.[17] In applying that principle, the seriousness of the breach remains an important (though it is no longer a decisive) factor. Hence the old cases on fundamental breach (many of which were decided before the development of the substantive doctrine) will continue to provide some guidance on the *scope* of the rule of construction. It is also necessary to consider its exact legal *effects*. The practical importance of the subject is now largely restricted to clauses which are outside the scope of the legislation to be considered later in this chapter. A party obviously cannot rely on a clause (however clearly expressed) if it is simply ineffective or not binding on the other party under that legislation; and where a clause is subject to the statutory reasonableness test, the right to rely on the

---

15 Post, pp 101–118.
16 *Suisse Atlantique Société d'Armement Maritime SA v Rotterdamsche Kolen Centrale NV* [1967] 1 AC 361; *Photo Production Ltd v Securicor Transport Ltd* [1980] AC 827; *George Mitchell (Chesterhall) Ltd v Finney Lock Seeds Ltd* [1983] 2 AC 803.
17 See ante, p 85. *George Mitchell (Chesterhall) Ltd v Finney Lock Seeds Ltd* [1983] 2 AC 803.

clause is more likely to depend on the application of that test than on the construction of the clause at common law.[18]

i   Scope of the rule

The scope of the rule of construction depends on three factors: the nature of the term broken, the effects of the breach and the manner in which the breach is committed.

So far as the first factor is concerned, we shall see in Chapter 16 that, as a general rule, relatively slight breaches give rise only to a right to damages, while more serious breaches give rise to a right to rescind the contract and also to a right to damages. But for the purpose of determining whether a breach gives rise to a right to rescind, the law further distinguishes between conditions, warranties and intermediate terms. Breach of a warranty or of an intermediate term does not, of itself, give the injured party the right to rescind the contract, and breaches of such terms are plainly not within the rule of construction here under discussion. Nor does that rule apply merely because the term broken is a condition, even though such a breach does normally give the injured party the right to rescind. But the rule does apply to the breach of what is known as a fundamental term; this is 'narrower than a condition'[19] and is so central to the purpose of the contract that its breach turns the performance rendered into one essentially different from the performance promised. The stock example of a breach of such a term is provided by the case of a seller who contracts to deliver peas but instead delivers beans:[20] exemption clauses have been construed so as not to cover breaches of such terms.[1] By contrast, in the *George Mitchell* case[2] a farmer bought seed for a crop of cabbage which totally failed because the seed was seriously defective. It was said that this was 'not a peas and beans case at all'[3] so that a clause limiting the seller's liability did, as a matter of construction, cover the breach.[4] The contract was evidently regarded as one for the sale of 'seed', and seed (though seriously defective seed) had indeed been delivered.

---

18   Eg *George Mitchell (Chesterhall) Ltd v Finney Lock Seeds Ltd* [1983] 2 AC 803.

19   *Smeaton Hanscomb & Co Ltd v Sassoon I Setty, Son & Co* [1953] 1 WLR 1468 at 1470.

20   *Chanter v Hopkins* (1838) 4 M & W 399 at 404.

1   Eg *Andrews Bros (Bournemouth) Ltd v Singer & Co Ltd* [1934] 1 KB 17.

2   *George Mitchell (Chesterhall) Ltd v Finney Lock Seeds Ltd* [1983] 2 AC 803.

3   [1983] 2 C 803, at 813.

4   But the clause did not protect the seller as it failed to satisfy the statutory reasonableness test: see post, p 107.

Whether the performance rendered is so fundamentally different from that promised, as to bring the case into the 'peas and beans' category, depends on two factors: the nature of the performance promised, and the extent to which the performance rendered differs from that promised. If, for example, the subject-matter of a sale is a car which turns out to be defective, one cannot classify the term broken simply by looking at the seriousness of the defects. One has to ask what the seller promised (expressly or by implication) at the time of sale. If he was a dealer who undertook that the car was in good running order, the defects necessary to constitute breach of a fundamental term will be relatively less serious than if the seller was a private person with no technical knowledge. Indeed, if the car were sold to an enthusiast as a wreck, which might or might not be coaxed into running order, there would be no breach at all.

In contracts for the carriage of goods by sea it is well established that the term as to the route is fundamental.[5] Hence the carrier loses the protection of an exemption clause if he deviates, that is, if without justification he departs from the agreed or customary route.[6] It makes no difference that the goods are ultimately carried to their destination, that the deviation was only slight, that the loss or damage was not caused by the deviation, or indeed that the deviation was 'for practical purposes irrelevant':[7] in other words, the *actual effects* of the deviation are not taken into account. The rule is based on the probable, or hypothetical, effect of the deviation: the owner of the goods may lose his effective insurance cover if the goods are carried by a different route from that covered by the policy,[8] and therefore it is thought necessary to give him a remedy against the carrier in spite of the exemption clause.[9] The situation may be contrasted with that in which the goods are damaged because the ship is unseaworthy; the mere fact that the carrier has in some way broken his obligation in relation to seaworthiness does not deprive him of the protection of an exemption clause.[10] The principle of the deviation cases has been extended to land carriage,[11] and to cases which have nothing to do with carriage at all. For example, it has been applied to the case of a

---

5   *Smealton Hanscomb & Co Ltd v Sassoon I Setty, Son & Co* [1953] 1 WLR 1468 at 1470.
6   *Joseph Thorley Ltd v Orchis Steamship Co Ltd* [1907] 1 KB 660; *Hain Steamship Co v Tate and Lyle Ltd* (1936) 41 Com Cas 350; for the continued existence of the rule, see post, p 93.
7   *Suisse Atlantique* case [1967] 1 AC 361 at 423.
8   Marine Insurance Act 1906, s 46(1).
9   *Hain Steamship Co v Tate and Lyle Ltd* (1936) 41 Com Cas 350. at 354.
10   *Kish v Taylor* [1912] AC 604.
11   *London and North Western Rly Co v Neilson* [1922] 2 AC 263.

warehouseman who agrees to store goods in one particular warehouse and stores them in another;[12] and to a person who undertakes to do certain work (eg of cleaning or repairing) personally and then lets the work out to a sub-contractor.[13]

In a second group of cases it is the *effect of the breach* (rather than the *term broken*) which is the crucial point. For example, failure to perform at the agreed time is always a breach of the same term, but a clause which covers a slight delay may not cover one that is serious and prolonged. Again, a person who supplies a defective car under a contract of sale or hire-purchase will often be in breach of an implied condition as to quality. This is not a fundamental term;[14] but in a number of cases it has been held that the supplier was not protected by exemption clauses where the defects were so serious as to make the vehicles for practical purposes useless to the customers.[15] What is stressed in these cases is the *effect* of the breach. This must either be such as to make the performance rendered 'totally different from that which the contract contemplates'[16] or (as in the defective car examples just given) merely cause *serious* prejudice to the injured party, without turning the performance rendered into something *totally* different from that promised. The degree of 'seriousness' required for this purpose cannot be precisely defined: all that can be said is that the difficulty of convincing the court that the clause covers a particular breach will increase with the gravity of that breach.

In a third group of cases the question whether an exemption clause applies turns on the *manner* (rather than on the *effect*) of the breach. Suppose that goods are entrusted to a person for safe-keeping or for carriage, and that person, in breach of contract, delivers them to someone who is not entitled to them, so that they are lost to the owner. Here a distinction is drawn: if the misdelivery is deliberate, an exemption clause is unlikely to protect the party in breach, because the probability is that 'the parties never contemplated that such a breach should be excused or limited';[17] but this reasoning does not apply where the misdelivery is merely negligent.[18] Nor would it apply where the goods were lost or damaged by a fire caused

12   *Woolf v Collis Removal Service* [1948] 1 KB 11 at 15; cf *United Fresh Meat Co Ltd v Charterhouse Cold Storage Ltd* [1974] 2 Lloyd's Rep 286 (chilled instead of frozen store).
13   *Davies v Collins* [1945] 1 All ER 247.
14   See ante, p 88.
15   *Yeoman Credit Ltd v Apps* [1962] 2 QB 508; *Farnworth Finance Facilities Ltd v Attryde* [1970] 2 All ER 774.
16   *Suisse Atlantique* case [1967] 1 AC 361 at 393.
17   [1967] 1 AC 361 at 435; *Alexander v Railway Executive* [1951] 2 KB 882.
18   *Hollins v J Davy Ltd* [1963] 1 QB 844.

by negligence:[19] such a breach would deprive the party in breach of the protection of the clause only if he had been guilty of some particularly serious deficiency in his precautions against fire. In all these cases the *effect* of the breach is the same, viz wholly to deprive the owner of his goods; and the question whether an exemption clause should be construed so as to cover the breach was sometimes held to depend on whether it had been committed deliberately. But the mere fact that it was so committed is no longer regarded as decisive. Thus a person will not be deprived of the benefit of an exemption clause merely because he is guilty of a deliberate delay of one day in loading a ship under a charterparty;[20] for the prejudicial effect of such a delay is assumed to be slight. In the present group of cases, in other words, the breach must be deliberate *and* its effects must be serious.

ii Legal effects of the rule

Where the breach is a serious one in the sense of the preceding discussion, the effect of the rule of construction is that an exemption clause will be construed so as to cover that breach only if it is 'most clearly and unambiguously expressed'.[1] At one time, the courts were inclined in applying this rule, to give a 'strained and artificial meaning'[2] to exemption clauses so as to exclude from their scope the serious breaches which had occurred. This approach no longer prevails;[3] but the court may still hold that general words which might seem to be capable of covering the breach should not be construed in this sense 'because this would lead to an absurdity or because it would defeat the main object of the contract ...'[4] Thus in one case[5] a contract for the carriage of goods by sea provided that the carrier's responsibility was to cease after the goods had been discharged. It was held that he was not protected when he delivered the goods to someone who (as the carrier knew) was not entitled to them. Even where clauses do apply to breaches of fundamental terms, they are nevertheless strictly construed. This point is particularly well illustrated by cases in which contracts for the carriage of goods by sea contained clauses permitting

19 Cf *Kenyon Son and Craven Ltd v Baxter Hoare & Co Ltd* [1971] 2 All ER 708.
20 *Suisse Atlantique* case [1967] 1 AC 361 at 435.
1 *Ailsa Craig Fishing Co Ltd v Malvern Fishing Co Ltd* [1983] 1 WLR 964 at 966.
2 *George Mitchell (Chesterhall) Ltd v Finney Lock Seeds Ltd* [1983] 2 AC 803 at 810.
3 [1983] 2 AC 803 at 814; *Ailsa Craig* case [1983] 1 WLR 964 at 966; *Photo Production Ltd v Securicor Transport Ltd* [1980] AC 827 at 851.
4 *Suisse Atlantique* case [1967] 1 AC 361 at 396.
5 *Sze Hai Tong Bank Ltd v Rambler Cycle Co Ltd* [1959] AC 576.

deviation. Prima facie such clauses were construed so as to permit deviation only so long as the ship proceeded in the general direction contemplated by the contract.[6] And even if they expressly permitted deviation 'in a contrary direction' they would not be taken absolutely literally: such a clause in a contract for the carriage of goods from London to Hamburg might justify a deviation to Newcastle, but not one to New York.[7]

It follows, however, from the status of the rule as one of construction that a clause can apply even to a breach of the most serious kind if that is the meaning of the words used: eg if the clause expressly covers 'fundamental breach'.[8] An express reference to fundamental breach is not, however, the only way of achieving this result. In the *Photo Production* case,[9] a security firm had been engaged to safeguard a factory which was totally destroyed as a result of the firm's breach of contract; and it was held that the firm was protected by an exemption clause which, though containing no reference to fundamental breach, was clearly worded so as to cover the breach which had occurred. Such a construction is even more likely to be adopted where the clause does not wholly exclude, but merely limits liability.[10] In the *Suisse Atlantique* case,[11] charterers under a long-term charterparty broke their part of the contract by causing the ship to be detained in port for very considerable periods; and the delays were so great as to amount to a 'fundamental breach'.[12] The contract provided that the charterers should pay $1,000 for each day of the delay; and the House of Lords held that the shipowners could not recover more by way of damages, even though their actual loss far exceeded the stipulated amount. The clause effectively limited the charterers' liability because on its true construction it applied even to the very serious delays which had occurred. Similarly, in the *George Mitchell* case[13] the seller's breach in supplying defective seed had the most serious consequence, in that the buyer's crop wholly failed. But the House of Lords nevertheless held that a clause limiting the seller's liability did, on its true construction, cover the breach.[14] The character of the rule as one of

6   *Glynn v Margetson & Co* [1893] AC 351.
7   Cf *Connolly Shaw Ltd v Nordenfjeldske Steamship Co* (1934) 49 Ll L Rep 183.
8   *The Antwerpen* [1994] 1 Lloyd's Rep 213 at 246.
9   *Photo Production Ltd v Securicor Transport Ltd* [1980] AC 827.
10   As in *George Mitchell (Chesterhall) Ltd v Finney Lock Seeds Ltd* [1983] 2 AC 803.
11   [1967] 1 AC 361.
12   [1967] 1 AC 361 at 396.
13   Supra, n 2.
14   But the seller was held fully liable because the clause did not satisfy the statutory test of reasonableness: see post, p 107.

construction is therefore firmly established; but three problems call for further consideration.

The first arises from the fact that a serious breach of the kind here under discussion normally gives the injured party two rights: a right to damages and a right to rescind the contract.[15] An exemption clause may be so drawn as to affect only one of these rights. Thus in the *Suisse Atlantique* case the clause limited the shipowner's right to damages but said nothing about his right to rescind. Conversely, a contract may contain a non-rejection or non-cancellation clause which excludes the right to rescind, but says nothing about the injured party's right to damages. Such a clause may take away the right to rescind even for a breach of a most serious kind; but this would not prevent the injured party from claiming damages for that breach. The right to rescind may also be lost in other ways, in particular if the injured party affirms the contract. Such affirmation does not affect the operation of a clause which excludes or limits only the right to damages: in other words, that right continues, even after affirmation, to depend on the construction of the clause.[16] Similarly, the construction of the clause is decisive where the clause excludes or limits only the right to damages and the injured party rescinds on account of the fundamental breach. In the *Photo Production* case,[17] the factory owners argued that they could get rid of the exemption clause by so rescinding the contract; but acceptance of this argument would have amounted to a virtual reintroduction of the former substantive doctrine of fundamental breach. The House of Lords therefore rejected the argument, holding that the exemption clause, on its true construction, covered the breach, and that rescission only affected *future* performance: hence it did not retrospectively deprive the security firm of the benefit of the clause with respect to loss suffered before rescission. This rule seems, however, not to apply where a carrier of goods by sea deviates; for in such cases the carrier does lose the benefit of exemption clauses even in respect of losses which had occurred *before* rescission by the cargo-owner. Such cases can be regarded as a special exception to the general rule that rescission does not retrospectively affect exemption clauses;[18] or they can be explained on the ground that this result follows as a matter of construction from the special commercial considerations which justify the treatment of deviation as a breach of a fundamental term.[19]

---

15 See ante, p 88, post, p 333.
16 As in the *Suisse Atlantique* case [1967] 1 AC 361.
17 [1980] AC 827.
18 [1980] AC 827 at 845.
19 Ie, from the fact that deviation deprives the cargo-owner of his insurance cover automatically 'as from the time of the deviation': see Marine Insurance Act 1906, s 46(1) and *The Good Luck* [1992] 1 AC 233, construing similar language in s 33(3) of the 1906 Act: post, p 343.

The second problem arises from the fact that the law distinguishes between very *serious* breaches and those which make the performance rendered *totally* different from that bargained for.[20] In theory, the seller in the *George Mitchell* case might have drafted a clause that would have protected him even if, instead of delivering seeds, he had delivered grass clippings; but in practice he would find it hard to persuade the court that a clause in a contract for the sale of seeds was intended to lead to such a surprising result. The point is illustrated by *The TFL Prosperity*[1] where a clause in a charterparty exempting the shipowners from liability for 'damage' was held not to protect them when the charterer suffered economic loss because the ship was simply not of the size stipulated in the contract. To hold that the clause applied to this kind of breach would give the shipowners so much discretion in the performance of the charterparty as to turn it into 'no more than a statement of intent by the owners',[2] thus destroying its essential character as a contract. Since this did not accord with 'the true common intention of the parties',[3] the House of Lords cut down the scope of the exemption clause so as to make it consistent at the very least with the purpose of the contract as a whole.

The third problem relates to the burden of proof where a clause is held, as a matter of construction, not to extend to certain serious breaches and it is alleged that such a breach has occurred. Suppose, for example, that a bailee, such as a cleaner or carrier, loses goods that have been entrusted to him. In such a case it is not up to the owner of the goods to show that the loss is due to a breach so serious as not to be covered by the clause. The burden is on the bailee to show that the loss was *not* due to such a breach.[4] The law takes this view because, in the case put the question whether the breach is sufficiently serious depends on the manner[5] in which it was committed, and the bailee is in a better position than the owner to prove just how the goods were lost. On the other hand, where the breach consists of delay and is serious because of its *effects*[6] (as in the *Suisse Atlantic* case) the burden is probably on the injured party, since he will be in a better position than the party in breach to show that the prejudice resulting from the delay was indeed of the required degree of seriousness.

20   See ante, p 90.
1   [1984] 1 WLR 48.
2   [1984] 1 WLR 48 at 58–59.
3   [1984] 1 WLR 48 at 59.
4   *Levison v Patent Steam Carpet Cleaning Co Ltd* [1978] QB 69.
5   See ante, p 90–91.
6   See ante, p 90.

3 COMMON LAW LIMITATIONS ON EFFECTIVENESS

a In general

Common law limitations on the effectiveness of standard terms remain important in cases not covered by the legislation to be discussed below;[7] and, even in cases which are so covered, common law rules may provide additional safeguards. One suggestion is that the courts will hold a party bound by a term only when it would be fair and reasonable to do so.[8] But if this were true as a general rule much of the legislation which now restricts the effectiveness of exemption clauses and other standard terms[9] would have been unnecessary. Such a common law rule would also be open to the objection that it would extend the requirements of reasonableness and fairness to cases from which the legislator had deliberately excluded them. The reasonableness or fairness of a clause may be relevant to the degree of notice of it that has to be given to *incorporate* it into the contract. But the better view is that there are at common law no such requirements for the *validity* of standard terms, save perhaps in highly exceptional circumstances. These may be illustrated by two examples concerning, not exemption clauses, but terms purporting to confer rights on the party relying on them. In a nineteenth-century case it was suggested that a term in a contract for the deposit of goods at a railway station would be void for unreasonableness if it provided that £1,000 was to be paid if the goods were not collected within 48 hours.[10] The extreme nature of the example indicates that the suggested exception will be of no more than minimal importance. In a more recent case[11] an advertising agency hired photographic transparencies; these were sent to it with a delivery note which provided that the hirer was to pay a 'holding charge' of £5 per day for each transparency retained for more than 14 days, when a reasonable charge would have been no more than £3.50 per week. One member of the court said that it would not be 'fair to hold [the hirer] bound by the condition in question';[12] but the actual ground for holding that the hirer was not bound by it was that adequate steps to incorporate it into the contract

---

7   See post, pp 101–119.
8   *Thornton v Shoe Lane Parking Ltd* [1971] 2 QB 163 at 170; *Levison v Patent Steam Carpet Cleaning Co Ltd* [1978] QB 69 at 79.
9   Post, pp 101–119.
10   *Parker v South Eastern Rly Co* (1877) 2 CPD 416 at 428.
11   *Interfoto Picture Library Ltd v Stiletto Visual Programmes Ltd* [1989] QB 433.
12   [1989] QB 433 at 445.

had not been taken.[13] The case is therefore not authority for the view that unfairness or unreasonableness is, of itself, a ground of invalidity.[14]

b   Exemption clauses

A number of limitations on the effectiveness of such clauses have been developed at common law.

First, a party cannot rely on an exemption clause if he has misrepresented the effect of the clause to the other party. This was held to be the position where a clause in a contract for the cleaning of a dress exempted the cleaner from liability for 'any damage, however arising' and the customer signed the contractual document after she had been told that the contract excluded only liability for damage to beads and sequins, and certain other specified risks.[15]

Secondly, the party in breach may, at the time of contracting, make an oral promise inconsistent with an exemption clause in a contractual document. That oral promise will then prevail: for example, where at an auction the auctioneer gives an oral assurance inconsistent with the printed conditions of sale.[16] A somewhat similar rule applies where a series of contracts is made under a 'master agreement'. An obligation imposed by that agreement may prevail over an exemption clause contained in one of the particular contracts made under it.[17]

Thirdly, the courts have held that there are certain kinds of conduct for which liability cannot be excluded. A party cannot exclude liability for his own fraud in performing the contract.[18] For example, a carrier would not be protected by a clause protecting him from liability for short delivery if he had himself stolen the missing goods. It is an open question whether a party can exclude liability for the fraud of his agent;[19] and even if he can do so he will only succeed by using 'clear and unmistakable' words to that effect.[20] A party also cannot exempt himself from liability for his own breach of fiduciary duty, for example, for breach of the duty which the promoter of a company owes to the company, not to make a profit

---

13   Ante, p 83.
14   See *Amiri Flight Authority v BAE Systems plc* [2002] EWHC 2481, [2003] 1 Lloyd's Rep 50 at [14] varied on other grounds [2003] EWCA Civ 1477, [2003] 2 Lloyd's Rep 767.
15   *Curtis v Chemical Cleaning and Dyeing Co Ltd* [1951] 1 KB 805.
16   *Couchman v Hill* [1947] KB 554; *Harling v Eddy* [1951] 2 KB 739.
17   *Gallagher v British Road Services Ltd* [1974] 2 Lloyd's Rep 440.
18   *S Pearson & Son Ltd v Dublin Corpn* [1907] AC 351 at 353, 362; *Walker v Boyle* [1982] 1 All ER 634.
19   *HIH Casualty and General Insurance Ltd v Chase Manhattan Bank* [2003] UKHL 6, [2003] 1 All ER (Comm) 349 at [16], [24], [82], [92], [122].
20   [2003] UKHL 6, [2003] 1 All ER (Comm) 349 at [16].

out of the promotion.[1] There is also some authority to support the view that a contract setting up a 'domestic tribunal' such as a private disciplinary body cannot effectively exclude the so-called rules of 'natural justice'.[2] These are rules of law designed to ensure that such a body exercises its powers fairly; in particular, by requiring the tribunal to give each party a fair hearing, and by disqualifying members of the tribunal who have a pecuniary interest in the dispute, or any other interest which is likely to bias them.

4 THIRD PARTIES

a Benefiting third parties

The starting principle, based on the common law doctrine of privity of contract,[3] was that third parties were not entitled to the benefit of exemption clauses. In the leading *Midland Silicones*[4] case, for example, a contract for the carriage of a drum of chemicals from New York to London contained a clause by which the liability of the carriers was limited. While the drum was being delivered to the consignees it was damaged as a result of the negligence of a firm of stevedores, who had been employed by the carriers to unload the ship. It was held that the stevedores were not protected by the limitation of liability contained in the contract between the carriers and the owners of the drum. The rule was an inconvenient one, for it meant that the injured party could often get round an exemption clause, by simply suing the other party's servant or agent, who then either had to discharge the liability himself[5] or look to his employer to 'stand behind' him and pay the damages. This may sometimes have been a useful way of protecting consumers against commercial suppliers of goods or services;[6] but such protection is no longer necessary now that legislation provides for the direct control of undesirable exemption clauses.[7] Between commercial entities contracting on equal terms, the rule gave rise to undesirable uncertainty and tended to falsify assumptions on which such parties base their decisions as to (for example) the risks against which each of them should insure. Hence, especially in relation to

1   *Gluckstein v Barnes* [1900] AC 240.
2   *Lee v Showmen's Guild of Great Britain* [1952] 2 QB 329 at 342.
3   Post, p 246.
4   *Scruttons Ltd v Midland Silicones Ltd* [1962] AC 446.
5   Hence in Canada it has been held that such third parties are protected: *London Drugs Ltd v Kuehne and Nagel International Ltd* [1992] 3 SCR 299.
6   Eg *Adler v Dickson* [1955] 1 QB 158.
7   See post, p 101 et seq.

international carriage, the rule has been modified by legislation extending the benefit of exemption clauses to the servants or agents of the protected party.[8] The Contracts (Rights of Third Parties) Act 1999[9] now contains a more general provision by which, where specified requirements are satisfied, a third party (C) can avail himself of a term in a contract between two others (A and B) which 'excludes or limits'[10] his liability to B. Even before the Act, the courts had given effect to express terms by which A declared himself to be acting as agent for C (typically a servant or agent or independent contractor engaged by A to render services for the purpose of performing A's contract with B) in order to secure for C the benefit of exemptions or limitations available under the contract between A and B to A himself. So long as the exemptions and limitations relied on by C were referred to in such a term,[11] and so long as the term was itself valid,[12] C was thus protected by them[13] if, while carrying out work under the contract between A and B on behalf of A,[14] he caused injury, loss or damage to B. The objection that C was not a party to the contract between A and B was overcome by arguing that, when C began to do the work, a new or collateral contract arose between B and C,[15] incorporating the exemptions of limitations contained in the contract between A and B. This reasoning survives the 1999 Act and can protect C in cases not covered by the Act: eg where the term on which C relies is not one which 'excludes or limits' liability.[16] The common law reasoning also differs from the rationale of C's protection under the Act: that rationale is that C can enforce a term of the contract between A and B,[17] while the common law reasoning is that C is protected by an independent contract between C and B. The common law further protected C on

---

8   Eg Carriage by Air Act 1961, Sch 1 Art 25A; Carriage of Goods by Sea Act 1971, Sch Art IVbis.
9   Post, pp 255–259.
10   Contracts (Rights of Third Parties) Act 1999, s 1(1), (6).
11   See *The Mahkutai* [1996] AC 650, where the clause relied on by C was *not* one of those referred to in the relevant term of the contract between A and B.
12   See *The Starsin* [2003] UKHL 12, [2004] 1 AC 715, where the term was invalid.
13   *The Eurymedon* [1975] AC 154; *The New York Star* [1980] 3 All ER 257; cf *Snelling v John G Snelling Ltd* [1973] QB 87.
14   *Raymond Burke Motors Ltd v Mersey Docks and Harbour Co* [1986] 1 Lloyd's Rep 155; *The Borvigilant* [2003] EWCA Civ 935, [2003] 2 Lloyd's Rep 520.
15   *The Eurymedon* [1975] AC 154 at 167–168; *The Starsin* [2003] UKHL 12, [2004] 1 AC 715 at [34], [93], [152], [153], and [196].
16   Eg, if it is an exclusive jurisdiction clause, as in *The Mahkutai*, but *is* referred to in the relevant term in the contract between A and B (as in that case it was not).
17   See s 1(1) of the 1999 Act.

other grounds, which may still be of use to him where the requirements of the 1999 Act are not satisfied. This possibility can be illustrated by supposing that A has undertaken to build a house for B and it is agreed between them that part of the work is to be done by a subcontractor C. If B suffers loss as a result of defects in C's work, C may be liable in tort to B if he has been negligent, ie for breach of a duty of care; and it has been suggested that an exemption clause in the contract between A and B might 'limit the duty of care'[18] and so provide C with a defence. Although the suggestion has been doubted[19] it seems to be a reasonable one since B has by the terms of his contract with A assented both to the clause and to A's employment of a subcontractor.

b Binding third parties

Here again the law starts with the principle that, under the doctrine of privity of contract, a person is not bound by an exemption clause in a contract to which he is not a party. The point may be illustrated by varying the example of the building contract just discussed and supposing that the exemption clause is contained, not in the main contract between A and B, but in the subcontract between A and C. Such a clause would not bind B,[20] and this seems to be a desirable result where B (who has no control over the terms agreed between A and C) has not assented to the clause. The example is based on the assumption that C has committed a *breach* of the subcontract. If he has *performed* that contract to the letter (eg by fitting the very components specified in it) he cannot be held liable merely because that performance turns out to be inadequate for B's purposes.[1] C can, in other words, rely on the subcontract as defining *what he has to do*, but not as excluding or limiting legal liability to a third party for *doing it defectively*.

The general rule that an exemption clause cannot bind a third party is subject to exceptions which have been developed in the interests of commercial convenience. One such exception exists

---

18 *Junior Books Ltd v Veitchi Co Ltd* [1983] 1 AC 520 at 524; *Southern Water Authority v Carey* [1985] 2 All ER 1077 at 1086; *Norwich City Council v Harvey* [1989] 1 All ER 1180.
19 *The Aliakmon* [1986] AC 785 at 817; cf *Muirhead v Industrial Tank Specialities Ltd* [1986] QB 507 at 525.
20 Cf *The Aliakmon* [1986] AC 785. In this context, B is the third party.
1   See *Junior Books Ltd v Veitchi Co Ltd* [1983] 1 AC 520, 534; *Simaan General Contracting Co v Pilkington Glass Ltd (No 2)* [1988] QB 758 at 782–783; cf *White v Jones* [1995] 2 AC 207 at 294.

where goods are handed over by their owner (B), eg to a cleaner or repairer (A), under a contract of bailment which allows A to employ a subcontractor (C) to do the work. Here B may be bound by an exemption clause in the subcontract between A and C if he has 'consented to the bailee [A] making sub-bailment containing those conditions'.[2] The cases have so far applied this exception only where B's claim is based on a bailment relationship between himself and C; and it seems not to extend to the situation in which C has never acquired the custody of B's goods but causes loss to B while rendering services to B in the course of performing a contract between A and C which contains an exemption clause.[3] In such cases, B might, however, be bound by the clause on other grounds: eg that A had acted as B's agent[4] when making the contract with C so far as it affected B; or that, when B requested C to render the services and C began to do so, an implied contract incorporating the clause sprang up between B and C.[5] In many commercial situations, this implied contract device would be a useful way of giving effect to the expectations of the parties, on which their insurance arrangements are likely to have been based.

The general rule that a person is not bound by an exemption clause in a contract to which he is not a party is based on the doctrine of privity of contract; and this aspect of the doctrine is not directly affected by the Contracts (Rights of Third Parties) Act 1999.[6] But where a third party seeks under s 1 of that Act to enforce a term in the contract against the promisor, then any defence available under the contract to the promisor against the promisee is available also against the third party.[7] Suppose that, in our building contract example, the subcontract between A and C provided that the term which specified the date by which C was to complete his part of the work was to be enforceable by B, and also validly limited C's liability to A for any breach to £1,000. That limitation could then be set up by C in an action against him by B for failure to meet the completion date. This

---

2   *Morris v C W Martin & Sons Ltd* [1966] 1 QB 716 at 729; *Singer Co (UK) Ltd v Tees and Hartlepool Port Authority* [1988] 2 Lloyd's Rep 164; *The Pioneer Container* [1994] 2 AC 324.

3   As in the *Midland Silicones* case [1962] AC 466 at 470, ante, p 97, where there was a limitation clause not only in the contract between A and B, but also in that between A and C.

4   *Pyrene Co Ltd v Scindia Navigation Co Ltd* [1954] 2 QB 402 at 423–425.

5   *Scruttons Ld v Midland Silicones Ltd* [1962] AC 446 at 471; *The Kapetan Markos NL (No 2)* [1987] 2 Lloyd's Rep 321 at 331. Implied contract can overlap with bailment: *Sandeman Coprimar SA v Transitos y Transportes Integrales SL* [2003] EWCA Civ 113, [2003] 3 All ER 108 at [63].

6   Post, p 262.

7   Contracts (Rights of Third Parties) Act 1999, s 3(2).

is true *only* where B's claim is made under the Act. If B made a claim against C in tort for negligently damaging the structure, then B would not, in general, be bound by the limitation clause since he was not a party to the contract in which it was contained.

5 LEGISLATIVE LIMITATIONS ON EFFECTIVENESS

The most important limitations on the effectiveness of standard terms are those contained in the Unfair Contract Terms Act 1977 and in the Unfair Terms in Consumer Contracts Regulations 1999. These two sets of provisions overlap so that some types of terms will be governed by both and others by only one of them. The following discussion will deal only with one technique used by both of them, which is simply to deprive certain terms of their legal force. Other legislative techniques will be considered at the end of this chapter.

a The Unfair Contract Terms Act 1977

This Act deals almost exclusively with exemption clauses;[8] it makes some such clauses ineffective in all circumstances and others ineffective unless they comply with a requirement of reasonableness.

i Terminology

In general, the Act applies only to terms affecting 'business liability', that is liability arising from things done or to be done in the course of a business, or from the occupation of business premises.[9] A person acting in the course of a business will in the following discussion be called B.

The Act gives special protection to a person who 'deals as consumer'. A person so deals if he does not make (or hold himself out as making) the contract in the course of a business, *and* the other party does make the contract in the course of a business.[10] The former party does not act in the course of a business in making a contract which is not part of its *regular* business, so that a company buying a car

---

8   It also deals in s 4 with indemnity clauses; for the close relationship between these and exemption clauses, see post, pp 105–106.
9   Unfair Contract Terms Act 1977, s 1(3). 'Business' includes a profession and activities of government departments and local or public authorities: s 14. Occupiers' Liability Act 1984, s 2 makes certain exceptions relating to access to premises for recreational or educational purposes.
10   Section 12(1)(a) and (b).

from a dealer for use by one of its directors may deal as consumer.[11] If the contract is for the supply of goods, there is the additional requirement that they must (except where the goods are supplied to an individual[12]) be of a type ordinarily supplied for private use or consumption.[13] A person dealing as consumer will in the following discussion be called C. Where neither party acts in the course of a business there can be no 'dealing as consumer'. For example, if a car is sold to a 'private' buyer by a 'private' seller neither party deals as a consumer.

The Act strikes at terms which 'exclude or restrict' liability. These words are not defined; but to the extent that the Act prevents exclusion or restriction of liability it also prevents a party from doing analogous things: for example, from imposing short time-limits on claims; or from excluding one remedy (eg rejection) without affecting another (eg damages).[14] A written arbitration agreement is not to be treated as excluding or restricting liability.[15]

While the Act prevents the parties from excluding or restricting *liabilities*, it generally leaves them free to define in their contract what *duties* each is undertaking. For example, if a seller promised to deliver goods by a certain date but made his promise 'subject to strikes', this qualification would not be within the Act. In certain cases, however, the Act specifically prevents a party from excluding or restricting duties. This is the position where a term purports to exclude the duty of care giving rise to liability in negligence,[16] or the duties arising out of terms implied by statute in contracts for the supply of goods.[17] Even in these cases, however, there may be a distinction between terms which exclude or restrict a duty and those which prevent one from arising. Once all the circumstances giving rise to the duty are shown to exist, the Act applies to a term which attempts to exclude or restrict the duty: this would be the position where goods were sold in circumstances giving rise to the implied condition that the goods were of satisfactory quality,[18] and the contract simply provided that the seller's liability for breach of that condition should be limited or excluded. On the other hand, if a seller expressly warned the buyer

---

11   *R & B Customs Brokers Co Ltd v United Dominions Trust Ltd* [1988] 1 All ER 847.
12   Section 12(1A).
13   Section 12(1)(c).
14   Section 13(1).
15   Section 13(2). Contrast the position under the Unfair Terms in Consumer Contracts Regulations 1999, Sch 2, para 1(q), post, p 117.
16   See the reference to ss 2 and 5 in s 13(1).
17   See the reference to ss 6 and 7 in s 13(1).
18   Under Sale of Goods Act 1979, s 14(1).

not to use goods for a particular purpose, the warning would negative any term, which might otherwise be implied, that the goods were fit for that purpose; and the warning would not be subject to the Act.[19] In borderline cases, the distinction between the two types of terms is hard to draw; and the courts will not allow a party to 'emasculate'[20] the Act by drafting what is in substance an exemption clause in terms which purport to define his duty.

ii Ineffective terms

In the first place, the Act makes ineffective any contract term or notice by which B seeks to exclude or restrict liability for death or personal injury resulting from negligence.[1] Terms or notices excluding or restricting *strict* liability[2] are not affected by this provision of the Act, but may be ineffective under some of its other provisions,[3] or under other legislation.[4]

Secondly, the Act strikes at exemption clauses in so-called manufacturers' guarantees of goods ordinarily supplied for private use or consumption. It provides[5] that in such guarantees B cannot exclude or restrict liability for loss or damage arising from defects in the goods while in 'consumer use', and resulting from the negligence of any person concerned in the manufacture or distribution of the goods. 'Consumer use' means use other than exclusively in the course of a business; thus it covers the case where a car is bought in the course of a business but also used partly for private purposes. A 'guarantee' is a written promise or assurance that defects will be made good. The present provision does not apply between the immediate parties to the contract for the supply of goods: exemption clauses in contracts between them are governed by the provisions to be discussed below.

Thirdly, a term is sometimes ineffective if it attempts to exclude or restrict liability for breach of undertakings implied by statute[6] in

19 *Wormell v RHM Agriculture (East) Ltd* [1987] 3 All ER 75.
20 *Smith v Eric S Bush* [1990] 1 AC 831 at 848.
1   Section 2(1). Cf Defective Premises Act 1972, ss 1(1) and 6(3); other legislation while not referring to negligence in practice deals with negligence liability: eg Public Passenger Vehicles Act 1981, s 29; Transport Act 1962, s 43(7).
2   Cf post, pp 313–315.
3   Eg ss 6 and 7.
4   See infra, at nn 11, 12.
5   Section 5. This section could apply to 'consumer guarantees' which take effect as contractual obligations owed by guarantor by virtue of Sale and Supply of Goods to Consumers Regulations 2002, SI 2002/3045, reg 15.
6   See ante, p 72.

contracts for the supply of goods. One group of such undertakings relates to the correspondence of the good with description or sample, and (when the supplier acts in the course of a business) to their quality or fitness for a particular purpose. A term excluding or restricting the liability of B to C for breach of any of these implied undertakings is ineffective.[7] Another group of such terms relates to the supplier's title to the goods and to his right to give possession. In contracts of sale or hire-purchase, an attempt to exclude or restrict liability for breach of these undertakings is invalid whether or not the supplier acted in the course of a business.[8] Attempts to exclude or restrict such liability are also invalid in certain other contracts for the transfer of goods (such as contracts of exchange), but only if the supplier acts in the course of a business.[9]

Fourthly, certain exemption clauses are made ineffective by other legislation. This relates to such disparate matters as producers' liability in respect of goods which are unsafe;[10] certain obligations of commercial suppliers of goods and services to consumers under 'distance contracts';[11] and the liability of unit trust scheme managers for failing to exercise due care and diligence in managing the scheme.[12]

iii   Terms subject to the requirement of reasonableness

A number of further terms are ineffective under the Act except in so far as they satisfy the requirement of reasonableness. Where this requirement applies, the burden of showing that it is satisfied lies on the party so claiming.[13]

The requirement applies, in the first place, where B by a contract term or notice seeks to exclude or restrict his liability for negligence giving rise to loss or damage *other than* death or personal injury.[14]

Secondly, the requirement applies in certain cases to terms purporting to exclude or restrict liability for breach of the undertakings implied by statute in contracts for the supply of goods. This is the position where B tries to exclude or restrict his liability to a person other than C for breach of the implied undertakings as to

---

7   Sections 6(2), 7(2).
8   Sections 6(1) and (4).
9   Sections 1(3) and 7(3A).
10   Consumer Protection Act 1987, ss 7, 10, 41(1) and (4).
11   Consumer Protection (Distance Selling) Regulations 2000, SI 2000/2334, regs 7–20, 25.
12   Financial Services and Markets Act 2000, s 253.
13   Unfair Contract Terms Act 1977, s 11(5).
14   Section 2(2).

the correspondence of the goods with description or sample or as to their quality or fitness for a particular purpose;[15] where a person, even though not dealing in the course of a business, tries to exclude liability for breach of the implied undertakings as to correspondence of the goods with description or sample in a contract of sale or hire-purchase;[16] and where B tries to exclude the implied undertakings as to his right to transfer possession under certain contracts for the supply of goods (such as contracts of hire) by which the property in the goods is not transferred or to be transferred.[17]

Thirdly, the requirement of reasonableness applies to a term by which B seeks to exclude or restrict his liability for breach of *any* contract (regardless of its type) if the contract is made (a) between B and C or (b) on B's 'written standard terms of business';[18] in the second of these cases the other party need not deal as consumer. This provision of the Act extends the requirement of reasonableness even to cases in which there is no breach at all: it applies to a term purporting to entitle B (i) to render a contractual performance substantially different from that which was reasonably expected of him, or (ii) to render no performance at all.[19] The first situation may be illustrated by a term in a contract between a tour operator and a carrier purporting to allow the carrier to change the itinerary or the ship at will;[20] the second by a term purporting to give a contracting party a free discretion whether to perform. However, contract terms entitling a party to refuse to perform in the event of the other party's failure to perform his part,[1] and terms restricting the duty to perform (eg by making it 'subject to strikes')[2] would not seem to be within the present provision of the Act.

Fourthly, the requirement of reasonableness applies to certain 'indemnity clauses'. These are clauses by which one contracting party undertakes to indemnify the other for any liability incurred by the latter in the performance of a contract: for example, where equipment

---

15 Sections 6(3), 7(3).
16 Sections 6(3) and (4).
17 Section 7(4), as amended by Supply of Goods and Services Act 1982, s 17(3); for similar terms in contracts of sale, hire purchase and in certain other contracts for the transfer of goods, see ante, p 104.
18 Sections 3(1) and (2)(a).
19 Section 3(2)(b).
20 Eg *Anglo-Continental Holidays Ltd v Typaldos (London) Ltd* [1967] 2 Lloyd's Rep 61; a contract of this kind between tour operator and tourist would now be governed by the Package Travel, Package Holidays and Package Tours Regulations 1992, SI 1992/3288.
1 See post, pp 320–321, 324–325.
2 Cf ante, p 102.

is hired out with a driver, and the contract provides that the hirer is to indemnify the owner for any liability incurred by the owner as a result of the driver's negligence. If the driver negligently injures, or causes damage to, a *third party*, and the hirer dealt as consumer, the owner's right to enforce the clause is subject to the requirement of reasonableness.[3] If the injury or damage was caused *to the hirer himself*, the clause will be invalid or subject to the requirement of reasonableness under provisions of the Act (already discussed)[4] even if the hirer did *not* act as consumer. Between these parties, the 'indemnity' is in substance an exemption clause:[5] there is no difference of substance between saying 'I am not liable to you' and saying 'you must indemnify me against any damages that I may have to pay to you'.

The requirement of reasonableness applies finally to any term purporting to exclude or restrict liability for misrepresentation inducing the making of a contract.[6] For this purpose the requirement applies to contracts of all types and whether or not one party acts in the course of a business or the other deals as consumer.

iv   *Rules relating to reasonableness*

The requirement of reasonableness makes it hard to foretell just when an exemption clause will be upheld. The Act contains a number of provisions which to some extent reduce this uncertainty. First, it provides that the issue of reasonableness is to be determined by reference to the time when the contract was made.[7] If at that time the term was a reasonable one to be included, it will not become invalid as a result of later events. Secondly, the Act lays down guidelines for determining reasonableness. Where the clause places a monetary limit on a person's liability, regard is to be had to his resources; and to the extent to which it was open to him to cover himself by insurance.[8] Where the contract is one for the supply of goods, the Act lays down further guidelines:[9] these include the relative bargaining positions

---

3   Section 4; if the hirer did not deal as consumer the indemnity clause is not subject to the requirement of reasonableness: see *Thompson v T Lohan (Plant Hire) Ltd* [1987] 2 All ER 631; *The Casper Trader* [1991] 2 Lloyd's Rep 550.

4   Ie s 2(1) and (2); ante, pp 103, 104.

5   *Phillips Products Ltd v Hyland* [1987] 2 All ER 620.

6   Misrepresentation Act 1967, s 3, as amended by Unfair Contract Terms Act 1977, s 8.

7   Section 11(1).

8   Section 11(4).

9   Section 11(2) and Sch 2; applicable by analogy also to other contracts: *Singer Co (UK) Ltd v Tees and Hartlepool Port Authority* [1988] 2 Lloyds' Rep 164.

of the parties and the customer's knowledge, or means of knowledge, of the existence and extent of the term. These guidelines are not decisive: for example, a warehouseman may be able to rely on an exemption clause even though he *could* have insured against loss of goods stored with him; for he may know so little about their value that it is not reasonable to expect him to insure them.[10] Nor do the guidelines specify all the factors which may be taken into account in deciding the issue of reasonableness: it is 'impossible to draw up an exhaustive list'[11] of such factors. In *Smith v Eric S Bush*[12] the House of Lords held that a term purporting to exclude the liability to house-buyers for negligence of surveyors engaged by a building society did not satisfy the requirement of reasonableness. Factors supporting this conclusion were that the houses in question were of modest value, and that it was therefore unreasonable to expect the buyers to commission their own survey. Terms incorporated in a contract after negotiations between commercial entities 'of equal bargaining power'[13] are unlikely to be struck down for unreasonableness; but even between such parties a term may be unreasonable if it was not the subject of negotiation between them.[14]

The reasonableness test and the common law rules of construction discussed earlier in this chapter are separate requirements of the effectiveness of exemption clauses. A clause which, under the common law rules, covers the breach may nevertheless fail to pass the statutory reasonableness test.[15] But the two concepts are related in that a term may fail that test precisely because it would, if valid, operate 'in respect of matters which the parties would have regarded as fundamental':[16] eg where ingredients sold to a manufacturer of beverages were so defective that the beverages were unsaleable. The assumption here is that the term does, as a matter of construction, cover the breach: if it did not, the issue of reasonableness would not arise.

Where the test of reasonableness applies, a term which satisfied the test remains effective even though the contract has been

---

10 *Singer Co (UK) Ltd v Tees and Hartlepool Port Authority* [1988] 2 Lloyd's Rep 164.
11 *Smith v Eric S Bush* [1990] 1 AC 831 at 858.
12 [1990] 1 AC 831.
13 *Watford Electronics Ltd v Sanderson CFL Ltd* [2001] EWCA Civ 317, [2001] 1 All ER (Comm) 696 at [55].
14 *Britvic Soft Drinks Ltd v Messer UK Ltd* [2002] EWCA Civ 548, [2002] 2 All ER (Comm) 321 at [26].
15 See the *George Mitchell* case [1983] 2 AC 803, ante, p 88; *Smith v Eric S Bush* [1990] 1 AC 831.
16 *Bacardi-Martini Beverages Ltd v Thomas Hardy Packaging Ltd* [2002] EWCA Civ 549, [2002] 2 All ER (Comm) 335 at [26].

terminated.[17] On the other hand, a term which does not satisfy the test remains ineffective even though the contract has been affirmed.[18]

v   *Partially effective terms*

Under the Act, a term may be effective in part. For example, a seller of goods may seek to limit liability for 'any breach'. This would not protect him from liability for breach of his implied undertaking as to title but could protect him from liability for breach of his implied undertaking as to quality if the buyer did not deal as consumer and the limitation was reasonable.[19] Moreover, a single clause might contain two terms: eg it might impose a reasonable time limit and an unreasonable financial limit on a claim. The former limit can then be upheld and the latter rejected.[20] But where the clause cannot be 'severed' in this way, the court could not vary it by, for example, substituting a reasonable limitation of liability for an unreasonable exclusion.[1]

vi   *Restrictions on evasion*

The Act strikes at two possible devices for evading its provisions.

First, a term excluding or restricting liability may be contained, not in the contract giving rise to the liability, but in a separate contract. The Act makes such a secondary contract ineffective so far as the rights which it tries to take away are rights to enforce 'another's liability', which under the Act cannot be excluded or restricted.[2] This provision of the Act applies where the 'liability' is that of a third party: ie where a contract between A and B provides that B is not to sue C for breach of a separate contract between B and C and this breach is one for which liability could not be limited or excluded under the Act.[3] It does not apply where the parties to both contracts are the same: eg where a genuine renegotiation of a contract between A and B results in a reasonable reduction of a previously agreed (and equally reasonable) limitation of liability; or where A and B reach a genuine out of court settlement of a claim for damages for breach of an earlier contract between them.

---

17 Section 9(1).
18 Section 9(2).
19 Cf *George Mitchell (Chesterhall) Ltd v Finney Lock Seeds Ltd* [1983] QB 284 at 303, 309; affd [1983] 2 AC 803.
20 *R W Green Ltd v Cade Bros Farms* [1978] 1 Lloyd's Rep 602 (decided under an enactment now superseded by s 6(3) of the 1977 Act).
1   *George Mitchell (Chesterhall) Ltd v Finney Lock Seeds Ltd* [1983] 2 AC 803 at 816; cf *Stewart Gill Ltd v Horatio Myer & Co Ltd* [1992] QB 600.
2   Section 10.
3   *Tudor Grange Holdings Ltd v Citibank NA* [1992] Ch 53 at 65–67.

Secondly, an attempt may be made to evade the Act by means of a 'choice of law' clause, subjecting the contract to the law of another country under which the effectiveness of exemption clauses is not similarly restricted. The Act applies even though the contract contains such a clause if it was imposed wholly or mainly to evade the Act; and also where one of the parties was habitually resident in the United Kingdom and dealt as consumer, and the essential steps for the making of the contract were taken there.[4] An EC Convention which has the force of law in the United Kingdom further restricts the efficacy of choice of law clauses by providing that such a clause in a contract for the supply of goods or services is not to deprive a consumer of the protection of mandatory rules of law of the country of his habitual residence.[5]

vii Cases not covered by the Act

Some contract terms are not covered by the Act because they simply do not fall within its scope. Thus generally terms excluding or restricting the liability of a person not acting in the course of a business are not affected by the Act.[6] Even terms excluding or restricting the liability of a person who does so act may be outside the scope of the Act. Suppose, for example, that B1 sold goods to B2 and the contract was not made on B1's written standard terms of business. The Act would not apply to a clause by which B1 excluded or limited his liability for late delivery.

In other cases, exemption clauses would be within the Act if the contracts in which they are contained were not to some extent specifically excepted from its scope. These exceptions are extremely complex; but some illustrations of them may be given. The Act does not apply to contracts of insurance, or to any contract so far as it relates to the transfer of an interest in land.[7] The ordinary contract for the sale of a house is thus excepted. Nor does the Act apply to contracts for the international supply of goods.[8] Certain contracts, particularly those relating to the international carriage of goods and persons, are governed by international conventions to which the United Kingdom

---

4 Section 27(2).
5 Contracts (Applicable Law) Act 1990, Sch 1, Art 5; for exceptions see Art 5(4); mandatory rules are those 'which cannot be derogated from by contract': Art 3(3).
6 Section 1(3); an exception is made by s 6(4), see ante, pp 104, n 8 and p 105, n 16.
7 Section 1(2) and Sch 1, para 1(a) and (b).
8 Section 26(1).

is a party, and which have been given the force of law.[9] These
conventions often limit the liability of one party but make void any
attempt further to reduce liability by contract. The 1977 Act preserves
this position and also excludes from its scope terms which are
'authorised or required' by legislation.[10] Finally, it often happens that
international commercial contracts which have no substantial
connection with England are governed by English law simply because
they contain an express provision to this effect. Most of the provisions
of the Act were not intended to apply, and do not apply, to such
contracts.[11]

b   The Unfair Terms in Consumer Contracts Regulations 1999

These Regulations, which give effect to an EC Council Directive,[12]
apply in relation to unfair terms which have not been individually
negotiated in contracts between commercial sellers or suppliers and
consumers.[13] Their central provision is that such unfair terms do not
bind the consumer.[14]

i   *Relation with Unfair Contract Terms Act 1977*

In some respects, the Regulations are narrower in scope than the Act.
They strike only at contract terms,[15] while the Act sometimes applies
to notices not forming part of any contract.[16] They apply only to terms
which have not been individually negotiated[17] while only one provision
of the Act is restricted in this way[18] (the others being potentially
applicable to individually negotiated contracts). And they apply only
where, in making the contract, one party acts for purposes relating to
his trade, business or profession and the other is a consumer,[19] while
the Act can apply where both parties act, or where neither party acts,
in the course of a business.[20] On the other hand, the scope of the

---

9   Eg Carriage of Goods by Road Act 1965, Sch; Carriage of Goods by Sea Act
     1971, Sch; International Transport Conventions Act 1983, s 1.
10   Unfair Contract Terms Act 1977, s 29.
11   Section 27(1).
12   93/13/EEC.
13   SI 1999/2083, regs 3(1), 4(1) and 5(1).
14   SI 1999/2083, reg 8(1).
15   Regulations 4(1), 8(1).
16   Sections 2, 5(1), 11(3) and 11(4).
17   Regulation 5(1).
18   Section 3(1).
19   Regulations 8(1) and 3(1) (definitions of 'seller' and 'supplier').
20   Eg ss 6(3), 7(3).

Regulations is wider than that of the Act in that they deal generally with unfair contract terms while the Act deals almost exclusively[1] with exemption clauses. For example, contract terms which enable a seller or supplier to increase his charges or to forfeit a deposit can fall within the Regulations,[2] but since such terms confer rights on the seller or supplier (as opposed to excluding or restricting his liability) they would not be affected by the Act.

ii Definitions

The Regulations define 'seller or supplier' as 'any natural or legal[3] person who, in contracts covered by these Regulations, is acting for purposes relating to his trade, business or profession'.[4] The Regulations do not specify what it is that the seller or supplier must supply; and, although their wording is not explicit on the point, it has been held that they apply to contracts relating to land, such as a lease granted by a local authority to a consumer.[5]

'*Consumer*' is defined to mean 'any natural person who in making contracts covered by these Regulations,[6] is acting for purposes which are outside his trade, business or profession'.[7] This definition differs in a number of ways from that of dealing as consumer under the 1977 Act. The two most significant differences are that a corporation can deal as consumer under the Act[8] but is not generally[9] a consumer under the Regulations; and that a person who does not in fact make the contract in the course of his business but holds himself out as doing so does not deal as consumer under the Act[10] but does seem to fall within the definition of consumer within the Regulations.[11]

The Regulations apply only[12] to terms which have *not been individually negotiated*; and they provide that a term 'shall always be

---

1   Ante, p 101.
2   See Sch 2, para 1(d) and (l), post, p 405.
3   Corporate sellers or suppliers are thus included, as are local authorities: *R (on the application of Khatun) v Newham London Borough Council* [2004] EWCA Civ 55, [2004] 3 WLR 417 at [88], [92].
4   Regulation 3(1).
5   *R (on the application of Khatun) v Newham London Borough Council* [2004] EWCA Civ 55, [2004] 3 WLR 417.
6   Cf n 13, supra.
7   Regulation 3(1).
8   *R & B Customs Brokers Co Ltd v United Dominions Trust Ltd* [1988] 1 WLR 321.
9   For an exception, see Arbitration Act 1996, ss 89–91.
10   Section 12(1)(a).
11   Regulation 3(1) ('is acting for purposes which are outside his trade, business or profession').
12   This seems to be the combined effect of Regulations 3(1), 4(1) and 5(1); cf Directive 93/13/EEC, Recital 12.

regarded as not having been individually negotiated where it has been drafted in advance *and* the consumer has therefore not been able to influence the substance of the term'.[13] The words 'in advance' presumably refer to a term drafted before the *beginning* of the negotiations leading to the contract. Where some parts of a contract have, but the rest of it has not, been individually negotiated, the Regulations apply to the rest of the contract if, viewed as a whole, it is a 'preformulated standard contract'.[14] The burden of proof on the issue whether a term has been individually negotiated is on the seller or supplier who seeks to rely on the term.[15]

iii   Unfairness and good faith

Two ideas are central to the definition of an 'unfair term'. The term must be 'contrary to the requirement of good faith' and it must cause a 'significant imbalance in the parties' rights and obligations arising under the contract, to the detriment of the consumer'.[16] The Regulations and the courts have sought in a number of ways to reduce the uncertainty which could result from these requirements.

First, the Regulations list factors to be taken into account deciding the issue of *unfairness*.[17] One is the nature of the goods or services, so that a term which was not fair in a contract for the sale of new goods might be fair if the goods were second-hand. Another is the 'circumstances attending the conclusion of the contract' as at the time of its conclusion: for example, the fact that the consumer had at that time examined the goods would be relevant. The court is also directed to take into account 'all the other terms of the contract': these words might make it fair for a supplier who undertook liabilities beyond those imposed by the general law to require notice of claims to be given within a shorter period than that normally allowed by law for claims in respect of defects in performance.

Secondly, certain *core provisions* are not subject to the requirement of fairness at all. The Regulations are not intended to operate as a mechanism of price or quality control.[18] They accordingly provide that 'the assessment of fairness of a term shall not relate (a) to the definition of the main subject-matter of the contract or (b) to the adequacy of the price or remuneration, as against the goods or services supplied in

13   Regulation 5(2) (italics supplied).
14   Regulation 5(3).
15   Regulation 5(4).
16   Regulation 5(1).
17   Regulation 6(1).
18   *Director General of Fair Trading v First National Bank plc* [2001] UKHL 52, [2002] 1 AC 481 at [12].

exchange …'.[19] A term is therefore not unfair merely because it fixes a price which is by some objective standard 'excessive'.[20] The parties can also define the subject-matter in such a way that what might objectively be regarded as a defect in it is not a breach: eg where the contract was one for the supply of 'seed' rather than 'cabbage seed' and the seed disappointed the buyer's expectation of yielding a crop of cabbages.[1] In these respects, the Regulations recognise the parties' freedom of contract with regard to the essential features of their bargain. Such core provisions must, however, be 'in plain intelligible language'.[2] An obscurely expressed term which entitled the supplier to increase a price prominently stated elsewhere in the contractual document could be an 'unfair' term. The courts are, moreover, reluctant to give too wide a scope to the concept of a 'core provision', since if they did so the object of the Regulations would be 'plainly frustrated'[3] by excepting too great a range of contract terms from their scope. For example, in a contract for the hire of a car to a consumer for a fixed period, the term specifying the rate of hire would no doubt be a 'core provision', but a term requiring him to pay a 'holding charge' for late return of the car is likely to be regarded as an 'ancillary'[4] rather than as a 'core provision' and so be subject to the Regulations.

Thirdly, attempts have been made to explain the requirement of *good faith*, which has been described by the House of Lords as 'one of fair and open dealing'.[5] Openness here refers to the way in which the terms are set out: they must be 'expressed fully, clearly and legibly' and give 'prominence to terms which might operate disadvantageously to the consumer'.[6] Fairness refers to matters of substance and means that the seller or supplier must not 'take advantage of the consumer's necessity, indigence, lack of experience, unfamiliarity with the subject-matter of the contract, [or] weak bargaining position'.[7] The Directive on which the Regulations are based[8] (and in the light of which they must be interpreted[9]) lists, among factors relevant to good faith, 'the

---

19 Regulation 6(2).
20 Thus preserving the common law principle that the court will not take the adequacy of consideration into account.
1   Example based on the *George Mitchell* case [1983] 2 AC 803, ante, p 88.
2   Regulation 6(2).
3   *Director General of Fair Trading v First National Bank plc* [2001] UKHL 52, [2002] 1 AC 481 at [52].
4   [2002] 1 AC 481.
5   *Director General of Fair Trading v First National Bank plc* [2002] 1 AC 481 at [17].
6   Ibid.
7   Ibid.
8   Directive 93/13/EEC.
9   Case 14/83 *Von Colson and Kamann v Land Nordrhein-Westfalen* [1984] ECR 1891.

strength of the bargaining positions of the parties, whether the consumer had an inducement to agreement to the term and whether the goods or services were supplied to the special order of the consumer'.[10]

Fourthly, the Regulations list *examples of prima facie unfair terms.*[11] The list is 'indicative and non-exhaustive',[12] so that a term of a type included in it is only *prima facie* unfair, while a term may be unfair even though it does not fall within any such type. The list in effect provides further guidelines on the issue of fairness. It includes many types of terms which would be classified as exemption clauses under the 1977 Act and, like the Act, it distinguishes terms which exclude or limit liability for death or personal injury (which are prima facie unfair[13]) from terms which exclude or limit other liability (which are prima facie unfair only if they 'inappropriately' do so).[14] Perhaps the most interesting aspect of the list is the inclusion in it of many types of terms which would not be exemption clauses under the Act or at common law because, far from excluding or limiting the liability of the seller or supplier, they confer rights on him. Some such clauses might, apart from the Regulations, be subject to legal control at common law: eg as penalty or forfeiture clauses.[15] But others are of a kind that are not subject to control at common law: for example a term automatically extending a determined term contract unless the consumer gives notice to terminate it, where the time for giving such notice is unreasonably early;[16] a term 'providing for the price of goods to be determined at the time of delivery';[17] and a term providing for such a price to be increased, if the final price is too high in relation to that originally agreed, without giving the consumer the right to cancel the contract.[18] These examples emphasise the point that the Regulations deal with all types of unfair standard terms while the Act deals almost exclusively with exemption clauses.

---

10   Directive 93/13/EEC, Recital 16.
11   Regulation 5(5) (terms 'which *may* be regarded as unfair') and Sch 2.
12   Regulation 5(5).
13   Schedule 2, para 1(a).
14   Schedule 2, para 1(b). There is no reference to negligence in para 1(a) or (b).
15   Post, pp 403, 405.
16   Schedule 2, para 1(h).
17   Schedule 2, para 1(l).
18   Schedule 2, para 1(l).

iv Excluded terms

The Regulations do not apply to terms which reflect 'mandatory statutory or regulatory provisions' of United Kingdom law:[19] eg to terms which a contract is required by legislation to contain.[20] The 1977 Act is subject to a similar, but broader, exception covering provisions '*authorised* or required'[1] by other legislation. Provisions which are merely so 'authorised' would not seem to be 'mandatory' and so to be within the Regulations; but the fact that they were 'authorised' would no doubt be taken into account in deciding whether they were unfair. The Regulations also do not apply to terms incorporated in a contract to comply with or reflecting 'the provisions or principles of international conventions to which the Member States or the [European] Community are party'.[2] This exclusion resembles (and goes somewhat beyond) the similar exclusion from the 1977 Act.[3]

v Excluded contracts

The Directive on which the Regulations are based lists a number of types of contracts which 'must be excluded'[4] from its scope. The most important of these are 'contracts relating to employment'; and although the list is not reproduced in the Regulations, such contracts seem to be excluded by force of the Directive.[5] They are wholly excluded, while the scope of their exclusion from certain provisions of the 1977 Act is limited in that it does not prevent the employee from relying on those provisions.[6] Other contracts are not or may not be covered because, though not specifically excluded, they simply do not fall within the inclusive provisions of the Regulations. Unlike the 1977 Act,[7] the Regulations can apply to contracts for the transfer of an interest in land, such as a lease granted by a local authority[8] or a sale of a house by a commercial developer; but the ordinary sale of a dwelling house by one home-owner to another would not be covered, since

---

19   Regulation 4(2)(a).
20   Eg post, p 118.
1   Section 29(1)(a).
2   Regulation 4(2)(b); 'Member States' and 'Community' are defined in reg 3(1).
3   Section 29(1)(b).
4   Directive 93/13/EEC, Recital 10.
5   Cf ante, p 113 at n 9,
6   1977 Act, Sch 1, para 4; the relevant provisions are those of s 2(1) and (2).
7   Schedule 1, para 1(b).
8   *R (on the application of Khatum) v Newham London Borough Council* [2004] EWCA Civ 55, [2004] 3 WLR 417; and see ante, p 111, n 3.

neither party to it would act as a commercial seller or supplier. Conversely, there was no need in the Regulations to exclude international supply contracts (which are specifically excluded from the Act[9]) since generally neither party to such a contract is a consumer. Contracts for the sale of intellectual property are excluded from the 1977 Act;[10] the most common sale of this kind to a consumer would be one to license the use of computer software and, as contracts of this type usually involve the transfer of a moveable physical object, they would be contracts for the supply of 'goods or services' within the Directive and so be covered by the Regulations.[11] Contracts of insurance (which are excluded from the 1977 Act[12]) are covered by the Regulations.[13]

vi   Drafting and interpretation

The Regulations require 'any written term of a contract' to be in 'plain, intelligible language';[14] but failure to use such language does not make the term even *prima facie* unfair (except under the provision which requires the price and main subject-matter of the contract to be stated in plain intelligible language).[15] The Regulations also provide that 'if there is doubt about the meaning of a written term, the interpretation which is most favourable to the consumer shall prevail':[16] this is no more than a legislative formulation of the common law principle of construction,[17] which can apply even where the language is plain and intelligible, but ambiguous. The repeated reference here to a 'written term' indicates that the Regulations can apply to oral contracts or terms but (curiously) these are not expressly required to be in 'plain, intelligible language'.[18]

vii   Effects of unfairness

An unfair term in a contract governed by the Regulation is 'not ... binding on the consumer'.[19] If the unfair term is an exemption clause,

9   Section 26.
10   Schedule 1, para 1(c).
11   Cf *St Albans City and District Council v International Computers Ltd* [1996] 4 All ER 481, where the question is discussed in relation to the 1997 Act.
12   Schedule 1, para 1(a).
13   See Directive 93/13/EEC, Recital 19.
14   Regulation 7(1).
15   Regulation 6(2), ante, p 113 at n 2.
16   Regulation 7(2).
17   Ante, p 85.
18   There does seem to be such a requirement under 1993/13/EEC, Recital 11.
19   Regulation 8(1).

the consumer will be able to enforce his rights under the contract as if the term had not been included. If the term is one purporting to confer rights on the other party, those rights will not arise. If effect has been given to those rights, the effects may have to be undone: for example, a deposit may have to be paid back. The term is binding on the other party: for example, he may be bound by an unfair arbitration clause[19a] if the consumer wants to enforce it.

The fact that the unfair term does not bind the consumer does not affect the binding force of the contract, even on him, if the contract 'is capable of continuing in existence without the unfair term'.[20] Thus the mere fact that the contract contains an unfair exemption clause does not relieve the consumer from liability for the price. But if the unfair term goes so much to the heart of the contract that the contract cannot without the term exist at all, the consumer would not be bound. If, for example, the term enabled the seller or supplier to raise the price, its unfairness[1] might support the view that the contract contained no price term and so was not binding on the consumer at all; an alternative possibility is that the contract would become one under which a reasonable price must be paid.

Where a term falls within the scope both of the 1999 Regulations and of the 1977 Act, the requirements of both schemes must be satisfied. For example, a term in a contract for the sale of goods to a consumer may contain a term limiting the seller's liability for breach of an implied term as to the quality of the goods. Such a term may be perfectly fair but the seller will not be able to rely on it because it is simply ineffective under the Act.[2] Where the Regulations impose a requirement of fairness and the Act one of reasonableness, a term which satisfied one of these requirements would normally also satisfy the other; but this is not necessarily so since the guidelines for determining reasonableness under the Act differ from the criteria for assessing fairness under the Regulations.[3] For example, under the Act a limitation clause may be reasonable on the ground that the party relying on it could not have covered himself by insurance,[4] but this guideline has no counterpart in the Regulations. It is possible, if unlikely, that such a clause would be reasonable under the Act but that it was nevertheless not binding on the consumer because it was unfair under the Regulations.

19a Certain arbitration clauses fall within Sch 2, para 1(q).
20 Regulation 8(2).
1 See Sch 2, para 1(l).
2 1977 Act, s 6(2).
3 Regulation 6, ante, p 113.
4 1977 Act, s 11(4).

viii Restrictions on evasion

The 1999 Regulations deal less fully than the 1977 Act[5] with this problem, but they do provide that the consumer is not to be deprived of his protection under them by means of a choice of law clause applying to the contract the law of a non-member state which, but for such a clause, would not apply to it.[6]

6   OTHER LEGISLATIVE TECHNIQUES

Three further legislative techniques for dealing with the problem of standard terms call for discussion.

The first is that of *supervised bargaining*: a court, or some other body, has to approve the clause to ensure that no undue advantage is taken of the weaker party. For example, the landlord's covenants to repair which are implied by statute in certain leases can be excluded only by a court order made with the consent of both parties.[7]

A second technique is to *prescribe the contents* of contracts of particular types. This possibility is illustrated by consumer credit agreements, the contents of which are to a considerable extent prescribed by the Consumer Credit Act and by delegated legislation: for example, the contract must give the debtor a cooling-off period and the right to earn certain rebates by making early payment.[8] Other types of contract, the contents of which are subject to similar legislative control, include contracts for the provision of package travel and similar facilities to consumers;[9] contracts with consumers concluded away from the trader's business premises;[10] and 'distance contracts' with consumers.[11]

A third technique is to use *administrative action* to control exemption clauses. Under the Enterprise Act 2002, one of the duties of the Office of Fair Trading (OFT) is to promote good consumer practices such as approving consumer codes;[12] and earlier legislation which remains in force makes it an offence for a commercial seller to use in

5   Section 27, ante, pp 108–109.
6   Regulation 9; for the definition of 'member state', see reg 3(1).
7   Landlord and Tenant Act 1985, ss 11 and 12.
8   Consumer Credit Act 1974, ss 67, 94, 95.
9   Package Travel, Package Holidays and Package Tours Regulations 1992, SI 1992/3288.
10 Consumer Protection (Cancellation of Contracts Concluded away from Business Premises) Regulations 1987, SI 1987/2117.
11 Consumer Protection (Distance Selling) Regulations 2000, SI 2000/2334, reg 10; see also Electronic Commerce (EC Directive) Regulations 2002, SI 2002/2013, esp regs 11 and 15.
12 Enterprise Act 2002, s 8.

a consumer sale an exemption clause made void by legislation discussed earlier in this chapter.[13] The Unfair Terms in Consumer Contracts Regulations 1999 also impose on the OFT[14] and on certain qualifying bodies a duty to consider complaints that any contract term drawn up for general use is unfair and to ask the court to restrain such use by injunction.[15] The OFT and qualifying bodies are also empowered to obtain information and obtain undertakings in respect of the use of any 'preformulated contract in dealings with consumers'.[16] Since individual consumers may well lack the means or energy to contest even plainly invalid terms, such 'pre-emptive challenges'[17] by public authorities may well be a more effective means, than private litigation, of controlling unfair standard terms in consumer contracts.

13 Consumer Transactions (Restrictions on Statements) Order 1976, SI 1976/1813; Consumer Transactions (Restrictions on Statements) (Amendment) Order 1978, SI 1978/127.
14 See Enterprise Act 2002, s 2(3), substituting the OFT for the (now abolished) Director General of Fair Trading.
15 Regulations 10–12.
16 Regulation 13(3)(a).
17 *Director General of Fair Trading v First National Bank plc* [2001] UKHL 52, [2002] 1 AC 481 at [33].

Chapter 8

Mistake

1 INTRODUCTION

The cases in which the validity of a contract may be affected by mistake fall into two main types. In the first, both parties make the same mistake: for example both believe that the thing about which they are contracting is in existence when it has in fact ceased to exist. In the second type of case, the parties make different mistakes, so that they misunderstand each other: for example, one party thinks that they are contracting about one thing and the other about a different one. In the first type of case, the parties reach agreement, but the effect of the mistake may be to deprive that agreement of its normal contractual effect: here the mistake *nullifies* consent. In the second type of case, the effect of the mistake is to put the parties at cross purposes, and the reason why there is no contract is that they never reach agreement at all: here the mistake *negatives* consent.

At first sight there might seem to be little similarity between situations in which mistake prevents the parties from reaching agreement, and those in which it deprives an agreement of the effect of a binding contract. There is, however, an important feature which is common to both situations and which justifies the treatment of them under one heading. This is the requirement that the mistake must be *fundamental.* The concept of fundamental mistake will be further elaborated below; but the basic idea is that the mistake must relate to some crucially important element in the contract. A person who has made a bad bargain can almost always say that he has made a 'mistake' of some kind; and it is obviously undesirable to allow him, merely on this ground, to escape from the contract. But the more important his 'mistake' becomes, the greater will be the hardship of holding him to the contract; and the law tries to strike a balance between this hardship and the uncertainty which may be caused by holding contracts invalid on the ground of mistake.

The striking of this balance is in itself a delicate task; and the difficulty of the subject is further increased by the different approaches to it at common law and in equity. The first main difference between the two approaches is that the common law, stressing the need for commercial certainty, gives relief only for a very narrowly defined range of mistakes. Equity, on the other hand, places greater emphasis on the factor of hardship to the mistaken party and gives relief for some kinds of mistake which are disregarded at common law. Secondly, the common law holds that, where its stringent test of mistake is satisfied, the contract is wholly void. The effect (if any) in equity of a mistake which does not satisfy this test is less drastic; in particular, the validity of the contract is not affected by it.

2 MISTAKES WHICH MAY NULLIFY CONSENT

Consent may be nullified if both parties at the time of entering into the contract (or purported contract) make the same mistake about the subject-matter. Two topics arise for discussion: the types of mistake which may thus affect a contract, and the legal effects of the mistake.

a Types of mistake

At common law, a mistake nullifies only consent if it is a fundamental one, but equity to a limited extent[1] gives relief for mistakes which do not satisfy this strict common law requirement.

i Fundamental mistake at common law

A mistake is most obviously fundamental where it relates to the existence of the subject-matter: for example, where a charter-party is made concerning a ship which (unknown to either party) had been previously sunk; where a contract is made to paint a portrait of a person believed to be alive but in fact deceased; or where a separation agreement is made between two persons who erroneously believed that they were married to each other.[2] A mistake as to the existence of the subject-matter of one contract may also affect a second, accessory contract: for example, where A gives B a guarantee of C's liability to B under a lease of machinery which, unknown to A and B, does not exist.[3] A mistake is also fundamental where the parties believe that it is possible to perform the contract when this is not the case. Thus, if a person agrees to buy a property from another, and neither of them

---

1 See post, p 129.
2 *Galloway v Galloway* (1914) 30 TLR 531.
3 *Associated Japanese Bank (International) Ltd v Crédit du Nord SA* [1988] 3 All ER 902.

knows that it already belongs to the buyer, there is a fundamental mistake, since a person cannot in law buy his own property.[4] Similarly, a contract for the sale of ten tons of potatoes to be grown on a particular field would be affected by a fundamental mistake if, unknown to either party, the field could not, even in the most favourable circumstances, produce more than two tons.[5] A mistake would also be fundamental where it related to the identity of the subject-matter, eg where at an auction sale *both* parties believed that one lot was 'under the hammer' when in fact it was another. This is a rare situation: confusion of this kind generally exists in the mind of one party only and thus *negatives* consent, if it has any effect at all.

The above cases are relatively straightforward, but greater difficulty arises where the mistake relates to some important quality of the subject-matter. Of course, if one of the parties *undertakes* that it has that quality, he is normally liable if the subject-matter in fact lacks the quality; and the other is in that event normally not bound to perform.[6] The difficult cases are those in which both parties simply *assume* that the thing has a certain quality which in fact it lacks: for example, if both buyer and seller of a horse believe it is sound, when it is not. It has been said that such a mistake is not fundamental.[7] The position was held to be the same where kapok was sold under a brand name and both buyer and seller believed that kapok of that brand was pure when it in fact contained an admixture of other materials and so was useless to the buyer;[8] and a mistake is also not fundamental if it merely makes the subject-matter less useful to the acquirer than he believed it to be.[9] In cases of this kind, it can be said either that the mistake was not important enough to affect the validity of the contract, or that it related to a matter in respect of which the party prejudiced by the mistake could have been expected to protect himself, by expressly stipulating that the quality must exist.

To be 'fundamental' in the narrow common law sense, the mistake must, it has been said, be one 'as to the substance of the whole consideration [ie of the subject-matter] going, as it were, to the whole root of the matter'.[10] This requirement was very strictly interpreted in

4   *Bell v Lever Bros Ltd* [1932] AC 161 at 218; *The Great Peace* [2002] EWCA Civ 1407, [2003] QB 679 at [126]–[128].
5   Cf *Sheikh Bros v Ochsner* [1957] AC 136.
6   *Associated Japanese Bank (International) Ltd v Crédit du Nord SA* [1988] 3 All ER 902; *Peco Arts Inc v Hazlitt Gallery* [1983] 3 All ER 193.
7   *Bell v Lever Bros Ltd* [1932] AC 161 at 224.
8   *Harrison & Jones Ltd v Bunten & Lancaster Ltd* [1953] 1 QB 646.
9   *The Great Peace* [2002] EWCA Civ 1407, [2003] QB 697.
10   *Kennedy v Panama New Zealand and Australian Royal Mail Co Ltd* (1867) LR 2 QB 580 at 588.

the leading case of *Bell v Lever Bros*.[11] In that case, Lever Bros wanted to terminate the service contracts of the chairman and vice-chairman of one of their subsidiary companies, and entered into an agreement to pay them £50,000 by way of compensation for loss of office. It was later discovered that the service contracts could legally have been terminated without paying any compensation at all, as the gentlemen in question had long ago committed breaches of duty which would have justified their summary dismissal. But these had been forgotten by them,[12] so that none of the parties to the compensation agreement was (when that agreement was made) aware of the possibility of terminating the service contracts without compensation. In the lower courts it was held that this mistake was fundamental; but the House of Lords reversed their decision. Lever Bros, it was said, had got exactly what they bargained for. Their only mistake was as to a quality of the subject-matter of the compensation agreement, viz as to the binding force of the underlying service contracts. Similarly, a mistaken belief that premises are suitable in the normal way for redevelopment, or free from rent control, or subject to a protected tenancy, is not fundamental in the common law sense; and the same conclusion has been reached where a claim on an insurance policy was settled in the belief that the policy was valid, when in fact it was voidable for misrepresentation.[13] Perhaps the most extreme illustration of the narrowness of the common law concept is to be found in an example given by Lord Atkin in *Bell v Lever Bros*: 'A buys a picture from B; both A and B believe it to be the work of an old master and a high price is paid. It turns out to be a modern copy. A has no remedy in the absence of representation or warranty.'[14]

The actual and hypothetical cases mentioned in the last paragraph so much restrict the concept of fundamental mistake that it has been doubted whether any mistake as to quality can ever be fundamental at common law. But one possible view is that *Bell v Lever Bros* was simply a 'quite exceptional case'[15] in which the House of Lords may have been influenced by the harshness of the rule that relatively minor breaches of duty were in law a ground for summary dismissal; and there are cases which fall on the other side of the line. In one such case[16] a

11 [1932] AC 161; contrast *Sybron Corpn v Rochem Ltd* [1984] Ch 112.
12 They were under no duty to disclose the breaches: see post, p 169.
13 *Amalgamated Investment and Property Co Ltd v John Walker & Sons Ltd* [1976] 3 All ER 509; *Solle v Butcher* [1950] 1 KB 671; *Magee v Pennine Insurance Co Ltd* [1969] 2 QB 507.
14 [1932] AC at 224.
15 *Associated Japanese Bank (International) Ltd v Crédit du Nord SA* [1988] 3 All ER 902 at 911.
16 *Griffith v Brymer* (1903) 19 TLR 434.

contract for the hire of a room for the purpose of viewing King Edward VII's coronation procession was made in ignorance of the fact that the procession had been cancelled; and it was held that the mistake was fundamental. In another case,[17] table napkins were put up for auction and described in the catalogue as 'with the crest of Charles I and the authentic property of that monarch'. They were in fact Georgian and worth much less than the buyer had paid for them; and it was said that the buyer could have treated the contract as void for mistake. One possible view of the case is that the contract was for the sale of 'table linen', in which case a mistake as to its age would not be fundamental. But it is equally possible to say that the contract was for the sale of 'a personal relic of Charles I'; and on this view the mistake would be fundamental.

This last case provides a clue to the common law concept of a fundamental mistake. A thing which is the subject-matter of a contract will have many qualities such as age, colour, size and so on. Usually the contracting parties will have one or more (but not all) of these qualities in mind when they deal with the subject-matter. If the quality about which they are mistaken is *the* one by reference to which they have actually *identified* the subject-matter, then, and then only, is the mistake fundamental at common law. A test for determining whether the mistake is as to an identifying quality is to imagine that one can ask the parties, immediately after the making of the contract, just what the subject-matter was. The mistake is fundamental only if, by reason of their mistake, their answer is wrong: for example if, in the case of the napkins, their answer were 'a Carolean relic', but not if it were 'antique table linen'. Similarly, in *Bell v Lever Bros* the mistake was not fundamental because the parties would have correctly said that they were contracting about 'service contracts' and the possibility of terminating those contracts without compensation would not have entered their thoughts as part of the process of identifying the subject-matter.

Although this test of *the identifying quality* appears to state the gist of the common law concept of fundamental mistake, some cases take a wider and others a narrower view of what amounts to a fundamental mistake. The first possibility is illustrated by a case in which an insurance policy on the life of a man called Death was sold in the belief that he was alive when he was in fact dead. This mistake (which of course affected the value of the policy) was regarded by one of the judges as fundamental.[18] Yet the parties no doubt identified the

---

17   *Nicholson and Venn v Smith Marriott* (1947) 177 LT 189.
18   *Scott v Coulson* [1903] 2 Ch 249 at 252.

subject-matter simply as an insurance policy', which it was. On the other hand, a person who had just paid ten million pounds for what both parties believed to be an old master would surely say that he had bought (for example) 'a Rembrandt'. It would be simply facetious for him to say that he had just bought 'a picture'; and the better view (though not one that is generally accepted) is that the mistake should be regarded as fundamental. The *effect* of such a mistake depends on further factors to be discussed below.[19]

ii Mistake of law

It used to be generally thought that the validity of a contract was not affected by a mistake of law, as opposed to one of fact.[20] But the distinction between the two types of mistake was sometimes hard to draw and often harder to justify. It was sometimes rejected[1] and sometimes mitigated in equity by an intermediate category of so-called mistakes as to 'private right', such as those which arose where, as a result of the misconstruction of a will, A was believed to be the owner of something that belonged to B.[2] More recently, the House of Lords has rejected the distinction in the context of the right to recover back money paid under a mistake and has held that this right extends to payments made under mistake of law, ie under a belief that the contracts under which payments were made were valid when actually they were void.[3] The distinction is also likely to be rejected in the present context,[4] so that a challenge to the validity of a contract on the ground of mistake will no longer fail merely[4a] because the mistake was one of law.

iii Mistakes for which equity gives relief

Recent developments have considerably curtailed equitable relief for mistake; but they have left open the availability of at least one form

19 Post, pp 126–127.
20 *British Homophone Ltd v Kunz* (1935) 152 LT 589 at 583; the same assumption underlies *Solle v Butcher* [1950] 1 KB 671.
1   *Allcard v Walker* [1896] 2 Ch 369.
2   Cf *Cooper v Phibbs* (1867) LR 2 HL 149, where the contract would now be regarded as void at law: cf supra, p 122 at n 4.
3   *Kleinwort Benson Ltd v Lincoln City Council* [1999] 2 AC 349.
4   See *Brennan v Bolt Burden* [2004] EWCA Civ 1017, (2004) Times, 27 August at [10], [17] and post, p 148; contrast *S v S* [2002] EWHC 223, [2003] Fam 1 at [70].
4a For other requirements, see *Shamil Bank of Bahrain v Beximo Pharmaceuticals* [2004] EWCA Civ 19, [2004] 2 Lloyd's Rcp 1 at [56]–[60] (mistake not fundamental); *Brennan v Bolt Burden*, supra n 4, at [23], [39] (risk of 'mistake' allocated by compromise agreement; cf post, pp 127-128).

of such relief. These developments will be discussed below.[5] Our present concern is with the point that, for the purpose of equitable relief, the mistake need not be 'fundamental' in the narrow common law sense discussed above.[6] Even in equity, however, the mistake must be more than merely slight:[7] it must go beyond the sort of 'mistake' of which anyone can complain when he has made a bad bargain. It must, moreover, relate to circumstances in existence at the time of contracting, and not merely to 'the expectation of the parties'.[8] For example, in one case[9] a contract was made for the sale of a London warehouse which the buyer intended to redevelop. Shortly afterwards it was listed as a building of special architectural or historic interest; this made it much less likely that permission to redevelop would be given, and substantially reduced the value of the property. It was held that the buyer's mistaken belief that the property was 'suitable for and capable of being redeveloped'[10] was not a sufficient ground for equitable intervention.

b   Effects of the mistake

i   Contract void at common law

The general rule of common law is that a fundamental mistake makes a contract void.[11] Neither party therefore comes under any obligation to perform; and any performance rendered (or its value) must be returned: for example, money paid under such a contract must be paid back.[12] The common law (subject to a possible exception mentioned below)[13] knows no half-way house between such complete voidness and complete validity. If the mistake is not fundamental, the contract is treated as fully binding, however much hardship this may cause to one of the parties.

---

5   Post, pp 128–129.
6   See, eg, *Solle v Butcher* [1950] 1 KB 671, post, pp 128–129.
7   *Debenham v Sawbridge* [1901] 2 Ch 98; *William Sindall plc v Cambridgeshire County Council* [1994] 1 WLR 1016 at 1041.
8   *Amalgamated Investment and Property Co Ltd v Walker & Sons Ltd* [1976] 3 All ER 509 at 516.
9   *Amalgamated Investment and Property* case [1976] 3 All ER 509.
10   [1976] 3 All ER 509 at 515.
11   *Associated Japanese Bank (International) Ltd v Crédit du Nord SA* [1988] 3 All ER 902 at 909, 912.
12   Eg *Griffith v Brymer* (1903) 19 TLR 434.
13   See post, p 128.

ii Risk of mistake taken by one party

A contract is not void for mistake if one or both parties have consciously taken the risk of the mistake. The point may be illustrated by referring again to the sale of a picture which is believed to be genuine but turns out to be a copy. If the seller has expressly undertaken that the picture is genuine, he will be in breach;[14] conversely if he makes it clear that the attribution is not guaranteed he will not be in breach and the buyer will have to pay the full price (which will no doubt reflect the seller's disclaimer). Between these extremes, there is the intermediate case in which the authenticity of the picture is a matter of dispute between experts. Here the seller will not be regarded as having impliedly undertaken that the picture is genuine;[15] and it would be inappropriate to give relief to either party on the ground of mistake even if both believed the picture to be genuine and even if such a mistake could be regarded as fundamental. The case would be one in which each party had taken a risk: the seller that of the picture's being worth more, and the buyer that of its being worth less, than the contract price.

There are many other cases which illustrate this process of contractual allocation of such risks. In one case, a seller of land sold 'my title, *if any*' to the land, and it was said that such a contract could be binding even if the seller had no title, unless the seller knew this.[16] Conversely, where land is sold expressly subject to any rights of neighbouring landowners, the buyer cannot claim relief for mistake because it turns out that a neighbour has the right to run a sewer under the land.[17] Similarly, marine insurance policies may contain 'lost or not lost' clauses, the effect of which is that both parties are bound even though the subject-matter is already lost at the time the policy was made: that is, the insurer is liable for the loss if it was covered by the policy; and the insured is liable for the premium, even though the loss which occurred was not covered by the policy. Again, a mistake as to the productive capacity of a quarry or mine may relieve the tenant from liability for failing to extract the agreed minimum quantity;[18] but if he promises to pay a fixed rent or royalty *in any event,* he will be liable in full, even though the capacity of the mine falls short of the stipulated quantity.[19] In some of these cases of conscious risk-taking it is, indeed, scarcely appropriate to talk of mistake: they

14 As in *Peco Arts Inc v Hazlitt Gallery Ltd* [1983] 3 All ER 193.
15 *Harlingdon & Leinster Enterprises Ltd v Christopher Hull Fine Art Ltd* [1990] 1 All ER 737.
16 *Smith v Harrison* (1857) 26 LJ Ch 412.
17 *William Sindall plc v Cambridgeshire County Council* [1994] 1 WLR 1016.
18 *Clifford v Watts* (1870) LR 5 CP 577.
19 *Bute v Thompson* (1844) 13 M & W 487.

are hardly cases in which both parties positively believed in one state of facts when a different one existed.

Even outside this area of conscious risk-taking the courts may impose the risk of a fundamental mistake on one of the parties and so hold him liable on the contract. In an Australian case[20] the Commonwealth Disposals Commission purported to sell the wreck of an oil tanker lying on a certain named reef. No such tanker had ever existed, but the Commission was held liable in damages to the buyer, on the ground that it had impliedly undertaken that a tanker such as that described did exist. A person may similarly be liable if he has no reasonable grounds for his mistaken belief.[1] Conversely, it is theoretically possible for the risk to be thrown on the buyer, so that he may have to pay the price even though the goods do not exist. In two English cases, however, such claims for the price were dismissed.[2] In one of these it was said that where specific goods were sold which did not exist, the case would not 'be treated as one in which the seller warrants the existence of these specific goods, but as one in which there has been failure of consideration and mistake'.[3] This view is reinforced by a provision in the Sale of Goods Act 1979 under which a contract for the sale of specific goods is void if, at the time when the contract was made, the goods had perished without the knowledge of either party.[4] It therefore seems that the courts would only throw the risk of a mistake as to the existence of the subject-matter on one of the parties in exceptional circumstances: for example, where he is somehow at fault in inducing the mistake in the other party's mind. This would be the position where the former party ought to have known that the subject-matter did not, or probably did not, exist and nevertheless entered into the contract without qualification. In this situation the party at fault would not be able to rely on the mistake, though the other party would probably be able to do so.

iii   Relief in equity

Mistakes which do not affect the validity of a contract at law because they are not fundamental may be grounds for relief in equity. This was formerly given in one of two ways.

---

20   *McRae v Commonwealth Disposals Commission* (1950) 84 CLR 377.
1   *Associated Japanese Bank (International) Ltd v Crédit du Nord SA* [1988] 3 All ER 902 at 913.
2   *Couturier v Hastie* (1856) 5 HL Cas 673; *Barrow Lane and Ballard Ltd v Phillip Phillips & Co Ltd* [1929] 1 KB 574.
3   *Barrow Lane & Ballard Ltd v Phillips & Co Ltd* supra at 582.
4   Sale of Goods Act 1979, s 6.

The first was by way of *rescission* of the contract by the party prejudiced by the mistake, on whom terms could in turn be imposed to ensure that justice was done to the other party. For example, where a flat was let in the mistaken belief that it was free from rent control, the contract was not void at law, but the court rescinded the lease and gave the tenant the option of staying in the flat on terms of paying the rent which the landlord could have charged, if he had known the true position in time.[5] In such cases, the equitable power to rescind no doubt alleviated the hardship to one of the parties which could result from the narrow common law concept of a fundamental mistake. But no satisfactory way was ever found of reconciling this equitable view with the common law rule established in *Bell v Lever Bros Ltd*;[6] and in *The Great Peace*[7] the Court of Appeal held that there was no longer any equitable power to rescind a contract which was valid at law because the mistake under which it was made was not fundamental. This conclusion was based on the need to restore doctrinal consistency;[8] no attempt was made to evaluate earlier cases exercising the equitable jurisdiction to rescind on their merits, or to meet the point that rescission in equity could 'on occasion be the passport to a just result'.[9] But the argument that a contract can be rescinded in equity for a mistake that is not fundamental in the narrow common law sense is now open only in the House of Lords.

The second form of equitable relief is refusal of the remedy of specific performance against the party prejudiced by the mistake.[10] This form of equitable relief for mistakes which are not fundamental at law is not affected by *The Great Peace*, which is concerned only with rescission. So, if an agreement for a lease were made under such a mistake prejudicial to the landlord, then the landlord could no longer rescind the contract in equity, but the court could take the mistake into account in deciding whether to order specific performance of the contract at the suit of the tenant. This possibility presents no acute conflict with the common law rules since refusal of specific performance (unlike rescission) does not affect the continued existence of the contract so that, in the above example, a claim for damages remains available to the tenant. The present form of equitable relief is, moreover, flexible: instead of simply refusing specific performance, the court may grant it *on terms*, those terms usually being designed to remove the

5   *Solle v Butcher* [1950] 1 KB 671.
6   [1932] AC 161, ante, p 123.
7   [2002] EWCA Civ 1407, [2003] QB 679.
8   [2003] QB 679 at [157].
9   *West Sussex Properties Ltd v Chichester District Council* [2000] All ER (D) 887 at [42] (CA).
10   *Jones v Rimmer* (1880) 14 Ch D 588.

prejudice which the mistake causes to one of the parties. For example where land sold is, because of some misdescription, supposed to be larger in area than it actually is, equity can grant specific performance on the terms that the price is reduced.[11]

Equitable relief, whether by way of refusal of specific performance or formerly by way of rescission, is (or was) available where the contract is valid at law *because the mistake is not 'fundamental'* in the narrow common law sense. There is (as we have seen) another reason why a mistake may not make a contract void, and this is that one party has, or is deemed to have, *taken the risk of the mistake.* In cases of this kind, relief is no more available in equity than it is at common law:[12] it would not, for example, be granted where the contract was one for the sale of a picture of disputed authenticity.[13]

The above discussion is concerned with the possibility of obtaining equitable relief, sometimes on terms, where the contract is *valid* at common law. Where the contract is *void* at common law, there is normally no need to seek equitable relief. The contract can simply be disregarded by either party. A court order may, however, be necessary where a person has mistakenly agreed to buy property, to which he is beneficially entitled under a trust, from the trustee who holds the legal title for him.[14] Such an order may also be necessary to secure a return to the pre-contract position: for example, where the 'seller' had improved the property the 'buyer' may be ordered to pay for the improvements.[15] Such liability does not arise from the supposed contract but is imposed simply to prevent the unjust enrichment that would result if the 'buyer' could keep the improvement for nothing.

3   MISTAKES WHICH MAY NEGATIVE CONSENT

Mistake is said to negative consent when it puts the parties so seriously at cross-purposes that they cannot be said to have agreed at all. We shall first discuss the types of mistake which are sufficiently serious to negative consent and then consider the legal effects of such mistakes. It cannot be too strongly emphasised that in this type of case a mistake, though serious enough to negative consent, will not normally affect the validity of the contract at all. For reasons to be discussed later in

---

11   *Aspinalls to Powell and Scholefield* (1889) 60 LT 595.
12   *William Sindall plc v Cambridgeshire County Council* [1994] 1 WLR 1016 at 1035.
13   See p 127, ante.
14   As in *Cooper v Phibbs* (1867) LR 2 HL 149.
15   *Cooper v Phibbs* (1867) LR 2 HL 149: this point was not disputed.

this chapter,[16] the mistake will only impair the validity of the contract in a number of somewhat exceptional situations.

a Types of mistake

The cases provide illustrations of three types of mistake which may negative consent: mistakes as to the subject-matter, as to the person, and as to the terms of the contract.

i Mistake as to the subject matter

Mistake will negative consent if one party intends to deal with one thing and the other with a different one. This principle is generally thought to explain the case of *Raffles v Wichelhaus*,[17] where a contract was made for the sale of '125 bales of Surat Cotton ... to arrive ex *Peerless* from Bombay'. Two ships called *Peerless* had left Bombay, one in October and the other in December. It was held that the buyer was not bound to accept the December shipment, as he had intended to buy the October shipment. On the assumption that the seller intended to sell the December shipment, consent would be negatived. If, on the other hand, both parties had intended to deal with the December shipment, consent would not have been negatived merely because either party was mistaken as to the quality of the goods. Such a mistake would not be 'fundamental' and so it would not create a misunderstanding sufficiently serious to negative consent.[18] The concept of a 'fundamental' mistake here is the same as that already discussed in relation to mistakes which nullify consent. A mistake of one party as to a quality of the subject-matter will negative consent only if it is a mistake as to *the* quality by which that party identified the subject-matter.

ii Mistake as to the person

This kind of mistake was not discussed above, in connection with mistakes which nullify consent. The reason for this is that the possibility of both parties making the *same* mistake about the identity or attributes of one of them is so remote as to be of no practical importance. But one party (A) may well make such a mistake about the other (B) and this most commonly happens where B makes some pretence about himself in order to induce A to contract with him, or

16 See post, pp 136–138.
17 (1864) 2 H & C 906.
18 *Smith v Hughes* (1871) LR 6 QB 597, see post, p 135.

to give him credit. Usually (though not always), B is an impecunious rogue who pretends to be a person of means, and the question once again is whether A's mistake about B is sufficiently fundamental to negative consent. If A's mistake is of this kind, its effect will (since B knows of it[19]) usually be to make the contract void at common law.

As between the two parties to the alleged contract (A and B) the question whether the mistake is sufficiently fundamental to make the contract void is of small practical importance. B's pretence will almost always amount to fraud, so that the contract (if any) between them will be voidable on account of that fraud, in accordance with the principles to be discussed in Chapter 9. But the question of mistake is of crucial importance where (as often happens) B obtains goods under the contract without paying for them and then sells them to X who buys them in good faith. If the contract between A and B is void for mistake, no title in the goods will pass to B who will thus be unable to confer any title on X. Hence A can recover the goods (or their value) from X. If, on the other hand, the contract between A and B is only voidable for fraud, B will get a voidable title to the goods, which A will be unable to avoid, once X has in good faith acquired the goods. It follows that X will, as against A, be entitled to retain the goods. The likely effect of holding a contract void for mistake is therefore to prejudice innocent third parties. This state of the law has been criticised both judicially[20] and by the Law Reform Committee,[1] who have recommended that the innocent third party (X) should be entitled to retain the goods even where the contract between A and B is void for mistake. But that recommendation has not been implemented; and the courts can only protect X by adopting a narrow definition of the kinds of mistake as to the person which will negative consent. For this purpose, a distinction has been drawn between mistakes as to identity and mistakes as to attributes. The former do, while the latter do not, negative consent.

In the leading case of *Cundy v Lindsay*,[2] Lindsay received an order for handkerchiefs from a rogue called Blenkarn, who signed his name so as to make it look like that of Blenkiron & Co, a respectable firm whom Lindsay knew by repute. Lindsay sent the handkerchiefs to the address given by Blenkarn, who did not pay for them and resold them to Cundy. It was held that the contract between Lindsay and Blenkarn was void, as Lindsay had made a mistake as to the identity of the other contracting party: they had dealt with Blenkarn when they thought

19　See post, p 137.
20　Eg in *Shogun Finance Ltd v Hudson* [2003] UKHL 62, [2004] 1 AC 919 at [5], [60], [84].
1　12th Report ((1966) Cmnd 2958) para 15.
2　(1878) 3 App Cas 459.

they were dealing with Blenkiron & Co. Hence the handkerchiefs remained Lindsay's property throughout, so that Lindsay recovered their value from Cundy.

In *Cundy v Lindsay* the crucial fact was that A (Lindsay) believed that he was dealing with B (Blenkiron & Co) when in fact he was dealing with C (Blenkarn). The position would be different if A's only mistake were about some attribute of B, but for the existence of which A would not have been willing to deal with B. Thus, in a later case,[3] a rogue called Wallis obtained goods on credit by using an impressive letter-head purporting to come from a firm called 'Hallam & Co' which was said to operate a large factory and various depots. There was in fact no such entity as 'Hallam & Co', which was simply an alias for Wallis. It was held that the sellers had not made a mistake as to the identity of the other contracting party, but only as to one of his attributes, namely his credit-worthiness. Accordingly, they were not entitled to recover the goods from an innocent third party to whom Wallis had resold them. As the sellers had sent goods on credit to a completely unknown customer, without taking any steps to find out whether he was a good credit risk, the decision is an eminently reasonable one.

It is obviously sensible for the law to take the view that a mistake as to the particular attribute of credit-worthiness should not suffice to negative consent. Any decision which one party makes as to the credit-worthiness of the other involves the deliberate taking of a commercial risk, and a person who takes such a risk should not be entitled to relief against an innocent third party. But the cases leave open the possibility that mistake as to some other attribute may negative consent. Here, an analysis similar to that used in defining a fundamental mistake as to the subject-matter may be adopted. A person has many attributes, and for the purpose of a particular contract he may be identified by any one or more of these. If the other party is mistaken about such an *identifying attribute*, consent may be negatived. For example, a company may identify persons with whom it wishes to deal simply as its 'shareholders'; or a jeweller may identify the person with whom he wants to deal as 'the wife of Z'.[4] If the persons dealt with lack those identifying attributes, then it is suggested that a mistake as to identity has been made. The question whether the attribute to which the mistake relates is an identifying attribute can give rise to considerable difficulty; but there are two ways in which this difficulty is, at least to some extent, mitigated.

3   *King's Norton Metal Co Ltd v Edridge, Merrett & Co Ltd* (1897) 14 TLR 98.
4   See *Lake v Simmons* [1927] AC 487.

134   *Mistake*

First, the law makes certain provisional assumptions about the way in which one contracting party identifies the other. One strong assumption is that parties who actually meet face to face have identified each other by the normal process of sight and hearing. This assumption is so strong that even a belief by the mistaken party that he is dealing (face to face) with a totally different person will not normally negative consent. In one case,[5] a jeweller sold a ring and delivered it on credit to a customer who had come into his shop and had falsely claimed to be Sir George Bullough, a wealthy man known by name to the jeweller. It was held that the contract was not void for mistake. In a contrasting case,[6] two ladies sold their car, and delivered it against a worthless cheque, to a person who had claimed to be 'PGM Hutchinson of Stanstead House, Stanstead Road, Caterham'. They did so only after one of them had checked in a telephone directory that there was such a person living at that address. It was held that the contract was void. The case had been judicially doubted,[7] but it can perhaps be justified on the ground that the normal assumption as to the process of identification between persons who deal face to face had been rebutted by the sellers' attempt to check the buyer's claimed identity in the directory. That assumption could also be negatived where the dishonest person adopted an actual physical disguise. Even in this type of case, however, a distinction must be drawn. If A is induced to contract with B, by a disguise which simply leads him to believe that B *is not B*, the contract is not void for mistake, though it is voidable for fraud. To make the contract void, the disguise must induce A to believe that B *is C* and C must be a distinct person either known to A or at least believed by A to exist. So long as A believes that there is a separately identifiable person called C, it seems to be immaterial that there is in fact no such person in existence: for example where, unknown to A, C had died before the transaction in question.

The difficulty of determining whether a mistake relates to an identifying attribute is secondly mitigated where the alleged contract is in writing. The question who the parties to the contract are then turns on the construction of the document and prima facie[8] they are the persons described as such in it. In the *Shogun Finance* case,[9] a

5   *Phillips v Brooks Ltd* [1919] 2 KB 243; cf *Lewis v Averay* [1972] 1 QB 198; *Whittaker v Campbell* [1984] QB 318 at 329.
6   *Ingram v Little* [1961] 1 QB 31
7   *Shogun Finance Ltd v Hudson* [2003] UKHL 62, [2004] 1 AC 919 at [87], [110], [185].
8   Ie, subject to the possibility that the person named as a party may have acted as agent for another.
9   *Shogun Finance Ltd v Hudson* [2003] UKHL 62, [2004] 1 AC 919; cf *Hector v Lyons* (1988) 58 P & CR 156.

rogue (X) obtained possession of a car under a written hire-purchase agreement by pretending to be Y, producing Y's driving licence (which X had improperly obtained) and forging Y's signature. The written agreement was expressed to be between Y and Z, a finance company which had checked Y's address and credit-rating before entering into the agreement; this provided that the hirer was, and was only, the person named in it as such. A majority of the House of Lords held that X was not a party to the agreement, so that a person who later in good faith bought the car from X acquired no title to it;[10] indeed, extrinsic evidence that X was a party was excluded by the parol evidence rule as it would have contradicted the writing.[11] An alternative ground for the decision was that, since Z's investigations into Y's credit-rating and address showed that Z intended to deal only with Y, there was no agreement between Z and X.[12] On this view, Z's mistake was one as to an identifying attribute of the rogue.

iii Mistake as to terms

Sometimes a mistake as to the terms of a transaction will negative consent. For example, in *Hartog v Colin and Shields*[13] a seller of rabbit skins intended to sell them at a fixed price per *piece* and the buyer to buy them at the same price per *pound*. There were about three pieces to the pound, and the contract was held void. It is obvious that in this case the parties were seriously at cross-purposes, but greater difficulty arises from the troublesome case of *Smith v Hughes*.[14] Oats were sold by a farmer to a trainer of racehorses, who was only interested in buying *old* oats and who refused to accept the oats which the farmer delivered, on the ground that they were in fact *new*. It was not an express term of the contract that the oats were old; and the buyer's mistaken belief that the oats *were old* would not have invalidated the contract, as this mistake as to quality would not be a fundamental one, within the principles already discussed. But it was said that a mistaken belief that the oats were *warranted to be old* would have negatived consent. It is not at all easy to see why a mistake of the latter kind should be so much more serious (than a simple mistake as to the age of the oats) as to negative consent; and another possible explanation of the decision will be put forward below.[15]

---

10 Under Hire Purchase Act 1964, ss 27, 29(4).
11 Ante, p 77.
12 [2003] UKHL 62, [2004] 1 AC 919 at [50]–[51].
13 [1939] 3 All ER 566.
14 (1871) LR 6 QB 597.
15 See post, p 138.

iv   Mistake must induce the contract

A mistake will not negative consent merely because it is fundamental. It must, in addition, be as to a point of some commercial significance to the mistaken party, and it must induce him to enter into the contract. Suppose, for example, that a person orders goods from a shop with which he has long had dealings, but does so in ignorance of the fact that the shop has just been taken over by a new owner. His mistake is certainly fundamental: he thinks he is dealing with the old owner when in fact he is dealing with the new one. But in the great majority of cases this mistake will not matter in the least to the customer, so long as he in fact gets goods which satisfy his needs. To negative consent, further facts must be shown. For example, in one case[16] the buyer was owed money by the former owner of the shop and he intended to set off this debt against the price of the goods which he had ordered, so as not to have to pay cash. In these circumstances, it was held that there was no contract between him and the new owner.

Just as a mistake may be fundamental without inducing the contract, so the converse may be true. There can be no stronger inducement than a mistake as to a person's creditworthiness, but such a mistake alone[17] will not negative consent. To produce this effect, the mistake must be fundamental *and* induce the contract, as (for example) in *Cundy v Lindsay*. The requirement of inducement is most commonly discussed in relation to cases of mistaken identity but it can also apply in relation to mistakes as to the subject-matter. Suppose that, in *Raffles v Wichelhaus*,[18] both *Peerlesses* had sailed (and arrived) on the same day. Probably, the validity of the contract would not have been affected by the fact that the buyer intended to buy goods arriving in the one ship and the seller to sell those arriving in the other.

b   Effects of the mistake

i   Contract generally valid at common law

The fact that a mistake has been made which negatives consent does not generally invalidate a contract at common law. This is so because, generally, the mistaken party (A) will have conducted himself in such a way as to induce the other party (B) reasonably to believe that he, A, is in fact agreeing to the terms proposed by B. Hence the objective test of agreement[19]

16   *Boulton v Jones* (1857) 2 H & N 564.
17   As in *Collings v Lee* [2001] 2 All ER 332, where no attempt was made to argue that the contract was void for mistake.
18   (1864) 2 H & C 906; see p 131, ante.
19   Ante, p 2.

is satisfied (even though there is no agreement in fact) and there is a good contract. Suppose, for example, that at an auction sale a person thinks he is bidding for one lot when he is actually bidding for another, which is knocked down to him. He will normally be bound by the contact of sale even though his mistake was fundamental and induced the contract. Similarly, the landlord may, as a result of a clerical error, offer to grant a tenancy at a monthly rent of £1,000, when he intended to charge £2,000. Once the tenant has accepted the offer, the landlord cannot treat the contract as void merely because he was under a mistake as to its terms.[20] Whenever the objective principle applies the contract is valid in spite of the fact that a mistake has been made. In such cases, it is therefore unnecessary to discuss the difficult question whether the mistake is 'fundamental' in the common law sense.[1]

ii   Contract exceptionally void at common law

A mistake which negatives consent affects the validity of a contract only in three exceptional situations. It is only in these situations that the mistake is *operative*, so as to make the contract void.

First, the circumstances may give rise to such *perfect ambiguity* that the objective test provides no solution. This was the position in *Raffles v Wichelhaus*.[2] A reasonable person would have had no ground for believing that the buyer had agreed to buy the cotton on the December, rather than that on the October, *Peerless*.

Secondly, the mistake of one party will make the contract void if that mistake is *known to the other party*. The objective test exists to protect a person against the prejudice which he may suffer by relying on an appearance of agreement, and he can hardly complain if he actually knows that that appearance is false. Thus in *Cundy v Lindsay* the mistake made by Lindsay was operative because Blenkarn knew that Lindsay intended to deal with Blenkiron & Co. The contract may also be void if the mistake, though not actually known to the other party, is so obvious that it ought to have been known to him. This was the position in *Hartog v Colin and Shields*[3] where it was held that the buyer must, in the light of market prices and conditions, have known that the seller could not have intended the quoted price to apply to pounds but only to pieces. It is important to stress that, where a mistake is, or ought to be, known to the other party, it must still be fundamental if it

---

20   *Centrovincial Estates plc v Merchant Investors Assurance Co Ltd* [1983] Com LR 158, approved in *Whittaker v Campbell* [1984] QB 318 at 327 and in *The Antclizo* [1987] 2 Lloyd's Rep 130 at 146; affd [1988] 2 All ER 513.
1   Eg *The Unique Mariner* [1978] 1 Lloyd's Rep 438 at 451–452.
2   See ante, p 131.
3   [1939] 3 All ER 566; see ante, p 135.

is to make the contract void. If, for example, A mistakenly believes that B is rich, B's knowledge of A's mistake will not make the contract void, since it is a mistake as to an attribute only. Similarly, in *Smith v Hughes*,[4] a mistaken belief on the part of the buyer (A) that the oats *were old* would not have made the contract void, even if it had been known to the seller (B), since such a mistake would be one as to a non-fundamental quality. To make the contract void, two elements would, in the court's view, have to be combined: (i) a mistaken belief on A's part that the oats were *warranted old*; and (ii) knowledge on B's part of *this* mistake.

It is (as suggested above) not altogether easy to see why a mistaken belief that oats were *warranted old* negatives consent, when a mistaken belief that they *were old* does not have this effect; and there may be an alternative explanation of *Smith v Hughes*. This is that the seller who knows of the buyer's belief that he is giving a warranty must be treated, on the objective principle, as if he (the seller) had actually given the warranty. Hence he would be in breach of contract if he delivered new oats, and the buyer would be justified in rejecting the goods.[5]

Thirdly, the mistake of one party may make the contract void if it was *negligently induced by the other*. This rule was applied where auction particulars were so obscure as to lead a bidder to make a mistake as to what he was bidding for; and the contract was accordingly held void.[6]

iii   *Equitable relief*

Here, as in relation to mistakes which nullify consent, two forms of equitable relief call for discussion: refusal of specific performance and rescission.

When the contract is valid at common law because the mistake is *not fundamental*, specific performance may nevertheless be refused. This principle has been discussed in relation to mistakes which nullify consent and nothing more need be said about it here.

The contract may also be valid at common law because the mistake, though fundamental, is (by reason of the objective principle) *not operative*. Here too, specific performance is sometimes refused in equity. In one case[7] a buyer at an auction bid for one lot in the mistaken belief that he was bidding for another, and specific performance was refused to the seller. But in another case of this kind, specific performance was granted to the seller where the buyer's only mistake

---

4   (1871) LR 6 QB 597; see ante, p 135.
5   'Warranty' at that time was often used to refer to what would now be called a 'condition': see post, p 327 for this distinction.
6   *Scriven Bros & Co v Hindley & Co* [1913] 3 KB 564.
7   *Malins v Freeman* (1836) 2 Keen 25.

was as to the extent of the land for which he was bidding. It was said that, where the contact was valid at law, specific performance would be refused only 'where a hardship amounting to injustice would have been inflicted upon [the mistaken party] by holding him to his bargain, and it was unreasonable to hold him to it'.[8] It follows from this statement that the *buyer* could have obtained specific performance, if he had been content with the smaller purchase. The court may also adopt the middle course of granting specific performance on terms. Thus, in one case,[9] a purchaser of a plot on an estate believed that the vendor had covenanted not to build a public house on the estate, when in fact such covenants had been given only by the purchasers of the other plots. It was held that the vendor could obtain specific performance only on the terms that he entered into a similar covenant.

In discussing the possibility of rescission in equity for mistakes alleged to have negatived consent, it is convenient to begin with the situation in which the mistake, though *fundamental*, is, under the objective principle, not *operative*. To refuse specific performance in such a case leaves it open to the non-mistaken party to seek his remedy in damages. But to rescind the contract would (subject to the possible imposition of terms) deprive that party of all rights under the contract. Since rescission would thus seriously undermine the objective principle, the remedy is not available when the mistake is not operative at common law.[10]

Where a contract is valid at law because the mistake is *not fundamental*, we have seen that the Court of Appeal has, in *The Great Peace*,[11] held that the remedy of rescission is no longer available in equity. Strictly speaking, that decision was concerned with the situation in which the mistake was alleged to have *nullified* consent and therefore does not conclude the question whether the remedy continues to be available in cases of the present kind, where the mistake is alleged to have *negatived* consent. But the reason for rejecting the remedy in *The Great Peace* was that doctrinal consistency or coherence would be destroyed[12] if courts could rescind contracts in equity for mistakes which were not fundamental in the common law sense (and so did not affect the validity of the contract). This reasoning applies with

---

8   *Tamplin v James* (1879) 15 Ch D 215 to 221.
9   *Baskcomb v Beckwith* (1869) LR 8 Eq 100.
10 *Riverlate Properties Ltd v Paul* [1975] Ch 133. In *Torrance v Bolton* (1872) 8 Ch App 118 the objective principle would not have applied as the one party's mistake was in part induced by misleading auction particulars issued on behalf of the other party.
11 [2002] EWCA Civ 1407, [2003] QB 679.
12 [2003] QB 679 at [157].

equal force where such a mistake is alleged to have negatived consent, so that any power which may once have existed to rescind contracts for such mistakes cannot, it is submitted, have survived the decision.

Where a contract is *void* at law because of a mistake which negatives consent, there is no scope for equitable intervention except to reverse any unjust enrichment that may have resulted from acts done in reliance on the mistake.[13] Specific performance will be refused simply because the contract is void and there is no power to impose terms. It was sometimes suggested[14] that the power to rescind contracts in equity extended even to cases such as *Cundy v Lindsay*, where the contract was void at law.[15] The attraction of this view is that it would enable the law to protect innocent third parties who had for value acquired an interest in the subject-matter. But where there is 'no contract at all',[16] there can be nothing to rescind, so that the better view is that there is no scope for this kind of relief in cases of this kind.

4   DOCUMENTS SIGNED UNDER A MISTAKE

a   The doctrine of non est factum

In general, a person who signs a contractual document is bound by its terms whether he has read the document or not.[17] But at the end of the 16th century, the law developed a special defence to protect illiterate persons who had executed deeds which had been incorrectly read over to them. This was the defence of non est factum, by which the signer pleaded that the instrument was 'not my deed'. In the 19th century, these cases were rationalised by saying that the alleged contract was void because 'the mind of the signer did not accompany the signature'.[18] But the mere fact that this is so does not suffice to make a contract void for mistake. Under the objective principle,[19] the contract will, on the contrary, generally be upheld. It will be void only in the exceptional situations discussed above;[20] and of these the only one likely to be relevant in the present context is that in which the mistake of one party is known to the other. Usually, the signature of the mistaken party is procured by some kind of fraud; and if the

---

13 See *Cooper v Phibbs* (1867) LR 2 HL 149, ante, p 130.
14 Eg, *Solle v Butcher* [1950] 1 KB 671 at 692.
15 (1873) 3 App Cas 459.
16 *Gallie v Lee* [1969] 2 Ch 17 at 33; affd [1971] AC 1004.
17 See ante, p 82.
18 *Foster v Mackinnon* (1869) LR 4 CP 704 at 711.
19 See ante, p 2.
20 See ante, pp 137–138.

document purports to be a contract between the mistaken and the fraudulent party, the contract may be held void without infringing the objective principle. More commonly, however, the document purports to be a contract between the mistaken party and some third party. This happens where A is induced by the fraud of B to sign a document addressed to C: for example B may wish to raise a loan from C and induce A to sign a guarantee in favour of C by representing that the document is an insurance proposal; or B may induce A to sign a promissory note in favour of C by representing that the signature is required for the purpose of witnessing a private document. In these cases, C may reasonably assume that A had agreed to the terms of the document; and to allow A to rely on the doctrine of non est factum would conflict with the objective principle and become a source of danger to innocent third parties.

b   Restrictions on the doctrine

To minimise the dangers described above, the law has developed the following restrictions on the doctrine.

i   *Persons who can rely on the doctrine*

The doctrine was originally devised to protect illiterate persons; and it might be thought that it should not apply at all to persons who could read the document but failed to do so. But in *Saunders v Anglia Building Society Ltd* the House of Lords rejected this perhaps somewhat Draconian view, and held that the doctrine could apply in favour of a person who has 'no real understanding' of the document 'whether ... from defective education, illness or innate incapacity'.[1] Adult persons of normal attainments and capacity will only rarely be able to rely on the doctrine.

ii   *Nature of the mistake*

The doctrine is, secondly, restricted by a requirement which resembles that of fundamental mistake, discussed earlier in this chapter. In *Saunders v Anglia Building Society* the House of Lords held that the plea was available only where the difference between the document actually signed, and the document as it was believed to be, was a 'radical' or 'essential' or 'fundamental' or 'substantial' one. In the actual case a widow of seventy-eight wanted to help her nephew to raise money for the purposes of his business, and to do so on the security of her

1   [1971] AC 1004 at 1016.

house. A document was presented to her which she did not read because her glasses were broken. She thought that it was a deed making a gift of the house to her nephew, but in fact it purported to be a sale of the house to an intermediary called Lee, through whom the nephew had arranged to raise the money. Lee then mortgaged the house to a building society, but did not pay the purchase price to the widow, nor did he pay over any money to the nephew in accordance with the arrangement between them. It was assumed that the widow was the sort of person who could rely on the doctrine of non est factum, but it was held that her mistake was not serious enough to bring the doctrine into operation. Her purpose in executing the document was to help her nephew to raise money on the security of her house, and the document was in fact intended to serve that purpose, though by a different route from that envisaged by her. It is worth noting that the effect of the decision was to protect an innocent third party (the building society) which had advanced money on the faith of the document.

iii   Carelessness

A further ground for the decision in *Saunders v Anglia Building Society Ltd* was that the doctrine of non est factum applied only if the person invoking it showed that he or she was not careless in signing the document. The standard of care here seems to be a subjective one, depending on the actual capacities of the signer; but even an elderly widow of moderate educational attainments should not sign a document transferring her house, without at least making sure that the transfer is in favour of the right person. Similarly, a person cannot rely on the doctrine if he signs a document containing blanks which are later filled in otherwise than in accordance with his directions.[2] The doctrine might, on the other hand, still apply if the signer could show that a person of his limited capacities could not have discovered the truth, even by reading the document.[3]

5   MISTAKES IN RECORDING AGREEMENTS

a   Rectification of documents

So far, we have been concerned with mistakes which affect consent and hence invalidate contracts. There is a further group of cases in

---

2   *United Dominions Trust Ltd v Western* [1976] QB 513.
3   *Saunders v Anglia Building Society Ltd* [1971] AC 1004 at 1023; cf *Lloyds Bank plc v Waterhouse* [1993] 2 FLR 97.

which mistakes affect only the process of *recording* agreements; and such mistakes may be corrected by means of the equitable remedy of rectification. This remedy is available where the parties fail to put into the document terms which were agreed, or put into it terms which were not agreed, or which differ from those which were agreed. In such cases, the court may order the wording of the document to be changed so as to bring it into line with the agreement. For example, if an oral agreement for the sale of peas were recorded in writing as a sale of beans, the document could be rectified by the substitution of 'peas' for 'beans'. Sometimes the court will simply treat a document as rectified, without making a formal order for rectification,[4] but it is useful to have such an order where the document records a long-term contract or where the benefit of it is likely to be transferred to a third party.[5]

b   Types of mistake

In general, the mistake on which a claim for rectification is based must be that of *both* parties. Hence the remedy is not available if the document accurately expresses the intention of one party but not that of the other. Suppose that a lease stipulated for a monthly rent of £1,000 and that this accurately expressed the intention of the tenant. It would be obviously wrong to allow the landlord to obtain rectification merely because he (and he alone) intended the rent to be £2,000;[6] for this would impose on the tenant a liability to which he had never agreed. In such a case the landlord could obtain rectification only if he could show both that the lease did not record his true intention and that the tenant was guilty of fraud or knew of the landlord's mistake or wilfully shut his eyes to it and tried to take advantage of it.[7] Even in the absence of such facts, it used to be thought that the landlord could force the tenant to choose between *either* having the lease rectified by the substitution of '£2,000' for '£1,000' *or* having it cancelled altogether.[8] But this view is inconsistent with the objective principle;[9] and it has accordingly been held that neither rectification nor rescission is available in such circumstances.[10]

4   *The Nile Rhapsody* [1994] 1 Lloyd's Rep 382.
5   Post, Chapter 14.
6   *Faraday v Tamworth Union* (1916) 86 LJ Ch 436; cf *The Ypatia Halcoussi* [1985] 2 Lloyd's Rep 364.
7   *Blay v Pollard and Morris* [1930] 1 KB 628 at 633; *Commission for the New Towns v Cooper (Great Britain) Ltd* [1995] Ch 259 at 277.
8   *Harris v Pepperell* (1867) LR 5 Eq 1; *Paget v Marshall* (1884) 28 Ch D 255.
9   See ante, p 2.
10 *Riverlate Properties Ltd v Paul* [1975] Ch 133; cf *The Nai Genova* [1984] 1 Lloyd's Rep 353.

A person who claims rectification needs to show only that the written document fails accurately to record the prior agreement. He does not have to establish that the prior agreement amounted to a *binding contract*. Thus if the prior agreement suffered from a formal defect, or was not intended to be legally binding until the written document was executed, the written document may still be rectified. All that is necessary is that the parties continued to entertain a common intention, evidenced by 'some outward expression of accord',[11] up to the time of the execution of the document, and that the document failed to record that intention.

On the other hand, if the written document does accurately record the prior agreement, it cannot be rectified on the ground that the prior agreement was itself made under some mistake; for equity does not rectify *contracts* but only *documents*.[12] If, for example, parties orally agreed on the sale of 'your picture of Salisbury Cathedral' and then reduced the contract to writing in these terms, the document could not be rectified on the ground that both parties believed the picture to be by John Constable, when in fact it was a copy. This would be so whether or not the mistake affected the validity of the contract.[13] Rectification is available for many mistakes which do not make the contract void at law and for some which are not even a ground for refusal of specific performance in equity: for example, in some cases for a mistake as to the legal effect of an agreement.[14] But the mistake must in all cases simply be one in *recording* the agreement. If the remedy were not limited in this way, it would indirectly subvert the principles which limit the kinds of mistake that affect the validity of contracts.

c   Restrictions

The remedy of rectification may be barred if it is not claimed within a reasonable time of the making of the contract; or by the intervention of third party rights (for example, where a third party in good faith acquires land which the seller had agreed to sell, but which was by mistake omitted from the conveyance). On the other hand, since

---

11 *Joscelyne v Nissen* [1970] 2 QB 86 at 98.
12 *Mackenzie v Coulson* (1869) LR 8 Eq 368 at 375.
13 Cf *Frederick E Rose (London) Ltd v William H Pim Jnr & Co Ltd* [1953] 2 QB 450.
14 *Jervis v Howle and Talke Colliery Co Ltd* [1937] Ch 67. Cf *Re Colebrook's Conveyances* [1973] 1 All ER 132; contrast *Nittan (UK) Ltd v Solent Steel Fabrication Ltd* [1981] 1 Lloyd's Rep 633 (legal effect fully explained to party alleging mistake).

rectification is intended to give effect to the agreement of the parties and not to restore them to their pre-contract position, the remedy is not barred by the fact that such restoration has become impossible.[15]

Mistakes in certain kinds of documents cannot be rectified, because the law provides other machinery for correcting such mistakes. For example, a settlement of property which is binding by virtue of a court order cannot be rectified: if a mistake has been made in drawing up such a settlement, it can be corrected by applying to the court which ordered the settlement to be made, rather than by applying to another court to rectify it.[16] Similarly, articles of association of a company cannot be rectified even if they contain an obvious mistake.[17] Once such a document is registered in accordance with the Companies Act, it can be altered only in the manner provided for by that Act.

A claim to rectification may be, and often is, preceded by a dispute as to the construction of a document. That is, a party may claim, first, that a document bears a certain meaning, and secondly, that, if it does not bear that meaning, it should nevertheless be rectified on the ground that the meaning alleged by him represented the common intention of the parties, as expressed in a prior agreement. A party who wants to take this line should put forward *both* claims in the alternative in the same proceedings for, if judgment is given against him on the point of construction, in proceedings in which he might have claimed rectification (but failed to do so), then his right to claim rectification will be barred. The purpose of this rule is to discourage multiple proceedings on substantially similar issues.[18]

---

15 Eg, *Johnson v Bragge* [1901] 1 Ch 28; contrast the position where rescission is claimed for misrepresentation (post, p 166).
16 *Mills v Fox* (1887) 37 Ch D 153.
17 *Scott v Frank F Scott (London) Ltd* [1940] Ch 794.
18 *Crane v Hegeman-Harris Co Inc* [1939] 4 All ER 68.

Chapter 9

Misrepresentation

Our concern in this chapter is with the remedies available to a person who has been induced to enter into a contract by a misleading statement. That person may then have a right to damages, or one to rescind the contract. He will, however, only have these rights if the statement is of a kind which the law recognises as giving rise to liability and if certain other requirements are satisfied. Similar remedies are also sometimes available where there has been no active misrepresentation, but only a failure to disclose material facts.

1 GENERAL REQUIREMENTS

a A representation of fact

As a general rule, relief for a misrepresentation, as such, will be given only in respect of statements of *existing fact*. These must be contrasted with statements of opinion or belief and statements as to the future; and a distinction was formerly drawn between statements of fact and statements of law.

i Statements of opinion or belief

These are sometimes so vague as to have no legal effect at all. Thus in one case,[1] a description of land as 'fertile and improveable' was held to give rise to no liability. Even statements which are more precise may fall into this category: in another case,[2] it was held that a seller of land was not liable for stating that it could support 2,000 sheep, as he had no personal knowledge of the facts and as the buyer knew this, so that it was understood that the seller could state no more than his belief. A statement is, however, likely to be treated as one of fact if the person making it had, or professed to have, some special knowledge or skill with regard to the matter stated.[3] Moreover, a statement of opinion or

1   *Dimmock v Hallett* (1866) 2 Ch App 21.
2   *Bisset v Wilkinson* [1927] AC 177.
3   Eg *Esso Petroleum Co Ltd v Mardon* [1976] QB 801.

belief will generally, by implication, contain a representation that the person making the statement actually holds the opinion or belief, and it may contain a further implied statement that he holds the opinion or belief on reasonable grounds. Thus, if a person says that he believes a picture to be an original when he actually believes it to be a copy, he misrepresents a fact, namely the state of his belief.[4] The same is true if the seller of a house says that it is 'let to a most desirable tenant', when the tenant has for a long time been in arrears with the rent.[5] In such a case it would not matter that the seller did not actually know this, since such a fact is one of which the buyer could reasonably have expected him to be aware.

ii Statements as to the future

A person who promises to do something in the future and then breaks that promise is, of course, liable for breach of contract if the promise amounted to a binding contract. But if the promise did not have contractual force he will not be subject to the remedies for misrepresentation, as he has not misrepresented an existing fact. For example, a person who obtains a loan of money by 'representing' that he *will* use it for one purpose is not liable for misrepresentation if he then changes his mind and uses the money for a different purpose. But he would be so liable if, when he made the representation, he had no intention of using the money for the stated purpose. In such a case, he would be misrepresenting a fact, namely his present intention. In the words of Bowen LJ: 'There must be a misstatement of existing fact; but the state of a man's mind is as much a fact as the state of his digestion ... A misrepresentation as to the state of a man's mind is, therefore, a misstatement of fact.'[6] A person would also be liable for misrepresentation if he coupled a statement as to the future with one of existing fact: for example, if he untruthfully said that he *had* sold certain goods and *would* pay over the proceeds.

iii Statements of law

A distinction was formerly drawn between misrepresentations of 'fact' and those of 'law' so that damages were not available for misrepresentations of law, though a deliberate misrepresentation of this kind could be a ground for rescission. An example of a representation of law would be one as to the content and meaning of

---

4   *Jendwine v Slade* (1797) 2 Esp 572 at 573.
5   *Smith v Land and House Property Corpn* (1884) 28 Ch D 7 at 15.
6   *Edgington v Fitzmaurice* (1885) 29 Ch D 459 at 482.

an Act of Parliament. On the other hand, in the case of a misrepresentation as to the effects of a private document, a distinction was drawn. If the misrepresentation related to the *content* of the document it would be one of fact, but if it related to the meaning of a document of known content it would be one of law, since the construction of a document is a question of law.[7] However, a misrepresentation as to 'private right'[8] would probably be treated as one of fact, even though it involved a misrepresentation as to the construction of a document. Sometimes, it was impossible to tell from the statement itself whether it was one of law or of fact. For example, a statement that a will made by A was valid might involve a representation that A was 18 years old (the age at which persons acquire capacity to make a will) when in fact A was only 16, or a representation that A, though only 16, had full testamentary capacity. The former would be a representation of fact; the latter one of law.

The courts' reluctance to give relief for representations of law was based on the theory that knowledge of the law is equally accessible to both parties: the representee ought not to rely on what the representor says about matters of law, but should rather take his own advice on such matters. In fact it is often quite unrealistic to expect the representee to do this; and while the effect of the distinction was mitigated by the refinements discussed above, these tended to blur the distinction to such an extent that it became hard to draw and impossible to justify. In the law relating to the recovery of payments made under a mistake, the distinction has been rejected by the House of Lords;[9] and it seems likely that it will no longer be applied in the present context,[10] so that the normal remedies including damages will be available for misrepresentation of law. If the representee did in fact take his own legal advice, these remedies would still be excluded on the principles to be discussed below.

b   Other conditions of liability

Where a misrepresentation has no contractual force, the remedies of damages or rescission in respect of it are available only when the following three further conditions are satisfied.

7   *Carmichael v National Power plc* [1999] 1 WLR 2042 at 2049–2050.
8   Cf ante, p 125.
9   *Kleinwort Benson Ltd v Lincoln City Council* [1999] 2 AC 249.
10   *Pankhania v Hackney London Borough Council* [2002] All ER (D) 22 (Aug), [2002] NLJ 1884; and see ante, p 125.

i Representation must be unambiguous

A representation may be capable of bearing two meanings, one of which is true and the other false. If the representor (A) honestly intended it to bear the true meaning, he is not guilty of fraud merely because the representee (B) rightly understood it in the sense which was false.[11] But if A intended the representation to bear a meaning which he knew to be false, and B reasonably so understood it, A is guilty of fraud. He cannot escape liability for fraud by showing that the statement was also capable of bearing another meaning, which was true; or even that, as matter of construction, it did bear such a meaning.[12]

ii Representation must be material

In the law of misrepresentation there is not (as in the law of mistake) any requirement that the misrepresentation must relate to a 'fundamental' matter. But relief for misrepresentation which relates to a matter of only minor importance may be denied because of the requirement that the misrepresentation must be material.[13] This means that the misrepresentation must relate to a matter which would influence a reasonable person in deciding whether or on what terms to enter into the contract: for example, on a sale of land a representation that the land yielded an annual rent of £4,000 when the actual rent was only £3,000, would be material;[14] but one that the vendor's age was 40 when in fact it was 30 would not be material. The requirement does not mean that it must have been reasonable for the representee to have relied on the representation, so that failure by the representee to make use of an opportunity to discover the truth is no bar to relief.[15] The requirement of materiality is, moreover, subject to a number of qualifications. First, it does not apply where the misrepresentation was made fraudulently.[16] Secondly, it does not apply where the contract induced by the misrepresentation provides that every representation (however unimportant) is to be material or to be the basis of the contract.[17] And there is, thirdly, no scope for the

---

11　*Akerhielm v De Mare* [1959] AC 789.
12　*The Siboen and The Sibotre* [1976] 1 Lloyd's Rep 293 at 318.
13　*Traill v Baring* (1864) 4 De GJ & Sm 318 at 326; *Industrial Properties Ltd v Associated Electrical Industries Ltd* [1977] QB 580; Marine Insurance Act 1906, s 20(2).
14　*Museprime Properties Ltd v Adhill Properties Ltd* [1990] 2 EGLR 196.
15　See further, post, pp 150–151.
16　*Smith v Kay* (1859) 7 HL Cas 750.
17　See further, post, p 172.

requirement where a professional adviser, such as a solicitor, misstates facts in advising a client, who consequently suffers loss.[18] The solicitor's liability in such a case is not for misrepresentation as such, inducing the contract between himself and the client. It is for breach of the earlier contract between them which gave rise to the solicitor's duty of care in giving the advice.

iii   Reliance on the representation

Even if a reasonable person would have relied on the representation, there will be no liability if the representor can show[19] that representee did not rely on it in fact.[20] This will obviously be the case if the representation never came to his attention; but it may come to his attention even though it was not made directly to him: eg if it was made to a third person with the intention that it should be repeated to the claimant, and if it was so repeated.[1] The position is the same where the representor could reasonably have anticipated that the representation would be so repeated: eg where a valuer's report on a house is commissioned by a building society and passed on to a mortgage applicant who relies on the report when buying the house.[2]

Reliance is also negatived if the true facts were actually known to the representee, or to his agent acting within the scope of his authority.[3] More difficulty arises where the representee did not actually know the truth but took, or could have taken, steps to discover it. If he actually took such steps, but failed to discover the truth, it could be said that he did not reply on the misrepresentation but rather on his own judgment. Accordingly, he should not be entitled to relief, and this view certainly applies where the misrepresentation is innocent. But to deny relief where the misrepresentation is fraudulent would put a premium on skilful deception, so that in such cases relief is not barred simply because of an unsuccessful attempt by the representee to discover the truth.[4] Where the representee had, but simply did not take, an opportunity to discover the truth, he is similarly entitled to relief where the representation is

---

18   See *Bristol and West Building Society v Mothew* [1998] Ch 1 at 10–11.
19   *Smith v Chadwick* (1884) 9 App Cas 187 at 196.
20   *The Mercandian Continent* [2001] EWCA Civ 1275, [2001] 2 Lloyd's Rep 563 at [26].
1   *Pilmore v Hood* (1838) 5 Bing NC 97.
2   *Smith v Eric S Bush* [1990] 1 AC 831.
3   *Strover v Harrington* [1988] Ch 390.
4   See *S Pearson & Son Ltd v Dublin Corpn* [1907] AC 351; *Gordon v Selico Co Ltd* (1986) 278 Estates Gazette 53 at 61.

fraudulent. According to the older authorities, this rule also applied where the representation was 'innocent'.[5] But when these cases were decided the law did not recognise any separate category of negligent misrepresentation, so that 'innocent' misrepresentations included all those which could not be proved to be fraudulent. Where the representor was wholly innocent or negligent, the test of liability should now be whether in all the circumstances it was reasonable for the representee to rely on the misrepresentation.[6] If, for example, the representation was made by a private seller of a car to a dealer, it might not be reasonable for the dealer to rely on the representation since he would normally be better placed than the seller to discover the truth. An express warning not to rely on the representation could also negative liability for innocent or negligent misrepresentation.

If the representee relied on the misrepresentation, he may be entitled to relief even though (as is often the case) there were also other factors which induced him to enter into the contract. A victim of fraud can recover damages in full even though the fraud was only one of the causes leading to the loss;[7] and it is no bar to such a claim that the representee would have acted in the same way even if the representation had not been made.[8] Where, however, the misrepresentation was not fraudulent, relief may be denied on the ground that the representee would have entered into the contract on the same terms even if he had known the truth.[9]

2 EFFECTS OF MISREPRESENTATION

Misrepresentation may give rise to certain claims for damages, to rescission, and to certain consequences under the doctrine of estoppel. Before these matters are discussed in detail, something must be said of the relationship between misrepresentation and mistake.

---

5 *Redgrave v Hurd* (1881) 20 Ch D 1.
6 *Smith v Eric S Bush* [1990] 1 AC 831.
7 *Standard Chartered Bank v Pakistan National Shipping Corpn (No 2)* [2000] 1 Lloyd's Rep 218; revsd on another point [2002] UKHL 43, [2003] 1 AC 959.
8 *UCB Corporate Services Ltd v Williams* [2002] EWCA Civ 555, [2002] 1 P & CR 168.
9 *Assicurazioni Generali SpA v Arab Insurance Group (BSC)* [2002] EWCA Civ 1642, [2003] 1 All ER (Comm) 140.

a   **Misrepresentation and mistake**

The relationship between these subjects can best be understood by distinguishing between three possible situations. First, a fundamental mistake may arise spontaneously, without any misrepresentation. In that case the remedies for misrepresentation do not apply. It is true that the cases sometimes refer to 'rescission' of a contract for mistake; but where the effect of mistake is to make a contract void there is no need to 'rescind', in the sense in which that word is used in the law of misrepresentation. Secondly, a misrepresentation may (and often will) induce a mistake which is not fundamental: eg where a racehorse is sold with a false pedigree.[10] Such a mistake will not make the contract void and the only remedies will be those for misrepresentation. Thirdly, there is an area of overlap in which a fundamental mistake is induced by a misrepresentation. Here both sets of remedies are available to the representee, who is entitled to choose that which is most favourable to him. This would, for example, be the position in cases of impersonation, such as *Cundy v Lindsay*,[11] discussed in Chapter 8.

b   **Damages**

There are no fewer than five separate legal grounds on which damages can be claimed for misrepresentation. After discussing each of these grounds, we shall consider the relationship between them, and finally refer, in the context of misrepresentation, to the power of a criminal court to make compensation orders.

i   *Damages for fraud*

A person who suffers loss by relying on a fraudulent statement can recover damages in an action of deceit. This is an action in tort, available quite irrespective of the existence of any contract; but one possible application of it is to the situation in which a person has been induced by fraud to enter into a contract. Actions of deceit are not commonly brought, as fraud is a serious charge which must be strictly substantiated. It must be shown that the person making the false statement *either* knew that it was false *or* had no belief in its truth *or* made it recklessly, not caring whether it was true or false.[12] Mere

10   *Naughton v O'Callaghan* [1990] 3 All ER 191.
11   (1878) 3 App Cas 459; see ante, p 132.
12   *Derry v Peek* (1889) 14 App Cas 337.

negligence in making a false statement does not amount to fraud, though it may entail liability in damages under two of the headings to be discussed below. Fraud requires some degree of conscious deception, that is, an 'intention to deceive'. But it is not necessary to show an 'intention to defraud'[13] in the sense of a bad motive or intention to cause loss. A person may say that a certain state of facts exists when he knows it does not exist; and such a person is guilty of fraud even though he in good faith believes that the facts asserted will come true and that the present and temporary falsity of his statement will not prejudice the representee.[14]

ii   *Damages for negligence at common law*

Liability for damages for negligent misrepresentation is again liability in tort, available irrespective of contract. It arises where a statement is made carelessly and in breach of a duty to take reasonable care that it is accurate. The question whether the statement has been made carelessly is one of fact. The major legal problem is to determine whether any duty of care exists at all. Obviously, a duty of care may arise out of a contract, for example, between a professional adviser such as an architect, or a solicitor, and his client. If such a duty is broken an action may be brought both for breach of contract, and in tort for negligence at a common law.[15] The difficult cases are those in which there is *no* contract between the representor and representee; and here it is said that a duty of care arises if there is a 'special' relationship between them, by virtue of which the representor assumes responsibility for the accuracy of the statement.[16] There are three essential elements of such a relationship: it must be reasonably foreseeable by the representor that the representee will rely on the statement; there must be sufficient 'proximity' between the parties; and it must be just and reasonable for the law to impose a duty.[17] There is obviously considerable overlap between these requirements,[18] but they can be illustrated by taking the case of an

13   See *Standard Chartered Bank v Pakistan National Shipping Corpn* [1995] 2 Lloyd's Rep 365 at 375; *Standard Chartered Bank v Pakistan Corpn (No 2)* [2000] 1 Lloyd's Rep 218, 221, 224, revsd on other grounds [2002] UKHL 43, [2003] 1 AC 959.
14   *Polhill v Walter* (1832) 3 B & Ad 114.
15   *Henderson v Merrett Syndicates* [1995] 2 AC 145.
16   *Hedley Byrne & Co Ltd v Heller & Partners Ltd* [1964] AC 465.
17   *Smith v Eric S Bush* [1990] 1 AC 831 at 854; *Caparo Industries plc v Dickman* [1990] 2 AC 605 at 617–618. It is an open question whether the requirement of 'assumption of responsibility' is additional or alternative to the three listed above.
18   [1990] 2 AC 605 at 632.

accountant or auditor making a report on the financial state of a company. If the report is prepared for the purpose of providing a potential investor with information on which his decision whether to put money into the company is to be based, then the accountant is likely to be under a duty of care to the investor.[19] But no such duty arises where an investor puts money into the company in reliance on an auditor's report which has been prepared simply to enable the company to perform its statutory duty to produce audited accounts; for in such a case there is no sufficient proximity between the auditor and the investor.[20] For the purposes of this chapter, however, it is generally unnecessary to show that such a duty exists. Our concern is with cases in which the misrepresentation induces a contract between misrepresentor and misrepresentee, and in such cases there is now a statutory liability in damages even in the absence of a 'special relationship'. Such liability is discussed in the immediately following section of this chapter. The question whether there is liability for negligent misrepresentation at common law only becomes acute where the misrepresentation does *not* lead to a contract between the representor and the representee.

iii   Damages under Misrepresentation Act 1967, section 2(1)

This subsection creates a statutory liability in damages which arises 'where a person has entered into a contact after a misrepresentation has been made to him by another party thereto'. This cause of action is, from the representee's point of view, more favourable than common law liability for negligence. In the first place, he need only show that he entered into a contract with the representor after the misrepresentation had been made:[1] he need *not* establish a 'special relationship' giving rise to a duty of care.[2] Section 2(1) would, for example, apply between buyer and seller, even though no 'special relationship' existed between them. Secondly, at common law the representee must prove negligence, but under section 2(1) the representor is liable 'unless *he proves* that he had reasonable ground to believe and did believe up to the time that the contract was made that the facts represented were true'. The burden of proof is thus

---

19   *Hedley Byrne & Co Ltd v Heller & Partners Ltd* [1964] AC 465, overruling *Candler v Crane Christmas & Co* [1951] 2 KB 164.

20   *Caparo Industries plc v Dickman*, supra; cf *Huxford v Stoy Hayward & Co* (1989) 5 BCC 421.

1   Unless he can show this, he has no claim under s 2(1): *Morin v Bonhams & Brooks Ltd* [2003] EWHC 467 (Comm), [2003] 2 All ER (Comm) 36; affd on other grounds [2003] EWCA Civ 1802, [2004] 1 All ER (Comm) 880.

2   *Howard Marine and Dredging Co Ltd v A Ogden & Sons (Excavations) Ltd* [1978] QB 574 at 596.

placed on the representor; and where, during negotiations for the hire of barges, the owner's agent misstated their dead-weight capacity in reliance on a wrong statement in Lloyd's Register, it was held that the burden had not been discharged, since documents in the owner's possession disclosed the true situation.[3] But the representor could discharge the burden by showing that he had no such means of discovering the truth and had merely repeated a representation by which he had himself been induced to buy the subject-matter;[4] or that he had reasonably relied on an expert report;[5] or that he had made due enquiries before making the statement.[6]

Section 2(1) imposes a statutory liability for misrepresentation which is 'essentially founded on negligence',[7] but it does so in a curious way, by a fiction of fraud. That is, it provides that, if the representor would be liable in damages if he were guilty of fraud, he shall be so liable even though he was not guilty of fraud. The point of the fiction may simply have been to make it clear that some liability in damages should exist, though for this purpose the fiction seems to be quite unnecessary. Another possible effect of the fiction is to make the statutory liability subject to rules which have been evolved in cases of actual fraud; and sometimes (eg in assessing damages) the courts appear to have given this effect to the fiction.[8] In other cases[9] they have, however, taken the preferable view that it would be quite inappropriate to apply these rules to situations in which the representor had acted in good faith and was liable simply because he could not disprove fault.

iv   Damages for breach of contract

A statement made before the conclusion of a contract may be a 'mere' representation inducing the contract. Alternatively, it may actually have the force of contract: in other words, the person making the statement may undertake or promise that it is true. If, in such a case,

---

3   *Howard Marine* case [1978] QB 574.
4   As in *Oscar Chess Ltd v Williams* [1957] 1 All ER 325 and in *Hummingbird Motors Ltd v Hobbs* [1986] RTR 276.
5   *Cooper v Tamms* [1988] 1 EGLR 257.
6   *William Sindall plc v Cambridgeshire County Council* [1994] 1 WLR 1016.
7   *Gran Gelato Ltd v Richcliff Ltd* [1992] Ch 560 at 573; cf *HIH Casualty and General Insurance Ltd v New Hampshire Insurance Co* [2001] EWCA Civ 735, [2001] 2 All ER (Comm) 39 at [137] (lack of negligence a defence).
8   See *Royscot Trust Ltd v Rogerson* [1991] 2 QB 297; *MCI Worldcom International Inc v Primus Telecommunications Inc* [2003] EWHC 2182 (Comm), [2004] 1 All ER (Comm) 138 at [68].
9   See *Gosling v Anderson* (1972) 223 Estates Gazette 1743.

the statement turns out to be untrue, the party to whom it is made is entitled to damages for breach of contract.

Where a descriptive statement is set out in a written contract, the question whether the maker undertakes that it is true is one of construction. Such a statement will generally be a term,[10] but the representor's intention to guarantee its truth may be negatived by express contrary provision, or by other circumstances. The statement may be a term even though the other party had not read the document and so could not have been induced by the statement to enter into the contract.

Where the statement is made in negotiations leading to a written contract, but is not set out in it, the question whether the statement has contractual force depends on the intention (objectively ascertained) with which it was made.[11] This is a question of fact, so that no 'rules' can be laid down on the point; but the cases do provide illustrations of factors which are taken into account in determining whether the requisite intention exists. Three such factors are of particular significance.

The first, and most obvious, factor is the *wording of the statement*. An express guarantee that it was true would clearly give it contractual force.[12] This situation may be contrasted with a case in which the seller of a car said that to the best of his knowledge and belief the odometer reading was correct. It was held that this statement had no contractual force, so that the seller was not liable merely because the odometer had (unknown to him) been tampered with before he had acquired the car.[13]

The second relevant factor is the *importance* which is attached by the representee to the statement. For example, a statement as to the quality of goods would be a term of the contract if, before the sale, the buyer had made it clear to the seller that he would not be interested in buying goods which did not have that quality.[14] The position is different where the statement merely affected the price which the buyer was willing to pay. Thus a representation as to the age of a car is (as will be seen below) not necessarily a term of the ensuing sale.

Thirdly, the courts stress the *relative abilities of the parties to determine the truth* of the statement. Two cases may be contrasted. In *Oscar Chess Ltd v Williams*[15] a private seller sold a car to a dealer in part exchange,

---

10 *Behn v Burness* (1863) 3 B & S 751.
11 *Howard Marine* case [1978] QB 574 at 595.
12 *The Larissa* [1983] 2 Lloyd's Rep 325 at 330.
13 *Hummingbird Motors Ltd v Hobbs* [1986] RTR 276.
14 *Bannerman v White* (1861) 10 CBNS 844.
15 [1957] 1 All ER 325.

representing in good faith that it was a 1948 model. It had been previously sold to him as such, with forged documents, but it was in fact a 1939 model. It was held that the seller had not warranted the car to be a 1948 model, and the main reason for the decision was that the buyer, as a dealer, was in at least as good a position as the seller to check the truth of the statement. But in *Dick Bentley Productions Ltd v Harold Smith (Motors) Ltd*[16] a dealer sold a Bentley car to a customer, representing that it had done only 20,000 miles since having a replacement engine fitted, when in fact it had covered 100,000 miles since then. Here the dealer was in a better position than the customer to check the truth of the statement, and it was held that the statement as to mileage was a term of the contract.

So far, it has been assumed that, if the statement is to have contractual force, it must be incorporated as a term in the contract which it has induced. It may be impossible for the statement to take effect in this way because it is oral and the contract is either in writing (so that extrinsic evidence cannot be used to add to it or to vary it[17]) or required by law to be in writing. In such cases it is nevertheless possible for the statement to take effect as a *collateral contract*. For example, in *Esso Petroleum Co Ltd v Mardon*[18] a person took a lease of a petrol station from an oil company in reliance on a statement, made by one of the company's salesmen, as to the potential turnover of the premises. This statement was held to be a collateral contract. For such a contract to arise, the representor must intend the statement to be binding as a *separate* contract (and not just as a term of the main contract).[19] The representee must also provide separate consideration for the promise contained in the statement, but this requirement would usually be satisfied by his entering into the main contract.[20]

v   Damages in lieu of rescission

Before 1967, the primary remedy for a 'mere' misrepresentation (not incorporated in the contract) was rescission, damages being available only in cases of fraud and, since 1963, in certain cases of negligence. This was an unsatisfactory state of the law; for it meant that the only remedy available to the victim of a wholly innocent misrepresentation was completely to set aside the contract, even though the misrepresentation related to some relatively minor defect. The victim

16   [1965] 2 All ER 65.
17   Because of the parol evidence rule: ante, p 75.
18   [1976] QB 801; cf *De Lassalle v Guildford* [1901] 2 KB 215.
19   Cf ante, p 80.
20   Cf *Brikom Investments Ltd v Carr* [1979] QB 467.

might prefer to keep the subject-matter of the contract with some monetary adjustment; while the representor might prefer to pay a sum of money instead of having the subject-matter of the contract thrown back on his hands. It was therefore provided by s 2(2) of the Misrepresentation Act 1967 that the court should have a discretion to uphold the contract and award damages in lieu of rescission 'where a person has entered into a contract after a misrepresentation has been made to him otherwise than fraudulently, and he would be entitled, by reason of the misrepresentation, to rescind the contract ...'.

The court's discretion to uphold the contract and to award damages in lieu of rescission is likely to be exercised where the representation related to a relatively minor matter,[1] and where the representor was not at fault. Damages can be awarded under the subsection even though the misrepresentation was wholly innocent (ie not even negligent) and even though no contractual undertaking as to its accuracy was given. But this extension of the power to award damages is, or may be, limited in a number of ways. First, the subsection gives no *right* to damages: it only gives the court a discretion to make such an award. Secondly, the damages are awarded in lieu of rescission. Thus the victim of a wholly innocent misrepresentation cannot rescind *and* claim damages;[2] by contrast both these possibilities are open to the victim of a fraudulent or negligent misrepresentation, and sometimes to the victim of a misrepresentation which has contractual force. If the victim of a wholly innocent misrepresentation wants to get rid of the subject-matter of the contract, he can sometimes, as part of the process of rescission, get what is called an indemnity. In this way he can rescind *and* get a sum of money, but the sum is (as we shall see)[3] assessed on more restricted principles than damages. A third limitation on the court's discretion under s 2(2) is more controversial. The right to rescind the contract is in certain cases lost[4] eg if the representee has disposed of the subject-matter so that he can no longer restore it to the representor. There is no very good reason why the court's discretion to award damages should be lost at the same time;[5] but the wording of s 2(2) does suggest that the court must have a real choice between rescission and damages, and that damages

---

1   *William Sindall plc v Cambridgeshire County Council* [1994] 1 WLR 1016 at 1036, 1043.
2   *HIH Casualty and General Insurance v Chase Manhattan Bank* [2001] EWCA Civ 1250, [2001] 2 Lloyd's Rep 483 at [51]; varied on other grounds [2003] UKHL 6, [2003] 1 All ER (Comm) 349.
3   See post, p162.
4   See post, pp 166–168.
5   *Thomas Witter Ltd v TBP Industries Ltd* [1996] 2 All ER 573 at 591.

therefore cannot be claimed after the right to rescind has been lost.[6]

vi   Relationship between the various rights to damages

The relationship between the above rights to damages gives rise to two questions: what facts must be shown to establish, or to defeat, any particular claim? and how much can the claimant recover under the various headings which have been discussed?

In discussing the first of these questions it will be helpful to take an example based on *Oscar Chess Ltd v Williams*,[7] and to suppose that a 1999 car is sold after a representation has been made that it is a 2003 model. If the buyer claims damages for fraud, he will have to show that the seller knew that his statement as to the age of the car was false, or at least that he was reckless in this respect. In practice the buyer will find it very hard to substantiate such a charge. To succeed in an action for negligence at common law, the buyer will have to show that there was a 'special relationship' giving rise to a duty of care at common law; and that the seller failed to take reasonable care to ensure that his statement as to the age of the car was accurate. If the buyer claims damages under s 2(1) of the Misrepresentation Act, his position is much more favourable: he need only show that the false statement was made, and it is then up to the seller to show that he believed on reasonable grounds that the statement was correct. In practice this is therefore the claim which the buyer is most likely to pursue. If the seller can discharge the burden of proof imposed on him by s 2(1), the buyer may still succeed in his claim for damages by showing that the statement had contractual force: fault is irrelevant in such an action. If there is no element of fault or contractual intention, the buyer has no *right* to damages, though he has the chance of obtaining a discretionary award of damages in lieu of rescission. But such damages cannot be awarded in addition to rescission so that where the buyer wants to return the car his only other remedy will be by way of an indemnity, and this is (as we shall see) unlikely to cover loss caused merely because he has relied on the representation. If the right to rescind has been lost, the buyer still has no remedy whatsoever for a wholly innocent misrepresentation which does not have contractual force.

6   This seems to be assumed in *The Lucy* [1983] 1 Lloyd's Rep 188 at 201–202 and *MCI Worldcom International Inc v Primus Telecommunications Inc* [2003] EWHC 2182 (Comm), [2004] 1 All ER (Comm) 138 at [76].
7   [1957] 1 All ER 325. See ante, pp 156–157.

The second question relates to the contents of the various rights to damages, ie to the amount recoverable in each type of claim. Here the leading distinction is between claims in tort and claims in contract. The basic difference is this: in tort the claimant gets such damages as will put him into the position in which he would have been if the tort *had not been committed,* while in contract he is entitled to be put into the position in which he would have been if the contract *had been performed.* Suppose for example that a person is induced by misrepresentation to buy a car for £5000 which would have been worth £7500 if the representation had been true but which is actually worth only £4000; and suppose further that the car has been delivered and paid for and that it cannot be returned. In tort, it is assumed that the buyer would, if the misrepresentation *had not been made,* not have bought the car at all. He would therefore still have his £5000 instead of a car worth £4000, and so he gets damages of £1000. In contract, the buyer is entitled to be put into the position in which he would have been if the representation *had been true.* In that event he would have had a car worth £7500 instead of having one worth £4000. His damages are therefore £3500. Of course if the buyer would have made a bad bargain even if the representation had been true, he may recover more in tort than in contract. This would be the position in the above case if the car would have been worth only £4250 even if the representation was true. Here the buyer still gets £1000 in tort but only £250 in contract. For the purpose of these distinctions a claim under s 2(1) of the Misrepresentation Act is treated in the same way as a claim in tort[8] by virtue of the fiction of fraud. A claim for damages in lieu of rescission under s 2(2) of the Act does not seem to be a claim either in contract or in tort, being independent of fault and contractual intention; and it is not at all clear on what principle such damages will be assessed.

In the above examples the representation is a positive assertion that the subject-matter has a certain quality. It may, however, be no more than an inaccurate estimate: for example, of the turnover of a business that has been put up for sale. In such a case, damages (whether for negligence or for breach of contract) will be assessed, not on the basis that the turnover would be as estimated, but on the basis of an estimate which had been prepared with due care.[9]

So far, we have considered only the loss which the buyer suffers because of the lower value of the subject-matter. He may also suffer

8   *Cemp Properties (UK) Ltd v Dentsply Research and Development Corpn* [1991] 2 EGLR 197; *The Siben (No 2)* [1996] 1 Lloyd's Rep 35 at 63.
9   *Esso Petroleum Co Ltd v Mardon* [1976] QB 801.

consequential losses, eg where he loses money in the course of running a business which he has been induced to buy by a misrepresentation as to its profitability.[10] Consequential loss may also in such cases take the form of failing to make a profit which would have been made if the representation had been true. Damages in respect of such a lost profit are recoverable in contract, but in tort the buyer can recover only the profits which he would have made out of *another* business in which he would have invested his money if he had not been induced by the misrepresentation to invest it in the defendant's business.[11] Consequential losses of either kind are, however, recoverable only if they are not 'too remote' and the rules as to remoteness (which are discussed in Chapter 18)[12] are more favourable to the claimant in tort than in contract, particularly if the defendant was (or is under s 2(1) of the 1967 Act treated as if he were) guilty of fraud.[13] This point has to be set against the possibility of recovering more in contract in respect of difference in value under the principles discussed above; so that the question whether the buyer should press his claim in contract or in tort will often be a finely balanced one. The stricter contract test of remoteness also applies where damages for consequential loss are claimed in lieu of rescission under s 2(2) of the 1967 Act.[14]

The distinction between contract and tort damages is most easily illustrated by cases of the above kind, in which a buyer claims damages from a seller in respect of a misrepresentation as to the quality of the subject-matter. It can apply also to a number of other situations: for example to that in which the seller's misrepresentation relates to the price at which he sells goods of the same kind to other buyers;[15] and to that in which a lender claims damages, not from the borrower, but from a valuer who has negligently overvalued the property on the security of which the loan was made.[16]

---

10 *Doyle v Olby (Ironmongers) Ltd* [1969] 2 QB 158; cf *Archer v Brown* [1985] QB 401.
11 *East v Maurer* [1991] 2 All ER 733. Damages are here recovered for loss of expectations which exist independently of the tort: see ante, p 5 and *White v Jones* [1995] 2 AC 207, post, p 252.
12 See post, pp 389–392.
13 *Doyle v Olby (Ironmongers) Ltd* [1969] 2 QB 158; *South Australia Asset Management Corpn v York Montague Ltd* [1997] AC 191 at 215–216; *Smith New Court Securities Ltd v Scrimgeour Vickers Ltd* [1997] AC 254 at 256, 267, 269.
14 *William Sindall plc v Cambridgeshire County Council* [1994] 1 WLR 1016 at 1038, 1048; the damages may be *less* than in contract (at 1038).
15 *Clef Aquitaine SARL v Laporte Materials (Barrow) Ltd* [2001] QB 488.
16 *Swingcastle Ltd v Gibson* [1991] 2 AC 223.

Damages for fraudulent misrepresentation are, in general, assessed by reference to the value of the subject-matter at the date of the transaction.[17] But this rule could cause hardship to the victim of the fraud: for example, where he had been induced by the fraud to buy shares for £30 which at the time of the sale were worth only £15 and then fell in value to £5. The general 'date of transaction' rule is therefore subject to exceptions where the victim has acted reasonably in keeping the shares after that date, or where he has, by reason of the matter misrepresented, been 'locked into' his purchase, or where the shares had fallen in value before discovery of the truth.[18] The general 'date of transaction' rule no doubt applies also where the misrepresentation was merely negligent; and in such a case the exceptions to it probably apply where the representor could reasonably have foreseen that loss due to further falls in the market would be suffered by the representee. He will then be entitled to compensation for loss due to falls in the market up to the time when he disposed, or acting reasonably should have disposed, of the subject.matter.[19]

The various rights to damages must be contrasted with the equitable right to an 'indemnity'. Equity did not award damages for misrepresentation, but it might order the representor to pay a sum of money to the representee, as part of the process of rescission. The object of this process was to restore each party so far as possible to the position he was in before the contract, so that sums expended under the contract had to be repaid. Suppose, for example, that by the terms of a lease a tenant is bound to pay rent to the landlord and rates to the local authority, and to repair the premises. Any money paid or spent by him in discharge of these obligations will be recoverable if he rescinds for misrepresentation. But this right to an indemnity exists only in respect of sums which the tenant *was bound under the lease* to disburse.[20] He cannot claim an indemnity in respect of his removal expenses, or injury suffered by him or his employees as a result of relying on the landlord's representations as to the physical state of the premises. Such losses result from his acts of moving in and using the premises, and these were not acts which he was under the lease bound to do. He can recover in respect of them only on a claim for damages; and he cannot both rescind *and* claim damages for a misrepresentation which was wholly innocent, and which was not a term of the contract.

---

17   *Smith New Court Securities Ltd v Scrimgeour Vickers (Asset Management) Ltd* [1997] AC 254 at 267, 283, 284.
18   *Smith New Court* case [1997] AC 254 at 267.
19   See *Downs v Chappell* [1997] 1 WLR 426.
20   *Whittington v Seale-Hayne* (1900) 16 TLR 181.

vii Compensation orders in criminal cases

Misrepresentation may involve criminal liability: for example, where property, services or a pecuniary advantage is obtained by deception, or where a false trade description is applied to goods.[1] When a person is convicted of such an offence (or indeed of any offence) he may be ordered to pay compensation for any personal injury, loss or damage resulting from the offence.[2] If the misrepresentation gives rise to both civil and criminal liability, any compensation paid under the order made by the criminal court is taken into account in later civil proceedings, so that the misrepresentor is not made liable twice over.[3]

c Rescission

The word rescission is confusingly used to describe a number of processes, of which three are relevant here. After these have been discussed, we shall consider the circumstances in which the right to rescind for misrepresentation may be lost.

i Rescission for misrepresentation

In the first sense, rescission refers to the process of setting a contract aside for misrepresentation. At common law this process was available only in cases of fraud, but equity extended it to all cases of innocent misrepresentation. Misrepresentation (unlike mistake) does not make the contract void.[4] It only gives the representee the option to avoid it. If he exercises the option, the contract is 'wipe[d] ... out altogether'[5] so that each party is relieved from his obligation to perform. In addition, the representee is entitled to recover what he has transferred on terms of restoring what he has received under the contract. For example, if a contract of sale is rescinded by a seller for misrepresentation he will get back the goods on terms of paying back the price.

The rule that the contract is voidable and not void has important effects on the rights of third parties. If a contract of sale is void because of a mistake as to the identity of the buyer, no property in the goods passes to the buyer, so that the goods can be recovered by the seller

---

1 Theft Act 1968, ss 15, 16; Theft Act 1978, ss 1, 5; Trade Description Act 1968, s 1(1)(a).
2 Powers of Criminal Courts (Sentencing) Act 2000, s 130(1)(a); cf Financial Services and Markets Act 2000, s 397.
3 Powers of Criminal Courts (Sentencing) Act 2000, s 134.
4 *Lonrho plc v Fayed (No 2)* [1991] 4 All ER 961 at 971.
5 *The Kanchenjunga* [1990] 1 Lloyd's Rep 191 at 198.

from an innocent third party to whom the buyer has resold them.[6] If, on
the other hand, the sale is induced by the fraud of the buyer (not
leading to a fundamental mistake), a voidable title nevertheless passes
to him and can be transferred to an innocent third party who buys the
goods without knowledge of the fraud, before the seller has rescinded
the contract.[7]

For the purpose of the rule just stated, it is crucial to know exactly
when the contract has been rescinded. Rescission may be effected by
taking legal proceedings; or extra-judicially, by giving notice to the
other party; or, where goods have been obtained by fraud, by retaking
them. Obviously none of these steps can be taken where the
fraudulent party has made off with the goods and cannot be traced. In
one such case, it was held that the defrauded seller of a car could
rescind the contract by simply notifying the police.[8] The unfortunate
result was that a third party who subsequently in good faith bought
the car from the rogue had to give it up to the true owner. In Scotland,
it has been held that a notice to the police cannot amount to rescission
in such circumstances.[9] This appears to be the preferable view, but a
recommendation that it should be adopted in England has not been
implemented.[10]

ii Rescission for breach

The victim of a breach of contract can always claim damages, and in
addition he can sometimes 'rescind' the contract. This topic is
discussed in Chapter 16; here it suffices to say that, as a general rule,
a breach must be *serious* to give rise to a right to rescind for the breach:
a *slight* breach gives rise only to a claim for damages. A representation
inducing a contract may be incorporated in it as one of its terms; and
s 1(a) of the Misrepresentation Act 1967 provides that such
incorporation does not affect the right to rescind for misrepresentation.
An incorporated misrepresentation may therefore give rise to a right
to rescind for misrepresentation even if it only leads to a slight breach,
ie to one which is not sufficiently serious to give rise to a right to
rescind for breach. However, in such a case, it is probable that the
court will exercise its discretion under s 2(2) of the Misrepresentation
Act to declare the contract subsisting, in which case the representee
will be limited to his claim for damages *either* for breach of the still

---

6 Eg *Cundy v Lindsay* (1878) 3 App Cas 459; see ante, p 132.
7 Eg *Lewis v Averay* [1972] 1 QB 198; cf ante, p 133.
8 *Car and Universal Finance Co Ltd v Caldwell* [1965] 1 QB 525.
9 *MacLeod v Kerr* 1965 SC 253.
10 Law Reform Committee 12th Report (1966) Cmnd 2958, para 16.

subsisting contract, *or* in lieu of rescission under s 2(2). Usually, the former will be the preferable claim.

If the incorporated misrepresentation leads to a breach which is sufficiently serious to give rise to a claim to rescind for breach, the representee has two rights to rescind, one for misrepresentation and one for breach. He will almost invariably exercise the latter right, since it has two advantages over the former. First, rescission for breach can be coupled with a claim for damages for the breach,[11] whereas rescission for misrepresentation probably extinguishes any claim for damages for breach,[12] and cannot be claimed together with damages in lieu of rescission. Secondly, a representee who wants, above all, to rescind runs the risk that, if he relies on misrepresentation as such, the court may exercise its discretion under s 2(2) to declare the contract subsisting and to award damages in lieu of rescission. Although the point is not entirely clear, it seems probable that this discretion only applies to rescission for misrepresentation and not to rescission for breach. Hence a person whose main interest is in rescission should, in the case of an incorporated misrepresentation, base his claim on breach.

iii *Misrepresentation as a defence*

A party who rescinds will often do so because he wants to get back what he gave under the contract. But he may not yet have performed his part and may wish to rely on the misrepresentation simply as a justification for his refusal to perform. This purely defensive use of the misrepresentation is sometimes referred to as rescission; but it is not in all respects governed by the same rules as the process by which a party seeks to get back what he gave under the contract. Such a claim will succeed only if the representee restores what he himself received under the contract. But this requirement of restoration is not always insisted upon where fraud is simply set up as a defence to a claim. Thus an insurance company can rely by way of defence on the fraud of the policyholder, without returning the premiums.[13] Similarly, a person who is induced by fraud to enter into a contract of sale with a buyer with whom he would not have dealt, if he had known the truth, can refuse both to deliver the goods and to pay back the price.[14] The rule does not apply where the representation is negligent or wholly

---

11 See post, pp 319, 344.
12 Cf supra, at n 5; and (in certain cases of non-disclosure) *The Star Sea* [2001] UKHL 1, [2003] 1 AC 469 at [52].
13 See *Feise v Parkinson* (1812) 4 Taunt 640 at 641; Marine Insurance Act 1906, s 84(1) and (3)(a).
14 *Berg v Sadler and Moore* [1937] 2 KB 158.

innocent. Its purpose seems to be to deter fraud,[15] particularly where the fraud is criminal; but it is far from clear why the criminal law is not considered to provide adequate deterrence.

iv   Limitations on the right to rescind

The right to rescind is a potential source of hardship to the representor and to third parties. Prejudice to third parties is avoided by the rule that, once an innocent third party has for value acquired an interest in the subject-matter, the contract cannot be rescinded so as to deprive him of that interest.[16] The other limitations on the right to rescind are designed to avoid hardship to the representor; and they can be discussed under three headings: restitution, affirmation and lapse of time.

The requirement of *restitution* means that a person seeking to rescind the contract must be able and willing to restore what he has received under it. This requirement may not, as we have just seen, apply where a victim of fraud simply pleads it as a defence. But if, for example, a buyer wants to rescind in order to get his money back, he must restore the goods; and conversely a seller claiming back his goods must pay back the price. The most difficult cases are those in which restoration is possible in some sense but not in the fullest sense: for example, because the subject-matter has deteriorated or been altered in some way; or because the representee has used it and cannot, strictly speaking, restore the benefit which he has derived from such use.

Deterioration may be due to one of a number of causes. If it is due to the very defect to which the misrepresentation relates, it should obviously not bar rescission: it is precisely on account of such deterioration that the right to rescind is most commonly exercised. Deterioration similarly does not bar the right to rescind where it is due to a wholly extraneous cause, as where goods are damaged by a third party, or where shares decline in value because of a fall in the market.[17] But the position is different where the alteration or deterioration is due to the voluntary act of the representee. Here the general principle is that the change in the subject-matter does bar rescission;[18] but this principle is subject to a number of qualifications. It does not apply at all where the deterioration occurs simply in the course of a reasonable test carried out to determine the accuracy of

---

15   *South Australia Asset Management Corpn v York Montague Ltd* [1997] AC 191 at 215.
16   Eg ante, p 132.
17   *Head v Tattersall* (1871) LR 7 Exch 7; *Armstrong v Jackson* [1917] 2 KB 822.
18   *Clarke v Dickson* (1858) EB & E 148.

the representation. And it is modified where the deterioration or alteration is relatively slight, so that substantial restoration remains possible. In such a case the representee can restore the thing as it is, provided that he also makes an allowance for any benefit which he has obtained as a result of its use. For example, in one case,[19] the purchaser of a phosphate-bearing island had worked it, but not worked it out; and it was held that he could rescind on terms of restoring the island and accounting for any profit derived from his operations there. A similar rule applies where the representee has not altered the subject-matter, but has simply used it. Thus, a purchaser of land may go into possession and then discover that there has been a misrepresentation. He will be entitled to rescind on terms of restoring the land and paying a rent for the period of his occupation. The principle of making a money allowance may also apply where a sale is induced by a misrepresentation on the part of the *buyer,* who then incurs expenses (beyond payment of the price) in performing other terms of the contract. A seller claiming rescission in such a case may be obliged, not only to repay the price, but also to make an allowance in respect of those other expenses incurred by the buyer.[20]

The right to rescind is, secondly, barred if the representee *affirms* the contract after he has discovered the truth. Such affirmation may be express, but it can also be inferred from failure to repudiate: for example, from retaining goods, or from staying in possession of land, with knowledge of the truth.[1] Here again, retention for a reasonable period to test the accuracy of the representation will not amount to affirmation of the contract; but further use of the subject-matter after the true facts have been discovered will have this effect. Acts done in ignorance of the true facts will not amount to affirmation and so will not, of themselves, bar the right to rescind *for misrepresentation,* though such acts may sometimes[2] bar the right to rescind for breach.

A third bar to rescission is *lapse of time.* Where the misrepresentation is fraudulent, time for this purpose begins to run from the discovery of the truth, lapse of time being in such cases regarded simply as evidence of affirmation. But where the misrepresentation is innocent, time begins to run from the conclusion of the contract, or perhaps from the time when the truth ought reasonably to have been discovered. In one case,[3] a buyer of a picture innocently said by the seller to be 'by J Constable', sought to rescind for misrepresentation

19   *Erlanger v New Sombrero Phosphate Co* (1878) 3 App Cas 1218.
20   *Spence v Crawford* [1939] 3 All ER 271.
1   Eg *Long v Lloyd* [1958] 2 All ER 402.
2   See post, p 338.
3   *Leaf v International Galleries* [1950] 2 KB 86.

five years after the sale. The claim was held barred by lapse of time, even though the buyer had acted promptly after discovering that the picture was a modern copy, so that he could not be said to have affirmed. In cases of innocent misrepresentation, lapse of time is therefore an independent bar to rescission.

In the circumstances discussed above, the right to rescind is absolutely barred; but it does not follow that rescission will be allowed merely because none of the bars to rescission has arisen. Under s 2(2) of the Misrepresentation Act 1967, the right to rescind for innocent misrepresentation is subject to the discretion of the court, to declare the contract subsisting and to award damages in lieu of rescission. The subsection enables the court to refuse to allow rescission in any case in which damages would, in its view, be the more appropriate remedy. However, it may still be in the interest of the party resisting rescission to show that one of the bars to rescission has arisen. For if he can show this rescission *must* be refused: the matter will not be at the discretion of the court.

d   Estoppel

Under the doctrine of estoppel by representation, a person who makes a precise and unambiguous representation of fact may be prevented from denying that the facts were as he stated them to be, if the person to whom the representation was made was intended to act on it, and did act on it to his detriment. It is generally said that the effect of such an estoppel is not to create a cause of action,[4] but only to give rise to a defence. Suppose, for example, that A induces B to hire a car by innocently representing that it is in good running order, and that the contract requires B to keep the car in repair. In such a case estoppel would not entitle B to damages if the car was in fact unroadworthy; but it could provide B with a defence if, immediately after the conclusion of the contract, A sued B for failing to remedy the very defects which the car had when it was handed over to him.

A further example, however, shows that estoppel may help a claimant no less than a defendant. Suppose that A is a warehouseman who says to B that there are goods belonging to C in the warehouse and promises to deliver those goods to B, for some consideration moving from B (eg payment of warehouse charges). If there are in fact no goods of C in the warehouse, A may be liable to B on the basis of estoppel. Here estoppel does not create B's cause of action (which is based on A's promise to deliver); but A's representation that C's

---

4   Eg *Low v Bouverie* [1891] 3 Ch 82 at 101.

goods were in the warehouse prevents him from relying on the defence that in fact no such goods were there.[5]

3 NON-DISCLOSURE

a Generally no duty of disclosure

So far in this chapter we have been concerned with active misrepresentations. Of course, such misrepresentations do not have to be made in so many words. They may be made by conduct, the stock example being the case where the seller of a house papers over the cracks.[6] A misrepresentation may also be impliedly made where a person states a misleading half-truth. In one case,[7] a solicitor employed by a vendor of land said that he did not know of any restrictive covenants affecting the land. This statement was literally true, but it was held to amount to a misrepresentation, as the solicitor had not given the reason for his ignorance, which was simply that he had failed to read the relevant documents.

Where there is no express or implied misrepresentation, the general rule is that there is no liability for non-disclosure.[8] Thus a seller is not bound to disclose facts known to him but not to the buyer which make the subject-matter less valuable than the buyer had supposed it to be; and conversely a buyer need not disclose facts known to him, but not to the seller, which make the subject-matter more valuable than the seller supposed it to be. 'Insider dealing' in securities is, indeed, a criminal offence,[9] but the mere commission of this offence does not affect the validity or enforceability of the resulting contract.[10] The general rule is justified partly by the argument that, in the absence of active misrepresentation, each party takes the risk that the subject-matter may turn out to be worse, or better, than he had supposed; and partly by the difficulty of determining the scope of a general duty of disclosure. It would, for example, be very hard to say just which of the many facts known by a seller about his house must be disclosed to the buyer.

---

5   *Griswold v Haven* 25 NY 595 (1862); *Coventry Sheppard & Co v Great Eastern Rly Co* (1883) 11 QBD 776.
6   Eg *Gordon v Selico* (1986) 278 Estates Gazette 53; cf Financial Services and Markets Act 2000, s 397(1)(b).
7   *Nottingham Patent Brick and Title Co v Butler* (1886) 16 QBD 778.
8   *Norwich Union Life and Pensions Ltd Co v Qureshi* [1999] 2 All ER (Comm) 707 at 717.
9   Criminal Justice Act 1993, Pt V, giving effect to Directive 89/592 EEC.
10 Criminal Justice Act 1993, s 63(2).

b   Exceptions

A duty of disclosure exists in the exceptional cases to be discussed below. In these cases the general rule is that a person need disclose only facts which were actually known to him (or his agent) at the time of the conclusion of the contract. Sometimes, however, the duty of disclosure ceases as soon as the parties are bound as a matter of business, even though there is as yet no binding contract. Thus, in contracts of insurance, it ceases when the insurer agrees to accept the risk by initialling a slip, even where there is no legally enforceable contract until the policy is executed.[11] Conversely, a contract may impose a duty of disclosure which continues after its formation and requires one party to inform the other as the occasion arises of certain facts, eg that he has been involved in an accident or convicted of a motoring offence.[12]

Failure to perform such a duty does not vitiate the formation of the contract but is a breach of it.

i   Change of circumstances

A person may, in the course of negotiations for the sale of a business, make a representation as to its profitability which is perfectly true when made. But if, before any contract is concluded, there is a radical change of circumstances which wholly falsifies that representation, he must disclose this change to the other party.[13] At least this is so if it is still reasonable for the latter to rely on the original representation. Where the negotiations have gone on for a very long time, it may no longer be reasonable for him to do this.

The same duty of disclosure has been held to exist where there was a 'change of intention': that is, where during negotiations one party made a statement as to his future commercial policy but changed that policy before the contract was made.[14] In a contrasting case,[15] a wife who had been left by her husband received an offer of financial provision from him after saying that she would not remarry. She later decided after all to remarry and then accepted the offer. It was held that she was not bound to disclose her change of mind as her original representation was one of *intention* as opposed to one of *fact*. A better

---

11   *Cory v Patton* (1872) LR 7 QB 304.
12   Cf post, p 173 at nn 8 and 9.
13   *With v O'Flanagan* [1936] Ch 575; cf Financial Services and Markets Act 2000, ss 81, 86.
14   *Traill v Baring* (1864) 4 De GJ & Sm 318.
15   *Wales v Wadham* [1977] 2 All ER 125, disapproved (but on another ground only) in *Livesey v Jenkins* [1985] AC 424.

ground for the decision would have been that a statement of intention not to remarry was so intrinsically likely to be changed that it was not reasonable for the husband to have relied on it. As a general principle, there seems to be no good reason for saying that a representation of intention should not be corrected if the representor changes his mind. A representation of present intention is generally regarded as one of fact;[16] and there is no difficulty in cases of this kind in specifying exactly what must be disclosed.

ii Latent defects

A seller is not bound to disclose a latent defect which merely affects the value of the subject-matter. But if he knows of a defect which causes further loss or injury to the buyer, he may be liable in negligence for failing to warn the buyer of its existence: the seller of a car would be liable on this ground if he knew that the car had defects which made it dangerous and if those defects led to an accident in which the buyer was injured.[17]

iii Custom

A duty of disclosure may arise by the custom of a particular trade or market.

iv Contracts uberrimae fidei

A duty of disclosure exists in relation to certain types of contracts on the ground that one party to them is in a much better position than the other to know material facts. Such contracts are known as contracts *uberrimae fidei* (of utmost good faith). The outstanding illustration of this category is the contract of insurance. Here 'the underwriter knows nothing and the man who asks him to insure knows everthing'.[18] Hence the latter is, as a general rule, bound to declare all facts which a reasonably prudent insurer would take into account in deciding whether to accept the risk, or what premium to charge.[19] The insured must, for example, disclose the fact that other underwriters had declined to cover the risk; in the case of life insurance he must disclose any illness from which he suffers; and he must disclose earlier losses of the kind to be covered by the policy. Such non-disclosure is a ground of avoidance if it was one of the factors (even if it was not a decisive

---

16 See ante, p 147.
17 *Hurley v Dyke* [1979] RTR 265 at 303.
18 *Rozanes v Bowen* (1928) 32 Ll L Rep 98 at 102.
19 Marine Insurance Act 1906, s 18(2).

one) which induced the insurer to enter into the contract.[20] Insurers often stipulate for an even greater degree of protection, by providing that all answers in the proposal form shall form the basis of the contract. The result of such clauses is to enable insurers to avoid liability for misstatements, even though they relate to quite trivial matters, which are not material at all, and even though they were made in the most perfect good faith; and this position has drawn much criticism.[1] Under a contract of insurance, a duty of disclosure may also be imposed on the underwriter: for example, if the insured property had already been destroyed when the policy was taken out, or if the insured had been deceived by his own broker, an underwriter who knows such facts is under a duty to disclose them to the insured.[2]

Certain agreements between members of a family for settling disputes as to the family property also fall within the class of contracts uberrimae fidei.[3]

v   Analogous contracts

In some contracts which are not *uberrimae fidei* there is a limited duty to disclose: that is, a duty which is not one to disclose all material facts, but a lower duty to disclose *unusual* facts. A creditor to whom a guarantee is given by a surety must, for example, disclose to the surety any *unusual* circumstances, such as terms of the principal contract which the surety would not normally expect it to contain.[4] Thus the duty of disclosure is less exacting under a contract of suretyship than it is under a contract of insurance.

A limited duty of disclosure may also arise in contracts for the sale of land. Here it has been said that a seller is bound to disclose defects, or at least unusual defects, of title.[5] Certain other cases in which there is a duty of disclosure have been discussed elsewhere in this book, in particular in relation to compromises of invalid claims and to exemption clauses.[6]

20 *Pan Atlantic Insurance Co Ltd v Pine Top Insurance Co Ltd* [1995] 1 AC 501.
1   The Law Commission has recommended that such clauses should cease to have this effect: Law Com 104 para 7.4; cf *The Star Sea* [2001] UKHL 1, [2003] 1 AC 469 at [50]. In consumer contracts such clauses may be open to challenge under the Unfair Terms in Consumer Contracts Regulations 1999.
2   See *Banque Keyser Ullmann SA v Skandia (UK) Insurance Co Ltd* [1991] 2 AC 249 at 268, 281.
3   *Greenwood v Greenwood* (1863) 2 De GJ & Sm 28.
4   *Cooper v National Provincial Bank Ltd* [1946] KB 1 at 7.
5   *Rignall Developments Ltd v Halil* [1988] Ch 190; *William Sindall plc v Cambridgeshire County Council* [1994] 1 WLR 1016 at 1023.
6   See ante, pp 39, 82–83.

vi Relationship of parties

In some cases, the duty of disclosure arises because there is a so-called *fiduciary* relationship between the parties. Such a duty is, for example, owed by an agent to his principal, and by a company promoter to the company. In yet other cases of fiduciary relationships the contract may be set aside, even though full disclosure has been made, unless further conditions to be discussed in Chapter 10 are satisfied.[7]

Our present concern is with non-disclosure which *induces* a contract; but a duty of disclosure may also arise in the *performance* of a contract: for example, an employee may be bound to disclose the fact that his fellow employees have defrauded the employer.[8] Failure to perform such a duty does not invalidate the contract of employment but amounts to a breach of it. The failure may, however, vitiate a second contract: eg one for the payment of compensation for the 'early retirement' of the employee.[9]

vii Statutory duties of disclosure

Many modern statutes require certain facts to be disclosed in relation to specific contracts. These requirements are designed to protect classes of persons such as investors, or borrowers, or consumers of certain kinds of goods. For example, the Financial Services and Markets Act 2000[10] imposes extensive duties of disclosure on persons who seek official listings of securities on the stock exchange or who issue a prospectus inviting subscriptions for unlisted securities.

c   The effects of non-disclosure

These effects depend on the following distinctions.

i   Inferred representations and pure non-disclosure

In the first group of cases to be discussed under this heading no misrepresentation is made in so many words, but one can be inferred from conduct or from such circumstances as failure to correct a statement which has been falsified by later events.[11] Such cases must

---

7   Post, p 180.
8   *Sybron Corpn v Rochem Ltd* [1984] Ch 112 at 126–127.
9   *Sybron Corpn v Rochem Ltd* [1984] Ch 112.
10 Sections 80, 86.
11 See ante, p 170.

be distinguished from those of 'pure' non-disclosure in which no such inference can be drawn, but the law nevertheless gives a remedy: eg in contracts of insurance or where a duty of disclosure is imposed by statute.

In the first of these groups of cases, non-disclosure gives rise to the same remedies (by way of damages and rescission) as express misrepresentation. But no such general statement can be made of the second group of cases, ie of those of 'pure' non-disclosure. In some such cases, the only remedy is by way of damages: this is, for example, true of breach of the statutory duty of disclosure described above.[12] On the other hand, it has been held that breach of the duty of disclosure which arises in the case of contracts *uberrimae fidei* gives rise only to a right to rescind and not to one to damages for negligence at common law.[13] The restricted effect of non-disclosure in these cases appears to be based on the policies underlying the rules which impose the duties of disclosure in such cases.

The distinction between the two types of cases is also relevant for the purposes of the Misrepresentation Act 1967, and here it is based simply on the wording of the Act. Liability in damages arises under s 2(1) where 'a misrepresentation has been made' and the same phrase is used in s 2(2), which gives the court power to award damages in lieu of rescission. It seems that the phrase does not cover 'pure' non-disclosure,[14] but that it can cover cases in which a misrepresentation, though not made in so many words, can be inferred from conduct or from other surrounding circumstances.

ii   Pre- and post-contractual non-disclosure

The right to rescind for non-disclosure can give rise to hardship: for example, where it enables an insurer to avoid all liability under a policy even though the non-disclosure which induces it was quite innocent and related to a matter of only trivial importance.[15] To mitigate this hardship, the courts have distinguished between cases in which the misrepresentation induces the making of the contract and those in which it occurs after the contract was made and amounts

---

12   At n 10. *Re South of England Natural Gas and Petroleum Co Ltd* [1911] 1 Ch 573, which seems to be unaffected by the Financial Services and Markets Act 2000, ss 90, 86.

13   *Banque Keyser Ullmann SA v Skandia (UK) Insurance Co Ltd* [1990] 1 QB 665 at 789–790; affd on this point [1991] 2 AC 249 at 288.

14   *Banque Keyser Ullmann SA v Skandia (UK) Insurance Co Ltd* [1990] 1 QB 665 at 779–781; affd sub nom *Banque Financière de la Cité SA v Westgate Insurance Co Ltd* [1991] 2 AC 249.

15   Ante, p 172.

to a breach of it:[16] for example, in the course of making a claim under a policy that was properly obtained. The insurer's right to rescind in cases of the latter kind is governed by the rules relating to the right to rescind for breach which differs in several ways from the right to rescind for non-disclosure or misrepresentation. In particular, the right to rescind for breach is, in general, available only where the breach causes serious prejudice to the injured party;[17] and the exercise of the right has, in general, no retrospective effect and so does not deprive the party in breach of rights which had accrued before rescission.[18] The latter rule is, in cases of the kind here under discussion, subject to an exception in cases of fraud, so that where an insured person makes a fraudulent claim, the insurer is entitled to reject, not only that claim, but also any lesser claim which the insured might honestly have made.[19] It is thought that, but for this exception, the insured would have nothing to lose by making fraudulent claims (though these could lead to criminal penalties).

16   *The Star Sea* [2001] UKHL 1, [2001] 1 AC 469.
17   Post, p 321.
18   Post, p 343.
19   *The Star Sea* [2001] UKHL 1, [2001] AC 469 at [62].

Chapter 10

Improper pressure

The law in a number of situations gives relief against contracts obtained by improper pressure. The crucial word here is 'improper'. Almost every contract is made under some form of economic pressure, and even where this pressure is considerable – where, in other words, one party is able to drive a hard bargain – the validity of the contract is not normally affected. But victims of certain forms of pressure are protected by the common law of duress and the equitable rules of undue influence, while further rules for the protection of particular classes of person have been developed in equity and by legislation.

1 DURESS

The original definition of duress was a very narrow one. It meant actual or threatened unlawful violence to, or constraint of, the person of the other contracting party.[1] Later cases reject this narrow view and recognise that a contract may be vitiated by 'economic duress':[2] eg where a person is forced to enter into a contract under a threat to burn his house down, or one to call his employees out on strike in breach of their contracts of employment, or one to refuse to perform an earlier contract (either between the same parties or with a third party).[3] Any threat *can* amount to duress so long as it is 'illegitimate', eg because what is threatened is a legal wrong (as in the above examples) or because of the nature of the threat itself (as in the case of a blackmailer's threat to reveal the truth about his victim).[4] Whether it *does* amount to duress then depends, not on what is threatened, but on the effect of the threat on the victim: it must produce 'coercion of

---

1 See *Latter v Braddell* (1880) 50 LJQB 166; affd (1881) 50 LJQB 448.
2 *The Universe Sentinel* [1983] 1 AC 366 at 383.
3 *The Siboen and The Sibotre* [1976] 1 Lloyd's Rep 293, and see the authorities cited in nn 4–6 below. This view would now prevail over cases such as *Skeate v Beale* (1840) 11 Ad & El, according to which contracts were not vitiated by 'duress of goods'.
4 *The Universe Sentinel* [1983] 1 AC 366 at 383; contrast *R v A-G for England and Wales* [2003] UKPC 22, [2003] EMLR 499, where the threat was lawful.

the will which vitiates consent'.[5] For example, a threat to break a contract was held to amount to duress where the consequence of its being carried out would have been economically so disastrous for the victim as to leave him with no reasonable alternative but to comply with it.[6] But the position was held to be different where a person who had made a contract with a company threatened to refuse to perform it unless the directors guaranteed that such performance would not cause him any loss. The directors, thinking that the risk was small and wanting to avoid adverse publicity, gave the guarantee; and the argument that they had done so under duress was rejected as their will had not been coerced.[7] A threat to *enforce* contractual rights, eg to call in a debt when due or one to refuse to enter into a contract will not normally amount to duress; for such threats are not 'illegitimate'.[8]

Where a contract is affected by duress the result is to make the contract voidable, not void.[9] Innocent third parties are therefore not prejudiced by the invalidity of the contract.

2   UNDUE INFLUENCE

a   Actual pressure

Equity sometimes gave relief where an agreement had been obtained by the actual exercise of some form of pressure, which fell outside the originally narrow common law definition of duress. In one line of cases, for example, contracts obtained by threatening to prosecute the promisor, or his spouse or close relative, for a criminal offence were set aside on the ground of undue influence.[10] Even now the equitable concept of actual pressure is wider than the common law concept of duress in that such pressure can be exercised without making any illegitimate threats, or indeed any threats at all.[11]

---

5   *Pao On v Lau Yiu Long* [1980] AC 614 at 616; cf *Huyton SA v Peter Cremer GmbH & Co* [1999] 1 Lloyd's Rep 620 at 638.

6   *B & S Contracts and Design Ltd v Victor Green Publications Ltd* [1984] ICR 419; cf *The Atlantic Baron* [1979] QB 705 and ante, p 45.

7   *Pao On v Lau Yiu Long* [1980] AC 614.

8   *CTN Cash and Carry Ltd v Gallaher Ltd* [1994] 4 All ER 714; *Alf Vaughan & Co Ltd v Royscol Trust plc* [1999] 1 All ER (Comm) 856.

9   *Pao On v Lau Yiu Long* [1980] AC 614 at 634; *The Universe Sentinel* [1983] 1 AC 366 at 383, 400.

10   Eg *Kaufman v Gerson* [1904] 1 KB 591.

11   Eg *CIBC Mortgages plc v Pitt* [1994] 1 AC 200, where the claim failed on the ground stated on p 181, post at n 18.

b   Presumed undue influence

Equity further grants relief where the circumstances in which a transaction was concluded gives rise to a 'presumption of undue influence'.[12] This, unfortunately ambiguous, phrase can refer either to the fact that such influence *exists* or that it has been *exercised*. To give rise to a claim for relief on the ground of presumed undue influence, two facts must be established.[13] The first is that there was a relationship between A and B by virtue of which B reposed trust and confidence in A; this requirement is further discussed below. The second is that the transaction from which B claims relief was one that 'calls for explanation'.[14] This requirement would, for example, be satisfied where B made a substantial transfer of property to A or guaranteed A's business debts, but not where B made an ordinary (or moderate) birthday present to A.[15]

The effect of establishing the above two facts is to give rise to a 'rebuttable evidential presumption'[16] that 'the transaction can only have been procured by undue influence'[17] – or, in other words, that such influence has been *exercised*. The word 'rebuttable' here refers to the point that the presumption can be displaced in one of the ways to be discussed below;[18] while the word 'evidential' seems to refer to the point that if A, after proof of the above two facts, introduces further evidence which leaves the court in doubt whether the transaction was procured by undue influence, then B will not (unless he can dispel that doubt) be entitled to relief.[19]

One way of establishing that B reposed trust and confidence in A is to show that the relationship between them was one of a group in which 'the law presumes, irrebuttably',[20] that A had influence over B. This is, for example, the position where the relationship is that between parent and child, doctor and patient, solicitor and client or trustee and beneficiary.[1] This presumption differs from the 'evidential presumption' discussed above in being irrebuttable and also in its

---

12   *Barclays Bank plc v O'Brien* [1994] 1 AC 180 at 189; *Royal Bank of Scotland v Etridge (No 2)* [2001] UKHL 44, [2002] 2 AC 773 (hereafter 'the *Etridge* case') at [16]

13   *Etridge* case at [13].

14   *Etridge* case at [14].

15   *Etridge* case at [24], [156].

16   *Etridge* case at [16], [153], [194].

17   *Etridge* case at [14].

18   Post, p 180.

19   *Etridge* case at [158]

20   *Etridge* case at [18]; cf at [104].

1   *Bullock v Lloyds Bank Ltd* [1955] Ch 317; *Radcliffe v Price* (1902) 18 TLR 466; *Wright v Carter* [1903] 1 Ch 27; *Ellis v Barker* (1871) LR 7 Ch App 104.

effect: while the evidential presumption is that undue influence has been *exercised,* the irrebuttable presumption is merely that the influence *exists.* A relationship giving rise to the latter presumption is not, of itself, a ground for relief; it would still be up to B to show that the transaction 'call[ed] for explanation'.[2] An ordinary Christmas present could not be set aside merely because it was made by a child to its parent.

A second way of establishing that A had influence over B is to show that this was in fact the position. This possibility covers a wide and flexible range of relationships of which examples can be given but which 'cannot be listed exhaustively'.[3] Examples of relationships in this group include those of husband and wife, banker and customer, financial adviser and client, and musical manager and an as yet unknown song-writer who later became a celebrity.[4] The mere fact that such influence is shown to exist does not give rise to any presumption that it has been exercised: the transaction must also (once again) be one which 'calls for explanation'.[5] Even where this is the position, it may be implausible to apply the presumption. A wife may, for example, provide security for her husband's business debts by a bank guarantee supported by a charge on the matrimonial home owned wholly or in part by her. In 'the ordinary course'[6] she is as likely to have acted from motives of affection or common interest with the husband as under his undue influence.[7] There is also the point that, although the wife's allegation of undue influence is levelled against her husband, the couple have a common interest in resisting the bank's attempt to enforce the security and so to turn them out of their home. For these reasons, there may be little or no scope in such cases for any presumption that the transaction was induced by undue influence.[8] But this reasoning would not apply to many other situations in which B could show actual undue influence and a transaction calling for explanation.[9] In such other situations, there is therefore still scope for the evidential presumption that the influence

2   *Etridge* case at [14].
3   *Etridge* case at [10].
4   *Etridge* case at [19]; *Lloyds Bank Ltd v Bundy* [1975] QB 326; *National Westminster Bank plc v Morgan* [1985] AC 686; *Tate v Williamson* (1866) 2 Ch App 55; *O'Sullivan v Management Agency and Music Ltd* [1985] QB 428.
5   *Etridge* case at [14]; *Barclays Bank plc v O'Brien,* [1994] 1 AC 180 at 189–190.
6   *Etridge* case at [30].
7   *Etridge* case at [45].
8   Hence in the *Etridge* case at [107] and [161] two members of the House of Lords rejected or doubted the existence of any such presumption in the husband and wife cases.
9   Eg, those illustrated by the last three examples given at n 4, supra.

induced the transaction. The presumption would not dispense with the need to show that the influence *existed* but would dispense with the need to show that it had been *exercised*. In this respect, a claim based on the presumption would stand a greater chance of success than one based on actual pressure.[10]

c   Rebutting the presumption

Where the facts giving rise to the presumption are established, the transaction will nevertheless be upheld if the party benefiting from it can rebut the presumption. The most usual (though not the only) way of doing this is by showing that the other party was independently and competently advised before entering into the transaction.[11] In some cases the party seeking to uphold the presumption must show that the transaction was fair: this is the position where a solicitor buys from his client or a trustee from his beneficiary.[12]

d   Bars to relief

Relief in cases of undue influence is barred on grounds similar to those discussed in relation to misrepresentation, such as inability to make restitution,[13] affirmation and lapse of time.

The only one of these bars to relief which calls for further discussion here is that relating to third party rights, since relief for undue influence is quite commonly sought against a third party: for example where A by undue influence induces B to mortgage B's house to C as security for A's debt to C. Here B can clearly set the mortgage aside if C actually knew of the undue influence; and B can also do so if C was 'put on enquiry'.[14] This means that, in the circumstances described below,[15] C must take reasonable steps to reduce the risk of B's entering into the transaction as a result of undue influence or other vitiating factor. C is under this duty even though no vitiating factor exists: the purpose of the requirement is to guard against the *risk* of B's consent having been improperly obtained.[15a] It follows that C's failure to take such steps is

---

10   This was the position in *Barclays Bank plc v Coleman*, one of the decisions under appeal in the *Etridge* case: see that case at [130]; and cf at [36].
11   *Allcard v Skinner* (1887) 36 Ch D 145 at 190; cf *Banco Exterior Internacional v Mann* [1995] 1 All ER 936.
12   *Wright v Carter* [1903] 1 Ch 27; *Thomson v Eastwood* (1877) 2 App Cas 215.
13   See *O'Sullivan v Management Agency and Music Ltd* [1985] QB 428 (*precise* restitution not necessary).
14   *Royal Bank of Scotland v Etridge (No 2)* [2001] UKHL 44, [2002] 2 AC 773 at [44].
15   Post, p 181, at nn 17–2.
15a *Etridge* case at [41].

not itself a ground for relief: it does not dispense with B's need to show that the transaction was procured by undue influence or to establish the facts giving rise to the 'evidential presumption'[16] that it was so procured.

The question whether C must take reasonable steps for the purpose described above depends on two factors. The first is the nature of the transaction. Thus the duty arises where B guarantees A's business debts (since such a guarantee does not on its face benefit B)[17] but not, in general, where C makes a loan to A and B jointly (since such a loan may well benefit B).[18] The second factor is the nature of the relationship between A and B. In many of the decided cases, B was A's wife, but C's duty can also arise in the converse case in which B is A's husband;[19] in 'the case of unmarried couples, whether heterosexual or homosexual';[20] and in other relationships of trust and confidence.[1] It may extend to all guarantee cases in which the relationship of B (the guarantor) and A (the debtor) is a non-commercial one.[2]

The principal step that C must take to protect B against the risk of undue influence is to tell B that C will require a solicitor acting for B to confirm in writing to C that the solicitor has, at a face-to-face meeting with B at which A was not present, explained to B the nature and effects of the documents to be signed by B.[3] If C takes the required steps, C will normally be entitled to rely on the solicitor's confirmation that the transaction has been duly explained to B.[4]

3 PROTECTION OF PARTICULAR GROUPS OF PERSONS

Even where there was no undue influence (actual or presumed) equity sometimes gave relief because one of the parties to a transaction was thought to require special protection; for example because he was poor or ignorant and unfair advantage had been taken of him.[5] This principle was, for example, applied where a wife, in the course of divorce proceedings, transferred her share in the matrimonial

16 Ante, p 178.
17 *Etridge* case at [48], [47].
18 *CIBC Mortgages plc v Pitt* [1994] 1 AC 200.
19 *Etridge* case at [47].
20 *Etridge* case; *Barclays Bank plc v O'Brien* [1994] 1 AC 180 at 196.
1   Eg *Credit Lyonnais Bank Neederland NV v Burch* [1997] 1 All ER 144.
2   *Etridge* case at [87].
3   *Etridge* case at [76], [79].
4   *Etridge* case at [56].
5   *Evans v Llewellin* (1787) 1 Cox Eq Cas 333.

home to her husband without independent advice and for a grossly inadequate consideration.[6]

One group of persons thought by the courts to need special protection were the so-called 'expectant heirs': that is, persons who raised money by selling reversionary interests in property before they were entitled to possession of it, or even by selling the bare expectancy of inheriting under someone's will or intestacy.[7] Originally such sales could be set aside merely on the ground of undervalue. But this rule was later reversed by legislation[8] and now relief will be given only if the undervalue is so gross as to make the transaction an unconscionable one.[9]

In a number of cases Lord Denning MR has relied on the equitable rules discussed in this chapter, and on a number of other instances,[10] in support of a general principle of 'inequality of bargaining power'. Under this principle, relief would be given against unfair transactions at the suit of a party 'whose bargaining power is grievously impaired by reason of his own needs or desires, or by his own ignorance or infirmity, coupled with undue influence or pressures brought to bear on him by or for the benefit of the other'.[11] The scope of this alleged principle is very wide: it seems to be intended to apply to such diverse transactions as a guarantee of a bank loan obtained from the borrower's father by a bank manager in whom the father placed implicit trust;[12] the renegotiation of a contract;[13] the settlement of a personal injury claim;[14] and the inclusion of an exemption clause in a standard form contract with a consumer.[15] However, the actual decisions in these cases can be explained on other grounds, and were so explained by other members of the court. Later decisions have rejected the general principle for two main reasons. First, its vagueness has drawn the criticism that it would be 'unhelpful because it would render the law uncertain'.[16] Secondly, the need for such a principle has been greatly reduced by the modern expansion of the concept of duress,[17]

6   *Creswell v Potter* [1978] 1 WLR 255n.
7   *Nevill v Snelling* (1880) 15 Ch D 679.
8   Sale of Reversions Act 1867; now Law of Property Act 1925, s 174.
9   *Fry v Lane* (1888) 40 Ch D 312 at 321.
10   Eg the restraint of trade cases, discussed post, p 201.
11   *Lloyds Bank Ltd v Bundy* [1975] QB 326 at 339.
12   *Lloyds Bank Ltd v Bundy* [1975] QB 326 at 339.
13   *D & C Builders Ltd v Rees* [1966] 2 QB 617.
14   *Arrale v Costain Civil Engineering Ltd* [1976] 1 Lloyd's Rep 98.
15   *Levison v Patent Steam Carpet Cleaning Co Ltd* [1978] QB 69 at 78.
16   *Pao On v Lau Yiu Long* [1980] AC 614 at 634.
17   Ante, p 176.

and by the fact that legislation has dealt with a number of specific instances in which inequality of bargaining power might be abused.[18]

One illustration of this legislative approach is to be found in the law relating to 'extortionate credit bargains'.[19] Since the repeal of the usury laws in 1854, there has been no legal restriction of the maximum rate of interest which a moneylender can charge. But under the Consumer Credit Act 1974 an extortionate credit bargain can be 'reopened' by the court. A credit bargain is extortionate if it requires the debtor to make payments which are grossly exorbitant, or if it otherwise grossly contravenes the principles of fair dealing.[20] The power to 'reopen' is a very flexible one. The court can order accounts to be taken, set aside any obligation undertaken by the debtor or by any surety, order the creditor to repay excessive amounts received by him, direct the return to a surety of property given as security, and even alter the terms of the credit agreement or of any security instrument executed in relation to it.[1]

Further protection against certain kinds of unfair bargains is provided by the legislation, discussed in Chapter 7, which restricts the validity of exemption clauses and of unfair terms in consumer contracts; while legislation giving consumers a 'cooling off' period during which they can cancel contracts gives them some protection against improvident contracts.[2]

---

18 *National Westminster Bank plc v Morgan* [1985] AC 686 at 708.
19 Consumer Credit Act 1974, ss 137–140.
20 Consumer Credit Act 1974, s 148(1); see *Coldunell Ltd v Gallon* [1986] QB 1184.
1   Consumer Credit Act 1974, s 139(2).
2   Eg Consumer Credit Act 1974, ss 67–68; Consumer Protection (Distance Selling) Regulations 2000, SI 2000/2334, reg 10.

Chapter 11

Illegality

The general principal that parties can make what contracts they please is subject to the obvious limitation that their contract must not involve the commission of a legal wrong. The law also denies full effect to contracts which, even though they do not involve the commission of a legal wrong, are said to be 'contrary to public policy'. Contracts which involve the commission of a legal wrong, or are contrary to public policy, are said to be illegal, or affected with illegality. In this chapter we shall first consider the various groups of contracts so affected; and we shall see that such 'illegality' can vary very much in seriousness from one type of contract to another. It follows that the effects of illegality on contracts are likewise far from uniform; and these effects will be discussed in the concluding section of this chapter.

1 CONTRACTS CONTRARY TO LAW

a Making of the contract forbidden by law

In some cases the very making of a contract is against the law: for example, where the making of the contract amounts to a statutory offence.[1] At common law, a contract to finance another person's litigation in return for a share in the proceeds was also illegal as it amounted to the crime of champerty.[2] Criminal liability in cases of this kind has been abolished, but the contract remains illegal,[3] though its scope has been restricted by the requirement that, to constitute champerty, the agreement must be a 'wanton or officious intermeddling with the disputes of other'.[4] By statute, moreover, a lawyer can in many cases validly contract with his client to provide advocacy or litigation services for a 'conditional' fee payable only if the litigation ends in the client's favour, and the fee may be a 'success

---

1 Eg, Dealing in Cultural Objects (Offences) Act 2003, ss 1 and 3.
2 *Re Thomas* [1894] 1 QB 747.
3 Criminal Law Act 1967, s 14; *Trendtex Trading Corpn v Crédit Suisse* [1982] AC 679.
4 *Giles v Thompson* [1994] 1 AC 142 at 164.

fee', that is, one increased above the normal fee by a percentage not exceeding that specified by the Lord Chancellor.[5] 'Contingency' fee agreements, by which the legal adviser is remunerated by a share in the amount recovered, remain illegal.[6]

Legislation may simply prohibit the making of a contract without rendering it criminal. The courts then have to decide whether it was the purpose of the legislation to make contracts which violate the prohibition illegal; and the task of discovering that purpose can obviously be a difficult one.[7] Some modern Acts of Parliament solve the problem by providing whether a contract made in breach of the statutory prohibition, is, or is not, to be illegal.[8] A contract which is not prohibited, but simply declared by statute to be void or voidable or unenforceable, is not illegal.[9]

b   Object of the contract contrary to law

A contract may be illegal because of its object. Obviously, a contract for the deliberate *commission of a crime* is illegal; indeed it falls under the previous heading as such a contract would be a criminal conspiracy. A contract may be illegal, even though there is no conspiracy, if one of the parties simply knows that the other intends to use the subject-matter for an illegal purpose: eg where the seller of a car knows that the buyer intends to use it for 'ram-raiding'. A contract may also have a criminal object where only one party has any criminal intent, or even, under modern criminal statutes, where neither party has such an intent. Here again, there is no criminal conspiracy, but the contract is often to some extent affected by illegality. The difficulties arising from such 'innocent illegality' will be discussed later in this chapter.[10]

Where the object of a contract is the deliberate *commission of a civil wrong*, the contract is often illegal. This would be the position where a contract was made to defraud or defame a third party. But where one of the parties is innocent, the better view is that he can enforce the contract: for example, a printer who innocently prints libellous matter

---

5   Courts and Legal Services Act 1990, s 58(4)(c); Conditional Fee Agreements Order 2000, SI 2000/823, reg 4 (up to 100%).
6   *Callery v Gray* [2001] EWCA 117, [2001] 3 All ER 833 at [6]; affd [2002] UKHL 28, [2002] 3 All ER 417.
7   Contrast *Harse v Pearl Life Assurance Co Ltd* [1904] 1 KB 558 with *Fuji Finance Inc v Aetna Life Insurance Co Ltd* [1994] 4 All ER 1025.
8   See post, p 211.
9   Eg Marine Insurance Act 1906, s 4(1); *Re London County Commercial Reinsurance Office Ltd* [1922] 2 Ch 67.
10   See post, pp 211–213.

can probably recover his charges.[11] Nor is the contract illegal where both parties are innocent: eg where A sells goods to B which they both believe to belong to A but which, in fact, belong to C. The contract is not illegal even though A or B (or both of them) may have committed a civil wrong, known as the tort of conversion, against C.

c   Method of performance contrary to law

A contract may be capable of being performed in several ways, some of which are lawful, while another involves the commission of an offence. For example, the law may require a seller of certain goods to be licensed, or to attach statements to them specifying their ingredients. In such cases there is nothing illegal in the sale as such: the illegality arises only if the seller does not in fact hold the licence or give the required information. The question whether this makes the contract illegal depends, in these cases, on the court's view of the purpose of the rule of law that is contravened. In one case[12] a shipowner overloaded his ship and so became liable to a fine under the relevant merchant shipping legislation. The owner of some of the goods on the ship argued that the contract of carriage was therefore illegal and that he was not liable to pay the agreed freight. If this argument had been accepted, two consequences would have followed. First, the shipowner would have been subjected to a very severe penalty (in addition to the fine) in the shape of loss of freight; and secondly, the owner of the goods (which in fact arrived safely at the agreed destination) would have obtained a totally undeserved windfall. The court therefore held that the shipowner was entitled to the freight, as the purpose of the legislation was to prohibit overloading and not to invalidate contracts of carriage.

Similar reasoning has been applied where an offence is committed by failing to comply with requirements of form imposed by statute. In one case,[13] a landlord committed an offence by failing to give his tenant a rent-book. It was held that the landlord was nevertheless entitled to sue for the rent, since the purpose of the legislation was simply to punish his failure to give the rent-book and not to invalidate the lease. A fortiori, where the landlord commits an offence by requiring an illegal premium the tenant can enforce the contract, but without having to pay the premium.[14]

---

11   *Clay v Yates* (1856) 1 H & N 73.
12   *St John Shipping Corpn v Joseph Rank Ltd* [1957] 1 QB 267.
13   *Shaw v Groom* [1970] 2 QB 504.
14   *Ailion v Spiekermann* [1976] Ch 158 – unless the tenant takes the initiative and 'tempts the [landlord] with a cheque book' (at 163).

A contract may be subject to a licensing or similar requirement under which its performance is legal only if the consent of some public body (such as an export licence or a building permit) has been obtained. Such a contract is not illegal so long as it is expressly or impliedly made subject to such consent.[15] It is illegal only if it is performed without the required consent;[16] or if the parties intend it to be performed even though that consent is not obtained.[17] A licence may also be required for carrying on some specified kind of business, as opposed to the making or performance of a particular contract. If a person carries on such a business without the required licence, the resulting contracts will be illegal if the legislation which imposed the requirement also expressly prohibited those contracts.[18] Such a prohibition may also be implied: this was held to be the position at common law where insurers carried on business without the required licence.[19] But in such cases the licensing requirement was imposed on only one party (the insurer) for the protection of the other (the insured); and the preferable solution, now adopted by statute,[20] is that the illegality does not deprive the latter of the right to enforce the contract.

d Promises contingent on the commission of an unlawful act

A contract may be made under which one party promises to pay the other a sum of money on the occurrence of one or more events, including the commission by the other of an unlawful act. In one case,[1] a person who had insured his life for £50,000 committed suicide, and it was held that his estate was not entitled to enforce the policy even though it expressly covered death by suicide. The actual reasoning is obsolete now that suicide is no longer a crime;[2] but the principle remains, that a promise to pay a sum of money to a person on the commission by him of a crime is generally illegal.

Problems of this kind commonly arise where one person promises to indemnify another against liability arising out of the commission of

---

15 Eg *Michael Richards Properties Ltd v Corpn of Wardens of St Saviour's Parish, Southwark* [1975] 3 All ER 416.
16 Eg *Dennis & Co Ltd v Munn* [1949] 2 KB 327.
17 Eg *Bigos v Bousted* [1951] 1 All ER 92.
18 Eg *Re Mahmoud and Ispahani* [1921] 2 KB 716; post, p 212.
19 See *Bedford Insurance Co Ltd v Instituto de Resseguros do Brasil* [1985] QB 966; *Phoenix General Insurance Co of Greece SA v Halvanon Insurance Co Ltd* [1988] QB 216 (where the statute had not been contravened).
20 Financial Services and Markets Act 2000, ss 26(1), 27(1).
1 *Beresford v Royal Insurance Co Ltd* [1938] AC 586.
2 Suicide Act 1961.

an unlawful act. Such liability may either be criminal or civil, and it may be incurred either deliberately (with guilty intent) or innocently; for the present purpose innocence will be taken to include negligence.

A promise to indemnify a person against *civil* liability innocently incurred is perfectly valid. Such a promise is made expressly whenever an insurance company undertakes to indemnify a person against civil liability (for example, for negligence); and a promise of this kind is enforceable against the insurer even if the negligent conduct also amounts to a crime – as it often does in the case of motor accidents.³ A promise to indemnify a person against civil liability may also be implied. For example, an agent who in good faith and with his principal's authority sells property which belongs to a third party, may be liable in conversion to the third party; and he is entitled to be indemnified by his principal against such liability.⁴ It seems that a promise to indemnify a person against *criminal* liability is also enforceable if the liability is incurred (as under modern legislation it quite commonly is) without guilty intent. For example a person may drive a car after being told by his insurance agent that he is properly insured. If this is not the case, the driver incurs criminal liability but he can nevertheless enforce the agent's implied promise to indemnify him against that liability.⁵

On the other hand, where the wrong is deliberately committed, the general principle is that the promise to indemnify is illegal.⁶ This is true whether the promise relates to criminal or to civil liability. If a passenger tells a taxi driver to break the speed limit and promises to pay the fine, the promise is not legally enforceable; and the same is true where a promise is made to indemnify a person against civil liability for deceit,⁷ or for publishing a statement which he knows to be defamatory.⁸ If a motorist deliberately causes injury to someone, he cannot recover from his insurer the damages which he has to pay the injured party.⁹ But the latter will often have a direct right against the motorist's insurer or against the Motor Insurers' Bureau;¹⁰ and this is not affected by the illegality which prevents the motorist himself from suing the insurer. If the injured party's right were so affected, the

---

3   *Tinline v White Cross Insurance Association* [1921] 3 KB 327.
4   *Adamson v Jarvis* (1827) 4 Bing 66.
5   *Osman v J Ralph Moss Ltd* [1970] 1 Lloyd's Rep 313.
6   *Gray v Barr* [1971] 2 QB 554.
7   *Brown Jenkinson & Co Ltd v Percy Dalton (London) Ltd* [1957] 2 QB 621.
8   *W H Smith & Sons Ltd v Clinton* (1908) 99 LT 840.
9   *Charlton v Fisher* [2002] QB 578.
10   See post, p 260; cf *Gardner v Moore* [1984] AC 548 at 560–561.

scheme of compulsory third party motor insurance would be seriously weakened.

2 CONTRACTS CONTRARY TO PUBLIC POLICY

Contracts are said to be contrary to public policy when they have a clear tendency to bring about a state of affairs which the law regards as harmful. Obviously, the attitude of the law towards such questions varies from time to time so as to reflect changing social attitudes and economic conditions. The resulting flexibility of the doctrine of public policy is a source of uncertainty, and it could, if carried to extremes, enable courts to invalidate any contracts of which they strongly disapproved. This danger has led some judges to take a somewhat restrictive view of the doctrine of public policy. Their attitude was summed up long ago in the statement that public policy is 'a very unruly horse and when once you get astride it you never know where it will carry you'.[11] Other judges have laid greater stress on the creative role of the courts in this area; and their attitude is, in turn, expressed in the statement that 'With a good man in the saddle the unruly horse can be kept in control'.[12] The present law is a compromise between these two attitudes.

On the one hand, the courts will not readily invent new 'heads' of public policy, that is, they will not generally apply the doctrine to contracts or clauses to which it has never been applied before. They are more reluctant to extend the doctrine in this way at the present time than they were when it was originally developed; and the reason for this is that the more important fields of public policy are now regarded as primarily a matter for Parliament.[13] It is, for example, unlikely that the courts in England would have made a significant contribution to solving the problem of racially discriminatory contracts. They would have regarded the problem as a political one, to be regulated mainly by Parliamentary legislation and not by judicial innovation.

On the other hand, 'where the subject-matter is "lawyer's law"'[14] the courts do still exercise a creative role in the field of public policy in a number of important ways. First, they have relatively little hesitation

---

11   *Richardson v Mellish* (1824) 2 Bing 229 at 252; *McFarlane v Tayside Health Board* [2000] 2 AC 59 at 100–101.

12   *Enderby Town Football Club Ltd v Football Association Ltd* [1971] Ch 591 at 606.

13   See *Cheall v Association of Professional, Executive, Clerical and Computer Staff* [1983] 2 AC 180 at 191; *Beavan Ashford v Geoff Yeandle (Contractors) Ltd* [1999] Ch 239 at 250.

14   *D v National Society for the Prevention of Cruelty to Children* [1978] AC 171 at 235.

in extending existing heads of public policy: for example once a contract falls within the general category of being in restraint of trade, the fact that it was made to further a policy of (for example) religious discrimination would quite probably lead to a holding that the restraint was not justified[15] and thus invalid. Secondly, the courts do still occasionally apply the doctrine of public policy to entirely new classes of contracts. For example, in one case[16] the doctrine was applied to a contract by which a trade journal promised not to comment on the affairs of a company, since this could prevent it from exposing even frauds committed by the company; and in another case[17] an agreement purporting to deprive an agricultural tenant of his statutory security of tenure was held to be contrary to public policy. There were no direct precedents for these decisions. Thirdly, the courts sometimes invalidate contracts, or terms of contracts, on grounds that are essentially based on public policy, but they forestall the criticism which an expansion of that doctrine would evoke by simply not mentioning it. The common law limitations on the effectiveness of exemption clauses,[18] and the rule that penalty clauses are invalid,[19] provide illustrations of this process.

The following types of contracts are at present regarded by the law as contrary to public policy. Contracts in restraint of trade also fall within this group, but give rise to problems of such complexity that it will be convenient to discuss them separately.

a   Immoral contracts

A contract is contrary to public policy if its object is to promote 'immorality'. In the present context, immorality seems to refer simply to extramarital sexual intercourse: the cases provide no illustration of any other kind of immorality which invalidates a contract. The principle most obviously makes illegal a promise to pay money for such intercourse; and the same is true of a contract which indirectly promotes this kind of immorality. For example a contract by which the owner of a brougham let it out to a prostitute, knowing that she intended to use it for the purpose of attracting customers, was held to be illegal.[20] And a contract of employment would be illegal if one of

15   Cf post, pp 199–202. For the prohibition of religious discrination in employment, see Employment Equality (Religion or Belief) Regulations 2003, SI 2003/1660.
16   *Neville v Dominion of Canada News Co Ltd* [1915] 3 KB 556.
17   *Johnson v Moreton* [1980] AC 37.
18   See ante, pp 96–97.
19   See post, pp 399–403.
20   *Pearce v Brooks* (1866) LR 1 Exch 213.

its terms were that the employee should procure prostitutes for the employer's clients.[1]

The law at one time took the view that all contracts which could be said to promote such immoral purposes were illegal; but it now recognises that 'cohabitation, whether heterosexual or homosexual, is widespread'.[2] It follows that, while the approach described above continues to govern contracts made for purely meretricious purposes, it no longer applies to the arrangements of persons who live together in a stable quasi-marital relationship without being married. Such an arrangement may, for example, confer legally enforceable rights in the accommodation which they share,[3] or in a joint bank account.[4] A contract between them to 'pool' their earnings would probably not be contrary to public policy;[5] and the same is true where the father of an illegitimate child promises to pay the mother money for its support.[6] Often the domestic arrangements of such parties will not be contracts for want of contractual intention;[7] but they will no longer be struck down on grounds of public policy.

b Contracts affecting the freedom and stability of marriage

The law of contract makes a number of assumptions about marriage, which are reflected in three sets of rules.

i Restraint of marriage

First, it assumes that everyone should be free to marry, so that a promise not to marry is *prima facie* invalid. The same is true of a promise by A to pay a sum of money by way of damages to B, in the event of A's marriage, this being in substance a promise not to marry.[8] In such cases the restraint on marriage is total, but if it were limited in such a way as to make it reasonable it might be valid: for example if a person promised not to marry before completing a course of training or study. Moreover, a contract which does not amount to an actual promise not to marry is not invalid merely because it may deter a person from marrying. This

---

1 See *Coral Leisure Group Ltd v Barnett* [1981] I CR 503 at 508.
2 *Barclays Bank plc v O'Brien* [1994] 1 AC 180 at 198; *Royal Bank of Scotland v Etridge (No 2)* [2001] UKHL 44, [2002] 2 AC 773 at [44].
3 Eg *Tanner v Tanner* [1975] 3 All ER 776; *Eves v Eves* [1975] 3 All ER 768; *Ghaidan v Mendoza* [2004] UKHL 30, [2004] 3 All ER 411.
4 *Paul v Constance* [1977] 1 All ER 195.
5 See the American case of *Marvin v Marvin* 557 P 2d 106 (1976).
6 *Horrocks v Forray* [1976] 1 WLR 230 at 239; cf *Ward v Byham* [1956] 2 All ER 318.
7 See ante, p 61.
8 *Lowe v Peers* (1768) 4 Burr 2225.

would be the position where a contract was made to pay an allowance until marriage, or where some other benefit under a contract was to cease on marriage.

ii   Marriage brokage

The law secondly takes the view that the arranging of marriages should not be made into a business; so that a contract to find a spouse for a client in return for a fee is invalid.[9] The law on the point is settled, but the harmful tendencies (if any) of such contracts are scarcely so clear as to justify their invalidation on grounds of public policy. It seems unlikely that 'computer dating' contracts would be held invalid.

iii   Protecting existing marriages

The law wants to protect existing marriages; and the law of contract plays some (though probably not a very significant) part in the pursuit of that aim. The overriding principle is that an agreement tending to weaken the marriage bond is invalid. This principle is the basis of three separate rules.

First, an agreement between husband and wife while they are living together, and providing for the terms of a possible future separation, is invalid; and the same is true where such an agreement is made even before marriage (as it sometimes was in the case of a 'shotgun' marriage).[10] The reasoning behind the rule is that, if such an agreement were valid, it might give one of the parties an incentive to break up the marriage. Obviously, this reasoning does not apply where the marriage has already broken up, so that separation agreements made *after* a separation has occurred are valid.[11] Moreover, an agreement for future separation is valid if made as part of the reconciliation of parties previously separated.[12] The purpose of this rule is to promote reconciliation, which might be less likely if the parties could not provide for future separation.

Secondly, the law at one time invalidated agreements which tended to facilitate divorce, for example by specifying the wife's rights to maintenance. Such agreements were thought to amount, or to lead, to collusion, which was formerly a bar to divorce. Now that collusion has ceased to be a bar to divorce, such agreements are no longer contrary to public policy,[13] and the law provides machinery for

9   *Hermann v Charlesworth* [1905] 2 KB 123.
10   *Brodie v Brodie* [1917] P 271.
11   *Wilson v Wilson* (1848) 1 HL Cas 538.
12   *Harrison v Harrison* [1910] 1 KB 35.
13   *Sutton v Sutton* [1984] Ch 184 at 194.

submitting them to the court for its approval.[14] An agreement of this kind will be invalid at common law only in the rare case where it amounts to a corrupt bargain, such as a conspiracy to deceive the court.

A third rule relates to promises by married persons to marry. A person who broke a promise to marry was formerly liable in damages for breach of contract. But this action for breach of promise in marriage could not be brought when the promisor was, to the knowledge of the promisee, already married when the promise was made.[15] In that case, the promise was said to have a tendency to break up the existing marriage and to lead to immorality, though it is far from clear how the promisor's immunity from liability for breach of promise protected his existing marriage. The action for breach of promise of marriage was abolished[16] by an Act of 1970; but that Act provides that 'where an agreement to marry is terminated'[17] the parties may have certain rights in each other's property. A party can assert such rights even though before the Act he could not have sued for breach of promise of marriage by reason of being already married when the promise was made;[18] and it seems to follow that the other (unmarried) party to the dissolved engagement must have the same rights. Difficult problems can obviously arise in balancing the rights of that party against those of the promisor's spouse: eg where a man had lived in the same house with his wife and then with a fiancée from whom he had later parted.

c Contracts excluding the jurisdiction of the courts

The parties to a contract may provide that disputes arising under it shall be settled extra-judicially, by arbitration; and that no action shall be brought on the contract until the decision of the arbitrator has been obtained.[19] Such arbitration clauses are generally speaking valid. Indeed, if one of the parties to the contract disregards such a clause and brings an action without going to arbitration, he is liable in damages at common law;[20] and by statute the court must, where arbitration agreement is in writing, generally stay the action,[1] and so in effect compel a party to resort to arbitration. The process of

---

14 Matrimonial Causes Act 1973, s 33A.
15 Eg *Spiers v Hunt* [1908] 1 KB 720.
16 Law Reform (Miscellaneous Provisions) Act 1970, s 1.
17 Law Reform (Miscellaneous Provisions) Act 1970, s 2(1).
18 *Shaw v Fitzgerald* [1992] 1 FLR 357.
19 *Scott v Avery* (1856) 5 HL Cas 811.
20 *Channel Tunnel Group Ltd v Balfour Beatty Construction Ltd* [1993] AC 334.
1   Arbitration Act 1996, ss 5(1), 9(4). For an exception in the case of certain arbitration agreements in contracts with consumers, see s 91.

arbitration is, however, subject to a considerable degree of judicial control: in particular the court may grant leave to appeal from an arbitrator on a point of law.[2] The original common law position was that any attempt by contract to exclude judicial control of arbitrations was contrary to public policy; for it might lead to the parties being bound by an arbitrator's decision even though it contravened some peremptory rule of law.[3] But the impossibility of excluding judicial control was a source of delay in arbitration proceedings; and the Arbitration Act 1996 states that, in general, parties should be 'free to agree how their disputes are to be resolved';[4] and it further enables parties to a written arbitration agreement to exclude by agreement the judicial control available under the Act.[5]

The rule that parties cannot effectively exclude the jurisdiction of the courts, has also been applied where a husband in matrimonial proceedings promises to pay his wife an allowance and she, in return, promises not to apply for maintenance. Here the wife's promise is invalid because her right to maintenance is a 'matter of public concern which she cannot barter away'.[6] It follows that she can still apply to the court in spite of her promise not to do so. Alternately she can, if the agreement is in writing, sue the husband for the promised allowance.[7]

The rule finally applies where the rules of an association purport to give exclusive power to the association to construe the rules. Since a question of construction is one of law, the attempt to deprive the courts of their jurisdiction over it is ineffective.[8]

d   Contracts which pervert the course of justice

The public has an interest in the enforcement of the criminal law, so that, as a general rule, criminal charges cannot validly be compromised by private agreement between the criminal and the victim. Sometimes, indeed, an agreement to stifle a prosecution may itself amount to the crime of concealing an arrestable offence[9] and be invalid on that

---

2   Arbitration Act 1996, s 69; under s 45 the court can also determine preliminary questions of law. For guidelines as to the exercise of the court's discretion to grant leave, see s 69(3), based on (but going slightly beyond) those laid down in *The Nema* [1982] AC 724.
3   *Czarnikow v Roth, Schmidt & Co* [1922] 2 KB 478.
4   Section 1(b); 'subject to such controls as are necessary in the public interest'.
5   Sections 69(1) and 45(1) ('unless otherwise agreed').
6   *Hyman v Hyman* [1929] AC 601 at 629.
7   Matrimonial Causes Act 1973, s 34: not where the agreement is oral, as in *Sutton v Sutton* [1984] Ch 184.
8   *Lee v Showmen's Guild of Great Britain* [1952] 2 QB 329.
9   Criminal Law Act 1967, s 5(1); and see Police and Criminal Evidence Act 1984, s 24(1) for the definition of 'arrestable offence'.

ground[10] but even where this is not the case (eg because the offence in question is not an arrestable one) the general principle is that the contract is illegal. For example, agreements to stifle prosecutions for riot, perjury and assaulting a police officer have all been held illegal.[11] On the other hand, it has been held that certain offences of a 'private' nature could be validly compromised. This rule has been applied to such disparate crimes as assaults by a husband and wife on each other and trade-mark offences.[12] In such cases, there was thought to be no strong public interest in prosecuting the offender; and the same may sometimes be true where the victim agrees not to prosecute the criminal, if the latter will make good any loss caused by the offence.

A contract may be illegal under the present heading even though it does not affect criminal proceedings. All that is necessary is that there should be a strong public interest in the outcome of the proceedings. An agreement to obstruct bankruptcy proceedings is accordingly illegal because of its tendency to prejudice creditors generally.[13] Corrupt agreements relating to matrimonial proceedings are likewise illegal, if they pervert the course of justice.

e Contracts to deceive public authorities

Such contracts often amount to criminal conspiracies but they may be illegal even where this is not the case, eg because one party is innocent. This was, for example, the position where a landlord drew up a lease in two documents so as to enable him to defraud the rating authorities, but the tenant did not know that this was the landlord's purpose.[14] A contract of employment would similarly be illegal if its purpose was to defraud the Revenue; eg by providing that the employee should receive 'expenses' in excess of those actually incurred,[15] or that part of his pay should be concealed from the tax authorities.[16] This rule applies only where there is an intention to defraud, so that a contract of employment can lawfully provide for the employee's pay to be 'free of tax', so long as the employer pays the revenue authorities the tax due.[17]

10 Ante, p 184.
11 *Collins v Blantern* (1767) 2 Wils 341; *Keir v Leeman* (1846) 9 QB 371; *Windhill Local Board v Vint* (1890) 45 Ch D 351.
12 *McGregor v McGregor* (1888) 21 QBD 424; *Fisher & Co v Apollinaris Co* (1875) 10 Ch App 297.
13 *Elliott v Richardson* (1870) LR 5 CP 744.
14 *Alexander v Rayson* [1936] 1 KB 169; contrast *21st Century Logistic Solutions v Madaysen Ltd* [2004] EWHC 231 (QB) (intention to evade VAT).
15 *Miller v Karlinski* (1945) 62 TLR 85; cf *Hyland v JH Barker (North West) Ltd* [1985] ICR 861.
16 Cf *Corby v Morrison* [1980] ICR 564.
17 See *Newland v Simons and Willer (Hairdressers) Ltd* [1981] ICR 521.

f   Contracts prejudicing the public service

Contracts for the sale of public offices, honours and commissions in the armed forces are illegal as they tend to lead to corruption or inefficiency in the public service.[18] On similar grounds, a contract purporting to bind a Member of Parliament to vote in accordance with the dictates of some person or body outside Parliament is illegal;[19] and a contract by which one party agrees to 'lobby' on behalf of the other for government contracts may be illegal.[20]

g   Trading with an enemy

It is a statutory offence to trade in time of war with an 'enemy', that is with a person voluntarily resident or carrying on business in enemy occupied territory. A contract which involves trading with an 'enemy' is illegal at common law, though the modern practice is to deal with the matter by war-time legislation.[1]

h   Contracts to break the law of a foreign country

A contract is illegal if its purpose is to do an act in a friendly foreign country which is contrary to the law of that country. On this ground, it has been held that a contract to smuggle whisky into the United States during the prohibition period was illegal.[2] and the same would be true of a contract which required goods to be illegally exported from their foreign country of origin in violation of its laws.[3] Such contracts are contrary to public policy as they are thought to prejudice good foreign relations. But if an English company sold arms to one foreign state, the contract would not be illegal merely because it was known that the arms were to be used in a war with a second foreign country.

---

18   *Morris v M'Cullock* (1763) Amb 432; *Garforth v Fearon* (1787) 1 Hy Bl 328; *Parkinson v College of Ambulance Ltd* [1925] 2 KB 1 (cf Honours (Prevention of Abuses) Act 1925).
19   *Amalgamated Society of Railway Servants v Osborne* [1910] AC 87.
20   *Lemenda Trading Co Ltd v African Middle East Petroleum Co Ltd* [1988] QB 448; contrast *Tekron Resources Ltd v Guinea Investment Co* [2003] EWHC 2577 (Comm), [2004] 2 Lloyd's Rep 26.
1   Trading with the Enemy Act 1939.
2   *Foster v Driscoll* [1929] 1 KB 470.
3   *Soleimany v Soleimany* [1999] QB 785 at 797.

i   Undue restrictions on personal liberty

In extreme cases, contracts may be illegal on the ground that they unreasonably restrict one party's personal freedom. This was held to be the position where a moneylending contract provided that the borrower should not, without the consent of the lender, change his job or his residence, borrow money elsewhere or dispose of any of his property.[4] Similarly, a contract by which a man assigned the *whole* of his salary, which was his sole means of support, has been held invalid.[5]

3   CONTRACTS IN RESTRAINT OF TRADE

The most important group of contracts contrary to public policy are those in restraint of trade. The law relating to these contracts provides a particularly good illustration of the flexible nature of the doctrine of public policy. It has undergone many changes in the course of history and is even today in a considerable state of flux. The overriding common law principle, however, is clear. Contractual provisions in restraint of trade are prima facie void, but they will be upheld if they are reasonable and not contrary to public interest. They can be divided into the following classes or categories.

a   Sale of a business and employment

The first group consists of provisions in contracts for the sale of a business by which the seller undertakes not to compete with the buyer; and of provisions in contracts of employment by which the employee undertakes that he will not, after leaving the employer, compete with him, or take up employment with a competitor. The validity of such restraints depends on three points.

i   A 'proprietary interest'

A person who sells a business sells, amongst other things, the goodwill, and the law will protect the buyer's interest in the goodwill by restraining the seller from canvassing the old customers of the business. It will do so even in the absence of a covenant in restraint of trade, for it regards the buyer as having acquired a 'proprietary interest' in the goodwill.[6] This 'proprietary interest' is the buyer's interest in

---

4   *Horwood v Millar's Timber and Trading Co* [1917] 1 KB 305.
5   *King v Michael Faraday & Partners* [1939] 2 KB 753.
6   Cf *Trego v Hunt* [1896] AC 7.

the business which he has bought. It does not extend to his interest in any other business which he already owned or which he hoped afterwards to carry on. If A owns a bookshop in Oxford and buys one from B in Cambridge, A can validly stipulate that B is not to set up another bookshop in Cambridge. But he cannot validly stipulate that B is not to set up a bookshop in Oxford or sell computers in Cambridge. Such restraints would not be related to the relevant proprietary interest, which is that in the goodwill of a bookselling business in Cambridge. Much less could A validly buy off competition by an independent contract not related to the sale of any business at all. If A owned a bookshop in Oxford and B simply threatened to set up a rival bookshop there, A would have no proprietary interest to which a restraint on B could be attached. An agreement by which A promised a sum of money to B, in consideration simply of B's not setting up a bookshop in Oxford, would therefore be invalid. Such an agreement is sometimes called a covenant 'in gross', an expression used to emphasise the point that it is not related to any 'proprietary interest'.

The 'proprietary interest' of an employer is more narrowly defined than that of the buyer of a business. The traditional reason for this distinction is that the courts in restraint of trade cases attach importance to disparity of bargaining power[7] and consider that an employee needs greater protection than the seller of a business. It is also the case that the buyer of a business pays for (amongst other things) freedom from competition, while an employer pays only (or very largely) for the services of the employee. The employer therefore does not have a 'proprietary interest' merely because the business in which the employee works would suffer from competition. He must go further and show one of two things: either that the employee has come into contact with the employer's customers or clients in such a way as to acquire influence over them; or that he has learned the employer's 'trade secrets' (such as secret processes and formulae and 'know-how')[8] or other confidential information. These interests are again 'proprietary' in the sense that the law protects them, even if there is no stipulation in restraint of trade. The employee can be restrained from soliciting the employer's customers *during employment* and from using or disclosing the employer's trade secrets *at any time*;[9] while the restriction on the use of confidential information is normally limited to the period of employment but may extend beyond it: eg where the employee copies or memorises lists of customers, or where

---

7   *A Schroder Music Publishing Co Ltd v Macaulay* [1974] 1 WLR 1308 at 1315.
8   *Caribonum Co Ltd v Le Couch* (1913) 109 LT 587; *Commercial Plastics Ltd v Vincent* [1965] 1 QB 623 at 642.
9   *Printers and Finishers Ltd v Holloway* [1964] 3 All ER 731; *Wessex Dairies Ltd v Smith* [1935] 2 KB 80.

he proposes actually to sell such information as opposed to using it to earn his living.[10] Employees in the public service are also under a lifelong duty to treat certain types of information as confidential.[11] In the absence of any such proprietary interest, a restraint cannot be imposed on an employee merely because he has, in the course of his employment, acquired some general skill,[12] eg because he has been trained by the employer as a skilled electrician or carpenter.

There are borderline cases in which the relationship does not fall into either the employer and employee, or into the vendor and purchaser category: for example, where a restraint is contained in a partnership agreement between solicitors or doctors, or in a contract between a writer or composer and his publisher. In such cases, courts have regard to the relative bargaining power of the parties: thus they would not subject the restraint in the partnership case to the stringent tests that govern the validity of a restraint between employer and employee;[13] while those tests were applied, even in the absence of an employment relationship where a young, and relatively unknown, song-writer promised not to dispose of his work except to a particular publisher.[14]

ii Reasonableness

Assuming that there is a 'proprietary interest', the next requirement of validity is that the restraint must be 'reasonable'. This does not mean that the scope of the covenant must be identical with that of the interest. If this were the law, covenants in restraint of trade would be pointless since a 'proprietary interest' is (by definition) protected even in the absence of such a covenant. The 'proprietary interest' of the buyer of a business is merely that the seller should not *solicit* his old customers: not that the seller should not *deal* with them if they come to him of their own accord. It is against such other competition that the buyer can protect himself by a covenant in restraint of trade.[15] The question whether the covenant is reasonable depends primarily on the relation between it and the interest protected; and the covenant will be unreasonable if it goes further than reasonably necessary for the protection of that interest in point of space, time or subject matter. For example, the buyer of a shop whose customers live within five miles can validly stipulate that the seller must not set up a similar

---

10   *Faccenda Chicken Ltd v Fowler* [1987] Ch 117 at 139.

11   *A-G v Guardian Newspapers Ltd (No 2)* [1990] 1 AC 109 at 264, 284; for express covenants to this effect, see post, p 201, n 5.

12   *Herbert Morris Ltd v Saxelby* [1916] 1 AC 688.

13   *Bridge v Deacons* [1984] AC 705 at 714; *Kerr v Morris* [1987] Ch 90.

14   See *A Schroeder Music Publishing Co Ltd v Macaulay* [1974] 1 WLR 1308.

15   See *John Michael Design plc v Cooke* [1987] ICR 445.

shop within that radius. But a covenant against competition within fifty miles would be void, however much the parties both wished to enter into it.[16] Where the nature of the business demands it, a very extensive restraint may be regarded as reasonably necessary. In the leading *Nordenfelt*[17] case, a world-wide restraint was imposed on the Swedish seller of an armaments business to an English company. The restraint was upheld, since the customers of the business included governments throughout the world; but such a restraint would not be upheld where the proprietary interest related only to business done in one country.[18] The question whether a covenant is excessive in point of time similarly depends on the length of time for which the business sold would normally be expected to retain its clientèle. So far as subject-matter is concerned, the covenant can validly restrain the seller from competing only with the type of activity carried on by the business sold. Thus it has been held that the seller of an *imitation* jewellery business cannot be restrained from competing with the buyer in the sale of *real* jewellery.[19]

The position is similar in employment contracts. Suppose that an employer has a 'proprietary interest' in trade secrets. It would be pointless for him to take a covenant against the use or disclosure of these secrets, since he is protected against such conduct even in the absence of the covenant. What he can do is to use the interest as a peg on which to hang a restraint against competition within reasonable limits of space and time. If this were not possible, it would be very hard for the employer to prove that his proprietary interests were being infringed. In particular, it would be hard for him to prove that his trade secrets were being exploited by the employee while working for a rival concern. On the other hand, where the proprietary interest consists of trade connections, a blanket restraint covering an entire area might be unreasonable, for it would prevent the employee from working in the whole of the area, even though the employer had only dealt with a relatively small number of persons within it. The law therefore distinguishes, in this group of cases, between *area* covenants and *solicitation* covenants. The latter restrain the employee only from dealing with the employer's customers or clients, and leave the employee free to compete in other respects. In employment cases, the current judicial trend is to strike down area covenants, but to uphold the less restrictive solicitation covenants. It may be a further

---

16   See *Empire Meat Co Ltd v Patrick* [1939] 2 All ER 85; cf *Spencer v Marchington* [1988] IRLR 392.
17   [1894] AC 535.
18   *Lansing Linde Ltd v Kerr* [1991] 1 All ER 418 at 425.
19   *Goldsoll v Goldman* [1915] 1 Ch 292.

requirement in such cases that the covenant must be confined to customers or clients with whom the employee came into contact in the course of his work for the employer;[20] but a solicitation covenant between partners in a firm of solicitors has been upheld even where this requirement was not satisfied.[1] All this is not to say that, even in employment cases, area covenants may not be upheld if the area covered is only a small one.[2] In 1921 the House of Lords still upheld a restraint on a solicitor's managing clerk against practising within seven miles of his principal's office after the end of his employment.[3] But this was before the distinction between area and solicitation covenants had achieved its present prominence; and such a restraint might now well be regarded as excessive.[4] A restraint in a contract of employment may further be unreasonable for excessive duration. Thus where the employer's clientèle was of a fluctuating nature, a five-year restraint was held to be too long;[4a] while, on the other hand, in the case of the solicitor's managing clerk (mentioned above) a life-long restraint was regarded as reasonable. Life-long covenants not to disclose information obtained in the course of employment can also be enforced since these do not prevent the employee from working for others.[5] Finally a restraint may be unreasonable because it relates to some form of activity in which the employee was not employed. On this ground, a restraint on a person employed as a tailor against working as a hatter has been held invalid.[6]

In deciding whether a restraint is reasonable, the court also has regard to the adequacy of the consideration given for it and to the relative bargaining strengths of the parties.[7] It follows that where a restraint is imposed on the weaker party the fairness of the bargain is a necessary condition of its reasonableness.[8] In determining the issue of fairness, the court has to take into account not only the extent of the restraint, but also the benefits which the contract as a whole confers

---

20 *G W Plowman & Son Ltd v Ash* [1964] 2 All ER 10; cf *T Lucas & Co Ltd v Mitchell* [1972] 2 All ER 1035; *Marley Tile Co Ltd v Johnson* [1982] IRLR 75 and see *Mason v Provident Clothing and Supply Co Ltd* [1913] AC 724; *Spencer v Marchington* [1988] IRLR 392.

1 *Bridge v Deacons* [1984] AC 705; cf ante, p 199.

2 *Hollis & Co v Stocks* [2000] UKCLR 685.

3 *Fitch v Dewes* [1921] 2 AC 158.

4 See *Fellowes & Son v Fishe* [1976] QB 122.

4ᵃ *M and S Drapers v Reynolds* [1956] 3 All ER 814; cf SI 1993/3053, reg 20(2), prescribing a maximum two-year period in the case of 'commercial agents'.

5 Eg, *A-G v Barker* [19990] 3 All ER 257 (covenant by employee of Royal Household); *A-G v Blake* [2001] 1 AC 688 (covenant by employee of security services).

6 *Attwood v Lamont* [1920] 3 KB 571.

7 *Nordenfelt v Maxim Nordenfelt Guns and Ammunition Co Ltd* [1894] AC 535 at 565; *A Schroeder Music Publishing Co v Macaulay* [1974] 1 WLR 1308 at 1316.

8 Ibid; *Clifford Davis Management Co Ltd v WEA Records Ltd* [1975] 1 WLR 61 at 65.

on the party subject to the restraint.[9] The requirement of fairness must be satisfied as well as those discussed above; ie the restraint must go no further than necessary for the protection of the interest *and* it must be fair. Where there is no inequality of bargaining power the additional requirement of fairness does not apply.

iii   Public interest

A restraint which is reasonable in relation to the interest meriting protection may, nevertheless, be invalid on the ground that it is clearly contrary to the public interest. This requirement is not always easily separable from that of reasonableness, since both are in the last resort imposed on account of the broad public interest in freedom to trade. But it is possible to imagine a case in which the restraint, though reasonable in the sense that it secures to the buyer no more than the clientèle of the business which he has bought, is one which nevertheless prejudices the public by depriving it of much needed additional services of the kind provided by the business.[10] This might be the position on the sale of a medical practice. A restraint on one of the partners would not be struck down merely on the ground that particular patients wished to continue to be treated by that partner;[11] but it might be contrary to the public interest if, in the area covered by it, there was a shortage of doctors.

iv   Other problems relating to employment

The above discussion of restraints in employment contracts is based on two assumptions. The first is that there is an undertaking not to compete; but it seems that the same rules may apply, even though there is no such undertaking, if the *effect* of the contract is to stifle competition. Thus the doctrine of restraint of trade was applied to a contract under which an employee was, on his retirement, promised a pension on the terms that it would cease to be paid if he competed with his employer.[12] The second assumption is that the undertaking comes into effect *after* the employment has come to an end, so that the rules as to restraint of trade do not normally apply to an undertaking not to compete during employment:[13] indeed, the

---

9   Cf *Alec Lobb (Garages) Ltd v Total Oil (GB) Ltd* [1985] 1 All ER 303; *Bridge v Deacons* [1984] AC 705 at 716.
10   cf *Dranez Anstalt v Hayek* [2002] EWCA Civ 1729, [2003] 1 BCLC 278 at [25].
11   *Kerr v Morris* [1987] Ch 90; cf *Bridge v Deacons* [1984] AC 705 at 720.
12   *Wyatt v Kreglinger and Fernau* [1933] 1 KB 793; cf *Stenhouse Australia Ltd v Phillips* [1974] AC 391; *Sadler v Imperial Life Assurance Co of Canada Ltd* [1988] IRLR 388.
13   Eg *Evening Standard Co Ltd v Henderson* [1987] ICR 588.

employee's implied undertaking of faithful service would normally rule out such competition.[14] But there may be exceptional cases in which a restraint operative during employment would be invalid. This would, in particular, be the case where the employment was a long term one, or one giving the employer options to renew, and where such provisions were in fact used to stifle competition.[15]

b Restrictive trading and similar agreements

Agreements regulating competition between commercial suppliers of goods or services are subject to the common law of restraint of trade. They differ from the types of restraint so far discussed in that the interest meriting protection does not have to be a 'proprietary' one, that is, one which the law would protect even in the absence of an agreement in restraint of trade. Purely commercial interests, such as 'stability in ... lists of customers'[16] have been regarded as sufficient to support the validity of agreements of this kind. Once such an interest was established (and there was rarely any difficulty in doing this) the agreement was subject to the usual requirements of validity: that is, it must be reasonable and not contrary to the public interest. In fact, the courts interpreted these requirements leniently in this class of cases, so that agreements of this kind were only ever held invalid in extreme cases: for example, if the effect of the agreement was to force a party out of business, or if it provided that he could not withdraw from his trade association without the consent of its committee.[17] The common law was reluctant to disturb trading agreements between parties who were supposed to have bargained on equal terms.

But this attitude, though perhaps defensible in disputes between those two parties, might cause hardship to third parties who suffered from the high prices or scarcities which such agreements could create. Where the validity of the agreement was contested by one of the parties to it, the law could to some extent take account of such hardships, by holding that they made the contact contrary to the public interest. For example, an agreement between employers not to give jobs to each other's former employees might be invalidated on the ground that it unreasonably restricted the employees' opportunities to find work.[18] But this line of attack did nothing to solve the most pressing problem of all, which arose from the fact that agreements of

14   *Faccenda Chicken Ltd v Fowler* [1987] Ch 117 at 135–136.
15   Cf *A Schroeder Music Publishing Co Ltd v Macaulay* [1974] 3 All ER 616.
16   *McEllistrim's Case* [1919] AC 548 at 564.
17   *McEllistrim's Case* [1919] AC 548.
18   *Kores Manufacturing Co Ltd v Kolok Manufacturing Co Ltd* [1959] Ch 108.

trade associations were rarely broken, since they benefited the parties to them. It was at one time thought that third parties who were prejudiced by such agreements had no remedy merely on that account. Hence it followed that, though the agreement might not be enforceable, the parties could not be prevented from acting in accordance with it, if they so desired.[19] More recently, the common law began in a few cases to allow third parties to challenge such agreements.[20] It has also been suggested that an injunction might be available against a professional association to a person who had been excluded from it on grounds not relevant to his capacity to work in that profession.[1] But it is doubtful whether this remedy is available to a person who has no cause of action against the association (eg because he has no contract with it);[2] and judicial intervention on this ground is in any event restricted to cases in which the 'right to work' (one of the interests traditionally stressed by the common law) is at stake.[3]

At common law, trade union rules were subject to the restraint of trade doctrine. But this state of the law was changed by legislation long ago; and the present position is that union rules are not unenforceable by reason only of their being in restraint of trade.[4] But they may be ineffective on other related grounds. In particular, an employee or person seeking employment has a statutory right not to be excluded or expelled from a union except in specified circumstances;[5] and union rules are unenforceable unless they satisfy one or more of a number of criteria laid down by the legislation: eg they may validly restrict membership by reference to qualifications for the type of work in question.[6]

19   Cf *Boddington v Lawton* [1994] ICR 478.
20   *Eastham v Newcastle United Football Club Ltd* [1964] Ch 413, allowing a professional footballer to challenge the 'retain and transfer system'. In *Union Royale Belge des Sociétés de Football Association ASBL v Bosman* Case C-415/93 [1996] All ER (EC) 97 the system was held to contravene Art 48 (now Art 39) of the European Community Treaty; cf *Greig v Insole* [1978] 3 All ER 449; *Newport Association Football Club Ltd v Football Association of Wales* [1995] 2 All ER 87.
1   *Nagle v Feilden* [1966] 2 QB 633, a case of sex discrimination which would now be unlawful under the Sex Discrimination Acts 1975 and 1986. Discrimination on, eg, religious or political grounds by a 'public authority' might give the excluded person a remedy by virtue of Human Rights Act 1998, s 6 and Sch I, Pt I, arts 9 and 14. For religious discrimination in employment, see ante, p 190, n 15.
2   *R v Disciplinary Committee of the Jockey Club, ex p Aga Khan* [1993] 2 All ER 853 at 875–876.
3   *Cheall v Association of Professional, Executive, Clerical and Computer Staff* [1983] 2 AC 180 at 191 ('no poaching' agreement between trade unions).
4   Trade Union and Labour Relations (Consolidation) Act 1992, s 11.
5   Trade Union and Labour Relations (Consolidation) Act 1992, ss 174–177.
6   Trade Union and Labour Relations (Consolidation) Act 1992, s 174(3).

c Exclusive dealing and service agreements

It commonly happens that a buyer of goods agrees to buy all his requirements from a particular seller, or that a seller undertakes to sell his whole output to a particular buyer, or that a person agrees to employ another as his 'sole agent'. At common law, the general view used to be that exclusive dealing agreements were not invalid for restraint of trade. But this view was challenged in a line of cases concerning the so-called 'solus petrol agreements'. Under such an agreement a garage proprietor would give a number of undertakings to an oil company, usually in return for financial help by way of loans or discounts or both. The purpose of the agreement would be to ensure that the company's brand of petrol, and no other brand, was to be sold from the garage in question. Hence the agreement would provide that the proprietor should buy all his petrol from the company; keep his garage open for the sale of petrol at all reasonable times; and, if he should sell the garage, that he should obtain similar undertakings from the buyer. In the leading *Esso* case[7] the House of Lords held that such agreements were within the doctrine of restraint of trade, and thus required justification. Solus agreements were later the subject of a report by the Monopolies Commission[8] and the practice with respect to them was governed by undertakings given by the oil companies after that report. But the decision in the *Esso* case is still important for the guidance which it provides as to the common law principles governing the validity of exclusive dealing agreements in general.

The first and most difficult question is which such agreements are within the common law doctrine of restraint of trade at all. This has been said to depend on such factors as whether the agreement restrains or only regulates trade; and whether it is of a kind that has 'passed into the normal currency of ... contractual relations'.[9] Under these tests sole agency distributorship agreements are normally outside the doctrine of restraint of trade; but in the *Esso* case the solus system was held to be within the doctrine, largely because it was a novel system which had not yet acquired settled and stereotyped features. However, even contracts which have acquired such features may be within the doctrine, especially if they are not freely negotiated but made between parties of greatly disparate bargaining power. For example, in one case an unknown song-writer undertook to give his

---

7   *Esso Petroleum Co Ltd v Harper's Garage (Stourport) Ltd* [1968] AC 269.
8   Now the Competition Commission: see Competition Act 1998, s 45; Enterprise Act 2002, s 185.
9   [1968] AC at 332–333.

services exclusively to a publisher who made no promise to publish his work. It was held that the contract was subject to the restraint of trade doctrine as it was 'capable of enforcement in an oppressive manner'.[10] It seems probable that in future the courts will hold exclusive dealing and service agreements to be within the restraint of trade doctrine if they contain novel or unusual features; or if there is disparity of bargaining power and the agreement is likely to cause hardship to the weaker party.

If an exclusive dealing agreement is within the restraint of trade doctrine, the usual requirements have to be satisfied. First, there must be an interest meriting protection. In the *Esso* case this was described as the oil company's 'network of outlets'[11] and it is clear that (in the terminology used above) a 'commercial' as opposed to a 'proprietary' interest is sufficient. Secondly, the agreement must be reasonable in relation to the interest. In the *Esso* case this was held to depend on the probable effect of breach of the agreement on the oil company's distribution system. A twenty-one-year agreement was held unreasonable, as it attempted to look too far into the uncertain future; but an agreement covering a period of only four and a half years was upheld. Where the restriction is imposed on the weaker party to a relationship of unequal bargaining power, the fairness of the contract is again, relevant to its reasonableness. This requirement was, for example, not satisfied in the case of the unknown song-writer mentioned above.[12] The agreement for his exclusive services was for a term of five years and was held to be unfair as it did not oblige the publishers either to publish songs which the composer was required to submit to them or to pay him more than nominal amounts. The position would be different where terms were negotiated between a composer of established reputation with the help of expert legal (or other professional) advice;[13] and where the party subject to the restriction obtained considerable benefits under it and the other party had not made any unfair use of its superior bargaining power.[14] Thirdly, the agreement must not be contrary to the public interest; failure to satisfy this requirement was another ground on which the twenty-one-year agreement was held invalid in the *Esso* case.

---

10 *A Schroeder Music Publishing Co Ltd v Macaulay* [1974] 1 WLR 1308 at 1314; cf *O'Sullivan v Management Agency and Music Ltd* [1985] QB 428.
11 [1968] AC 269 at 329.
12 *A Schroeder Music Publishing Co ltd v Macaulay* [1974] 1 WLR 1308; cf *Watson v Prager* [1991] 3 All ER 487 (where boxing manager's and promoter's conflict of interest made the agreement unfair).
13 *Panayiotou v Sony Music Entertainment (UK) Ltd* (1994) Times, 30 June.
14 *Alex Lobb (Garages) Ltd v Total Oil (GB) Ltd* [1985] 1 WLR 173 (a 'solus' case).

d Restrictions on the use of land

Land is often sold subject to covenants which restrict its use: for example, by prohibiting building, or the carrying on of some particular trade, or of any trade at all. Such restrictive covenants are commonly enforced, and in the *Esso* case it was said that they were not subject to the doctrine of restraint of trade. The reason for this was said to be that the purchaser of the land 'had no previous right to be there at all, let alone to trade there, and when he takes possession of that land, subject to a negative restrictive covenant, he gives up no right or freedom which he previously had'.[15] It follows that even a solus agreement entered into by a purchaser of land as a term of the purchase is perfectly valid, irrespective of its extent. The reasoning seems to ignore the possibility that a solus agreement in a contract of sale may offend the public interest, just as much as one which is contained in a mortgage raised by a person who already owned the garage premises; and there is no doubt that a restriction in such a mortgage is within the doctrine of restraint of trade.[16] Even a restrictive covenant imposed on the sale of land may, by a special statutory provision, be modified or discharged on a number of grounds, one of which is that the continued existence of the covenant 'would impede some reasonable user of the land for public or private purposes'.[17] Since the purchaser will probably have paid less for the land on account of the restriction, he may be ordered to pay compensation as a condition of being released from the covenant or of having it modified.

e Other agreements

It has been said that the categories of restraint of trade are not closed;[18] for an agreement may restrain trade even though it falls outside the types so far considered. This would, for example, be true of an agreement by one manufacturer not to produce certain goods in competition with another; and of restrictions on the use of intellectual property imposed by an agreement for the settlement of disputes relating to it.[19] This is not to say that such agreements would be invalid,[20] but merely that they would have to be justified in accordance

---

15 [1968] AC 269 at 268.
16 *Texaco Ltd v Mulberry Filling Station Ltd* [1972] 1 WLR 814.
17 Law of Property Act 1925, s 84 (amended by Law of Property Act 1969, s 28).
18 *Esso* case [1968] AC 269 at 337.
19 *World Wide Fund for Nature v World Wrestling Federation* [2002] EWCA Civ 196, [2002] UKCLR 388 at [40]–[42].
20 The agreement in the *World Wide* case, supra, n 19, was held valid.

with the usual requirements of the doctrine. Two further types of agreements are covered by special statutory provisions. Price maintenance agreements were valid at common law, but may now be void under legislation discussed below.[1] Agreements between two or more persons not to bid against each other at an auction were likewise valid at common law; but if at least one of the parties to the agreement is a dealer, they may be guilty of a statutory offence.[2] If the agreement not to bid amounts to a crime, it is no doubt illegal and any resulting contract of sale between one of the parties and the owner of the auctioned property can be set aside by the latter.

f   Competition law

The common law relating to restrictive trading agreements gives only limited protection to third parties.[3] This problem is now dealt with by the Competition Act 1998 which, in provisions based on (and to be interpreted in accordance with the same principles as[4]) corresponding provisions of the European Community Treaty. The Act and the Treaty prohibit agreements between undertakings, decisions by associations of undertakings or concerted practices which may (a) affect trade and (b) have as their object the prevention, restriction or distortion of competition within (under the Act) the United Kingdom or (under the Treaty) the common market.[5] Prohibited agreements include those which 'directly or indirectly fix purchase or selling prices or any other trading conditions'.[6] Prohibited agreements are void[7] unless exemption is granted by the relevant United Kingdom or Community bodies.[8] The Act makes claims for compensation available to persons who have suffered loss or damage as a result of the infringement of these prohibitions.[9] If such persons are consumers, the claims can be brought on their behalf by persons or bodies appointed by the Secretary of State.[10]

A full account of this complex topic is beyond the scope of this book; but two points must be made about the relationship between

1   Infra at n 6.
2   Auctions (Bidding Agreements) Acts 1927–1969.
3   Ante, pp 203–204.
4   See Competition Act 1998, s 60(1), where the rule is qualified by the words 'having regard to any relevant differences between the provisions concerned'.
5   1998 Act, s 2; Treaty, Art 81 (formerly 85); the Treaty has the force of law in the UK by virtue of European Communities Act 1972, s 2.
6   1998 Act, s 2(2)(a); Treaty, Art 81(1)(a).
7   1998 Act, s 2(4); Treaty, Art 81(2).
8   1998 Act, s 6; Treaty, Art 81(3).
9   1998 Act, s 47A.
10   1998 Act, s 47B.

the above prohibitions and the common law of restraint of trade. First, an employee is not for their purposes an 'undertaking'[11] so that the common law relating to restraints in employment contracts is not affected by them. Secondly, the prohibitions apply only where the agreement (etc) has an 'appreciable' effect on competition and not where that effect is 'insignificant'.[12] The crucial factor is the percentage of the market share affected by it: for example 0.02% has been held insufficient[13] and it seems that less than 5% would be so regarded.[14] Many of the agreements dealt with under the common law of restraint of trade would not have a sufficiently significant effect to be prohibited and made void by the 1998 Act or the Treaty. An agreement may therefore fail to satisfy the requirements of validity imposed by the common law of restraint of trade without contravening the Treaty or the 1998 Act: for example, where the agreement was one between undertakings and affected trade but had no anti-competitive object or effect.[15] But to promote uniformity within the Community in this respect,[16] an agreement which for such reasons is valid under the Treaty cannot be struck down in England merely because it falls foul of the domestic common law restraint of trade rules.[17] Those rules, however, continue to apply to agreements which do not fall within the Treaty provisions at all: eg because of their geographical scope or because they are not agreements between 'undertakings'.

4   THE EFFECTS OF ILLEGALITY

The most common effect of illegality is to prevent the enforcement of the contract, either wholly or in part. It may also bar claims for restitution in respect of benefits conferred under it; and it may invalidate collateral transactions.

11   See *Suiker Unie v Commission* [1975] ECR 1663 at paras 539, 554.
12   *Völk v Vervaeke* Case 5/69 [1969] CMLR 273.
13   *Völk v Vervaeke* Case 5/69 [1969] CMLR 273; cf *Passmore v Morland plc* [1998] 4 All ER 468; affd [1999] 3 All ER 1005.
14   See, eg, *Miller GmbH v EC Commission* Case 19/77 [1978] ECR 131.
15   *Days Medical Aids Ltd v Pihsiang Machinery Manufacturing Co Ltd* [2004] EWHC 44 (Comm), [2004] 1 All ER (Comm) 991 at [236], [242]–[243].
16   See Council Regulation 1/2003 of 16 December 2002, [2003] OJ L1/1, Recital 8 ('to create a level playing field').
17   *Days Medical Aids* case [2004] 1 All ER (Comm) 991 at [262]–[265]; Art 3(1) and (2) of the Regulation cited in n 16, supra and implemented in the UK by The Competition Act 1998 and Other Enactments (Amendment) Regulations 2004, SI 2004/1261. The latter Regulations do not deal with the relationship between the common law rules and *the 1998 Act*, perhaps because the 'level playing field' argument (supra, n 16) has little force in relation to agreements affecting trade only in the UK.

a   Enforcement of the contract

The law relating to the enforcement of illegal contracts is in a complex and not very satisfactory state. The basic rule is that a guilty party cannot enforce the contract while an innocent party may be able to do so.

i   *A guilty party cannot enforce the contract*

Cases illustrating this rule have already been mentioned: for example, the owner of a brougham who knowingly let it to a prostitute to help her to attract clients could not recover the agreed hire.[18] It makes no difference that the other party is (as in that case) equally guilty. The defendant to an action on an illegal contract thus gets a windfall, but the rule has been justified on the ground that 'the courts will not lend their aid to such [ie a guilty] a plaintiff'.[19]

The rule, as so far stated, assumes that the illegality arises by reason of the object of the contract. Where it arises by reason of the method of performance, a party is not 'guilty' for the present purpose merely because he breaks the law. We have, for example, seen that a shipowner may be entitled to enforce a contract of carriage by claiming freight in spite of the fact that he had overloaded his ship.[20] He would have been a 'guilty' party only if he had intended all along to perform the contract in an unlawful way, ie if at the time of entering into the contract he had known that he could not perform it lawfully, but only by overloading. If the cargo-owner had 'participated' in the scheme, he, too, would have been a 'guilty' party for the purpose of the present rule. This would have been the position if he had known of the unlawfulness in the method of performance and assented to it in order to benefit from it by saving any extra expense which might be incurred by having his goods lawfully carried.[21]

A party may be 'guilty' for the purpose of the present rule even though he is ignorant of or mistaken about the law, so that he is morally quite innocent. In such cases, the rule can work harshly[22] and at one time the courts took the view that it should apply only where it would be 'an affront to the public conscience'[1] to allow the guilty party to sue. But the vagueness of this test makes it 'very difficult to

---

18   *Pearce v Brooks* (1866) LR 1 Exch 213.
19   *Holman v Johnson* (1775) 1 Cowp 341 at 342.
20   *St John Shipping Corpn v Joseph Rank Ltd* [1957] 1 QB 267; cf *Coral Leisure Group Ltd v Barnett* [1981] ICR 503.
21   As in *Ashmore, Benson, Pease & Co Ltd v A V Dawson Ltd* [1973] 2 All ER 856.
22   The rule is, nevertheless, not affected by Human Rights Act 1998, Sch 1 Pt II: *Shanshal v Al Kishtaini* [2001] EWCA Civ 264, [2001] 2 All ER (Comm) 601.
1   *Euro-Diam Ltd v Bathurst* [1990] 1 QB 1 at 35.

apply'[2] and has led to its rejection by the House of Lords.[3] The rule that the guilty party cannot enforce the contract therefore survives. But its severity is relaxed where a contract can be performed in several ways only one of which is (unknown to the parties) unlawful. If, on discovering that the intended method is unlawful, they actually perform in another, lawful, way, the contract is not affected by illegality;[4] or, to put the point in another way, neither party is treated as a 'guilty' party. The rule that the guilty party cannot sue may also be excluded by the statute which gives rise to the illegality; and many modern statutes contain express provisions to this effect: for example, where a motor vehicle is supplied which does not comply with statutory safety requirements, the supplier commits an offence, but the validity of the contract is unaffected.[5]

ii An innocent party may be able to enforce the contract

An innocent party, that is, one who is mistaken about, or ignorant of, the *facts* which constitute the illegality can often enforce the contract. He can obviously do so where the illegality arises under a statute which expressly provides that the commission of the offence is not to invalidate the contract;[6] but his right is not limited to cases of this kind. In *Archbolds (Freightage) Ltd v Spanglett Ltd*[7] a contract was made for the carriage of a consignment of whisky; and, in attempting to perform it, the carrier committed an offence, as the vehicle which he used was not properly licensed to carry goods belonging to third parties. But, as the owner of the whisky did not know this, it was held that he was entitled to damages for breach of the contract of carriage. In the view of the court, the purpose of the statute which had imposed the licensing requirement was 'sufficiently served by the penalties prescribed for the offender; the avoidance of the contract would cause grave inconvenience and injury to innocent members of the public without furthering the object of the statute'.[8] Similar reasoning has prevailed where the contract contravened legislation passed for the protection of a class of persons. This situation is illustrated by cases in which insurers carried on business without the requisite licences; and, according to some of these cases, the contracts were then illegal

---

2   *Pitts v Hunt* [1990] 3 All ER 344 at 362.
3   *Tinsley v Milligan* [1994] 1 AC 340 at 358–361, 363–364.
4   *Waugh v Morris* (1873) LR 8 QB 202.
5   Road Traffic Act 1988, s 65(1) and (4); s 75(7); cf Fair Trading Act 1973, s 26; Consumer Protection Act 1987, s 41(3); Criminal Justice Act 1993, s 63(2).
6   Supra, n 5.
7   [1961] 1 QB 374.
8   [1961] 1 QB 374 at 390; cf *Skilton v Sullivan* [1994] 21 LS Gaz R 41.

and could not be enforced even by the innocent insured.[9] But the purpose of the legislation was scarcely promoted by denying a remedy to the very class of persons whom it was designed to protect. Legislation now provides that, where A provides financial services to B without having the requisite authorisation, the contract is unenforceable against (but not by) B;[10] and if A's contravention of the legislation is innocent, the court may, exceptionally, also allow the contract to be enforced by him.[11]

iii Cases in which the innocent party cannot enforce the contract

In another group of cases, it was held that even an innocent party could not enforce the illegal contract. The leading case arose under war-time legislation making it an offence to buy or sell (amongst other things) linseed oil without a licence. A contract for the sale of such oil was made between a seller who had a licence and a buyer who fraudulently pretended to the seller that he had one. It was held that the seller could not get damages for breach of the contract, even though he did not know of the facts constituting the illegality.[12] Similarly, it has been held that a builder doing work in the honest, but mistaken, belief that the requisite licences had been obtained could not recover the agreed price of the work.[13]

These cases are very hard on the innocent party. They can be justified (if at all) on the ground that, in this group of contracts, it would 'further the object of the statute' to deny even an innocent party a remedy on the contract. In a sense such a denial always has this effect. It might induce an innocent party to take greater care, before entering into the contract, to make sure that it was not illegal; and also to back out of the contract if, before he had performed it, he discovered its illegality. It may be asked why this reasoning should apply to some cases of contracts affected by illegality but not to others. One possible answer is that in the sale and building contracts mentioned above the claimants asked to be put into the position in which they would have been if the contract had *been performed*; while in the *Archbolds* case they asked to be put into the position in which they would have been if the contract had *never been made*. The purpose of

---

9   Contrast *Stewart v Oriental Fire and Marine Insurance Co Ltd* [1985] QB 988 with *Phoenix General Insurance Co of Greece SA v Halvanon Insurance Co Ltd* [1988] QB 216.

10   Financial Services and Markets Act 2000, ss 26(1), 27(1).

11   2000 Act, s 28(3)–(6).

12   *Re Mahmoud and Ispahani* [1921] 2 KB 716; cf *Bedford Insurance Co Ltd v Instituto de Resseguros do Brasil* [1985] QB 966 at 982.

13   *Dennis & Co Ltd v Munn* [1949] 2 KB 327.

the statute is, in general, more likely to be defeated by allowing a claim of the former than of the latter kind.

iv Other remedies of the innocent party

Where the innocent party cannot enforce the illegal contract, the courts have sometimes alleviated the hardship to him by giving him some other remedy.

If he has been induced to enter into the illegal contract by a misrepresentation as to its legality, he may be able to recover damages in tort for the misrepresentation. Such a claim was for example upheld where the claimant had been induced by the defendant's fraud to buy a house in Spain and the contract was illegal because payments under it violated exchange control regulations then in force.[14] This remedy differs from an action on the contract in that it will give the claimant only the amount by which he is worse off as a result of the misrepresentation and not the amount by which he would have been better off if the contract had been performed. In other words, it will not give him damages for loss of his bargain.[15]

Alternatively, the innocent party may be able to claim damages for breach of a 'collateral contract' to the effect that the principal contract is lawful. In one case[16] this device was used to allow builders who had, in all innocence, done unlicensed work, to recover the value of the work; and it seems that they recovered exactly the same amount in this action as they would have recovered if they had been able to sue on the illegal contract. The rule is a strange one, for it makes very little sense to say that the public interest precludes enforcement of the contract but does not preclude another remedy which is just as good. In fact, the builders in our case were not careless in failing to see that licences had been obtained (since the owner was an architect on whose word they reasonably relied); and it was too late for them to back out, as they had finished the work. But in these circumstances it would have been better to recognise that there was no public interest against allowing them to sue on the main contract itself. The collateral contract device in the present context is an unnecessary complexity, and it gives the law a strange air of inconsistency.

Innocence may finally be relevant to claims (to be discussed later in this chapter) for the restitution of benefits conferred under illegal contracts.

---

14   *Shelley v Paddock* [1980] QB 348; cf *Burrows v Rhodes* [1899] 1 QB 816; *Saunders v Edwards* [1987] 2 All ER 651 (some of the reasoning of which is open to doubt since *Tinsley v Milligan* [1994] 1 AC 340, ante, p 201 at n 3).
15   Cf ante, p 160; post, pp 375–377.
16   *Strongman (1945) Ltd v Sincock* [1955] 2 QB 525.

b   Severance

Where only part of a contract is illegal, it may be possible to sever that part and to enforce the rest of the contract. Two situations require discussion.

i   Severance of illegal promises

Suppose that A buys a bookshop in Cambridge from B, and B promises not to engage in the bookselling business in Cambridge or in Oxford. Here B's promise is valid so far as it relates to Cambridge but invalid so far as it relates to Oxford; and the question is whether A can sever the valid from the invalid part and prevent B from opening a new bookshop in Cambridge. He can do so if three conditions are satisfied.

First, the illegal promise must not be so seriously illegal as to contaminate the whole contract. Severance would, for example, not be possible where a lawful promise was combined with one deliberately to commit a crime, or to do an immoral act.[17] If a man promised to serve another as a valet and as a pickpocket, he could obviously not be sued for failing to perform even his duties as valet.

Secondly, the so-called 'blue pencil' test must be satisfied. It must be possible to sever the illegal part by simply deleting words in the contract. The court will not add words, or substitute one word for another, or rearrange words, or in any other way redraft the contract. For example, a promise not to compete within ten miles of a particular place cannot be severed by deleting 'ten' and substituting 'five', even though a five-mile restraint would have been perfectly reasonable. Where the contract is drawn up by laymen, this rule can cause hardship to the party for whose benefit the restraint was intended. On the other hand, it gives little protection to the other party since a draftsman who knows of the 'blue pencil' rule can easily draw up the restraint so as to neutralise its operation.

A promise cannot be severed merely because the 'blue pencil' test is satisfied. The courts have laid down a third requirement: that severance must not change the nature of the covenant. The requirement is illustrated by a case[18] in which a general outfitter's business was divided into several departments, and the person employed as head of each department covenanted not to compete with the employers, after leaving their service, in the business of *any* of the departments. The effect of the covenant was thus to prevent the head of the tailoring department from competing as a hatter or

---

17   See *Bennett v Bennett* [1952] 1 KB 249 at 254.
18   *Attwood v Lamont* [1920] 3 KB 571.

milliner, and so forth, while the only reasonable restraint would have been one against competing as a tailor. It was held that the covenant could not be severed (even though the 'blue pencil' test was satisfied). The covenant was 'one covenant for the protection of the entire business'[19] so that to sever the references to all trades except tailoring would be to alter its entire nature. The courts are more ready to sever covenants between vendor and purchaser[20] than between employer and employee; but it should not be supposed that they will always sever covenants of the former kind, or that they will not, in any circumstances, sever covenants of the latter kind. The requirement that severance must not alter the nature of the covenant is easy enough to state, but its operation is hard to predict. It turns on subtle questions of degree, and even of personal impression.

In the situations so far discussed, the question was whether invalid parts of the promise not to compete could be severed. Even where this cannot be done, the rest of the contract generally remains binding. Thus the fact that a contract contains an invalid promise not to compete will not normally justify breaches of other unrelated terms of the contract, for the contract as a whole will not, merely because of the invalidity of one of its terms, have 'so changed its character as not to be the sort of contract that the parties intended to enter into at all'.[1] The illegality will only invalidate the contract as a whole where one of the main objects of the contract was to secure the restraint.[2] The question in such cases is not whether severance of parts of an illegal covenant will alter the nature of *that covenant*, but whether deletion of the covenant will alter the nature of *the contract as a whole*, by leaving it without subject-matter or by substantially altering its intended subject-matter.[3]

ii Severing illegal parts of the consideration

So far we have considered the question whether the legal part of a promise can be enforced *against* the person making a promise which is partly legal and partly illegal. An action may also be brought *by* such a person to enforce the (wholly legal) counter-promise which he has received for it. For example, a builder might have performed his undertaking to do work of which a part was licensed, and the rest unlicensed and therefore illegal. If he sued for the agreed price, the client would argue that part of the consideration for his promise to

19 [1920] 3 KB 571 at 593.
20 As in *Goldsoll v Goldman* [1915] 1 Ch 292.
1 *Alec Lobb (Garages) Ltd v Total Oil (GB) Ltd* [1985] 1 All ER 303 at 320; cf *Carney v Herbert* [1985] AC 301.
2 *Royal Boskalis Westminster NV v Mountain* [1999] QB 674 at 693.
3 Eg *Amoco Australia Pty Ltd v Rocca Bros Motor Engineering Co Pty Ltd* [1975] AC 561.

pay was illegal, while the builder might argue that that part should be severed.

Here again, severance is not allowed if the illegal part of the consideration is immoral, or if the illegality arises from a deliberate violation of the law.[4] In our example, the builder would not be entitled to recover anything if he knew that part of the work was unlicensed; but severance might be possible if he were innocent of the illegality. Whether it actually is possible depends on the importance of the illegal part of the consideration in relation to the contract as a whole. A promise cannot be enforced if a *substantial* part of the consideration for it is an illegal counter-promise;[5] but if the *main* part of the consideration for a promise is lawful, then the promise can be enforced even though there was also some subsidiary illegal consideration. This would normally be the position where an employee agreed to an unreasonably wide stipulation in restraint of trade. He could nevertheless sue for his wages since the main consideration for the employer's promise to pay them would be the employee's promise to work, or the performance of it.[6]

The case last put is not strictly one of severance, for the result in such a case is that the employee recovers the *whole* of his wages. This result is probably due to the fact that the illegal part of the consideration (ie the excessive part of the restraint) cannot be precisely valued. Where such valuation is possible, there may be true severance, leading to recovery of so much of the promised payment as is supported by lawful consideration. Thus in one case,[7] a builder innocently did work worth nearly £1,200 when the owner held a licence for work up to only £1,000; and it was held that the builder could recover the latter sum.

c   Restitution of money or property

Where one party to a contract completely fails or refuses to perform it, the other normally has a choice of remedies. He can try to 'enforce' the contract; or to 'undo' it by claiming restitution in respect of money paid or property transferred by him under the contract.[8] In the case of an illegal contract, there is (as we have seen) often no right to enforce the contract; and it is also the general rule that money paid or property transferred under such a contract cannot be claimed back.[9]

---

4   *Bennett v Bennett* [1952] 1 KB 249 at 254.
5   *Lound v Grimwade* (1888) 39 Ch D 605.
6   *Carney v Herbert* [1985] AC 301 at 311; *Marshall v NM Financial Management Ltd* [1997] 1 WLR 1527.
7   *Frank W Clifford Ltd v Garth* [1956] 2 All ER 323.
8   See generally Ch 18, post, pp 375–380.
9   Eg *Scott v Brown* [1892] 2 QB 724.

The rule is supposed to operate as a further deterrent against the making of illegal contracts, by leaving one party entirely at the mercy of the other. On the other hand, it is capable of producing very harsh results, especially where an illegal contract is innocently made; and there are situations in which the purpose of the rule of law which has made the contract illegal is better served by allowing, than by denying, the recovery of money or property. The general rule against non-recovery is therefore subject to the following exceptions.

i   Statutes for the protection of a class

The illegality of a contract may arise under a statute passed for the protection of a class of people, such as tenants, or borrowers from moneylenders. Some such statutes expressly provide that a member of the protected class can get back money paid, or property transferred, under the contract; for example, under the Rent Act a tenant can get back money (such as a premium or an excess rent) which he could not legally be required to pay.[10] He can recover an illegal premium even though he paid it quite willingly so as to secure preferential treatment for himself.[11] A member of the protected class can get back money or property in these situations at common law, even though there is no express statutory provision to that effect;[12] and he can do so even though the other party has performed his part of the illegal bargain.

ii   Illegal contract made under pressure

Recovery of money paid or property transferred has sometimes been allowed on the ground that the claimant was 'forced' to enter into the contract by some form of pressure. In one case,[13] an insolvent debtor wanted to make a composition with his creditors, but one creditor would not join in unless the debtor first paid him £50. The debtor was allowed to claim back this £50 on the ground that he had been 'forced' to agree to defraud the other creditors. The result was clearly desirable since the £50 thus became available for distribution among all the creditors.

A person may be 'forced' to enter into an illegal contract, not only by the other party, but also by extraneous circumstances. This is another

---

10   Rent Act 1977, ss 57, 94, 125; cf Financial Services and Markets Act 2000, ss 26(2), 27(2), subject to s 28(3)–(6).
11   *Gray v Southouse* [1949] 2 All ER 1019.
12   *Kiriri Cotton Co Ltd v Dewani* [1960] AC 192; cf *Nash v Halifax Building Society* [1979] Ch 584.
13   *Atkinson v Denby* (1862) 7 H & N 934.

218   *Illegality*

reason why a tenant who pays an illegal premium during a housing shortage can get the money back.[14] But the pressure must be of a kind which makes it, in the view of the court, excusable to enter into the illegal transaction. In *Bigos v Bousted*[15] a father made an illegal contract to acquire foreign currency because he wanted to send his daughter abroad as a cure for her recurrent attacks of pleurisy. It was held that he had not been 'forced' to make the illegal contract and that he could not get back securities which he had deposited with the other party to the illegal contract.

iii   Fraud or mistake inducing the illegal contract

Money paid or property transferred under an illegal contract can be reclaimed by a person who was induced to enter into the contract by the other party's fraudulent representation that the contract was lawful. Under this rule, premiums paid under an illegal insurance have been recovered by an innocent policyholder who was deceived by the insurance company's agent into believing that he had an insurable interest in the subject-matter, when in fact he had none.[16] The rule does not apply where the misrepresentation was innocent,[17] though there might in such a case, be a right to rescind for misrepresentation;[18] and if this right were exercised it would follow that money paid or property transferred could be claimed back.

In an old case[19] a policy of insurance was taken out on goods in Russia at a time when neither party knew (or could have known) that war had broken out between this country and Russia. This made the policy illegal, but the policy-holder recovered back the premium as he had paid it under a mistake of fact affecting the legality of the contract.

iv   Repentance

'Public policy', it has been said, 'is best served by allowing a party to repent before it is too late, and to prevent the completion of the illegal purpose by reclaiming the money paid by him in pursuance of it'.[20] Two points arising out of this statement call for comment.

14   *Kiriri Cotton Co Ltd v Dewani* [1960] AC 192 at 205.
15   [1951] 1 All ER 92.
16   *Hughes v Liverpool Victoria Legal Friendly Society* [1916] 2 KB 482.
17   *Harse v Pearl Life Assurance Co* [1904] 1 KB 558; *Edler v Auerbach* [1950] 1 KB 359.
18   Ante, p 163.
19   *Oom v Bruce* (1810) 12 East 225.
20   *Harry Parker Ltd v Mason* [1940] 2 KB 590 at 609.

First, the claimant must 'repent' – that is, he must voluntarily abandon the illegal purpose. If that purpose is simply frustrated by the other party's failure or refusal to perform, there is no 'repentance' and hence no recovery. This was the position in the case of *Bigos v Bousted*,[1] mentioned above. The party who had agreed to supply the foreign currency simply failed to do so; and the argument that the other party had repented (and that he could recover his securities on this ground) was accordingly rejected.

Secondly, the repentance must come 'before it is too late'. Obviously, it is too late once the illegal purpose has been achieved; and the position is the same if the illegal purpose has been partly performed, at least if the part that has been performed is substantial. On the other hand, the mere fact that acts have been done in preparation for performing the illegal purpose will not prevent recovery. Thus property transferred under a scheme to defraud creditors can be reclaimed if the scheme is not in fact used to defraud any creditor.[2] But in another case[3] money was paid under a scheme to interfere with the course of justice. It was held that the money could not be recovered as some such interference (though less than that bargained for) had actually taken place.

v   No reliance on the contract or its illegality

A person may be able to recover money paid or property transferred under an illegal contract if he can establish his right to it without relying on the contract or on its illegality.[4] The law on this subject is complex, technical and not very satisfactory. It approaches the problem by reference to the rules which govern the transfer of proprietary or possessory rights in the subject-matter of illegal contracts; and it pays little attention to the more important question whether the purpose of the rule giving rise to the illegality would be promoted or defeated by allowing recovery.

One group of cases concerns the hire or hire-purchase of goods under illegal contracts. Suppose that a television set is hired under such a contract for twelve months. During that period, the owner cannot claim it back. The contract would give the hirer the right to keep possession of it, and the owner could not rely on the illegality of the contract to negative that right.[5] But after the end of the twelve months,

1   [1951] 1 All ER 92, ante, p 218.
2   *Taylor v Bowers* (1876) 1 QBD 291; *Tribe v Tribe* [1996] Ch 107.
3   *Kearly v Thomson* (1890) 24 QBD 742.
4   *Bowmakers Ltd v Barnett Instruments Ltd* [1945] KB 65 at 71; *Tinsley v Milligan* [1994] 1 AC 340 at 366, 369, 370.
5   Cf *Taylor v Chester* (1869) LR 4 QB 309 (pledge).

the owner could claim back the set by simply saying that it was his property. His title would exist, quite apart from the contract or its illegality. This is a relatively straightforward case, but variations of it give rise to more difficulty. Suppose first that, after one month, the hirer sells the set. This will amount to a repudiatory breach of contract,[6] as a result of which the hirer's right to keep possession of the set can be brought to an immediate and premature end by the owner. Once this has happened the owner will be able to claim damages for conversion from the hirer, by simply relying on his ownership; while the hirer will no longer be able to rely on his right to keep possession as that right will have come to an end with the contract. Suppose next that the hirer had simply failed to pay the first month's rent; that a clause in the contract entitled the owner, on such failure, to give notice terminating the contract; and that such notice had been given. Here again, the hirer's right to keep possession of the set would have terminated prematurely, but only as a result of action taken by the owner under a term of the contract. Hence it would seem that the owner was relying on the illegal contract, and in a sense trying to enforce one of its terms, if he claimed the set before the end of the twelve months. In one case of this kind[7] the owner's claim nevertheless succeeded as he relied, not on the contract or its illegality, but simply on his title. It may be objected that this reasoning deprived the rule against enforcement of the illegal contract of much of its practical importance; for the remedy of claiming the goods back will be equally available against a defaulting hirer whether the contract is legal or illegal. But the actual decision can be justified on the ground that the owner's violation of the law was innocent and that the policy of the relevant legislation (which was to regulate the allocation of scarce resources in time of war) was promoted rather than defeated by allowing the owners' claim.

The position of an owner who has let out goods under a contract of hire or hire-purchase is much more favourable than that of a seller who has sold the goods outright. Here the position is that the entire property in the goods can pass from the seller to the buyer, notwithstanding the illegality of the contract, in accordance with the usual rules which govern the passing of property under a contract of sale.[8] If under these rules the property has passed, the seller cannot get the goods back, since he has no title left on which he can rely. Indeed, if the seller or a third party takes the goods away from the buyer, the latter is legally entitled to claim them back.[9] The same

6   *North Central Wagon and Finance Co Ltd v Graham* [1950] 2 KB 7.
7   *Bowmakers Ltd v Barnet Instruments Ltd* [1945] KB 65 (hire purchase).
8   *Belvoir Finance Co Ltd v Stapleton* [1971] 1 QB 210.
9   *Sagan Singh v Sardara Ali* [1960] AC 167; *Belvoir Finance Co Ltd v Stapleton* [1971] 1 QB 210.

principle applies where the claim is based on an equitable (as opposed to a legal) title. In *Tinsley v Milligan*[10] a house was bought by two women (A and B), with money provided by both of them and intended to be owned jointly; but it was conveyed into the name of A so as to enable B to make false claims for social security benefits. When the parties later quarrelled, it was held that B was entitled to a half share in the house by virtue of the presumption which normally arises in equity, where B buys, or provides money for the acquisition of, property which is conveyed to A. That presumption is that the property is to be held, to the appropriate extent, in trust for B, who therefore relied, not on any illegality but simply on the presumption. But in certain relationships the presumption is the other way: for example, where a father provides money for the acquisition of property by his child, he is presumed to have made a gift. Hence in such a case the father could not reclaim the property on the strength of his title since he would have to rely on the illegality to rebut the presumption of gift.[11] It would, of course, be open to him to rely on one of the other exceptions to the general rule of non-recovery: eg, where he had 'repented' of the illegal purpose before it was too late.[12]

A person who has paid money under an illegal contract is very unlikely to be able to get it back by relying simply on his title. When money is paid over, the payor's entire property in it almost invariably passes to the payee. The only significant exception to this rule occurs where money is deposited with a stakeholder. If money has, for example, been so deposited under an illegal wager, the depositor can claim it back from the stakeholder, so long as the latter has not paid it over to the other party to the wager.[13]

A person may be able to establish a right to money due under an illegal transaction without relying on the illegality. This was sometimes held to be the position where a contract was made on his behalf by an agent who received money on his (the principal's) behalf from the other party to that contract.[14] He could establish his right to it by simply showing that it had been received by his agent on his behalf; and it was not necessary for him to rely on the illegal contract under which it had been received by the agent. There are, however, limits to the principle that a party to an illegal contract can recover money or property obtained under it by relying merely on his title. The principle probably does not apply where a party who has obtained property by means of a criminal

10   [1994] 1 AC 340.
11   *Chettiar v Chettiar* [1962] AC 294.
12   *Tribe v Tribe* [1996] Ch 107; ante, p 219 at n 2.
13   Cf *O'Sullivan v Thomas* [1895] 1 QB 698.
14   Eg *Bone v Ekless* (1860) 5 H & N 925.

fraud makes a claim in respect of 'the very proceeds of the fraudulent conduct';[15] and many statutes provide for the making of confiscation or similar orders in respect of the proceeds of criminal conduct.[16]

vi   Recovery allowed under certain illegal contracts

The general rule against recovery of money or property is by no means an obviously or universally desirable one; and some of the older authorities, particularly in equity, took the view that recovery should generally be allowed.[17] Traces of this view can still be seen today in the rule that money paid in advance by a client under a marriage brokage contract can be claimed back.[18] Obviously, the policy of the rule against these contracts is better served by making the marriage bureau pay back the money even if it has made efforts to promote a match, than by allowing it to keep the money in spite of the fact that it has done nothing. This reasoning suggests that, in cases not yet covered by authority, the court should not mechanically apply the general rule of non-recovery. Rather, it should ask itself whether the policy of the rule making the contract illegal is better served by denying or by allowing the recovery of money paid or property transferred under the contract.

d   Recompense of services

A person who has done work under a void contract is normally entitled to a reasonable sum for that work;[19] and such a claim is not barred merely because the contract is both void under one rule of law and also illegal under another.[20] The position would be different where illegality was the *only* ground of invalidity: eg where a person had introduced clients to a solicitor under a prohibited fee-sharing agreement, his claim for a reasonable remuneration for that work was dismissed.[1] To allow such a claim would subvert the policy of the rule of law making such agreements illegal. But even in such a situation a person who is innocent of the illegality can recover a reasonable sum in respect of *other* work lawfully done, such as translation services provided in relation to the same clients.[2]

---

15   *Thackwell v Barclays Bank plc* [1986] 1 All ER 676 at 689.
16   Eg Powers of Criminal Courts (Sentencing) Act 2000, s 143.
17   Eg *Morris v M'Cullock* (1763) Amb 432.
18   *Hermann v Charlesworth* [1905] 2 KB 123.
19   Post, p 422.
20   *Cotronic (UK) Ltd v Dezonie (t/a Wendaland Builders Ltd)* [1991] BCLC 721.
1   *Mohamed v Alaga & Co* [1999] 3 All ER 699 at 707.
2   [1999] 3 All ER 699 at 707, 710, as explained in *Awwad v Geraghty & Co* [2001] QB 570 at 596.

e   Collateral transactions

The illegality of a principal contract may infect an intrinsically lawful
collateral transaction if that transaction is intended to help a party to
the illegal contract to perform it, or if enforcement of the collateral
contract could amount to indirect enforcement of the illegal one.
Thus a loan of money would be illegal if the lender knew that the
money was going to be used to pay off another loan which was illegal.[3]
But the mere existence of some remote connection between the two
transactions will not invalidate the collateral contract. It has, for
example, been held that a policy of insurance on diamonds was not
invalid merely because the insured had, in the course of acquiring
the diamonds, committed a breach of a foreign revenue law;[4] for he
had not benefited from the breach,[5] nor had it in any way contributed
to the loss.

3   *Spector v Ageda* [1973] Ch 30; *The American Accord* [1983] 1 AC 168.
4   *Euro-Diam Ltd v Bathurst* [1990] 1 QB 1.
5   Contrast *Geismar v Sun Alliance and London Insurance Ltd* [1978] QB 383 (no
    action on insurance on goods smuggled into this country).

Chapter 12

Contractual capacity

1 MINORS

A minor is a person below the age of majority, which is reached at 18.[1] The main purpose of the legal rules regulating the contracts of such persons is to protect them from their inexperience, which may lead them to enter into contracts on unfavourable terms, or into contracts which, though perfectly fair, are simply improvident. On the other hand, the law also wants to prevent undue hardship to adults who deal fairly with minors. One way of achieving both aims would be to require minors' contracts to be made with the authorisation of their guardians. But this expedient was not adopted in English law; instead minors' contracts were divided into a number of classes, ranging from those which are valid to those which do not bind the minor but nevertheless may subject him to certain extra-contractual liability.

In the nineteenth and early twentieth centuries (when the age of majority was 21) a good deal of litigation arose out of cases in which young men of 'good family' ran up large tradesmen's bills or borrowed substantial sums of money. Such 'quaint examples of a bygone age'[2] have no direct counterpart in modern litigation. But the question whether minors are bound by contracts can still arise today: for example, out of employment contracts, out of the contracts of young professional athletes or entertainers, and out of contracts made by minors who pretend to be of age. Claims may also be made *by* the minors either to enforce the liability of the other contracting party or to reclaim money or property with which the minor has parted under the contract. The practical importance of the topic, though reduced by changes in social conditions, remains by no means negligible.

a Contracts which are binding

A minor is bound by contracts for necessaries, and by contracts of employment and analogous contracts.

1   Family Law Reform Act 1969, s 1.
2   *Allen v Bloomsbury Health Authority* [1993] 1 All ER 651 at 661.

i Necessaries

A minor's liability for necessaries was originally said to exist for his own good: the theory was that he could not get necessaries (except for ready cash) unless the law made him liable.[3] However, some of the relevant rules of law make the position of the supplier so precarious that no reasonable person would rely on them in giving credit to a minor; while others fairly obviously exist for the benefit of the supplier and not for that of the minor.

This is, for example, true of the legal definition of necessaries, which is not confined to necessities. They include all goods and services (such as education[4] or medical or legal advice) which are 'fit to maintain the particular person in the state, station and degree ... in which he is'.[5] Thus in one old case, even a livery for a minor's servant was held to be a necessary.[6] Obviously, the purpose of this wide definition was to protect persons who gave credit to wealthy minors in respect of goods or services which, in the view of the court, it was reasonable for the minors to have.

Not surprisingly, juries (consisting traditionally of twelve shop-keepers) were inclined to push this broad definition of necessaries beyond its legitimate limits. In one case, 'an Oxford jury held that champagne and wild ducks were necessaries to an ... under-graduate'.[7] The courts countered this trend by distinguishing between 'luxurious articles of utility' and 'mere luxuries'.[8] The latter could not, as a matter of law, be necessaries; and the courts reserved to themselves the right to determine whether, as a matter of law, the goods were *capable of being* necessaries.[9] It was only if this preliminary question was answered in the affirmative that the case could properly be left to the jury, who then decided whether the goods *actually were* necessaries. This depended partly on the nature of the goods (so that, for instance, a racehorse could never be a necessary); and partly on the minor's actual needs (so that clothes could be necessaries but would not be if the minor already had an adequate supply). So far as the latter requirement was concerned, the law insisted that the goods must actually be necessaries both when they were sold and when they were delivered to the minor.[10] It was up to the supplier to prove the

3   *Ryder v Wombwell* (1868) LR 4 Exch 32 at 38.
4   *Sherdley v Sherdley* [1988] AC 213 at 225.
5   *Peters v Fleming* (1840) 6 M & W 42 at 46.
6   *Hands v Slaney* (1800) 8 Term Rep 578.
7   HL, 219 Official Report (3rd Series) Col 1225 (1874).
8   *Chapple v Cooper* (1844) 13 M & W 252 at 258.
9   *Ryder v Wombwell* (1868) LR 4 Exch 32.
10 *Nash v Inman* [1908] 2 KB 1; Sale of Goods Act 1979, s 3.

difficult negative proposition that the minor was not adequately supplied at both times; and if the minor had an adequate supply, the supplier's action would fail, even though he did not know this.[11] No doubt these rules were developed to control juries, who were too much inclined to find verdicts against minors; and they have survived, although today contract cases are no longer tried by jury.

Even where a minor is liable for necessaries, he is not bound to pay more than a reasonable price.[12] The fact that the minor is not bound to pay the agreed price has given rise to the view that his liability for necessaries is not contractual at all. It is said to be a liability imposed by law, not because he has agreed, but because he has been supplied.[13] From this it is thought to follow that, if he has not been supplied, he cannot be liable under a contract for necessaries to be supplied in the future. In other words, if a minor ordered a dress to be delivered and paid for in a month's time she could cancel the order without being liable for the price or for damages. This view makes little sense if liability for necessaries exists for the minor's own good, and it makes even less sense if such liability exists for the protection of adults who agree to supply minors with their reasonable needs. In one case where the necessaries consisted largely of education (in the art of playing professional billiards), a minor was held liable for repudiating the contract when it remained partly unperformed.[14]

A minor may find that the supplier of necessaries will not give him credit, but that a third person will, either by paying the supplier or by lending money to the minor. A person who pays the supplier can recover the amount so paid (at least if the amount was reasonable) from the minor,[15] who is no worse off than he would be if he had to pay the supplier. A person who lends money to a minor to enable him to pay for necessaries can, however, recover only so much of the loan as was actually used for that purpose.[16] His right is restricted in this way because of the danger that the loan might be misapplied.

The common law rules relating to liability for necessaries are not mentioned in, or directly affected by, the legislation which imposes on an absent parent the duty to maintain a child or empowers courts to make orders against parents for financial relief in respect of children.[17] But the operation of this legislation may result in the minor's being adequately supplied with necessary goods and services;

11   *Barnes & Co v Toye* (1884) 13 QBD 410.
12   Sale of Goods Act 1979, s 3.
13   *Nash v Inman* [1908] 2 KB 1 at 8.
14   *Roberts v Gray* [1913] 1 KB 520.
15   *Earle v Peale* (1711) 10 Mod Rep 67.
16   *Marlow v Pitfeild* (1719) 1 P Wms 558.
17   Child Support Act 1991, s 1(1); Children Act 1989, s 15 and Sch 5.

and to this extent it may indirectly affect the minor's contractual liability.

ii Employment and analogous contracts

The employment of children is regulated by legislative provisions which restrict the age from which children may be employed, and specify conditions and hours of work.[18] Subject to such provisions, the common law rule is that a minor is bound by a contract of employment (including one of apprenticeship[19]) so long as it is *on the whole* for his benefit. This depends on the terms generally available in the type of employment and locality in question. If the minor is employed on terms which are usual from this point of view, they will normally bind him in spite of the fact that some of them are disadvantageous to him.[20] But they will not bind the minor where they are harsh and oppressive, even though they are no worse than those offered to adults.[1]

These rules also apply to two further groups of contracts. First, they apply to contracts ancillary to contracts of employment, such as contracts to dissolve contracts of employment. Secondly, they apply to contracts which are not strictly contracts of employment but which are analogous to such contracts in enabling the minor to make a living. For example, in one case[2] an under-age heavyweight boxer was held to be bound by a term in a contract by which he forfeited his 'purse' if he was disqualified. This term was *on the whole* for his benefit, as it encouraged clean fighting. Similarly, a contract giving a firm of publishers the exclusive right to publish the memoirs of a minor was held binding (in spite of the contents of the book) as it would help him 'to make a start as an author'.[3] On the other hand, a contract is not binding on a minor merely because it is for his benefit and because it helps him to make a living. In particular, a minor is not liable on a 'trading contract'. This means primarily a contract by which the minor buys or sells goods as a dealer,[4] but it also extends to certain contracts for the provision of services. An under-age haulage contractor has been held to be a trader. Hence he was not liable on a contract to hire-

---

18 Eg Employment of Children Act 1973.
19 See *Gadd v Thompson* [1911] 1 KB 304.
20 *Clements v London and North Western Rly Co* [1894] 2 QB 482.
1 *De Francesco v Barnum* (1889) 43 Ch D 165; cf *Godwin v Uzoigwe* [1993] Fam Law 65.
2 *Doyle v White City Stadium Ltd* [1935] 1 KB 110.
3 *Chaplin v Leslie Frewin (Publishers) Ltd* [1966] Ch 71 at 95.
4 *Cowern v Nield* [1912] 2 KB 419.

purchase a lorry;[5] nor would he have been liable for breach of contract to carry goods in the lorry.

b   Contracts which are binding unless repudiated

In some cases the contract binds both parties, but the minor (though not the other party) can escape liability by repudiating the contract. This rule applies where a minor agrees to buy or sell land,[6] or to take or grant a lease of land;[7] where a minor enters into a marriage settlement;[8] and where he incurs liability for calls on shares in a company,[9] by either subscribing for the shares or by buying partly paid up shares from a previous holder. It also applies to the relations between a minor and persons with whom he enters into a partnership, in the sense that he is not entitled to any share in the profits of the partnership unless he discharges his obligations under it to the other partners.[10] He is not liable to third parties who deal with the partnership. These cases have been explained on the not wholly satisfactory ground that the minor has acquired an interest in a subject-matter of a permanent nature; and that it would be unjust to allow him to retain this, unless he discharged the obligations attached to it.

The repudiation may take place either during or after minority. If it takes place during minority it can still be withdrawn either before the minor comes of age or within a reasonable time thereafter.[11] Repudiation after minority is effective only if it takes place within a reasonable time. This begins to run from the date on which the minor reaches full age and not from the time of the making of the contract or from the time at which the former minor discovered his right to repudiate.[12] The effect of repudiation is to relieve the minor from all future liability under the contract, such as liability for future rent or future calls on shares. On the other hand repudiation is probably not retrospective: it does not free the minor from liabilities which had accrued at the time of repudiation. Nor does repudiation enable the minor to get back money which he has paid under the contract, unless there has been a 'total failure of consideration'. In one case,[13] a minor

---

5   *Mercantile Union Guarantee Corpn Ltd v Ball* [1937] 2 KB 498.
6   *Whittingham v Murdy* (1889) 60 LT 956.
7   *Davies v Benyon-Harris* (1931) 47 TLR 424.
8   *Edwards v Carter* [1893] AC 360.
9   *North Western Rly Co v M'Michael* (1850) 5 Exch 114.
10   *Lovell and Christmas v Beauchamp* [1894] AC 607. The Limited Liability Partnerships Act 2000 does not refer to minors.
11   *North Western Rly Co v McMichael* (1850) 5 Exch 114 at 127.
12   *Edwards v Carter* (1893) AC 360.
13   *Steinberg v Scala (Leeds) Ltd* [1923] 2 Ch 452.

had applied for shares in a company. The shares were allotted to her and then fell sharply in value. The minor repudiated and thus escaped liability for calls but it was held that she could not get back the money which she had already paid. There had been no 'total failure of consideration' as she had got the very shares for which she had bargained. If there is such failure of consideration, even an adult can get back money paid.[14] A minor's position is, however, more favourable than an adult's in that the minor can get back money paid even though the total failure was brought about by his own act. This would, for example, be the position if a minor, having paid a deposit under a lease to commence on a future date, repudiated before that date.

A minor may borrow money to enable him to make payments under a contract within the present group and actually use the money for this purpose. He is not bound by the contract of loan, but the lender has rights similar to those of a lender for necessaries.[15]

c Contracts which are not binding on the minor

Here we are concerned with contracts which do not fall within the groups so far discussed. For example, a minor might contract to buy goods which are not necessaries, or to sell goods as a trader, or to go on a luxury world cruise, or he might borrow money or enter into a contract of service which was not beneficial, or into a contract of insurance. Such contracts do not bind the minor; but the fact that he is not bound does not prevent his promise from being good consideration for that of the adult party. That party is therefore bound by the contract,[16] though the remedy of *specific* performance is not available against him.[17] The present group of contracts differs from group **b** above, in that the minor does not have to repudiate to escape liability: if he does nothing, he is not bound. He will, however, become liable on the contract if, after reaching full age, he 'ratifies' it[18] by either declaring himself bound by it or by behaving in such a way as to show that he regards himself as bound.

The minor may perform his part of the contract without being bound to do so: eg by paying for goods which were not 'necessaries'.

---

14 Post, p 418.
15 Ante, p 226, *Nottingham Permanent Benefit Building Society v Thurston* [1903] AC 6.
16 See *Bruce v Warwick* (1815) 6 Taunt 118; *Wilson v Kearse* (1800) Peake Add Cas 196; *Corpe v Overton* (1833) 10 Bing 252 at 259; *Williams v Moor* (1843) 11 M & W 256.
17 *Flight v Bolland* (1828) 4 Russ 298.
18 See *Williams v Moor* (1843) 11 M & W 256.

He is not entitled to the return of the payment merely because the contract did not bind him by reason of his minority.[19] The only circumstances in which he is entitled to get his money back are the same as those in which an adult would be so entitled: eg if he had paid in advance and the goods were never delivered to him, so that thee was a 'total failure of consideration';[20] or if the goods were defective and he justifiably rejected them on that ground.[1]

Performance of the contract will also generally involve some dealing with the subject-matter: eg goods which are not 'necessaries' may be delivered by an adult seller to the minor. The property in such goods can pass to the minor (though the contract does not bind him) by such delivery,[2] coupled with the seller's intention to pass the property to the minor. It is true that where a contract is void for mistake as to the identity of the other contracting party, property does not pass;[3] but this situation differs from that in which the contract does not bind the buyer because of his minority. In the mistake case there is no intention to pass property to the recipient. In the case of the under-age buyer there is such an intention, though it may (if the seller does not know the law) be based on a mistaken view of the binding force of the underlying contract. The view that property passes is also the more desirable one; for to hold the contrary would prejudice innocent third parties who had in turn bought the goods from the minor, and who might have done so long after the minor had come of age.

Property can pass *from*, no less than *to* the minor under a contract which does not bind him: for example, where he delivers goods sold by him as a trader; or where he transfers his copyright in a book or in a musical composition under a contract which does not bind him because it is not, on the whole, beneficial to him.[4]

d   Liability in tort

Minors (except for very young children) are subject to the law of tort in the ordinary way: eg they are liable for negligently causing injury or damage, or for converting property that does not belong to them. But

---

19   *Wilson v Kearse* (1800) Peake Add Cas 196; *Corpe v Overton* (1833) 10 Bing 252 at 259.
20   Post, p 418.
1   Eg post, p 327.
2   *Stocks v Wilson* [1913] 2 KB 235 at 246; the same assumption underlies the Minors' Contracts Act 1987, s 3(1), post, p 231.
3   *Cundy v Lindsay* (1878) 3 App Cas 459; see ante, p 132.
4   See *Chaplin v Leslie Frewin (Publishers) Ltd* [1966] Ch 71 (where the contract was held to be binding: ante, p 227).

a tort is often at the same time a breach of contract: for example where a minor negligently damages a car which he has hired. The law in such cases will not allow the adult to get round the minor's immunity from contractual liability, by suing in tort.[5] But the minor could be held liable in tort if he did something which was wholly outside the acts envisaged by the contract: for example, if he entered the hired car for a stock-car race, or if he sold it.[6]

e Liability in restitution

A minor may be made liable in restitution where he has obtained benefits under a contract but cannot be made to pay for them because the contract is not binding on him. Section 3(1) of the Minors' Contracts Act 1987 gives the court a wide discretion to impose such liability; but this is expressly said to be without prejudice to any other remedy available to the adult.[7] Other restitutionary remedies therefore still need to be discussed, though generally the adult will make his claim under s 3(1) since the conditions imposed by the subsection are less onerous than those imposed by the earlier rules of equity and common law.

i *Minors' Contracts Act 1987, s 3(1)*

The subsection applies where a contract has been made with a minor and is unenforceable against him because of his minority. In such a case, the court 'may, if it is just and equitable to do so, require [the minor] to transfer to the [other party] any property acquired by the [minor] under the contract, or any property representing it.' The operation of the subsection can be illustrated by supposing that the minor has bought a diamond ring for £500, that the ring has been delivered to him, but that he has not paid the price. The court can then order the minor to return the ring to the seller. Moreover, if the minor were to exchange the ring for a necklace, the court could order the minor to transfer the necklace to the seller as 'property representing' the ring. Similarly, if the minor sold the ring for £400 the court could order the minor to transfer the £400 to the seller;[8] and if the minor used the £400 to buy a bracelet the court could order the minor to transfer the bracelet to the seller. On the other hand, if

---

5   *Fawcett v Smethurst* (1914) 84 LJKB 473.
6   Cf *Burnard v Haggis* (1863) 14 CBNS 45; *Ballett v Mingay* [1943] KB 281.
7   Section 3(2).
8   'Property' in s 3(1) seems to include money: Law Commission Report on Minors' Contracts (Law Com No 134) para 4.21.

the minor had spent the £400 on a party to celebrate his coming of age, the court could not make an order under s 3(1) since the minor no longer has either 'the property acquired' or any 'property representing' it; if he had spent £250 out of the £400 on the party, the court could order him to transfer no more than the remaining £150. The fact that the minor may have *other* assets is irrelevant. The court's discretion under s 3(1) exists only to prevent the minor from being enriched by retaining the 'property' obtained under the contract or its identifiable proceeds: to extend the restitutionary remedy beyond this point would come too close to making him liable on a contract that does not bind him. The crucial point is that the minor does not come under a *personal* liability, enforceable against his assets generally. The remedy is *proprietary* in the sense of being enforceable only against a particular asset, ie the property obtained under the contract, or another asset into which it has been transformed. So long as this restriction on the scope of the remedy is observed, it is immaterial that the *measure* of liability is identical with what was due under the contract. If, in our example of the diamond ring, the minor had happened to resell the ring for exactly the £500 that he had agreed to pay for it, he could be ordered to transfer the whole of that sum, so long as it was still in his hands.

The examples considered in the preceding discussion are relatively straightforward. It is easy to imagine more complex situations in which the minor sells the 'property acquired', pays the money into an active bank account which is already in credit, and (perhaps a month later) draws on the account to make a substitute purchase. In such cases, the process of 'tracing' property into its product can be extremely complex and technical; but the detailed rules governing the process need not be considered here since the discretion conferred on the court by s 3(1) seems to be designed to avoid their complexities. In exercising that discretion, the court can take account of the difficulties of 'tracing' and can refuse to order the minor to 'restore' unless it is clear that the property in respect of which the order is sought does indeed represent the property acquired under the contract.

ii   *Effects of fraud*

A minor might induce an adult to enter into a contract with him by some fraud: for example, he might procure a loan of money, or the delivery of goods on credit, by fraudulently pretending to be of age. At common law, he could not be made liable on the contract merely because he had procured it by fraud;[9] nor could the adult get round

9   Eg *Bartlett v Wells* (1862) 1 B & S 836.

the minor's immunity from contractual liability by claiming the amount of the loan, or the value of the goods, as damages in tort for deceit.[10]

These rules unduly favoured fraudulent minors: and equity redressed the balance by ordering a minor who had fraudulently misrepresented his age to restore benefits obtained under the resulting contract. There seems to be no reason now for the adult to resort to this equitable remedy; for it is available only in cases of fraud while the statutory remedy under s 3(1) of the Minors' Contracts Act 1987 is not so restricted. The statutory remedy is, moreover, clearly available, not only in respect of the very thing obtained under the contract, but also in respect of its proceeds; while it was disputed whether the equitable remedy was available in respect of such proceeds.[11] One clear limitation on the scope of the equitable remedy is illustrated by a case[12] in which a minor had, by fraudulently pretending to be of full age, obtained a loan of £400. It was held that he could not be made to 'restore' that amount in the absence of evidence that he still had the money or its identifiable proceeds. Once he had dissipated the money, he could not be ordered to pay an equivalent sum out of his other assets. Such authorities on the scope of the equitable remedy are now of interest chiefly as illustrating the sort of circumstances in which the court is, or is not, likely to exercise its discretion to order the minor to make a transfer under s 3(1) of the 1987 Act. The common principle underlying the equitable and the statutory remedy is that both remedies are *proprietary* rather than *personal* (in the sense already explained): they are available only in respect of identifiable property , and not in respect of the minor's assets generally.

iii   Common law liability restitution

Where one party to a contract has paid a sum of money to the other for some counter-performance, which then is not rendered, he is normally entitled to recover that payment in a restitutionary action for money paid on a total failure of consideration.[13] Generally, the payer's liability in such an action is *personal*, in the sense discussed above. It should therefore not be imposed on a minor who has failed to perform a contract which does not bind him. His liability should be restricted to one to restore the actual money or its traceable proceeds: in other words, he should be liable to a *proprietary* remedy only.[14] Unless

10 *R Leslie Ltd v Sheill* [1914] 3 KB 607.
11 [1914] KB 607 at 619, doubting *Stocks v Wilson* [1913] 2 KB 235.
12 *R Leslie Ltd v Sheill* [1914] 3 KB 607.
13 Post, pp 418–419.
14 *R Leslie Ltd v Sheill* [1914] 3 KB 607.

his liability were restricted in this way, the policy which limits his contractual capacity would be fundamentally subverted.

The common law restitutionary remedy is available as of right: in this respect it is preferable (from the adult's point of view) to the remedy under s 3(1) of the Minors' Contracts Act 1987, which is discretionary. On the other hand, the common law remedy is subject to two limitations. First, it is (according to one case[15]) available only against a minor who is guilty of fraud. Secondly, it is available only in respect of *money* and not in respect of *goods* after they have been delivered, and the property in them has passed, to the minor. Formerly, these limitations could lead to the regrettable result that a minor could keep something for nothing: for example, where he had simply not paid for goods obtained under a contract which did not bind him, or where he had not delivered goods for which he had been paid. But in such cases he can now be ordered to make restitution under s 3(1) of the 1987 Act, so that the practical importance of the limitations on the scope of the quasi-contractual remedy has been virtually eliminated.

2   MENTAL PATIENTS

A contract with a mental patient is valid;[16] but to this rule there are two exceptions. First, the contract can be avoided by the patient if the other party knew of his inability to understand the transaction.[17] Secondly, if the patient's disorder is so serious that his property is made subject to the control of the court, any contract amounting to an attempt by him to dispose of the property does not bind him, though it binds the other party.[18] A contract which does not bind the patient becomes binding on him, if he ratifies it after he is cured.[19]

Even where the patient cannot be sued on the contract, he is liable to pay a reasonable price for necessaries supplied to him.[20] Necessaries include services, so that the patient would be liable for the reasonable price of medical treatment given in circumstances in which a charge would normally be made. This would obviously exclude free treatment under the National Health Service; cases of this kind more commonly

---

15   *Cowern v Nield* [1912] KB 419.
16   *Hart v O'Connor* [1985] AC 1000.
17   *Imperial Loan Co v Stone* [1892] 1 QB 599.
18   *Re Walker* [1905] 1 Ch 160.
19   *Manches v Trimborn* (1946) 115 LJ KB 305.
20   Sale of Goods Act 1979, s 3, the relevant part of which is to be replaced by cl 7 of the Mental Capacity Bill 2004.

raise the question whether the treatment is lawful without the patient's consent than the question of liability to pay for it.[1]

3 DRINK AND DRUGS

A person cannot avoid liability on a contract merely because, when he made it, his commercial judgment was befuddled by drink; though in equity the remedy of specific performance has occasionally been refused, where one party took advantage of the other's intoxication.[2] The contract is voidable by the latter party only if he was so drunk that he could not understand the transaction and if the other party knew this.[3] Even then, the contract becomes binding if it is ratified when the effects of drink have worn off.[4] A drunken person is also liable for necessaries supplied to him while he is suffering from his temporary incapacity to contract.[5] These rules could perhaps be applied by analogy to persons whose judgment was impaired by drugs.[6]

4 CORPORATIONS

a Charter corporations

Some corporations (such as many Universities and Colleges) are created by Royal Charter. The charter will specify the purposes for which the corporation was created; but such provisions do not restrict the corporation's contractual capacity.[7] Thus a contract may be valid, although it was not authorised, or was prohibited, by the charter. If the corporation makes such a contract, it runs the risk of having its charter revoked, and its members may take legal proceedings to stop it from entering into contracts which expose it to this risk.[8] But this does not affect the validity of any such contract which the corporation has actually made.

---

1   *Re F* [1990] 2 AC 1; *Re C* [1994] 1 All ER 819 at 824; and see new provisions dealing with this problem in the above Bill.
2   *Malins v Freeman* (1836) 2 Keen 25 at 34.
3   *Gore v Gibson* (1845) 13 M & W 623.
4   *Matthews v Baxter* (1873) LR 8 Exch 132.
5   Sale of Goods Act 1979, s 3.
6   See *Irvani v Irvani* [2000] 1 Lloyd's Rep 412 at 425.
7   *Jenkin v Pharmaceutical Society of Great Britain* [1921] 1 Ch 392 at 398.
8   *Jenkin v Pharmaceutical Society of Great Britain* [1921] 1 Ch 392.

b   Statutory corporations

It will be convenient to consider first the contractual capacity of corporations which have been created by special Acts of Parliament; and then to discuss the position of the great majority of commercial corporations which have, since 1862, been created by using the machinery provided for this purpose by legislation such as the Companies Acts.

i   Corporations created by special statute

Where a corporation is created by special statute, the objects of the corporation will be set out in that statute, and contracts made by the corporation which fall outside those objects are ultra vires and void.[9] This ultra vires doctrine can be a source of hardship to persons who deal with the corporation in ignorance of the terms of its incorporating statute; and this hardship has been mitigated in various ways. First, the company can validly make contracts reasonably incidental to the specified objects: for example, it can grant short leases of premises not immediately required for its stated objects.[10] Secondly, a contract, eg one to borrow money, may on its face be quite neutral. Such a contract is not invalid merely because the money is used for an ultra vires purpose: it would be invalid only if the lender had notice of that purpose when he made the loan.[11] Thirdly, the incorporating statute may, after specifying the objects of the corporation, go on to give it power to do anything 'calculated to facilitate' or 'incidental or conducive to' those objects.[12] Such a power must be exercised for the purpose of the objects; and if it is exercised for other purposes the resulting contract is beyond the powers of the directors and cannot be enforced by a third party with notice that it has been so exercised;[13] but it can be enforced by a third party who has no such notice.

A third party who is prevented by the ultra vires doctrine from enforcing the contract has a number of other remedies. If he pays money under an ultra vires contract, he can recover it (on returning anything that he may have received under the contract) as money paid under a void contract.[14] An ultra vires contractor may also have a remedy against an officer of the company who has induced him to

9   *Ashbury Railway Carriage and Iron Co Ltd v Riche* (1875) LR 7 HL 653.
10   *Foster v London, Chatham and Dover Rly Co* [1895] 1 QB 711.
11   Cf *Re Jon Beauforte (London) Ltd* [1953] Ch 131.
12   *Den Norske Creditbank v Sarawak Economic Development Corpn* [1988] 2 Lloyd's Rep 616 (where the incorporating legislation was a Malaysian Ordinance).
13   *Rolled Steel Products (Holdings) Ltd v British Steel Corpn* [1986] Ch 246, where the distinction stated in the text was developed in the context of companies incorporated under the Companies Acts.
14   Post, p 420.

enter into the contract by representing that it was intra vires. The remedy would be in tort if the officer was guilty of fraud or negligence. If the representation was wholly innocent the officer would still be liable in contract, for breach of a so-called 'implied warranty' that he had authority to make the contract on behalf of the company.[15]

The above discussion is concerned with the rights of the ultra vires contractor. The further question arises whether the company itself can enforce an ultra vires contract. If the contract is still unperformed on both sides, it probably cannot be enforced by the company, for such enforcement could hardly be ordered without requiring the company to perform its part, and thus sanctioning ultra vires expenditure. If, on the other hand, the contract has been performed by the company, little harm could be done by allowing the company to enforce the contract. Probably it can do so,[16] though strictly the purpose of the ultra vires doctrine would be better served by allowing the company to claim back any money paid or property transferred by it under the contract.

ii Companies created under the Companies Acts

The objects of such a company have to be stated in its memorandum of association, a document which is registered in the Companies Register where it is open to public inspection. The original common law position was that the contracts of such companies were subject to the ultra vires doctrine. The purpose of the doctrine was to protect investors in the company by giving them some assurance that money invested in one kind of business should not be used for a wholly different one. On the other hand the hardship which the doctrine could cause to outsiders who contracted with the company attracted much criticism; and this hardship was substantially removed by legislative reforms in 1989.

This legislation in the first place enables a company incorporated under the Companies Acts to state its objects in very broad terms so as to enable it to carry on 'any trade or business whatsoever'[17] and also to alter its objects for any purpose whatsoever.[18] These points would in themselves make it hard to apply the ultra vires doctrine to such a company.

Secondly, the 1989 legislation provides that any act done by a company is not (as a general rule[19]) to be called into question on the ground of lack of the company's capacity by reason of anything in (or,

15 *Firbank's Executors v Humphreys* (1886) 18 QBD 54; see p 308, post.
16 *Bell Houses Ltd v City Wall Properties Ltd* [1966] 2 QB 656 at 694.
17 Companies Act 1985, s 3A.
18 Companies Act 1985, s 4.
19 For exceptions, see Companies Act 1985, s 35(4) and Charities Act 1993, s 64 (charitable companies and certain transactions with directors).

presumably, not in) its memorandum.[20] It follows that neither the company nor a party contracting with it can any longer rely on the argument that the contract is void for lack of capacity because it is not authorised by the company's memorandum. This would not of itself entitle a third party to sue the company since a contract which is not authorised by the memorandum is necessarily beyond the powers of the directors. Further protection is therefore given by a provision that 'in favour of a person dealing with the company in good faith, the power of the board of directors to bind the company, or to authorise others to do so, shall [as a general rule[1]] be deemed to be free of any limitation under the company's constitution'.[2] The third party is not bound to enquire whether the transaction is permitted by the memorandum or whether the powers of the directors are limited in respect of it;[3] is presumed to have acted in good faith till the contrary is proved;[4] and is not to be regarded as having acted in bad faith 'by reason only of his knowing that an act is beyond the powers of the directors under the company's constituton'.[5] This last provision allows for the possibility that it may be in the interest of the company to take advantage of a commercial opportunity by making a contract which is technically outside its objects. Obviously, on the other hand, a contract would not be saved by the present provision if it was not only beyond the powers of the directors but also amounted to a collusive attempt between them and the third party to bind the company by a transaction that was contrary to its interests.

The 1989 legislation also to some extent protects members of the company by giving them the right to bring proceedings to restrain an act which would (but for the provisions stated above) be beyond the company's capacity[6] or beyond the powers of the directors.[7] But no such proceedings lie in respect of an act to be done in fulfilment of a legal obligation arising from a previous act of the company.[8] It follows that a member cannot restrain the company from performing a contract which can be enforced against it in spite of its lack of capacity and in spite of the fact that it was beyond the powers of the directors.

---

20 Companies Act 1985, s 35(1).
1   For exceptions similar to those stated in n 19, supra, see the references to Charities Act 1993 there given and Companies Act 1985, s 35A(6).
2   Companies Act 1985, s 35A(1).
3   Companies Act 1985, s 35B.
4   Companies Act 1985, s 35A(2)(c).
5   Companies Act 1985, s 35A(2)(b).
6   Companies Act 1985, s 35(2).
7   Companies Act 1985, s 35A(4).
8   Companies Act 1985, ss 35(2), 35A(4).

iii Limited liability partnerships

Such partnerships become bodies corporate on the registration of specified documents.[9] They then have 'unlimited capacity',[10] so that the ultra vires doctrine does not apply to them.

---

9 Limited Liability Partnerships Act 2000, ss 1 and 2.
10 Limited Liability Partnerships Act 2000, s 1(3).

Chapter 13

The parties to a contract

So far, we have assumed that a contract is made simply between two parties, each consisting of one person. Occasionally reference has been made to multilateral contracts between more than two parties: for example, to the situation in which three or more persons agree to compete in a race and to obey certain rules. Here again it is assumed that each party to the contract consists of one person. It is, however, also possible to have more than one person on each side of the contract. Four such situations call for discussion. First, there may be more than one debtor, as where A and B make a promise to X; secondly, there may be more than one creditor, as where A makes a promise to X and Y; thirdly, A may make a contract with X for the benefit of Y; and fourthly, the question may arise whether a contract between A and X can bind Y.

1 PROMISES BY MORE THAN ONE PERSON

Suppose that A and B promise to pay X £10. One possibility is that each makes an entirely *separate* promise, in which case X can claim £10 from each of them ie £20 in all.[1] Another possibility is that A and B promise *together* to pay X £10, in which case X cannot get more than £10 in all. The exact legal effect of such a promise depends on whether it is *joint* or *joint and several*. A joint promise is a single promise made by a number of persons; a joint and several promise consists of such a single promise coupled with a separate promise by each promisor. Promises by a number of persons are deemed to be joint unless they provide the contrary, eg by being framed in the form 'we promise jointly and severally' or 'we, and each of us, promise'.

a Similarities between joint, and joint and several, promises

Whether the promise is joint or joint and several, each promisor is fully liable to the promisee: ie X can recover the full £10 from either

1   Eg *Mikeover Ltd v Brady* [1989] 3 All ER 618.

A or B (but not from both). But if one debtor, being liable to pay the whole,[2] pays more than his share, he is entitled to contribution from the other. This is assessed by dividing the debt by the number of debtors who are solvent when the right to contribution arises.[3] Thus if A, B and C promise to pay £18 to X and A pays the whole sum, he can recover £6 from B and £6 from C. But if C is bankrupt at the time of the payment, A can recover £9 from B. These rules are subject to contrary provision, express or implied, in the contract. If, for example, A is a principal debtor while B and C are sureties, obviously A cannot recover contribution from B and C. On the contrary, if B or C or both of them pay the debt, they are entitled to be wholly indemnified by A.

If the creditor releases one of the co-debtors, the general rule is that the others are also released;[4] for if they could still be sued they would then be able to claim contribution from the one who was released and so deprive the release of its practical force.[5] But this rule applies only where X's release of A contains no express or implied reservation of X's rights against B.[6] Where the release on its true construction does contain such a reservation, the court will give effect to the intention of the parties as so expressed, and B will remain liable.[7] A similar principle of construction applies where A and B are not co-debtors but are persons who have broken entirely separate contracts with X.[8]

If one debtor raises a defence to the claim, this will not avail the others, if it was personal to him: for example, if one successfully pleads that he is a minor the others are not released.[9] The position is different if one debtor's defence goes to the root of the whole claim: for example, if the defence is that the creditor had not performed his part of the contract.[10] One special problem is whether a guarantor, who generally undertakes joint and several liability with the principal debtor, can rely on a defence available to the latter. The solution to this problem depends on the policy of the rule giving the debtor his defence. Thus, a guarantee of an illegal contract cannot be enforced, since to allow

2 For this requirement, see *Legal and General Assurance Society Ltd v Drake Insurance Co Ltd* [1992] QB 887.
3 *Hitchman v Stewart* (1855) 3 Drew 271.
4 *Nicholson v Revill* (1836) 4 Ad & El 675; *Deanplan Ltd v Mahmoud* [1993] Ch 151.
5 *Jenkins v Jenkins* [1928] 2 KB 501 at 508.
6 See *Deanplan v Mahmoud* [1993] Ch 151; cf *Gardiner v Moore* [1969] 1 QB 55 (where the liability was in tort).
7 *Johnson v Davies* [1999] Ch 117 at 127–128.
8 *Heaton v Axa Equity and Law Life Assurance Society plc* [2002] UKHL 15, [2002] 2 AC 329.
9 *Lovell and Christmas v Beauchamp* [1894] AC 607.
10 *Pirie v Richardson* [1927] 1 KB 448.

enforcement would tend to undermine the rule giving rise to the illegality.[11] On the other hand, an adult is liable where he guarantees a debt which cannot be enforced against the principal debtor by reason of the latter's minority.[12] The rule that the minor cannot be sued for the debt exists for his protection alone, and its purpose would not be furthered by allowing the adult to escape liability on the guarantee.

Similar problems used to arise where the principal debt was incurred by a corporation under an ultra vires contract. If the corporation is incorporated by special statute, so that the ultra vires doctrine still applies to it,[13] there seems to be no good reason why the guarantor should be able to escape liability by relying on the invalidity of the principal debt.[14] If the principal debtor is a company incorporated under the Companies Act, it will normally be liable for the principal debt even though this arose under a contract which was beyond the powers of its directors.[15] The company will not, however, be liable to a third party who had dealt with it in bad faith[16] and the analogy of the illegality rule (stated above) suggests that such a party should not be allowed to enforce the guarantee, any more than he can enforce the principal contract.

b Differences between joint, and joint and several, promises

At common law, the so-called doctrine of survivorship applied to joint, but not to joint and several, promises. Under this doctrine, if A and B made a joint promise to X and A died, his liability passed to B. If B paid the debt, he could get contribution from A's estate,[17] but X had no right against the estate. The result might be that, if A died and B became bankrupt, X had no substantial rights against anyone. The rule was inconvenient in commercial cases and equity in some such cases refused to follow it.[18] It no longer applies to partnership debts;[19] and it is arguable that the topic was one in which there was a conflict between common law and equity, so that the equitable rules now prevail by virtue of the general principle which gives them primacy in cases of such conflict.[20]

11 *Swan v Bank of Scotland* (1836) 10 Bli NS 627.
12 Minors' Contracts Act 1987, s 2; see ante, p 229.
13 Ante, p 236.
14 *Yorkshire Railway Wagon Co v MacLure* (1882) 21 Ch D 309; see pp 236–237, ante.
15 Ante, pp 237–238.
16 Ante, p 238.
17 *Batard v Hawes* (1853) 2 E & B 287.
18 *Thorpe v Jackson* (1837) 2 Y & C Ex 553.
19 Partnership Act 1890, s 9.
20 Judicature Act 1873, s 25(11); now Supreme Court Act 1981, s 49(1).

There were also procedural distinctions between the two types of promises; but these have lost much of their former importance. At common law, an action on a joint contract had to be brought against all the debtors, whereas one on a joint and several contract could be brought against all the debtors or against any one of them. But the rule in the case of joint debtors is relaxed in some cases: for example, if one of the debtors is abroad, or cannot be traced, or is bankrupt. In all these cases the others can be sued without that one.[1] And in an action against one liable jointly and severally with others the court may order the others to be made parties to the proceedings,[2] so that (for example) contribution between them can be assessed once for all in a single action. Moreover, the rule that all joint debtors had to be sued together, applied only if the one who was sued expressly pleaded the creditor's failure to join the others as parties to the action. There was thus the possibility that judgment might be obtained against only one of the co-debtors; and if that judgment was not satisfied, the creditor would wish to take further proceedings against the others. At common law he could do so only where the debt was joint and several[3] but by statute he can now also do so in the case of joint debts.[4]

2   PROMISES TO MORE THAN ONE PERSON

If A promises to pay £10 to X and Y, he may make two separate promises to pay them £10 each, in which case, his total liability is to pay £20. But the promise may be a single promise to pay no more than £10 in all. Here it is necessary to distinguish between cases in which the promise is made to X and Y jointly and those in which it is made to them severally.

a   Joint promises

If a promise is made to X and Y jointly they are together entitled to the whole of the promised performance. Suppose that A is tenant of a house owned by X and Y and promises to pay rent of £2,000 per annum to them jointly. As against A neither of the landlords is entitled to any particular share of the £2,000. A is not concerned with any

---

1   *Wilson, Sons & Co Ltd v Balcarres Brook Steamship Co* [1893] 1 QB 422; *Robinson v Geisel* [1894] 2 QB 685; Insolvency Act 1986, s 345(4).
2   CPR, r 19.2(2)(a).
3   *Blyth v Fladgate* [1891] 1 Ch 337; contrast *Kendall v Hamilton* (1879) 4 App Cas 504 (joint debt).
4   Civil Liability (Contribution) Act 1978, s 3.

3　PROMISES IN FAVOUR OF A THIRD PARTY

This situation differs from the one just discussed in that A makes no promise directly to Y. The only contract is between A and X, and Y is merely an intended, or third party, beneficiary. Suppose that X takes out an insurance policy with the A company in favour of Y. Here Y is not a party to the contract between A and X but a third party beneficiary. An arrangement involving A, X and Y may, moreover, be so constituted that Y is not a beneficiary at all.[19] Suppose that A sells goods to X who directs A to deliver them at Y's warehouse. Here the intention is in all probability not to confer any benefit on Y but simply to tell A how to perform his promise to X. There is a further possibility: Y may not be a mere beneficiary of a contract between A and X, but an immediate party to a *separate* contract between himself and A. An arrangement involving three parties may in law be analysed as consisting of two contracts: a main contract between A and X and a collateral contract between A and Y. Such an analysis has, for example, been adopted where a car belonging to Y was damaged in a road accident and repaired by A (a garage) on the instructions of X (an insurance company). It was held that the main contract to repair the car was between A and X, but that there was also a collateral contract between A and Y under which A was liable in damages for undue delay in carrying out the repairs.[20]

Assuming, however, that the arrangement in question is a contract for the benefit of a third party, the question then arises as to the legal effects of such a contract. The starting principle of English law is contained in the common law doctrine of privity of contract. This doctrine is subject to many judge-made and statutory exceptions, including the 'general and wide-ranging'[1] one created by the Contracts (Rights of Third Parties) Act 1999.

a　Privity of contract at common law

As a general rule, rights arising under a contract can be enforced only by the parties to it.[2] For example, in *Beswick v Beswick*[3] X transferred his business to his nephew, A, who promised X that after X's death he

---

19　Cf *Thavorn v Bank of Credit and Commerce International SA* [1985] 1 Lloyd's Rep 259.

20　*Charnock v Liverpool Corpn* [1968] 3 All ER 473; cf ante, p 35.

1　Law Commission, *Privity of Contract: Contracts for the Benefit of Third Parties*, Law Com No 242 (1886), § 5.16, and see § 13.2.

2　*Tweddle v Atkinson* (1861) 1 B&S 393; *Dunlop Pneumatic Tyre Co Ltd v Selfridge & Co Ltd* [1915] AC 847 at 853.

3　[1968] AC 58.

would pay £5 per week to X's widow, Y. It was assumed by the House of Lords that Y could not enforce A's promise as this had been made, not to her, but to X. One reason for the general common law rule was that Y normally provided no consideration for A's promise. Another was that if Y acquired rights under the contract, the power of A and X to put an end to their contract would be lost or severely limited.

b Other effects of the contract

Although a contract between A and X for the benefit of Y cannot generally be enforced by Y, it remains binding between A and X. The fact that the contract was made for the benefit of a third party does, however, give rise to a number of special problems.

i *Promisee's remedies*

X may be entitled to an order of specific performance, and if such an order is made A will be compelled to perform in favour of Y. This is what happened in *Beswick v Beswick*. On X's death, his widow Y became his administratrix and so for legal purposes represented him. In that capacity she obtained an order directing the nephew (A) to make the promised payments to her in her personal capacity. The result was that a promise in favour of a third party was enforced exactly in accordance with its terms. But this result can only be reached if A's promise is of such a kind that it is specifically enforceable: this requirement would, for example, exclude the remedy where A had promised X to render personal services to Y.[4] Moreover, enforcement of the promise in favour of Y *requires the co-operation of X*. If X refuses to sue A, Y cannot force him to do so; nor can Y force X to sue for specific performance if X chooses to pursue some other remedy.

The most obvious other remedy is for X to claim damages from A. Such a claim will clearly succeed where A's failure to pay Y had caused loss to X. This would be the position where X owed money to Y and looked to the payment by A to Y as a means of discharging that debt. The difficult cases are those in which A's breach, at least at first sight, causes loss only to Y and not to X, for the general rule is that X can recover damages for breach of contract only in respect of his own loss and not in respect of loss suffered by Y.[5] Thus in *Beswick v Beswick* it was

4   See post, p 411.
5   *Woodar Investment Development Ltd v Wimpey Construction (UK) Ltd* [1980] 1 WLR 277; *Panatown Ltd v Alfred McAlpine Construction Ltd* [2001] 1 AC 518 at 522, 563, 572, 580–581.

said that the damages recoverable by X's estate would have been no more than nominal since A's breach had caused no loss to the estate, but only to Y.[6] This position can be 'most unsatisfactory'[7] in giving rise to a 'legal black hole',[8] that is, to a situation in which A has committed a plain breach of his contract with X but loss is suffered only by Y, so that no-one has a substantial remedy in respect of the breach. The law has therefore created many exceptions to the general rule. For example, where a person books a family holiday or orders a meal in a restaurant for himself and one or more guests, he can probably recover damages in respect of loss suffered by other members of the party;[9] a trustee may be able to recover damages in respect of loss suffered by his beneficiary, an agent in respect of loss suffered by his undisclosed principal, and a shipper of goods (X) can recover damages for breach of his contract with the carrier (A) in respect of loss suffered by the consignee (Y) to whom A has sold the goods and who has not acquired any rights under the contract between A and X.[10] The principle of these carriage cases has been extended to cases in which breach of a building contract between a builder (A) and an employer (X) caused loss to a third party (Y) to whom the site was later transferred by X;[11] and even to the situation in which the site already belonged to Y when the contract was made.[12] One justification for this outcome (the 'narrower ground'[13]) was that it was simply an application of the principle of the carriage cases to building contracts.[14] A second justification (the 'broader ground'[15]) was that X had himself suffered loss by being put to the cost of remedying the defects or deficiencies in A's performance;[16] on this reasoning X recovers damages in respect of his own (and not in respect of Y's) loss. Neither justification extends to the situation in which Y has his own contractual rights against A under a separate contract between them. In such a case, the 'narrower

---

6   [1968] AC 58, especially at 102.
7   *Woodar Investment Development Ltd v Wimpey Construction (UK) Ltd* [1980] 1 WLR 277 at 291.
8   *Darlington Borough Council v Wiltshier Northern Ltd* [1995] 1 WLR 68 at 79.
9   *Woodar* case [1980] 1 WLR 277 at 283.
10 Post, pp 253, 305; *Dunlop v Lambert* (1839) 6 Cl & Fin 600 at 627, as qualified by *The Albazero* [1977] AC 774.
11 *Linden Gardens Trust Ltd v Lenesta Sludge Disposals Ltd* [1994] 1 AC 85 ('the *Linden Gardens* case').
12 *Darlington Borough Council v Wiltshier Northern Ltd* [1995] 1 WLR 68; approved in *Panatown Ltd v Alfred McAlpine Construction Ltd* ('the *Panatown* case') '[2001] 1 AC 518 at 531, 566.
13 *Panatown* case at 575.
14 *Linden Gardens* case at 114.
15 *Linden Gardens* case at 532.
16 *Linden Gardens* case at 96–97.

ground' would not apply since there would be no 'legal black hole' and hence no need[17] for any exception to the general rule that X can recover damages in respect only of his own loss. Nor would the 'broader ground' apply where Y has such rights, since if that were the position X would have no financial interest in curing the defects in A's work.[18] The 'broader ground' is probably also restricted to cases in which 'the repairs have been or are likely to be carried out',[19] or in which X is contractually liable to Y to carry them out. It is so restricted to avoid the 'unattractive result' of enabling X to 'put the money [ie the damages] in his own pocket',[20] as he would be entitled to do where he recovered the cost of cure, under the 'broader ground', as damages for his *own* loss.[1]

The above carriage and building cases are concerned with defective performance of promises to perform services. It is an open question whether a promisee should be entitled to damages in respect of the third party's loss for other breaches: eg for A's failure to perform a simple promise to X to pay a sum of money to Y. This was the position in *Beswick v Beswick*,[2] where there was no 'black hole' because X was able specifically to enforce A's promise to pay the money to Y. But if no such remedy were available to X, if no loss had (as in that case) been suffered by X, and if Y had no contractual remedy of his own against A, then the need to avoid a 'black hole' should now[3] generate a remedy at the suit of X in respect of Y's loss.

As an alternative to damages, X might claim the return of any payment he had made under the contract: for example, where X insures his life in favour of Y and Y cannot enforce the policy against A (the insurer),[4] X he might sue A for the return of his premiums; or he might claim that A should pay X the policy moneys, ie the sums which under the contract A had promised to pay to Y. But a claim for the return of premiums will often be less advantageous than one for the policy moneys; and if the contract say as that these are to be paid to Y then they can be successfully claimed by X or his estate only if the contract is on its true construction one to pay Y or as X shall direct,[5] or

---

17 *Panatown* case at 575 ('because it was not needed'); *The Albazero*, [1977] AC 774 at 846–848.
18 *Panatown* case at 574, 577.
19 *Linden Gardens* case at 97.
20 *Panatown* case at 571.
1 The rule requiring the promisee to hold the damages for the third party (post, p 250) applies only where they are recovered in respect of that party's loss.
2 [1968] AC 58, ante, p 246.
3 Ie, after developments of the law in the *Linden Gardens* and *Panatown* cases, supra nn 11 and 12.
4 See, eg, *Re Sinclair's Life Policy* [1938] Ch 799.
5 *The Spiros C* [2000] 2 Lloyd's Rep 319 at 331.

perhaps in other exceptional circumstances: eg if Y is convicted of having murdered X.[6]

An action by X for damages in respect of his own loss, for return of the money paid by him, or for the sum agreed to be paid under the contract, will not be of any help to Y: the success of such an action would simply lead to a judgment for a sum of money in favour of X. But in the exceptional cases in which X can recover damages in respect of loss suffered by Y, those damages must be held for Y.[7]

ii   Position between promisee and third party

Where A has actually performed in favour of Y, for example by making the promised payment to him, X might claim that Y should hand that payment over to X. It is unlikely that X himself will make such a claim, since this would defeat his intention to benefit Y. But if X has gone bankrupt or died the claim may be put forward for the benefit of his creditors or of the persons entitled under his will. As a general rule claims of this kind will fail, so that Y can keep the money for his own benefit. X (or someone standing legally in his shoes) can claim the money from Y only if Y received it as X's nominee. In such a case Y would not be a true third party beneficiary, but merely a person to whom A was authorised to make a payment (or to render some other performance) due under the contract to X.[8]

X may also claim the money before it has actually been paid over to Y. Often A is quite willing to pay either X or Y, so long as the payment is made in such a way as to discharge him from his liability under the contract. Since our present assumption is that Y has no enforceable rights under the contract, there is nothing to stop A and X from agreeing to vary the contract, so as to make the money payable to X. Such a variation, however, requires the consent of *both* parties to the contract: A is not bound to pay X merely because X asks him to do so. He would normally[9] be bound to do this only if the contract on its true construction obliged him to pay Y, or such other person (including X), as X might direct.[10] The answer to this question of construction would probably depend on whether it mattered to A whether the payment was received by Y or by someone else. If A is an insurance company, the destination of the payment will usually not matter in

---

6   Infra at n 9.
7   *Jackson v Horizon Holidays Ltd* [1975] 1 WLR 1486 at 1473; *The Albazero* [1977] AC 774 at 845; cf (in tort) *Hunt v Severs* [1994] 2 AC 350 at 363.
8   As in *Coulls v Bagot's Executor and Trustee Co Ltd* [1967] ALR 385.
9   For an exception to the normal rule, see *Cleaver v Mutual Reserve Fund Life Association* [1892] 1 QB 147, where Y had been convicted of murdering X.
10   *The Spiros C* [2000] 2 Lloyd's Rep 319 at 331.

the least to the company, whose only concern will be to ensure that its obligation to pay is effectively discharged. On the other hand, if A is Y's close relation, A may have an interest in seeing that the payment is made to Y, since, if it were diverted to X, A might feel obliged to make some other provision for Y's support.[11]

c Scope of the doctrine of privity

The doctrine of privity prevents a person from enforcing rights (or relying on defences) which *arise under* a contract to which he is not a party. It does not mean that he may not indirectly benefit from the contract: for example, payment by A of part of Y's debt to X, which X accepts in full settlement, may discharge that debt.[12] The contract between A and X may also be one of the circumstances giving Y a right to sue A in tort. Two such situations call for discussion.

i Liability in negligence

A contract between A and X may give rise to a relationship between A and Y in which A owes a duty of care to Y: eg if it results in Y's goods being carried in A's ship. If, in the course of performing that contract, A negligently damages those goods, he will be liable in tort to Y.[13] On the same principle, professional advisers, such as surveyors and solicitors, have been held liable in tort to persons other than the clients who had engaged them.[14] A detailed discussion of the circumstances giving rise to such liability in tort is beyond the scope of this book; but something must be said about ways in which such liability differs from liability for breach of contract. First, A's liability in tort depends on fault, while contract liability is often strict.[15] Secondly, A is liable in tort only if his negligence in performing his contract with X causes loss to Y: there is in general[16] no such liability if A simply fails or refuses to perform that contract.[17] Thirdly, A is liable to Y in tort only if there is a relationship of 'proximity' between them in which it is foreseeable that the breach of A's contract with X will cause loss to Y and it is just as reasonable to impose on A a duty of care to Y,[18] while if Y can establish a contract with A, that is sufficient to give rise to A's duty to perform. Fourthly, in a tort

---

11 Cf *Re Stapleton-Bretherton, Weld-Blundell v Stapleton-Bretherton* [1941] Ch 482.
12 *Hirachand Punamchand v Temple* [1911] 2 KB 330.
13 *The Antonis P Lemos* [1985] AC 711.
14 Eg *Smith v Eric S Bush* [1990] 1 AC 831; *White v Jones* [1995] 2 AC 207.
15 Post, p 314.
16 For exceptions, see the 'disappointed beneficiary' cases, infra at n 4.
17 Cf *The Zephyr* [1985] 2 Lloyd's Rep 529 at 538.
18 Eg *The Nicholas H* [1996] AC 211; cf ante, pp 153–154.

action Y must often show that he suffered physical harm, as opposed to purely financial loss,[19] such as the loss of profit which Y, the owner of a fishing boat, suffered as a result of defects in an engine supplied by A to X, the maker of the boat, under a contract to which Y was not a party.[20] The physical harm must, moreover, relate to something other than the very thing supplied by A to X: hence if A sells goods to X and X resells them to Y, A is not liable to Y in tort merely because the goods disintegrate because of a defect amounting to a breach of A's contract with X.[1] Finally, in a contractual action damages are recoverable to put the claimant into the position in which he would have been if the contract had been performed,[2] while such damages are not, in general, recoverable in an action in tort. For example, where defective building work is done under a contract between A and X in a flat which is later let to Y, then Y cannot in a tort action against A recover the cost of making the defects good.[3] This general principle, however, does not apply to a group of so-called 'disappointed beneficiary'[4] (and closely analogous[5]) cases in which X instructs his solicitor A to draw up a will in favour of Y, and A fails to do so, or to do so effectively. A is then liable in tort for the amount that Y would have received under the will if X's instructions had been carried out. One way of distinguishing this 'unusual class of cases'[6] from the building contract cases is to say that in those cases Y's complaint is that he has not received the benefit of the builder's performance, while in the disappointed beneficiary cases the benefit of which Y was deprived was not to be created by the solicitor's work but existed independently of it. Another possible explanation of the disappointed beneficiary cases is that, if a duty to Y is to be imposed on the solicitor, the only realistic measure of damages is the value of the lost benefit.

---

19   *Tate & Lyle Industries Ltd v Greater London Council* [1983] 2 AC 509 at 530–531; the present rule does not apply to the misrepresentation cases discussed at pp 153–154 ante, or where the contract between A and X gives rise to an 'assumption of responsibility' by A to Y: see *White v Jones* [1995] 2 AC 207 at 274; *Lennon v Metropolitan Police Commissioner* [2004] EWCA Civ 130, [2004] 2 All ER 266 at [20], [34].

20   *The Rebecca Elaine* [1999] 2 Lloyd's Rep 1 at 8; cf *Simaan General Contracting Co v Pilkington Glass Ltd (No 2)* [1988] QB 758.

1   *Aswan Engineering Establishment Co v Lupdine Ltd* [1887] 1 WLR 1.

2   Ante, pp 5–6, post, pp 375–377.

3   *D & F Estates Ltd v Church Comrs for England* [1989] AC 177, restricting (at 204) to its 'unique facts' the contrary decision in *Junior Books Ltd v Veitchi Co Ltd* [1983] 1 AC 520.

4   *White v Jones* [1995] 2 AC 207.

5   Eg *Carr-Glynn v Frearsons* [1999] Ch 326; *Gorham v British Telecommunications plc* [2000] 1 WLR 2129.

6   *Goodwill v Pregnancy Advisory Services* [1996] 1 WLR 1397 at 1403.

ii Intimidation

The tort of intimidation is committed where A, by threats of unlawful conduct directed at X, induces X to act to the detriment of Y. For this purpose, a breach of contract is an unlawful act,[7] so that A would be liable for intimidation to Y if, by threatening to break his contract with X, he induced X to stop doing business with Y. In such a case, Y is not enforcing the contract between A and X:[8] his claim is for damages for the loss which A has inflicted on him by means of his unlawful threat against X.

d Exceptions to the doctrine of privity

Although the doctrine of privity can to some extent be explained on both theoretical and practical grounds,[9] it is also open to criticism. It can cause inconvenience where it prevents enforcement of the contract by the person (Y) who had the greatest interest in enforcing it: this would often be the result of a strict application of the doctrine to commercial transactions involving (as they commonly do) more than two parties. Worse still, it can cause injustice, for it may enable the promisor (A) to break his contract with relative impunity, since there may be no effective remedy against him: this might be the position if X's only remedy were in damages and these were no more than nominal because the breach had caused him no loss.[10] These defects have led to much criticism of the doctrine,[11] culminating in a report issued by the Law Commission in 1996 and implemented (with minor modifications) by the Contracts (Rights of Third Parties) Act 1999. Earlier exceptions to the doctrine survive the Act[12] and so still call for discussion.

i Agency, assignment and land law

Under the law of agency, an agreement between A and X can give rise to a contract between A and Y if X, in making the agreement, acted on behalf of and with the authority of either A or Y. This exception is discussed in Chapter 15. Another exception arises where a contractual

---

7   *Rookes v Barnard* [1964] AC 1129.
8   [1964] AC 1129 at 1168, 1208.
9   See ante, p 247.
10   See ante, p 248.
11   *Beswick v Beswick* [1968] AC 58 at 72; *Woodar Investment Development Ltd v Wimpey Construction (UK) Ltd* [1980] 1 WLR 277 at 281; *Swain v Law Society* [1983] 1 AC 598 at 611; Law Com No 242 (1996).
12   See s 7(1).

right between A and X is transferred to Y, who thus becomes entitled to enforce it against A. This process is called assignment and is discussed in Chapter 14. Further exceptions to the doctrine of privity exist in land law. Accounts of them will be found in works on that subject; they relate mainly to covenants in leases and to restrictive covenants, such as covenants not to build on specified land.

ii   *Trusts of promises*

When A makes a promise to X for the benefit of Y, X is sometimes regarded as trustee for Y of the benefit of A's promise. Y can then sue A on the promise; though he must join X to the action so that A is not exposed to the risk of being sued twice on the same promise. This trust device was for example applied where a broker (Y) negotiated a charterparty in which the shipowners (A) promised the charterer (X) to pay a commission to Y. It was held that X was trustee for Y of A's promise, which could therefore be enforced by Y against A.[13] Such a trust may be created even though the contract does not contain the word 'trust' or 'trustee'. The crucial factor, in determining whether there is a trust, is the intention of the parties to the contract and primarily that of the promisee (X).[14]

The first requirement of such a trust is that X must intend to take the promise for the benefit of Y. It follows that there will be no trust in favour of Y where X took the promise for his own benefit[15] or where it is as consistent with the facts that he took the promise for his own benefit as for that of Y.[16] Conversely, the fact that X did *not* intend the promise to be for his own benefit may support the conclusion that there was a trust in favour of Y.[17]

Secondly, the intention of X to benefit Y must be final and irrevocable. Thus where X took out a life insurance policy for the benefit of his godson Y it was held that there was no trust in favour of Y since the policy contained an option entitling X to surrender it for his own benefit.[18] On the other hand, a trust is not negatived merely because the contract names several beneficiaries between whom X can choose. In one case[19] A promised X to pay an annuity after X's death to his widow or (if X so directed) to his children. It was held (in

---

13   *Affréteurs Réunis SA v Leopold Walford (London) Ltd* [1919] AC 801.
14   *Swain v Law Society* [1983] 1 AC 598 at 620.
15   *West v Houghton* (1879) 4 CPD 197.
16   *Vandepitte v Preferred Accident Insurance Corpn of New York* [1933] AC 70.
17   *Lyus v Prowsa Developments Ltd* [1982] 2 All ER 953.
18   *Re Sinclair's Life Policy* [1938] Ch 799.
19   *Re Flavell* (1883) 25 Ch D 89.

the absence of a direction to pay the children) that there was a trust in favour of the widow.

Thirdly, a trust will not be created merely because an intention to benefit the third party is shown and no power to revoke that benefit is reserved. There must be an 'intention to create a trust' and this most elusive requirement appears, in principle, to involve an intention on the part of X, both to confer a benefit on Y, and also to assume fiduciary responsibilities towards him. But the decided cases do not make it at all clear when this requirement is satisfied. One pair of cases will suffice to illustrate the point. In the nineteenth-century case of *Re Flavell*,[19a] A and X were carrying on business in partnership. On X's retirement, A promised X to provide after X's death for his widow, Y. It was held that there was a trust of the promise in favour of Y. But more recently in *Re Schebsman*[20] a similar promise, made by A to his retiring employee X for the benefit of the latter's widow Y, was held not to create a trust in her favour (though this decision did not prejudice her as A was in fact ready to make the promised payment to her). Such cases suggest that the courts have become less willing than they once were to apply the trust device. The reason for this change of attitude is that the implication of a trust in favour of Y would make it impossible for A and X to vary or rescind the contract by mutual consent; and the courts are reluctant to deprive them of this right, unless the intention to create a trust is clearly shown to exist. Such an intention will not readily be inferred where X is under some legal obligation to provide for Y: for example where Y is X's employee, the contract of employment requires X to insure Y against accidents and X effects such insurance with company A for Y's benefit.

iii   Contracts (Rights of Third Parties) Act 1999

Third party's right of enforcement. The main purpose of this Act is to give a third party (Y) the right to enforce a term of a contract to the extent that the parties to it, ie the promisor (A) and the promisee (X) so intend. Section 1 of the Act therefore provides that Y can enforce a term of a contract between A and X in two situations. First, he can do so if the contract 'expressly provides that he may'.[1] The effect of these words is to create a new drafting device for conferring rights on Y. This device could, for example, be used to simplify the drafting of terms intended to make exemption clauses available for the benefit of third parties;[2] for under the Act 'enforcing' a term includes Y's

19a   Supra, n 19.
20   [1944] Ch 83.
1   1999 Act, s 1(1)(a).
2   Ante, p 98.

availing himself of such a clause.[3] Secondly, Y can enforce a term of the contract if 'the term purports to confer a benefit on him'[4] unless 'on a proper construction of the contract it appears that the parties [A and X] did not intend the term to be enforceable by' Y.[5] These provisions can obviously give rise to difficult questions of construction: eg where A is a sub-contractor engaged by X to work on a house belonging to Y. In cases of doubt, the burden of proving that 'the parties' did not intend a term which purports to *benefit*Y to be *enforceable* by Y is on A and it is up to him to show that *both* parties (ie A and X) did not so intend. To acquire rights under s 1, Y must also be 'expressly identified' in the contract either 'by name, as a member of a class or as answering a particular description'.[6] This requirement would, for example, be satisfied where A promised X to pay £1,000 to each of X's children. Such a term could be enforced even by a child born after the time when the contract was made, for the Act provides that the third party 'need not be in existence'[7] at that time. On the other hand, there would be no such identification of Y where A contracted with X to build a house on X's land and the house was later sold to Y. Y's right of enforcement is also subject to 'any other relevant term of the contract' which may either limit that right, eg by providing that it must be exercised within a year; or negative it altogether, eg by providing that the Act was not to apply to the contract.

Where Y is entitled to enforce a term of the contract between A and X, all remedies are available to him that would have been so available, if he had been a party to the contract.[8] He can therefore recover damages for loss of bargain[9] even though the bargain was made, not with him but with X, and he is also entitled to specific relief. His rights are subject to the usual limitations: for example, he cannot recover damages in respect of loss which is too remote;[10] though in claims under s 1 the test of remoteness will be whether loss to Y (not loss to X) was within A's reasonable contemplation.

Rescission and variation of the contract. The courts were reluctant to give Y rights of enforcement under the rules relating to trusts of promises as they did not want unduly to restrict the power of A and X to rescind or vary their contract.[11] The Act deals with this problem by way of a

---

3   Section 1(6).
4   Section 1(1)(b).
5   Section 1(2).
6   Section 1(3).
7   Section 1(3).
8   Section 1(5).
9   Ante, p 5, post, p 376.
10   Post, p 389.
11   Ante, p 255.

compromise which applies where Y has acquired rights under s 1. The general rule, stated in s 2(1), is that A and X cannot then by agreement rescind or vary the contract so as to 'extinguish or alter' Y's entitlement if *either* Y has communicated his assent to the term to A *or* Y has relied on the term and A was (or reasonably should have been) aware of such reliance. But this general rule can be displaced by the terms of the contract which may provide that A and X may rescind the contract without Y's consent or (on the other hand) that Y's consent is required in circumstances other than those specified in s 2(1).[12] It is also open to the court to dispense with Y's consent (on payment of 'compensation' to Y[13]) if his consent cannot be obtained because he cannot be found or if he is mentally incapable of giving his consent, or if it cannot reasonably be ascertained whether Y has relied on the term.[14]

Defences. Section 3 is concerned mainly with the extent to which, in an action by Y in reliance on s 1, A can rely by way of defence or set-off on matters which would have been available to A, if the action had been brought by X. The general principle is that A can rely on such a matter if it 'arises from or in connection with the contract [between A and X] and is relevant to the term' and would have been available to X in proceedings brought by X to enforce the term.[15] A could, for example, rely against Y on a valid exemption clause in the contract between A and X or on the fact that X's breach of that contract justified A's refusal to perform. The general principle can be excluded or extended by an express term of the contract.[16] Subject to contrary agreement, A can also rely against Y on defences and counterclaims that would have been available to A, if Y had been party to the contract.[17] Where Y seeks to 'enforce' an exemption clause in the contract between A and X (in the sense of availing himself of it), he can do so only if he could have done so, had he been a party to the contract.[18] Y could therefore not rely on the clause if (for example) it was invalid, or did not satisfy the requirement of reasonableness, under the Unfair Contract Terms Act 1977.

Exceptions. Section 6 of the Act lists a number of exceptions to Y's entitlement under s 1. In the first group of exceptions, Y has prima facie no right under other rules of law, so that cases within this group

12 Section 2(3).
13 Section 2(6).
14 Section 2(4) and (5).
15 Section 3(2).
16 Section 3(3) and (5).
17 Section 3(4) and (5).
18 Section 3(6).

continue to be governed by the common law doctrine of privity. Where, for example, A is X's employee, any promise by A to X cannot be enforced under the Act by Y, even if it is intended to confer a benefit on Y.[19] In the second group, Y can acquire rights against A under other legislation. This is, for example, the position where Y is the transferee of a bill of lading containing or evidencing a contract for the carriage of goods by sea made between A (the carrier) and X (the shipper). The 1999 Act does not apply[20] since the transfer of contractual rights in such a case is governed by other legislation,[1] the scheme of which would be disrupted if Y could also enforce terms of the contract under the 1999 Act.

Third party's other rights. The 1999 Act does not affect any rights or remedies that the third party has apart from its provisions.[2] If Y has no rights under the Act (eg because its requirements are not satisfied or because the case falls within one of the exceptions just described), he may nevertheless enforce rights available to him under some other exception to the doctrine of privity. Such rights are clearly not subject to the provisions of the Act. It is also possible for Y to have rights both under the Act and apart from it: eg where the same facts not only satisfy the requirements of s 1 but also give rise to a trust in favour of Y[3] or where the benefit of an exemption clause in a contract between A and X is available to Y both at common law and under the Act. In such cases Y can choose between enforcing the term under the Act, subject to its provisions, and doing so apart from the Act, not so subject. The latter course could be more advantageous to him than the former; and it is this possibility which gives point to the continued discussion of the earlier mitigations and qualifications of the common law doctrine of privity.

Promisee's rights. The fact that the third party has acquired rights under the 1999 Act also does not affect any right of the promisee to enforce any term of the contract.[4] On A's failure to perform in favour of Y, it is therefore open to X to claim damages, the agreed sum or specific relief, to the extent to which these remedies would be available to X apart from the Act.[5] This possibility gives rise to the risk of A's being made liable twice over for the same loss: eg where A is sued by Y after

19   Section 6(3)(a).
20   Section 6(5).
1   Ie, the Carriage of Goods by Sea Act 1992.
2   1999 Act, s 7(1).
3   Eg *Nisshin Shipping Co Ltd v Cleaves & Co Ltd* [2003] EWHC 2602 (Comm), [2004] 1 Lloyd's Rep 38.
4   1999 Act, s 4.
5   Ante, pp 247–250.

X has recovered damages in respect of Y's loss[6] or in respect of expenses incurred by X in making good deficiencies in A's performance.[7] In such cases, the court must therefore reduce any award to Y to such extent as it thinks appropriate to take account of the sum recovered by X.[8] This reduction does not prejudice Y since he will either be entitled to the damages recovered by X[9] or have received the benefit of the expenses incurred by X.

Nature of third party's rights. The 1999 Act does not, in general,[10] treat Y as if he were a party to the contract between A and X. In particular, it provides that Y is not to be so treated for the purposes of other legislation.[11] Suppose, for example, that a contract between A and X were made on A's standard terms of business and contained (i) a term enforceable by Y under the Act and (ii) a term excluding or restricting A's liability for defects in the performance to be rendered by A to Y. The requirement of reasonableness under the Unfair Contract Terms Act 1977[12] would not apply in favour of Y since he was not a party to the contract; it would apply only in favour of X. There is, however, an exception or quasi-exception to this general rule. A contract between A and X in favour of Y may impose a duty of care to Y on A and A's defective performance of the contract may make A liable in negligence to Y. If the negligence results in the death of, or personal injury to, Y, then a term in the contract excluding or restricting A's liability for such harm so inflicted is void, under the 1977 Act,[13] not only against X, but also against Y.[14] The exception reflects the strong policy reasons against contract terms excluding or restricting liability for harm of this kind.

iv Insurance

Legislation has created many exceptions to the doctrine of privity in relation to contracts of insurance.[15] It is, for example, common for

6   Under the 'narrower ground' in the *Linden Gardens* case [1994] 1 AC 85 (ante, p 248); cf 1999 Act, s 5(a).

7   Under the 'broader ground; in the *Linden Gardens* case (ante, p 248); cf 1999 Act, s 5(b).

8   1999 Act, s 5 ('tailpiece').

9   Ante, p 250.

10   For exceptions, see, eg, ss 1(5), 3(6).

11   Section 7(4).

12   Unfair Contract Terms Act 1977, s 3(1) and (2)(a).

13   1977 Act, s 2(1).

14   Section 7(2) of the 1999 Act disapplies only s 2(2) of the 1977 Act, which deals with harm other than death or personal injury. See Law Com No 242 (1996) § 13.12.

15   See Contracts (Rights of Third Parties) Act 1999, s 7(1) for the survival of these exceptions.

motor insurance policies to cover not only the policyholder, but also any person driving the car with his consent. By statute, such a person is entitled to the benefit of the policy.[16] Moreover, such a policy must (and other policies may) cover the policyholder against certain liabilities to third parties. Here the insurance company (A) does not promise the policyholder (X) to pay the accident victim (Y). A's promise is rather to pay X any amount which X has to pay Y. But Y has a substantial interest in the performance of A's promise; and by statute Y may in certain circumsances[17] enforce X's right against A.[18] Where Y is the victim of a motor accident, he has further rights under an agreement originally made between the Motor Insurers' Bureau and the Minister of Transport.[19] Under this agreement, the Bureau undertakes to pay the victim any amount due to him which he cannot recover from the driver or insurer, 'in respect of any liability which is required to be covered by a policy of insurance' under the statutory scheme of compulsory third party motor insurance. This agreement may not technically be enforceable by the accident victim.[20] But it can be enforced by the appropriate Minister;[1] and the Bureau has never relied on the doctrine of privity to escape liability under the agreement.

Under the Solicitors Act 1974 a scheme has been set up for the compulsory insurance of solicitors against liability for professional negligence. This takes the form of a contract by which insurers promise the Law Society to provide such insurance for solicitors. The scheme gives rise to rights and duties between the insurers and solicitors, by way of exception to the doctrine of privity.[2]

A further exception to the doctrine exists in relation to life insurance. A person may insure his or her life for the benefit of his or her spouse or children; and by statute such a policy creates 'a trust in favour of the objects therein named'.[3]

A final group of cases which fall under this heading are those in which several persons have an interest in the same property. If that property is insured by one of them, he may be able to recover in full from the insurer, but have to pay over to the other persons interested

---

16 Road Traffic Act 1988, s 148(7).
17 See *Bradley v Eagle Star Insurance Co Ltd* [1989] AC 957; *Eagle Star Insurance Co Ltd v Provincial Insurance plc* [1994] 1 AC 130.
18 Third Parties (Rights against Insurers) Act 1930, s 1; Road Traffic Act 1988, ss 151–153.
19 *Hardy v MIB* [1964] 2 QB 745 at 770; *White v London Transport* [1971] 2 QB 721.
20 See *Gardner v Moore* [1984] AC 548 at 556.
1 See *Gurtner v Circuit* [1968] 2 QB 587.
2 *Swain v Law Society* [1983] 1 AC 598.
3 Married Women's Property Act 1882, s 11.

any amount exceeding his own loss.[4] Similarly, by statute the benefit of insurance on property may be available to persons, other than the insured, who have interests in the property. For example, if premises are let to a tenant and insured by him against fire, the landlord can claim under the policy; and vice versa.[5] Again, where property is sold and then destroyed or damaged before completion of the sale, any insurance money received by the seller must be paid over to the buyer on completion of the purchase, thus indirectly giving him the benefit of the seller's insurance.[6]

v   Law of Property Act 1925, s 56(1)

This subsection provides that '*A person may take* an immediate or other interest in land or other property, or *the benefit of any* condition, right of entry, covenant or *agreement over or respecting land or other property, although he may not be named as a party to the conveyance or other instrument.*' The italicised words might appear at first sight to suggest that the subsection had abolished the doctrine of privity in all cases of written agreements affecting 'property'. Moreover, the Act provides that, unless the context indicates the contrary, 'property' includes 'any thing in action'.[7] Since a promise by A to X is a 'thing in action', it was at one time argued that a written promise by A to X to pay money to Y could be enforced by Y against A, by virtue of section 56(1).[8] But this view was rejected by the House of Lords in *Beswick v Beswick*.[9] It was there held that s 56(1) gave the widow no rights in her personal capacity to enforce the promise to pay her an annuity, which had been made to her husband by his nephew. This interpretation appears to be supported by the wording of the subsection, which says that a person may take the benefit of an agreement over or respecting property, although he may not '*be named as a party*': not although he may not *be a party*. The general view is that the subsection only applies in favour of persons to whom the instrument purports to make a grant, or with whom it purports to make a covenant:[10] such persons

---

4   *Waters and Steel v Monarch Fire and Life Assurance Co* (1856) 5 E & B 870; *Hepburn v A Tomlinson (Hauliers) Ltd* [1966] AC 451.

5   Fires Prevention (Metropolis) Act 1774, s 83; *Portavan Cinema Co Ltd v Price and Century Insurance Co Ltd* [1939] 4 All ER 601; cf *Mark Rowlands Ltd v Berni Inns Ltd* [1986] QB 211; *Lonsdale & Thompson Ltd v Black Arrow Group plc* [1993] Ch 361.

6   Law of Property Act 1925, s 47 (now commonly excluded by contract: Law Com No 191, para 3(2)).

7   1925 Act, s 205(1)(xx); cf post, pp 266–267.

8   Eg in the Court of Appeal in *Beswick v Beswick* [1966] Ch 538.

9   [1968] AC 58; see ante, p 246.

can take the benefit of the instrument even though it does not actually name them. A covenant in favour of 'the owner of Blackacre' would thus fall within its provisions, at least if the owner was an ascertainable person at the time when the covenant was made.[11] But the great majority of promises in favour of third parties are not covered by the subsection.

4   PROMISES PURPORTING TO BIND A THIRD PARTY

a   The general rule

As a general rule, a contract between A and X does not bind Y. Where the contract purports to impose some positive obligation on Y, the rule may seem to be too obvious to need stating. Clearly Y cannot be liable to pay A £10 merely because A and X have made a contract to this effect. This follows from the nature of contractual obligations, which are essentially based on consent. But the rule can also apply where the contract between A and X simply purports to deprive Y of rights, for example, where a contract between A and X contains an exemption clause purporting to protect A against liability to Y. The general rule (discussed in Chapter 7) is that Y is not bound by such a clause if he is not a party to the contract.[12]

The general rule that a person is not bound by a contract to which he is not party is regarded as an aspect of the doctrine of privity. It is subject to a number of exceptions; and there is also an important group of cases which falls outside the scope of the rule.

b   Exceptions to the general rule

Most of the exceptions to the doctrine of privity only entitle a third party to the benefit of a contract and do not subject him to any obligations under it. No one has, for example, suggested that a third party can be bound by a contract under the trust exception; nor is a third party so bound by virtue of the Contracts (Rights of Third Parties) Act 1999.[13] But under some of the other exceptions, a person can be bound (no less than entitled) under a contract to which he is not directly a party. The most important of these is agency (to be discussed in Chapter 15): it is perfectly possible for Y to become liable to A

---

10   *White v Bijou Mansions Ltd* [1937] Ch 610; affd [1938] Ch 351.
11   *Re Ecclesiastical Comrs for England's Conveyance* [1936] Ch 430.
12   See ante, p 99.
13   Law Com No 242 (1996), §§ 10.32, 7.6.

under a contract made between A and X, if X in making the contract acted as A's or Y's agent. Agency is also one of the grounds, discussed in Chapter 7, on which exemption clauses can, exceptionally, bind third parties.[14]

c Scope of the general rule

The general rule states that Y is not bound by a contract between A and X, so that its terms cannot be enforced against him. But the existence of the contract may restrict Y's freedom of action in a number of other ways. The most important of these are as follows:

i *Contracts creating proprietary interests or possessory rights*

This class of cases is best discussed by reference to two illustrations, which are not intended to be exhaustive. Suppose first that X agrees to sell a Rembrandt to A and then agrees to sell the same painting to Y. Since the contract between X and A is specifically enforceable,[15] its effect in equity is to confer on A a proprietary interest in the painting; and this would prevail against Y if he bought with notice of the earlier contract.[16] Similar reasoning applies where possession of the subject-matter is transferred under the contract. Suppose that X hires his car out to A and then sells it to Y. Although Y is not bound to perform any obligations which X may have undertaken in his contract with A, he is nevertheless bound to respect A's right to retain possession of the car in accordance with the terms of A's contract with X.

ii *Interference with contractual rights*

In the cases put above, A had, under his contract with X, acquired a proprietary interest in, or possession of, the subject-matter of the contract. Greater difficulty arises where A has no such proprietary or possessory interest, but does have some commercial interest in the disposition of the subject-matter. This possibility is illustrated by the following further examples.

14   See ante, p 100.
15   Post, p 409.
16   Cf *Swiss Bank Corpn v Lloyds Bank Ltd* [1982] AC 584 at 598, 613 (where the actual decision was that there was *no* specifically enforceable agreement): *The Stena Nautica (No 2)* [1982] 2 Lloyd's Rep 336 (where specific enforcement was again refused).

First, A may enter into a contract with X which imposes restrictions on subsequent dealing with the subject-matter. In one case,[17] X bought a new car and covenanted with A (the British Motor Trade Association) not to resell the car for one year, without first offering it to A at a price not above the list price. The purpose of the covenant was to stop profiteering at a time when cars were in short supply. Within the year, Y, with knowledge of the covenant, bought the car from X and he was held liable to A. The liability was not for breach of contract, but in tort for knowingly interfering with A's contractual rights against X, ie with A's right to have the car offered to him. Put generally, the point is that contracts do not only create rights and duties between the contracting parties. They also impose a duty on third parties to abstain from interfering with the performance of contractual duties of which they are aware. But this principle cannot impose positive obligations on Y: for example, if in the above case X had promised to pay A £1,000 on the sale of the car, that promise could not have been enforced against Y even if he knew of it when later acquiring the car.[18]

A second type of contract which may affect a third party is one which requires the *use* of a particular thing for its performance. The most common commercial illustration is the time or voyage charterparty. Under such a contract the charterer does not get possession of the ship. The contract amounts simply to an undertaking by the shipowner to provide a service: namely to carry cargo in the chartered ship. Now a ship may first be chartered by X to A and then (while the charterparty is still in force) she may be sold by X to Y. The question then arises whether A can enforce his rights under the charterparty in any way against Y. One case supports the view that the charterparty between A and X gave A an equitable interest in the ship which he could enforce by restraining a purchaser with notice of the charterparty from using the ship inconsistently with it.[19] But this view was criticised, particularly because an equitable interest can be enforced against a purchaser with only 'constructive notice' of it: that is, against somebody who did not actually know of the contract between A and X, but who could have discovered it by making reasonable enquiries. This doctrine of constructive notice works well enough in relation to contracts for the acquisition of interests in land which are concluded and performed only after careful investigations. But its

---

17   *British Motor Trade Association v Salvadori* [1949] Ch 556.

18   *Law Debenture Trust Corpn plc v Ural Caspian Oil Corpn Ltd* [1993] 1 WLR 138; for a successful appeal on another point, see [1995] Ch 152.

19   *Lord Strathcona Steamship Co v Dominion Coal Co Ltd* [1926] AC 108; it is now clear that such an interest only arises where the contract is specifically enforceable: see ante, p 263.

introduction into the field of commercial contracts, which are much more quickly made and performed, is generally regarded as undesirable. Hence, in a later case of the same kind, the argument that the charterer had an equitable interest in the ship was rejected.[20] But the case leaves open two further possibilities. One is that A may be able to obtain the purely negative remedy of an injunction to restrain Y from using the subject-matter inconsistently with the contract between A and X, without being able to enforce against Y any positive obligation that X may have undertaken towards A.[1] In the charterparty example given above, this means that Y could be prevented from using the ship for his own purposes if he had bought with knowledge of the charter; but he would not be liable for failing to render the services to be provided under that contract by X to A. The second possibility is that Y may be liable in tort for wrongfully interfering with the contract between X and A.[2] This would again have the purely negative effect described above, and be restricted to the situation in which Y at the time of his contract[3] with X had actual knowledge of the earlier contract between A and X. Hence the doctrine of constructive notice is kept out of this branch of the law; while justice is done by preventing Y from using the ship inconsistently with a charterparty of which he knew at the time of his purchase, and the existence of which presumably affected the price he paid.

20 *Port Line Ltd v Ben Line Steamers Ltd* [1958] 2 QB 146.
1   *De Mattos v Gibson* (1858) 4 De G & J 276, 282; cf ante, p 246 at n 18.
2   Ante, p 264 at n 17.
3   See *Swiss Bank Corpn v Lloyds Bank Ltd* [1979] Ch 548 at 568–569, 569–573; varied [1982] AC 584 at 598; affd [1982] AC 584 at 610.

Chapter 14

Transfer of contractual rights

A contract is both the source of an obligation and an asset. Suppose that A buys goods from X for £100 payable in a month's time. From one point of view, the effect of the contract is to oblige A to pay X £100. From another point of view, A's promise to pay is an asset with which X can deal, for example by asking his banker Y to advance money at once, on the strength of A's promise to pay the £100. If Y agrees to do this, he may ask X to transfer to him the rights which X has against A under the original contract of sale. This process of transferring contractual rights is called 'assignment'. It is effected by a transaction between only two parties. In the above example, these are X, the creditor or assignor, and Y, the assignee. The important point is that the debtor (A) is not a party to the transaction: in other words, an assignment does not require the consent of the debtor.[1] The effect of an assignment is to transfer the assignor's rights to the assignee, who thus becomes entitled to sue the debtor on the contract.

The development of the law on this topic has been profoundly influenced by the different approaches to it adopted at common law and in equity. Even today, the subject cannot be understood without some knowledge of the position before the merger of common law and equity in 1875, when the Judicature Act 1873 came into force.

1 LAW AND EQUITY

Before 1875 common law and equity had different substantive rules on the subject of assignment. The two systems were also administered in separate courts, and this gave rise to procedural difficulties in enforcing an assignee's rights.

a Substantive differences

We must begin by distinguishing between *choses in possession* and *choses in action*. The former are things that can be physically seized; the

---

1 *Mulkerrins v PricewaterhouseCoopers* [2003] UKHL 41, [2003] 4 All ER 1 at [15].

latter are rights that can be asserted only by bringing legal proceedings. A contractual right, eg to the payment of £100, is a chose in action. If the debtor does not pay, the creditor cannot simply seize the money; he must bring an action for it. At common law, choses in action could not be assigned. It was thought (or said) that such assignment might lead to officious intermeddling in litigation;[2] and such intermeddling formerly constituted a wrong, known as 'maintenance', or as 'champerty' if the intermeddler was to share in the proceeds of the litigation.[3] Equity, however, did not regard the assignee as an officious intermeddler,[4] but rather as a person who had acquired an interest in the property. It therefore enforced assignments of choses in action. Hence the basic rule was that choses in action were not assignable at common law, but were assignable in equity.

There were, however, exceptions to the common law rule; and these still exist in the present law. The most important relates to negotiable instruments. The nature of such instruments will be more fully explained later in this chapter;[5] the only point to be made here is that they were regarded as transferable at common law. The common law, moreover, recognises at least three methods by which someone other than the original creditor can become entitled to sue the original debtor. The first of these is *novation*. This is a tripartite contract between debtor, creditor and transferee, by which it is agreed that the debt will henceforth be owed, not to the creditor, but to the transferee.[6] Assuming that the transferee has provided consideration for the debtor's new promise to pay him, he can enforce that promise. The second common law method has no accepted technical name but may be called *acknowledgment*. The creditor asks his debtor to pay a third party and the debtor agrees to do so and notifies the third party. The third party can then sue the debtor; and it seems that he can do so even though he has not provided any consideration for the debtor's promise.[7] Thirdly, the creditor can give the third party a *power of attorney*, making him his agent to sue the debtor and freeing him from an agent's usual liability to account to his principal (the creditor) for the

2   *Fitzroy v Cave* [1905] 2 KB 364 at 372.
3   Ante, p 184, see now Criminal Law Act 1967, ss 13, 14.
4   *Wright v Wright* (1750) 1 Ves Sen 409 at 411.
5   See post, pp 279–280.
6   Since the transferee is a party to the tripartite contract, he is not a 'third party' for the purposes of the Contracts (Rights of Third Parties) Act, 1999: see s 1(1).
7   *Shamia v Joory* [1958] 1 QB 448. On such facts, the debtor's promise might now give rise to a contract which the third party could enforce by virtue of the Contracts (Rights of Third Parties) Act 1999 if the requirements of s 1(1) and (2) (ante, pp 255–256) were satisfied.

proceeds of the action. None of these common law methods, however, quite does the work of assignment. The first two require the consent of the debtor; and the third has two disadvantages: as a general rule, it is revocable by the creditor, and it is often revoked by his death.[8]

b   Procedural difficulties

To understand these difficulties it is first necessary to draw yet a further distinction, namely that between legal and equitable choses in action. A legal chose in action was one which could be sued for in a common law court, such as a debt due under a contract. An equitable chose in action was a right which could be sued for only in the Court of Chancery, such as the right to receive the income of a trust fund. Where the assignment was of an equitable chose, there was no procedural difficulty in enforcing it. The assignee could simply sue the trustee in the Court of Chancery for the income which had been assigned; and if the trustee were later sued in the same Court by the assignor, he could make good his defence by relying on the assignment and on his payment to the assignee. Where, on the other hand, the assignment was of a legal chose, the position was more complicated. Equity could not simply allow the assignee to sue the debtor for the debt in the Court of Chancery. For one thing, that court did not enforce ordinary legal debts. For another, such a course could cause hardship to the debtor. If he were later sued again in a common law court by the assignor for the same debt, he would have to go to the trouble of taking separate proceedings in Chancery to restrain the common law action. To avoid these difficulties, equity allowed the assignee to use the name of the assignor for the purpose of suing the debtor in a common law court; and if the assignor refused to allow his name to be used for this purpose the Court of Chancery could compel him to do so. In this way effect was given to the assignment without exposing the debtor to the risk of a second action by the assignor, whose right against the debtor would have been consumed by the original action, brought in his name.

2   EFFECTS OF THE JUDICATURE ACT 1873

This Act affected the law as to assignment in two ways.

---

8   See post, pp 309–310.

a   Removal of procedural difficulties

The procedural difficulties described above disappeared when the High Court (created by the Act) took over the functions of the old courts of common law and equity, and administered both systems concurrently. The assignee of a chose in action could now sue for it in the High Court. He could do so whether the chose was a legal or an equitable one, since all Divisions of the High Court now recognised both legal and equitable claims. Nor need the debtor fear a subsequent action in a different court, since there was now only a single system of courts. Hence the requirement that the assignee of a legal chose must sue in the name of the assignor became obsolete;[9] though, as we shall see, it is still sometimes desirable to have the assignor as well as the assignee before the court in any action brought by either of them against the debtor.

b   Statutory assignment

The state of affairs outlined above was recognised by a provision in the Judicature Act 1873 which is now reproduced in s 136(1) of the Law of Property Act 1925. This provides that an assignment of a 'debt or other legal thing in action' transfers to the assignee the legal right to the debt or thing in action; and that the assignee can sue for the debt in his own name. The assignment, however, only has these effects if three conditions laid down in s 136(1) are satisfied: the assignment must be 'absolute', it must be 'by writing under the hand of the assignor', and written notice of the assignment must have been given to the debtor. If these requirements are *not* satisfied the assignment may still be valid under the old rules of equity. It is therefore still necessary to distinguish between statutory assignments and equitable assignments. An equitable assignment may be an assignment of a legal or of an equitable chose: it is simply one which fails to comply with the statutory requirements. The most important effect of the distinction is this: if the assignment is statutory, the assignee can sue the debtor *alone*, but if it is equitable he may have to *join the assignor* to the action. He formerly had to do so where the chose was a legal one, so that under the old rules of equity he had to sue in the name of the assignor. In this situation, the joinder requirement has become a mere historical survival and the courts no longer insist on it.[10] But the assignee must still join the assignor where the latter retains an interest

---

9   *Weddell v J A Pearce & Major* [1988] Ch 26 at 40.
10   *The Mount I* [2001] EWCA Civ 68, [2001] 1 Lloyd's Rep 597 at [60].

in the subject-matter. Here the joinder requirement reflects an important principle: that both assignor and assignee must be brought before the court when the absence of one of them might prejudice the debtor. This principle has been carried into effect by judicial interpretation of the requirement stated in s 136(1) that the assignment must be 'absolute'.

i   *'Absolute assignment'*

The courts have tended to classify assignments as absolute or non-absolute with an eye on the consequences. When it was desirable to have the assignor before the court, they have said that the assignment was not absolute – with the result that the assignment was only equitable so that the assignor had to be joined to the action. A convenient starting point for the discussion is the distinction, drawn in s 136(1), between absolute assignments and assignments 'by way of charge'. The distinction may be illustrated by supposing that A is X's tenant at a rent of £1,000 per month, that X borrows £5,000 from Y and that, as security for the loan, he assigns to Y his right to the monthly rent due from A. Obviously, X and Y do not intend that A is to go on paying Y after Y's loan to X (together with interest) has been repaid; and they may provide for this in one of two ways. First, they may say that A is to pay Y '*until Y's loan to X has been repaid*'. In this case, neither A nor the court could (in the absence of X) tell how much (if anything) ought to be paid by A to Y. For X might have used money from another source to pay off the loan to Y and the question whether he has done so cannot be satisfactorily determined either by A or by the court in the absence of X. As it is thus desirable to have X before the court, the assignment will be classified as not absolute (but by way of charge), with the result that X must be joined to the action.[11] Secondly, X and Y may say that, when Y's loan to X has been repaid, the right to receive the rent from A is *to be reassigned* to X. Here A and the court have (even in the absence of X) no difficulty in knowing whether A is bound to pay X or Y. For the crucial point is not whether X has paid off the loan made by Y, but simply whether Y has reassigned to X the right to receive the rent from A. The reassignment will only bind A when he receives notice of it: until then he can safely pay Y, and the court can safely give judgment in favour of Y, even in the absence of X. As X is not a necessary party to the action, the assignment is absolute so that Y can sue A without joining X as a party to the action.[12] If the debt has been repaid, Y's failure to reassign might be a breach of contract

---

11   Cf *Durham Bros v Robertson* [1898] 1 QB 765.
12   Cf *Tancred v Delagoa Bay and East Africa Rly Co* (1889) 23 QBD 239.

between him and X; but such a breach would not affect the question whether A was bound to pay X or Y.

The reason why an assignment by way of charge is not absolute is that it will *automatically* come to an end on the occurrence of a condition subsequent, viz, the discharge of the assignor's debt to the assignee. The same reasoning can apply to other conditions: eg if X assigns rent due from A to his son Y 'so long as Y continues his studies at Oxford'. Here A will want to have the question whether Y is still continuing those studies settled in such a way that neither X nor Y can subsequently dispute it. Hence it is desirable to have both X and Y before the court; and the assignment will be classified as not absolute in order to produce this result. Similar reasoning would apply where the condition was precedent:[13] eg where the assignment was expressed to take effect only 'when Y begins his studies at Oxford'.[14]

It is also settled that an assignment of part of a debt is not absolute.[15] When X assigns to Y £50 out of the £100 which A owes to X, A does not have any difficulty in determining how much he is bound to pay respectively to X and Y. But if Y could sue A without joining X, A might be prejudiced in another way; for he might want to deny that he was liable to pay at all. Suppose that Y made a claim and A wanted to raise the defence that the contract had been procured by fraud, or that he was exonerated by X's breach. Even if he could establish such a defence in the absence of X, he would then have to establish it all over again if he were later sued for another £50 by X. Obviously, this hardship would be even more severe if X by a series of assignments had split the debt into (say) ten or more parts. To avoid this hardship *all* the interested parties must join in the action. It follows that even the original creditor cannot sue for his part without joining the assignee or assignees.[16]

ii   'Debt or other legal thing in action'

A 'debt' within s 136(1) is a fixed sum due under contract or otherwise. The phrase 'other legal thing in action' means any right (including an equitable chose in action) which, though formerly not assignable at common law, was assignable in equity by the ordinary process of equitable assignment.[17] But where some special statutory provision

---

13 See ante, p 28 for the distinction between conditions precedent and subsequent.

14 Cf *The Halcyon the Great* [1984] 1 Lloyd's Rep 283.

15 *Williams v Atlantic Assurance Co Ltd* [1933] 1 KB 81 at 100; *Deposit Protection Board v Dalia* [1994] 2 AC 367 and at 392.

16 *Walter and Sullivan Ltd v J Murphy & Sons Ltd* [1955] 2 QB 584.

17 *Torkington v Magee* [1902] 2 KB 427 at 430 (revsd on another ground [1903] 1 KB 644).

governs the transfer of rights, only that provision has to be complied with. Thus s 136(1) need not be complied with to transfer bills of lading, policies of life and marine insurance, or shares in companies, all such transfers being regulated by special statutory provisions.[18]

iii   *Assignor disputing validity of the assignment*

The assignor may want to dispute the validity of the assignment: for example, on the ground that it was procured by fraud, or made in pursuance of a contract which was broken by the assignee or which was ineffective. Here the substantial dispute will be between assignor and assignee, the debtor being concerned only to pay whichever of them turns out to be entitled to the debt. In such a case s 136(1) provides for a form of proceedings in which the debtor drops out of the dispute and the issue is left to be contested by the real protagonists in the case ie the assignor and the assignee.

3   ASSIGNMENT AND AUTHORITY TO PAY

An assignment is a transfer of a debt to the assignee. So long as the assignor's intention to make such a transfer is clear, no particular words need be used to constitute an assignment. Generally an assignment takes the form of a transaction between assignor and assignee; but it can also take the form of a direction to the debtor by which he is 'given to understand that the debt has been made over by the creditor to some third person'.[19] Where the assignment takes this form, it must, however, also be communicated to the assignee.[20] The exact reason for this requirement is obscure, though it can perhaps be justified as preserving the essential nature of an assignment as a transaction between assignor and assignee.

Although an assignment may take the form of a direction to the debtor, it is not every such direction that amounts to an assignment. The direction may amount only to an authority to the debtor to pay the third party. This means that the debtor will be discharged if he pays the third party, but the third party will not acquire any rights against the debtor. The point may be illustrated by reference to the common case of a person who draws a cheque on his bank in favour of

18   Policies of Assurance Act 1867; Companies Act 1985, s 182(1) and see post, p 276; Carriage of Goods by Sea Act 1992 Marine policies may be assigned under either s 136(1) or Marine Insurance Act 1906, s 50: *The Mount I* [2001] EWCA Civ 68, [2001] 1 Lloyd's Rep 597 at [74].
19   *William Brandt's Sons & Co v Dunlop Rubber Co Ltd* [1905] AC 454 at 462.
20   *Re Hamilton* (1921) 124 LT 737.

a third party. This is regarded as a direction to the bank to pay the third party, so that the bank is justified in debiting the customer's account if it pays the third party; and if it refuses to pay him it may be liable to the customer for breach of contract. But the cheque is not an assignment of part of the customer's bank balance, so that the payee does not acquire any right which he can enforce directly against the bank.[1]

4 FORMALITIES

A statutory assignment must be 'by writing under the hand of the assignee'.[2] An assignment which is not statutory may, however, still be effective as an equitable assignment.

Equity laid down no formal requirements for assignments, and the general rule is that no writing or other form is necessary for the validity of an equitable assignment. Such an assignment can therefore be made orally. This general rule is, however, subject to a number of exceptions. By statute a 'disposition of an equitable interest' has to be in writing,[3] and this requirement will generally apply to assignments of equitable choses. Other statutes provide for the registration of certain assignments:[4] the purpose of these provisions is to safeguard a person's creditors against the risk that he may secretly assign away all (or a class) of the debts owed to him. Finally, a contract may provide that any assignment of rights arising under it must be in writing; and it seems that such a provision must be complied with before an effective assignment can be made.

5 NOTICE TO THE DEBTOR

An equitable assignment is perfectly valid between assignor and assignee even though no notice of it has been given to the debtor.[5] Nevertheless there are three reasons why notice to the debtor should, if possible, be given.

First, the notice may turn the assignment into a statutory assignment and so enable the assignee to sue the debtor without joining the

1 Cf Bills of Exchange Act 1882, s 53(1); *Deposit Protection Board v Dalia* [1994] 2 AC 367 at 400.
2 Law of Property Act 1925, s 136(1).
3 Law of Property Act 1925, s 53(1).
4 Companies Act 1985, ss 395, 396; Insolvency Act 1986, s 344.
5 *Holt v Heatherfield Trust Ltd* [1942] 2 KB 1.

assignor as a party to the action. To have this effect, the notice must be in writing. It may be given by either the assignor or the assignee.[6]

Secondly, the notice perfects the assignee's title as against the debtor.[7] Once the debtor has received notice of the assignment, he is bound to pay the assignee. If he disregards the notice and pays the assignor, he runs the risk of having to make a further payment to the assignee even though the assignment is only equitable:[8] eg because it is not absolute or because the notice to the debtor is not in writing. For this purpose, the notice does not have to be in any particular form: it may thus be given orally.

Thirdly, notice is important to determine questions of priorities between competing assignees. Suppose that a debt of £100 is assigned to Y as security for a loan of £75 and then to Z as security for a further loan of £75. The rule is that Y and Z rank in the order in which they give notice to the debtor.[9] If the right which is assigned is equitable, the notice must be in writing;[10] but where the chose is legal even an oral notice will secure priority.

6 CONSIDERATION

An assignment is primarily a transfer of property, and as such it may be valid without consideration. Just as X can make a gift of a car to Y, so X can make a gift to Y of the £100 which A owes to X. Nevertheless, there is much dispute on the question exactly when a gratuitous assignment of a chose in action is binding. There are two reasons why this question gives rise to so much difficulty. The first is that it is often hard to tell the difference between an actual assignment of a chose in action and a promise to make such an assignment. A mere promise to give is, of course, binding only if the requisites of a valid contract are fulfilled. Secondly, an attempt to make a gift may fail because the steps required by law to make it effective have not been taken. Here the general rule is that equity will not perfect an imperfect gift. Recent cases have somewhat mitigated the rigour of this rule;[11] but it still applies where a gift is ineffective by reason of the donor's failure to take steps which only he could have taken to make it effective.[12] The

---

6   *Holt v Heatherfield Trust Ltd* [1942] 2 KB 1.
7   *Warner Bros Records Inc v Rollgreen Ltd* [1976] QB 430.
8   *Brice v Bannister* (1878) 3 QBD 569.
9   *Dearle v Hall* (1828) 3 Russ 1.
10   Law of Property Act 1925, s 137(3).
11   *T Choithram International SA v Pagarani* [2001] 1 WLR 1; *Pennington v Waine* [2002] EWCA Civ 227, [2002] 1 WLR 2075.
12   *Milroy v Lord* (1862) 4 De G F & J 264.

donor will then not be compelled to take those steps unless his attempt to make the gift could be construed as a promise to make a gift, *and* that promise was binding as a contract. Here again, consideration would be necessary and, since Equity would not aid a 'volunteer',[13] the mere presence of nominal consideration, or of a deed, was not enough to induce equity to perfect an imperfect gift.

Consideration may therefore be necessary for the effectiveness of an assignment; but this is not a point which can be taken by *the debtor*.[14] He has to pay the debt in any event and is concerned only to ensure that all possible claimants are before the court, so that he does not run the risk of having to pay twice. Our concern, therefore, is with cases in which *the assignor* disputes the validity of the assignment on the ground that it is gratuitous: in other words, with claims that the debt should be paid, not to the assignee, but to the assignor (or, more probably, to those who legally represent the assignor on his death or bankruptcy). The cases may be divided into the following three categories.

a Attempts to assign future rights

An assignment is the present transfer of a contractual right, and there can be no such transfer of a right which does not yet exist. An attempt to assign such a right can operate only as a promise to assign and will therefore have to be supported by consideration.[15] This would, for example, be the position where a person purported to assign the benefit of a contract which he had not yet made but merely expected to make. On the other hand a present right under an existing contract to a future payment can no doubt be assigned.[16] For example, a landlord can assign rent which will become due on a future day under an existing lease. Such an assignment is effective without consideration if it amounts to a completed gift, in accordance with the rules and distinctions to be discussed below.

b Incomplete gifts

The notion of an incomplete gift can most readily be understood by reverting to the simple case of the gift of a chattel, such as a picture. Here the law provides two ways in which the gift may effectively be

13   See ante, p 33.
14   *Walker v Bradford Old Bank Ltd* (1884) 12 QBD 511.
15   *Glegg v Bromley* [1912] 3 KB 474.
16   Eg *Hughes v Pump House Hotel Co* [1902] 2 KB 190.

made: by delivery or by deed of gift.[17] If the donor fails to make the gift in one of these two ways, the gift is incomplete. This would, for example, be the position if the donor simply wrote to the donee, saying 'I hereby give you the picture hanging over my mantelpiece'. Similar reasoning may apply to the gift of incorporeal property. In the leading case of *Milroy v Lord*[18] the owner of shares in a company wanted to make a gift of them and for that purpose executed a deed of gift. This purported gift was incomplete since the donor could, as a matter of law, transfer the title to the shares only by executing a proper 'instrument of transfer'. The same reasoning applies whenever *something more must be done by the donor to transfer the subject-matter* of the gift to the donee.

Now any attempt to apply this reasoning to the assignment of an ordinary contractual right comes up against this difficulty. At common law there could be no assignment, and hence no transfer at all, of a chose in action. In equity, there were no rules specifying *how* an assignment must be executed, except for the statutory requirement that a disposition of an equitable interest must be in writing.[19] At first sight, one might therefore suppose that *any* assignment (or in the case of an equitable interest any written assignment) was sufficient to transfer the right to the assignee and that consideration was *never* necessary. On the other hand where the assignment was of a legal chose it could be said that the assignor always had to do 'something more' to transfer it, namely to allow his name to be used in an action against the debtor in a common law court. This argument at first sight leads to the view that consideration should *always* be necessary for the validity of an assignment of a legal chose. In fact, the courts did not accept either of these arguments. They sometimes upheld and sometimes struck down gratuitous assignments of choses in action. The test of validity was not whether the assignee could sue without the co-operation of the assignor. The test was whether the assignor had made a completed gift.

c   Completed gifts

The question whether an assignment is a completed gift is one to which no simple answer can be given. The answer depends on whether the assignment is statutory or equitable; and, if equitable, on the reason why it falls into this category.

17   *Cochrane v Moore* (1890) 25 QBD 57.
18   (1862) 4 De G F & J 264.
19   Law of Property Act 1925, s 53(1), reproducing Statute of Frauds 1677, s 9.

i Statutory assignment

A statutory assignment is a completed gift, so that consideration is not necessary for its validity.[20] As the statute provides that such an assignment transfers the legal right to the chose in action to the assignee, there is nothing more that the assignor needs to do to transfer the property.

ii Equitable assignments

An assignment may be equitable (as opposed to statutory) for one or more of three reasons.

First, written notice of the assignment may not have been given to the debtor. In this case the assignment may be valid without consideration.[1] The reason is that notice may be given by the assignee, so that there is nothing more that the assignor *must* do to transfer the property.

Secondly, the assignment itself may not be in writing. Here one possible view is that the assignor has not done all that he needs to do to transfer the property since he has not executed a statutory assignment (or a document which the assignee can turn into such an assignment by giving notice). Hence, it is said, the gift is incomplete.[2] The other view is that, although the statute specifies a way in which a transfer of a chose in action *may* be made, it does not in terms say that such a transfer *must* be made in that way. Hence an oral assignment may still be a completed gift in equity, if the intention to make such a gift is clear.[3] The latter seems to be the preferable view, since there is nothing in the statute to restrict the effects of assignments in equity; and equity laid down no requirements as to the manner of making assignments. It will be recalled that a gift of a chattel may be made in two ways, and it would not be surprising or odd if a gift of a chose in action could also be made in two ways, by statutory and by equitable assignment.

Thirdly, the assignment may not be absolute. Where it is not absolute because it is one of part of a debt, there seems to be no reason in principle why the assignment should not be a completed gift. This could, for example, be the position where X assigned to Y half the rent due to him from A. Where the assignment is by way of charge, on the other hand, it would not be intended as a gift at all, but

20 *Harding v Harding* (1886) 17 QBD 442.
1   *Holt v Heatherfield Trust Ltd* [1942] 2 KB 1.
2   *Olsson v Dyson* (1969) 120 CLR 365.
3   *German v Yates* (1915) 32 TLR 52.

as security for a loan by the assignee to the assignor. This would usually provide consideration for the assignment: the consideration would consist either in the making of the loan or, if it had already been made, in the assignee's forbearance to enforce the loan.[4] An assignment might also fail to be absolute because it is made subject to some other condition. Here the position would seem to be that the assignment can be a complete gift if the condition can be performed without the co-operation of the assignor; but, if the condition requires some further act of the assignor, the gift would be imperfect until that act had been done. For example, an assignment executed to pay for work *already* done by the assignee (and so constituting past consideration) would not be a completed gift if it were made 'subject to inspection and approval' of the work by the assignor.[5]

7 THE ASSIGNEE'S TITLE

The basic principle is that the position of the assignee, as against the debtor, should be no better than that of the assignor. The object of the principle is to safeguard the debtor from the prejudice which he would suffer if he had to pay more to the assignee than he would have had to pay to the assignor. Hence the rule is that an assignee takes 'subject to ... equities'.[6] The phrase is a little misleading, in that the debtor can rely against the assignee on legal no less than on equitable defences. The rule and its limits can be illustrated by the following examples.

Suppose that A agrees to buy a car from X for £8,000 and X assigns to Y the benefit of A's promise to pay the £8,000. In an action by Y, A can rely on such defences as the following: that he was induced to buy the car by the fraud of X;[7] or that X had failed to deliver the car;[8] or that (before A received notice of the assignment) A and X had rescinded the contract by mutual consent. A more difficult situation arises if the car which is delivered to A lacks qualities which X said it had, with the result that A suffers loss. The untruth of X's statement about the car may amount to a breach of contract or only to a misrepresentation. In the former case, there is no doubt that A can reduce his liability to Y by the amount of the loss.[9] In the latter case, A

---

4   See ante, pp 39–40.
5   Cf *Re McArdle* [1951] Ch 669.
6   *Mangles v Dixon* (1852) 3 HL Cas 702 at 732.
7   Cf *William Pickersgill & Sons Ltd v London and Provincial Marine and General Insurance Co Ltd* [1912] 3 KB 614 (non-disclosure).
8   Cf *Tooth v Hallet* (1869) 4 Ch App 242.
9   Cf *Newfoundland Government v Newfoundland Rly Co* (1888) 13 App Cas 199.

is entitled to rescind the contract and, if he does so, he can avoid liability to Y. But he may have lost the right to rescind, and in a case where this was the position it was held that A could not rely against Y on the loss which he had suffered as a result of the fraud of X.[10] This seems to be a regrettable result as it cuts across the policy that the right assigned should not be worth more in the hands of the assignee than it would have been worth in the hands of the assignor; and the preferable view is that A should be able to rely *by way of defence* on loss suffered through the fraud of X, even in an action brought by Y. Of course, if, in the above cases, A suffers loss in excess of £8,000 he cannot *claim* the excess from Y since Y himself is not guilty of breach of contract or of fraud. The loss can be relied on only to reduce or extinguish Y's claim. Any excess must be claimed from X. A similar rule applies where, after A has paid Y, a breach is committed by X which entitles A to the return of the money: again such a claim can be made only against X and not against Y.[11]

So far it has been assumed that the only transaction between A and X is the contract, the benefit of which has been assigned to Y. But A may wish to set up against Y a debt due to him from X under a second, independent transaction. For example, X may lend £100 to A and assign the debt to Y. Later, A may sell goods to X for £125; and when A is sued by Y for the £100 he may rely on the fact that £125 has become due to him from X (and has not been paid) under the sale. In substance A is here relying on the sale as a kind of payment of the original loan; so that the rules (already discussed)[12] as to payment by the debtor to the assignor after notice of the assignment will determine the effect of the later transaction. In other words, A's defence will succeed if he entered into the sale before he had notice that the original debt of £100 had been assigned, but not if he entered into the sale after he had such notice.[13] In the latter case A suffers no hardship. He cannot expect to pay off the £100 which X had lent him by delivering goods to X under a contract of sale made after having had notice that the £100 was no longer owed to X but was owed to Y.

8   NEGOTIABILITY

Certain documents are, by the custom of merchants, negotiable instruments. The most important such document is the bill of

---

10   *Stoddart v Union Trust Ltd* [1912] 1 KB 181, viewed with scepticism in *Banco Santander SA v Bayfern Ltd* [2000] 1 All ER (Comm) 776 at 778–779.
11   *The Trident Beauty* [1994] 1 All ER 470.
12   See ante, p 274.
13   Cf *Stephens v Venables* (1862) 30 Beav 625.

exchange. This takes the form of a written order by X (the drawer) on A (the drawee), requiring A to pay a sum of money either to the order of X or of a named third person (the payee) or to bearer. When A accepts the order he becomes liable as acceptor on the bill. A cheque is a bill of exchange drawn on a banker payable on demand[14] but is usually deprived of negotiability by being crossed 'a/c payee'.[15] The rules which regulate the transfer of a negotiable instrument differ in a number of ways from those which govern the ordinary assignment of a chose in action.

First, a negotiable instrument is transferable by delivery. If it is payable to bearer, delivery is all that is necessary. If it is payable to the order of a named person, the transfer requires both endorsement (ie the payee's signature) and delivery. The transfer does not need to be in writing, nor is it necessary to give written notice to the debtor.

Secondly, the transferee of a negotiable instrument does not take 'subject to equities' if he is a 'holder in due course'. Such a holder is a person who has in good faith given value for the instrument, provided that it is valid and regular on its face, not overdue and not to the holder's knowledge dishonoured. There is a presumption that a holder is a holder in due course. This presumption does not apply where the instrument is affected by fraud, duress or illegality, but even then the holder can sue on the instrument if he proves that he gave value for it in good faith.[16] The reason for all these rules is that, in commercial practice, a bill of exchange is treated almost as cash, so that it would be most undesirable to allow the validity of such an instrument to be disputed on some ground that was not apparent on its face.

Thirdly, consideration is not necessary for the validity of *the transfer* of a negotiable instrument[17] so that the transferor cannot deny the validity of the transfer on the ground it was gratuitous. Consideration is, however, necessary for the validity of *the original contract* contained in the instrument, though even this requirement is modified in two ways in relation to bills of exchange. Past consideration, in the shape of an antecedent debt, or liability, is sufficient; and a holder of the bill can enforce it if consideration has at *any* time been given for the bill, even though the holder himself provided no consideration.[18]

14   Bills of Exchange Act 1882, s 73.
15   Bills of Exchange Act 1882, s 81A; *Esso Petroleum Co Ltd v Milton* [1997] 1 WLR 938 at 946.
16   Bills of Exchange Act 1882, ss 29, 30.
17   *Easton v Pratchett* (1835) 1 Cr M & R 798 at 808.
18   Bills of Exchange Act 1882, s 27(1) and (2).

9 LIMITS ON ASSIGNABILITY

The law in general treats contractual rights as assignable; but it only treats them in this way so long as this does not prejudice the debtor or offend some public interest.

a Prejudice to the debtor

The cases in which assignment may cause prejudice to the debtor can be grouped under two heads.

i Personal contracts

In general it is thought to make no difference to a contracting party in whose favour he performs. This is most obviously true in the case of a money debt. If A owes £100 to X he normally suffers no prejudice if instead of having to pay X he has to pay an assignee, Y. This is assumed to be true even where X is an indulgent and Y an exacting creditor. If A wants to protect himself against having to perform in favour of anyone except X, he can do so by expressly providing in the original contract that its benefit is not to be assignable.[19]

There is, however, a group of contracts which are said to be 'personal'. These are contracts in which it would be unreasonable to expect one party (A) to perform in favour of anyone except the other (X). Where this is the case, the benefit of A's obligations cannot be assigned. The leading common law illustration of this principle is provided by the rule that an employer cannot assign the benefit of his employee's obligation to serve. The purpose of the rule is said to be to protect the employee's right freely to choose whom he will serve,[20] though this freedom is somewhat illusory where the employer is a company, the *shares* in which are acquired by another company in the course of a takeover bid. If, however, the employer company sells its *business*, then at common law the contract of employment was brought to an end,[1] but legislation now provides that, in certain transfers of this kind, the contract remains in being as if it had originally been made between employee and transferee.[2] The employee can, however, avoid this consequence by giving notice (to the transferor or to the

19 *Helstan Securities Ltd v Hertfordshire County Council* [1978] 3 All ER 262; *Linden Gardens Trust Ltd v Lenesta Sludge Disposals Ltd* [1994] 1 AC 85.
20 *Nokes v Doncaster Amalgamated Collieries Ltd* [1940] AC 1014 at 1026.
1 *Re Foster Clark Ltd's Indenture Trusts* [1966] 1 WLR 125.
2 Transfer of Undertakings (Protection of Employment) Regulations 1981, SI 1981/1794, as amended by Trade Union Reform and Employment Rights Act 1993 and later legislation.

transferee) that he objects to being employed by the transferee,[3] and in this way he can preserve his legal right to choose whom he will serve. Another illustration of the principle is that a person who has taken out a policy of motor insurance cannot assign the benefit of the policy. The contract is 'personal' in the sense that the insurance company will probably have relied on the policy-holder's driving record in issuing the policy.[4]

Problems of this kind can also arise where A makes a long-term contract to supply X with raw materials for the purpose of X's business, and that business is later taken over by Y (a much larger concern) to whom X purports to assign the benefit of the contract with A. In a sense the contract is 'personal' since A may have relied on his estimate of X's requirements in entering into the contract, or in fixing his price. Nevertheless, if the contract can be construed to require A to supply only the quantity of goods which X could reasonably have required, it will normally be regarded as assignable.[5] But it will not be so regarded if its terms confer other benefits on A which he would lose if the contract could be assigned. In one case[6] A undertook to supply X with all the eggs which X should need in his bakery for one year, and X agreed not to buy eggs elsewhere during the year. X sold his business to Y, to whom he purported to assign the benefit of the contract with A. It was held that A was not bound to supply eggs to Y since X's promise not to buy eggs elsewhere could not be enforced against Y, and it would be unjust to subject A to all the burdens of the contract while depriving him of one of its important benefits.

ii   *Danger of maintenance or champerty*

Equity rejected the common law's view that assignments in general were invalid on the ground that they *might* lead to maintenance or champerty.[7] In equity, an assignment was, however, regarded as invalid if it was *in fact likely* to lead to undesirable interference by one person in litigation which was properly the concern of another. The principle has survived the abolition of maintenance and champerty as legal wrongs. It is most clearly illustrated by the rule that rights of action in tort cannot, in general, be assigned.[8] Thus if A defames X or negligently injures him, X cannot assign to Y his right to claim damages

---

3   See the 1993 amendments of the 1981 Regulations, *supra*.
4   *Peters v General Accident Fire and Life Assurance Corpn Ltd* [1937] 4 All ER 628.
5   *Tolhurst v Associated Portland Cement Manufacturers (1900) Ltd* [1903] AC 414.
6   *Kemp v Baerselman* [1906] 2 KB 604.
7   See ante, p 267.
8   *Defries v Milne* [1913] 1 Ch 98.

from A. To allow such assignments would, it is thought, lead to undesirable speculation in claims of this kind. Where there is no such danger the assignment may be allowed. This accounts for a well established exception to the general rule: an insurance company which has compensated the victim of a tort can take an assignment of the victim's rights against the tortfeasor.[9] Indeed, to the extent to which it has compensated the victim, it can assert his rights against the tortfeasor even without assignment.[10]

Rights to damages which cannot be assigned are sometimes called 'mere' rights of action; but the phrase is not particularly helpful in distinguishing between those contractual rights which can and those which cannot be assigned. The distinction certainly does not depend on the existence of a dispute as to liability: it is clear that a debt can be assigned even though the debtor denies liability to pay it.[11] There can, moreover, be an assignment not only of a right to a fixed sum of money but also of a right to some other performance: for example, a buyer can assign his right to receive the goods. Even where a contract has already been broken, the right to claim damages for the breach can then be assigned, so long as the assignment is not in fact likely to lead to undesirable interference in litigation which is properly the exclusive concern of the assignor.[12] Thus a seller of land can validly assign to the buyer his (the seller's) right to damages against a tenant of the land for breaches of covenant in the lease.[13] Such an assignment does not lead to maintenance or champerty as the outcome of the litigation is no longer primarily the concern of the seller, but rather that of the buyer (ie the assignee) since the sale gives him a proprietary interest in the land. Similar reasoning may apply where the assignee has 'a genuine commercial interest'[14] in the outcome of the litigation. This could be the position where a bank takes an assignment from one of its customers of the latter's claim to damages for breach of a contract of sale which had been financed by the bank.[15] But such an assignment is champertous and void if it is taken for the express purpose of enabling the bank to resell the claim with a view to sharing the profit to be made from it.[16]

---

9 *King v Victoria Insurance Co Ltd* [1896] AC 250.
10 *Hobbs v Marlowe* [1978] AC 16 at 37.
11 *County Hotel and Wine Co v London and North Western Rly Co* [1918] 2 KB 251 at 258.
12 *Weddell v JA Pearce & Major* [1988] Ch 26 at 43.
13 *Ellis v Torrington* [1920] 1 KB 399.
14 *Trendtex Trading Corpn v Crédit Suisse* [1982] AC 679 at 703.
15 *Brownton Ltd v Edward Moore Inbucon Ltd* [1985] 3 All ER 499 at 506, 509.
16 This was the outcome in *Trendtex Trading Corpn v Crédit Suisse* [1982] AC 679.

b Public policy

The assignment of certain rights is invalid on grounds of public policy. For example, a wife cannot assign a right to the payments which her husband may be ordered to make to her in matrimonial proceedings: if she could do this she might anticipate the allowance and be left without means of support.[17] It has also been held that a 'public officer' cannot assign his salary.[18] This rule is said to be necessary to enable such a person to maintain the dignity of his office, but this argument now looks decidedly old fashioned. Another possible justification for the rule is that it prevents corruption, but the rule does not seem to be a very powerful instrument for this purpose, especially as it does not apply to officers paid out of local funds.[19] The assignability of many other payments out of public funds is expressly forbidden by various statutory provisions.[20]

10 INVOLUNTARY ASSIGNMENT

So far, we have considered the assignment of rights by act of the creditor. Assignment may also come about by operation of law on the death or bankruptcy of one of the contracting parties.

a Death

When a contracting party dies, his rights pass to his personal representatives who can claim any performance due to the deceased under the contract, or damages for its breach. Where the contract has not been fully performed by the deceased, the personal representatives may be entitled to complete its performance so as to earn the sum to be paid to the deceased: for example, the personal representatives of a deceased seller may deliver the goods and claim the price. But they will not be entitled to complete the performance of an obligation of the deceased which was 'personal' in the sense discussed later in this chapter,[1] ie such that the other contracting party would be entitled to refuse to accept performance from anyone except the deceased.

17 *Watkins v Watkins* [1896] P 222.
18 *Liverpool Corpn v Wright* (1859) 28 LJ Ch 868.
19 *Re Mirams* [1891] 1 QB 594.
20 Eg Social Security Administration Act 1992, s 289.
1   Post, p 289.

b Bankruptcy

On the bankruptcy of a contracting party, contractual rights to which he was entitled at the time of the bankruptcy are 'deemed to have been assigned' to his trustee in bankruptcy.[2] The trustee can claim performance of the contract, or damages for its breach; or he may be entitled to complete performance of the bankrupt's obligations so as to earn the agreed sum. Once again, the trustee cannot take this last course if the contract is 'personal' in the sense described above. But, since the bankrupt is still available to perform the contract, the trustee may employ him to do so; and, if the other party in this way gets what he bargained for, he will have to pay the agreed sum to the trustee.[3] The rule that the bankrupt's choses in action pass to his trustee is, however, subject to a number of limitations.

First, certain rights do not pass on the ground that they are 'personal'. The word is here used in a sense quite different from that discussed above: namely, to refer to the personal affairs of the bankrupt. For example, the bankrupt's right to damages for breach of a contract to render him medical services does not pass to his trustee.[4] The underlying theory is that the bankrupt's creditors are entitled to his property, but not to any sum due to him as compensation for injury to his person. This rule has survived the statutory definitions of the bankrupt's 'property' (which vests in his trustee) so as to include 'things in action'.[5]

Secondly, special provisions apply to the bankrupt's right to payments in the nature of income (eg under a contract of employment). These may not vest in the trustee because they will often not arise until after the commencement of the bankruptcy.[6] But the trustee can apply to the court for an order directing such income to be paid to him; and in deciding how much of the income is to be paid to the trustee the court will take into account 'what appears ... to be necessary for meeting the reasonable domestic needs of the bankrupt and his family'.[7] The rule is designed to encourage the bankrupt to work so as to maintain himself and his family.

2   Insolvency Act 1986, s 311(4).
3   *Ex p Shrine* [1892] 1 QB 522.
4   *Beckham v Drake* (1849) 2 HL Cas 579 at 627; *Mulkerrins v PricewaterhouseCoopers* [2003] UKHL 41, [2003] 4 All ER 1 at [17], [22].
5   Insolvency Act 1986, ss 306, 436; see *Re Landau* [1998] Ch 223.
6   1986 Act, s 283(1)(a).
7   1986 Act, s 310(2).

11 ASSIGNMENT DISTINGUISHED FROM TRANSFER OF LIABILITIES

Assignment is the transfer of a *right* without the consent of the debtor. The law does not recognise any converse process by which a liability can be transferred without the consent of the creditor.[8] Suppose that X has lent £100 to A. He cannot be deprived of his right to sue A merely because B has contracted with A to pay the debt. Moreover, as a general rule the assignee of a contractual right does not become liable to perform any obligations which the assignor may have owed to the debtor under the contract. Suppose, for example, that a builder assigns to his bank monies due or to become due to him under a building contract. The bank does not, by virtue of the assignment, become liable to the builder's client for any breach of contract by the builder; though the client may be able to rely on such a breach by way of defence to the bank's claim.[9]

There are, however, cases in which one person becomes liable to perform an obligation originally undertaken by another, or discharges such an obligation by actually performing it. These are discussed below; it will be seen that in none of them is there any true transfer of liability.

a Novation

We have seen that novation can be used so as to substitute one creditor for another and so in a sense to do the work of assignment.[10] Similarly, A, B and X can enter into a contract whereby A's obligation to X is discharged and B agrees to perform what A had undertaken. Strictly this is not a transfer of A's liability. What happens is that A's obligation ceases to exist and a new one is undertaken by B. This new obligation would not, for example, necessarily be affected by any defence which A had against X.

b Benefit and burden

The assignee of a contractual right may incur liabilities under the contract by virtue of the so-called principle of benefit and burden. This principle most commonly applies where the discharge of a

---

8   *Linden Gardens Trust Ltd v Lenesta Sludge Disposals Ltd* [1994] 1 AC 85 at 103.
9   See *Young v Kitchin* (1878) 3 Ex D 127; *The Trident Beauty* [1994] 1 All ER 470 at 474, 479.
10   See ante, p 267.

burden is made a condition of the enjoyment of a benefit: eg where a right to extract minerals from land is made subject to a duty to pay compensation for subsidence. In such a case, the compensation may be payable by an assignee of the right in the sense that he will have to forgo the right unless he discharges the burden.[11] Under the so-called 'pure principle of benefit and burden,[12] the same rule may also apply where the burden is imposed by the contract giving rise to the benefit, even though discharge of the burden is *not* made a condition of the enjoyment of the benefit. But this 'pure principle' could all too easily come into conflict with the general rule that an assignee does not become liable under the contract; and the 'pure principle' is therefore restricted in two ways. First, the burden 'must be relevant to the exercise of the right':[13] that is, there must be a necessary connection between them. The 'pure principle' therefore did not apply where the owner of a house had covenanted to keep the roof of an adjoining cottage in repair and both properties were then sold: there was no necessary connection between the right to occupy the house and the duty to repair the cottage roof.[14] Secondly, it must be the intention of assignor and assignee to subject the assignee to the burden;[15] and it follows from this requirement the 'pure principle' will not apply to the ordinary case where only a contractual right is assigned. Even where it does apply, the liability is not strictly *transferred*: the assignor is not released by it from his original liability under the contract.

c Operation of law

Sometimes contractual liabilities are, in a sense, transferred by operation of law. For example, the personal representatives of a deceased contracting party are bound to apply his assets in discharging his contractual liabilities. Similarly, the trustee of a bankrupt contractor is bound to distribute his assets among his creditors. In these cases the personal representative or trustee in bankruptcy is not, of course, *personally* liable on the contracts, so that strictly speaking there is no transfer of liabilities. The administrative receiver of a company can become personally liable on its contracts by 'adopting' them, but this liability arises from a new contract rather than from a transfer of the company's liability.[16]

---

11   Eg, *Aspden v Seddon* (1876) 1 Ex D 496.
12   *Tito v Waddell (No 2)* [1977] Ch 106 at 302.
13   *Rhone v Stephens* [1994] 2 AC 310 at 322.
14   *Rhone v Stephens* [1994] 2 AC 310.
15   As in *Tito v Waddell (No 2)* [1977] Ch 106 at 302.
16   Insolvency Act 1986, s 44; *Powdrill v Watson* [1995] 2 AC 394.

The lawful holder of a bill of lading evidencing a contract for the carriage of goods by sea can acquire rights under that contract;[17] and he may also become liable under it.[18] But as the original shipper remains so liable, no liability is transferred.[19]

The burden as well as the benefit of a contract of employment can be transferred as a result of the transfer of the undertaking with which the contract was made.[20] But the employee can by notice avoid being bound to serve the transferee; and perhaps because (in this sense) the consent of all three parties is necessary, the process has been described as a 'statutory novation'[1] of the contract.

d   Vicarious performance

A's obligation to X may be discharged if B performs it. This is most obviously true where X actually agrees to accept performance from B in discharge of A's obligation. Suppose that A owes £100 to X and that B, with A's authority,[2] offers to pay this sum (or a smaller sum) to X in satisfaction of A's debt. If X accepts the payment on these terms, A's debt is discharged.[3]

X may, however, be unwilling to accept performance from B and wish to insist on personal performance from A. The general rule is that he is not entitled to do so. In one case[4] A let out railway wagons to X and agreed to keep them in repair for 7 years. During that period A transferred the benefit of the contract to B, to whom he also delegated the task of performing the obligation to repair. It was held that X could not object to B's performance of this obligation so long as B did the work efficiently. But X is entitled to object to vicarious performance in two types of cases.

First X can object to performance by B if the contract expressly or by implication provides that the obligation in question will be performed by A and by no one else. This was the position where a dry-cleaning contract contained the words 'whilst every care is exercised in cleaning ... garments ...'. The cleaner (A) was not entitled to delegate performance of the cleaning operation to a subcontractor

---

17   Carriage of Goods by Sea Act 1992, s 2(1)(a).
18   1992 Act, s 3(1); *The Berge Sisar* [2001] UKHL 17, [2002] 2 AC 205.
19   1992 Act, s 3(3).
20   Ante, p 281–282; *Litster v Forth Dry Dock and Engineering Co Ltd* [1990] 1 AC 546 at 555.
1   *Newns v British Airways plc* [1992] IRLR 575 at 576.
2   See *Crantrave Ltd v Lloyds Bank plc* [2000] QB 917, where this requirement was not satisfied.
3   *Hirachand Punamchand v Temple* [1911] 2 KB 330.
4   *British Waggon Co v Lea & Co* (1880) 5 QBD 149.

(B), since A could not take care of the garment while it was being cleaned by B.[5]

Secondly, the creditor can object to vicarious performance of an obligation which is 'personal' in the sense that it is unreasonable to require him to accept performance from anyone except the other contracting party.[6] For example, an employee is not entitled to perform his duties as such by a substitute. Similarly, it has been held that the duties of a warehouseman under a contract to store goods and those of an estate agent instructed to find a purchaser for a house cannot be delegated to a third party.[7] The same may even be true of a contract for the sale of goods: for example where the buyer has entered into the contract in special reliance on the seller's reputation as a manufacturer or supplier of goods of a particular quality.[8]

Vicarious performance is sometimes called 'assignment of liabilities'. But this is a concept which the law does not recognise;[9] and even where vicarious performance is allowed, there is no *transfer* of liability. In one case[10] A contracted to repair X's car. He delegated performance of the work to a subcontractor, B, who did the work defectively, so that X was injured. As X had consented to the employment of a subcontractor, he could not have refused to accept vicarious performance. But this did not relieve A from liability under the contract,[11] so that A was held liable to X for B's defective workmanship. On the other hand, B would not have been under any contractual liability to X for simply refusing to do the work, unless the contract by which A had engaged B was drawn up so as to give X enforceable rights as a third party under it.[12] If that contract conferred no such rights on X, B's only liability to him would have been in tort if B had been negligent in doing the work.

---

5   *Davies v Collins* [1945] 1 All ER 247.
6   *Robson v Drummond* (1831) 2 B & Ad 303.
7   *Edwards v Newland & Co* [1950] 2 KB 534; *John McCann & Co v Pow* [1975] 1 All ER 129.
8   *Johson v Raylton, Dixon & Co* (1881) 7 QBD 438.
9   Ante, p 286.
10 *Stewart v Reavell's Garage* [1952] 2 QB 545.
11 If A had undertaken, not to do the work, but only to procure it to be done, A would not have been liable for defects in B's work so long as he had exercised reasonable care and skill in selecting B: *Raflatac Ltd v Eade* [1999] 1 Lloyd's Rep 507 at 509.
12 By virtue of Contracts (Rights of Third Parties) Act 1999, s 1; ante, p 255.

Chapter 15

Agency

1 INTRODUCTION

Agency is both a general principle of the law of contract and a special contract. The *general principle* is that, where an agent is authorised by a principal to make a contract on the principal's behalf with a third party, and does so, then a contract is created between principal and third party. Generally the relationship of principal and agent results from an agreement between them; and that agreement often amounts to a *special contract* giving rise to rights and duties on either side. Our sole concern in this book, however, is with agency as a general contract principle.

There is an important difference between the legal and the commercial concept of agency. In a commercial sense, it is, for example, common to refer to a car dealer as 'agent' for a particular manufacturer. But when such a dealer sells a car to a customer, he does not normally make a contract of sale between the customer and the manufacturer. What he usually does is to buy the car from the manufacturer and to resell it to the customer. Hence, if the car is defective, the customer's only remedy under the contract of sale is against the dealer; though he may have a remedy against the manufacturer in contract under the latter's 'guarantee', or in tort[1] if the defect results in personal injury or in loss of, or damage to, the customer's other property. The dealer may also act partly on his own and partly on someone else's behalf. This is commonly the position where a car is supplied on hire-purchase, the bulk of the purchase price being provided by a finance company, which may buy the car from the dealer and then let it out on hire-purchase to the customer. Here the dealer is considered to act on his own behalf (and not as the customer's agent) when he sells the car to the finance company;[2] but he may be the agent of the finance company to accept the customer's

---

1   For negligence at common law, and irrespective of negligence under the Consumer Protection Act 1987, Pt I.
2   *Mercantile Credit Co Ltd v Hamblin* [1965] 2 QB 242 at 269; cf Consumer Credit Act 1974, s 56(3)(a).

offer to enter into a hire-purchase agreement, and for various other purposes.[3] Similarly an estate agent instructed to negotiate the sale of a house by private treaty may act on his client's behalf for certain purposes: eg for the purpose of making representations about the property.[4] But for other purposes he is not an agent in the legal sense. For example, he has normally no power to make a contract of sale between his client and a prospective purchaser; nor does he normally act on the client's behalf when receiving a precontract deposit from such a purchaser. The agent holds such a deposit on trust for the purchaser;[5] and if the purchaser asks for its return (as he is entitled to do at any time before a binding contract has been concluded) the liability to repay it falls on the agent and not on his client.[6] All this is only 'normally' true; it is possible, if unusual, for the client expressly to authorise the agent to make a contract on his behalf,[7] or to receive a deposit.[8]

A person who makes a contract between two others is sometimes the agent of both of them. An auctioneer is the agent of the seller for the purpose of making a contract of sale between him and the highest bidder. But he is also the agent of the highest bidder for the purpose of signing any document required to make the sale binding.[9]

2 CREATION OF AGENCY

In the normal case, agency arises by agreement:[10] that is the principal actually authorises the agent to act on his behalf and the agent agrees to do so. But sometimes agency arises by operation of law, even though the principal has not actually authorised the agent to act on his behalf; and it may arise ex post facto by ratification.

a Actual authority

Actual authority may be express or implied.

3 *Northgran Finance Ltd v Ashley* [1963] 1 QB 476; Consumer Credit Act 1974, ss 57(3), 69(6) and 102.
4 *Sorrell v Finch* [1977] AC 728 at 753.
5 Estate Agents Act 1979, s 13(1)(a).
6 *Sorrell v Finch* [1977] AC 728; for interest on the deposit, see the Estate Agents Act 1979, s 15.
7 Cf eg *Spiro v Lintern* [1973] 1 WLR 1002 at 1006.
8 Eg *Ryan v Pilkington* [1959] 1 All ER 689, as explained in *Sorrell v Finch* [1977] AC 728 at 750.
9 *Wilson & Sons v Pike* [1949] 1 KB 176; *Leeman v Stocks* [1951] Ch 941.
10 *Garnac Grain Co Inc v HMF Faure and Fairclough Ltd* [1968] AC 1130n at 1137.

i   *Express authority*

An agent's authority is express to the extent to which it is conferred in so many words. An express appointment need not take any particular form. It may be oral even though the contract which the agent is authorised to make has to be in, or evidenced in, writing.[11] But authority to execute a deed must itself be conferred by a deed, known as a power of attorney.[12]

ii   *Implied authority*

The terms of an express appointment may not exhaustively specify all that the agent is authorised to do. He may have implied authority to do acts which are reasonably incidental to the execution of his express authority. The scope of this incidental authority depends on the facts of each case. These, for example, determine whether an agent who is employed to sell property has authority to sign a document to make the sale binding; or to give an undertaking as to the quality of the subject-matter. Generally an agent who is authorised to sell has no implied authority to receive payment.[13]

Where an agent is authorised to make a contract in a particular market he further has implied authority to act in accordance with any relevant custom of the market. This is so whether or not the principal knows of the custom. But the agent has such customary authority only if the custom is 'reasonable'. This means that the custom must not be actually inconsistent with the express instructions given to the agent or with the relationship of principal and agent. Where an agent is employed to buy for the principal, a custom of the market entitling him to buy on his own account and then to resell to the principal is unreasonable.[14] It converts the agent into a seller, thus giving him an incentive to secure the highest possible price from the principal, while his duty as agent is to buy for the principal as cheaply as he can.

In the situations so far considered, implied authority supplements an authority which has been expressly conferred. It is also possible for the very existence of the authority to be implied: for example, a wife may have implied authority to pledge her husband's credit for household necessaries.[15] A similar implication may arise even though

11   *Heard v Pilley* (1869) 4 Ch App 548. In the case of a contract with a 'commercial agent' within SI 1993/3053, each party is entitled on request to a written record of the terms of the contract: reg 13.

12   Powers of Attorneys Act 1971, s 1; *Gregory v Turner* [2003] EWCA Civ 183, [2003] 2 All ER 1114 at [66].

13   *Butwick v Grant* [1924] 2 KB 483.

14   *Robinson v Mollett* (1875) LR 7 HL 802.

15   *Jewsbury v Newbold* (1857) 26 LJ Ex 247.

the partners in a joint household are not married.[16] Now that household supplies are normally paid for on delivery or on credit terms requiring the debtor's personal signature, these rules are of little importance, but they could still apply where services are rendered to the household. A child, as such, has generally no authority to pledge the credit of either parent;[17] though a child who was nearly of age could have implied authority as manager of a household.

The implied authority here discussed is *actual* authority. It can therefore be negatived by express contrary instructions from the principal. But the mere fact that the principal has given such instructions may not exonerate him from liability on contracts made by the agent: he may still be liable under the rules discussed below.

b Authority by operation of law

In the following situations, a principal may be liable on contracts which he has not actually authorised, and even on those which he has expressly forbidden.

i *Apparent authority*

An agent (A) who in fact has no authority to contract on behalf of the principal (P) may nevertheless *appear* to the third party (X) to have such authority. P may then be bound by the contract if the appearance of authority resulted from his words or conduct. In one case[18] P owned a jeweller's shop and regularly paid X for goods ordered by his manager A for resale in the shop. A then left P's employment, ordered more jewellery from X, and made off with it. It was held that P was liable to X on the ground that A still appeared to X to have authority to bind P. In such a case, A is said to have *general* apparent authority, extending to all transactions which the manager of a shop normally has authority to conclude.[19] Even where A has no such authority by virtue of the position into which P has placed him, he may have *specific* apparent authority by virtue of an express representation by P that A had authority to enter into a particular contract on his behalf.[20] To avoid liability after an appearance of authority has been created in either of these two ways, P must give notice to X that A no longer has authority to bind P.

16 *Blades v Free* (1829) 9 B & C 167.
17 *Mortimore v Wright* (1840) 6 M & W 482.
18 *Summers v Solomon* (1857) 7 E & B 879; cf *United Bank of Kuwait v Hammoud* [1988] 3 All ER 418.
19 *The Ocean Frost* [1986] AC 717 at 777.
20 Ibid (where a claim on this basis failed).

This doctrine of apparent authority applies if the following conditions are satisfied. First, the representation must be made *by the principal*: P is not liable merely because A has represented that he has an authority that he actually lacks;[1] though this requirement is relaxed where P expressly or by conduct induces X to believe that he has authorised A to make further representations on his behalf[2] or to communicate what purports to be P's approval of A's actually unauthorised transaction to X.[3] Secondly, the representation must be made *to the third party* with whom the agent has purported to contract: that party cannot rely on a representation made to someone else. Both these rules may be illustrated by supposing that, in the case of the jeweller, A had ordered jewellery on credit from a new supplier, Y, alleging that he had P's authority to do so. Here P would not be liable to Y, since Y could not rely either on the representation made *by* A or on that made *to* X. Thirdly the doctrine does not entitle X to rely on the fact that he has misconstrued the document by which A was appointed and so has formed the mistaken view that A had an authority which he in fact lacked. Fourthly, the third party must have *relied on the representation*; and this requirement can be satisfied only if the representation was actually known to him.[4] Fifthly, the third party cannot invoke the doctrine of apparent authority if he *knew that the representation was false*, or if he had a reasonable opportunity of discovering the truth but failed to take it. This would be the position if he was shown a document setting out the limits of the agent's authority but did not read it.[5]

Under the fourth of the above rules *actual knowledge of the representation* is necessary to establish apparent authority; but under the fifth rule apparent authority is negatived where the third party *ought to have known the truth*. These requirements have given rise to particular difficulties in relation to contracts with companies. Such contracts are necessarily made through agents whose authority may be set out in the company's memorandum and articles of association. At common law, a third party was deemed to know what was in these documents[6] as they are open to public inspection; and this doctrine of 'constructive notice' could operate in favour of the company but not against it.[7] That is, it could *prevent* apparent authority from arising

---

1   *A-G for Ceylon v Silva* [1953] AC 461; *The Ocean Frost* [1986] AC 717 at 778.
2   *United Bank of Kuwait v Hammoud* [1988] 1 WLR 1051.
3   *First Energy (UK) Ltd v Hungarian International Bank Ltd* [1993] 2 Lloyd's Rep 194.
4   *The Ocean Frost* [1986] AC 717 at 778.
5   *Jacobs v Morris* [1902] 1 Ch 816.
6   *Mahony v East Holyford Mining Co* (1875) LR 7 HL 869.
7   See *Rama Corpn Ltd v Proved Tin and General Investments Ltd* [1952] 2 QB 147.

on the ground that the third party was taken to know of any limitation on the agent's authority; but it could not *establish* apparent authority where the third party had not read the memorandum or articles. This state of the law could cause considerable hardship to third parties; and two important changes were made in 1989 to the Companies Act 1985. First, the doctrine of constructive notice of the company's registered documents has been abolished;[8] and although a third party may still be 'affected by notice of any matter by reason of a failure to make such enquiries as ought to be made'[9] he is not bound to enquire whether the transaction is permitted by the memorandum or whether the board of directors had power to bind the company to the transaction or to authorise others to do so.[10] Secondly, as already noted in Chapter 12, in favour of a person who deals in good faith with the company, the power of the board of directors to bind the company is 'deemed to be free of any limitation under the company's constitution'.[11] Under this provision the company may be liable even if there is *no* apparent authority, for a person may act in good faith even though he knows that the act is beyond the powers of the company.[12] The company may also be liable under the common law principles of apparent authority where the third party relies, not on the apparent *existence* of the powers, but on their apparent *exercise*. This could be the position where the board of directors has power to appoint to an office and represents to the third party that the person with whom the third party deals as holder of that office has been appointed to it when in fact no such appointment has been made.[13]

A principal may sometimes be liable for his agent's forgery on the basis of apparent authority. This was held to be the position where a solicitor's clerk obtained money from a client on the security of forged title deeds; for the solicitor had impliedly represented that the clerk had authority to conclude mortgage transactions on his behalf.[14] But the third party cannot rely on the doctrine of apparent authority where the agent forges the principal's signature. In such a case the third party's belief is not that the agent had authority to sign *on the principal's behalf,* but that the signature actually was that of the principal.[15]

---

8   Companies Act 1985, s 711A(1). Contrast Limited Liability Partnerships Act 2000, s 6(3)(b) (termination of authority by notice to Registrar of Companies).
9   1985 Act, s 711A(2).
10 1985 Act, s 35B.
11 1985 Act, s 35A(1), ante, p 238.
12 1985 Act, s 35A(2)(b).
13 *Freeman and Lockyer v Buckhurst Park Properties (Mangal) Ltd* [1964] 2 QB 480.
14 *Uxbridge Permanent Benefit Building Society v Pickard* [1939] 2 KB 248.
15 Eg *Ruben v Great Fingall Consolidated* [1906]] AC 439.

Even where the requirements of apparent authority are not satisfied, a person may sometimes be liable on an analogous ground. For example, where a person 'stands by' knowing that his signature has been or will be forged, he may be estopped from denying that the signature was genuine.[16] The same principle was applied where a wife purported to enter into a contract to sell her husband's house although she had no authority, actual or apparent, to do so. At this stage the husband would not have been bound by the contract. But later he met the buyer, led him to believe that there was a binding contract, and allowed him to have work done on the house. It was held that the husband was estopped from denying his wife's authority to enter into the contract, as he had induced the buyer to believe that she had such authority, and to act to his prejudice in reliance on that belief.[17]

ii   Usual authority

This expression sometimes refers to certain cases of either implied or apparent authority. But it is also used in a third sense, illustrated by a case in which A, the manager of P's public house, had in his own name bought cigars from X for the purposes of the business. A had no actual authority to make the contract as P had told him not to make such purchases from third parties. Nor was the case one of apparent authority, as X did not believe that A was P's agent but thought that A was buying on his own account. P was nevertheless held liable for the price of the cigars, on the ground that the contract was within the class of acts 'usually confided to an agent of that character'.[18] The decision, though controversial, seems on the whole to promote justice. Where the contract is made in the course of the principal's business, he will generally benefit from it; and it seems reasonable that he should equally be liable in the exceptional cases where the contract is to his disadvantage, whether as a result of the agent's dishonesty or for some other reason.

iii   Authority of necessity

A person who acts for another in an emergency is sometimes said to have authority of necessity, and so to have become the latter's agent. Three illustrations of the principle may be given.

---

16   Greenwood v Martins Bank Ltd [1933] AC 51. For estoppel, see ante, p 168.
17   Spiro v Lintern [1973] 3 All ER 319 at 323; Worboys v Carter [1987] 2 EGLR 1.
18   Watteau v Fenwick [1893] 1 QB 346 at 348–349.

First, the master of a ship may find it necessary to raise money quickly, for example to make repairs without which the ship cannot pursue her voyage. If he cannot get instructions from the shipowner in time, he has authority to borrow on the shipowner's credit or on the security of the ship or cargo, and even to sell part of the cargo.[19]

Secondly, a power of sale is conferred by statute on a bailee of uncollected goods if he has given notice to the bailor of his intention to sell, or if he has failed to trace the bailor after having taken reasonable steps to do so.[20]

Thirdly, agency of necessity may arise where one person intervenes to save another's life or property, and in certain analogous cases. The outstanding illustration of this rule is to be found in the law of maritime salvage, under which a person who goes to the aid of a ship in distress at sea[1] and saves life or property is entitled to some payment for his efforts; and if he takes the salvaged goods to a place of safety he has authority of necessity to warehouse them there, so as to prevent them from deteriorating.[2] Occasionally, the courts have been prepared to apply this principle outside the area of maritime salvage. For example, in *Great Northern Rly Co v Swaffield*[3] a railway company spent money on feeding and stabling a horse which the owner had failed to collect; and it was held that the owner was liable to reimburse the company. The decision is based on obvious humanitarian grounds; but the general rule is that a person who, without authority, preserves another's property is not entitled to any recompense: it is thought that the owner should not be subjected to obligations without his consent.[4] A distinction must, however, be drawn between the mere preservation of property and its improvement. Where the owner claims the return of property which has actually been improved, he often has to make some allowance for an increase in value which is due to the improver's efforts.[5]

As the above cases show, authority of necessity produces three quite different consequences. First, it may enable the 'agent' to make a contract between the 'principal' and a third party. This is its effect where a shipmaster borrows on the owner's credit. Secondly, it may enable the 'agent' to dispose of the principal's property either wholly

19 See *Notara v Henderson* (1872) LR 7 QB 225.
20 Torts (Interference with Goods) Act 1977, ss 12 and 13 and Sch 1.
1 See *The Goring* [1988] AC 831.
2 *The Winson* [1982] AC 939.
3 (1874) LR 9 Exch 132.
4 *Falcke v Scottish Imperial Assurance Co* (1886) 34 Ch D 234 at 248.
5 See *Munro v Wilmott* [1949] 1 KB 295, the facts of which would now be covered by ss 12 and 13 and Sch 1 of the Torts (Interference with Goods) Act 1977; cf (in cases of mistake) s 6 and *Greenwood v Bennett* [1973] QB 195.

or by way of security: this is illustrated by the shipmaster's power to borrow on the security of the ship or to sell the cargo, and by the bailee's power to sell uncollected goods. Thirdly, it may entitle the agent to recompense or reimbursement, as in the salvage and analogous cases. Strictly, our only concern in this chapter should be with the first of these consequences. This alone involves an application of the general contract principle that an agent can make a contract between his principal and a third party, and it has been suggested that the phrase 'agency of necessity' should be used to refer only to cases of this kind.[6] But such a narrow use of the phrase obscures the fact that often the same circumstances which produce one of the consequences just described will also lead to another. Thus in the *Swaffield* case the actual question was whether the railway company was entitled to be reimbursed; but if the company had made a contract with a livery stable on the owner's behalf, that contract might well have bound the owner on the ground that the company had authority of necessity.

iv   Other cases of agency by operation of law

In a number of other cases an agent is attributed to a person by operation of law. Thus when a company is first formed its original directors are, by statute, declared to be its agents.[7] Sometimes the court can appoint an agent for a person: for example it does so when it appoints someone to manage the affairs of a mental patient.[8]

c   Ratification

Where an agent makes a contract without being authorised to do so, the principal may become a party to that contract by subsequent ratification. This may be express, where the principal says in so many words that he adopts the agent's act. It may also be inferred from conduct: for example where the agent without authority buys goods which the principal then uses or resells. It may even be inferred from failure to repudiate the contract where the third party believes the agent's act to have been authorised and the principal knows of this belief.[9] It is, however, essential for the principal to have a free choice

---

6   *The Winson* [1982] AC 939 at 958.
7   Companies Act 1985, s 282.
8   *Plumpton v Burkinshaw* [1908] 2 KB 572.
9   *Suncorp Insurance and Finance v Milano Assicurazioni SpA* [1993] 2 Lloyd's Rep 225 at 241.

in the matter. Suppose that an agent without authority enters into a contract for the repair of the principal's property. Ratification cannot be inferred merely from the fact that the principal takes back his own property on which the work has been done.[10]

i Conditions to be satisfied

Ratification can take effect only if the following conditions are satisfied.

First, the agent must purport to act for the principal. This does not mean that he must intend to act for the principal, who may be able to ratify even though the agent intended to act for his own benefit and in fraud of the principal.[11] What the rule does mean is that the agent must make it appear to the third party that he was acting for a principal. The principal does not have to be named, so that an unauthorised contract made by an agent simply 'on behalf of my principal' can be ratified. But ratification is not possible where an agent makes an unauthorised contract *in his own name*, so that the third party thinks that he is dealing with the agent and with no one else.[12]

Secondly, the principal must have been in existence when the unauthorised contract was made. This rule looks logical, but it leads to the awkward result that a company cannot ratify contracts made by its promoters on its behalf before its incorporation.[13] As a practical matter it is often necessary to make such contracts; and various attempts have been made to circumvent the rule. None of these wholly solves the problem of creating mutually binding obligations between the company and the third party. By statute, the contract takes effect (subject to contrary agreement) as a contract between the agent and the third party;[14] but this provision does not confer rights or impose liabilities on the company itself. Rights can be acquired by the company by virtue of the Contracts (Rights of Third Parties) Act 1999;[15] but if the company chooses not to enforce those rights it cannot be required to discharge liabilities under the contract.

Thirdly, the principal must have had the capacity to enter into the unauthorised contract when it was made. At common law, a corporation cannot ratify its agent's unauthorised act in entering into

---

10 *The Liddesdale* [1900] AC 190.
11 *Re Tiedemann and Ledermann Frères* [1899] 2 QB 66.
12 *Keighley Maxsted & Co v Durant* [1901] AC 240.
13 *Kelner v Baxter* (1866) LR 2 CP 174.
14 Companies Act 1985, s 36C(1).
15 Section 1(3) ('need not be in existence').

an ultra vires contract.[16] This rule still applies to companies incorporated by special statute. But there are two reasons why it no longer applies to companies incorporated under the Companies Acts. First, the validity of an act done by such a company can no longer be called into question on the ground of lack of capacity by reason of anything in the company's memorandum.[17] Secondly, it is expressly provided that an act can be ratified even where it was done by the directors of such a company in breach of their duty to observe limitations on their powers contained in the memorandum of association.[18] Such a ratification would also prevent the company from denying the effectiveness of the ratified transaction on the ground that it was beyond the powers of the board of directors.[19]

Fourthly, there is a group of rules which limits the time for ratification. The general rule is that ratification must come within a reasonable time.[20] Ratification is also too late if it comes after the time fixed for performance.[1] There is some conflict of opinion on the question whether an unauthorised insurance can be ratified after loss.[2] The preferable view is that such ratification should be possible since its effectiveness could scarcely prejudice an insurer who expected to be bound and did not know of the agent's want of authority.

Fifthly, a nullity (such as a contract prohibited by statute)[3] cannot be ratified. This principle is sometimes used to explain the rule that a principal cannot ratify his agent's act in forging his signature.[4] A better reason for this rule is that the agent pretends, not that he is signing *on behalf* of the principal, but that the signature *actually is* that of the principal. Hence he does not purport to act on behalf of the principal within the first of our ratification rules. A principal may, however, be liable on a forged signature on the ground of estoppel.[5]

---

16 *Ashbury Rly Carriage and Iron Co Ltd v Riche* (1875) LR 7 HL 653.
17 Ante, pp 237–238 (where certain exceptions are stated).
18 Companies Act 1985, s 35(3).
19 1985 Act, s 35A(1).
20 *Re Portuguese Consolidated Copper Mines Ltd* (1890) 45 Ch D 16.
1   *Dibbins v Dibbins* [1896] 2 Ch 348.
2   Contrast *Grover & Grover Ltd v Mathews* [1910] 2 KB 401 with Marine Insurance Act 1906, s 86 and *National Oilwell (UK) Ltd v Davy Offshore Ltd* [1993] 2 Lloyd's Rep 582 at 607–608.
3   *Bedford Insurance Co Ltd v Instituto de Resseguros do Brasil* [1985] QB 966 at 986.
4   *Brook v Hook* (1871) LR 6 Ex 89.
5   See ante, p 296.

ii   Relation back

Ratification gives the unauthorised act the same effect as it would have had, if it had been originally authorised. In the leading case,[6] A without authority purported to buy a house from X on P's behalf. X repudiated the transaction and P then ratified. It was held that the ratification related back to the time of the unauthorised transaction between A and X, so that X was liable to P. This doctrine of 'relation back' has been criticised on the ground that it gives P the option of holding X to the contract while X has no corresponding option to hold P. But if P does not ratify, X has (as we shall see) a remedy against A;[7] and, as soon as X discovers A's lack of authority, he can force the issue by calling on P to ratify promptly. Any undue delay by P at this stage would make the ratification too late under the time rules discussed above.[8] Further, if A and X are conscious of a doubt as to A's authority, they can contract expressly 'subject to ratification'; and if they do so, the doctrine of 'relation back' does not apply.[9] Nor does it apply if A and X by mutual consent agree to cancel the contract before P ratifies.[10] The doctrine is subject to the further restrictions that it cannot be used so as unfairly to deprive a third party of an accrued property right,[11] and that it does not apply where the unauthorised act is a nullity.[12] In view of all these limitations on its scope, the doctrine of 'relation back' does not seem to be unjust in its practical operation.

3   EFFECTS OF AGENCY

The most important effects of agency as a general contract principle[13] are first that the agent can make a contract between principal and third party; and secondly that the agent himself is not a party to this contract. The following discussion deals with the operation of these rules and with exceptions to them.

---

6   *Bolton Partners v Lambert* (1889) 41 Ch D 295.
7   See post, pp 308–309.
8   Ante, p 300 at n 20.
9   *Watson v Davies* [1931] 1 Ch 455.
10   *Walter v James* (1871) LR 6 Exch 124.
11   *The Borvigilant and Romina G* [2003] EWCA Civ 935, [2003] 2 Lloyd's Rep 520 at [70]–[86].
12   Supra at n 4.
13   See ante, p 290.

a   Relations between principal and third party

It will be convenient to consider first the rights and secondly the liabilities of the principal. These depend in part on a distinction between disclosed and undisclosed principals. A *disclosed* principal is one of whose existence the third party was aware at the time of contracting. He is called a named principal if the third party also knew his name, and an unnamed principal if the third party knew of his existence but did not know his name. A principal is *undisclosed* if at the time of contracting the third party was unaware of his existence. In this situation the agent, though carrying out the principal's instructions, does not reveal this fact to the third party, who thinks that he is dealing with the agent and with no one else.

i   Rights of principal

As a general rule, the principal is a party to the contract[14] and so entitled to enforce it against the third party.[15] Where the principal is disclosed, this rule causes no injustice to the third party, since he knows at the time of contracting that he is undertaking a liability towards someone other than the agent. But where the principal is undisclosed, his intervention might prejudice a third party who at the time of contracting thought that he was dealing only with the agent. The mere possibility of such prejudice will not exclude the undisclosed principal's right where (as is often the case in a commercial context) it is a matter of indifference to the third party whether his contract is with the agent or with the principal.[16] The risk of such prejudice is also reduced by the rule that the third party can set up against the undisclosed principal any defence that he could have raised against the agent.[17] This rule, however, does not deal adequately with two situations in which personal considerations enter into the contract. First, the third party may have wanted to deal with the agent *and with no one else*, for example because the contract was 'personal' – ie of a kind that could not be assigned or vicariously performed.[18] If this is the position, the third party is not bound to accept and pay for performance from the undisclosed principal. Secondly, the third party, though willing to deal with persons other

14   Hence his rights are not affected by the Contracts (Rights of Third Parties) Act 1999: see s 1(1) ('not a party').
15   *Langton v Waite* (1868) LR 6 Eq 165.
16   *Siu Yin Kwan v Eastern Insurance Co Ltd* [1994] 2 AC 199 at 208.
17   *Browning v Provincial Insurance Co of Canada* (1873) LR 5 PC 263 at 272.
18   *Collins v Associated Greyhound Racecourses Ltd* [1930] 1 Ch 1.

than the agent, *may not have wanted to deal with the undisclosed principal.*
In one case[19] the managers of a theatre had refused to sell a first night
ticket to a dramatic critic who had been hostile to them in the past.
The critic then sent a friend to buy the ticket, ostensibly for the latter's
own use; and it was held that the critic had acquired no rights under
the resulting contract. Although the authorities on the point are not
easy to reconcile, it seems that the undisclosed principal cannot
intervene *if he knew* that the third party did not want to deal with him.
If the principal *did not know* this, he could probably intervene unless
it could be inferred from the 'personal' nature of the contract, or
from its express or implied terms, that its benefit was not to be
assigned.

A third party from whom money is due under the contract may pay
this money to the agent; and the agent may abscond or become insolvent
before he has paid the money over to the principal. The question
then arises whether the third party is discharged by the payment, or
whether he must make a second payment to the principal. If at the
time of the payment the principal was still undisclosed, the third
party is discharged, for he has paid the only creditor of whose existence
he knew.[20] But if at that time the principal was disclosed, the third
party is not discharged:[1] he knows that his creditor is the principal
and if he pays someone else he does so at his own risk. Payment to an
agent for a disclosed principal will discharge the third party only if
the agent has authority (whether actual, apparent or usual) to receive
payment.

The agent may, before the contract was made, have incurred a debt
to the third party; and the third party may try to set this off against the
principal's claim. Suppose that A owes X £20 and then on P's behalf
sells and delivers goods to X for a price of £100. The extent of X's
liability to P depends on whether P was at the time of contracting a
disclosed or an undisclosed principal. If P was a disclosed principal,
X must pay P the full £100.[2] But if P was an undisclosed principal, X
need only pay P £80; for in this case X believed that he was dealing
with A alone, and he could therefore reasonably expect that the price
of the goods would be reduced by the amount that A owed him.[3] If X
simply did not know whether A was acting for a principal or on his

19   *Said v Butt* [1920] 3 KB 497; see also *Nash v Dix* (1898) 78 LT 445; *Dyster v Randall & Sons* [1926] Ch 932.
20   *Curlewis v Birkbeck* (1863) 3 F & F 894.
1   *Linck, Moeller & Co v Jameson & Co* (1885) 2 TLR 206.
2   Cf *Mildred v Maspons* (1883) 8 App Cas 874.
3   Cf *George v Clagett* (1797) 7 Term Rep 359.

own behalf, this reasoning does not apply; and in such a case he is once again liable to pay the full £100 to P.[4]

ii   Liabilities of principal

The general rule is that the principal is liable to the third party under the contract. This is so whether the principal was disclosed or undisclosed. The rules which limit the undisclosed principal's rights under the contract exist only to protect the third party and therefore do not limit the liability of the principal. A third party who discovers the existence of an undisclosed principal thus gets a benefit for which he did not bargain, in that he can sue two persons (the principal and the agent) on the contract.[5] But the principal can hardly complain about this as he initiated the transaction. Of course if the alleged 'agent' contracted solely on his own behalf (and not for a principal at all) he alone will be liable on the contract.[6]

Further problems arise where the principal gives his agent the money to pay the third party, and the agent fails to pay it over and absconds or becomes insolvent. The general rule is that the principal must then make a second payment to the third party.[7] This rule clearly applies where the principal is disclosed; and the better view is that it also applies where the principal is undisclosed.[8] It may be hard on the principal to have to pay twice; but generally a debtor must see that his creditor is paid, and he bears any risk inherent in the method that he has chosen for transmitting the payment. The principal is only discharged by a payment to the agent if the third party has expressly requested (or has otherwise induced) him to pay in this way.[9]

b   Relations between agent and third party

As a general rule an agent is not a party to the contract that he makes between his principal and the third party. But there are many exceptions to this rule, and the agent may also be liable to the third party where he acts without authority.

4   *Cooke & Sons v Eshelby* (1887) 12 App Cas 271.
5   This does not mean that he will be *paid* twice over: see post, pp 307–308.
6   *J H Rayner (Mincing Lane) Ltd v Department of Trade and Industry* [1989] Ch 72 at 190–191; affd [1990] 2 AC 418 at 515.
7   *Irvine & Co v Watson & Sons* (1880) 5 QBD 414.
8   *Heald v Kenworthy* (1855) 10 Exch 739; *Armstrong v Stokes* (1872) LR 7 QB 598, contra, is doubted in *Irvine & Co v Watson & Sons* (1874) 5 QBD 414.
9   *Smyth v Anderson* (1849) 7 CB 21; cf *Wyatt v Hertford* (1802) 3 East 147.

i   Agent may be a party to the contract

The first group of cases in which the agent is a party to the contract are those in which he intends to undertake personal responsibility. Where the contract is in writing, the question whether the agent had this intention is one of construction; and the answer to it depends on the way in which the agent is described in the body of the document and on the way in which he signs it. Obviously he is not a party if he is described, and signs, as agent. But where the document is not clear a distinction has to be drawn between 'words of representation', which negative the intention to assume personal liability, and words which merely describe the professional or commercial capacity of the agent. Words which are merely descriptive[10] are perfectly consistent with an intention to assume personal liability; and even the words 'as agents' may be descriptive when they are used in their commercial and not in their strictly legal sense.[11] Normally a person who signs an order on company notepaper with the addition 'Director' would not be personally liable; but in one case[12] a director who in this way signed an order for repairs to *his own* boat was held personally liable on the contract. Words such as 'on behalf of' will generally be regarded as words of representation; but they may simply mean that the person on whose behalf the agent has signed *is*, and not that the agent is *not*, to be a party to the contract.[13] Where the agent is, under the above rules, personally liable he can normally also enforce the contract. But if the parties so intend it is possible for him to be liable without at the same time being entitled; or entitled without being liable so long as he provides some consideration for the third party's promise:[14] eg by making payments under the contract on behalf of the principal.

Secondly, the agent is a party to the contract (so that he can both sue and be sued on it) where the principal is undisclosed.[15] The rule does not apply where the principal is only unnamed.[16] In such a case the rights and liabilities of the agent depend on the principles stated in the preceding paragraph; though it may be relatively easier to infer that he intended to undertake personal responsibility where the principal is unnamed than where he is named.[17]

10   *Burrell v Jones* (1819) 3 B & Ald 47 ('we, as solicitors, undertake').
11   *Parker v Winlow* (1857) 7 E & B 942; cf ante, pp 290–291.
12   *The Swan* [1968] 1 Lloyd's Rep 5.
13   *The Sun Happiness* [1984] 1 Lloyd's Rep 381.
14   *Punjab National Bank v de Boinville* [1992] 3 All ER 104.
15   *Sims v Bond* (1833) 5 B & Ad 389 at 393.
16   See *Universal Steam Navigation Co Ltd v James McKelvie & Co* [1923] AC 492.
17   See *N & J Vlassopulos Ltd v Ney Shipping Ltd* [1977] 1 Lloyd's Rep 478.

Thirdly, the agent may be a party to the contract where he purports to act for a principal but in fact acts on his own behalf. It has accordingly been held that the agent can enforce the contract where he intends to act for himself but purports to act for an unnamed principal, eg by buying 'on behalf of my principal'.[18] But the position is different where he names the principal: ie where he buys 'on behalf of my principal P'. Here the third party may have relied on P's commercial reputation in entering into the contract, so that he could be prejudiced by having to perform in favour of the agent.[19] Where the principal is unnamed, the possibility of such prejudice to the third party is remote; though it might arise in a situation (similar to that discussed above) in which the third party was willing to contract with *anyone except* the agent.[20]

Fourthly, the agent may be a party to the contract if he intends and purports to contract for a non-existent principal. This is the position where an agent purports to make a contract on behalf of a company which does not yet exist: by statute the contract has effect as a contract entered into by the agent, who is liable on it accordingly;[1] he is also entitled.[2] The statutory rule can be excluded by contrary agreement, but the agent will not escape liability merely by contracting 'as agent'.[3] He must establish that there was an agreement exonerating him from liability. This is a question of fact in each case.[4]

So far it has been assumed that the agent purports to act on behalf of the unformed company, as where he signs the contract 'A, on behalf of P plc'. But it is also possible for him simply to sign the contract in the company's name, as where he signs 'P plc, A (director)'. In the latter case he does not say that he is contracting on behalf of the company, but that the signature *is* that of the company. The statutory rule stated above[5] applies also to this situation, so that (unless otherwise agreed) the agent will be entitled and liable under the contract.[6] But the rule does not apply to the converse situation in which the company had once existed and had been dissolved before

---

18   *Schmaltz v Avery* (1851) 16 QB 655; criticised in the Scottish case of *Hill Steam Shipping Co v Hugo Stinnes Ltd* 1941 SC 324.
19   *Bickerton v Burrell* (1816) 5 M & S 383; *Fellowes v Gwydyr* (1829) 1 Russ & M 83.
20   Ante, pp 302–303; cf *The Remco* [1984] 2 Lloyd's Rep 205.
1   Companies Act 1985, s 36C(1).
2   See infra at n 6.
3   *Phonogram Ltd v Lane* [1982] QB 938 at 944.
4   Cf the common law position as stated in *Black v Smallwood* [1965] ALR 744.
5   Supra, at n 1.
6   *Braymist Ltd v Wise Finance Co Ltd* [2000] EWCA Civ 127, [2002] Ch 273.

the contract was made. The contract is then a nullity and cannot be enforced by the 'agent' who had purported to act for the company.[7]

Finally, an agent may acquire rights or be subject to liabilities under the contract by virtue of a relevant custom or usage, or by special statutory provision.[8]

ii Position where agent is a party to the contract

Where the agent is a party to the contract, the principal may, and often will, also be a party; but this does not mean that the third party is either liable or entitled twice over.

So far as the third party's *liabilities* are concerned, the first rule is that if he performs in favour of the principal, he is under no further liability to the agent. If, on the other hand, the third party performs in favour of the agent he is discharged only if the principal was undisclosed, or if the agent was authorised to receive performance: the rules on this topic have been discussed above.[9] Under these rules a third party who pays the agent may have to make a second payment to the principal.

So far as the third party's rights are concerned, the first question is whether the agent's undertaking was merely one of *personal*, or also one of *exclusive*, liability. If it was of the latter kind, the third party has no rights against the principal at all.[10] But more commonly both principal and agent will be liable on the contract: this is, for example, the position where the agent contracts for an undisclosed principal. There are then three possibilities. First, the third party may have actually received performance from either the principal or the agent; and in that case he cannot sue the other. Secondly, the third party may have 'elected' to hold either the principal or the agent liable; and the effect of this is again that the third party cannot then sue the other.[11] What amounts to 'election' is a question of fact. If the third party took legal proceedings against the agent, this would be strong (though not conclusive) evidence of election to hold the agent liable.[12] The reason for this doctrine of 'election' appears to be that the third party's conduct in (for example) claiming performance from the agent might lead the principal to believe that no claim would be made against him, and accordingly to settle his own accounts with the agent.[13] If there has

7   *Cotronic (UK) Ltd v Dezonie (t/a Wendaland Builders Ltd)* [1991] BCLC 721.
8   Eg Insolvency Act 1986, s 4(1).
9   See ante, p 303.
10   Eg *Thomson v Davenport* (1829) 9 B & C 78.
11   *Debenhams Ltd v Perkins* (1925) 133 LT 252 at 254.
12   See *Scarf v Jardine* (1882) 7 App Cas 345.
13   Eg *Davison v Donaldson* (1882) 9 QBD 623.

been no such action in reliance, it is hard to see in what way a principal (or agent) is prejudiced by the third party's unsuccessful attempt to obtain payment from the agent (or principal). In practice the courts can, when there is no such prejudice, refuse to apply the doctrine by finding as a fact that the conduct of the third party does not amount to election.[14] Thirdly, the third party may have actually obtained judgment against principal or agent; and if their liability was joint it used to be the law that the third party could not then sue the other even though the judgment was not satisfied.[15] Now the mere fact that the third party has obtained a judgment against principal or agent is no longer a bar to proceedings against the other;[16] though it might, presumably, still amount to an 'election'.

iii   Agent acting without authority

An agent who purports to enter into a contract on behalf of a principal is taken to represent that he had authority to make the contract. If he had no such authority and knew this, he is liable in tort to the third party for fraud; and he might be liable in negligence if he ought to have known of his want of authority. But the law goes further and holds the agent liable even though he in good faith and without negligence believed that he had authority when he had none. He is said to have impliedly warranted that he had the authority which he purported to have; and liability for breach of the implied warranty is independent of fault in the sense of fraud or negligence.[17] Thus an agent would be liable if his authority had come to an end as a result of the principal's death or insanity, even though he did not know and could not reasonably have known of these events.[18] This rule can cause hardship to the agent, who may have acted in the most perfect good faith. The hardship is alleviated by a special statutory provision under which the agent is not liable to the third party if he acts under a power of attorney in ignorance of the fact that it has been revoked.[19]

The agent's liability for breach of implied warranty of authority is further limited by a number of rules of common law. He is, in the first place, not liable if the third party knew (or must be taken to have known) that the agent had no authority.[20] Secondly, the agent is not liable if, though he had no actual authority, the principal is

14   Eg *Clarkson Booker Ltd v Andjel* [1964] 2 QB 775.
15   See ante, p 243.
16   Civil Liability (Contribution) Act 1978, s 3.
17   *Collen v Wright* (1857) 8 E & B 647.
18   *Yonge v Toynbee* [1910] 1 KB 215.
19   Powers of Attorney Act 1971, s 5(1).
20   *Halbot v Lens* [1901] 1 Ch 344.

nevertheless liable to the third party under the rules relating to apparent or usual authority;[1] or if the principal ratifies. In such cases the third party can sue the principal, so that the agent's want of authority does not cause the third party any loss. Thirdly, the traditional view is that he is not liable if the representation was one of law (including one as to the construction of the document conferring his authority);[2] but this view is open for reconsideration now that the distinction between mistakes and representations of 'law' and of 'fact' is, in other contexts, discredited.[3] Finally, it has been held that the doctrine of breach of implied warranty of authority does not apply to agents of the Crown.[4] The reason for this limitation on the scope of the doctrine seems to be that it would be most unreasonable to make civil servants personally liable for the very large sums often involved in government contracts. The effect of these statutory and common rules is certainly to mitigate the harshness of the doctrine of implied warranty of authority; but it would be more satisfactory to confine the doctrine to cases in which the agent knew, or was negligent in not knowing, of his want of authority.

An agent is also liable to the third party in tort for misrepresentations which relate to matters other than his authority: for example, an estate agent may be so liable to a purchaser for misrepresentations about the property.[5] Such liability differs from liability for breach of warranty of authority in that it arises only if the agent is guilty of fraud or negligence. An estate agent who makes misleading statements about the property may also be guilty of a criminal offence.[6]

4 TERMINATION OF AGENCY

Agency is often a contract, and any event which terminates that contract will bring the relation of principal and agent to an end. To take the most obvious cases: the parties may terminate the relation by mutual consent; or the contract may provide that it is to expire at the end of a fixed time.

A common way of terminating agency is by notice, which may be given by either party to the other. Where a contract of agency prescribes

---

1 *Rainbow v Howkins* [1904] 2 KB 322; but see *Yonge v Toynbee* [1910] 1 KB 215.
2 *Rashdall v Ford* (1886) LR 2 Eq 750.
3 *Kleinwort Benson Ltd v Lincoln City Council* [1999] 2 AC 349, ante, pp 125, 148.
4 *Dunn v Macdonald* [1897] 1 QB 555.
5 *McCullagh v Lane Fox & Partners Ltd* (1994) 138 Sol Jo LB 54.
6 Property Misdescriptions Act 1991, s 1.

a period of notice, the giving of such a notice will terminate the agency; where no period of notice is specified, a reasonable period of notice will have the same effect.[7] A notice which specifies too short a period is a breach of contract, giving rise to liability in damages, but it is nevertheless *effective*: that is, it terminates the relation of principal and agent.[8] We are not in this book concerned with the financial consequences of termination between principal and agent since these are an aspect of agency, not as a general contract principle, but as a special contract.[9]

At common law, agency may come to an end by operation of law on the death or total disability of either party; on the bankruptcy of the principal; and on that of the agent if it makes him unfit to perform his duties.

The events listed above terminate the relationship of principal and agent and the agent's actual authority (whether express or implied) to contract on behalf of the principal. They do not necessarily put an end to authority which exists independently of the principal's consent. For example, a principal who terminates the agent's actual authority by notice to the agent may still be liable on the basis of apparent authority on contracts made by the agent after receipt of the notice. To avoid such liability, the principal must further give notice *to the third party* that he has terminated the agent's authority. There is considerable confusion in the authorities on the exact effects at common law of the principal's death or incapacity; but the better view seems to be that these events, too, terminate only actual authority and do not affect apparent authority unless the third party has notice of them.[10] Where the agent's authority is conferred by a power of attorney, a third party who deals with the agent without notice of revocation can, by statute, treat the transaction as valid as if the power had still been in existence.[11]

Agency is sometimes 'irrevocable' in the sense that an attempt by the principal to revoke it is not merely wrongful, *but ineffective*, in the sense that it survives such events as the principal's death, legal disability or bankruptcy. Such irrevocability can affect the relations both between principal and agent and between either of them and a third party. At

---

7   *Martin-Baker Aircraft Co Ltd v Canadian Flight Equipment Ltd* [1955] 2 QB 556.
8   *Denmark Productions Ltd v Boscobel Productions Ltd* [1969] 1 QB 699.
9   Cf ante, p 290.
10   *Drew v Nunn* (1879) 4 QBD 661; contrast *Yonge v Toynbee* [1910] 1 KB 215; *Blades v Free* (1829) 9 B & C 167.
11   Powers of Attorney Act 1971, s 5(2).

common law, authority is irrevocable where it is 'coupled with an interest'.[12] For this purpose it is not sufficient to show that the agent has an interest in earning his commission; for, if it were, all commercial agencies would be irrevocable. The rule refers to cases in which the agency is created to protect some *previously existing* interest of the agent. It could, for example, apply where P owed money to A and then authorised A to sell some of P's property and to repay himself out of the proceeds. The authority would not be irrevocable if P's indebtedness to A arose only *after* the authority had been conferred.[13] There are, finally, statutory restrictions on the revocability of certain powers of attorney. Such a power is irrevocable if it expressly so provides and if it is given to secure a proprietary interest or the performance of an obligation.[14] And a power of attorney which is expressed to continue in spite of the principal's supervening incapacity[15] is not revoked by such incapacity, but only in that event suspended till registered with the court.[16] Such an 'enduring power' can then only be revoked with the consent of the court;[17] and the agent and the third party are protected if in good faith they act in ignorance of the incapacity, and in certain other cases.[18]

---

12   *Carmichael's Case* [1896] 2 Ch 643.
13   *Smart v Sandars* (1848) 5 CB 895.
14   Powers of Attorney Act 1971, s 4.
15   Enduring Powers of Attorney Act 1985, s 2, to be repealed and replaced by provisions for 'lasting' powers of attorney if the Mental Capacity Bill 2004 is passed in its present form.
16   1985 Act, s 1(1)(a) and (b), 6.
17   1985 Act, ss 7(1)(a), 8(3).
18   1985 Act, ss 1(1)(c), 9.

Chapter 16

Performance and breach

Every contract imposes obligations on at least one of the parties. If the contract is unilateral, it imposes an obligation on only one of the parties. In the more common case of a bilateral contract, obligations are imposed on both parties, and each of the parties may be subject to more than one obligation. Under an ordinary contract for the sale of goods, for example, the seller is obliged to deliver the goods, and he may be obliged to ensure that they are of a certain quality, or fit for a particular purpose. The buyer, on the other hand, is obliged to accept the goods and to pay for them.

A party who fails to perform his obligations under the contract will generally be in breach, so that performance and breach can be regarded as two sides of the same coin. But failure to perform is not invariably a breach. It may be excused either under the doctrine of frustration (to be discussed in Chapter 17) or for reasons stated later in the present chapter. Our concern here will be with four topics: the nature of the duty to perform; the rules governing the method of performance; the effects of failure to perform (not amounting to frustration); and repudiation before performance has become due.

1 THE DUTY TO PERFORM

a Terms of the contract

It goes almost without saying that the extent of the duty to perform depends primarily on the terms of the contract. Performance must be exactly in accordance with these terms. It will not suffice for the party who is under the duty to do something else that is as good, or almost as good, or even better. If some latitude is required, the contract must expressly provide for it: for example, by saying that a seller is to deliver 'about' a certain quantity of goods, or that a ship is 'expected to arrive' at 'about' a stated time. Such stipulations are common in commercial contracts. Unless they are included, failure to perform exactly in accordance with the contract is prima facie a breach.

So far it has been assumed that the terms of the contract clearly specify the duties of the party alleged to be in breach. But there may be, and often is, dispute as to the meaning of terms in the contract which impose these obligations; and sometimes a more fundamental question arises, namely whether the defendant is under any duty at all, or under any duty of the kind which he is alleged to have broken. There may be no such duty: in one case[1] a carrier agreed with the Admiralty that, for eleven years, he would convey from Dover to Calais such mail as he should be asked to carry. It was held that the Admiralty was under no duty to give him any mail to carry but only under one to pay him at the contract rate for such mail as he actually carried. Similarly, a contract by which A binds himself to supply B with such quantities of (for example) steel as B may order, or as B may require in his business, does not bind B to order any steel, or to carry on his business in such a way that any relevant requirements will arise. On the other hand, obligations which are not expressly stated can sometimes be implied. A contract of employment, for example, may simply say that the employer is to pay wages without making it clear whether he must actually provide work. The traditional view is that the employer need only pay,[2] so that he is not in breach if he sends the employee home on so-called 'garden leave' with full pay.[3] But there are exceptions to this general rule: for example, an actor who has been engaged for a play must be given an opportunity of appearing;[4] and it has been suggested that, at least in the case of a skilled worker, the law now recognises a 'right to work'.[5] In such cases, an employee may lose that chance of maintaining or enhancing his reputation or skill if he is not given work, so that the employer may be liable in damages for breach of contract if he sends the employee home, even on full pay. There is also a 'right to return' after statutory maternity, parental or paternity leave.[6]

b   Standard of duty

Once it has been determined *what* each contracting party must do, the next question is this: is a party liable for *any* failure in performance, or only for a failure which can, in some sense, be said to be due to his fault?

---

1   *Churchward v R* (1865) LR 1 QB 173.
2   *Turner v Sawdon & Co* [1901] 2 KB 653; cf *Delaney v Staples* [1992] 1 AC 687 at 692.
3   *Delany v Staples* [1992] 1 AC 687 at 692.
4   *Herbert Clayton and Jack Waller Ltd v Oliver* [1930] AC 209.
5   *Langston v Amalgamated Union of Engineering Workers* [1974] 1 All ER 980.
6   Employment Rights Act 1996, Pt VIII.

Contractual liability is in many cases strict: that is, it arises quite independently of fault. The point is most clearly illustrated by the case of a buyer who cannot pay the agreed price for goods simply because his bank has failed: there is no doubt that he is in breach of contract.[7] Similarly, a seller of goods may be unable to deliver because he is let down by his suppliers or because he is unable to find shipping space to get the goods to their agreed destination:[8] again he is in breach even though his inability to deliver was not due to any failure on his part to take reasonable steps to secure performance. The same principle can apply to defects of quality. In one case[9] it was held that a seller of contaminated milk was in breach of contract even though he had taken all reasonable precautions to ensure that the milk was pure. Perhaps the most striking case of all was one in which a bottle of lemonade was supplied by manufacturers to a shopkeeper who sold it to a customer. The lemonade contained carbolic acid and it was held that the shopkeeper (though in no moral sense at 'fault') was liable to the customer for breach of contract.[10] The principle of strict liability seems also to apply where goods are supplied under a contract other than one of sale: eg under a contract of hire.[11]

There are, however, other situations in which fault is relevant to the issue of contractual liability. First, a supervening event may discharge a contract under the doctrine of frustration; but a party cannot rely on such an event as a ground of discharge if he has himself voluntarily brought it about, or (generally) if its occurrence is due to his negligence.[12] Secondly, there are some contracts which do not impose a strict duty to produce a specified result, but only a duty to use reasonable care and skill, or best endeavours to bring it about. This standard of liability commonly applies where a person contracts to supply a service in the course of a profession or business.[13] Thus a doctor who contracts to provide medical treatment is not normally understood to guarantee its success:[14] he need only show reasonable care and skill.[15] The same is true of contracts calling for the exercise

7   Cf *Universal Corpn v Five Ways Properties Ltd* [1979] 1 All ER 552.
8   *Lewis Emanuel & Son Ltd v Sammut* [1959] 2 Lloyd's Rep 629; *Intertradex SA v Lesieur-Tourteaux SARL* [1978] 2 Lloyd's Rep 509.
9   *Frost v Aylesbury Dairy Co* [1905] 1 KB 608.
10   *Daniels and Daniels v R White & Son Ltd* [1938] 4 All ER 258. Lack of fault is, however, a defence to a claim in respect of failure of the goods to comply with a 'public statement' about their 'specific characteristics' contrary to the Sale of Goods Act 1979, s 14(2D) and (2E) (a).
11   See Supply of Goods and Services Act 1982, ss 4, 9; cf Supply of Goods (Implied Terms) Act 1973, ss 9–11.
12   Post, pp 362–364.
13   Supply of Goods and Services Act 1982, s 13.
14   See *Eyre v Measday* [1986] 1 All ER 488; *Thake v Maurice* [1986] QB 644.
15   Eg *Gold v Haringey Health Authority* [1987] 2 All ER 888.

of some other professional skills, for example as a solicitor.[16] Architects occupy an intermediate position: they are only liable for negligence in respect of errors of supervision,[17] but may be strictly liable for defects of design.[18] The principle of strict liability was also applied where a firm had contracted to repair a car and in the course of so doing fitted connecting rods supplied by a reputable manufacturer. The rods suffered from latent defects and gave way, causing extensive damage; and the repairers were held liable even though they had taken all reasonable care.[19] The distinction between this case and those of the professional services is that the car-repairing contract contains both a supply and a service element.[20] Liability for defects in the components *supplied* is strict, by analogy to sale. Liability for short-comings in the *service* element probably depends on fault, ie on failure to use reasonable care and skill.

Fault is finally relevant in the case of those conditional contracts, in which one party impliedly undertakes to bring about the occurrence of the condition.[1] For example, a contract may be made to sell goods for overseas delivery and both parties may know that the goods cannot be exported without licence. In such a case, the seller is not normally bound to do more than to make reasonable efforts to get the licence.[2] If such efforts are made and fail, the seller will not be in breach merely because he cannot lawfully deliver the goods in accordance with the contract.

The standard of duty normally imposed by law can be varied by the terms of contract. Thus it is possible (if unlikely) for a medical practitioner to guarantee the success of his treatment; while conversely the parties can (subject to legislative restrictions)[3] reduce a duty which is prima facie strict to one of reasonable diligence.

c Excuses for non-performance

Not every failure to perform a contractual promise is a breach. The failure may be excused by some rule of law, or by the terms of the contract.

---

16 *Clark v Kirby-Smith* [1964] Ch 506.
17 *Bagot v Stevens, Scanlan & Co Ltd* [1966] 1 QB 197.
18 *Independent Broadcasting Authority v EMI Electronics Ltd* (1980) 14 BLR 1. Cases of strict liability at common law are preserved by Supply of Goods and Services Act 1982, s 16(2)(a).
19 *G H Myers & Co v Brent Cross Service Co* [1934] 1 KB 46.
20 See *Young and Marten Ltd v McManus Childs Ltd* [1969] 1 AC 454.
1 Ante, p 28.
2 *Re Anglo-Russian Merchant Traders Ltd* [1917] 2 KB 679.
3 See ante, pp 101 et seq.

One situation in which an excuse can be said to be provided by law is that in which the duty to perform has not yet arisen. If, for example, goods are sold for cash on delivery and the seller has failed to deliver, then obviously the buyer need not pay. But even after the duty to perform has come into existence, excuses for non-performance may be provided by supervening events outside the control of the parties. Such an event may so seriously affect performance as to frustrate the contract. It will then discharge *both* parties from *all* their obligations under the contract.[4] But a supervening event may also have less drastic effects. For example, an employee who does not go to work because he is temporarily ill is not in breach. The illness operates as an excuse for non-performance. But it does not frustrate the contract unless it is so serious as to make effective resumption of work impossible.[5] Except in such a case, the employee is bound to go back to work when his illness is over. In the meantime the employer is prima facie bound to go on paying wages,[6] unless his obligation to do so is excluded by the express or implied terms of the contract.[7]

Excuses provided by the contract take two common forms. First, the contract may contain a clause entitling a party to cancel or to terminate. Hire-purchase agreements, for example, often expressly (or by statute[8]) confer on the hirer the right to terminate by notice. If the hirer exercises that right his failure thereafter to pay instalments is obviously not a breach – though he will be in breach if he simply fails to pay without going through the motions of terminating in accordance with his right to do so. Secondly, a contract which would normally impose a strict duty may provide that, if one party cannot perform for some reason beyond his control, he is to be excused. For example, a charterparty prima facie imposes a strict duty on the charterer to provide the agreed cargo, but it may contain an 'exception' for failure to perform this duty in circumstances not due to the charterer's fault. If such circumstances arise, the charterer's failure to perform is excused and does not constitute a breach.[9]

A party relying on an excuse for non-performance must show that it existed at the time of his refusal or failure to perform.[10] If he can show this, he is not in breach even though at that time he did not state the excuse (or even know of it) but gave some other, insufficient

4　Post, pp 350, 364.
5　Eg, *Marshall v Harland and Wolff Ltd* [1972] 2 All ER 715, post, p 353.
6　*Marrison v Bell* [1939] 2 KB 187; Employment Rights Act 1996, s 64(1).
7　*Mears v Safecar Security Ltd* [1983] QB 54.
8　Consumer Credit Act 1974, s 99.
9　*The Angelia* [1973] 2 All ER 144.
10　See *British and Beningtons Ltd v North Western Cachar Tea Co Ltd* [1923] AC 48.

ground.[11] For example, if a seller tenders goods which suffer from a defect justifying their rejection the buyer has the right to reject them; and if he exercises that right it makes no difference that at the time of rejection he did not specify the defect, or alleged the existence of another defect which he could not substantiate.[12] In support of the rule, it can be said that it prevents the party in breach (the seller in our example) from benefiting from concealment of defects. On the other hand, the seller may be as ignorant of the defects as the buyer, and in such a case the rule can cause him considerable surprise and hardship. It therefore does not apply where failure to specify the defect deprives him of the chance of putting matters right:[13] eg by making a second tender of conforming goods within the period fixed for delivery; or where his conduct is in some other way affected by the buyer's failure to specify the true ground for rejection: eg where he spends time or money in investigating or trying to put right a different objection which the buyer raises at the time of rejection, but later fails to substantiate.[14] The buyer will also be unable to rely on a defect which would have justified rejection if at the time of rejection his right to reject had already been barred on one of the grounds to be discussed later in this chapter: eg by acceptance.[15]

2 METHOD OF PERFORMANCE

Performance is generally due without demand[16] but this rule is subject to a number of qualifications. It obviously does not apply where the contract provides for performance 'on demand'.[17] A demand is also necessary where, without it, a party cannot reasonably be expected to know that performance is required: for example, where a landlord who has covenanted to keep premises in repair has no means of knowing that they are in need of repair until a notice to this effect has been given to him by his tenant.[18]

Often performance by one party (such as payment or delivery) cannot be completed unless the other party co-operates by accepting

11 Eg *Ridgway v Hungerford Market Co* (1835) 3 Ad & El 171.
12 Eg *Arcos Ltd v E A Ronaasen & Son* [1933] AC 470.
13 *André et Cie v Cook Industries Inc* [1987] 2 Lloyd's Rep 463.
14 Cf *The Lena* [1981] 1 Lloyd's Rep 68 at 79; *The Eurometal* [1981] 1 Lloyd's Rep 337 at 341.
15 *Panchaud Frères SA v Etablissements General Grain Co* [1970] 1 Lloyd's Rep 53, as explained in *B P Exploration Co (Libya) Ltd v Hunt (No 2)* [1979] 1 WLR 783 at 810–811; affd [1983] 2 AC 352.
16 *Walton v Mascall* (1844) 13 M & W 452.
17 See *Bank of Baroda v Panessar* [1987] Ch 335.
18 *Calabar Properties Ltd v Stitcher* [1984] 1 WLR 287 at 298.

it. In such cases, the obligation of the former party is to tender performance. A tender of money requires actual production of the money: a statement that the debtor is ready and willing to pay is only an offer to tender. A tender of less than the amount due is bad;[19] and the same is true where a debtor tenders more than is due and asks for change.[20]

A payment by cheque is generally regarded as a conditional payment which becomes absolute when the cheque is honoured.[1] On the other hand, where goods or services are paid for by credit card or charge card, such payment is regarded as absolute. Hence if the card issuing company should fail to pay the supplier, the latter's sole remedy is against the company.[2] He is not entitled to claim the price from the customer, since it would be unjust to make the customer liable for immediate full payment in cash when he had contracted on credit terms. The customer's only liability is to the company, in accordance with the agreement under which it issued the card to him.

A contract may specify not only the nature but also the manner of the performance required: for example it may state how, where and when goods are to be delivered and paid for. A tender of performance which does not comply with the contract is defective; but if it is rejected on that ground and a second 'good' tender is made within the contract period, the good tender must normally be accepted.[3]

A troublesome type of provision is one which allows for alternative methods of performance without making it clear which party has the right to choose between them. The law in some cases resolves the uncertainty by more or less arbitrary rules: for example if a loan is repayable in 'one or two years' the option is the borrower's;[4] if a lease is for seven, fourteen or twenty-one years, the option is the tenant's.[5] In other cases there is no general rule. For example a contract may provide for delivery of goods 'in April' without stating whether it is the buyer or the seller who is entitled to specify the exact delivery date. The question in such cases is one of construction, depending on the nature and terms of the contract as a whole.

---

19   *Dixon v Clark* (1848) 5 CB 365.
20   *Betterbee v Davis* (1811) 3 Camp 70.
1   *Sayer v Wagstaff* (1844) 14 LJ Ch 116 treats the condition as precedent; *Jameson v Central Electricity Generating Board* [2000] 1 AC 455 at 478 treats it as subsequent.
2   *Re Charge Card Services Ltd* [1989] Ch 497; *Customs and Excise Comrs v Diners Club Ltd* [1989] 1 WLR 1196.
3   *Tetley v Shand* (1871) 25 LT 658.
4   *Reed v Kilburn Co-operative Society* (1875) LR 10 QB 264.
5   (1875) LR 10 QB 264 at 265.

3 RESCISSION FOR FAILURE IN PERFORMANCE

Failure to perform a contract is generally a breach. As such it gives rise to the usual remedies for *enforcing* the contract, either specifically or by an award for damages. These remedies are discussed in Chapter 18. But a person who does not get what he bargained for may also seek to *undo* the contract by 'terminating' or 'rescinding' it, and he may be entitled to do this even though the other party's failure to perform was not a breach.[6] 'Rescission' here does not mean that the contract is wholly brought to an end, much less that it is retrospectively annulled, as in cases of misrepresentation.[7] In particular, where the failure in performance amounts to a breach, rescission for that breach does not deprive the injured party of his right to damages for the breach.

Rescission for breach (or other failure in performance) refers to three different, though related, processes. The first is a simple refusal to perform, as where a buyer of defective goods refuses to accept and pay for them. The second is a refusal to accept further performance, as where a buyer of goods by instalments refuses to accept further deliveries on the ground that those already made are not in accordance with the contract. The third is a claim by the injured party to be returned, so far as possible, to the pre-contract position: for example, where a buyer rejects defective goods and asks for his money back.

Such claims to rescind the contract are sometimes more advantageous to the injured party than claims for enforcement. For one thing, refusal to perform, or to accept performance, is a kind of self-help, free from the delays and risks of legal proceedings. For another, it will often be more reasonable to allow a buyer to whom defective goods are tendered to reject them, rather than to require him to accept and pay, and then to seek his remedy in damages.

On the other hand, rescission is also used for the more questionable purpose of enabling a party to get out of a bad bargain. Suppose that A has sold goods to B at a price of £100, to be delivered and paid for in six months. When the goods are delivered they are found to be defective in some way which reduced their value by 10 per cent; but by this time the market value of such goods has declined to £40. If B were entitled to rescind, he could save himself £60 by buying equivalent goods elsewhere; while if his only claim were one for

---

6   Eg because he had an excuse for non-performance: see ante, p 315.
7   Ante, p 163, for criticism of the terminology, see *Photo Production Ltd v Securicor Transport Ltd* [1980] AC 827 at 844–851; for its continued use, see eg *Bunge Corpn v Tradax SA* [1981] 2 All ER 513 at 548, 549; *Berger & Co Inc v Gill & Duffus SA* [1984] AC 382 at 390, 391.

damages it would yield no more than £4. Conversely, the value of the goods at the time fixed for delivery may have risen to £200 and A may seek to rescind on the ground that B has failed strictly to perform the terms as to payment. This failure may not cause A any appreciable loss at all, but if it entitles him to rescind he will be able to avoid his liability to deliver the goods for the original price. This desire to get out of a bad bargain appears as the motive for rescission in many of the reported cases on this topic. Rescission can also lead to another kind of hardship where a party has performed in part but cannot complete. He may by such part performance have conferred benefits on the other party which the latter cannot restore. This would be the position where A contracts to paint B's house for a lump sum payable on completion, but only manages to do three-quarters of the work. To allow B to refuse to make *any* payment can cause hardship to A.

There may thus be strong practical reasons both for and against allowing rescission; and the courts have had much difficulty in balancing the competing interests of the parties. This difficulty accounts for the complexity of the rules which determine the availability of rescission and the grounds on which the right to rescind may be barred.

a   The order of performance

The right to rescind, in the sense of simply refusing to perform, depends in the first place on the provisions of the contract with regard to the order in which the parties are to perform. The possible situations are best discussed by taking some simple examples. First, A agrees to work for B at a monthly salary payable in arrear. Here A's performance is said to be a *condition precedent* to B's duty to pay. This means that B does not become liable to pay the agreed salary until the end of the month; and B will not be bound to make the payment if, before then, A has repudiated the contract by refusing to do the work.[8] Secondly, A agrees to sell goods to B for cash on delivery (and in the absence of a contrary provision it will be assumed that a sale is on these terms).[9] Here delivery and payment are said to be *concurrent conditions*: that is, neither party need perform until the other is ready and willing to do so; and if, before such an exchange of the goods for the price has taken place, one party repudiates the contract, the other will be entitled to rescind so as to be permanently relieved of his

---

8   *Miles v Wakefield Metropolitan District Council* [1987] AC 539 at 561, 574; *Wiluszynski v Tower Hamlets London Borough Council* [1989] ICR 493 at 498.
9   Sale of Goods Act 1979, s 28.

obligations under it. Thirdly, performance by one party may be due in spite of a breach by the other. For example, a landlord is not entitled to refuse to perform his covenant to repair simply because the tenant is in arrears with his rent.[10] The obligations of the parties in these cases are sometimes said to arise out of *independent covenants.*

The rule that B need not perform if A has failed to perform a condition precedent or concurrent condition is qualified where, before performance from A became due, B has without justification indicated that he would refuse to accept A's performance. This would amount to a repudiation by B and, if A accepts that repudiation, he thereby puts an end to his own duty to perform. It follows that A is then entitled to damages for wrongful repudiation from B without having to show that he has (or could have) performed his part of the contract.[11]

b   Requirement of serious failure

Performance may be in the agreed order, but be deficient in quantity or quality, or may be tendered after the agreed time. The general rule in such cases is that the right to rescind depends on the seriousness of the failure in performance. The question is said to be whether the failure deprives the injured party of 'substantially the whole benefit',[12] which it was intended that he should obtain; or whether it 'goes to the root'[13] of the contract. If it does, the injured party can rescind. If its effect is less serious, the injured party in general has to accept and pay for the defective performance, and his remedy (if the failure is a breach) is in damages. The requirement that the failure must be serious is subject to many exceptions which are discussed later in this chapter. Our present concern is with the requirement itself, which is often expressed in vague phrases, such as those quoted above. But behind this façade of vague language the courts have applied a number of essentially practical tests.

i   Adequacy of damages

The first of these tests is this: will the injured party be adequately protected by an action for damages, or does he *need* the more drastic

---

10   *Taylor v Webb* [1937] 2 KB 283.
11   *British and Beningtons Ltd v North Western Cachar Tea Co Ltd* [1923] AC 48; *Berger & Co Inc v Gill & Duffus SA* [1984] AC 382; contrast *The Simona* [1989] AC 788 where the repudiation was *not* accepted.
12   *Photo Production Ltd v Securicor Transport Ltd* [1980] AC 827 at 849.
13   *Poussard v Spiers and Pond* (1876) 1 QBD 410 at 414.

remedy of rescission? This point is well illustrated by a line of cases concerning breaches by sellers of contracts for the sale of land. If the breach simply is that the seller cannot convey the whole area of land comprised in the contract, then compensation in money may be an adequate remedy, at least where the reduction in area does not seriously interfere with the use to which the purchaser intended to put the land.[14] But where such interference does result from the deficiency, so that compensation for the breach is hard to assess, the injured party is entitled to rescind as damages are then an inadequate remedy.[15] The same test was applied where the English distributor for a French tile manufacturer was persistently (but only slightly) late in making payments under the contract. It was held that the French manufacturer could not rescind since he suffered no loss except a small amount of interest on the sums paid late; and this could easily be made good by an award of damages.[16]

ii   Reasonableness of accepting further performance

A second test, which has been applied to contracts calling for continued performance over a period of time, is whether it is reasonable to require the injured party to continue to accept performance of the contract in the light of the failure that has occurred. One factor relevant to this issue is the ratio of the failure to the performance that was bargained for. Thus in one case[17] 100 tons of rag flock were sold for delivery by instalments and it was held that defects in only 1½ tons did not justify the buyers' refusal to accept further deliveries. In another case[18] a tenor had been engaged for the 1875 season at Covent Garden, which was to last for three and a half months; and it was held that his failure (on account of illness) to attend rehearsals on four out of the six days before the season opened did not justify his dismissal. Another important factor is that the failure may give rise to uncertainty as to future performance. The case of the tenor may, from this point of view, be contrasted with one in which a soprano had been engaged to take the leading female part in a new opera. She was ill on the opening night and this fact was held to justify her dismissal, as the illness 'was a serious one of uncertain duration'.[19]

14   Eg *Aspinalls to Powell and Scholefield* (1889) 60 LT 595.
15   *Flight v Booth* (1834) 1 Bing NC 370; cf *Walker v Boyle* [1982] 1 WLR 495.
16   *Decro-Wall International SA v Practitioners in Marketing Ltd* [1971] 2 All ER 216.
17   *Maple Flock Co Ltd v Universal Furniture Products (Wembley) Ltd* [1934] 1 KB 148.
18   *Bettini v Gye* (1876) 1 QBD 183.
19   *Poussard v Spiers and Pond* (1876) 1 QBD 410 at 415.

The same test has been applied to determine whether failure to remedy the unseaworthiness of a chartered ship justifies rescission of the charterparty.[20]

No exhaustive list can be given of the factors which influence decisions in cases of this kind. In an American case,[1] rescission of a contract to supply milk to State schools and hospitals for a year was held to be justified on the ground that on three occasions in the first two weeks live maggots or dirt had been found in the milk. All that one can say about such a case is that the court found the breach so shocking as to conclude that the State could not reasonably be expected to take further supplies from this source.

iii Ulterior motives

A third test which the courts sometimes apply is this: was the injured party really rescinding because of the prejudice caused to him by the failure in performance, or was he using the failure as an excuse for getting out of a bad bargain? If the latter was his real motive the courts are reluctant to hold that the failure was sufficiently serious; for 'contracts are made to be performed and not to be avoided according to the whims of market fluctuation'.[2] In one case[3] a ship which had been chartered for twenty-four months was unseaworthy and needed extensive repairs. When these were completed, the charterparty had seventeen months to run. Meanwhile there had been a 'catastrophic fall' in freight rates.[4] There was no evidence that the unseaworthiness and consequent delays had caused the charterer any loss; on the contrary, they benefited him as he did not, under the terms of the contract, have to pay the (very high) rate of agreed hire while the ship was undergoing repairs. In these circumstances the court refused to allow the charterer to rescind. The decision may well have been influenced by the fact that, under a long-term charterparty, the commercial risk of a fall in freight rates is on the charterer; and this risk should not be thrown back on the shipowner in consequence of breaches which caused the charterer no (or no serious) loss. This flexible and realistic approach to the problem of rescission should be contrasted with that which is adopted in cases falling within the exceptions to the requirement of serious failure, to be discussed in the following paragraphs.

---

20   *Hong Kong Fir Shipping Co Ltd v Kawasaki Kisen Kaisha Ltd* [1962] 2 QB 26; *The Hermosa* [1982] 1 Lloyd's Rep 570.
1   *Hershey Farms v State* 110 NYS 2d 324 (1952).
2   *The Hansa Nord* [1976] QB 44 at 71.
3   *Hong Kong Fir Shipping Co Ltd v Kawasaki Kisen Kaisha Ltd* [1962] 2 QB 26.
4   [1962] 2 QB 26 at 39.

c Exceptions to the requirement of serious failure

It is often hard to predict whether a failure in performance will be regarded as sufficiently serious to justify rescission. To promote greater certainty, the law therefore allows rescission in a number of situations irrespective of the seriousness of the failure. These exceptions to the requirement of serious failure can, however, lead to injustice. For example, they may allow a party to rescind even though this will lead to his being unjustly enriched,[5] and even though his motive for rescinding is simply to get out of a bad bargain.[6] The risk of such injustice has in turn led to judicial and legislative restrictions on the scope of the exceptions.[7]

i *Express terms*

A contract may contain an express term giving one party the right to cancel in specified circumstances. Such terms are, for example, often found in charterparties, hire-purchase agreements, leases and contracts for the sale of land. The law starts with the principle that, in the interests of commercial certainty, such terms can be literally enforced, so that rescission will be allowed for even a quite trivial breach[8] eg for a purchaser's delay of just one minute in completing a contract for the sale of land.[9] But the resulting hardship to the party in breach is mitigated in four ways. First, the express term may be narrowly interpreted so as not to cover a purely trivial breach.[10] Secondly, the rescinding party must act exactly in accordance with the term giving him the right to cancel: he cannot, for example, cancel *before* the specified event has occurred, merely because its occurrence has become virtually certain.[11] Thirdly, the law sometimes grants the party in breach relief against the express term: for example, by allowing a defaulting tenant or hire-purchaser extra time in which to perform his obligations.[12] It is, however, a necessary (though not a sufficient[13]) condition of such 'relief against forfeiture' that rescission would, if it were allowed, deprive the party in breach of 'proprietary or possessory

---

5 See post, pp 325, 326, 340–341.
6 See post, p 328.
7 See post, pp 329–332, 341–342.
8 *The Laconia* [1977] AC 850; *The Chikuma* [1981] 1 All ER 652; *The Scaptrade* [1983] 2 AC 694.
9 *Union Eagle Ltd v Golden Achievement Ltd* [1997] AC 514.
10 See *Rice v Great Yarmouth BC* [2001] 3 LGLR 4.
11 *The Afovos* [1983] 1 WLR 195; cf *The Mihalis Angelos* [1971] 1 QB 164.
12 Eg Law of Property Act 1925, s 146; Consumer Credit Act 1974, s 88.
13 *Union Eagle Ltd v Golden Achievement Ltd* [1997] AC 514.

rights'[14] acquired by him under the contract: eg where it would deprive a tenant or hire-purchaser of the premises or goods which were the subject matter of the contract. It is not available merely because rescission would deprive the party in breach of *contractual* rights, such as a charterer's rights to services to be performed by the shipowner under a long-term charterparty.[15] A cancellation clause may finally be open to challenge under legislation restricting the validity of standard terms in consumer contracts,[16] and perhaps even at common law.[17]

ii   Entire and severable obligations

A party is sometimes entitled to refuse to perform if performance by the other has not been *fully* completed. He can do this if the obligation left partly unperformed is *entire*, but not if it is *severable*. The distinction is most easily illustrated by reference to contracts for the carriage of goods by sea. If the contract provides that the freight is to be paid at the agreed destination, the carrier cannot recover anything for carrying the goods part of the way: the obligation to get the goods to the destination is entire.[18] On the other hand if the contract provides that freight is to be paid at the rate of so much *per ton* the obligation is severable with regard to the quantity carried, so that the carrier can recover a proportionate part of the freight if he carries less than the agreed amount to the agreed destination.[19] And if the carrier carries the cargo to the agreed destination but it arrives damaged, he is entitled to full freight unless the damage is so serious as to make the goods quite useless to the cargo-owner.[20] Of course, in all these cases the carrier is liable in damages if his failure in performance amounts to a breach. A contract for the sale of goods imposes an entire obligation with regard to *quantity*. Hence the general rule is that if the seller delivers too little (or too much) the buyer is entitled to reject.[1] But this rule does not apply where the contract provides for a

---

14 *The Scaptrade* [1983] 2 AC 694 at 702.
15 See the authorities cited in n 8, supra; cf *Sport International Bussum BV v Inter-Footwear Ltd* [1984] 1 WLR 776; contrast *BICC Ltd v Burndy Corpn* [1985] Ch 232.
16 Unfair Terms in Consumer Contracts Regulations 1999, ante, pp 111, 114; but such clauses do not seem to be within s 3(2) of the Unfair Contract Terms Act 1977 (see ante, p 105).
17 *Timeload Ltd v British Telecommunications plc* [1995] EMLR 459 at 467.
18 *St Enoch Shipping Co Ltd v Phosphate Mining Co* [1916] 2 KB 624.
19 *Ritchie v Atkinson* (1808) 10 East 295.
20 *Dakin v Oxley* (1864) 15 CBNS 646 at 667.
1   Sale of Goods Act 1979, s 30(1).

margin;[2] where the discrepancy is only minimal;[3] or where the buyer does *not* deal as consumer and the discrepancy, though not minimal, is 'so slight that it would be unreasonable' for the buyer to reject,[4] but the parties can by contrary agreement exclude this limitation on the right to reject delivery of the wrong quantity.[5] Such a contract does not, however, impose an entire obligation with regard to *quality*: the right to reject for defects of quality depends on different distinctions to be discussed below.[6] A contract of employment which provides for payment at the end of a fixed period or periods imposes an entire obligation to serve for the stipulated period: thus if the contract provides for payment monthly in arrear and the employee leaves in breach of contract (or is justifiably dismissed) before the end of the month, he is not entitled to his agreed pay for that month; nor, at common law, to any part of it.[7] But if, in the course of the month, he has committed some minor breach of contract, eg by doing bad work, he may be entitled to his pay, less damages for the breach.[8] A similar distinction exists in the case of building contracts. In *Sumpter v Hedges*[9] a builder contracted with a landowner to build two houses on the latter's land for a lump sum of £560; but he was unable to complete the work as he ran out of money. It was held that the builder could not recover the agreed sum as the obligation to complete was entire; nor, for reasons to be discussed later, could he recover the reasonable value of his work. In practice the resulting hardship to the builder is mitigated by stipulations for progress payments; and in *Sumpter v Hedges* itself substantial payments on account had in fact been made to the builder. Moreover, if the houses had been completed late, or defectively, the landowner could not have refused to pay merely on account of these breaches: his right to rescind in such a case would have depended on the seriousness of the breach.[10]

---

2   1979 Act, s 30(5).

3   Eg *Shipton, Anderson & Co v Weil Bros & Co* [1912] 1 KB 574.

4   Sale of Goods Act 1979, s 30(2A).

5   Sale of Goods Act 1979, s 30(5).

6   See post, pp 327 et seq.

7   *Boston Deep Sea Fishing and Ice Co v Ansell* (1888) 39 Ch D 339; and cf ante, p 305. For possible rights under the Apportionment Act 1870, see post, p 341.

8   *Miles v Wakefield Metropolitan District Council* [1987] AC 539 at 570; for restrictions on the right to deduct damages from wages, see Employment Rights Act 1996, Pt II. For the position where the employee's breach amounts to a *repudiation*, see post, p 340.

9   [1898] 1 QB 673.

10   *Hoenig v Isaacs* [1952] 2 All ER 176.

iii   Conditions, warranties and intermediate terms

The availability of rescission may turn on the question whether the term which is not performed is a condition, a warranty or an intermediate term. A warranty (in modern legal usage) is a term which affects some relatively minor or subsidiary aspect of the subject-matter of the contract. Breach of it gives rise to a right to claim damages but not, in general, to a right to rescind the contract.[11] A condition, on the other hand, is a term which affects an important aspect of the subject-matter. Breach of it entitles the victim not only to claim damages but also, in general, to rescind the contract. An intermediate term is one which falls between the categories of conditions and warranties. Breach of such a term justifies rescission only where it leads, or amounts, to a serious failure in performance; where the breach does not have this effect, the injured party's only remedy is in damages.

'Condition' as used here must be distinguished from the sense in which the same word was used earlier in this chapter in discussing 'conditions precedent' and 'concurrent conditions'.[12] There 'condition' meant the *performance* of an obligation; here it means a *term* of a contract. There the effect of one party's failure to perform the 'condition' was that the other party's obligation simply did not arise; here the effect of a breach of condition is to give the injured party an option to rescind, and he must take steps to *exercise* that option in order to get rid of his obligation to perform.[13]

The distinction between conditions and warranties is in some cases based on the intention of the parties, as expressed in the contract. Thus a provision giving the buyer the right to reject goods if they did not possess a specified quality would be classified as a condition, as this would give effect to the intention of the parties.[14] But the mere use of the word 'condition' is not decisive, for the word may have been used in a non-technical sense to mean simply a term of the contract (as in the phrase 'our conditions of contract'). In one case[15] a four-year distributorship agreement made it a 'condition' that the distributor would visit six named customers once a week. It was held that the contract could not be rescinded merely because this term

---

11   In insurance law, 'warranty' is still used in a sense similar to that now generally given to 'condition': *The Good Luck* [1992] 1 AC 233, post, p 343.
12   Ante, pp 320–321; *State Trading Corpn of India Ltd v M Golodetz Ltd* [1989] 2 Lloyd's Rep 277 at 284.
13   *The Good Luck* [1992] 1 AC 233 at 262.
14   Eg *Bannerman v White* (1861) 10 CBNS 844; cf *Bergerco USA v Vegoil Ltd* [1984] 1 Lloyd's Rep 440.
15   *L Schuler AG v Wickman Machine Tool Sales Ltd* [1974] AC 235.

had been broken. The parties could not have intended rescission to be available if only one out of a possible 1,400 or so visits was not paid; indeed they had elsewhere in the contract laid down a procedure for 'determination' for 'material breach'.

Often, however, the words of the contract gave no clue as to the intention of the parties in this respect; and in such cases the distinction between conditions and warranties was originally based on the seriousness of the failure to perform. Where the term broken was so important that it was unreasonable to require the injured party to accept and pay, it was classified as a condition. Where it was less important, so that damages were an adequate remedy, it was classified as a warranty. Unfortunately, however, the distinction between conditions and warranties came to be overlaid with technicalities, so that to some extent its original purpose was obscured. This development took place because the courts came to classify terms as conditions or warranties by reference to authority, rather than by reference to their importance in individual contracts. Certain commonly found terms thus became conditions as a matter of law, and had to be so treated irrespective of the effects of failure to perform them in a particular case.[16] It was, for example, held to be a condition in a contract for the sale of goods that the goods must correspond with the contractual 'description'; and this rule has received statutory recognition in the Sale of Goods Act.[17] The buyer can therefore reject goods which do not answer the contractual description, even though their failure to do so does not prejudice him seriously, or at all.[18] Goods may, for example, be sold on the terms that they are to be shipped (or have been shipped) in a specified period, eg as a 'September shipment'. Such words are part of the description of the goods[19] so that the buyer can reject if the goods were shipped on 1 October even though this does not prejudice him in the least and even though his motive for rejecting is that the market has fallen. This type of reasoning, whereby any breach of a term justifies rescission, once that term has been classified as a condition, is particularly common in relation to contracts for the supply of goods, in which many terms are classified as conditions by statute.[19a] But it is by no means confined to such contracts. It is for example settled that in a charterparty a statement that the ship is at the time of the contract in a particular port, or one that she will sail on a named day, is a

16   *Bunge Corpn v Tradax Export SA* [1981] 1 WLR 711 at 724; cf ibid at 715–716, 718.
17   Originally enacted in 1893; see now Sale of Goods Act 1979, s 13.
18   Eg *Arcos Ltd v EA Ronaasen & Son* [1933] AC 470.
19   *Bowes v Shand* (1877) 2 App Cas 455.
19a   See post, p 331 at n 15.

condition.[20] Breach of such a term will therefore automatically and as a matter of law justify rescission.

Judicial or statutory classification of terms as warranties is less common. Of the many terms implied by the Sale of Goods Act into contracts for the sale of goods, only one is classified as a warranty: namely the implied term that the goods are free from charges in favour of third parties.[1] Damages (enabling the buyer to pay off the charge) will generally be an adequate remedy for breach of this term.

Where a term has been classified by law as a condition its breach gives rise at common law[2] to an automatic right to rescind even though there is no evidence that the parties so intended, even though the breach did not prejudice the injured party seriously or at all, and even though his motive in rescinding was simply to escape from a bad bargain. This position has been described as 'excessively technical';[3] and the courts have mitigated its rigours by sometimes placing terms not previously classified as conditions or warranties into the category of intermediate terms.[4] The point may be illustrated by reference to a charterparty under which the shipowner fails to provide a seaworthy ship. Such a failure amounts to a breach of an intermediate term, so that the charterer is not entitled to rescind merely because the ship is unseaworthy;[5] but he may be entitled to do so on one of the other grounds discussed in this chapter: eg if the unseaworthiness leads to a delay which causes him serious prejudice, or which brings a cancelling clause into play. Certain terms in contracts for the sale of goods have similarly been classified as intermediate. In one case,[6] citrus pulp pellets were sold under a contract which provided that they were to be 'shipped in good condition'. Some of the goods were not so shipped, and the buyer purported to reject the whole consignment. Later he re-acquired it through an intermediary for little more than a third of the original contract price and used it (as he had intended all along) to manufacture cattle food. The court was clearly unwilling to allow the buyer in this way to escape from a bad bargain. It held that the broken term was not a condition but an intermediate term and that the effect of the breach was not sufficiently serious to justify rescission. Such decisions raised the difficult problem of determining when previously unclassified terms will be classified as intermediate terms and when as conditions.

20   *Behn v Burness* (1863) 3 B & S 751; *Glaholm v Hays* (1841) 2 Man & G 257.
1   Sale of Goods Act 1979, s 12(2) and (5A).
2   For statutory exceptions, see post, pp 331–332.
3   *Reardon Smith Line Ltd v Hansen Tangen* [1976] 1 WLR 989 at 998.
4   As in *Federal Commerce and Navigation Ltd v Molena Alpha Inc* [1979] AC 757.
5   *Hong Kong Fir Shipping Co Ltd v Kawasaki Kisen Kaisha Ltd* [1962] 2 QB 26.
6   *The Hansa Nord* [1976] QB 44.

On the one hand, classification of terms as intermediate can be said to promote justice, by preventing a party from rescinding for ulterior motives where the breach has not caused him any serious loss. Accordingly, a number of cases support the view that previously unclassified terms should be classified as intermediate,[7] unless a contrary intention clearly appears from the terms of the contract.[8]

On the other hand, classification of terms as conditions can be said to promote certainty; for it will enable an injured party in a future case to know, as soon as the term has been broken, that he is entitled to rescind: he will not need to go into the difficult question whether the breach has serious effects. This point has often been stressed when the term in question is one which specifies a fixed time for performance in a commercial contract. Such a term is likely to be classified as a condition because punctual performance is often vital in dealings with commodities which fluctuate rapidly in value. In one case of this kind, goods were sold on the terms that they were to be delivered on board a ship to be provided by the buyers, who were to give at least 15 days' notice of the ship's readiness to load. The House of Lords held that the latter term was a condition, so that the sellers were entitled to rescind simply on the ground that the notice of readiness had reached them five days too late.[9] This classification promoted certainty by making it unnecessary for the sellers to show that the delay had caused them serious prejudice: they could safely rescind as soon as the buyers had failed to give the notice by the specified day. Obviously, this reasoning cannot apply where the term does not specify a *precise* time or interval but is itself vague. Accordingly, a term requiring notice of prohibition of export to be given 'without delay' has been held to be only an intermediate term.[10] Even a term which did specify a precise time for an act to be done has been held not to be a condition where it related to a matter of only trivial importance.[11] Such cases illustrate the continuing validity of the view that 'the courts should not be too ready to interpret contractual clauses as conditions'[12] and that they should 'lean in favour'[13] of classifying

---

7   Eg *Bremer Handelsgesellschaft mbH v Vanden Avenne-Izegem PVBA* [1978] 2 Lloyd's Rep 109 at 113 (so far as it relates to cl 22 of the contract); *Tradax International SA v Goldschmidt SA* [1977] 2 Lloyd's Rep 604.

8   Eg *Tradax Export SA v European Grain and Shipping Ltd* [1983] 2 Lloyd's Rep 100.

9   *Bunge Corpn v Tradax Export SA* [1981] 1 WLR 711; *Toepfer v Lenersan-Poortman NV* [1980] 1 Lloyd's Rep 143; *The Naxos* [1990] 1 WLR 1337.

10   *Bremer Handelsgesellschaft mbH v Vanden Avenne-Izegem PVBA* [1978] 2 Lloyd's Rep 109 (so far as it relates to cl 21 of the contract).

11   *State Trading Corpn of India Ltd v M Golodetz Ltd* [1989] 2 Lloyd's Rep 277.

12   *Bunge Corpn v Tradax Export SA* [1981] 1 WLR 711 at 715.

13   *Tradax International SA v Goldschmidt SA* [1977] 2 Lloyd's Rep 604 at 612.

terms as intermediate. The cases in which time clauses have been classified as conditions may qualify, but have not rejected, that view.

The conflict between certainty and justice is further illustrated by two statutory restrictions on the right of a buyer of goods to rescind for breach of condition. The first, introduced in 1994,[14] applies where the buyer does *not* deal as consumer and the seller is in breach of one of the conditions implied by the Sale of Goods Act 1979 as to the correspondence of the goods with their description or with a sample, or as to their quality.[15] If the seller can show that the breach is 'so slight that it would be unreasonable' for the buyer to reject the goods, then the breach is not to be treated as one of condition but as one of warranty so that the only remedy for it will be in damages.[16] The exception also applies to other contracts for the supply of goods (such as contracts of hire and hire-purchase)[17] but in all other significant respects its scope is limited. It does not affect the right to rescind for breach of condition in other contracts (such as voyage charterparties[18]), or for breach of condition by a *buyer*,[19] or for breach by the seller of an *express* condition or of statutorily implied conditions other than those listed above.[20] It is also excluded where 'a contrary intention appears in, or is to be implied from, the contract'.[1] Such an implication might be based on the nature of the contract so as to preserve the common law principle that, in a commodity contract, a buyer can reject for breach of a stipulation as to the time of shipment (which forms part of the description of the goods). In cases which do fall within the exception, the buyer will be deprived of his right to reject only if the breach is 'slight' *and* it would be 'unreasonable' for him to reject. These requirements do not turn the implied conditions to which the exception refers into intermediate terms; for a breach may be more than 'slight' without being sufficiently serious to justify rescission for breach of an intermediate term. But they do make it hard to predict just when the exception will apply and so give force to the criticism that the exception undermines the certainty which classification of a term as a condition is meant to provide. On the

---

14 By amendments to the Sale of Goods Act 1979 made by the Sale and Supply of Goods Act 1994.
15 Ie, the conditions implied under Sale of Goods Act 1979, ss 13, 14 and 15.
16 Sale of Goods Act 1979, s 15A.
17 Supply of Goods (Implied Terms) Act 1973, s 11A and Supply of Goods and Services Act 1982, s 5A.
18 See ante, p 329 at n 20.
19 As in *Bunge Corpn v Tradax Export SA* [1981] 1 WLR 711.
20 Eg under the Sale of Goods Act 1979, s 12(1) (such a breach might be 'slight' if it related only to part of the goods).
1 Sale of Goods Act 1979, s 15A(2).

other hand, the partial operation of the exception leaves it open to the objection that it scarcely goes far enough to satisfy the requirements of justice: for example, rescission by a *seller* can cause just as much injustice as rejection by a buyer. The exception seems therefore to have sacrificed certainty without attaining justice.

The second exception, introduced in 2002,[2] applies where the buyer does deal as consumer. Such a buyer now has certain 'additional rights',[3] including one to require the seller to repair or replace[4] 'non-conforming' goods, ie goods in respect of which the seller is in breach of the statutorily implied terms as to correspondence with description or sample or as to quality, or of an express term.[5] Where the buyer asks for repair or replacement he must not reject for breach of condition until the seller has had a reasonable time to comply with the request.[6] If by the end of that time the seller has not so complied, the buyer has a right to 'rescind' the contract.[7] This right is, in effect, subject to the discretion of the court, which may instead give effect to another of the buyer's 'additional rights', such as a price reduction.[8] But there is nothing to compel the buyer to resort to these rights. Hence if he chooses not to claim repair or replacement, his right simply to reject for breach of condition remains unimpaired.

There are, finally, three situations in which rescission may be available as a remedy for breach of warranty. First, a statement of fact which induced the making of the contract may later be incorporated in it as a warranty. Such incorporation does not affect the right to rescind *for misrepresentation*.[9] Secondly, a seller may deliver to a buyer who deals as consumer goods which are not in conformity with an express term of the contract. Under the legislation described in the preceding paragraph,[10] the buyer may then have a right to rescind the contract, even though the term is a warranty. In both these situations, however, the court has a discretion to disallow rescission and instead to award damages[11] or allow a price reduction;[12] and it

---

2   By amendments to the Sale of Goods Act 1979 made by the Sale and Supply of Goods to Consumers Regulations 2002, SI 2002/3045, which also amend legislation relating to contracts for the supply of goods otherwise than by way sale.
3   Heading to Pt 5A of the 1979 Act.
4   1979 Act, ss 48A(2)(a) and 48B; for limitations see s 48B(3) and (4).
5   1979 Act, s 48F.
6   1979 Act, s 48D(1), (2)(a).
7   1979 Act, s 48C(2); the right is also available where limitations on the right to repair or replace apply by virtue of s 48B(3).
8   1979 Act, s 48E(3) and (4).
9   Misrepresentation Act 1967, s 1(a); ante, p 164.
10 Supra, at nn 5, 7.
11 Misrepresentation Act 1967, s 2(2), ante, p 157.
12 Supra, at n 8.

will probably take this course where the breach does not cause the buyer serious prejudice.[12] Thirdly, there is the possibility that a breach of warranty may in fact cause very serious prejudice: eg if a breach of warranty in a contract to supply a wedding dress made the dress useless on the day of the wedding. There is some support for the view that rescission would then be available even though the term broken was only a warranty.[13] If this is right, a warranty differs from an intermediate term only in that it *generally* does not give rise to a right to rescind: not in that it can *never* do so.

iv Breach of fundamental term

In Chapter 7 we saw that a breach of a fundamental term justified rescission; and normally such a breach will amount to a serious failure in performance. But this is not invariably true, since the concept of fundamental term has, like that of condition, become technical. Sometimes, a term is fundamental merely because it has been so classified by authority; and any breach of it then justifies rescission. This is, for example, true where a carrier of goods by sea deviates:[14] it makes no difference that the deviation is 'for practical purposes irrelevant'.[15] Hence, paradoxically, the right to rescind for breach of a fundamental term sometimes constitutes an exception to the requirement of serious failure in performance.

v Manner of breach

A breach which is in itself trivial will not justify rescission *merely* because it was deliberate. A shipowner would not, for example, be entitled to rescind a charterparty merely because the charterer had deliberately delayed loading for a single day.[16] But where the breach is deliberate it may justify rescission (even though its effects are not such as to satisfy the normal requirement of serious failure in performance) on the ground that its deliberate nature was evidence of the guilty party's 'intention no longer to be bound by the contract'.[17] Thus the effects

---

13 *Astley Industrial Trust Ltd v Grimley* [1963] 1 WLR 584 at 599; *The Hansa Nord* [1976] QB 44 at 83.
14 See ante, p 89.
15 *Suisse Atlantique Société D'Armement Maritime SA v Rotterdamsche Kolen Centrale NV* [1967] 1 AC 361 at 423. Cf, in another context, *Pilbrow v Pearless de Rougemont & Co* [1999] 3 All ER 355 at 360.
16 *Suisse Atlantique* case [1967] 1 AC 361 at 435.
17 *Freeth v Burr* (1874) LR 9 CP 208 at 213 (sale); *Laws v London Chronicle Ltd* [1959] 2 All ER 285 (employment); *The Product Star* [1993] 1 Lloyd's Rep 397 at 407 (charterparty).

of unseaworthiness may not in themselves be so serious as to justify rescission of a time charterparty; but if the shipowner, before delivery of the ship, refused to remedy the unseaworthiness, the charterer would (so long as the defect was not trivial) be entitled to rescind on that ground.[18] However, the deliberate nature of the breach is not necessarily evidence of the guilty party's intention no longer to be bound by the contract. Thus in one case[19] a buyer of land refused to perform, believing in good faith and in reliance on legal advice that his refusal was justified. The advice turned out to be wrong; but it was held that the buyer had not repudiated since he had throughout declared that he would perform if his belief, that he was not bound to do so, should turn out to be mistaken.

It does not follow from the above cases that a deliberate breach will justify rescission *only* where it is evidence of the guilty party's intention no longer to be bound by the contract. Even if that party intended to keep the contract alive, the breach may be sufficiently serious to justify rescission.[20] There is then no need to invoke any *exception* to the requirement of serious failure in performance.

vi Unilateral contracts and options

So far we have been concerned with cases in which the failure of one party to perform a promise justifies the refusal of the other to perform his counterpromise. This analysis, however, does not fit the case of a unilateral contract in which only one party makes a promise. Where A promises to pay B £100 if B walks from London to York, B makes no promise and is not bound to do anything. But A can refuse to pay if B gives up the walk before he reaches York. B's completing the walk is here a condition of A's liability; and B must strictly comply with that condition. If he abandons the walk so much as one mile short of York, A can refuse to pay. This rule is particularly important in relation to options which also only bind one of the parties (though their exercise will generally lead to a contract binding both). It goes without saying that an option to purchase can be exercised only within the stipulated time; and the other conditions of its exercise must also be strictly performed.[1] In one case[2] a tenant was given an option to renew his

---

18 *Hong Kong Fir Shipping Co Ltd v Kawasaki Kisen Kaisha Ltd* [1962] 2 QB 26 at 56–64; cf (in the employment context) *Cantor Fitzgerald International v Callaghan* [1999] 2 All ER 411.
19 *Woodar Investment Development Ltd v Wimpey Construction (UK) Ltd* [1980] 1 All ER 571; cf *Mersey Steel and Iron Co v Naylor Benzon & Co* (1884) 9 App Cas 434.
20 *Federal Commerce and Navigation Ltd v Molena Alpha Inc* [1979] AC 757.
1 *Hare v Nicoll* [1966] 2 QB 130.
2 *West Country Cleaners (Falmouth) Ltd v Saly* [1966] 3 All ER 210.

lease provided that *all* the covenants of the lease had been duly performed. He purported to exercise the option but it was held that the landlord was not bound to renew as the tenant was in breach of some of the covenants of the original lease. The landlord would have been bound to renew only if the tenant had cured those breaches by the time he came to exercise the option.[3]

d Stipulations as to time

Stipulations as to the time of performance are divided by law into two kinds. Some such stipulations are treated as being 'of the essence of the contract'. Failure to perform a stipulation of this kind gives rise of itself to a right to rescind. Others are regarded as less important. Failure to perform these does not of itself give rise to a right to rescind, though it may do so under one of the headings already discussed: eg because the delay amounts to a serious failure in performance. The distinction may be illustrated by reference to contracts for the sale of goods, in which prima facie a stipulation as to the time of making delivery is of the essence of the contract;[4] but one as to the time of taking delivery,[5] or of payment, is not.[6] In other words, a buyer can rescind if delivery is not made within the agreed time but a seller cannot rescind merely because the buyer delays in taking delivery or in paying for the goods. These are only prima facie rules. They can be excluded by express provisions that time is (or is not) to be of the essence, and also by other circumstances. For example, a stipulation as to the time of payment is of the essence if the goods are perishable,[7] and one as to the time of taking delivery is of the essence where the contract requires the buyer to provide a ship on which the goods can be loaded within a specified time.[8]

At common law, time was of the essence of contracts for the sale of land. Hence if the buyer was not ready to pay, or the seller to convey, at the agreed time, then the other party could rescind. Equity did not follow this rigid rule. It generally regarded time as a matter of subsidiary importance in such contracts, and it therefore enforced them, even after the time fixed for performance,[9] so long as the delay

---

3   *Bass Holdings Ltd v Morton Music Ltd* [1987] 2 All ER 1001.
4   *Hartley v Hymans* [1920] 3 KB 475 at 484.
5   *Woolfe v Horne* (1877) 2 QBD 355.
6   Sale of Goods Act 1979, s 10(1).
7   *Ryan v Ridley & Co* (1902) 8 Com Cas 105.
8   *The Osterbek* [1973] 2 Lloyd's Rep 86; *Bunge Corpn v Tradax Export SA* [1981] 1 WLR 711.
9   *Parkin v Thorold* (1852) 16 Beav 59; *Graham v Pitkin* [1992] 2 All ER 235.

did not amount to a serious breach. By statute, the equitable rule now prevails,[10] so that rescission is no longer available to one party merely because the other has failed to perform at the agreed time. Thus a party who refuses to perform on account of the delay can be sued for specific performance or damages.[11] But the delay remains a breach, so that, if no attempt is made to rescind, and the contract is performed late, the victim of the delay will be entitled to damages.[12] A party can avoid the risk of being held to the contract in spite of the other's delay by expressly providing that time is to be 'of the essence' or that he is to be entitled to rescind in the event of the other's failure to perform within the agreed time.[13] Even if time is not originally of the essence, the injured party is not bound to wait indefinitely for performance. He can (as soon as the other party is in default)[14] give notice to that party calling for performance by the end of a specified period. A contract for the sale of land generally stipulates how much notice must be given for this purpose; failing that, the period of notice must be reasonable.[15] If *either* party then fails to perform by the end of that period, the other can rescind.[16]

Even in equity time is of the essence of a contract for the sale of land if delay in performance is in fact likely to have a serious effect. This is, for example, the position where the subject-matter of the contract is a short leasehold, since such a property tends to depreciate rapidly.[17] Similarly, time is of the essence in so-called 'commercial' contracts for the sale of land, such as a contract for the sale of business premises as a going concern, or one for the sale of land intended for rapid commercial development.[18] Now that land and houses fluctuate violently in value, the distinction between these 'commercial' and other contracts begins to look artificial.[19] But it seems that, in the case of a contract for the sale of ordinary domestic premises as a private residence, time would still not be of the essence unless the contract expressly so provided. Time may, finally, in a sense be of the essence where the contract is conditional and specifies a time by which the condition is to be satisfied: eg where the contract is subject to planning

---

10   Law of Property Act 1925, s 41 (re-enacting the Judicature Act 1873, s 25(1)); *United Scientific Holdings Ltd v Burnley Borough Council* [1978] AC 904 at 940.
11   *Stickney v Keeble* [1915] AC 386 at 404.
12   *Raineri v Miles* [1981] AC 1050.
13   *Union Eagle Ltd v Golden Achievement Ltd* [1997] AC 514.
14   *Behzadi v Shaftsbury Hotels Ltd* [1992] Ch 1.
15   *Stickney v Keeble* [1915] AC 386.
16   *Finkielkraut v Monohan* [1949] 2 All ER 234; *Quadrangle Development and Construction Co Ltd v Jenner* [1974] 1 All ER 729.
17   *Hudson v Temple* (1860) 29 Beav 536.
18   *Lock v Bell* [1931] 1 Ch 35; *Bernard v Williams* (1928) 44 TLR 437.
19   *Union Eagle Ltd v Golden Achievement Ltd* [1997] AC 514 at 519.

permission being obtained in six months. Here the stipulation as to time is not one as to the performance of the contract. It affects the more fundamental question whether a binding contract of sale is to come into existence at all; and this question must be resolved within the stipulated time.[20]

e Limits on rescission

The right to rescind a contract for failure in performance may be lost, or the exercise of the right may be limited, on one of the following grounds:

i Waiver

The injured party may know that a breach has occurred which gives him the right to rescind. But if he indicates that he will nevertheless perform the contract, or that he will accept late or defective performance, then he will be taken to have 'waived' his right to rescind for the breach in question, in the sense of having elected to affirm the contract.[1] This type of waiver differs from that discussed in Chapter 3, by which a party purports wholly to relinquish contractual rights.[2] That type of waiver gives rise to problems of consideration, since a party's promise to abandon rights under a contract does not at first sight benefit that party or subject the other to any detriment. The present type of waiver, by which the injured party merely elects not to rescind, does not raise any problems of consideration, since performance, coupled with damages for the breach, *may* be more beneficial than rescission. It follows that the element of reliance by the other party, which serves as a substitute for consideration in the type of waiver discussed in Chapter 3,[3] is not necessary for waiver in the sense of election not to rescind for breach.[4] All that is necessary for this kind of waiver is that the injured party should have known that he had the right to rescind[5] and that he should by some 'unequivocal act or statement'[6] have indicated that he would not exercise that right.

---

20   *Aberfoyle Plantations Ltd v Cheng* [1960] AC 115.
1   *Bentsen v Taylor Sons & Co (No 2)* [1893] 2 QB 274; *The Kanchenjunga* [1990] 1 Lloyd's Rep 391 at 397–398; Sale of Goods Act 1979, s 11(2).
2   *The Happy Day* [2002] EWCA Civ 1068, [2002] 2 Lloyd's Rep 487 at [64]; *Super Chem Products Ltd v American Life & General Insurance Co Ltd* [2004] UKPC 2, [2004] 2 All ER 56 at [21]; and see pp 47–49, ante; cf ante, pp 68–69.
3   Ante, p 48.
4   See *Peyman v Lanjani* [1985] Ch 457 at 493, 500–501; *The Kanchenjunga* [1990] 1 Lloyd's Rep 391 at 399; *Oliver Ashworth (Holdings) Ltd v Ballard (Kent) Ltd* [2000] Ch 12 at 27.
5   *Peyman v Lanjani* [1985] Ch 457.
6   *The Mihalios Xilas* [1979] 2 All ER 1044 at 1049.

ii   *Part performance of the contract*

Rescission often causes hardship to the party in breach, and this hardship tends to become more severe the further performance or purported performance of the contract has gone. Suppose that a seller has delivered goods at a distant place, or that a shipowner has sent his ship half-way round the world to begin performance of a charterparty, or that a builder has nearly completed a house which he had contracted to build. Such persons would clearly suffer hardship if at this stage the buyer or charterer or landowner could still rescind; and as a general guide it can be said that the courts become less ready to allow rescission, the further performance has gone. This does not mean that the right to rescind is lost merely because the contract has been partly performed, as a backward glance at *Sumpter v Hedges*[7] will show; but there can be no doubt about the general policy. A particularly clear illustration of it is to be found in the rule that a buyer of goods cannot reject them for breach of condition after he has 'accepted' them.[8] Acceptance is here a technical concept. A buyer is deemed to have accepted the goods in three situations: when he intimates to the seller that he accepts them; when they have been delivered to him and he does an act inconsistent with the ownership of the seller, such as reselling the goods and delivering them to a sub-buyer; and when he retains them for more than a reasonable time without intimating to the seller that he rejects them.[9] In the first two of these situations the buyer is not deemed to have accepted the goods until he has had an *opportunity* of examining them,[10] but in any of them he may have accepted without *actually* knowing of the breach. In this respect the requirements of acceptance differ strikingly from those of waiver.

A buyer may have the right to reject all the goods even though only some of them are not in conformity with the contract. If in such a case he accepts some of the goods, he does not thereby lose the right to reject the rest.[11]

'Acceptance' only bars the right to rescind *for breach of condition*. There are two cases in which a buyer who has 'accepted' may still be able to rescind.

First, the seller may have made a misrepresentation inducing the contract. In that case, the buyer may be able to rescind the contract

7   [1898] 1 QB 673; ante, p 326; cf also such cases as *Hershey Farms v State* 110 NYS 2d 324 (1952), p 323, ante; *Thorpe v Fasey* [1949] Ch 649 appears to take a contrary view but to be explicable on the ground that there was no sufficiently serious breach,.

8   Sale of Goods Act 1979, s 11(4).

9   Sale of Goods Act 1979, s 35(1) and (4).

10   Sale of Goods Act 1979, s 35(2).

11   Sale of Goods Act 1979, s 35(4).

even though the misrepresentation has become a term of the contract,[12] and the right to rescind *for misrepresentation* is probably not lost merely because the buyer has 'accepted' the goods. It may be lost on analogous grounds discussed in Chapter 9, such as affirmation and lapse of time.[13] But these could be more favourable to the buyer than the rules as to acceptance: in particular, affirmation presupposes knowledge of the truth. On the other hand, the right to rescind for misrepresentation is subject to the discretion of the court[14] while the right to rescind for breach can be exercised as of right.

Secondly, the seller may have committed a breach which is more serious than a breach of condition and it seems that the right to rescind for such a breach will not be barred merely by 'acceptance'. Suppose that peas are sold by sample, that the seller delivers peas in bags, and that the peas are not in accordance with the sample. If the buyer keeps the peas for more than a reasonable time without opening the bags he will be deemed to have 'accepted' them and so to have lost his right to rescind for breach of condition. But if the bags contain beans, the buyer will not lose his right to rescind by 'acceptance', for in this case the seller's breach goes beyond a mere breach of condition: it amounts to a total failure to perform.[15] The right to rescind for such a failure may, however, be lost if, after discovering the truth, the buyer indicates that he will keep the beans. In such a case he can be said to have 'waived' the right to rescind, or possibly to have made a new contract to buy beans.

iii Terms of the contract

Commercial suppliers of goods often try to protect themselves against rescission by clauses which provide that certain breaches by the supplier shall give rise only to a claim for damages and not to a right to reject or rescind. Similarly, contracts for the sale of land may provide that errors and misdescriptions shall not annul the sale but shall give rise to a claim for compensation only. Such non-rejection or non-cancellation clauses are prima facie effective. They are, however, regarded as exemption clauses; and accordingly they are subject to the common law rules[16] and to the legislation[17] (discussed in Chapter 7) which restrict the scope and limit the validity of such clauses.

12 Misrepresentation Act 1967, s 1(a).
13 See ante, p 167.
14 Misrepresentation Act 1967, s 2(2).
15 See *Chanter v Hopkins* (1838) 4 M & W 399 at 404; and ante, p 88.
16 Eg *J Aron & Co Inc v Comptoir Wegimont* [1921] 3 KB 435 (construction).
17 See pp 101 et seq, ante; *Walker v Boyle* [1982] 1 All ER 634.

iv   New contract

Where performance by one party (A) is incomplete or defective, the other (B) may be entitled to rescind *the contract*. But B may nevertheless be under some liability to A in respect of the performance actually rendered.

This is most obviously so where A's failure to complete performance is due to B's wrongful refusal to accept it. In one case[18] A agreed to write a serial for B's magazine; and, when A had done a substantial part of the work, B discontinued the publication. A was not entitled to the *agreed remuneration* but recovered a reasonable recompense for the work he had done.

A similar liability also arises where A fails to complete performance in accordance with the contract but B nevertheless voluntarily accepts A's partial or defective performance. The point may be illustrated by further reference to *Sumpter v Hedges*[19] where the builder was not entitled to the agreed price as the unperformed obligation to complete the two houses was an entire one. His claim for the reasonable value of his work also failed as the landowner had not accepted it *voluntarily*: the partly completed houses were on his land and so he really had no choice in the matter. On the other hand the landowner had also used building materials left lying loose on the site by the builder. As he had voluntarily accepted these materials he was held liable for their reasonable value. A similar distinction exists where a carrier by sea fails to carry goods to the agreed destination and delivers them at an intermediate port. A new contract may be inferred if the carrier so delivers the goods at the request of their owner,[20] but no such inference will be drawn merely because the owner of the goods takes possession of them at an intermediate port where they have been unloaded without his consent.[1] A similar problem arises where an employee in the course of an industrial dispute refuses to perform his duties under the contract. He is not entitled to his pay in respect of periods in which he does no work at all;[2] and the same is true if he continues to work but refuses to carry out specified tasks and the employer declines to accept such partial performance of the contract.[3] The employer may, alternatively, 'accept' such work (falling short of what is due) because he has no practical

18   *Planché v Colburn* (1831) 8 Bing 14.
19   [1898] 1 QB 673; see ante, p 326.
20   *Christy v Row* (1808) 1 Taunt 300.
1   Cf *Hopper v Burness* (1876) 1 CPD 137.
2   *Miles v Wakefield Metropolitan District Council* [1987] AC 539; *British Telecommunications plc v Ticehurst* [1992] ICR 383.
3   *Wiluszynski v Tower Hamlets London Borough Council* [1989] ICR 493.

choice in the matter; and there is a difference of judicial opinion on the question whether the employee is then entitled to a reasonable sum in respect of the work that he has actually done.[4] This difference of opinion reflects a conflict of policies. On the other hand, the purpose of the rule that the acceptance must be voluntary is to protect the injured party against having to pay for a performance different from that for which he bargained. This may be particularly necessary where damages would not adequately compensate him for the loss which he has suffered. On the other hand the rule may lead to unjust enrichment where the value of the performance received by the victim exceeds the loss caused by the breach. Under the rule in *Sumpter v Hedges* the landowner could get a nearly completed building for nothing. There appears to be an element of penalty in this rule; and it would be better if the party in breach could recover the value to the victim of the performance actually rendered and retained, less any loss suffered by the victim in consequence of the failure to complete performance.[5]

v Both parties in breach

Each party to a contract may simultaneously commit a breach (such as a breach of condition) which justifies rescission. Normally *each* party is then entitled to rescind;[6] but a different rule was said to apply in a group of arbitration cases, where A's breach consisted in undue delay in prosecuting his claim and B's breach in failure to avoid the consequences of that delay by taking steps to expedite the proceedings. In such cases it was said that *neither* party could rescind;[7] but now that arbitrators have a statutory power to dismiss arbitration claims for want of prosecution[8] the reasoning of these cases has become largely obsolete. It should no longer be followed, for no good purpose is served by holding parties to a contract after each of them has committed a repudiatory breach of it.

vi Apportionment Act 1870

This Act provides that certain 'periodical payments in the nature of income' shall, unless the contract otherwise provides, 'be considered

---

4   *Miles v Wakefield Metropolitan District Council* [1987] AC 539 at 552, 553, 561.
5   See Law Commission Paper 121; not to be implemented: Law Commission, 19th Annual report, para 2.11.
6   *State Trading Corpn of India Ltd v M Golodetz Ltd* [1989] 2 Lloyd's Rep 277 at 286.
7   *Bremer Vulkan Schiffbau und Maschinenfabrik v South India Shipping Corpn Ltd* [1981] AC 909 at 987.
8   Arbitration Act 1996, s 41(3).

as accruing from day to day and shall be apportionable in respect of time accordingly'.[9] The Act applies to such payments as rents, annuities, dividends, salaries and pensions.[10] If, for example, a person who was entitled to a monthly salary died in the third week of the month, he would be entitled to a proportionate part of his month's pay. The terms of the Act are wide enough to lead to the same result even where the employee leaves in breach of contract or is lawfully dismissed during the month; but judicial opinion is divided on the question whether a party in breach can take advantage of the provisions of the Act.[11]

f   The option to rescind

At this stage we shall assume that there has been a failure in performance which justifies rescission. Four further points now require discussion.

i   No automatic termination

A breach of contract gives the injured party an option to rescind. It does not automatically discharge the contract[12] (even if this says that it is to become 'void' on breach[13]); for if it had this effect a party could rely on his own breach of the contract to deprive the other of rights under it. The general rule, therefore, is that discharge occurs only at the election of the injured party. That party's freedom of choice is, however, to some extent curtailed by law. Suppose, for example, that an employee is wrongfully dismissed in breach of contract. The dismissal may determine the employment *relationship*,[14] but it does not automatically terminate the *contract*,[15] though the damages which

9   Sections 2, 7.
10   Section 5.
11   *Clapham v Draper* (1885) Cab & El 484; *Moriarty v Regent's Garage Co* [1921] 1 KB 423; on appeal [1921] 2 KB 766.
12   *Heyman v Darwins Ltd* [1942] AC 356 at 361; *Photo Production Ltd v Securicor Transport Ltd* [1980] AC 827; *Rigby v Ferodo Ltd* [1987] ICR 457; *The Simona* [1989] AC 788 at 800. Contrast the position in cases of frustration: post, p 350, 364.
13   See *Davenport v R* (1877) 3 App Cas 115; *New Zealand Shipping Co Ltd v Société des Ateliers et Chantiers de France* [1919] AC 1. Contrast *Cheall v Association of Professional Executive Clerical and Computer Staff* [1983] 1 All ER 1130 (breach of agreement with third party); *Thompson v ASDA-MFI Group plc* [1988] 2 All ER 722 (no breach).
14   See *Delaney v Staples* [1992] 1 AC 687 at 692; *Wilson v St Helens Borough Council* [1998] ICR 1141 at 1152.
15   *Gunton v Richmond-upon-Thames London Borough Council* [1981] Ch 448; *Dietman v Brent London Borough Council* [1987] ICR 737; for the converse situation (repudiatory breach by employee) cf *Evening Standard Co Ltd v Henderson* [1987] ICR 588; *Miles v Wakefield Metropolitan District Council* [1987] AC 539.

the employee can recover will be reduced to the extent that he failed to mitigate his loss. If he mitigates by taking another job, he will have put it out of his power to perform the original contract and so be taken to have exercised his option to rescind that contract.[16] The mitigation rules do not compel the injured party to exercise that option, but they provide him with a strong incentive to do so.[17] They may, conversely, provide him with an incentive to accept a performance which he was entitled to reject: for example where a seller on a rising market offers delivery after the agreed time, and it would be reasonable for the buyer to accept such delivery. Although the buyer is not *bound* to accept the late delivery, his unreasonable refusal to do so will be taken into account in reducing his damages.[18]

There is one well-established exception to the rule that breach does not result in automatic discharge. In the law of insurance, certain undertakings by the insured (eg that he will not take a ship into a war zone) are known as 'warranties'. This word here bears a meaning similar to that of 'condition' in the sense discussed earlier in this chapter; and the effect of breach of such a term is to discharge the insurer from liability, without the need for any election on his part.[19]

ii Effects of rescission

The effects of rescission are best considered by looking in turn at the position of the injured party and at that of the party failing to perform.

The injured party is released from future obligations under the contract: for example, a buyer who exercises his right to rescind an instalment contract need not accept and pay for future deliveries. But he is not released from obligations already accrued at the time of rescission:[20] he must, for example, pay for instalments already delivered before that time, except to the extent that they are themselves defective and are lawfully rejected. If they are so rejected, the buyer is entitled to get back the money paid for them: to this extent rescission operates retrospectively.

The party who has failed to perform is also released from future (but not from accrued) obligations *to perform*. If, for example, a party to whom instalment payments are due under a contract lawfully rescinds for the other party's breach, the latter cannot be sued for instalments

16 As in *Dietman's case* [1987] ICR 737.
17 *Gunton's case* [1981] Ch 448 at 468.
18 *The Solholt* [1983] 1 Lloyd's Rep 605 cf post, p 394.
19 Marine Insurance Act 1906, s 33(3); *The Good Luck* [1992] 1 AC 233.
20 *The Dominique* [1989] AC 1056.

which would have become due *after* the date of rescission.[1] But he is
not released from his liability to pay instalments which had become
due *before* that date.[2] Nor is he released from liability in *damages* if his
failure to perform amounted to a repudiatory breach, giving the other
party the right to rescind. Thus if a hire-purchase agreement is
wrongfully repudiated by the hirer, the owner can rescind and recover
not only any payments due at the time of rescission, but also damages
for wrongful repudiation.[3] These can include compensation for loss
suffered after rescission: eg because the owner can only let the subject-
matter out to another customer for less money than he was entitled to
receive under the original contract with the defaulting party.[4] Damages
can similarly be recovered where a contract for the sale of goods or of
land is rescinded by one party on account of the other's breach.[5]
There is no inconsistency between rescinding for breach and claiming
damages: in this respect rescission for breach differs from rescission
for misrepresentation.[6] The reason for the difference seems to be
that misrepresentation affects the formation of the contract, so that a
party who rescinds on this ground in effect says that there was never a
properly formed contract. A party who rescinds for breach makes no
similar allegation: his complaint is simply that the contract has not
been properly performed.

The above rules governing the effects of breach can be excluded
by express contrary agreement or by other evidence of contrary
intention.[7] In particular, the rule that rescission discharges future
obligations does not apply to certain 'ancillary' obligations such as
those relating, not to the performance due under the contract, but to

1   Cf *Financings Ltd v Baldock* [1963] 2 QB 104 at 110 (hire-purchase); *UCB
     Leasing Ltd v Holtom* [1987] RTR 362.
2   *Hyundai Shipbuilding and Heavy Industries Co Ltd v Pournaras* [1978] 2 Lloyd's
     Rep 502; *Hyundai Heavy Industries Ltd v Papadopoulos* [1980] 2 All ER 29;
     Moschi v Lep Air Services Ltd [1973] AC 331 at 354–355; for an exception see
     post, p 405.
3   There is no such liability where the injured party rescinds under an express
     term for a breach not amounting to a repudiation: *Financings Ltd v Baldock*
     [1963] 2 QB 104; the contrary decision reluctantly reached in *Lombard
     North Central plc v Butterworth* [1987] QB 527 can perhaps be explained on
     the ground that the term broken was a condition.
4   *Yeoman Credit Ltd v Waragowski* [1961] 3 All ER 145; *Photo Production Ltd v
     Securicor Transport Ltd* [1980] AC 827 at 849.
5   *Millar's Machinery Co Ltd v David Way & Son* (1935) 40 Com Cas 204;
     Buckland v Farmer and Moody [1978] 3 All ER 929; *Johnson v Agnew* [1980] AC
     367; *Berger & Co Inc v Gill & Duffus SA* [1984] AC 382; *The Blankenstein*
     [1985] 1 All ER 475.
6   See ante, p 163.
7   *Yasuda Fire and Marine Insurance Co of Europe Ltd v Orion Marine Insurance
     Underwriting Agency Ltd* [1995] 1 Lloyd's Rep 525.

the machinery for resolving disputes under it. Arbitration clauses thus survive rescission.[8]

iii Effects of affirmation

If the injured party affirms (or simply fails to rescind) the obligations of both parties remain in force.[9] For example, an employee may commit a breach justifying his dismissal; but if he is not dismissed and the employer accepts his continued performance of duties under the contract, then the employer will be liable to pay such part of the employee's salary or wages as has become due, less any damages caused by the breach.[10]

A distinction must, however, be drawn between the continued existence of contractual *obligations* and the *remedies* for their enforcement. A party who elects to keep the contract alive may in fact be prevented (by the other's wrongful repudiation) from performing his own obligations: for example a wrongfully dismissed employee may be prevented from doing the work that he was engaged to do. In such a case, his only remedy will be by way of damages: he will not be entitled to the agreed wages.[11] Even where the wrongful repudiation does *not* prevent the injured party from performing, affirmation of the contract will not necessarily enable him to secure remedies for the *specific* enforcement of the other's obligation. The circumstances in which such remedies are available will be discussed in Chapter 18.[12]

iv Change of course

An injured party who first rescinds cannot then affirm and claim performance. This follows from the rule that rescission releases the other party from his obligation to perform. The result may also be justified on the ground that that party may have acted in reliance on the belief that, after rescission, he would no longer be called on to perform. If, on the other hand, the injured party first affirms, the guilty party is clearly not released; nor will the injured party's efforts to secure performance of themselves amount to an 'unequivocal act or statement' that he will in no circumstances rescind, so as to give

8 *Heyman v Darwins Ltd* [1942] AC 356; cf Arbitration Act 1996, s 7.
9 *Segap Garages Ltd v Gulf Oil (Great Britain) Ltd* (1988) Times, 24 October; *The Simona* [1989] AC 788.
10 See *Sim v Rotherham Metropolitan Borough Council* [1987] Ch 216; and cf *Miles v Wakefield Metropolitan District Council* [1987] AC 539 on the question how much has become due (ante, p 341).
11 See post, p 407.
12 See post, pp 406–416.

rise to a waiver.[13] Hence if those efforts prove fruitless the injured party can still rescind.[14] This is so even if he has actually gone to court and obtained an order of specific performance, with which the guilty party has failed to comply. It is then open to him to apply to the court to dissolve the order, to put an end to the contract, and to claim damages for its breach.[15]

4   ANTICIPATORY BREACH

One of the parties to a contract may, before performance is due, *renounce* the contract by indicating that he will refuse to perform it, or *disable himself* from performing it by some act or omission making such performance impossible. He is then said to commit an 'anticipatory' (as opposed to an actual) breach. The other party can either 'accept' the breach or keep the contract alive by continuing to press for performance.[16]

a   Accepting the breach

The injured party can 'accept' the breach by bringing an action on the contract, by other conduct known to the other party,[17] or by giving notice to that party. The legal effects of accepting the breach are as follows.

i   Rescission

Acceptance of an anticipatory breach amounts to a rescission of the contract. For the purpose of this rule it is assumed that the breach is one that would, if it were actual, justify rescission: ie that it would be of the degree of seriousness discussed earlier in this chapter,[18] or that it would fall within an exception to that requirement, eg because it would amount to a breach of condition.[19] However, where the right to rescind arises *only* under an express provision for cancellation,[20] it cannot be exercised on account of a merely anticipatory breach. Suppose that a charterparty gives a charterer the right to cancel if the

---

13   See ante, p 337.
14   See *Stocznia Gdanska SA v Latvian Shipping Co (No 3)* [2002] EWCA Civ 889, [2002] 2 All ER (Comm) 768 at [100].
15   *Johnson v Agnew* [1980] AC 367 at 394.
16   *Michael v Hart & Co* [1902] 1 KB 482.
17   *The Santa Clara* [1993] 2 Lloyd's Rep 301.
18   See ante, pp 321–323.
19   See ante, p 327; that a breach of condition suffices for this purpose is assumed in *Universal Cargo Carriers Corpn v Citati* [1957] 2 QB 401.
20   See ante, p 324.

ship is not at the port of loading by 1 June. He is not entitled to cancel on 25 May even though on that day the ship is so far from the port of loading that she cannot possibly reach it in less than ten days.[1]

In cases of anticipatory breach, the injured party may rescind before the time fixed for performance; and at the time of rescission the effects of the breach may still lie in the future. The question then arises whether it is enough for the injured party to show that, at the time of rescission, he *reasonably believed* that the breach would, by the time fixed for performance, have become such as to give rise to a right to rescind, or whether this must at the time of rescission have been *already certain*. This depends on the type of anticipatory breach in question. In the case of an alleged *renunciation*, a refusal to perform will be inferred from conduct where the party in breach has 'acted in such a way as to lead a reasonable man to conclude that [he] did not intend to fulfil [his] part of the contract'.[2] Whether a reasonable man would draw this conclusion is to be judged by reference to the time of rescission.[3] But the position is different where the ground on which one party rescinds is that the other has *disabled* himself from performing (without having refused to perform). The injured party may at the time of rescission reasonably believe that the other party will be unable to perform in accordance with the contract, and that the resulting actual breach will be sufficiently serious to justify rescission. Nevertheless if it turns out that the other party can perform or that his breach is not of the required degree of seriousness, rescission will not be justified.[4] This rule is likely to be inconvenient in practice since normally the injured party, when faced with an anticipatory breach, will want to know at once whether he remains bound by the contract, or whether he is free to make alternative arrangements. The rule does not apply where there has been an *actual* breach and the only doubt relates to the prospective effects of that breach. In such a case, the injured party is entitled to rescind if, when he did so, he reasonably believed that the effects of the breach would be of the required degree of seriousness.[5]

Where the injured party justifiably rescinds, both parties are released from their duty to perform future obligations, but the guilty

---

1   *The Mihalis Angelos* [1971] 1 QB 164; a dictum in *The Afovos* [1983] 1 All ER 449 at 455, limiting the doctrine of anticipatory breach to 'fundamental' breaches occurs in the context of such express provisions and should be restricted to this situation.
2   *The Hermosa* [1982] 1 Lloyd's Rep 570 at 580.
3   [1982] 1 Lloyd's Rep 570 at 573; *The Sanko Iris* [1987] 1 Lloyd's Rep 487.
4   *Universal Cargo Carriers Corpn v Citati* [1957] 2 QB 401 at 449–450.
5   *Hong Kong Fir Shipping Co Ltd v Kawasaki Kisen Kaisha Ltd* [1962] 2 QB 26 at 57.

party is liable in damages. To make good his claim for damages, the injured party need not perform, or even show that he could have performed, his own future obligations;[6] for after rescission his failure or inability to perform them can no longer amount to a breach. *Other* future events may, however, affect the damages to which he is entitled, and even reduce them to a nominal amount: this possibility is explained in Chapter 18.[7]

ii Damages

The most striking feature of the doctrine of anticipatory breach is that a victim who 'accepts' the breach can sue for damages *at once*.[8] He does not have to wait until the time fixed for performance arrives. Suppose that A on 1 January agrees to employ B with effect from 1 October and that on 1 February A repudiates the contract. B can immediately claim damages, and, if the case comes to trial quickly, he may even get his damages before 1 October. This result is open to the objection that A's obligation is accelerated: he may have to pay damages before he was due to perform. But the doctrine of anticipatory breach is nevertheless generally regarded as a convenient one. Its merit is that it tends to reduce loss by making it possible for the parties to have their dispute determined with a minimum of delay.

Once the victim has accepted the breach, his right to damages is not defeated by actual or possible supervening events. In the case put, A could not avoid liability by at this stage indicating that he was, after all, ready to employ B;[9] or by arguing that he or B might die before 1 October, and that the contract would then be frustrated.[10] Subsequent events may affect the amount recoverable,[11] but not the right to damages itself.

b   Keeping the contract alive

The victim of an anticipatory breach may elect to keep the contract alive, in the hope of securing its actual performance: this is likely to be more beneficial in practice than even a successful lawsuit. By taking this course, the victim also keeps open the possibility of being able to claim specific performance or the agreed sum.[12] His damages may

6   *British and Beningtons Ltd v North Western Cachar Tea Co Ltd* [1923] AC 48.
7   Post, p 389.
8   *Hochster v De la Tour* (1853) 2 E & B 678.
9   Cf *Danube etc Rly v Xenos* (1863) 13 CBNS 825.
10   Cf *Synge v Synge* [1894] 1 QB 466.
11   Cf supra at n 7.
12   See post, pp 406–414.

also be assessed on a basis more favourable to him than damages for an accepted anticipatory breach.[13] On the other hand he will not receive anything until (at the earliest) the time fixed for performance; and he runs the risk of losing his rights under the contract as a result of events occurring after the anticipatory breach: for example, on account of some supervening event which frustrates the contract,[14] or which entitles the other party to cancel the contract under one of its express terms.[15]

If the refusal to perform persists after the demand for performance, the injured party may then wish to rescind. He can certainly do so if the breach has become actual;[16] and he can probably do so if the breach is still anticipatory, so long as the change of course does not cause undue prejudice to the party in breach.[17] Such prejudice might, for example, be caused if, in response to the demand, that party had continued to make efforts to perform within the time allowed by the contract.

---

13 See post, pp 388–389.

14 *Avery v Bowden* (1855) 5 E & B 714; (1856) 6 E & B 953.

15 *The Simona* [1989] AC 788.

16 Cf ante, pp 345–346.

17 For conflicting views on this point, see *Stocznia Gdanska SA v Latvian Shipping Co* [1997] 2 Lloyd's Rep 228 at 235 (set aside [1998] 1 WLR 574 at 594) and *Stocznia Gdanska SA v Latvian Shipping Co (No 3)* [2002] EWCA Civ 889, [2002] 2 All ER (Comm) 768 at [97]–[100].

Chapter 17

Frustration

We saw in Chapter 16 that a contracting party may be in breach even though his failure to perform is not due to any want of care or diligence on his part. For example, a seller who undertakes to ship goods from a named port within a stated time may be liable in damages if he fails to do so, even though his failure is simply due to the fact that no ship which could carry the goods left that port within the time.[1] On the other hand, the seller would not be liable if, before the relevant time, the port were destroyed by an earthquake. In that case the contract is said to have been frustrated by supervening impossibility. The distinction between the two cases is an obvious, almost intuitive, one, which it is not altogether easy to put into words. In our first case the seller undertakes that there will be a ship, perhaps realising that there is an element of risk about such an undertaking. But in the second he does not undertake that there will be a port: this is simply assumed by both parties. When a fundamental assumption of this kind is falsified by subsequent events the doctrine of frustration comes into play.

The effect of the doctrine is to discharge the contract by operation of law. It follows that *both* parties are discharged, even though only one party's obligation has become impossible to perform. In our last example, both seller and buyer are discharged, even though it remains possible for the buyer to pay the price. The law regards the contract as a kind of common venture, having as its object the *exchange* of the goods for the price; and if fulfilment of that 'common object' becomes impossible, then both parties are at once discharged from all their obligations under the contract. This automatic and total discharge of the contract is a somewhat drastic solution of a difficult problem. It can occasionally lead to hardship and inconvenience almost as great as the opposite view (formerly held, but now abandoned, by the law) that a contract is not discharged by supervening impossibility of performance. Accordingly, the doctrine of frustration has been kept within narrow limits by two trends, one judicial and the other commercial. The judges have insisted that the doctrine applies only

---

1   See ante, p 314.

where the assumption which has been falsified was a *fundamental* one; and they have also limited the scope of the doctrine in a number of other ways. Businessmen have, for their part, taken steps to 'draft out' frustration. In other words they have, where possible, said in the contract what was to happen if supervening events interfered with performance. Where they have done so, these provisions will generally apply and will exclude the doctrine of frustration.

1   OPERATION OF THE DOCTRINE

A contract may be frustrated if it becomes impossible to perform; or if its purpose is frustrated; or if performance becomes illegal.

a   Impossibility

Supervening events may make performance impossible in the following situations:

i   *Destruction of the subject-matter*

The most obvious cause of impossibility is the destruction of the subject-matter of the contract. In *Taylor v Caldwell*[2] the Surrey Gardens and Music Hall were hired out by the defendants 'for the purpose of giving four grand concerts' on four named days in June, July and August 1861. Before the first of those days the Music Hall was accidentally burnt down. The hirers claimed damages in respect of their wasted advertising expenses, but the claim failed as the destruction of the Music Hall had frustrated the contract. The case shows that the destruction need not be total for the Surrey Gardens (with their many attractions) appear to have survived undamaged. In other words, 'destruction' in the present context does not mean complete physical destruction, but destruction of the commercial characteristics of the subject-matter.

Even the destruction of the subject-matter will not always frustrate a contract; for it may be governed by rules of law which place the 'risk of loss' under certain types of contract on one party or the other. The point may be illustrated by supposing that A has agreed to install machinery in B's factory. If, before the work is completed, the *factory* is destroyed the contract is frustrated.[3] But if only the *machinery* is

---

2   (1863) 3 B & S 826.
3   *Appleby v Myers* (1867) LR 2 CP 651.

destroyed, A must do the work again at no extra cost;[4] for under a building contract the risk of such loss is (unless otherwise agreed) on the builder until completion.

ii   Death or incapacity

A contract is frustrated by the death of a party who had undertaken a 'personal' obligation. A contract of employment, for example, can be frustrated by the death of either party; and the same would be true if either party were permanently incapacitated from performance.

iii   Unavailability

A contract may also be frustrated where the subject-matter, though not destroyed, ceases to be available for the purpose of performing the contract. A contract for the sale of goods may thus be frustrated if the goods are requisitioned,[5] and a charterparty may be frustrated if the ship is requisitioned or detained, or if cargo is unavailable by reason of a strike. In such cases, further problems can arise if the unavailability is only temporary. Frustration will most obviously result where time is of the essence so that the contract can be performed *only* on the specified day or days over which the temporary impossibility extends: for example a contract to give a musical performance on a particular day may be frustrated by the performer's illness on that day.[6] Even where time is not of the essence, the contract may be frustrated where performance after the end of the delay would 'become as a matter of business a different thing'[7] from that originally undertaken. This might be so either because performance at a later time would be useless *to* the party to whom it was to be rendered, or because it would be severely more burdensome for the party *by* whom it was to be rendered. The first possibility is illustrated by supposing that a ship had been chartered to carry spring vegetables and was then requisitioned, and not released till the autumn.[8] The second possibility is illustrated by a case in which delivery under a contract for the sale of goods was interrupted for three years by lack of shipping space during the First World War. It was held that the contract was discharged because, when it became possible to resume delivery, conditions in the business had fundamentally changed.[9] In other

---

4   (1867) LR 2 CP 651 at 660.
5   *Re Shipton Anderson & Co* [1915] 3 KB 676.
6   *Robinson v Davison* (1871) LR 6 Exch 269.
7   *Bank Line Ltd v Arthur Capel & Co* [1919] AC 435 at 460.
8   Cf *Jackson v Union Marine Insurance Co Ltd* (1874) LR 10 CP 125 at 140.
9   *Acetylene Corpn of Great Britain v Canada Carbide Co* (1921) 6 Ll L Rep 468.

cases, the question is not whether the *whole* of the originally promised performance should be rendered later, but whether any *balance* remaining possible should be rendered after the end of the delay, but still during the original contract period. The contract will obviously be frustrated if *no* performance then remains (or is likely to remain) possible: this is why charterparties were held to have been frustrated when ships were detained for long periods during the Gulf War between Iran and Iraq.[10] Where *some* performance remains possible, the result will depend on the proportion which the interruption bears (or is likely to bear) to the whole of the promised performance. For example during the First World War the requisition of a ship which was under a five-year charter did not frustrate the charterparty since it seemed likely, when the ship was requisitioned, that she would be released in time to render substantial services under the contract.[11] The same principle determines whether illness of an employee frustrates his contract of employment. It can have this effect if the illness is so serious as to make it unlikely that performance can be resumed.[12] A less serious illness may give the employee an excuse for non-performance[13] and may entitle the employer to terminate;[14] but it will not discharge both parties automatically under the doctrine of frustration.

iv Failure of a particular source

A contract may be frustrated if its subject-matter is to be taken from a source which fails. Thus where a farmer contracted to sell potatoes out of a crop to be grown on his land, it was held that the contract was frustrated when the crop was attacked by disease and failed.[15] But a contract is not frustrated merely because a source contemplated by only *one* of the parties (but not by the other) has failed. In one case a seller of timber expected to get supplies from abroad but the buyer did not know this. It was held that the contract was not frustrated when the seller was cut off by war from his foreign source of supply.[16] Where *both* parties contemplate the source that fails, the contract may

---

10   Eg *The Evia (No 2)* [1983] 1 AC 736; *The Wenjiang (No 2)* [1983] 1 Lloyd's Rep 400.

11   *FA Tamplin Steamship Co v Anglo-Mexican Petroleum Products Co* [1916] 2 AC 397.

12   See *Condor v The Barron Knights Ltd* [1966] 1 WLR 87; *Marshall v Harland and Wolff Ltd* [1972] 2 All ER 715; *Hart v A R Marshall & Sons (Bulwell) Ltd* [1978] 2 All ER 413; *Notcutt v Universal Equipment Co (London) Ltd* [1986] 3 All ER 582.

13   See ante, p 316.

14   *Poussard v Spiers and Pond* (1876) 1 QBD 410; ante, p 322.

15   *Howell v Coupland* (1876) 1 QBD 258.

16   *Blackburn Bobbin Co Ltd v TW Allen & Sons Ltd* [1918] 2 KB 467.

be frustrated even though the contract does not actually refer to that source; but there would be no frustration if it would have been commercially reasonable to provide against such failure: eg by contracting 'subject to availability' or 'subject to shipment'.

v   Method of performance impossible

Where a contract provides that it is to be performed in a particular way, impossibility in the method of performance may frustrate it. This was for example held to be the position where goods were to be carried in a named ship in January, and the ship was stranded and so unable to carry the goods in that month.[17] Here the stipulation as to the method of performance was considered to mean that the contract was to be performed *only* in the specified manner. Where this is not the case, the contract will not be frustrated *merely* because performance by the agreed method becomes impossible. For example a contract of carriage would not be frustrated merely because part of the agreed route was blocked, so long as there was still some other (and commercially reasonable) way of reaching the agreed destination. The contract would be frustrated only if performance by the available method differed *fundamentally* from that originally agreed or from that which both parties expected to be used. The judicial approach to questions of this kind is illustrated by a group of cases which arose out of the closing of the Suez Canal in 1956 and again in 1967. In one of these cases goods were sold at inclusive prices covering the cost of the goods and their carriage from Red Sea ports to European ports. The sellers had, no doubt, fixed the price on the assumption that they would be able to ship the goods via Suez. Shipment via the Cape of Good Hope was twice as expensive and would reduce the seller's expected profit. Nevertheless it was held that the contract was not frustrated by the closing of the Canal.[18] Similar decisions were reached in cases involving contracts of a carriage which had been made on the assumption that the ship would use the Canal.[19] If the contract was one to carry the goods to an agreed destination for a fixed charge, it would be the carrier who would suffer hardship in consequence of having to use a longer and more expensive route. If, on the other hand, the contract provided for payment at so much per day, the owner of the goods would suffer hardship in having to pay an unexpectedly large amount for getting the goods to the agreed destination. Yet in neither of these situations would the contract

17   *Nickoll and Knight v Ashton, Edridge & Co* [1901] 2 KB 126.
18   *Tsakiroglou & Co Ltd v Noblee Thorl GmbH* [1962] AC 93.
19   *The Eugenia* [1964] 2 QB 226; *The Captain George K* [1970] 2 Lloyd's Rep 21.

normally be frustrated. It would require very strong facts (such as, perhaps, a contract to carry perishable goods from Port Sudan to Alexandria and the subsequent closure of the Canal) to bring about such a result.

vi Impossibility contrasted with impracticability

Attempts are sometimes made to argue that a contract is frustrated because supervening events have greatly increased the expense of performance to one party. In such cases performance, though not impossible, is said to be 'impracticable'.[20] But in English law such impracticability is not generally recognised as a ground of frustration. Thus it has been said in the House of Lords that 'a wholly abnormal rise or fall in prices'[1] would not affect the bargain. The point is illustrated by a case[2] in which a builder had agreed to build council houses for a local authority for a fixed price, but found that (as a result of delays due to labour shortages) he could complete the work only at a substantial loss. His argument that the contract was frustrated was rejected by the House of Lords. A severe increase in cost may discharge a contract when combined with temporary impossibility,[3] or with supervening illegality;[4] or it may excuse a party under an express contractual provision for supervening events.[5] But it will not of itself discharge the contract under the common law doctrine of frustration.

Problems of this kind are particularly acute when long-term contracts are made for the supply of some commodity and the costs to the supplier increase, sometimes to many times the contract price. Paradoxically, the supplier's position is relatively favourable where the contract does not specify any time limit; for in such a case he is normally entitled to terminate the contract by reasonable notice: this was held to be the position where a contract had been made to supply water to a hospital 'at all times hereafter' for a fixed charge, and in the course of some 56 years the cost to the supplier had risen to over 18 times the contract price.[6] But no such avenue of escape is open to the

20 Eg, *Horlock v Beal* [1916] 1 AC 486 at 492; American Restatement, 2d *Contracts* § 261.
1   *British Movietonews Ltd v London and District Cinemas Ltd* [1952] AC 166 at 185.
2   *Davis Contractors Ltd v Fareham UDC* [1956] AC 696.
3   Ante, pp 352–353.
4   As in *William Cory & Son Ltd v London Corpn* [1951] 1 KB 8; affd [1951] 2 KB 476.
5   Eg *Tradax Export SA v André & Cie SA* [1976] 1 Lloyd's Rep 416 at 423.
6   *Staffordshire Area Health Authority v South Staffordshire Waterworks Co* [1978] 3 All ER 769; contrast *Watford Borough Council v Watford Rural District Council* (1987) 86 LGR 524 (contract to contribute to cost of maintaining cemetaries).

supplier where the contract is expressed to last for a fixed period, such as ten years, nor can the supplier in such a case rely on an increase in cost as a ground of frustration.[7] In practice he is likely to protect himself by express provisions for 'flexible pricing'.

Events falling short of impossibility may also discharge a contract on grounds other than hardship to either party. The point is illustrated by a case in which sugar had been sold by a Cuban to a Chilean state trading organisation. There was then a total breakdown of diplomatic and commercial relations between those two countries; and the contract was held to have been discharged simply because, both parties being state-controlled enterprises, there was no longer any realistic possibility of securing its performance.[8]

b Frustration of purpose

In cases to be discussed under this heading, performance is, again, not impossible; but one party argues that the contract ought to be discharged because the other's performance is no longer of any use to him. The argument was accepted in a series of cases which arose when the coronation of King Edward VII was postponed because of the sudden illness of the King. Before then, many people had bought seats on stands or hired rooms which overlooked the routes of the coronation processions; and it remained physically possible for them to sit on the stands or to use the rooms. But the contracts were nevertheless held to be frustrated, except where they expressly provided for the event.[9] They were not regarded simply as contracts to provide seats or rooms at high prices, but as contracts to provide facilities for watching the processions.

The application of the doctrine of frustration to these 'coronation seat' cases may seem sensible enough; but the courts were not prepared to extend the doctrine beyond this point. Many other contracts were made in the expectation that the coronation, and related festivities, would take place as planned. But by no means all such contracts were frustrated. For example in one case[10] a contract was made for the hire of a pleasure boat to watch the naval review which was to be held at Spithead at the time of the coronation, and for a day's cruise around the fleet. The review was cancelled but the fleet remained at Spithead; and it was held that the contract was not

---

7   *Kirklees Metropolitan Borough Council v Yorkshire Woollen District Transport Co Ltd* (1978) 77 LGR 448.
8   *The Playa Larga and The Marble Islands* [1983] 2 Lloyd's Rep 171.
9   Post, p 360.
10 *Herne Bay Steam Boat Co v Hutton* [1903] 2 KB 683.

frustrated. Its terms made it impossible to regard it as a contract to provide facilities for watching the review. It was simply a contract for the hire of a boat, though the cancellation of the review may have defeated the hirer's expectation of profiting from it. As a general rule, a contract is not frustrated merely because supervening events prevent a party from putting the subject-matter to its intended use. For example, a contract to buy property for redevelopment is not frustrated merely because between contract and completion the property is listed as being of special architectural or historic interest, so that redevelopment becomes impossible or more difficult, and the value of the property is very considerably reduced.[11] Nor is a contract for the sale of goods frustrated merely because the buyer's purpose to export them from, or to import them into, a particular country is defeated by export or import restrictions.[12] The doctrine of frustration does not enable a party to escape from a contract merely because it has turned out for him to be a bad bargain. There must, as in the coronation cases, be a 'cessation ... of [a] ... state of things going to the root of the contract and essential to its performance'.[13]

c Supervening illegality

A contract may be discharged if its performance becomes illegal. Thus a contract would be frustrated if it provided for the export of goods to (or the import of goods from) a place which, in the course of a war, became enemy territory;[14] or if its performance was prohibited by legislation.[15] Such discharge is not based on the injustice of holding the parties to the contract in the changed circumstances, but rather on public policy: if the parties were not discharged they might be tempted to perform the contract and so to break the law. It should follow that supervening illegality in respect of even a subsidiary obligation should operate as an excuse for the non-performance of that obligation,[16] though it would not frustrate the whole contract. It would only have this effect if it defeated the main purpose of the contract.[17] The test to be applied here is the

---

11 *Amalgamated Investment and Property Co Ltd v John Walker & Sons Ltd* [1976] 3 All ER 509.
12 Eg *Congimex Companhia Geral de Comercio Importadora e Exportadora SARL v Tradax Export SA* [1983] 1 Lloyd's Rep 250.
13 *Krell v Henry* [1903] 2 KB 740 at 748.
14 *Fibrosa Spolka Akeyjna v Fairbairn Lawson Combe Barbour Ltd* [1943] AC 32; cf *Re Badische Co Ltd* [1921] 2 Ch 331.
15 Eg *Denny Mott and Dickson Ltd v James B Fraser & Co Ltd* [1944] AC 265.
16 See post, p 359.
17 As in *Denny Mott and Dickson Ltd v James B Fraser & Co Ltd* [1944] AC 265.

same as that already discussed in relation to partial destruction of the subject-matter.[18]

d Alternatives

Where a contract gives a party the right to choose between two or more specified performances, it is not discharged by supervening impossibility or illegality of one or more of those alternatives so long as at least one of them remains possible and lawful. If, for example, a charterparty gives the shipowner the option of providing ship A or ship B and one of those ships is lost, he must provide the other.[19] Such a contract must be distinguished from one which requires the shipowner to provide ship A but gives him the liberty to substitute ship B. Here the contract is discharged if A is lost before the substitution has been made:[20] the obligation is not a true alternative (under which one cannot at the time of contracting tell whether A or B is due) but is one under which A is due unless and until the liberty has been duly exercised.[1]

e Time of frustration

As a general rule, the effect of supervening events on a contract must be assessed by reference to the time when they occur, so that the rights of the parties are not left indefinitely in suspense.[2] Thus a contract of carriage can be frustrated if, as a result of war, it becomes highly probable that the only possible route will be blocked; and it makes no difference that the route is then, unexpectedly, reopened within the time fixed for performance.[3] But this rule must be qualified where the alleged ground of frustration is a delay which may turn out to be either slight or serious. In such cases the contract is not frustrated as soon as the delay begins, but only when it has gone on for so long that a reasonable person would conclude that it was likely to interfere fundamentally with performance.[4]

---

18 Ante, p 351.
19 *The Super Servant Two* [1990] 1 Lloyd's Rep 1; cf *The Furness Bridge* [1977] 2 Lloyd's Rep 367 (alternative ports of loading).
20 *The Badagry* [1985] 1 Lloyd's Rep 395.
1 *The Marine Star* [1993] 1 Lloyd's Rep 329.
2 *Bank Line Ltd v Arthur Capel & Co* [1919] AC 435 at 454.
3 *Embiricos v Sydney Reid & Co* [1914] 3 KB 45.
4 *The Nema* [1982] AC 724; *The Wenjiang (No 2)* [1983] 1 Lloyd's Rep 400 at 403.

f Leases of land

The doctrine of frustration can apply to leases of land,[5] but such leases will only rarely be frustrated. One reason for this is that they are often long-term transactions; and a temporary interruption of the tenant's use of the premises may well not be long enough to bring about frustration.[6] Another is that potentially frustrating events are often dealt with by the terms of the lease, such as covenants to insure or repair structures that are later damaged or destroyed; and such terms will exclude frustration.[7] It is also paradoxically in the tenant's interest to argue against frustration; for if the lease is frustrated he will have to surrender a valuable site to the landlord many years before the agreed expiry date. These factors account for the narrow scope of the doctrine of frustration in this context. Thus it has been held that leases were not frustrated by the destruction[8] or requisitioning[9] of the premises, or by legislation which prevented the tenant from using the premises as he had intended;[10] and a 10-year lease of a warehouse was held not to have been frustrated when the only access road was closed by a local authority for 20 months some four years before the end of the tenancy.[11] But there could be frustration of a short lease for a particular purpose: eg if a person took a lease of a furnished house for six months and the house was then burnt down.

Even where the whole lease is not frustrated, supervening events may give a party an excuse for non-performance of a particular term in the lease. Thus if either party undertakes to do building work which becomes illegal, failure to do the work at the agreed time will be excused[12] even though the lease remains in being.

g Sale of land

A contract for the sale of land can be frustrated;[13] but the scope of the doctrine of frustration in relation to such contracts is limited by the

5 *National Carriers Ltd v Panalpina (Northern) Ltd* [1981] AC 675, and see infra at n 11.
6 See ante, p 353.
7 Post, p 360.
8 *Denman v Brise* [1949] 1 KB 22.
9 *Matthey v Curling* [1922] 2 AC 180.
10 *London and Northern Estates Co v Schlesinger* [1916] 1 KB 20; *Cricklewood Property and Investment Trust Ltd v Leighton's Investment Trust Ltd* [1945] AC 221.
11 *National Carriers Ltd v Panalpina (Northern) Ltd* [1981] AC 675.
12 *Sturke v S W Edwards Ltd* (1971) 23 P & CR 185 at 190, criticising *Eyre v Johnson* [1946] KB 481, contra.
13 This is assumed in *Amalgamated Investment and Property Co Ltd v John Walker & Sons Ltd* [1976] 3 All ER 509.

rule that risk of loss passes, unless otherwise agreed, as soon as the contract is made.[14] Under this rule, the purchaser of a house remains liable for the price even though the house is destroyed between contract and completion. In practice he will commonly protect himself either by insurance or by an express provision in the contract leaving the risk with the seller until completion.

2   LIMITATIONS ON THE DOCTRINE

Supervening events which are capable of frustrating a contract will not necessarily have this effect; for the doctrine of frustration may be excluded by the following factors.

a   Contractual provisions

The common law relating to frustration leads to 'all or nothing' solutions. If the doctrine applies, the contract is completely at an end; if it does not apply the contract remains in full force. The parties may well prefer to provide for intermediate solutions. In some of the coronation seat cases, for example, the contracts provided that, if the procession were postponed, the tickets should be valid for the day on which the procession eventually did take place; or that the ticket-holders should get their money back less a small sum to cover the other party's expenses.[15] When the coronation was postponed, these provisions took effect to the exclusion of the doctrine of frustration.

Where a contract contains a provision of this kind, it is, however, a question of construction whether the provision does indeed cover the events which have occurred. In one case[16] a contract to build a reservoir in six years provided that the builder should have an extension of time for delays 'however occasioned'. This provision was interpreted as giving him a period of grace only in the event of non-frustrating delays. It did not cover the delays which had actually occurred when government intervention in the First World War brought the work to a halt, and forced the builder to sell his construction plant. Hence the builder's plea of frustration succeeded. Moreover, the mere fact that the contract makes *some* provision for a supervening event will not exclude frustration if the provision is not *complete*. A charterparty may, for example, provide that the *shipowner* is

---

14   *Paine v Meller* (1801) 6 Ves 349; for risk of loss, see ante, p 351.
15   *Victoria Seats Agency v Paget* (1902) 19 TLR 16; *Clark v Lindsay* (1903) 19 TLR 202.
16   *Metropolitan Water Board v Dick Kerr & Co* [1918] AC 119.

not liable for delays due to certain events beyond his control. Such a clause will not prevent the *charterer* from relying on such a delay (if long enough) as a ground of frustration. The reason is that the provision deals only with *one* possible consequence of the delay, namely its effect on the liability of the shipowner for breach. It says nothing about the liabilities of the charterer, which can therefore still be discharged by frustration.[17]

A contractual provision for the event will not exclude frustration in certain cases of supervening illegality. For example if one of the contracting parties becomes an alien enemy the contract would not be saved by even the clearest express provision for that event; for the parties cannot 'contract out' of the particularly strong public policy against aiding the enemy economy in time of war.[18] On the other hand, clauses dealing with export or import prohibition are commonly upheld:[19] they assume that the prohibition will be observed and do not subvert its purpose.

There is, finally, the converse possibility that a contract may expressly provide for discharge on the occurrence of specified events (such as strikes or other obstacles to performance), whether or not these events bring about a change of circumstances which would be sufficiently fundamental to frustrate the contract. Such clauses are meant to reduce the *uncertainty* which can result from the difficulty of deciding whether the change is of this kind; and also to mitigate the *hardship* which a party may suffer where the change is not fundamental so that he would (but for the clause) remain bound even though the contract had become unexpectedly burdensome to him.[20] If the specified event occurs, the contract is discharged under the express term and not under the doctrine of frustration.

b Foreseen and foreseeable events

In many frustration cases, the courts have stressed the unexpected nature of the supervening event.[1] These statements suggest that there can be no frustration if, at the time of contracting, the parties actually foresaw that the event would, or was likely to, occur. This view is based

---

17 See *Jackson v Union Marine Insurance Co Ltd* (1874) LR 10 CP 125; cf *The Adelfa* [1988] 2 Lloyd's Rep 466 at 471.
18 *Ertel Bieber & Co v Rio Tinto Co* [1918] AC 260.
19 Eg *Johnson Matthey Bankers Ltd v State Trading Corpn of India Ltd* [1984] 1 Lloyd's Rep 427.
20 Eg in the Suez cases (ante, p 354); for a 'Suez clause' designed to avoid this hardship, see *DI Henry v Wilhelm G Clasen* [1973] 1 Lloyd's Rep 159.
1 Eg *Krell v Henry* [1903] 2 KB 740 at 752.

on the assumption that, in these circumstances, the parties freely took the risk that the event might occur. Such a risk would no doubt be reflected in the contract price; and if the parties did not want to take the risk, they could easily provide against it. Of course, for the purpose of this argument, it is necessary to define exactly what it is that the parties foresaw. The fact that they foresaw *a* delay does not prevent frustration if *the* delay which occurred was of a wholly different order of magnitude and was not foreseen. Nor is the doctrine of frustration excluded merely because the parties (or one of them) could, as a remote contingency, have foreseen that the event would occur. No doubt it was, in this sense, 'reasonably foreseeable' that King Edward VII (who was then 60 years old) might fall ill at the time fixed for his coronation, but this did not prevent the doctrine of frustration from applying in the coronation cases. Some judicial statements go even further and assert that a contract can be frustrated even by an event which was precisely foreseen.[2] But it is hard to see why, in such cases, the courts should reallocate contractual risks which have been consciously undertaken; and the preferable view seems to be that, if parties contract with reference to risk of which they were aware, they should not normally be able to rely on the doctrine of frustration. They should be able to do so only if the contract indicates that they had *not* intended to provide for the risk: eg by stipulating that, if the event were to occur, they would 'leave the lawyers to sort it out'.[3] If the lawyers' efforts to do so ended in deadlock, the contract could be frustrated.[4]

Special considerations apply where a contract is frustrated because its performance would, after the outbreak of war, involve trading with the enemy. Here the contract is discharged on grounds of public policy even if the event was clearly foreseen. Thus a contract for the export of goods from this country to Germany made in August 1939 would have been frustrated by the outbreak of war on September 3, however much that event was anticipated by both parties.

c   Self-induced frustration

A party cannot rely on 'self-induced' frustration,[5] that is on an obstacle to performance brought about by his own voluntary conduct. This is

---

2   *W J Tatem Ltd v Gamboa* [1939] 1 KB 132 at 138; *The Eugenia* [1964] 2 QB 226 at 239; *Nile Co for the Export of Agricultural Crops v H & J M Bennett (Commodities) Ltd* [1986] 1 Lloyd's Rep 555 at 582.
3   *The Eugenia* [1964] 2 QB 226 at 234.
4   Cf *Autry v Republic Productions Inc* 180 P 2d 888 (1947).
5   *Bank Line Ltd v Arthur Capel & Co* [1919] AC 435 at 452.

most obviously true where that conduct is in itself a breach of the contract. Thus a charterer who in breach of contract orders the ship into a war zone, with the result that she is detained there, cannot rely on the detention as a ground of frustration.[6] The doctrine similarly does not apply where the breaches of *both* parties contribute to an allegedly frustrating delay.[7] Nor can a party rely as a ground of discharge on an event which was due to his deliberate act, even though that act is not itself a breach.[8] For example, a singer who had contracted to give a concert on a specified day could not rely on inability to perform as a result of his imprisonment for unlawfully dealing in drugs. Even negligence in bringing about the event would generally exclude frustration: for example, the defendants in *Taylor v Caldwell*[9] would not have been able to rely on the doctrine if the fire had been due to their negligence. In principle the position should be the same where a singer was unable to perform because she had carelessly caught cold; but as the effect of such conduct on a person's health is hard to foresee it may be that the contract would be frustrated in such a case.[10]

The purpose of the rule that a party cannot rely on self-induced frustration is to deprive that party of the benefit of the doctrine of discharge: the rule must not be allowed to prejudice the *other* party. It follows that the party whose conduct has brought about the event cannot rely on it as a ground of discharge: but the other party may be able to do so. For example, an employee who is prevented from working by a sentence of imprisonment cannot rely on this fact as frustrating the contract;[11] but his employer could so rely on it, with the result that he would not be liable for unfair dismissal.[12]

The question whether frustration is indeed due to the voluntary act of a party can also arise where A enters into several contracts with different parties and the supervening event deprives him of the power of performing some, but not all, of those contracts. Suppose A has planted a crop of potatoes in a field which is normally expected to yield 200 tons. He agrees to sell 100 tons of this expected crop to X and 100 tons of it to Y; but, as a result of events beyond his control, the total yield is only 100 tons. One view, for which there is considerable

---

6   *The Eugenia* [1964] 2 QB 226.
7   *The Hannah Blumenthal* [1983] 1 AC 854.
8   *Denmark Productions Ltd v Boscobel Productions Ltd* [1969] 1 QB 699.
9   (1863) 3 B & S 826, ante, p 351.
10 See *Joseph Constantine Steamship Line Ltd v Imperial Smelting Corpn Ltd* [1942] AC 154 at 166–167.
11 Cf *Sumnal v Statt* (1984) 49 P & CR 367 (imprisonment of tenant no excuse for failing to perform covenant to reside in farmhouse).
12 *F C Shephard & Co Ltd v Jerrom* [1987] QB 301.

support in the authorities,[13] is that if A delivers the 100 tons to X, his contract with Y will not be frustrated since his failure to perform it was due to A's voluntary act; and that for the same reason his contract with X would not be frustrated if he delivered the 100 tons to Y. Yet it seems inconsistent with the principle of frustration to hold A liable for a shortfall due to an event beyond his control, which would have provided him with an excuse if he had agreed to sell the whole quantity to only one buyer. So long as A acts reasonably in allocating the actual yield (eg in delivering the 100 tons to the first of the two buyers to have contracted with him[14]) he should be under no further liability. It might also be reasonable for him to allocate 50 tons to each buyer. He could then rely by way of excuse on an express contractual provision for the event,[15] but probably not on the common law doctrine of frustration, since the effect of that doctrine is generally said to be to bring about the *total* discharge of the contract.[16]

3 LEGAL CONSEQUENCES OF FRUSTRATION

a In general

Frustration brings the contract automatically to an end.[17] No steps to 'rescind' it need be taken by either party; and the obligations of both are immediately terminated. Hence the odd result sometimes comes about, that a party actually makes a profit out of the frustrating event. Suppose that a ship is chartered for 12 months and then requisitioned. Normally one would expect the *charterer* to claim frustration, as he does not get the services of the ship. But if the compensation for requisition is more than the agreed hire, the *shipowner* may claim frustration so as to get the larger sum; and such claims have sometimes been allowed.[18] It might be better if the doctrine were to discharge only the party prejudiced by the event, in the sense of failing to get the performance promised to him. This is, indeed, the position in cases of 'self-induced' frustration, where the party bringing about the event cannot rely on it as a ground of discharge, while the other party can do so.[19]

---

13   *Maritime National Fish Ltd v Ocean Trawlers Ltd* [1935] AC 524; *The Super Servant Two* [1990] 1 Lloyd's Rep 1.
14   See *Bremer Handelsgesellschaft mbH v C Mackprang Jnr* [1979] 1 Lloyd's Rep 221 at 224; *Intertradex SA v Lesieur Tourteaux SARL* [1978] 2 Lloyd's Rep 509.
15   See *Bremer Handelsgesellschaft mbH v Continental Grain Co New York* [1983] 1 Lloyd's Rep 269.
16   See *The Super Servant Two* [1990] 1 Lloyd's Rep 1 at 8.
17   *Hirji Mulji v Cheong Yue Steamship Co Ltd* [1926] AC 497 at 505.
18   Eg *Bank Line Ltd v Arthur Capel & Co* [1919] AC 435.
19   *F C Shephard & Co Ltd v Jerrom* [1987] QB 301; ante, p 363.

b The Law Reform (Frustrated Contracts) Act 1943

At common law, frustration does not retrospectively annul the contract: it brings the contract to an end only as from the occurrence of the frustrating event. This rule gives rise to problems of adjustment where only one party has, or should have, performed some or all of his obligations before the time of frustration. Considerable powers to make such adjustments are given to the courts by the Law Reform (Frustrated Contracts) Act 1943.

i Prepayment of money

Suppose that under a contract of sale payment is due on August 10 and delivery on October 10. The contract is frustrated on September 10, when payment has not yet been made. As frustration does not operate retrospectively one might suppose that the buyer would remain liable to pay, while the seller's obligation to deliver was discharged. But this result would often be very unjust. Section 1(2) of the 1943 Act therefore provides that money due but not paid before frustration ceases to be payable; and that, if the money has actually been paid, it must be paid back. Thus frustration is given some retrospective effect. But this may in turn lead to injustice where the person to whom the prepayment was due has incurred expenses, eg in manufacturing the goods, or in packing them up for despatch. The subsection therefore goes on to provide that a person to whom a prepayment was made (or due) may be allowed, at the court's discretion, to keep (or recover) a reasonable sum not exceeding the amount of the prepayment to cover his expenses. What is a reasonable sum depends on all the circumstances. The crucial question will be whether the expenses have not only been incurred but wasted. For example, where manufacturing expenses have been incurred, the test will be whether the thing which has been made can be readily sold to another customer. The court cannot under the subsection allow more than the amount actually expended or more than the amount which has been (or should have been) prepaid. Thus if £100 was prepaid and £75 expended the court cannot allow more than £75; and if £100 was prepaid and £150 expended the court cannot allow more than £100.

ii Other benefits

Payments of money made before the time of frustration present relatively little difficulty, since money can be paid back. But greater difficulty can arise where, before frustration, one party has conferred on the other some benefit in kind. Suppose that A, a builder agrees to install a central heating system in B's house under a contract providing for payment on completion; and that, when the work is nearly finished, the house is accidentally burnt down. In such a case the builder cannot recover *the agreed sum*. But he may have a remedy under s 1(3) of the 1943 Act. This provides that if one party (B) has 'obtained a valuable benefit ... before the time of discharge' as a result of anything done by the other party (A) in or for the purpose of the performance of the contract, then A can recover from B such sum as the court thinks just, not exceeding the value of the benefit. Under this subsection, the court must first identify and value the benefit obtained by B: it does so by reference to what has been received by B, not to the cost incurred by A. Secondly, the court must determine what is the 'just' sum to be awarded to A: here the cost of performance to A can be taken into account; and where the cost incurred by A was less than the value of the benefit received by B that cost formed the basis of the award.[20] A further problem in our example is that the benefit received by B was destroyed by the frustrating event. Although the contrary has been suggested,[1] it is submitted that this fact is not relevant to the question whether B has obtained a valuable benefit; for in order to determine this question the Act requires the court to look at the position as it was *before* the frustrating event. Thus the fact that the house was burnt down does not affect the court's *power* to award something under s 1(3); though it is a factor which may be taken into account when the court assesses the 'just' sum actually to be awarded.[2]

iii Severability

Suppose that A agrees to install a central heading system in B's house on the terms that £300 is to be paid when the pipes are laid, a further £300 when the radiators are installed and a final £400 when the boiler has been installed *and* the system is in operation. After the boiler has been installed but *before* it is connected, the house is accidentally burnt down. If nothing has been paid, A is entitled to the first two instalments (ie £600) in full. He can, in addition, recover such sum as the court thinks just in respect of the 'valuable benefit' conferred on B by work done during the third stage of the contract; for the 1943 Act provides[3] that the provisions of s 1 (discussed above) shall apply to each severable part of a contract as if it were a separate contract.

---

20   *B P Exploration Co (Libya) Ltd v Hunt (No 2)* [1979] 1 WLR 783; affd [1983] 2 AC 352.
1   *B P Exploration Co (Libya) Ltd v Hunt (No 2)* [1979] 1 WLR 783 at 801.
2   Law Reform (Frustrated Contracts) Act 1943, s 1(3)(b).
3   Section 2(4).

iv Exceptions

The Act can be excluded by contrary agreement:[4] for example by a provision that money paid under a contract is not to be refundable in any event.[5]

The Act does not apply to contracts for the carriage of goods by sea, to contracts of insurance, and to contracts for the sale of specific goods where the cause of frustration is the perishing of the goods.[6] In these cases the effects of frustration were, before the Act, governed by well settled rules. For example, if freight was paid in advance no part of it could be reclaimed even though the contract was frustrated before the goods reached the agreed destination;[7] if freight was payable at the destination nothing could be recovered for any 'valuable benefit' conferred by carrying the goods (before frustration) to an intermediate port;[8] if goods were insured for three months against fire no part of the premium could be reclaimed merely because after one month the goods were destroyed by water;[9] and the effect of the destruction of specific goods was governed by special rules in the Sale of Goods Act 1979.[10] It was thought more important to preserve the certainty of all these rules than to extend the powers of adjustment created by the 1943 Act to cases of this kind. In relation to contracts for the sale of goods, this reasoning is not wholly convincing since the wording of the Act in this context gives rise to some strange distinctions. For example, a person who has agreed to buy *specific* goods and has paid for them in advance may, because the Act is excluded, get the *whole* price back if the goods are destroyed.[11] But if the goods are *not* specific he may (under the Act) get back his price *less* an allowance for the seller's expenses; and this is also the position if the cause of frustration is not the destruction of specific goods but their requisition. It is hard to see any justification for these distinctions.

---

4   Section 2(3)(a). See *B P Exploration Co (Libya) Ltd v Hunt (No 2)* [1983] 2 AC 352 (where the contract was held not to have excluded the Act).
5   A term of this kind is probably excepted from the Unfair Contract Terms Act 1977 by s 29 of that Act (ante, p 110). Such a term may be subject to the Unfair Terms in Consumer Contracts Regulations 1999 as the 1943 Act is not 'mandatory' within reg 4(2)(a) (ante, p 115); but the fact that the Act expressly allowed the parties to exclude it would be relevant to the issue of fairness of the term under the Regulations.
6   Section 2(5).
7   *Byrne v Schiller* (1871) LR 6 Exch 319.
8   See ante, p 325.
9   Cf *Tyrie v Fletcher* (1777) 2 Cowp 666 at 668.
10   Sections 7 and 20 (originally enacted in 1893).
11   Under the common law rule laid down in the *Fibrosa* case [1943] AC 32.

Chapter 18

Remedies for breach of contract

1 CLASSIFICATION

Remedies for breach of contract can be divided into judicial and non-judicial remedies. Judicial remedies are those that must be sought by taking proceedings in a court of law or before an arbitrator; non-judicial remedies are those that are sought in some other way. In some situations, an important non-judicial remedy is self-help: for example the owner of goods which are wrongfully detained by another person may be entitled simply to seize those goods. In this sense, self-help is not generally available as a remedy for breach of contract. Suppose that A agrees to sell a car to B for £5,000. If B does not pay, A cannot simply seize £5,000 belonging to B; nor can B, if A refuses to deliver, seize the car, at least so long as A remains owner of it. The purely defensive 'remedy' of refusing to perform on account of the other party's breach is a kind of self-help. This has been discussed in chapter 16. Our present concern is with judicial remedies.

Judicial remedies can further be subdivided into criminal and civil remedies. Occasionally, the same conduct may amount to a breach of contract and to a criminal offence: for example, where a landlord cuts off his tenant's gas supply.[1] In the criminal proceedings, the offender may be ordered to pay compensation for any personal injury, loss or damage resulting from the offence.[2] This power may be exercisable in a contractual context – eg where a person has been induced to buy goods because a false trade description has been applied to them.[3] But generally a breach of contract is purely and simply a civil wrong, and our concern will be with civil remedies for breach.

Civil remedies may further be subdivided according to the nature of the relief claimed. The injured party may claim specific relief, damages or restitution.

1 Protection from Eviction Act 1977, s 1; *McCall v Abelesz* [1976] QB 585.
2 Powers of Criminal Courts (Sentencing) Act 2000, s 130.
3 Trade Descriptions Act 1968, s 1(1)(a). The offence is committed when the false descriptions is *applied*, even though no sale results.

A claim for specific relief is one for the actual performance of the defaulting party's undertaking. It is usually associated with the so-called equitable remedies of specific performance and injunction but a common law action to recover the agreed sum due under a contract (eg an action for the price, or for wages) is also a claim for specific relief.

A claim for damages is one for money to compensate the injured party for the fact that he has not received the agreed performance. Our account of remedies begins with it since it is the remedy which is most frequently discussed in the reported cases on the subject.

A claim for restitution arises when the claimant has, in performing his part of the contract, conferred a benefit on the defendant and seeks to get back that benefit or its value. For example, a buyer who has paid in advance but has not received delivery may claim the return of his money. Where precise restitution is physically impossible, the court may award the reasonable value of the benefit: for example, the value of services rendered in partial performance of a contract which cannot be fully performed because it has been frustrated. As the last example shows, claims for restitution are by no means limited to cases of *breach* of contract; but, as they are sometimes available on breach, it is convenient to discuss them in this chapter.

2 DAMAGES

Damages are always available, and can be claimed as of right, whenever a contract has been broken. In this respect they differ from claims for specific relief or restitution, which may be subject to the discretion of the court and to other restrictions to be discussed later in this chapter. Even if the injured party has not proved any loss, he is entitled to nominal damages. Such damages may be claimed simply to establish the existence of a legal right; but an action for a declaration is now a more appropriate remedy for this purpose. Our sole concern will be with the principles governing awards of substantial damages.

a The compensatory principle

The purpose of damages is, in general, to compensate the injured party. The following points arising from this 'compensatory principle' call for discussion.

i   Loss to claimant or gain to defendant?

As a general rule, damages are based on loss to the claimant[4] and not on gain to the defendant. For example, an employee who in breach of contract left his job to take up a better-paid one elsewhere would not have to hand over his extra earnings in the new job to the original employer: he would be liable for no more than the loss (if any) which the latter had suffered in consequence of the breach.[5]

The distinction between loss to the claimant and gain to the defendant is further illustrated by the situation in which the defendant in breach of contract uses the claimant's property. The defendant is then liable for the reasonable rental value of the property even though the claimant would not himself have used it or let it out to anyone else.[6] This liability is based, not on gain to the defendant, but on the fact that the breach has deprived the claimant of the chance of letting the property out to some person of his choice. This 'loss of a bargaining opportunity'[7] was also the basis on which damages were assessed where a developer built houses in breach of a restrictive covenant entered into for the benefit of an adjoining landowner. The breach did not reduce the value of the adjoining land but damages were nevertheless awarded amounting to 5% of the developer's profit, this being the amount which the landowner could reasonably have demanded for releasing the covenant.[8] The basis of such awards is not that the defendant has made a profit from the breach, but that the claimant has suffered loss; and if in a particular case the lost bargaining opportunity has no value, then the damages may be no more than nominal.[9]

Gain to the defendant is, however, exceptionally taken into account in a number of situations. If the defendant in breach of contract abuses a 'fiduciary' position (eg if an agent makes a profit by using confidential information acquired in his capacity as agent) he must account for any profit so made.[10] On the conclusion of a contract for the sale of land, the vendor is regarded as trustee of the land for the

---

4   Or, in certain exceptional cases, to a third party: see ante, pp 247–250.
5   Cf *The Siboen and the Sibotre* [1976] 1 Lloyd's Rep 293 at 337 (charterparty).
6   *Penarth Dock Engineering Co Ltd v Pounds* [1963] 1 Lloyd's Rep 359.
7   See *A-G v Blake* [2001] 1 AC 268 at 281.
8   *Wrotham Park Estate Co v Parkside Homes Ltd* [1974] 1 WLR 798; cf *Jaggard v Sawyer* [1995] 2 All ER 189.
9   *Surrey County Council v Bredero Homes Ltd* [1993] 3 All ER 705, doubted in *A-G v Blake* [2001] 1 AC 268 at 283, but see also at 291.
10   *Regal (Hastings) Ltd v Gulliver* [1942] 1 All ER 378; cf *A-G v Guardian Newspapers Ltd (No 2)* [1990] 1 AC 109 at 262, 268; *A-G for Hong Kong v Reid* [1994] 1 AC 324; *Mathew v T M Sutton Ltd* [1994] 4 All ER 793. Partnership Act 1890, ss 29, 30.

purchaser and if in breach of the contract the vendor resells the land to a third party at a profit, the purchaser is in equity entitled to that profit.[11] Liability in these cases is not based on breach of contract as such, but on equitable principles.

A more general, if limited, exception to the compensatory principle was recognised in *A-G v Blake*.[12] In that case, George Blake, a member of the security services, had disclosed secret information to the Soviet Union, in breach of the terms of employment and of the Official Secrets Act 1911. Having been convicted of an offence under the Act, he escaped from prison and fled to Moscow. Some 20 years later, in further breach of the terms of his employment, he there entered into, and performed his part of, a contract with an English publisher for the publication of his memoirs. By then, the information in the book was no longer confidential, so that the qualifications to the compensatory principle discussed above[13] did not apply; no confiscation order[14] could be made in criminal proceedings as Blake was beyond the reach of English criminal law; there was no point in seeking an injunction as the book had been published; and compensatory damages were not a sufficient remedy as the publication had not caused any material loss to the Crown. The House of Lords nevertheless (by a majority) held Blake liable to account to the Crown for the amounts due to him from his publishers. It did so on the ground that, where no other sufficient remedy was available, the court should 'exceptionally' be able to grant the 'discretionary'[15] remedy of requiring the defendant to account for benefits derived by him from the breach. No clear answers can, however, yet be given to the questions exactly when this new discretion will be held to exist or when it will be exercised. The 'general guide', that the injured party must have a 'legitimate interest'[16] in preventing the profit-making activity, does little to dispel the resulting uncertainty since every person to whom a contractual promise is made can be said to have such an interest in its performance. Uncertainty is not, indeed, a ground for criticising the outcome in *Blake*'s case itself; for there is no merit in the argument that, in deciding to break his contract with the Crown, Blake should have been able to rely on the rule that damages are compensatory. But in a wider commercial context the uncertainty created by the new discretion does give rise to concern. This is to

---

11 See *Lake v Bayliss* [1974] 2 All ER 1114.
12 [2001] 1 AC 268.
13 Supra, at n 10.
14 See ante, p 222.
15 [2001] 1 AC 268 at 284–285.
16 [2001] 1 AC 268 at 285.

some extent alleviated by statements that the discretion will not be
exercised merely because the breach is 'cynical and deliberate' or
'enabled the defendant to enter into a more profitable contract
elsewhere'.[17] There is normally no good reason for transferring this
profit by way of windfall to the injured party. The court is, in particular,
unlikely to order a discretionary account of profits where that party
can be adequately protected by compensatory damages, eg for loss of
a bargaining opportunity.[18]

ii   Meaning of 'loss'

In the present context, 'loss' means any harm to the person or property
of the claimant, and any amount by which his wealth is diminished in
consequence of the breach.[19] Suppose that a seller has contracted to
deliver a car on October 1, and in breach of contract he delivers it a
month later. The buyer has suffered loss in not having the car for a
month and this would be so even if the car would not have been of any
use to him during that month, eg because he was ill or abroad for the
whole of it. Such factors could affect the *amount* of loss suffered, but
the claimant is not generally deprived of his right to damages merely
because it is shown that he would (or would not) have used the subject-
matter of the contract in a particular way. Exceptionally, the fact that
the claimant had resold the subject-matter may be relevant for the
purpose of showing that he suffered no loss: this point is further
discussed below.[20]

In determining whether the claimant has suffered loss, regard
must be had to his overall position in consequence of the breach.
Suppose that a seller who has not been paid fails to deliver on a
falling market. No doubt the buyer is deprived of the goods which
were due to him; but at the same time he is released from his obligation
to pay the price, and he can buy substitute goods more cheaply in the
market. Hence he has not suffered any overall loss. Similarly, the
buyer will suffer no loss if he accepts goods which are not in accordance
with the contract but which are no less valuable than the goods which
the seller ought to have delivered.

Even where the claimant has suffered loss, his overall position is
similarly taken into account in determining the extent of the loss.
Benefits which he obtains in consequence of the breach are therefore

17   [2001] 1 AC 268 at 286.
18   See *Experience Hendrix LLC v PPX Enterprises Inc* [2003] EWCA Civ 323,
     [2003] 1 All ER (Comm) 830.
19   For loss of bargaining opportunity, see ante, p 370.
20   See post, p 383.

set off against the prejudice that he suffers; and it is the difference between these two amounts which constitutes his loss. Thus an employee who is wrongfully dismissed must set off against his lost wages any amounts earned in substitute employment. The court will not generally award damages which will actually put the injured party into a better position than that in which he would have been, if the breach had not occurred.[1] But an exception may be made to this principle where its strict application would create a practical dilemma for that party. The exception is illustrated by a case[2] in which A rebuilt his factory after it had been burnt down as a result of B's breach of contract. It was held that A could recover the whole cost of rebuilding without making any allowance for the fact that he now had a new factory, worth more than the old one which had been destroyed. To take this benefit into account would, in effect, have forced A to spend money on improvements which he might not have wanted, or which he could not have afforded; for he had no reasonable alternative but to rebuild and had done so in order to mitigate his loss.[3]

iii No punitive damages

In tort cases, the courts occasionally mark their disapproval of the defendant's conduct by awarding damages in excess of the claimant's loss. They may, for example, do so where a person publishes a book, with a view to profit, knowing that it contains defamatory matter.[4] Such punitive (or exemplary) damages cannot be awarded in a purely contractual action.[5] However, the same conduct may amount both to a breach of contract and to a tort: for example, where a landlord unlawfully evicts his tenant. In such cases, the injured party can recover punitive damages if he frames his claim in tort.[6]

iv Injury to feelings

Punitive damages must be distinguished from damages for injured feelings. The latter are awarded not to punish the defendant, but to compensate a claimant for an injury which he has actually suffered,

---

1   *Philips v Ward* [1956] 1 All ER 874; *Perry v Sidney Phillips & Son* [1982] 3 All ER 705.
2   *Harbutt's Plasticine Ltd v Wayne Tank and Pump Co Ltd* [1970] 1 QB 447 (overruled, but on another point, in *Photo Production Ltd v Securicor Transport Ltd* [1980] AC 827); *Watts v Morrow* [1991] 4 All ER 937.
3   Post, p 393.
4   *Cassell & Co Ltd v Broome* [1972] AC 1027.
5   *Perera v Vandiyar* [1953] 1 WLR 672.
6   *Drane v Evangelou* [1978] 2 All ER 437.

even though it may not be an economic one. Although such damages are often awarded in tort actions, their availability for breach of contract is limited: a person cannot recover damages merely because the breach of a contract made in the course of his business causes him distress;[7] and it has been held that a wrongfully dismissed employee cannot recover extra damages because the manner of his dismissal was 'harsh and humiliating'.[8] But this last rule is now open for reconsideration;[9] and there are many other indications of a growing judicial willingness to award damages of this kind. In particular, damages for injured feelings or distress can be recovered in a contractual action where it is the very object of the contract to promote the enjoyment or comfort of the injured party. Such damages have, for example, been awarded against package tour operators for failing to provide holiday accommodation of the standard required by the contract;[10] and against a solicitor whose negligence resulted in his client's losing the custody of her children;[11] and (in California) against embalmers whose efforts failed to achieve the degree of preservation required by the contract.[12]

Damages are also sometimes awarded for inconvenience, as opposed to distress: for example against a surveyor who negligently fails to draw his client's attention to defects in a house which the client later buys as his home.[13] It can obviously be hard to distinguish between those two types of loss. In one case,[14] damages for 'loss of amenity' were awarded where a contract to build a swimming pool for the customer's own use was broken by building it to less than the stipulated depth. In another,[15] the purchaser of a house recovered damages from his surveyor whom he had asked to report on the extent to which the house was affected by

7   *Hayes v James & Charles Dodd* [1990] 2 All ER 815; *Johnson v Gore Wood & Co* [2002] 2 AC 1.

8   *Addis v Gramophone Co Ltd* [1909] AC 488 at 493; *Shove v Downs Surgical plc* [1984] 1 All ER 7; *Bliss v South East Thames Regional Health Authority* [1987] ICR 700.

9   See *Johnson v Unisys Ltd* [2001] UKHL 13, [2001] ICR 480 at [2], [43]; *Eastwood v Magnox Electric plc* [2004] UKHL 35 at [11]; [2004] 3 WLR 322. But damages for injured feelings cannot be included in an award of compensation available by statute for unfair (as opposed to wrongful) dismissal: *Dunnachie v Kingston upon Hull City Council* [2004] UKHL 36, [2004] 3 WLR 310.

10   *Jarvis v Swans Tours Ltd* [1973] QB 233.

11   *Hamilton Jones v David & Snape* [2003] EWHC 3147 (Ch), [2004] 1 All ER 657.

12   *Chelini v Nieri* 196 P 2d 915 (1948).

13   *Perry v Sidney Phillips & Son* [1982] 3 All ER 705; *Watts v Morrow* [1991] 4 All ER 937.

14   *Ruxley Electronics and Construction Ltd v Forsyth* [1996] AC 344.

15   *Farley v Skinner* [2001] UKHL 49, [2002] 2 AC 732.

aircraft noise and who, in breach of contract, failed to provide accurate information on this point. The breach did not in either case cause any material loss, and it is just as plausible to describe the damages as compensation for inconvenience as of distress.

Damages for injured feelings must further be distinguished from damages for 'anxiety'. The reason why damages of the latter kind cannot generally be recovered in a contractual action[16] is that some uncertainty always exists about the performance of a contract; so that 'anxiety' is a risk to which anyone who enters into a contract voluntarily exposes himself. Such damages have, for example, been refused where a bank in breach of contract wrongfully debited its customer's account.[17] Damages can, however, be recovered where the very object of the contract is to remove a pre-existing state of anxiety: for example, from a solicitor who failed to take necessary steps in non-molestation proceedings, so that the molestation of his client continued.[18]

Damages for injured feelings must further be distinguished from so-called 'stigma' damages: that is, damages for injury to reputation. Such damages are, for example, recoverable where an employer's breach of the contract of employment prejudices his former employee's future employment propects;[19] or where a banker's breach of contract prejudices his customer's business reputation[1] or credit rating.[2] They are recoverable for the injured party's economic loss and not for the injury to his feelings that may incidentally be caused by such breaches.[3]

b   Kinds of loss recoverable

A breach of contract may cause different kinds of loss and we have to ask for which of these compensation will be given.

i   Expectations

The first, and most important, principle is that the law protects the expectations created by a contract. Damages are therefore awarded to

---

16 *Cook v Swinfen* [1967] 1 All ER 299.
17 *McConville v Barclays Bank* (1993) Times, 30 June.
18 *Heywood v Wellers* [1976] QB 446.
19 *Malik v BCCI SA* [1998] AC 20.
1 *Rolin v Steward* (1854) 14 CB 595 at 605.
2 *Kpohraror v Woolwich Building Society* [1996] 4 All ER 119 at 124.
3 Hence the claims for 'stigma' damages in the *Malik* case [1998] AC 20 eventually failed for want of proof that the stigma had resulted in rejection of job applications: *BCCI SA v Ali* [2002] EWCA Civ 82, [2002] ICR 1258.

put the claimant into the position in which he would have been if the contract had actually been performed;[4] he is entitled to damages for loss of his bargain. It is therefore necessary to determine exactly what the injured party has bargained for, or (in other words) the scope of the duty undertaken by the party in breach. The point can be illustrated by supposing that A intends to lend money on the security of property belonging to X and engages B to value that property. B negligently values the property at £9 million when it is actually worth no more than £6 million; in reliance on that valuation, A lends £7 million to X, who defaults on the loan; and at the time of that default the property has fallen in value so that it yields no more than £2.5 million. A's total loss is therefore £4.5 million but B is liable to him for no more than the £3 million by which B had overvalued the security.[5] The underlying principle is that a wrongdoer is liable only for 'those consequences which are attributable to that which made the act wrongful';[6] and where the wrong is a breach of contract, 'that which made the act wrongful' depends on the definition of what should have been done under the contract. In the case put, B's contractual duty was merely one to *provide information* and he was therefore liable only for the loss which flowed from his having failed to take reasonable care to give accurate information. The position would have been different if B had undertaken to *advise* A as to whether to make the loan to X on the security of the property. Failure to take reasonable care in giving that advice would then have made B liable for the whole of A's loss.[7] The difference between the outcomes in these two examples follows from the fact that the scope of B's duty is not the same where he merely undertakes to provide information as it is where he advises A to take a course of action. It 'has nothing to do with questions of causation or any limit or "cap" [such as remoteness] upon damages which would otherwise be recoverable'.[8] Obviously, however, the distinction is sometimes hard to draw.[8a] On the one hand, certain kinds of professional 'advice' may amount to no more than the giving of information; while, on the other, a statement that the brakes of a car have been repaired may mean that it can safely be driven and so amount both to information and advice.

4   *Robinson v Harman* (1848) 1 Exch 850 at 855.
5   *South Australia Asset Management Corp v York Montague Ltd* [1997] AC 191 ('the *SAAMCO* case'); *Nykredit Mortgage Bank plc v Edward Erdman Group Ltd* [1997] 1 WLR 1627 ('the *Nykredit* case').
6   *SAAMCO* case [1997] AC 191 at 213.
7   [1997] AC 191 at 214.
8   *Nykredit* case [1997] 1 WLR 1627 at 1638; for remoteness, see post, p 389.
8ᵃ   Cf *Aneco Reinsurance Underwriting Ltd v Johnson & Higgins Ltd* [2001] UKHL 51, [2001] 2 All ER (Comm) 929 at [10]–[12].

The protection of expectations created by the contract is the feature which distinguishes contractual actions from actions in tort;[9] and it is particularly important where the claimant has made a good bargain. Suppose that A agrees to sell goods to B for £100. At the time fixed for delivery they are worth £150. If A fails to deliver, B's damages will be based on the value of the goods that he ought to have received: ie the damages will be £150 if B has already paid for the goods and £50 if he has not. The same principle applies where A warrants that the goods are of 'grade 1' quality and he delivers goods of 'grade 2' quality. If B 'accepts' the goods, his damages will be based on the difference in value between what he has actually received (grade 2 goods) and what he ought to have received (grade 1 goods). The position is different where A does not *warrant* but only *represents* that the goods have a certain quality. Here B may be entitled to damages in tort for misrepresentation and in such an action expectations created by the representation are not protected.[10]

ii Reliance

Expenses may be incurred or other losses suffered in reliance on the contract. For example, a buyer may be required by the contract to collect the goods, and if he takes steps to do so but the seller fails to provide the goods, then the buyer will have wasted the costs of collection. Expenses may also be wasted if the claimant incurs them for the purpose of making use of the subject-matter, even though he is not required by the contract to incur them. For example a buyer's costs of installing machinery may turn out to be useless because it is not up to the standard laid down in the contract. Subject to restrictions to be stated below,[11] damages can be recovered in respect of such reliance loss. This may be true even where the expenses are incurred *before* the contract. In one case[12] a television company incurred preliminary expenses of £2,750 for the purpose of making a film. They then engaged an actor for the leading part, and he later repudiated the contract. He was held liable for the £2,750 as reliance loss. The company had relied on their contract with him, not in incurring the expenditure, but in allowing it to be wasted: that is, in forbearing to look for someone else to play the part.

---

9   See ante, p 5. In the 'disappointed beneficiary' cases discussed ante, p 252, damages for loss of expectations are recoverable in tort, but the expectations in question exist independently of the contract and are not created by it.
10   See ante, p 160.
11   See post, p 379 at n 18.
12   *Anglia Television Ltd v Reed* [1972] 1 QB 60.

iii   Restitution

The nature of a claim for restitution has already been explained.[13] Such a claim may arise where the injured party has, in performing his part of the contract, conferred a benefit on the other party. It is, for example, available where the defaulting party has wholly failed to perform his part of the contract. Thus if a seller has been paid in advance and then refuses to deliver the goods, he is liable to *restore* the price to the buyer. The effect of such a claim is to put both parties into the position in which they would have been if the contract had never been made. In this respect it differs from a claim for loss of expectations, which is meant to put the claimant into the position in which he would have been if the contract had been performed. It also differs from a claim for reliance loss: this may put the injured party into the position in which he would have been if the contract had never been made, but it will often leave the guilty party in a worse position; and it may be available even though that party has not received any benefit. As a general rule,[14] restitution is available only in respect of such benefits. A claim for restitution is not strictly one for 'damages',[15] but it is mentioned here so that its relation to claims for damages for expectation and reliance loss can be discussed.

iv   Relation between expectation, reliance and restitution claims

This is a complex subject, but three leading principles are clear.

First, the claimant can often choose whether to base his claim on expectation, reliance or restitution. The defendant has no similar choice: he cannot insist that the claimant should get only reliance loss or restitution. If the defendant could do this, it would be too easy for him to get out of a bad bargain: for example, a seller who had sold goods for less than they were worth could simply pay back the price. Obviously in such a case the buyer would not want his money back, but damages for loss of his bargain.

Secondly, the claimant's choice is in some respects limited. Sometimes he cannot claim for loss of expectation. Where the value of his expectation is so speculative that it cannot be satisfactorily proved, he will be able to claim only reliance loss and restitution.[16] In many cases the claimant cannot get restitution. For example, a claim to get back money paid under a contract may be rejected if the breach

---

13   See ante, p 369.
14   For an exception see post, p 423.
15   *A-G v Blake* [2001] 1 AC 268 at 284.
16   *McRae v Commonwealth Disposals Commission* (1950) 84 CLR 377 at 411.

is not sufficiently serious to amount, or to give rise, to a 'total failure of consideration'.[17] Where this requirement is satisfied, restitution can be claimed even though it will leave the claimant better off than he would have been if the claimant has made a bad bargain. Suppose he has paid £100 in advance for goods which are worth only £75. If the seller fails to deliver, the buyer will get back the whole of his £100. The law will not limit the seller's liability to £75 for, if it did this, the end result would be that the seller would keep £25 for doing absolutely nothing. On the other hand, the court will *not* award the claimant his *whole reliance* loss if this would clearly leave him better off than he would have been if the contract had been performed.[18] Suppose A contracts to sell aero engines to B for £100m, and that he has incurred development expenses of £150m when B repudiates the contract. Here A cannot get more than £100m even if he claims reliance loss. Any further loss to A is the result, not of B's breach, but of the fact that A has made a bad bargain; and there is no compelling reason in this example for shifting that loss to B, since B will not (as in our previous example) be enriched if a ceiling of £100m is placed on his liability. It does not follow that a claim for reliance loss can never yield more than one for loss of expectation: it may do so where the claimant cannot prove the value of his expectation; or where the value of the expectation is speculative. In the case of the television film mentioned above, the company's profits might or might not have exceeded the £2,750 recovered as reliance loss. The company did not have to prove what these profits would be. Its claim for reliance loss would have been reduced to the level of its expectations only if the actor could have proved that the profits would *certainly* have been less than the amount of the reliance expenditure.[19]

Thirdly, although the claimant *may* be able to choose between expectation, reliance and restitution, it does not follow that he *must* choose: in other words, the various claims can sometimes be combined. In one case[20] machinery was delivered and paid for, and installed by the buyer. It was then found not to be in accordance with the contract and the buyer recovered the price he had paid (restitution), his installation expenses (reliance) and the net profits which he had lost because his productive capacity was reduced in consequence of the breach (expectation). Of course the buyer could not get the restitution and reliance items plus his *gross* profits, for this would give him these profits plus the costs of earning them, and so in

17 See post, pp 418–420.
18 *C and P Haulage v Middleton* [1983] 3 All ER 94.
19 *CCC Films (London) Ltd v Impact Quadrant Films Ltd* [1985] QB 16.
20 *Millar's Machinery Co Ltd v David Way & Son* (1935) 40 Com Cas 204.

effect give him damages twice over for the same loss.[1] But, so long as this danger of duplicating damages is avoided, there is no reason why claims of the kind here described should not be combined.

v   Consequential and incidental loss

The expression 'consequential loss' is used in the law of contract in several senses. First it is used simply to refer to loss of profits, that is to an element of expectation loss. Secondly, it is used to refer to reliance loss, such as expense wasted by a buyer in attempting to collect goods which the seller wrongfully refuses to deliver. But our present concern is with a third meaning of the expression. The breach may not merely deprive the claimant of what he bargained for; he may suffer further harm as a result of the defect in the defendant's performance. Suppose that the seller of a cow in breach of contract delivers an animal that is diseased. The buyer is entitled to the difference in value between this cow and a healthy one as damages for loss of his bargain. But he may also have put the diseased cow with his other cattle which in consequence were infected and died. He can recover the value of those cattle as a consequential loss in the present sense.[2] Yet it is hardly realistic to say that the buyer expected not to lose the other cattle or that he put the cow which he had bought with the others in reliance on her not being diseased. The possibility of injury to the other cattle may simply not have crossed his mind. His right to such consequential loss does not fit easily into the categories of expectation and reliance.

The same is true of a further type of loss. Suppose a seller fails to deliver and the buyer makes a substitute purchase. Even if the price of the substitute is the same as that of the goods originally bought, the buyer will have suffered some loss: namely, the administrative expenses of making the second contract. There is no doubt that he can recover such loss[3] which (following an American usage) may be called incidental loss.[4]

c   Valuing the loss

For the purpose of an award of damages, the claimant's loss has to be translated into money terms. This process of valuation or assessment gives rise to many problems.

---

1   *Cullinane v British Rema Manufacturing Co Ltd* [1954] 1 QB 292; *TC Industrial Plant Pty Ltd v Robert's Queensland Pty Ltd* [1964] ALR 1083.
2   *Smith v Green* (1875) 1 CPD 92.
3   *Robert Stewart & Sons Ltd v Carapanayoti & Co Ltd* [1962] 1 All ER 418.
4   Uniform Commercial Code, s 2–715(1).

i The bases of assessment

The first of these is to determine the basis on which the assessment is to be made. Where the claim is for reliance loss, the basis is the cost to the claimant of his action or forbearance in reliance on the contract. Where the claim is for restitution, the basis is the benefit obtained by the defendant. But where the claim is for expectation loss, or for consequential loss (in the third of the above senses) there are at least two possible bases of assessment. These will be called 'difference in value' and 'cost of cure'.

In some cases both of these bases of assessment will lead to the same result. Where a seller of goods fails to deliver, the buyer is entitled to damages based on the cost of substitute goods; and this can be described either as the difference in value between what he has got (nothing) and what he should have got (the goods), or as the cost of 'curing' the seller's breach. But (as the following discussion will show) there are other cases in which the choice between the two bases can be of crucial importance. The choice between them is not governed by any fixed or general rule: there are only prima facie rules, and even these are not rigidly applied. Two illustrations must suffice.

First a seller in breach of contract delivers defective goods. The Sale of Goods Act 1979 here states that prima facie the damages are based on the difference between the actual value of the goods and the value which they would have had, if they had been in accordance with the contract.[5] The rule is probably based on the assumption that the defect is one that cannot be cured: for example, that the goods are of a different commercial grade from that contracted for. The buyer can then resell those goods and, with the proceeds of sale together with damages based on difference in value, acquire goods of the contract quality. The rule is only a prima facie one: if the defect is one that can be cured (for example, if the sale is of a car with defective brakes) the court would probably award the cost of cure.[6]

Secondly, a builder in breach of contract fails to complete the work which he has contracted to do, or to execute it in accordance with the specifications. Here the law starts with the assumption that the damages will be based on cost of cure.[7] This is reasonable since normally the —

<hr>

5   Section 53(3). If the price has not been paid, the buyer can reduce it by the above amount: s 53(1)(a). The price reduction available under ss 48A(2)(b)(i) and 48C(1)(a) to a buyer who deals as consumer is a concept taken from the Civil law and will probably give the buyer, not the difference in value *as such,* but a reduction of *the price* in proportion to that difference.

6   Cf *Charterhouse Credit Co Ltd v Tolly* [1963] 2 QB 683 at 711–712 (hire-purchase).

7   *Hoenig v Isaacs* [1952] 2 All ER 176; *Tito v Waddell (No 2)* [1977] Ch 106 at 333; *Radford v de Froberville* [1978] 1 All ER 33; *Dean v Ainley* [1987] 3 All ER 748.

owner will in fact need to cure the defects: a house without a roof, or a central heating system which does not work, is of no use to him. A more difficult problem arises where the breach does not make the building appreciably less useful or valuable to the owner but is nevertheless very expensive to cure. This was the position where a builder broke a contract to build a swimming pool for some £38,500 by making its maximum depth nine inches less than that specified in the contract. This did not significantly affect the value of the pool; nor did it make the pool unserviceable or unsafe, so that the high cost of rebuilding it to the stipulated depth would have been wholly disproportionate to any benefit that the customer would have obtained from this operation. Hence there was no 'difference in value', nor could the customer recover the high 'cost of cure'[8] because it would have been unreasonable, and in conflict with the principle of requiring him to mitigate his loss,[9] for him to incur this cost. He recovered only a much smaller sum as compensation for 'loss of amenity'.[10]

Where the cost of cure basis applies, the starting principle is that the claimant can use the damages in any way he pleases and so does not need to show that he has undertaken cure or proposes to do so.[11] But the fact that he has already at the time of the claim decided not to effect cure may indicate that it would not have been reasonable for him to incur the cost of cure and so to lead to the rejection of a claim based on that cost.[12] If it is clear for some other reason that the breach will not be cured, then this fact may induce the court to apply the difference in value basis: for example, where the claimant, instead of curing the breach, has disposed of the subject-matter.[13]

ii   Relevance of market values

Where damages are based on difference in value, or on the cost of a substitute, the question arises whether they are to be based on the *actual* difference or cost, or on market values. The question will here be discussed by taking the common cases of failure by a seller to deliver goods, or by a buyer to accept and pay for them. There is said

---

8   *Ruxley Electronics and Construction Ltd v Forsyth* [1996] AC 344.
9   Post, p 394.
10   Ante, p 374.
11   *Ruxley Electronics and Construction Ltd v Forsyth* [1996] AC 344 at 359; and cf at 372.
12   As in the *Ruxley Electronics* case.
13   *Perry v Sidney Phillips & Son* [1982] 3 All ER 705; *Calabar Properties Ltd v Stitcher* [1984] 1 WLR 287 at 299.

to be a 'market' for goods if there is a place in which they can be bought and sold at a price fixed by supply and demand.[14]

Where a seller wrongfully fails to deliver, the buyer is entitled to the value of the goods, less the price if he has not yet paid it. If there is no market the court has to assess that value as best it can. Relevant factors include the cost of a reasonably close substitute, and the price at which the buyer may have resold the goods to a sub-buyer at or about the time of the seller's breach. If there is a market, the value of the goods is prima facie assessed by reference to it so that the buyer (assuming that he has not yet paid) will be entitled to the amount (if any) by which the market price exceeds the contract price.[15] The reason for the rule is that 'the buyer is entitled to the expense of putting himself in the position of having those goods, and this he can do by going into the market and purchasing them at the market price'.[16] This principle applies where goods are bought for resale, no less than where they are bought for use. Suppose that A sells 100 tons of wheat to B for £x per ton and B then sells 100 tons of wheat to C for £x + 3 per ton, intending to deliver to C the wheat that is due from A. Later A fails to deliver the wheat; and at this time the market value of the wheat is £x + 5 per ton. B's damages will prima facie be £5 per ton and not £3 per ton.[17] The theory is that, as B saw the market rise, he might have bought another 100 tons of wheat (say at £x + 1) to supply to C, and still have had the benefit of his contract with A. Similar reasoning applies in the converse situation. If the sale to C was at £x + 5 and the market price at the date of breach was £x + 3, B's damages will prima facie be £3 per ton, for he could have bought at £x + 3 to supply C.[18] But such reasoning does not apply where B is bound to deliver to C the very same wheat that he bought from A. Suppose that A sells to B the cargo of wheat *of a named ship* at £x per ton and B resells *that cargo* to C for £x + 5 per ton. Here B's loss will be £5 per ton even if the market price of similar wheat at the date of A's default was £x + 3 per ton. The point is that B could not pass on to C *other* wheat bought in the market at £x + 3 per ton since C was only bound to accept, and to pay £x + 5 per ton for, the particular cargo in question.[19]

Similar principles apply where a buyer wrongfully fails to accept and pay for the goods. Here the assumption is that, on the buyer's

14 *Dunkirk Colliery Co v Lever* (1878) 9 Ch D 20.
15 Sale of Goods Act 1979, s 51(3).
16 *Williams Bros v ET Agius Ltd* [1914] AC 510 at 531.
17 *Williams Bros v ET Agius Ltd* [1914] AC 510.
18 *Williams v Reynolds* (1865) 6 B & S 495.
19 *Williams Bros v ET Agius Ltd* [1914] AC 510 at 523; it is assumed that the resale is not too remote a consequence: see post, pp 389–392, and *Re R and H Hall Ltd and W H Pim Jnr & Co's Arbitration* (1928) 139 LT 50.

default, the seller will sell the goods to someone else, and his damages will be based on the proceeds of the substitute sale. If there is no market, the damages will be based on the actual proceeds so long as the substitute sale was, in all the circumstances, one which it was reasonable to make. If there is a market, the damages are prima facie assessed by reference to it so that the seller will be entitled to the amount (if any) by which the contract price exceeds the market price.[20] The fact that the seller has actually resold above or below the market price is again irrelevant, unless the sale is of particular goods as opposed to a sale of a quantity of some generic marketable commodity.

The rules stated above are concerned only with valuing one of the claimant's expectations, namely his expectation of getting the performance promised to him. They do not necessarily lay down the limits of his recovery, for he may also have another expectation, that of getting a profit out of the subject-matter. This is obvious enough where the seller is in breach and the buyer loses profits which he expected to make out of the use of the goods. He may lose such profits during the time it takes him to get a substitute; if so, he can recover damages even though the actual cost or market price of the substitute does not exceed the contract price. A somewhat similar possibility exists where the buyer is in breach. Suppose that a car dealer (A) agrees to sell a new car to a customer (B) for £9,000 and that B wrongfully refuses to accept and pay. A thereupon sells the car to C for £9,000 and claims damages from B for the loss of his profit on the contract with him. A's case is that he would, if B had not defaulted, have made two sales and two profits and that he has lost one of these. Such a claim will succeed if A can show that he would, but for B's breach, have performed not only his contract with B, but also that with C: eg if A could have got twenty cars from the manufacturers and have found only ten customers, including B and C. The result of B's default in such a case is that A loses one sale.[1] But A would not be entitled to damages for loss of his profit on the contract with B in the converse case in which he can only get ten cars but can find twenty customers.[2] Here A will still make the maximum number of ten sales in spite of B's default. The only loss he suffers is a small amount of incidental loss, that is, the extra expense of negotiating the sale with C. The position is the same if the sale is of a unique object (such as a second-hand car): here there can obviously be only one sale and one profit, and this is not lost if C buys for the same price that B had agreed to pay.[3]

---

20   Sale of Goods Act 1979, s 50(3).
1   *W L Thompson Ltd v Robinson (Gunmakers) Ltd* [1955] Ch 177.
2   *Charter v Sullivan* [1957] 2 QB 117.
3   *Lazenby Garages Ltd v Wright* [1976] 2 All ER 770 (BMW car).

iii Speculative damages

A breach of contract may deprive the claimant of the chance of gaining some benefit; and where the chance is a 'substantial' one,[4] damages can in principle be recovered for the loss of it. Damages have, for example, been awarded for loss of the chance of taking part in the final stages of a beauty contest;[5] for loss of the chance of earning tips,[6] and for loss of the chance of getting pension benefits which depended on the exercise of discretion by a government department.[7] Damages are also commonly awarded for 'loss of profits' even though there was only a chance, and not any certainty, that such profits would be made. In all these cases the value of the chance is to some extent a matter of speculation. The court not only has to value the expected benefit but also to take into account the likelihood of its being actually received by the claimant. Suppose that a tennis player is, in breach of contract, excluded from a tournament in which the winner is to get a prize of £50,000. The damages for loss of the chance of winning will be less than £50,000. The amount will depend on the stage at which the player was excluded and on his chance of winning; obviously the top seed excluded from the final will get more than an unseeded player excluded from the first round. The fact that the chance cannot be valued precisely is, in these cases, no ground for saying that it has no value at all. But sometimes the chance is so highly speculative that the court cannot sensibly value it. The court will then refuse to award damages for loss of the chance (which is a form of expectation) and instead confine its award to one for reliance loss.[8]

iv Taxation

Damages in a contractual action may be claimed for loss of some benefit which would, if the claimant had received it, have been taxable in his hands. This is most obviously true where an employee claims damages for wrongful dismissal. Such damages are based on the amounts which the employee would have earned under the contract. To award him those amounts in full might result in his making a profit out of the breach; for if he had earned his salary or wages he might have had to pay income tax, while the damages may be tax free. In such circumstances, the claimant will therefore recover the amount that he

---

4   As in *Equitable Life Assurance Society v Ernst & Young* [2003] EWCA Civ 1114, [2003] 2 BCLC 603.
5   *Chaplin v Hicks* [1911] 2 KB 786.
6   *Manubens v Leon* [1919] 1 KB 208.
7   *Scally v Southern Health and Social Services Board* [1992] 1 AC 294.
8   *McRae v Commonwealth Disposals Commission* (1950) 84 CLR 377 at 411.

would have earned under the broken contract less any tax that he would have had to pay on those earnings.[9] The exact amount of tax to be deducted will depend on his personal circumstances in each case.

Two conditions must be satisfied before the claimant's tax liability is taken into account in assessing damages. First, the benefit which he has lost must be one which would, if he had received it, have been taxable in his hands. Loss of income would, but the mere failure to get a capital asset would not, be such a benefit.[10] Thus the incidence of taxation would be irrelevant where a seller wrongfully failed to deliver goods and the buyer made a claim for damages based on the extra cost of obtaining substitute goods. Secondly, the damages themselves must not be taxable, for if the claimant has to pay tax on the damages he will obviously not make any profit out of the breach by being awarded his gross loss. Damages for wrongful dismissal are taxable to the extent to which they exceed £30,000.[11] Hence the claimant's damages must be reduced by reference to his tax liability where his lost income is less than £30,000; where it is more, the court will first assess his net loss and then award such sum as will, after tax on the sum so assessed, be equal to that loss.[12]

v *Alternatives*

Suppose that A agrees to sell to B for £50 'a ton of coal or a ton of coke'. At the time fixed for delivery a ton of coal is worth £55, and a ton of coke £51. If A refuses to deliver, B's damages will depend on who had the right to choose between the two performances. The general rule is that damages will be assessed on the assumption that each party will exercise the choice most advantageous to himself:[13] hence the damages will be £1 if A had the right to choose but £5 if the contract gave that right to B. But this rule will not be rigidly applied so as to produce absurd or inconvenient results. If, in our example A had the right to choose and had in fact chosen coal before refusing to deliver, the damages would be assessed on that basis.[14] Again, suppose

9   *Beach v Reed Corrugated Cases Ltd* [1956] 2 All ER 652; cf in tort *British Transport Commission v Gourley* [1956] AC 185.

10   Cf *Spencer v Macmillan's Trustees* 1958 SC 300.

11   Income and Corporation Taxes Act 1988, ss 148, 188(4).

12   *Parsons v BNM Laboratories Ltd* [1964] 1 QB 95; *Shove v Downs Surgical plc* [1984] 1 All ER 7.

13   *Kaye Steam Navigation Co Ltd v W & R Barnett Ltd* (1932) 48 TLR 440; *The Rijn* [1981] 2 Lloyd's Rep 267; cf *Paula Lee Ltd v Robert Zehil & Co Ltd* [1983] 2 All ER 390.

14   *Toprak Mahsulleri Ofisi v Finagrain Cie Commerciale Agricole et Financière SA* [1979] 2 Lloyd's Rep 98; *Shipping Corpn of India v Naviera Letasa SA* [1976] 1 Lloyd's Rep 132 at 137–138.

A sells goods to B on the terms that they are to be delivered in a given month on any day to be chosen by A. If by the end of the month A has not delivered, damages will be assessed by reference to the market price on the last day of the month – not by reference to the market price on the particular day of the month on which that price was lowest.[15] The latter basis would lead to too much uncertainty, whatever its theoretical merits might be.

vi   Time for assessment

As costs and prices fluctuate, the exact amount of damages will depend on the point of time by reference to which the assessment is made. The law starts with the principle of assessment by reference to the time of breach. This principle is, for example, stated in the Sale of Goods Act 1979. Where a buyer fails to accept and pay (or where a seller fails to deliver), damages are prima facie based on the market price at the time when the goods ought to have been accepted (or delivered), or, if no time was fixed, at the time of the refusal to accept (or deliver).[16] The injured party may, however, be given a reasonable time to consider the position, and damages may then be assessed by reference to the end of that reasonable time and not by reference to the very day of breach.[17] Even with this qualification, the principle of assessment by reference to the time of breach is not an inflexible one; and it will not be applied in the following situations.

First, the breach may not be known to the injured party as soon as it is committed. In that case damages will normally be assessed by reference to the time when the breach was, or reasonably should have been, discovered. This rule would, for example, apply where defects in building work became apparent only some considerable time after the work was done.[18]

Secondly, the injured party may know of the breach but be unable at once to act on that knowledge. Suppose that a seller has dispatched goods to the buyer, and that, while they are en route, the buyer wrongfully refuses to pay. If the seller cannot resell the goods while they are in transit, his damages may be assessed by reference to the

15   Cf *Harlow and Jones Ltd v Panex (International) Ltd* [1967] 2 Lloyd's Rep 509; *Phoebus D Kyprianou Co v Wm H Pim Jnr & Co* [1977] 2 Lloyd's Rep 570 (both cases on buyer's breach).
16   Sections 50(3), 51(3); cf *The Texaco Melbourne* [1994] 1 Lloyd's Rep 473 at 476 (breach by carrier of goods).
17   *C Sharpe & Co v Nosawa Co* [1917] 2 KB 814; cf *Bremer Handelsgesellschaft mbH v Vanden Avenne-Izegem PVBA* [1978] 2 Lloyd's Rep 109 at 117.
18   *East Ham Borough Council v Bernard Sunley & Sons Ltd* [1966] AC 406.

market value of the goods as soon as the transit is over, or as soon thereafter as it is reasonable for him to resell.

Thirdly, it may in all the circumstances be quite unreasonable to expect the injured party to act on his knowledge of the breach by making a substitute contract. He cannot be expected to do so where he continues, after breach, to negotiate in the hope of securing eventual performance, or where he is actually suing for specific performance of the contract. In such cases damages are assessed by reference to the time when it becomes clear that performance will not be obtained: ie when the negotiations break down,[19] when the court refuses to order specific performance,[20] or when it becomes clear that the defendant will not comply with an order for specific performance and the claimant elects instead to seek damages.[1]

vii Anticipatory breach

The victim of an anticipatory breach can either continue to press for performance or rescind the contract by 'accepting' the breach.[2]

If he takes the former course, the time for assessment is governed by the same rules that apply in cases of actual breach. It follows that damages will (subject to the exceptions just discussed) be assessed by reference to the time when the contract ought to have been performed, and not by reference to the time of repudiation.[3]

The prima facie rule of assessment by reference to the time of breach also applies where the victim 'accepts' the breach;[4] but here it is subject to the important qualification that, on 'accepting' the breach, the injured party must mitigate his loss.[5] This means that he will be expected to make a substitute contract on, or within a reasonable time of, his acceptance of the breach.[6] Thus the damages will be assessed by reference to any relevant market when that substitute contract should have been made – not when the original contract should have been performed. However, the burden of proving that such a substitute contract could have been made lies on the party in

---

19 *Radford v de Froberville* [1978] 1 All ER 33; *Toprak Mahsulleri Ofisi v Finagrain Cie Commerciale Agricole et Financiere SA* [1979] 2 Lloyd's Rep 98; *The Aktion* [1987] 1 Lloyd's Rep 283 at 314.
20 *Wroth v Tyler* [1974] Ch 30 as explained in *Radford v de Froberville*, supra; *Domb v Isoz* [1980] Ch 548 at 559; *Meng Leong Development Pte Ltd v Jip Hong Trading Co Pte Ltd* [1985] AC 511.
1 *Johnson v Agnew* [1980] AC 367 at 401.
2 Ante, p 346.
3 *Tai Hing Cotton Mill Ltd v Kamsing Knitting Factory* [1979] AC 91.
4 *Roper v Johnson* (1873) LR 8 CP 167.
5 See post, pp 393–396.
6 *L Roth & Co Ltd v Taysen, Townsend & Co* (1895) 1 Com Cas 240.

breach;[7] and, if he cannot show this, the damages will be assessed by reference to the market when he should have performed. The further question arises whether, in applying the principle of looking to that time, the court can take into account events (other than market movements) occurring, or likely to occur, after the anticipatory breach and before the time fixed for performance. Where the victim has rescinded the contract by 'accepting' the anticipatory breach, the court clearly cannot take into account the probability that the victim himself might subsequently have committed a breach justifying the guilty party's repudiation; for the victim's rescission of the contract relieves him from his obligation to perform in the future, so that his failure to do so can no longer be a breach.[8] But the contract may give the guilty party a right to cancel on the occurrence of an *event* (such as the late arrival of a chartered ship) even though that event did not amount to a *breach* by the victim. If the guilty party can show that, when the breach was accepted, such an event was already *certain* to occur, and that he would have exercised his right to cancel on account of it, then the contract will be of no value to the injured party, whose damages will therefore be nominal.[9]

d Methods of limiting damages

A breach of contract may be a starting point of a series of events which cause loss to the claimant; but the law does not hold the defendant liable for all such loss. Our concern in this section is with rules by which the law limits such liability.

i Remoteness

The first of these rules is that damages will not be awarded for loss that is 'too remote'. This principle is illustrated by the leading case of *Hadley v Baxendale*,[10] where a shaft in a mill at Gloucester broke and had to be sent to the makers at Greenwich to serve as a pattern for a new one. The defendants undertook to carry the shaft to Greenwich, but in breach of contract delayed its delivery for a few days, during which the mill was kept idle. The millers claimed damages for the resulting loss of profits but the court regarded this loss as too remote a consequence of the breach. The underlying idea is that it is

---

7   *Roper v Johnson* (1873) LR 8 CP 167.
8   *Berger & Co Inc v Gill & Duffus SA* [1984] AC 382 at 391; ante, p 321; contrast *The Simona* [1989] AC 788 (breach not accepted).
9   *The Mihalis Angelos* [1971] 1 QB 164 at 210; cf ante, p 347.
10   (1854) 9 Exch 341.

undesirable to make a defendant pay for such remote loss, for to hold him so liable might either deter him from entering into contracts at all, or lead him unduly to raise his charges to meet such liability. He will be liable only if one of two rules laid down in *Hadley v Baxendale* is satisfied.

First, the loss must arise 'naturally, ie, according to the usual course of things, from such breach of contract itself'.[11] This test was not satisfied in *Hadley v Baxendale* because 'in the great multitude of cases'[12] a carrier's delay in delivering a broken mill shaft would not keep the mill idle: the millers might have had, or been able to get, a spare shaft. In the contrasting *Victoria Laundry*[13] case, a large boiler had been sold to a laundry and was, in breach of contract, delivered 22 weeks late, so that the buyers could not use it (as they had intended to do) to expand their business. It was held that the sellers were liable for the general loss of profits suffered by the buyers. Having regard to the subject-matter, the likelihood of such loss was obviously very much greater in the *Victoria Laundry* case than in *Hadley v Baxendale*.

Secondly, the defendant may be liable if the loss was such 'as may reasonably be supposed to have been in the minds of both parties at the time they made the contract as the probable result of the breach'.[14] Liability under this rule depends in the first place on what the defendant knew of the claimant's circumstances; and in *Hadley v Baxendale* the defendants did not know enough to make them liable under this rule. It seems that they knew that the mill was stopped, but not that it would remain idle until the new shaft arrived from Greenwich.[15] In the *Victoria Laundry* case the defendants knew that the buyers were in the laundry business; but not that the buyers wanted the boiler for the purpose of some exceptionally lucrative government contracts. Hence the defendants were not liable for the actual loss suffered because the buyers could not perform *those contracts*, but only for loss of ordinary profits.

Under the second rule in *Hadley v Baxendale* the defendant is not liable if he is unaware of the special circumstances; but it does not follow that he will be liable *merely* because he knows of them. To impose this degree of liability there must be 'some knowledge *and acceptance* by one party of the purpose and intention of the other in entering into the contract'.[16] No doubt the claimants' purpose in

11   (1854) 9 Exch 341 at 354.
12   (1854) 9 Exch 341 at 356.
13   *Victoria Laundry (Windsor) Ltd v Newman Industries Ltd* [1949] 2 KB 528.
14   *Hadley v Baxendale* (1854) 9 Exch 341 at 354.
15   See the report in 18 Jur 358.
16   *Weld-Blundell v Stephens* [1920] AC 956 at 980.

making the contract of carriage in *Hadley v Baxendale* was to get their mill started again; but, even if the defendants had known all the facts, they could scarcely be said to have accepted this purpose as the basis of the contract. Such acceptance could, however, be inferred where A contracts to carry B's goods to a particular market in which B wishes to sell such goods. In *The Heron II*[17] the defendants agreed to carry a cargo of sugar belonging to the claimants from Constanza to Basrah 'with all convenient speed'. The claimants intended to sell the sugar on the sugar market in Basrah; and, although the defendants did not know this, they did know that there was a sugar market there, and they must have known that it was not unlikely that the claimants would want to sell the sugar in that market.[18] In breach of contract the defendants called at various ports out of the direct route, taking on and discharging cargo, so that they took twenty-nine instead of twenty days to reach Basrah. During the extra nine days, the price of sugar at Basrah fell so that the claimants sold the sugar for some £4,000 less than they would gave got if the ship had gone straight to Basrah. The House of Lords held the defendants liable for this loss, since, in the light of their knowledge of the circumstances, it was one which they should reasonably have had in their contemplation. And in the circumstances it seems correct to say that they not only knew of the claimants' purpose but 'accepted' it in the sense above discussed: that is, that they contracted to get the cargo to the particular market without undue delay. On the other hand, they could not have contemplated the terms of individual transactions: accordingly, if the delay had prevented the claimants from performing an exceptionally profitable contract of sale for more than the market price, the defendants would not have been liable for this loss.[19]

Before *The Heron II* it was sometimes said that a loss was not too remote if it could reasonably have been foreseen; and the references in that case to the contemplation of the parties suggest that the House of Lords was applying a foreseeability test of some kind. Nevertheless, the case marks a change of emphasis. Reasonable foreseeability is also established as a test of remoteness in the law of tort; and in that branch of the law a reasonable person is credited with the capacity to foresee some consequences which are by no means obvious or even very probable. In the law of contract a much higher degree of foreseeability is required. There must, as it was put in *The Heron II* be

---

17 [1969] 1 AC 350.
18 [1969] 1 AC 350 at 382; cf *The Baleares* [1993] 1 Lloyd's Rep 215.
19 Cf *The Rio Claro* [1987] 2 Lloyd's Rep 173; *Seven Seas Properties Ltd v Al-Essa (No 2)* [1993] 3 All ER 577.

a 'serious possibility' or a 'real danger'[20] that the loss will occur; and references to 'foreseeability' as a test of remoteness in contract must be understood in this sense. This test was, for example, satisfied where defects in a pig-food hopper supplied by the defendants caused the claimants' pigs to die of a rare intestinal disease: there was a 'serious possibility' that the pigs would become ill.[1]

The requirement of a higher degree of foreseeability in contract than in tort can be justified on the ground that a contracting party can often draw unusual risks to the other party's attention before the contract is made (and so make him liable for them); while the victim of a tort has no such opportunity as he usually has no previous relations with the wrongdoer.[2] But this justification would lose its force where a contracting party in fact had no such opportunity to protect himself; nor would it make sense to maintain different tests where the same facts gave rise to a cause of action both in contract and in tort.[3] In either of these situations the claimant could probably rely on the (to him) more favourable tort test. In other cases the more restrictive test stated in *The Heron II* will continue to apply to damages for breach of contract.[4]

ii   Causation

A claimant can recover damages only if there is some causal connection between the breach and his loss. Suppose that a ship founders in a storm and it is later discovered that she was technically unseaworthy because she was not carrying a proper medicine chest.[5] The unseaworthiness would be a breach of any contract which the shipowner may have made to carry goods in that ship. But the owner of those goods would not be entitled to damages merely on that account because such a breach would not normally have caused the ship to sink.[6]

On the other hand, the claimant may recover full damages even though the breach is not the sole cause of the loss. If the breach 'is one of two causes, both co-operating and both of equal efficacy, it is sufficient to carry a judgment in damages'.[7] In the leading *Monarch Steamship*[8]

---

20   [1969] 1 AC 350 at 414, 415, 425.
1   *H Parsons (Livestock) Ltd v Uttley Ingham & Co Ltd* [1978] QB 791 at 812.
2   *The Heron II* [1969] 1 AC 350 at 386.
3   Cf *Archer v Brown* [1985] QB 401 at 418.
4   *The Pegase* [1981] 1 Lloyd's Rep 175 at 181.
5   For this example of 'unseaworthiness', see *Hong Kong Fir Shipping Co Ltd v Kawasaki Kisen Kaisha Ltd* [1962] 2 QB 26 at 62.
6   *Monarch Steamship Co Ltd v A/B Karlshamns Oljefabriker* [1949] AC 196 at 226.
7   *Heskell v Continental Express Ltd* [1950] 1 All ER 1033 at 1048; cf *The Silver Sky* [1981] 2 Lloyd's Rep 95.
8   Supra, n 6.

case a contract was made in April 1939 to carry goods from Manchuria to Sweden. The ship was delayed by unseaworthiness and so failed to get to Sweden before the outbreak of war in September 1939. Instead she was ordered to a Scottish port where the goods had to be transferred to neutral vessels. The carriers were held liable for the cost of transhipment even though the loss was caused by a combination of unseaworthiness and the acts of the British authorities. Neither factor was the sole cause of the loss, and both could be said to have operated with 'equal efficacy'. Similarly, a ship does not usually sink *merely* because she is unseaworthy; and the shipowner will often be liable if the loss is caused by a combination of unseaworthiness and ordinary sea perils. On the other hand, it was said in the *Monarch Steamship* case that the shipowner would not be liable if the ship had been delayed by unseaworthiness and then been struck by a typhoon, for in that case the unseaworthiness would have had no 'real' but only a 'fortuitous' connection with the loss.[9]

iii Mitigation

The victim of a breach of contract is said to be under a 'duty to mitigate' his loss. The word 'duty' is here used in an unusual sense. It merely means that the victim is not entitled to recover damages for a loss that he should have avoided: not that he is liable for failing to avoid it. This 'duty' has two aspects.

First, the injured party must take all reasonable steps to minimise his loss. One application of this principle has already been considered. When a buyer fails to accept and pay for goods, or a seller to deliver them, the injured party is expected to go into the market and to make a substitute contract at the relevant time, which is prima facie the time of breach. If he fails to do so and the market then moves against him, he cannot recover the extra loss which he suffers, as this is due to his failure to mitigate.[10] Another application of the principle is that an employee who is wrongfully dismissed must make reasonable efforts to find another comparable job. The crucial point is that the injured party must, and need only,[11] act reasonably. Thus an employee who is wrongfully dismissed is not bound to take another job if this will involve an appreciable reduction in status;[12] nor is he bound to accept an offer of re-employment from an employer who has wrongfully

---

9   [1949] AC 196 at 215, approving a statement in the lower (Scottish) court: 1947 SC 179 at 193.
10   See ante, pp 382–384; cf *The Elena d'Amico* [1980] 1 Lloyd's Rep 75 at 79.
11   See *London and South of England Building Society v Stone* [1983] 3 All ER 105.
12   *Yetton v Eastwoods Froy Ltd* [1966] 3 All ER 353.

dismissed him in circumstances of personal humiliation.[13] But sometimes a party may be required to accept an offer of performance from the party in breach even on terms other than those originally agreed. In one case[14] a person who had agreed to sell crepe de chine on credit refused to deliver except for cash, and the buyer immediately bought against him in the market, which had risen. It was held that the buyer should have mitigated by accepting the seller's offer to deliver for cash. Where a seller cannot deliver on time, the buyer may similarly be required to mitigate by accepting an offer of late delivery.[15] In such cases the injured party remains entitled to damages for any loss suffered by him as a result of the difference between the newly offered performance and that originally bargained for; and if the defaulting party's offer purports to take away that right, it need not be accepted.[16]

The 'duty' to mitigate requires the injured party to make a *substitute* contract to replace that which has been broken. So far we have assumed that the new contract is indeed a true substitute for the broken one. But suppose that A reserves one of the hundred rooms in B's hotel and then in breach of contract cancels the reservation. C now wishes to book a room in the hotel. If the other ninety-nine rooms in the hotel are taken, B is bound to mitigate by letting A's room to C; but if less than ninety-nine rooms are taken, B can put C into one of the empty rooms and so claim damages from A.

The second aspect of the 'duty' to mitigate is that the injured party must not take unreasonable steps actually to increase the loss.[17] In the case just put, it would probably not be reasonable for B to spend money in getting the room ready for A's occupation *after* A had cancelled his reservation. But there are other cases in which it would be reasonable for the injured party to incur expenses after the breach – particularly if he was bound by commercial or moral obligations to third parties to do so. The point is strikingly illustrated by a case[18] in which an English firm had printed banknotes for the Bank of Portugal, and in breach of contract allowed them to get into the hands of a rogue who put them into circulation. The Bank then cancelled the notes and bought them up in exchange for good notes, even though it was not legally bound to do so. It was held that the printers were

13 *Payzu Ltd v Saunders* [1919] 2 KB 581 at 589.
14 *Payzu Ltd v Saunders* [1919] 2 KB 581.
15 *The Solholt* [1983] 1 Lloyd's Rep 605.
16 *Strutt v Whitnell* [1975] 2 All ER 510.
17 *The Borag* [1981] 1 All ER 856.
18 *Banco de Portugal v Waterlow & Sons Ltd* [1932] AC 452.

liable for the face value of the notes, and not merely for the cost of reprinting, as the Bank had acted reasonably, having regard to its commercial obligations.

The 'duty' to mitigate normally arises only after the claimant has become aware of the breach.[19] But it can probably also arise where he had, but failed to take, a clear opportunity of discovering the breach: eg where a buyer of goods is warned by the seller of the need to test them before use but fails to do so.

So far we have considered the *duty* to mitigate. The law also recognises a distinct, though related, idea: that the loss is *in fact* mitigated if the claimant has, as a result of the breach, obtained a benefit or avoided loss. This can happen in various ways. First, the claimant may benefit by being relieved of his own obligations under the contract. If a seller fails to deliver, the buyer need not pay, and the amount so saved is taken into account in assessing his loss. Secondly, he may benefit from performing his 'duty' to mitigate: for example, a wrongfully dismissed employee may get a substitute job and so receive wages. As such benefits are taken into account even if they are not obtained, it is obvious that they must equally be taken into account if they are obtained. Thirdly, he may benefit as a result of something which he did in consequence of the breach even though he was not required to do so in performing his 'duty' to mitigate. A skilled worker may be wrongfully dismissed and, if he cannot find comparable employment, he may take a job as an unskilled labourer. His actual earnings as a labourer will be taken into account in assessing damages.[20]

This example should be contrasted with a case[1] in which a contract of employment restricted the employee's right to invest in competing companies. On wrongful dismissal, the employee was freed from this restriction, and made such an investment. It was held that his profit on the investment was 'not a direct result of his dismissal' but a 'collateral benefit',[2] and that it should not be taken into account. The distinction between the two types of benefit has given rise to difficult questions of causation.[3] The claimant need not, however, bring into account benefits which he has received under a policy of insurance

---

19 *The Superhulls Cover Case (No 2)* [1990] 2 Lloyd's Rep 431 at 461.
20 Cf *Edwards v Society of Graphical and Allied Trades* [1971] Ch 354. Cf, in cases of *unfair* dismissal (which does not usually involve any *breach* of contract), Employment Rights Act 1996, s 123(4).
1 *Laverack v Woods of Colchester Ltd* [1967] 1 QB 278.
2 [1967] 1 QB 278 at 290.
3 Eg *British Westinghouse Electric and Manufacturing Co Ltd v Underground Electric Rlys Co of London Ltd* [1912] AC 673.

taken out by him against the loss caused by the breach[4] or under some other contract with a third party to compensate him for that loss.[5]

iv   *Default of the victim*

Where the victim of a breach of contract fails to mitigate, the loss is partly due to his default in the sense that he *failed to avoid* the consequences of an event brought about by the other party's breach. There is, however, another group of cases in which the event causing loss is *partly brought about* by conduct of the victim. Goods on board a ship may be damaged partly because the carrier failed to stow them properly and partly because the shipper did not provide adequate packing; or the hirer of a car may be injured partly because the brakes were defective and partly because he drove too fast. In the law of tort such conduct on the part of the victim is known as contributory negligence. At common law its effect was to bar the claim completely if the claimant had the 'last opportunity' of avoiding the accident; but where the defendant had the last opportunity the claimant recovered in full. This unsatisfactory 'all or nothing' solution was altered by the Law Reform (Contributory Negligence) Act 1945, which provides that where a person suffers loss partly as a result of his own 'fault' and partly as a result of the 'fault' of the defendant, he can nevertheless recover damages; but the court can reduce his damages in proportion to the effect which his fault had in causing the loss. 'Fault' is defined in the Act to mean 'negligence ... or other act or omission which gives rise to liability in tort or would, apart from this Act, give rise to the defence of contributory negligence'. The question arises whether the contributory negligence rules can be applied to contractual actions.

For the purpose of answering this question, the cases must be divided into three categories. First the defendant's conduct is careless and constitutes both a breach of contract and a tort: for example, where a carrier for reward failed to observe the duty of care which he owed to a passenger both under the contract and under the general law. If the passenger were injured partly as a result of this breach of duty and partly as a result of his own carelessness, then the contributory negligence rules would apply.[6] They would similarly apply where the defendant was in breach of a duty of care arising from a contract to

---

4   *Bradburn v Great Western Rly Co* (1874) LR 10 Exch 1; *The Yasin* [1979] 2 Lloyd's Rep 45; contrast *Mark Rowlands Ltd v Berni Inns Ltd* [1986] QB 211, where the rule was excluded by the terms of the contract.

5   *Gardner v Marsh and Parsons* [1997] 1 WLR 489.

6   Cf *Sayers v Harlow UDC* [1958] 2 All ER 342; *Sole v W J Hallt Ltd* [1973] QB 574.

render professional services;[7] for such a breach generally gives rise to liability in both contract and tort.[8] Secondly, the defendant is in breach of contract without being in any way careless.[9] In such a case the Law Reform (Contributory Negligence) Act could not apply because the definition of 'fault' in the Act connotes some degree of carelessness; and the question whether the defendant was liable in full or not at all would depend on the principles of causation discussed earlier in this chapter. Thus in one case[10] a dealer supplied a defective trailer coupling to a customer who went on using it, after it was obviously broken, until there was an accident. It was held that the dealer was not liable as the accident had been caused by the customer's use of the coupling when he knew that it was broken, and not by the fact that it was defective when sold. Thirdly, the defendant is liable for breach of a contractual duty of care, but that carelessness does not make him liable in tort. Conflicting views have been expressed in the cases on the question whether the Act applies to such a situation.[11]

In the situations so far discussed, the loss is caused partly by the defendant's (A's) breach of contract and partly by the claimant's (B's) careless conduct; but B's conduct does not amount to a legal wrong against A. Where B's conduct does amount to such a wrong[12] and each party suffers loss, those losses may be apportioned (quite apart from the Act) on the ground that they resulted from two independent actionable wrongs. Each party can then recover to the extent that his loss was caused by the other's wrongful act.[13] Thus if responsibility for the event were equally divided between the parties, each would be liable for half the loss suffered by the other.

7   *De Meza v Apple* [1974] 1 Lloyd's Rep 508 (auditor); affd [1975] 1 Lloyd's Rep 498 where the applicability of the 1945 Act was left open; *Forsikringsaktieselskapet Vesta v Butcher* [1989] AC 852; affd without reference to this point at 880 et seq.

8   *Esso Petroleum Co Ltd v Mardon* [1976] QB 801 at 819; *Midland Bank Trust Co Ltd v Hett Stubbs & Kemp* [1979] Ch 384; *Henderson v Merrett Syndicates Ltd* [1995] 2 AC 145; except where the contract exhaustively defines the defendant's duty: *Greater Nottingham Co-operative Society Ltd v Cementation Piling Foundations Ltd* [1989] QB 71.

9   See ante, p 314.

10   *Lambert v Lewis* [1982] AC 225; cf *Barclays Bank plc v Fairclough Building Ltd* [1995] 1 All ER 289.

11   Contrast *De Meza v Apple* [1974] 1 Lloyd's Rep 508; affd [1975] 1 Lloyd's Rep 498 (where the point was left open) and *Quinn v Burch Bros (Builders) Ltd* [1966] 2 QB 370 at 380–383 with *Forsikringsaktieselskapet Vesta v Butcher,* supra, n 7; the Law Commission has recommended that there should be power to reduce damages in such cases: Law Com No 219 (1993).

12   See *Raflatac v Eade* [1999] 1 Lloyd's Rep 506, where this requirement was not satisfied.

13   *Tennant Radiant Heat Ltd v Warrington Development Corpn* [1988] 1 EGLR 41.

v   Failure to pay money

The obvious remedy for failure to pay a fixed sum of money when due
is an action for that sum; but a breach of this kind gives rise to the
further problem whether interest or other damages can be recovered
in respect of such a breach. The general rule of common law is that
interest can be recovered only if the contract provides for it to be
paid; but this rule is subject to two statutory modifications. First, there
is a right to 'statutory interest' where the contract is one for the supply
of goods or services between parties acting in the course of a business.[14]
Secondly, the court has a discretionary power (applicable to all
contracts) to award interest so long as the action for recovery of the
principal sum is begun before that sum has been paid.[15] If the contract
is not one under which there is a right to 'statutory interest' and if the
payment is simply made late, the person to whom it was due cannot
then claim interest unless the contract so provides. The common law
rule can work hardship in times of high interest rates or tight credit
but it survives in spite of repeated criticism.[16] It used, moreover, to be
thought that no further damages (other than interest) could be
recovered for failure to pay money when due.[17] But this rule, too, was
hard to justify;[18] and it no longer prevents a claimant from recovering
special damages if he can show that he has suffered a particular loss
which is not too remote.[19] Thus in one case[20] the defendant was late
in making a substantial payment, knowing that the claimant needed
it to complete the purchase of a farm as his home. As a result of the
delay, the claimant incurred extra charges in connection with this
purchase; and he recovered these as damages for late payment.
Damages can similarly be recovered where a bank wrongfully refuses
to honour a customer's cheque;[1] and where a person fails to perform
an undertaking to subscribe for debentures in a company,[2] or to
provide a letter of credit under a contract for the sale of goods.[3]

---

14   Late Payment of Commercial Debts (Interest) Act 1998.
15   Supreme Court Act 1981, s 35A.
16   *London Chatham and Dover Rly Co v South Eastern Rly Co* [1893] AC 429 at
      437; *La Pintada* [1985] AC 104; Law Com No 88 (partly implemented by the
      1998 Act, supra, n 14).
17   *Fletcher v Tayleur* (1855) 17 CB 21 at 29.
18   *Wallis v Smith* (1882) 21 Ch D 243 at 257 ('not quite consistent with reason').
19   *The Lips* [1988] AC 395 at 423, 429; *International Minerals and Chemical
      Corpn v Karl O Helm AG* [1986] 1 Lloyd's Rep 81.
20   *Wadsworth v Lydall* [1981] 2 All ER 401, approved in *La Pintada* [1985] AC
      104 at 127.
1   *Prehn v Royal Bank of Liverpool* (1870) LR 5 Exch 92.
2   *Wallis Chlorine Syndicate Ltd v American Alkali Co Ltd* (1901) 17 TLR 656.
3   *Trans Trust SPRL v Danubian Trading Co Ltd* [1952] 2 QB 297.

e Penalties and liquidated damages

Under the rules so far discussed, the amount which will be recoverable on breach of contract is often hard to predict. The parties may try to remove this uncertainty by providing that a fixed sum is to be paid[4] on breach. If the sum is a reasonable estimate of the probable loss, the provision will at common law[5] be valid; a provision of this kind is known as a *liquidated damages* clause. Sometimes, however, the purpose of the provision is not to make a genuine pre-estimate of loss but to bring pressure to bear on one of the parties to perform his part of the contract. Such a provision is known as a *penalty* clause and is invalid.

i Rules for distinguishing between them

The category into which a particular clause falls depends on the construction of the clause as a whole. Thus the mere fact that the parties have called it a 'liquidated damages' or 'penalty' clause is not decisive either way. In the leading case of *Dunlop Co Ltd v New Garage Ltd* [6] four rules of construction were formulated for distinguishing between the two types of provisions.

The first, and most important, rule is that a clause is penal 'if the sum stipulated for is extravagant and unconscionable in amount in comparison with the greatest loss that could conceivably be proved to have followed from the breach'. An illustration given in one of the cases, though far-fetched, catches the spirit of the rule: it would be a penalty if a builder promised to pay £1 million on failure to do building work worth £50.[7]

The second rule is that a provision will be regarded as a valid liquidated damages clause if 'the consequences of breach are such as to make precise pre-estimation an impossibility'; and if the actual amount also bears a reasonable relation to the probable consequences of breach. In the *Dunlop* case itself, a contract for the sale of tyres imposed numerous restrictions on resales and provided that the buyer should pay the seller £5 for every tyre sold or offered in breach of these restrictions.[8] This provision was held valid since such breaches

---

4   Or that a 'payment in kind' or a share transfer at an undervalue is to be made: see *Jobson v Johnson* [1989] 1 All ER 621.

5   For possible effects of the Unfair Terms in Consumer Contracts Regulations 1999, see post, p 403.

6   [1915] AC 79 at 87–88 (the order in which the rules are stated in the text differs, for purposes of exposition, from that in the *Law Reports*).

7   *Clydebank Engineering Co Ltd v Don Jose Ramos Yzquierdo y Castaneda* [1905] AC 6 at 10.

8   For the possible effects of competition law on such agreements, see ante, p 208.

had a general tendency to disrupt the seller's business organisation, though the exact loss flowing from each breach was almost impossible to quantify.

The third rule lays down a presumption that a clause is penal if it makes the same sum payable on one or more of several breaches which must cause different amounts of loss. For example in one case[9] a lease provided that the tenant should pay £3 'for every ton of *hay or straw* which shall be sold off the premises during the last twelve months of the tenancy'. This was held to be a penalty because hay was worth more than straw. Similarly, a provision in a hire-purchase agreement would be a penalty if it provided that three-quarters of the hire-purchase price should be paid on the hirer's default as compensation for depreciation; for the depreciation would obviously be greater if the hirer defaulted in the twelfth month than it would be if he defaulted in the first.[10] The rule can, however, give rise to some very odd results. If it applies, the clause is invalid even though the actual breach is quite a serious one, and one for which the stipulated sum would be a reasonable pre-estimate.[11] But there are various ways of avoiding this result. One is for the court to construe the clause so as to apply only to the serious breach which has actually occurred.[12] Another is to disregard remote possibilities, in which (had they occurred) the stipulated sum would have greatly exceeded the claimant's loss, and to uphold the clause if at the time of contracting that sum was reasonable in relation to the *probable* consequences of the breach.[13] It is finally possible to circumvent the rule by proportioning the sum payable to the seriousness of the breach, or to its probable effects. In the hire-purchase cases, for example, the amount payable as compensation for depreciation can be increased in proportion to the time for which the hirer has had the goods (making allowance for payments which he has made under the agreement).[14] Similarly, where the breach consists of delay, the contract may provide that a fixed sum is to be paid for each week (or other period) of delay.[15]

The fourth rule deals with the situation in which the breach consists only in not paying a fixed sum of money and the contract provides in that event for the payment of a greater sum: eg for the payment of

---

9   *Willson v Love* [1896] 1 QB 626.
10   *Landom Trust Ltd v Hurrell* [1955] 1 All ER 839.
11   *Ariston SRL v Charly Records Ltd* (1990) Financial Times, 21 March.
12   See *Webster v Bosanquet* [1912] AC 394 'any part' held to mean 'any *substantial* part').
13   *Philips Hong Kong Ltd v A-G of Hong Kong* (1993) 61 BLR 41.
14   Eg *Phonographic Equipment (1958) Ltd v Muslu* [1961] 3 All ER 626.
15   *Clydebank Engineering* case [1905] AC 6.

£1,000 on failure to pay £50 when due. Such a provision is penal, but this obviously sensible result could be explained simply on the ground that the sum of £1,000 was 'extravagant and unconscionable'. Taken literally, however, the fourth rule can apply even where this is not the case, eg where £55 is due on failure punctually to pay £50. The view that such a provision was penal was formerly based on the view that no damages (other than interest) could ever be awarded for failure to pay money when due. But special damages can now be recovered for such a breach if the creditor can show that the delay has caused a particular loss which is not too remote;[16] and it may be that the present rule too, will no longer apply where it was likely, at the time of contracting, that late payment would cause such loss. Unless the rule is so limited, it can invalidate perfectly reasonable bargains, and it has therefore been interpreted restrictively. It does not, for instance, apply to a provision which merely accelerates the liability of a debtor (by providing that on his failure punctually to pay one instalment, the others shall at once become due).[17] Nor does the rule apply to a term which, in the event of a borrower's default, provides for a 'modest' increase in the rate of interest payable by him; for the fact of default makes him a less good credit risk and so provides a 'good commercial reason'[18] for such an increase. The rule can also be circumvented by providing for a discount for early payment: such a term is not a penalty.

ii Effects of the distinction

At common law, a provision for liquidated damages is fully effective. Thus on the one hand the injured party can recover the stipulated amount even though it exceeds his actual loss. On the other hand, the injured party cannot recover more than the stipulated amount even though his actual loss is greater.[19] In the latter situation, the liquidated damages clause operates to limit liability, but its legal nature is nevertheless distinct from that of a limitation of liability clause. Under a limitation clause the injured party recovers his loss up to the stipulated amount. Under a liquidated damages clause, on the other hand, the injured party simply recovers the stipulated amount and the amount of his loss (if any) is irrelevant.[20]

---

16 See ante, p 398.
17 *Protector Loan Co v Grice* (1880) 5 QBD 592; *The Angelic Star* [1988] 1 Lloyd's Rep 122.
18 *Lordsvale Finance plcv Bank of Zambia* [1966] QB 762 at 763, 767.
19 *Cellulose Acetate Silk Co Ltd v Widnes Foundry (1925) Ltd* [1933] AC 20.
20 For this reason, such clauses are probably not affected by the Unfair Contract Terms Act 1977; cf ante, p 102.

By contrast, a penalty clause is disregarded for all purposes. The injured party will therefore recover his loss in accordance with the normal rules. Usually the sum thus assessed will be less than the penalty; but the rule applies equally if the loss is greater than the penalty.[1] There are two reasons why this apparently paradoxical situation may arise. First, the question whether a stipulation is a penalty has to be determined by reference to the time of *contracting* and it is possible for a sum which was 'extravagant and unconscionable' at that time to fall short of a loss which arises at the time of *breach*. Secondly, a clause may be penal under the third or fourth of the rules of construction discussed above even though it is not 'extravagant and unconscionable' at all; and in such a case the stipulated amount may well fall short of the loss which is actually suffered and recoverable under the normal rules.

iii   Scope of the distinction

The distinction between penalties and liquidated damages only applies to sums payable *on breach*. In one case[2] a professional footballer suffered an injury which was thought to have put him permanently out of the game; and he was paid £500 under a policy of insurance on the terms that the money was to be repaid if he again played professional football. This was not a penalty since the player had made no promise not to play again and therefore committed no breach by so doing. More difficulty arises when the same sum is payable on several events of which some are breaches while others are not. For example a hire-purchase agreement may require the hirer to bring his payments up to a minimum sum if the agreement is terminated; and the agreement may be terminated *either* by the owner on account of the hirer's breach *or* by a notice given by the hirer. Here the distinction between penalties and liquidated damages applies if the agreement is terminated for breach, but not if it is lawfully terminated by notice.[3] The paradoxical result is that the hirer who terminates his contract lawfully may be worse off than one who breaks it; for in the former case he is liable for the whole of the stipulated sum, while in the latter he may be able to avoid such liability if he can show that the stipulation is a penalty. In the case of a 'regulated' consumer credit

---

1   *Wall v Rederiaktiebolaget Luggude* [1915] 3 KB 66.
2   *Alder v Moore* [1961] 2 QB 57; cf *Export Credits Guarantee Department v Universal Oil Products Co* [1983] 2 All ER 205 (distinction inapplicable to sums payable under one contract on breach of another contract with a third party).
3   *Campbell Discount Co Ltd v Bridge* [1961] 1 QB 445. On appeal, the House of Lords was evenly divided on the point: [1962] AC 600.

agreement,[4] the hirer has a statutory right to terminate on payment of half the hire-purchase price, and if he exercises this right the court may, instead of the statutory minimum payment, award such sum as will adequately compensate the owner for his loss.[5] But cases not falling within this special provision are still governed by the unsatisfactory common law rule that the distinction between penalties and liquidated damages applies only where there has been a breach.

iv Unfair Terms in Consumer Contracts Regulations 1999

Under these Regulations a standard term in a contract between a commercial seller or supplier and a consumer is prima facie unfair, and so does not bind the consumer,[6] if it requires him on failure to fulfil his obligation 'to pay a disproportionately high sum in compensation'.[7] Such a term is likely also to be invalid as a penalty at common law; but a term could be unfair under the Regulations even though it was not a penalty at common law because it was payable on an event other than a breach.[8] This could, for example, be the position where the event on which the payment was to be made was an authorised extension by the consumer of the contract period: eg where a contract of hire gave him the option to retain the goods after the end of that period on payment of an unduly high 'holding fee'.[9]

f Advance payments

One of the parties to a contract may make, or agree to make, an advance payment to the other. If the payee then fails to perform he must pay the money back. But if the payor defaults after making the payment the rights of the parties with respect to it depend on the distinction between a deposit and a part payment.

A deposit is a sum paid 'as a guarantee that the contract shall be performed'.[10] The law starts with the principle that the payee can keep the deposit[11] (unless the contract otherwise provides). But it also makes use, in this context, of the principle on which the

---

4   Ante, p 63.
5   Consumer Credit Act 1974, s 100(1) and (3).
6   Ante, p 116.
7   SI 1999/2083, Sch 2, para 1(e).
8   Ante, p 402.
9   Cf *Interfoto Picture Library Ltd v Stiletto Visual Programmes Ltd* [1989] QB 433, where the hirer would *not* now be a 'consumer' within the Regulations.
10   *Howe v Smith* (1884) 27 Ch D 89 at 95.
11   See *Howe v Smith* (1884) 27 Ch D 89.

distinction between penalties[12] and liquidated damages[13] is based. In one case[14] a contract for the sale of land provided for the payment of a deposit of as much as 25 per cent. This was held to be a penalty as it bore no relation to the vendor's likely loss and therefore had to be repaid to the purchaser on his default. By statute, the court has a discretion to order the repayment of a deposit paid under a contract for the sale of property[15] The current view is that the discretion will be exercised only 'in exceptional circumstances',[16] so that the court will not order the return of the normal 10 per cent deposit to a purchaser of land who simply defaults.[17] A provision for the forfeiture of such a deposit is also valid at common law, even though it does not bear any relation to the vendor's loss.[18]

A part payment is simply a payment on account of the price. Whether such a payment must be returned depends in the first place on the nature of the contract under which it was made. If repayment would restore both parties to their precontract position, the money must be paid back. This is the position where a part payment is made by a buyer under a contract of sale:[19] the buyer will get his money back and the seller will keep (or get back) the subject-matter of the sale. On the other hand, where the part payment is in respect of work done by the payee under the contract, then he cannot be restored to his precontract position; and so he is entitled to keep the part payment.[20]

Again these rules can be excluded by express contrary provisions. These give rise to particular difficulty where a contract of sale provides for payment by instalments and allows the vendor to rescind the contract and to forfeit instalments already paid if the purchaser defaults. If the purchaser has made substantial payments, the operation of such forfeiture clauses can be extremely harsh. The courts will often give him 'relief against forfeiture', usually by allowing

12   See *Public Works Comr v Hills* [1906] AC 368.
13   *Pye v British Automobile Commercial Syndicate Ltd* [1906] 1 KB 425.
14   *Workers' Trust & Merchant Bank Ltd v Dojap Investments Ltd* [1993] AC 573.
15   Law of Property Act 1925, s 49(2).
16   *Omar v El-Wakil* [2001] EWCA Civ 1090, [2002] 2 P & CR 3 at [37], where it was not argued that a 31% deposit was penal; for an illustration of 'exceptional circumstances' see *Tennaro Ltd v Majorarch* [2003] EWHC 2601 (Ch); for an earlier, wider, view of the discretion, see *Schindler v Pigault* (1975) 30 P & CR 328 at 336.
17   *Michael Richards Properties Ltd v Corpn of Wardens of St Saviour's Parish, Southwark* [1975] 3 All ER 416; *Safehaven Investments Inc v Springbok Ltd* (1995) 71 P & CR 59,
18   *Workers' Trust* case [1993] AC 573 at 578.
19   *Dies v British and International Mining and Finance Corpn* [1939] 1 KB 724.
20   *Hyundai Shipbuilding and Heavy Industries Co Ltd v Pournaras* [1978] 2 Lloyd's Rep 502; *Hyundai Heavy Industries Co Ltd v Papadopoulos* [1980] 2 All ER 29; cf *The Scaptrade* [1983] 2 AC 694 at 703.

him extra time to pay.[1] But if, at the end of that time, he still cannot pay, the general view is that the vendor can enforce the forfeiture so long as he was not guilty of unconscionable conduct in procuring the contract.[2] Another view, however, is that the vendor cannot take this step if it would be unconscionable for him to keep the part payment;[3] and where the forfeited amount is excessive in relation to the vendor's actual loss this would certainly be the fairer view. Certain forfeiture clauses in standard form consumer contracts may also be subject to the Unfair Terms in Consumer Contracts Regulations 1999[4] and hence not be binding on the consumer if they are 'unfair'.

Where a deposit or part payment has been promised but not paid when due, the person to whom it was promised may rescind the contract on account of the non-payment, and the question then arises whether he can nevertheless sue for the promised payment. This depends on whether the payment, if it had been made, would have been one that he was entitled to keep under the rules just stated. Thus he can generally sue for the promised payment if it was a deposit,[5] for rescission does not retrospectively affect accrued rights. But he could not sue for the payment if, exceptionally, the deposit was one that he was liable to restore. This would be the position where the deposit was penal, or such that the court would order its return in the exercise of its discretion to do so under a contract for the sale of land.[6] Similarly, the prospective payee could not sue for a part payment due under such a contract; for it would be absurd to allow him to recover the payment in one action when he would have to return it in another.[7] But where the contract is one under which a part payment, if made, could be retained, then a promise to pay it remains enforceable after rescission of the contract.[8]

1   *Starside Properties Ltd v Mustapha* [1974] 2 All ER 567; for another form of relief, see *Jobson v Johnson* [1989] 1 All ER 621.
2   *Mussen v Van Diemen's Land Co* [1938] Ch 253; *Galbraith v Mitchenall Estates Ltd* [1965] 2 QB 473.
3   *Stockloser v Johnson* [1954] 1 QB 476 at 485, 491; cf Law Commission Working Paper No 61 Pt V.
4   SI 1999/2083 (ante, p 110), especially Sch 2, para 1(d).
5   *Dewar v Mintoft* [1912] 2 KB 373; *Millichamp v Jones* [1983] 1 All ER 267; *The Blankenstein* [1985] 1 All ER 475 at 488 (disapproving *Lowe v Hope* [1970] Ch 94).
6   See ante, p 404.
7   *McDonald v Dennys Lascelles Ltd* (1933) 48 CLR 457; *Johnson v Agnew* [1980] AC 367 at 396; cf ante, p 404 at n 19.
8   *Stocznia Gdanska SA v Latvian Shipping Co* [1998] 1 WLR 574.

3   ACTION FOR AN AGREED SUM

One of the parties to a contract generally undertakes to pay a sum of money: for example a buyer promises to pay an agreed price, or an employer promises to pay agreed wages. An action for such an agreed sum is one for specific relief,[9] and also differs from an action for damages in its practical effect, for it may lead to a different measure of recovery. Of course this is not always the case. If a seller of goods has delivered and the buyer has not paid, it makes no difference whether the seller claims the price or his loss, since his loss is in fact the amount of the price. But if damages were claimed by the seller in respect of further loss caused by the breach, it might be argued that part of that loss was not recoverable because (for example) it was too remote; or a dispute might arise as how the loss should be quantified. On a claim for an agreed sum, such issues are irrelevant, though an issue of mitigation may (as we shall see) sometimes arise. It is therefore important to know when an action for an agreed sum can be brought. This depends on three factors.

First and most obviously it depends on whether, under the terms of the contract, the duty to pay the agreed sum has arisen. Suppose an employee is under his contract entitled to wages monthly in arrears. If he is wrongfully dismissed on the second day of the month, he is entitled only to damages, and not to his agreed wages. On the other hand, goods may be sold on the terms that they are to be paid for on 1 November and to be delivered a month later. If the buyer fails to pay on 1 November, the seller can sue for the price.[10]

The right to bring an action for the price may, secondly, be restricted by rules of law. The contract may define the point at which the *duty* to pay the agreed sum arises; but it does not follow that the *action* for the price is always available at that point. Suppose that goods are sold on the terms that they are to remain the seller's property till paid for, and that they are to be paid for by cash on delivery. If the buyer wrongfully rejects the seller's tender of delivery he can be sued for damages but not for the price. Under the Sale of Goods Act 1979 the *duty* to pay arises on tender of delivery; but where no day is fixed for payment the *action* for the price becomes available only when the property in the goods has passed to the buyer.[11] The purpose of making the seller claim damages (and not the price) is to encourage him to mitigate by making efforts to resell the goods elsewhere.

---

9   See ante, p 369 and post, p 409.
10   Sale of Goods Act 1979, s 49(2).
11   Section 49(1); *Stein, Forbes & Co v County Tailoring Co* (1916) 86 LJKB 448; but see *Workman, Clark & Co Ltd v Lloyd Brazileno* [1908] 1 KB 968.

The right to sue for the agreed sum depends, thirdly, on the conduct of the injured party in relation to the other party's breach. We saw in Chapter 16 that, on wrongful repudiation, the injured party may elect either to terminate the contract or to keep it alive. If he elects to terminate, he loses any right which might otherwise have accrued to him in the future to claim the agreed sum.[12] If he elects to keep the contract alive, there are some cases in which he is clearly entitled to sue for the agreed sum. This is the position where he has already done all that is required of him to make the action available: for example, if a seller of goods at the time of the buyer's repudiation has already transferred the property in them to the buyer.[13] On the other hand, the injured party will not be entitled to sue for the agreed sum if he has not yet done all that is required of him to make the action available, and if he cannot do the required acts without the co-operation of the other party. An employee who is wrongfully dismissed cannot sue *for his wages* merely because he has throughout the period of employment declared his readiness to go back to work.[14] These are clear cases, but the position is more controversial where, at the time of breach, the injured party has not yet done what is required to make the action available, and can do it without the co-operation of the party in breach. In *White and Carter (Councils) Ltd v McGregor*[15] A agreed to advertise B's garage business for three years. B purported to cancel the contract on the day on which it was made, but A nevertheless displayed the advertisements and his claim for the agreed price was upheld by a majority of the House of Lords. A possible objection to the decision is that A should have mitigated by reletting the advertising space. If he had done this, B would not have been forced to pay for something which he did not want; and A (it is said) would have been no worse off, for he could have recovered by way of damages any amount by which the proceeds of reletting fell short of the sum to be paid by B. The argument is sound in principle, but on the facts of the case it was probably not substantiated. It assumes that the demand for advertising space exceeded the supply, so that A could have relet the space intended for B; but it was up to B to show this and the decision can be explained on the ground that B had failed to prove that A could or should so have mitigated.[16] The argument also assumes that A had no other 'legitimate interest'[17] in going ahead with

---

12 See ante, pp 343–344.
13 See preceding paragraph.
14 *Denmark Productions Ltd v Boscobel Productions Ltd* [1969] 1 QB 699; *Roberts v Elwells Engineers Ltd* [1972] 2 QB 586.
15 [1962] AC 413.
16 Cf ante, p 394.
17 *White and Carter* case [1962] AC 413 at 431.

performance. Such an interest might have arisen by reason of commitments to third parties. This was, for example, the position where a charterparty was wrongfully repudiated by the charterer. The shipowner was held entitled to insist on continued performance, and so to sue for the agreed hire; and one reason for this conclusion was that he had assigned the hire to his bank, to whom he therefore owed a duty to keep the contract in being.[18] On the other hand, where there is no such legitimate interest in insisting on continued performance, the mitigation rules can apply even to an action for the agreed sum. This view is supported by another charterparty case[19] in which the charterer undertook to make certain repairs to the ship before redelivery and to pay the agreed hire till then. He failed to do the repairs; but it was held that the owner had no legitimate interest in refusing to accept redelivery, and claiming the agreed hire, until the repairs had been done. As the cost of the repairs far exceeded the value which the ship would have had after they had been done,[20] he should have mitigated by accepting redelivery of the unrepaired ship; and his only remedy was in damages.

4   SPECIFIC ENFORCEMENT IN EQUITY

A contract is specifically enforced when the court orders the defendant actually to perform his undertaking. Such an order may be positive or negative according to the nature of the undertaking. The court may (positively) order the defendant to do something, for example to convey a house, or to deliver a picture. Such an order is known as one of specific performance. Alternatively, the court may (negatively) order the defendant to forbear from doing something which he has promised not to do, for example it may restrain him from competing with the claimant. Such an order is known as an injunction.

Disobedience of an order of specific performance or of an injunction is contempt of court, and can be punished in the last resort by imprisonment of the defendant. This drastic effect of the remedy[1] is one factor that accounts for restrictions on its scope. But it is not decisive where effect can be given to the court's order in other ways, without putting the defendant under personal constraint:[2] for

18   *The Odenfeld* [1978] 2 Lloyd's Rep 357.
19   *Attica Sea Carriers Corpn v Ferrostaal Poseidon Bulk Reederei GmbH* [1976] 1 Lloyd's Rep 250; cf *The Alaskan Trader* [1983] 2 Lloyd's Rep 645.
20   Cf ante, p 382.
1   *Co-operative Insurance Society Ltd v Argyll Stores (Holdings) Ltd* [1998] AC 1 at 12.
2   *Miliangos v George Frank (Textiles) Ltd* [1976] AC 443 at 494, 497; *The Messiniaki Tolmi* [1983] 2 AC 787.

example, by ordering the delivery of conveyance of something to the claimant. Recognition of this point accounts for some expansion in the scope of the remedy; but this continues to be limited by other factors which make specific enforcement undesirable or impracticable on grounds to be discussed below. These factors[3] do not, however, restrict the availability of the action for an agreed sum. Although this is a form of specific enforcement, it results merely in an award of money which can be enforced by levying execution on the defendant's property.

a   Specific performance

The common law did not specifically enforce obligations except those to pay money. With this exception, there was, and is, no *right* to specific performance: the remedy is equitable and (like most such remedies) discretionary. Its scope is limited in a number of ways, of which the following are the most important.

i   Damages must be 'inadequate'

Specific performance will not be ordered where the claimant can be adequately protected by an award of damages. This will generally be the case where he has bought shares or generic goods which are available in the market.[4] On the seller's default, the buyer can go into the market, get a substitute, and recover any extra cost by way of damages. Specific performance will, on the other hand, be ordered where no satisfactory substitute can be obtained: for example where the sale is of land or of a house (however ordinary), or of 'unique' goods such as an heirloom or a great work of art.[5] Cases which formerly took a narrow view of this category[6] are open to question now that the courts tend to ask, not whether damages are 'adequate', but whether specific performance is the more appropriate remedy.[7] The category of 'unique' goods has been expanded to include such 'commercially

---

3   Post, pp 410–414. The 'adequacy' of damages (infra at n 4) may, however, be relevant in an action for the agreed sum to the issue of 'legitimate interest' (ante, pp 407–408).
4   *Re Schwabacher* (1907) 98 LT 127 at 128.
5   Eg *Pusey v Pusey* (1684) 1 Vern 273.
6   *Cohen v Roche* [1927] 1 KB 169 (set of Hepplewhite chairs not 'unique').
7   *Beswick v Beswick* [1968] AC 58; *Evans Marshall & Co v Bertola SA* [1973] 1 WLR 349 at 379; *Rainbow Estates Ltd v Tokenhold Ltd* [1999] Ch 64 at 72–73.

unique' things as ships or machinery[8] for which no satisfactory substitute is available to the claimant[9]; and specific relief has been ordered even of a contract to supply generic goods needed by the buyer for his business and not available from another source because of a temporary shortage of supply.[10] Damages may also be regarded as the less appropriate remedy for other reasons, such as the difficulty of assessing them. Thus a contract to execute a mortgage as security for a loan,[11] and a contract that a debt is to be repaid out of specific property[12] can be specifically enforced since the exact value of having such security rights is uncertain. Damages are also unlikely to be the most appropriate remedy for a consumer who has bought an appliance that does not work. Specific performance is therefore available against a commercial seller of goods to a consumer where the goods are defective by reason of the seller's breach and the buyer seeks their repair or replacement.[13]

ii   Discretion of the court

The court has a discretion to refuse specific performance even where this remedy would be a more appropriate one than damages. This discretion (which cannot be excluded by the terms of the contract[14]) is, however, 'to be governed as far as possible by fixed rules and principles'.[15] In particular, there are three grounds on which the remedy may be refused.

The first is undue hardship to the defendant. On this ground specific performance may be refused where the cost of performance to the defendant is wholly out of proportion to the benefit which performance will confer on the claimant;[16] or where, as a result of severe financial misfortune and incapacitating illness, specific performance would cause exceptional personal distress to the

---

8   *Behnke v Bede Shipping Co Ltd* [1927] 1 KB 649; *The Oro Chief* [1983] 2 Lloyd's Rep 509 at 520–521.
9   See *Société des Industries Metallurgiques SA v Bronx Engineering Co Ltd* [1975] 1 Lloyd's Rep 465; *The Stena Nautica (No 2)* [1982] 2 Lloyd's Rep 336.
10   *Sky Petroleum Ltd v VIP Petroleum Ltd* [1974] 1 All ER 954 (petrol during 1973–1974 energy crisis).
11   *Ashton v Corrigan* (1871) LR 13 Eq 76.
12   See *Swiss Bank Corpn v Lloyds Bank Ltd* [1982] AC 584 (where the contract was held to contain no such term).
13   Sale of Goods Act 1979, s 48E(2); for limitations, see s 48E(3).
14   *Quadrant Visual Communications Ltd v Hutchison Telephone (UK) Ltd* [1993] BCLC 442.
15   *Lamare v Dixon* (1873) LR 6 HL 414 at 423.
16   *Tito v Waddell (No 2)* [1977] Ch 106 at 326; cf *Redland Bricks Ltd v Morris* [1970] AC 652.

defendant.[17] But specific performance would not be refused merely because the vendor of a house was caught on a rising market and so had difficulty in buying another house with the proceeds of sale.[18]

Secondly, specific performance may be refused because the contract itself was grossly unfair. For this purpose it is not enough for a seller to show simply that the price was too low; but the remedy will be refused if, in addition, the buyer took unfair advantage of his superior knowledge or if he exploited his superior bargaining strength by rushing the other party into the transaction. Thus where an antique dealer bought valuable china jars from a widow for a fifth of their real value it was said that he could not specifically enforce the contract.[19] Specific performance can similarly be refused on the ground that the claimant's failure to disclose his own breach has reduced the value of the subject-matter.[20]

Thirdly, specific performance may be refused if the court in some other way disapproves of the claimant's conduct: for example, if he refuses to perform a promise which was neither binding contractually (because it was not so intended) nor operative as a misrepresentation (because it related to the future).[1] Unfair conduct of the claimant may suffice even if it does not amount to a breach of any promise. Thus specific enforcement of a solus agreement[2] against a garage was refused where the oil company, by giving discounts to other garages, had made it impossible for the defendant to trade except at a loss.[3]

iii Personal service

The court will not specifically enforce a contract of personal service.[4] One reason for this rule was that to order the employee to work would unduly interfere with his personal liberty; and it is now provided by statute that no court shall compel an employee to do any work by ordering specific performance of a contract of employment or by restraining the breach of such a contract by injunction.[5] Conversely it was thought that to order specific enforcement against the employer would be a futile attempt to enforce the continuance of a 'personal'

---

17 *Patel v Ali* [1984] Ch 283.
18 *Mountford v Scott* [1975] Ch 258.
19 *Falcke v Gray* (1859) 4 Drew 651.
20 *Quadrant Visual Communications Ltd v Hutchison Telephone (UK) Ltd* [1993] BCLC 442.
1 *Lamare v Dixon* (1873) LR 6 HL 414.
2 See ante, p 205.
3 *Shell UK Ltd v Lostock Garage Ltd* [1976] 1 WLR 1187.
4 *Johnson v Shrewsbury and Birmingham Rly Co* (1853) 3 De GM & G 914.
5 Trade Union and Labour Relations (Consolidation) Act 1992, s 236.

relationship against the wish of one of the parties. the principle is maintained in the law relating to unfair dismissal (which may not be a breach of contract at all). The employer may be ordered to reinstate or re-engage the employee;[6] but if he refuses to do so, the employee's remedy, in the last resort, is an award of compensation. The same is true of statutory rights such as the right to return to work after maternity, parental or paternity leave[7] and the right not to be excluded or expelled from a trade union.[8]

As a practical matter, however, an employer may actually be forced to reinstate an employee whom he would rather dismiss; or to dismiss one whom he is quite willing to keep. The courts have recognised these changes in the nature of the employment relationship. In one case[9] an employer was forced by union pressure to dismiss an employee in breach of contract. The court restrained the dismissal and thus in effect reinstated the employee. Reinstatement can also be ordered where the relation between the parties is not a purely contractual one: for example where a public employee is dismissed in violation of statutory conditions governing his employment.[10] The Visitor of a university also has power to order the reinstatement of a lecturer who has been dismissed in violation of the university's statutes.[11]

iv Other contracts

Specific performance will not be ordered of a promise without consideration, even though it is binding at law because it is made by deed.[12] The reason for the rule is that equity will not aid a 'volunteer' (ie a person who has given no consideration).[13] A contract will not be specifically enforced against a party who has the right to terminate it, for he could, by exercising that right, make the order of court nugatory.[14] A contract which is sufficiently certain to be legally binding

---

6   Employment Rights Act 1996, ss 113–117. Reinstatement or re-engagement is in practice rare: *Johnson v Unisys Ltd* [2001] UKHL 13, [2003] 1 AC 518 at [23], [78].

7   Employment Rights Act 1996, Pt VIII.

8   Trade Union and Labour Relations (Consolidation) Act 1992, ss 174–177.

9   *Hill v CA Parsons & Co Ltd* [1972] Ch 305; cf *Irani v Southampton and South West Hampshire Health Authority* [1985] ICR 590; *Powell v Brent London Borough Council* [1988] ICR 176.

10   *Malloch v Aberdeen Corpn* [1971] 2 All ER 1278.

11   *Thomas v University of Bradford* [1987] AC 795 at 824; *Pearce v University of Aston in Birmingham (No 2)* [1991] 2 All ER 469 at 475.

12   See *Cannon v Hartley* [1949] Ch 213.

13   Ante, pp 33, 275.

14   *Sheffield Gas Consumers Co v Harrison* (1853) 17 Beav 294; *Gregory v Wilson* (1852) 9 Hare 683.

may yet be too vague to be specifically enforceable. As disobedience of an order of specific performance may lead to imprisonment, the defendant must be told by the order exactly what he is to do. Thus a contract to publish an article cannot be specifically enforced if the text has not been agreed.[15]

v   *Difficulty of supervision*

Specific performance is sometimes refused on the ground that the defendant has undertaken continuous duties, the performance of which the court cannot, or is unwilling to, supervise. On this ground, specific performance has been refused of a landlord's undertaking to have a porter 'constantly in attendance';[16] of a contract to deliver goods by instalments;[17] and of a contract to do building work.[18] In the leading *Argyll Stores* case,[19] the House of Lords similarly refused specifically to enforce a covenant in a 31-year lease of a supermarket to keep the premises 'open for retail business' at the usual hours. This refusal was, however, based not merely on difficulty of supervision, but also on the ground that it was not in the public interest to force the defendant to carry on trading at a loss when damages were a suitable alternative remedy. This reasoning suggests that 'difficulty' of supervision is no longer decisive but must be balanced against the claimant's interest in specific enforcement. Thus where the duties are not to be performed by the defendant personally, he can be ordered to enter into a contract to procure their performance: such an order has been made against a lessor of luxury flats who had covenanted to employ a resident porter to perform certain specified tasks.[20] And contracts to build can be specifically enforced if the work to be done is sufficiently defined, the defendant is in possession of the land, and damages would not adequately compensate the claimant.[1] In such cases, the court will not need to supervise the building operation. It will merely have to 'examine the finished work'[2] and, where this is alleged to be defective, such supervision can be carried out by an expert appointed by the court instead of by the court itself.

---

15   *Joseph v National Magazine Co Ltd* [1959] Ch 14.
16   *Ryan v Mutual Tontine Westminster Chambers Association* [1893] 1 Ch 116.
17   *Dominion Coal Co Ltd v Dominion Iron and Steel Co Ltd* [1909] AC 293.
18   *Flint v Brandon* (1803) 8 Ves 159.
19   *Co-operative Insurance Society Ltd v Argyll Stores (Holdings) Ltd* [1998] AC 1.
20   *Posner v Scott-Lewis* [1987] Ch 25.
1   Eg *Wolverhampton Corpn v Emmons* [1901] 1 KB 515; *Jeune v Queens Cross Properties Ltd* [1974] Ch 97; cf *Channel Tunnel Group Ltd v Balfour Beatty Construction Ltd* [1993] AC 334; Landlord and Tenant Act 1985, s 17.
2   *Argyll Stores* case [1998] AC 1 at 13.

vi   Impossibility

The court will not order specific enforcement of an obligation, the performance of which is impossible. If, for example, a husband agreed to sell land belonging to his wife, he could not be ordered to convey it.[3] Nor will the court specifically enforce an agreement to assign a lease if (under the terms of the lease) the assignment requires the consent of the landlord, and he refuses to give his consent.[4]

vii   Mutuality of remedy

Under the so-called doctrine of mutuality of remedy, specific performance will not be ordered if the court cannot at the same time ensure that the unperformed obligations of the claimant will also be specifically performed.[5] Suppose that A promises to convey a house to B in return for B's promise to work for A for 10 years. Here B cannot get specific performance against A because his own promise to work cannot be specifically enforced against him. The reason why the court will not force A to convey the land is that it cannot ensure that he will receive the services from B. If the court did order A to convey and B then refused to do the work, A could only claim damages; and if B were insolvent this remedy would be worth very little. Obviously this reasoning would not apply if B claimed specific performance *after* he had done the work; and in such a case B's claim would succeed.[6] As our example shows, the question whether the requirement of mutuality is satisfied has to be determined by reference to the state of affairs at the time of the hearing[7] – not (as was formerly thought) to that at the time of contracting.

b   Injunction

Where a contract contains a negative promise (such as a promise not to build, or not to compete), the breach of that promise may be restrained by injunction. Such an order is known as a prohibitory injunction where it directs the defendant not to break the promise in the future; and as a mandatory injunction where it directs the defendant to undo a breach committed in the past: eg to pull down a house built in breach of a restrictive covenant.[8]

3   See *Castle v Wilkinson* (1870) 5 Ch App 534. Cf *Watts v Spence* [1976] Ch 165.
4   *Warmington v Miller* [1973] QB 877.
5   *Price v Strange* [1978] Ch 337 at 367–368.
6   *Price v Strange* [1978] Ch 337; cf *Sutton v Sutton* [1984] Ch 184.
7   *Price v Strange* [1978] Ch 337.
8   As in *Wakeham v Wood* (1982) 43 P & CR 40.

The principles governing injunctions to some extent resemble those governing specific performance. An injunction may, for example, be refused where its grant would be oppressive to the defendant and where damages could readily be assessed and would adequately compensate the claimant.[9] An injunction will also be refused if its practical effect would be to compel the performance of a contract which is not specifically enforceable. For example an injunction will not be granted to restrain an employee from breaking his obligation to work[10] or (normally[11]) to restrain an employer from dismissing the employee.[12] This would be so even if the contract contained a provision which was negative in form, such as a promise 'not to resign' or 'not to dismiss' for a given period.

A contract which is not specifically enforceable may, however, contain a narrower negative promise. In the leading case of *Lumley v Wagner*[13] the defendant agreed to sing at the claimant's theatre twice a week for three months, and she also promised not to use her talents at any other theatre during that period. She was restrained by injunction from breaking this negative promise. In such cases the effect of the injunction may be to put some pressure on the defendant to perform the positive obligation. But that is no objection to the granting of the injunction unless the pressure is so severe as to be, for practical purposes, irresistible. In one case[14] a film actress was restrained from breaking a promise not to act for third parties: it was said that she could still earn her living by doing other work. But in a contrasting case[15] a pop group had appointed the claimant as their manager for five years and promised not to make recordings for anyone else. An injunction to restrain the group from breaking this promise was refused as it would 'as a practical matter' force them to continue to employ the claimant. Where an employee promises not to work *in any capacity* except for the employer, an injunction to restrain the breach of that promise will normally be refused;[16] for were it granted the only 'choice' left to the employee would be one between remaining idle and performing his positive obligation to work. The employer can, however obtain an injunction if he undertakes that,

9   *Jaggard v Sawyer* [1995] 2 All ER 189; cf ante, p 410 (undue hardship).
10 *Whitwood Chemical Co v Hardman* [1891] 2 Ch 416.
11 For an exception see ante, p 412.
12 *Chappell v Times Newspapers Ltd* [1975] 2 All ER 233.
13 (1852) 1 De CM & G 604.
14 *Warner Bros Pictures Inc v Nelson* [1937] 1 KB 209.
15 *Page One Records Ltd v Britton* [1968] 1 WLR 157; cf *Warren v Mendy* [1989] 3 All ER 103.
16 *Ehrman v Bartholomew* [1898] 1 Ch 671.

while the injunction is in force, he will go on paying the employee[17] and give him the opportunity of continuing to work for the employer where this is necessary to maintain the employee's skill and reputation.[18]

The fear of putting too much pressure on an employee is further reflected in the rule that an injunction will be issued against him only where the contract contains an *express* negative promise. But where no question of employment is involved, the courts will sometimes *imply* a negative promise in a contract which is not specifically enforceable. If, for example, A makes a promise (positive in form) to buy *all* his requirements of coal from B for a specified period, a negative promise (not to buy elsewhere) can readily be implied, and be enforced by injunction.[19] This may, indeed, put pressure on him to buy from B. But, in cases of sale, direct specific performance is refused, not because it is *undesirable* in itself (as a form of undue personal constraint), but simply because it is thought to be *unnecessary* (damages being regarded as an appropriate remedy). Hence the objection to indirect specific performance through an injunction is less strong in the sale than in the employment cases.

c   Damages and specific performance or injunction

Power to award damages in addition to or 'in substitution for ... specific performance' or injunction was conferred on the Court of Chancery by an Act of 1858 and is now vested in the High Court.[20] That court has power to grant all remedies to which a party is entitled:[1] eg to award damages as well as, or instead of, specific relief. Normally there is therefore little point in invoking the power created by the 1858 Act, but there are still situations in which it may be to the claimant's advantage to do so. In particular, damages may be awarded under the Act even though there is as yet no cause of action at law: eg where an anticipatory breach has *not* been 'accepted'[2] and specific performance is sought before the time fixed for performance.[3]

There was also formerly some support for the view that, while at common law damages were to be assessed by reference to the time of

17   *Evening Standard Co Ltd v Henderson* [1987] ICR 588; cf *Delaney v Staples* [1992] 1 AC 687 at 692–693.
18   *Provident Financial Group plc v Hayward* [1989] ICR 160.
19   Cf *Metropolitan Electric Supply Co Ltd v Ginder* [1901] 2 Ch 799.
20   Supreme Court Act 1981, s 50.
1   Supreme Court Act 1981, s 49.
2   See ante, p 348.
3   For specific performance in such a case, see *Hasham v Zenab* [1960] AC 316.

breach,[4] under the Act they were to be assessed by reference to the time of judgment.[5] This was thought to follow from the fact that under the Act damages were awarded '*in substitution* ... *for* specific *performance*'; for if the value of the subject-matter had risen between the time of breach and the time of judgment damages assessed by reference to the time of breach would, it was said, be no true substitute for performance. But the common law also pursues the general objective of putting the claimant into the position in which he would have been '*if* the contract had been *performed*'.[6] This seems to mean much the same as the words quoted from the 1858 Act; and we have also seen that the common law does not invariably assess damages by reference to the time of breach.[7] The House of Lords has therefore held that, where the same breach gives rise to a claim for damages at common law and is also one in respect of which the court has power to order specific relief,[8] then the damages for that breach are to be assessed in the same way under the Act as at common law.[9] In particular, if the claimant ought to have made a substitute contract, damages will be assessed by reference to the time when that contract should have been made. The claimant cannot, on a rising market, inflate his damages by asking for them to be assessed under the Act at the later time of judgment; for to allow him to do so would conflict with the requirement that he must take all reasonable steps to mitigate his loss.[10]

5 RESTITUTIONARY REMEDIES

A claim for restitution on breach of contract is a claim for the return of the injured party's performance, or one for its reasonable value. Assuming that the injured party is entitled to restitution, the nature of his remedy depends on the kind of benefit which he has conferred on the party in breach. If the injured party has made a payment of money, he can get it back; if he has rendered some other performance, he is entitled to its reasonable value.

---

4   See ante, p 387.
5   *Wroth v Tyler* [1974] Ch 30.
6   *Robinson v Harman* (1848) 1 Exch 850 at 855; ante, p 376.
7   See ante, pp 387–388.
8   See *Jaggard v Sawyer* [1995] 2 All ER 189; *Surrey County Council v Bredero Homes Ltd* [1993] 3 All ER 705, where the right to specific relief had been lost by lapse of time; for this case, see ante, p 370, n 9.
9   *Johnson v Agnew* [1980] AC 367 at 400.
10 See ante, p 393.

a   **Recovery of money**

A person who has paid money under a contract can recover it back in the following circumstances.

i   'Total failure of consideration'

First, he can do so if there has been a 'total failure of consideration'. The word 'consideration' is here (rather confusingly) used in a sense different from that which it bears in relation to the formation of contracts. There it can, and often does, refer to a promise to perform. Here it generally refers to the *performance* of the promise.[11] There is a 'total failure of consideration' if the claimant has not received any part of the performance for which he bargained. This would be the position if a buyer of goods paid in advance and the seller failed to deliver. In such a case the buyer can, at his option, claim damages or the return of his money. He will take the former course if the market has risen and the latter if it has fallen. As a general rule, money can be only reclaimed if the failure of consideration is *total* and not if it is only *partial*.[12] The failure would, for example, be partial where A paid B in advance for a month's work and B left in breach of contract after ten days. In such a case it would be unfair to allow A to get back all his money when he had had the benefit of B's work for the ten days; and it might not be satisfactory to allow him to get back a proportionate part, since the hardest part of B's work might have come at the beginning. Where there is no such difficulty in making an apportionment, the person making the advance payment may sometimes be able to get back part of it. Suppose that A pays B £100 in advance for five tons of coal and B delivers only three tons. Here A can keep the three tons and get back £40.[13] The position is the same where the promise which is performed only in part is one by a borrower of money to make payments due under the contract of loan.[14]

There may, moreover, be a 'total' failure of consideration even though the claimant has received *some* benefit under the contract, if that was not *the* benefit for which he bargained. Suppose that A sells a car to B, and that at the time of the sale A and B in good faith believe that the car belongs to A. But in fact it belongs to X, who, some months later, traces it and claims it from B. Here B has had the use of the car

11   *Fibrosa* case [1943] AC 32 at 48, a point apparently overlooked in *Re Goldcorp Exchange Ltd* [1995] 1 AC 74 at 103.
12   *Whincup v Hughes* (1871) LR 6 CP 78.
13   Cf *Ebrahim Dawood Ltd v Heath Ltd* [1961] 2 Lloyd's Rep 512.
14   *Goss v Chilcott* [1996] AC 788, where restitution was claimed because the contract was no longer enforceable.

during the intervening period; but it has been held that this is not *the* benefit for which he bargained, namely, a car to which he would have title as owner. Hence there is a total failure of consideration, and B can get back the *whole* of the price from A.[15] One view is that this result is unjust since B gets the use of the car for nothing; and that B's claim for the return of the price should be reduced by an allowance for the use of the car.[16] But it is not easy to see why B should, in effect, pay A for having had the use of a car which belonged to X, particularly as B might be liable to X in tort for the value of the use of the car. In such a case, the present rule, allowing B to get back the whole price, seems to be as fair as any of the alternatives which have been suggested. The position would be different if all claims of X in relation to the car had been settled by A (or by some earlier person in a chain of sellers and buyers). In one case,[17] A in good faith acquired a car, not knowing that it was subject to a hire-purchase agreement under which X (a finance company) was its owner. A sold the car to B, who kept it for nearly a year before it was claimed by X. At this stage, B claimed the price back from A, and the claim succeeded in full, even though, after it was made, the original hire-purchaser had paid off X, so that B could have safely kept the car. Had he done so, he would have suffered no loss; and the actual outcome of the case was that he had nearly a year's use of the car for nothing. Since there was no longer any risk of his being sued by X, this result seems to be unnecessary for B's protection. Where B does have to return the car to X, his claim against A is not limited to one for the return of the price. He can, in addition, recover other loss (such as money spent on repairing the car) by way of damages.[18]

ii   Rescission of the contract

Even where the claimant has received some part of the benefit for which he bargained, he may be entitled to rescind the contract, either for misrepresentation or for breach.[19] One consequence of such rescission is that the claimant is entitled to refuse to accept or (where it is physically possible to do so) to return the defendant's performance. If he can in this way bring about a total failure of

15   *Rowland v Divall* [1923] 2 KB 500; cf *Baltic Shipping Co v Dillon* (1993) 176 CLR 344 (pleasure cruise ending in shipwreck).
16   Law Reform Committee, 12th Report (Cmnd 2958) para 36; but Law Commission Paper No 160, para 6.5 comes to no conclusion on the point.
17   *Butterworth v Kingsway Motors Ltd* [1954] 2 All ER 694; *Barber v NWS Bank plc* [1996] 1 All ER 906.
18   *Mason v Burningham* [1949] 2 KB 545.
19   See ante, pp 163 et seq, and 319 et seq.

consideration, he can get his money back: for example, a buyer to whom short delivery has been made can generally reject it and recover the whole of the price. The claimant's use of the subject-matter may bar his right to rescind;[20] but where it does not have this effect, the question whether it prevents the failure of consideration from being total depends on the tests already stated. Suppose that the hire-purchaser of a car keeps it for two months and then lawfully rejects it because it is defective. Here the failure of consideration will not be total since, for the two months, the hirer had what he bargained for: namely the use of the car and a valid option to purchase it. Hence his remedy is in damages;[1] these may be based on the instalments paid, but any benefit obtained by the hirer from the use of the car is also taken into account.[2] On the other hand, he could get his money back in full if he had never had a valid option to purchase at all: eg because the other party to the contract did not own the car.[3]

iii Frustration

The rights of a party to recover back money paid under a frustrated contract have been discussed in Chapter 17. The only point to be made here is that under the Law Reform (Frustrated Contracts) Act 1943[4] a payment can be reclaimed even though the failure of consideration was not total. This does not lead to injustice to a payee who has performed in part; for under the Act the court can make adjustments in his favour in respect of expenses incurred, and valuable benefits conferred, by the payee under the contract.

iv Invalid contracts

Money can be recovered back on the ground that the contract under which it was paid was wholly void eg by statute,[5] or for mistake,[6] or under the ultra vires doctrine,[7] or because one of the parties to it was

---

20 See ante, pp 166–167, 338–339.
1   *Yeoman Credit Ltd v Apps* [1962] 2 QB 508.
2   Eg *Charterhouse Credit Co Ltd v Tolly* [1963] 2 QB 683; strictly, the damages should be based on the *value* of the subject-matter and not on the *price* paid.
3   Cf *Warman v Southern Counties Car Finance Corpn Ltd* [1949] 2 KB 576.
4   See ante, p 365.
5   *Re London County Commercial Reinsurance Office* [1922] 2 Ch 67.
6   Eg *Branwhite v Worcester Works Finance Ltd* [1969] 1 AC 552.
7   Ante, p 236; *Westdeutsche Landesbank Girozentrale v Islington London Borough Council* [1994] 4 All ER 890 [1994] 1 WLR 938, revsd in part on another ground [1996] AC 669.

a company not yet in existence.[8] The better view is that there is, in such cases, no separate requirement of 'total failure of consideration', so that part performance of the purported contract is no bar to recovery of the payment;[9] for such a bar would tend to defeat the policy of the rule making the contract void.[10]

The special rules which govern the recovery of money paid under contracts affected by personal incapacity or illegality are discussed in Chapters 12 and 11.

b Recovery in respect of other benefits

A person who has conferred a benefit on the other contracting party by rendering a service, or by transferring property, will normally claim the sum of money which the other party has agreed to pay for that performance. The court will then normally enforce the agreement to pay according to its terms. It will not award a party either more than the agreed sum merely because his performance was unexpectedly onerous;[11] or less merely because the agreed sum was excessive; nor will it award anything at all if the event on which payment was to be made has not occurred.[12] The reason for all these rules is that, generally speaking, the court must enforce the contract which the parties have made and not make a different contract for them. But in some cases this reasoning does not apply, while in others there are good reasons for departing from it. In such situations a party who is not entitled to the agreed sum may nevertheless have a claim for a reasonable remuneration.

First, he may have such a claim where, though the parties have clearly entered into a contract, no sum is ever agreed. Thus if a contract for the sale of goods does not fix the price, the seller is entitled to a reasonable price;[13] and if a contract for services does not fix the remuneration, a reasonable sum must be paid.[14] The same result may be reached where the failure to fix a price has the effect that no contract is ever concluded: if the parties nevertheless believe that there is a contract, or that one will come into existence,

---

8   *Rover International Ltd v Cannon Film Sales Ltd (No 3)* [1989] 3 All ER 423.
9   *Westdeutsche Landesbank* case [1994] 1 WLR 938 at 953; cf [1994] 4 All ER 890 at 929; *Kleinwort Benson Ltd v Birmingham City Council* [1997] QB 380 at 394.
10 See *Kleinwort Benson Ltd v Lincoln City Council* [1999] 2 AC 349 at 387, 415–416.
11 *Gilbert & Partners v Knight* [1968] 2 All ER 248.
12 See ante, pp 325–326.
13 Sale of Goods Act 1979, s 8(2).
14 Supply of Goods and Services Act 1982, s 15.

a reasonable sum must be paid for goods or services supplied in that belief.[15]

Secondly, there may be a claim for a reasonable sum where the parties have agreed on the amount to be paid but have done so under a contract which was void. In one case,[16] such a claim was allowed where a managing director's appointment was void because neither he nor those who appointed him held the necessary qualification shares in the company. Similar claims have been allowed where a purported contract with a company was void because, when it was made, the company did not yet exist[17] or had already been dissolved.[18]

Thirdly, a reasonable remuneration may be payable under a contract which has been frustrated. Where a valuable benefit (other than money) is conferred on one of the parties *before* frustration, the other can claim a 'just' sum under the Law Reform (Frustrated Contracts) Act 1943.[19] Sometimes, however, the parties may continue to act under a contract, believing that it remains in force, when, as a matter of law, it has been frustrated. It seems that a party who in this belief confers a benefit on the other *after* frustration can recover a reasonable sum.[20]

Fourthly, it may sometimes be proper for the court to disregard a valid express contract and to award a reasonable sum. Thus where necessaries have been sold and delivered to a minor, he is liable only for a reasonable price and not for any higher price that he may have agreed to pay.[1]

Finally, the court may sometimes award a reasonable sum even though the event on which payment was to be made has not occurred. If one party is prevented by the other's breach from completing performance of an entire obligation, he can claim a reasonable sum for the performance which he has actually rendered. This would be the position where a house-owner in breach of contract refused to

15   *Peter Lind & Co Ltd v Mersey Docks* [1972] 2 Lloyd's Rep 234; *British Steel Corpn v Cleveland Bridge and Engineering Co Ltd* [1984] 1 All ER 504; contrast *Regalian Properties plc v London Docklands Development Corpn* [1995] 1 All ER 1005, where the party rendering the services took the risk that no contract might be formed.

16   *Craven-Ellis v Canons Ltd* [1936] 2 KB 403; contrast *Guinness plc v Saunders* [1990] 2 AC 663, where the contract, if valid, would have given rise to a conflict of interest and duty.

17   *Rover International Ltd v Cannon Film Sales Ltd (No 3)* [1989] 3 All ER 423.

18   *Cotronic (UK) Ltd v Dezonie (t/a Wendaland Builders)* [1991] BCLC 721.

19   See ante, p 366.

20   *The Massalia* [1961] 2 QB 278; overruled on the issue of frustration, but not on the present point, in *The Eugenia* [1964] 2 QB 226.

1   Sale of Goods Act 1979, s 3; see ante, p 226.

allow a builder to complete the agreed work. Where performance is prevented by the other party's breach, recompense is available in spite of the fact that no benefit has been received by the defendant.[2] Even if the failure to complete was due to the claimant's own breach, he can nevertheless recover a reasonable sum, or a pro rata payment, if the other party has 'voluntarily' accepted the partial performance.[3] Such acceptance is sometimes treated as evidence of a 'new contract' without any express term as to remuneration.

2   Eg *Planché v Colburn* (1831) 8 Bing 14.
3   Ante, pp 340–341.

Index